All about Almodóvar

ALL ABOUT
Almodóvar

A PASSION FOR CINEMA

BRAD EPPS and DESPINA KAKOUDAKI
Editors

University of Minnesota Press
Minneapolis
London

An earlier version of chapter 5 was previously published as "Heart of Farce: Almodóvar's Comic Complexities," *New Cinemas* 5, no. 2 (July 2007): 127–38. Chapter 7 was previously published as "Melancholy Melodrama: Almodovarian Grief and Lost Homosexual Attachments," *Journal of Spanish Culture Studies* 5 (2004): 273–86; published by Taylor and Francis, http://www.tandf.co.uk. An earlier version of chapter 8 was published as "World without Strangers: The Poetics of Coincidence in Pedro Almodóvar's *Talk to Her*," *Camera Obscura* 68, vol. 23, no. 2 (August 2008); published by Duke University Press. Chapter 9 was previously published in Leo Bersani and Ulysse Dutoit, *Forms of Being: Cinema, Aesthetics, Subjectivity* (London: British Film Institute, 2004); reprinted with kind permission from the British Film Institute.

The illustrations in this book from Pedro Almodóvar's films are reproduced courtesy of El Deseo, S.A.

Published by the University of Minnesota Press
111 Third Avenue South, Suite 290
Minneapolis, MN 55401-2520
http://www.upress.umn.edu

Library of Congress Cataloging-in-Publication Data

All about Almodóvar : a passion for cinema / Brad Epps and Despina Kakoudaki, editors.
    p.   cm.
Includes bibliographical references and index.
Includes filmography.
ISBN 978-0-8166-4960-0 (hc : alk. paper) — ISBN 978-0-8166-4961-7 (pb : alk. paper)
    1. Almodóvar, Pedro—Criticism and interpretation.   I. Epps, Bradley S.
II. Kakoudaki, Despina.
    PN1998.3.A46A24 2009
    791.4302'33092—dc22

                                                      2009002608

Printed in the United States of America on acid-free paper

The University of Minnesota is an equal-opportunity educator and employer.

15   14   13   10   9   8   7   6   5   4   3   2

For our loves, David and Linda

CONTENTS

THE AUTEUR IN CONTEXT   [IV]

CODA

Approaching Almodóvar Thirty Years of Reinvention

BRAD EPPS AND DESPINA KAKOUDAKI

Para Lola García, Paz Sufrategui y Jean Claude Seguin

For me, making movies is essentially a passion.
—Pedro Almodóvar, *"Volver:* A Filmmaker's Diary"

Pedro Almodóvar is something of a paradox—scintillatingly so. Celebrated and denigrated by critics as serious and superficial, political and apolitical, moral and immoral, feminist and misogynist, experimental and sentimental, universal and provincial, Almodóvar has charted a path from the countercultural margins of his native Spain to an international mainstream which, while still consistent with the Institutional Mode of Representation as developed and criticized by Noël Burch, is not reducible to its dominant Hollywood modality. In an international context characterized by major studio consolidations, streamlined formulas, blockbuster productions, and, as noted, the global dominance of Hollywood, Almodóvar is an independent director who works—and insists on working—outside the United States, but whose steady productivity, exacting aesthetic standards, and consistent return to a loyal team of collaborators bring to mind the work habits of powerful directors of the studio era. With their offbeat characters,

With Rossy de Palma and Verónica Forqué on the set of Kika *(1993). Copyright El Deseo.*

kitschy interiors, sexually transgressive themes, labyrinthine plots, and mixing of cinematic genres, his films would appear, however, to be the antithesis of standard Hollywood fare. Yet despite his status as a Hollywood outsider, Almodóvar has managed, with the steady advice and guidance of his brother and producer Agustín, to take advantage of the opportunities of the so-called new global order, using revitalized film festival circuits, national subsidies (particularly in the wake of the "Miró Law" that aimed to buttress Spanish productions), and new patterns of distribution to reach new audiences and to garner the attention and appreciation of Hollywood itself. His Academy Awards for Best Foreign Film for *All about My Mother* (1999) and Best Original Screenplay for *Talk to Her* (2002) are only the most visible of the many international nominations, awards, and retrospectives that he has received in recent years for his work as both a director and a screenwriter. Accordingly, while seeming to work against the grain of traditional narrative patterns and at a remove from the long-standing centers of cinematic power (Paris, London, and Berlin are in many respects even more "distant" from his work than Hollywood), Almodóvar has developed into a rather exceptional and, as noted, paradoxical figure: a commercially viable auteur with an inimitable personal style, a director who has been lauded as a standard-bearer of complex postmodern sensibility, but whose work has also, to our eyes, come to announce the return of a revitalized cinematic modernism.[1]

This volume of critical essays aims to elucidate Almodóvar's work from a range of perspectives that mirror, amid breaks and refractions, the stylistic and thematic diversity of his films. In many ways, the provocative paradoxes and eclectic procedures of Almodóvar's career necessitate such a collective, heterogeneous approach, the first one in English since Kathleen Vernon and Barbara Morris's *Post-Franco, Postmodern: The Films of Pedro Almodóvar* (1995), the most notable precursor of the present volume. Heterogeneity is here critical. In the last thirty years, Almodóvar has been, by turns, an experimental voice of the Spanish *Movida*, a social and political provocateur, a cultural iconoclast, an enfant terrible, a punk, a queer, and a quirky genius whose appeal transcends national boundaries and generic formations. In less personally implicating terms, Almodóvar has become virtually synonymous with innovative, campy, cutting-edge filmmaking in which entertainment and critique mutually reinforce each other.[2] Our collective task in this volume has been to explore Almodóvar's artistic and cinematic accomplishments in ways that attend to the wide range of styles and subjects that the director has employed, as well as the equally wide range of spectatorial, critical, and theoretical questions that his films present for our consideration. Admittedly, and perhaps thankfully, it is not possible to offer an evaluative overview of an artist whose work is still very much in progress. Despite the general sense of viewers, reviewers, and critics that Almodóvar's films have lately reached a new level of sophistication and maturity (two terms that tend to do a disservice, we submit, to his earlier work, "sophisticated" in its own right), his recent work remits to and sheds new light on the ambition, subtlety, and craft of his earlier films. Almodóvar continues to take calculated risks with each film, often returning to an iconography of stylistic and sexual experimentation and social provocation that echoes his early cinematic experiments. Perhaps rather than some vague sense of "maturation," then, it is the cinematic self-consciousness of his recent work—though cinematic self-consciousness is at play in the opening shots of a work as early as *What Have I Done to Deserve This?* (1984)—that has come more resolutely to the fore, as if each film complemented or revised the subjects and styles of earlier projects. As the essays in this volume demonstrate, Almodóvar's international success (evident, among other ways, in the publication of volumes such as ours) has partly depended on his deployment of auteurism, understood as both a theoretical and a descriptive category that would account for the director's stylistic signature and as a motivating impetus that leads him to mine and re-create a personal archive.

Although it is beyond the scope of this introduction to offer a full account of Almodóvar's auteurism, Marvin D'Lugo notes that the "patronage" of Andrés Vicente Gómez's Iberoamericana Films for Almodóvar's fifth feature film, *Matador* (1986), "effectively reframed the local filmmaker as a transnational auteur through the refiguring of Spanish culture itself. Further, it gave Almodóvar a decisive lesson in the international promotion of his films, planting the seeds for his own production company, El Deseo S.A." (*Pedro Almodóvar* 46). Indeed, scarcely a year after *Matador*, Almodóvar produced the groundbreaking "gay" melodrama *Law of Desire* (1987, though actually written before *Matador*) in El Deseo, whose name *coincidentally* echoes that of the first film there produced. As momentous as the activities of the mid-1980s were in helping to establish Almodóvar's independent, international profile, the truth is that he began to see himself as a budding auteur quite a bit earlier, in the heady days of that irreverent cultural and artistic movement known, for better or worse, as the *Movida*. A self-made artist who understands the importance of working closely with others, Almodóvar has sustained an impressively devoted and effective team at El

Deseo, which has increasingly expanded its power and purview to produce a number of films by other directors.[3]

The relative stability of Almodóvar's production arrangements since the mid-1980s fuels his experiments with new and old ideas alike. Finding delight and inspiration in Hollywood classics, "high art" European cinema, and the quasi-folkloric and nationally oriented *Españolada,* Almodóvar defies generic distinctions and moves deftly between comedy, melodrama, the thriller, film noir, metafiction, farce, and so on. Voraciously "catholic" in his interests, he brings together material from religious schools, fashion shows, gay bars, women's magazines, bullfights, television, theater, boleros, and a vast etcetera. In one interview after another, in one film after another, he cites, either verbally or visually, a diverse array of directorial influences that includes Douglas Sirk, Billy Wilder, Howard Hawks, Frank Tashlin, Ernst Lubitsch, Alfred Hitchcock, King Vidor, Nicholas Ray, Michael Curtiz, Luchino Visconti, Vittorio De Sica, Rainer Werner Fassbinder, Jean Cocteau, John Waters, Andy Warhol, Luis Buñuel, Florián Rey, Luis García Berlanga, and a host of others.[4] Eclectic, vivid, and retro-modern, Almodóvar's style perhaps seemed to be no style at all at first, with early films described—and often as not, dismissed—by critics as punkish reactions against normative storytelling, as pastiche, or as kitschy mergers of preexisting mannerisms. All of this soon changed, of course, as audiences and critics increasingly came to find something compelling, funny, sexy, moving, and/or smart in the sexually charged scenarios of his films. Over the course of his many interviews, as well as in his own sporadic publications (such as the "film diary" of *Volver* included at the end of the present volume), Almodóvar has engaged in self-evaluations, alternatively revealing and concealing himself. These impressionistically marked theorizations of his own processes and products, most memorably voiced by his alter ego Patty Diphusa (from *patidifuso,* meaning "bewildered" or "astounded"), struck a cord with viewers, who came to appreciate the director's gifts as a writer. Any account of the last three decades, even one as retrospectively "introductory" as ours, thus cannot help but intertwine notions of Almodóvar's authorial development as a director and a screenwriter alike, that is to say, as an artist of both the image and the word.

Accolades and expressions of admiration aside, few contemporary directors have enjoyed such speedy entry not just into some popular transnational imaginary but also, and more densely, into the once high-culturalist confines of the academy. Although film critics and scholars of Spanish cinema

Almodóvar on the set of Bad Education *(2004). Photograph by Diego López Calvín.*
Copyright Diego López Calvín/El Deseo.

and culture were among the first to engage Almodóvar's work critically (the
former often publishing far from glowing reviews of his films in newspapers
and magazines and the latter, working both in Spain and abroad, often publishing glowing, highly theoretical readings of his films in specialized journals and books), they were soon followed by a healthy cadre of critics working in queer theory and gender studies, cultural studies, film studies, and
philosophy.[5] What we might somewhat ironically call Almodóvar's "critical
canonization" has been, however, the work of a number of assiduous scholars
(and, it bears mentioning, fans), many of whom are among our contributors
here. Paul Julian Smith's brilliant *Desire Unlimited* (first published in 1994),
Frédéric Strauss's informative collection of interviews titled *Almodóvar on
Almodóvar* (first published in French in 1994, and in English in 1996), and
Peter Evans's finely tuned book-length analysis of *Women on the Verge of a
Nervous Breakdown* (1988) (published in the BFI "Film Classics" series in
1996) set the standard for subsequent critical approaches. More recently,
Mark Allinson's *A Spanish Labyrinth* (2001), which offers a distinctive and
comprehensive perspective on the thematic and stylistic development of
Almodóvar's work; Marvin D'Lugo's *Pedro Almodóvar* (2006), which sheds
new light on the interactions between visual and narrative experimentation

and historical context; and Ernesto R. Acevedo-Muñoz's *Pedro Almodóvar* (2008), which offers detailed overviews of Almodóvar's feature films, have confirmed the trend. The previously mentioned collection by Vernon and Morris likewise proposed a critical agenda—albeit a necessarily hetero- geneous one, as already indicated—for considering the films amid a net- work of historical, theoretical, and cultural concerns. Primary among them was the association of stylistic innovation, theorized under the once ubiqui- tous rubric of postmodernism and pastiche, with the historical and political conditions of Spain after Franco.

In interviews and critical analyses alike, this presumably originary "post- Francoist" moment—characterized by a fairly widespread desire to be done once and for all with the dictator, to forget and ignore him—is typically discussed in the context of the *Movida,* which many critics take as having inspired and supported Almodóvar's creative emergence. With its origins in the "drug culture" of rock, punk, and new wave music, the *Movida* was a recalcitrant, somewhat oblivious heir to the artificial paradises of the late nineteenth century and the countercultural hallucinations of the 1960s and 1970s, albeit with a lighter, flightier take on consumer indulgence.[6] As the old dictatorial order gave way to a new democratic order, it was again excit- ing, and fashionable, to be young and "on the move"—and young and on the move Pedro Almodóvar and his friends certainly were. Although pres- ent in Vigo, Barcelona, and other cities, the *Movida* was most energetically located in Madrid, a landlocked and long lethargic city that Italian philoso- pher Gianni Vattimo, drunk on the excitement of the country's newfound sense of freedom, provocatively designated as the capital of the twentieth century—in a playful allusion to Walter Benjamin's designation of Paris as the capital of the nineteenth century.[7] Exaggerated as Vattimo's assessment surely was, it tapped into the willful sense of exaggeration and excess that accompanied the renewed sense of freedom, however fractured and con- tested, that came in the wake of the Generalísimo's protracted death (the sub- ject, as many American readers may remember, of a series of comic send-ups on the NBC TV show *Saturday Night Live*).

When Almodóvar, steeling away time from his "day job" at the telephone company, first burst on the local scene in the late 1970s and early 1980s with Super-8 shorts like *La Caída de Sódoma (The Fall of Sodom,* 1975), *Salomé* (1978), and *Folle . . . folle . . . fólleme Tim (Fuck, Fuck, Fuck Me Tim,* 1978) and his first feature film, the raucous *Pepi, Luci, Bom and Other Girls on the Heap* (1980), Spain was indeed fertile ground for this gleefully erratic and anx-

iously self-expressive movement. And express himself Almodóvar repeat-
edly did. For instance, in Paula Willoquet-Maricondi's *Pedro Almodóvar:
Interviews,* Almodóvar, speaking in 1981,[8] describes his style in *Pepi, Luci,
Bom* as a matter of both necessity and choice, "the kind of style that you're
bound to adopt when you don't have any type of funding" and that is "the
product of a language compelled by circumstances" (3). In this account,
Almodóvar seems to present the film as emerging from the *Movida* itself.
The film "was born," he recounts, "when some people from the *Star* magazine
ask [him] to write a lewd and somewhat parodic story of the punk movement, sometime around 1977. Then the story began to grow and develop
into a script" (4). Yet just a bit later, he reverses the order, claiming that "the
Madrid 'new wave' didn't exist" at the time that he wrote the story in 1978
and that his friends had been "living 'pop' with a certain parodic meaning
for at least ten years" (5). In another interview, this time with Nuria Vidal
from around 1987 or 1988, Almodóvar spoke in more matter-of-fact terms
of a group of people who "worked in Madrid doing very modern things in
some very specific years: 1977–1982" and explicitly rejected the *Movida* as a
creation of the mass media (39, translation ours). Arguably more unified in
critical histories than in personal practices, the *Movida* is awash in ambiguous, ambivalent meanings.

Whatever its reality, and whatever the reality of Almodóvar's relation to
it (as chronicler, leader, participant, critic, independent artist, or naysayer),
the *Movida* is ultimately perhaps little more than a placeholder for a conge-
ries of acts and activities that range from pop, punk, and new wave music to
comic books, celebrity gossip magazines, photo-novels, and advertising—in

*With Fabio McNamara
on the set of* Labyrinth
of Passion *(1982).
Copyright El Deseo.*

other words, some of the venues of the very mass media that Almodóvar fit-fully claims to have created the *Movida* as a whole. Perhaps it is only in hazy retrospect, then, that the *Movida* can be seen as absorbing Almodóvar or, better yet, that Almodóvar can be seen as absorbing the *Movida*. Regardless, for many of those most persistently linked to the *Movida,* the margins gradually bled into the mainstream, as Almodóvar, singer Fabio or Fanny McNamara (Fabio de Miguel), singer Alaska (Olvido Gara), photographer Ouke Lele, the rock group Radio Futura, the ubiquitous semi-clandestine graffiti artist Muelle, and influential foreigners like Lou Reed, David Bowie, Boy George, Andy Warhol, and John Waters became, albeit to markedly dif-ferent degrees, emblematic of a countercultural identity that was increas-ingly popular—and increasingly marketable.

No current work on Almodóvar, and certainly not one comprised of a variety of perspectives like *All about Almodóvar,* can quite shake the sense of the ways in which the director's cinematic work and self-presentation have, for all their repetitions, changed over time. As viewers and critics, we have, amid the changes, generally come to recognize Almodóvar's command of his craft and, increasingly, his meditative, introspective, and serious bent, in evidence at least since *The Flower of My Secret* (1995), one of his most delicate, understated films. While earlier films such as *Labyrinth of Passion* (1982), *Kika* (1993), *Matador,* and *Tie Me Up! Tie Me Down!* (1990) more or less made light of everything from incest to sadomasochism to rape and murder (and were often roundly upbraided in the press for doing so),[9] in recent years, Almodóvar's films evince an interest in socially charged sto-ries involving traumatic, even "unspeakable" events: the death of a child and HIV-AIDS in *All about My Mother* (1999); mental and physical incapacita-tion and nonconsensual sex in *Talk to Her;* child abuse in the Catholic church, drug addiction, and murder in *Bad Education* (2004), and sexual assault and defensive murder in *Volver* (2006)—a film that, while marking the director's "return" to lighter comic material and to working with Carmen Maura, star of the breakaway hit *Women on the Verge of a Nervous Breakdown,* is by no means bereft of seriousness.[10]

This is not to say that all was fun and games in *Dark Habits* (1983), where a lesbian mother superior pines over a woman she can never have; or in *What Have I Done to Deserve This?,* where a working mother pops uppers to keep going and kills her husband in a moment of frustration and rage; or in *Law of Desire,* where an obsessive love affair between two men leads to murder, suicide, and general heartbreak; or, for that matter, even in *Pepi, Luci, Bom,* where a fascist policeman brutally beats his masochistic wife. While continuing to engage socially loaded phenomena, the more recent films have assumed a more cautious stance and, as Almodóvar himself states in his film diary on *Volver* included in the present volume, are more deeply marked by the director's personal memories and by a sense of loneliness amid solidarity and friendship. To cite only two examples of how things have changed over the years: where drug use is a source of humor in *Dark Habits*, it is the source of devastation in *Bad Education;* where rape is played for laughs in *Kika,* its very threat issues in a rather matter-of-fact and feminist-inflected justification of murder in *Volver.* At issue in the changes is not merely Almodóvar's more informed take on filmmaking (when he was young, he could not study at Spain's Official School of Cinematography and found inspiration instead in the Telephone Company at which he worked), but also his more complex understanding of himself and his country.

As powerful and influential as Almodóvar has become in the international cinematic scene, his films issue from and remit to a lucidly evoked and idiosyncratically inflected national history—that of a once giddy post-Francoist and now firmly consolidated democratic Spain. In many respects, the aforementioned changes in Almodóvar's cinema run parallel to changes in Spanish society, which is, as noted, solidly democratic—not withstanding the tendency to authoritarianism in the prominent Partido Popular, or Popular Party, that Almodóvar has publicly scorned and to which he has on more than one occasion attributed some of his most somber work, most notably *Bad Education.*[11] The effusive sense of possibility that attended a royal decree that lifted media censorship in 1977 and that stimulated the *destape* (literally, "the uncovering," a "movement" that had arguably begun in the final years of the dictatorship and that manifested itself in a surge in the production, distribution, and consumption of erotic and quasi-pornographic materials) meant, among other things, that Spaniards no longer had to go across the border to Perpignan or Biarritz to see *Last Tango in Paris* (Bernardo Bertolucci, 1972) and, in fact, that they could see a great deal of the female form (the male form remained altogether more discreet) plastered openly on kiosks across the country.[12] The situation for film was not very different. As critic Daniel Kowalsky notes, "[f]ilms of the *destape* are best described as light Iberian sex comedies, usually concerned with a middle-aged man afflicted with satyriasis" (190).

The coming to power of the Socialists in 1982 constituted another landmark, a tangible sign that the much-touted Transition or Change (*Cambio,* in Spanish), though too smooth for some and too abrupt for others, was more than mere rhetoric. A very old country, Spain was also, insofar as constitutional democracy was concerned, a very young country. The coexistence of political signs both old and young, of notions of the nation as mythically rooted in the past (the Francoist obsession with the Cid, the Reconquest, and the Catholic Kings is notorious) and as "just now" coming into its own, meant that the country was susceptible to nearly wholesale inclusion into a much-ballyhooed postmodernity of rights and identities. Symbolically thrown into a new order and a new old world, Spain became the poster child for postmodernity and postmodernism precisely *because* it had not fully experienced modernity—or so a certain well-known story goes. Whatever the case, Spain was finally international news for reasons other than states of emergency, suspended civil liberties, and polemical executions. Indeed, if in the late 1970s and early 1980s it was again exciting and fashionable to be young in Spain, it was also, and more broadly, exciting, and fashionable, to be Spanish.[13]

The excitement and fashion of things Spanish: many of the earliest critical studies of Almodóvar participated, whether advertently or inadvertently, in the promotion and diffusion of a Spanish director with international appeal. A boon to nationally oriented cultural agents, Almodóvar became the paradoxical embodiment of Francoist Minister Manuel Fraga Iribarne's astonishingly successful tourist slogan "Spain is different": paradoxical because what Almodóvar embodied was virtually anything and everything *but* the national Catholicism of the nearly forty-year-old regime. Almodóvar was also a boon to a number of professional Hispanists, particularly in the United States and Britain, who had long been frustrated with the seemingly unending diet of oligarchs, priests, and petty bureaucrats, rogues and mystics, Quixotic dreamers and inquisitors, seducers and flamenco dancers that populated earlier eras of Spanish culture. Almodóvar's irreverent but sensitive take on these old stereotypes; his creation of new and unexpected characters and character types; his novel yet historically informed treatment of cinematic form, and his seemingly effortless ability to position himself as the undisputed star of the *Movida* and a rising auteur quickly set him apart from most of his predecessors—Luis Buñuel is an insistent exception—and contemporaries alike. In all his various guises, Almodóvar proved himself to be adept at building on his early cult status and at extricating himself and his work from the "perpetual crisis" of Spanish cinema.[14]

As Paul Julian Smith noted in *Desire Unlimited*, Almodóvar soon proved himself to be unexpectedly profitable as well, with El Deseo, once it became established, coming to produce some of the top-grossing Spanish films of all time (4).[15] *Women on the Verge of a Nervous Breakdown* is generally accepted as Almodóvar's commercial "breakthrough," a venture that smashed box-office records throughout Spain and achieved an international visibility long thought impossible for a Spanish film. The film's critical fortunes matched its box-office success, for it was nominated for an Academy Award for Best Foreign Film and received nominations and awards in a number of European and International film festivals. Impressive as the reception of *Women on the Verge* was, Almodóvar's star had been on the rise since the release of the neo-neorealist *What Have I Done to Deserve This?*, if not indeed before. Almodóvar's "profitability," which a number of die-hard early fans of *Pepi, Luci, Bom, Labyrinth of Passion,* and *Dark Habits* considered to be tantamount to treason, meant that his films were attractive to Spanish, European and North and South American film distributors and exhibitors, to academics, critics and students, and to general and not-so-general audiences for a variety of intersecting and mutually reinforcing reasons: his enviable mixture of stylistic consistency, innovation, and productivity; his lush visual designs and intricate and engaging plots; his loving, almost fetishistic, attention to detail (handbags, nail polish, lipstick, earrings, shoes, notebooks, telephones, food, clocks, backdrops, lighting, music); his almost unparalleled knack for bringing marginal figures center stage and for advancing a sense of transgression without overt political attitudinizing; his social sensibility and theoretical sophistication; his nonjudgmental take on sexuality, desire, affect, and emotion, and his nuanced understanding of characterization and spectatorial identification.

Almodóvar's films, originally produced on shoestring budgets with minimal technical support, came, in short, to embody a new and dynamic Spain firmly at home in Europe and far from the relative isolationism that characterized Francoism. As our own presentation indicates, Almodóvar has been read both inside and outside Spain in relation to the opening, unfolding, and deepening of a democratic project in which difference and diversity—cinematically embodied in strung-out nuns, sadomasochistic lesbians, queer terrorists, pill-popping housewives, incestuous dry cleaners, garrulous Argentinean psychoanalysts, impotent detectives, sassy pre-ops, troubled porn stars, paraplegic ex-cops, murderous ex-matadors, and erstwhile telephone repairmen— were and remain prominent if still contested values.[16] He has also been seen in relation to more specific projects, most compellingly the women's movement and the lesbian, gay, bisexual, and transgender movement, even though many of his films, with a seemingly willful disregard for political correctness (the butt of a joke, for instance, in *Talk to Her* about the "proper" way to describe a character's sexuality), have rankled a number of feminist and queer critics and delighted even more. Put a bit differently, Almodóvar's work has sparked transnational debates about everything from male-directed feminism and misogyny to the intersections of gay liberation and queer commodification to the politics of diversity and the ethics, and economics, of international fame. It has also sparked debates about the "paradox" that Almodóvar's "apparently progressive stance on issues of gender or sexual orientation enmasks a failure to invest in more committed ideological affiliations," a paradox that has even led some particularly obdurate critics to see him a providing "a luscious cultural alibi for the Right" (Marsh 53).[17] However these debates are read, however they play themselves out, one thing is certain: Almodóvar is a director who continues to give a place of privilege— and employment—to women and queers alike. As Lynn Hirschberg put it in a cover story on the director for the *New York Times Magazine*, "Pedro Almodóvar has sanctified society's transgressors, rescued Spanish surrealism and liberated international cinema." And as David Denby put it in a lengthy paean in the *New Yorker*, "the most readily enjoyable of all art-house directors—a natural-born entertainer—Almodóvar . . . may be something unprecedented in movie history."

Academic critics of the caliber of Smith, Marsha Kinder, Kathleen Vernon, Marvin D'Lugo, and Peter Evans would seem to be in agreement with Denby and Hirschberg, and were among the first to examine, in English, the cross-cultural tensions in, and critical reception of, Almodóvar's work (the first major work on Almodóvar in Spanish is Nuria Vidal's *El cine de Pedro Almodóvar*). Happily for us, and for the reader, Smith, Kinder, Vernon, D'Lugo, and Evans are all part of the present work, where they continue to refine their critical vocabularies and hermeneutical protocols. In the face of an international entertainment industry that seemed all too eager to generalize and denationalize Almodóvar's work, these and other writers, many of them literary Hispanists turned film critics (Kinder is the exception), insisted on the director's specifically Spanish representational and cultural heritage. *Post-Franco, Postmodern: The Films of Pedro Almodóvar*, edited by Kathleen Vernon and Barbara Morris, continued the trend of culturally sensitive readings and included a variety of approaches to Almodóvar's work, unified under a critical agenda that engaged broad efforts in the study of gender, sexuality, history, culture, politics, and representation. Of course, as time passed, and as Almodóvar's international fame grew, other academic critics—journalists had been active long before—joined in the analysis of Almodóvar's work and prompted, from within other disciplinary spheres, a subtle repositioning of critical and analytic methodologies. It is along these lines that the contributions by Linda Williams, Despina Kakoudaki, and Leo Bersani and Ulysse Dutoit attest to the tensions between national context and international impact (none is, strictly speaking, a scholar of Spain) as well as to the relative significance of a formal language of film criticism and theory and the culturally specific knowledge necessary to an understanding of the nuances of these thoroughly interdisciplinary films.

The internationalization of Almodóvar and of the critical writing on him is part and parcel of a complex dynamic that runs from Spanish state interventions in the form of subsidies to collaborative ventures in the European Union to the "indie revolution" that rocked—and in some respects paradoxically reinvigorated—the hegemony of Hollywood. Along with a small cadre of other filmmakers, Almodóvar proved that irreverent but well-wrought films had a place in the expanded geography of filmic production characterized, at its best, by titles like *Blue Velvet* (David Lynch, 1986), *sex, lies, and videotape* (Steven Soderbergh, 1989), *Ju Dou* (Zhang Yimou, 1990), and, of course, *Women on the Verge of a Nervous Breakdown*. On the sidelines of the blockbusters that characterize the era, international film festivals, critics' conventions, revitalized independent festivals such as Sundance, and new film production and distribution companies stirred new synergies. As Peter Biskind and others have noted, the success of smaller, unconventional films such as *sex, lies, and videotape* and *The Crying Game* (Neil Jordan, 1992) spurred the rise of new companies such as Miramax that participated not merely in the distribution but also in the production of independent films. The two main distributors of Almodóvar's films in the United States, Orion Classics (1983–92) and Sony Pictures Classics (1992–present), have helped ensure that Almodóvar's name circulates alongside those of more established European directors like Federico Fellini, Jean-Luc Godard, or Rainer Werner Fassbinder, or alongside those of American directors like Woody Allen and John Cassavetes, and that his personal appearances in cities the world over generate an outpouring of fans and reporters alike.[18]

Perhaps it would not be inaccurate to describe Almodóvar's dealings with such international distributors as one of his many "crossover" acts, one that has contributed to the renewal of an energetic form of storytelling while productively complicating and expanding the very meaning of national and independent cinema. In an important respect, the recurring presence of the Spanish capital in Almodóvar's films has itself shifted from a matter of necessity to one of newly found choice. The protean presence of Madrid— dull and suffocating in *What Have I Done to Deserve This?*, glimmering and hectic in *Women on the Verge of a Nervous Breakdown*—was, as Marvin D'Lugo observed in 1995, "the result of the centralization of much of the film industry in and around the capital, which made it financially expedient to locate certain narratives in and near the city" ("Almodóvar's City" 127). And yet, more than a decade later, when he has secured the clout to set up shop pretty much wherever he would like, and when internationalization has reconfigured though by no means trumped centralization, Almodóvar refuses to move to Hollywood, or anywhere else for that matter, and thereby demonstrates—as if he needed to demonstrate—that he continues to be committed to his native country and, more specifically, his adopted city.[19]

The ties and tensions between the local, national, and international, the past and the present, are only some of the issues examined in this new collection of essays on Almodóvar's cinema, the first of its kind in English since the publication of *Post-Franco, Postmodern*. Needless to say, much has happened since then, not least of which is the creation of some of the Spanish director's best work. The contributors to our volume, many of whom have been writing on Almodóvar for years (and a number of whom participated in *Post-Franco, Postmodern*), set their sights on a diverse but coherent array of topics, including the director's collaborations in El Deseo and his love of writing; his use of television and popular music; his deployment of comic conventions; his penchant for melodrama and its relations to melancholy, violence, and coincidence; his intricate questioning of sexual and national identity; his mobilization of local spaces; his blend of autobiography and metafiction; his sophisticated inquiry into visuality and its limits, and his increasingly complex understanding of history and memory.[20] At once local, national, and international, Almodóvar's cinema is also as at once cutting-edge and mainstream, structurally complex and narratively accessible, contestatory and conciliatory, commercial and artful, effusive and controlled.

As significant as all of these ties and tensions are, there are, however, others that bear on the relation between the critic(s) and the director himself. Critical approaches to Almodóvar share the emphasis on personal and authorial signature that, as we want to suggest, also characterizes Almodóvar's own codification of his craft from the beginning. It seems indeed that the multivalent and hybrid form of Almodóvar's films not only inspires critics from a variety of disciplines, but also demands of them a doggedly inter-disciplinary approach, as if the films advocated breaking the boundaries of academic disciplines in much the same way that they push against cinematic and generic boundaries. This productive friction has become harder to discern, partly because Almodóvar's has successfully entered into a circuit that includes art films and independent productions and partly because academic circles have come to value interdisciplinary inquiry.

Given such a robust critical tradition, one wonders whether there is something fundamentally elusive in Almodóvar's work despite the seeming proliferation of commentaries, overviews, and approaches. Indeed, while the people at El Deseo have worked tirelessly to bring Almodóvar's films into global cultural prominence, Almodóvar himself oscillates between playing to the mainstream and provoking its sensibilities. This doubleness of purpose was already evident in Frédéric Strauss's interviews with Almodóvar conducted in the early 1990s. In his insightful comments, Strauss finds himself doubly captivated by Almodóvar: first, through repeated viewings of *Law of Desire* and *Women on the Verge of a Nervous Breakdown,* the two breakthrough films that brought Almodóvar to the attention of European and American critics and audiences, and then, in the course of the interview itself, by his eloquent subject, who delivers an "impassioned and rational story of a life dedicated to film" (ix). Strauss refers to the "two spirits" that, for him, characterize Almodóvar and his films: "the one is frank, innocently candid, passionate and rebellious," while "the other is serene, judicious, stubborn, exacting and constantly at work" (xi). Signaling "sense and sensation, intelligence and expressiveness" (ibid.) as qualities of Almodóvar's work, Strauss worries that his admiration for the director may be at odds with a critical appreciation of the films. As Strauss rather anxiously puts it, "nothing aroused my suspicions more than a director who not only possessed such attractive, if admittedly flashy, credentials, but could also touch my emotions. I was clearly in danger of being manipulated" (ix). Strauss's interviews with Almodóvar, like those by Marsha Kinder and many others, do indeed tend to revolve around passion and reason, eccentricity and intensity, and offer, for all their inevitable faults and fractures, a surprisingly coherent tale of Almodóvar's artistic "development." In a prescient critical move that elides the rhetoric of postmodernism with which Almodóvar was at the time so densely associated, Strauss describes the director's work as an experiment in the baroque, one that brings together "in one gesture all the great artistic adventures of the century" (xiii).

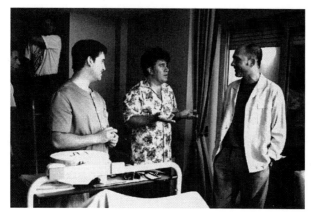

With Javier Cámara and Dario Grandinetti on the set of Talk to Her *(2002). Photograph by Miguel Bracho. Copyright Miguel Bracho/ El Deseo.*

The essays included in this volume could be said to create their own "baroque" or "neobaroque" approach to Almodóvar's oeuvre, making reference to melodrama, comedy, tragedy, horror, science fiction, pornography, and film noir, music, song, television, video, photography, design, and the visual arts. But there is another link here at work: Strauss's worries about not being sufficiently worried about the director and his work, about not being *properly* critical (cold, distant, self-assured, and relentlessly attentive to aesthetic, political, ethical, and other problems), are in some measure our own. His concerns that admiration and attraction are the bedmates of manipulation and a loss of critical acumen are thus well taken, and might serve as a tonic to the effusiveness with which we have opened a volume that purports to be "all about Almodóvar." Then again, we also share Strauss's implicit assumption that criticism that is so *properly* oriented, so fixated on ferreting out the negative, is itself in need of criticism. We would be the first to admit that the brand of criticism included in this volume is passionate about its subject.

What criticism cannot be, however, is complete. It is in this sense that what Leo Bersani and Ulysse Dutoit say in their article in this volume about the title of Almodóvar's *All about My Mother* can be said, mutatis mutandis, of the title of the present volume: it "makes promises that can be neither easily defined nor easily fulfilled." Such difficultly defined and difficultly fulfilled promises, part and parcel of an "epistemological fantasy," may serve, however, as an emblem of any work—perhaps especially a monograph comprised of inevitably disparate essays—that would give a full and exhaustive account of its subject of inquiry. Our choice of title is most decisively *not* a gambit on behalf of some ultimately graspable truth, that most extreme form of "epistemological fantasy," but on behalf of the dizzyingly citational and performative plays that engage, without confining themselves to, artistic production. Clearly echoing the title of one of Almodóvar's most celebrated films, the book strives both to locate and to lose itself in a web of work that emerges from academic fields such as film and visual studies, cultural studies, gay and lesbian studies, gender studies, literary studies, Hispanic studies, and that, of course, outstrips the academy altogether. This ongoing critical expansion, whatever its methodologies and elective affinities, is the effect of the ongoing creative expansion of Almodóvar himself, an expansion whose intensity is such that criticism, try as it might, cannot but remain, happily, incomplete. *All about Almodóvar* should not be taken, that is, as offering exhaustive readings of *all* of Almodóvar's filmography or biography, but as grappling with a diversity of issues, *all* of which provide an admittedly *partial* but hopefully productive view of his work and life.

The first section of the book, centered rather loosely on "Forms and Figures," addresses this diversity of registers and influences and offers a variety of readings of some of the director's iterative styles and persistent themes, from his use of television and music to his interest in the interplays between violence and desire, the turns of identity, the vagaries and varieties of performance, and the complexities of comedy. In "Almodóvar on Television: Industry and Thematics," Paul Julian Smith, one of the most prolific and informed authorities on the director, tracks some of the multivalent relations between cinematic and televisual media, which here range from satirical references to the ubiquitous commercialism of the small screen to collaborations between El Deseo and Spanish and European television and cable channels. Writing from an "industrial perspective" that understands the films in their globally fractured historical and economic contexts, Smith brings to the fore Almodóvar's complex stance toward this much-maligned but immensely influential medium. If television is, as Smith puts it, "the dark continent of Almodóvar's oeuvre," it is also a profusely productive continent, one that is more heterogeneous (as Smith notes, Almodóvar incorporates "commercials, variety shows, news, reality shows, and feature films" into his own feature films) and more significant (in its ability, for instance, to confuse presentation and representation and to implicate the act of looking in optical technologies) than is often recognized. Although he gestures to some of the theoretical implications of bringing different visual media together (film, TV, video, DVD, etc.), Smith is more concerned with such matters as the

mass appeal of television and its pervasive role in the construction, maintenance, and transformation of a popular imaginary, questions that are of signal importance to a director who shuttles between aesthetic refinement and
commercial success.

Kathleen Vernon traces Almodóvar's deployment of a similarly wide
range of cultural meanings in her beautifully crafted "Queer Sound: Musical Otherness in Three Films by Pedro Almodóvar." As Vernon argues,
Almodóvar's attention to the structural and emotional potential of songs,
scores, and sound tracks (their ability to convey a sense of continuity, to signal and accentuate affects and attitudes, and at times to contest the ascendancy of the visual itself) attests to a deep and abiding appreciation of the
relation between music and narrative cinema. The director's investment in
melodrama, which constitutes the focal point of other essays in this collection, is borne out in his investment in the *melos* of melodrama, that is to say
in music. More than a specific genre or modality is here at stake, however,
for, as Vernon notes, ambient sound and the maternal voice contribute to a
"queer" rendition of musicality that is more inclusive than exclusive, more
ambivalent and moving than univocal and fixed. Building on her previous
explorations of the aural landscapes of Almodóvar's cinema, Vernon turns
her ear—and eye—to performances in *All about My Mother, Talk to Her,*
and *Bad Education,* films that, even as they mark a departure from the Latin
American love songs and punk-pop idioms of earlier endeavors, draw on an
increasingly wide array of musical styles: from Ismaël Lô to Caetano Veloso,
from Gioacchino Rossini to Sara Montiel, from "Moon River" to liturgical
compositions. For Vernon, the "ambiguously charged potential of music"
can have supple yet decisive effects on visual representation and can activate both utopian promises of freedom and fulfillment and dystopian fears
of loss and entrapment.

The play of the psyche, its rich and contested vocabulary of drives
and complexes, libidinal stages and perverse acts, talking cures and bou-
doir scenarios, has long suggested something theatrical, something in line
with the Freudian notion of the unconscious as an *anderer Schauplatz* (an
other showplace), in short, something performative. Isolina Ballesteros, in
"Performing Identities in the Cinema of Pedro Almodóvar," deepens the
interrogation of Almodóvar's thematic (dis)continuities by way of a detailed
overview of the variegated if virtually ineluctable places of performance.
Within the general performative condition of the cinema, Ballesteros hones
in on some of the more deceptively visible renditions of performativity in

the guise of "musicians, singers, stage and screen actors, dubbers, television personalities, drag queens, bullfighters, and others." Paying special attention to the reiterations, replays, and rehearsals of sexual and personal identity, Ballesteros articulates an antiessentialist view of the subject that actualizes, as it were, the venerable notion that the world, all of it, is a stage. Moving elegantly across a wide roster of films, Ballesteros explores performance as a strategy of identification and disidentification with both conformist and disruptive implications.

There are, of course, more eye-grabbing topics and themes in Almodóvar's cinema, and it is to some of these that Peter Evans turns. Almodóvar's pre-occupations with violence and sexuality, which are on display in *Tie Me Up! Tie Me Down!*, *Matador*, *Kika*, and *Live Flesh* (1997), but present to varying degrees in virtually all of his films, are the focus of Evans's "Acts of Violence in Almodóvar." Another seasoned scholar of Almodóvar, Evans moves skillfully between metacritical commentary and close analysis, offering new insights into the director's forays not into comedy, farce, and melo-drama (the genres with which he is most consistently associated) but into horror and science fiction. Almodóvar's self-conscious reworking of these

With Cecilia Roth and Rosa Maria Sardà on the set of All about My Mother *(1999). Photograph by Teresa Isasi. Copyright Teresa Isasi/El Deseo.*

genres is of a piece with his often tongue-in-cheek redeployment of a sadomasochistic aesthetics that remits to Pauline Réage and even to Leopold von
Sacher-Masoch: tongue-in-cheek, because the director has explicitly rejected
the sadomasochistic prism through which some of his films were broadly
received and insisted on calling one of them "almost a romantic fairy-tale"
(Strauss 102). In keeping with the psychosymbolic heritage of these and
other amalgamations of aggression and desire, Evans advances a reading
that attends to the tense interplays between phallic and anti-phallic power,
narcissism, *jouissance,* and the death drive.

Continuing the exploration of Almodóvar's forays into different cinematic and narrative genres, Andy Medhurst queries the director's deployment of comic modalities. The centrality of comedy, satire, and even slapstick in Almodóvar's early films had a structuring effect on early critical
approaches, inspiring critics to associate his plots with the supposedly anar-
chic and unruly tenets of comedy in general and, more specifically, with
the absurd treatments of the body found in surrealism and, less portent-
ously, the *Movida.* As Medhurst proposes, however, comic modes continue
to inform even Almodóvar's most serious and dramatic ventures, and pose
new challenges to his "canonization" within the more highbrow rubrics of art,
queer, and international cinema. Comedy, to Medhurst's eyes, accentuates the
psychosexual migrations that run throughout Almodóvar's films and underscores the limits of verbal and cultural translation (many of Almodóvar's
jokes and puns are specific to the Spanish language), allowing us to see the
director's famous intergeneric versatility in a more local and "grounded"
light. In recent films, especially *Volver,* Almodóvar returns to the humor
that characterized many of his earlier endeavors and injects elements of
comedy and farce into the dramatic core of the film, highlighting rather
than diminishing its seriousness. For Medhurst, Almodóvar's "return" to the
comedic reaffirms his commitment to breaking and revising generic boundaries and challenges, moreover, an apparently widespread critical tendency to
incorporate Almodóvar into an amorphously global dynamic that would discount his ongoing "conversation" with Spanish culture and cinema.

The second section of the book, "Melodrama and Its Discontents," offers
a more concentrated take on the director's use of generic conventions, specifically those of melodrama, for although Almodóvar first came to notice as
a comedian, melodrama has indeed proved to be more insistent in his work.
Taking the tension between genre (as a codified "industry-driven product")
and auteurism (as a sign of authorial originality) as his starting point, Mark

Allinson, in "Mimesis and Diegesis: Almodóvar and the Limits of Melodrama," quickly comes to center his discussion on the relations between
melodrama and tragedy and the relatively "lower" and "higher" modes of
seriousness that they respectively entail. Drawing on a rich body of historical and genre criticism, Allinson reminds us that melodrama is not only
drama accompanied by music but drama in which music strives to compensate for the suppression of the spoken word (as in censorship) and for the
inviability of the spoken word (as in silent cinema, whose technical limits
have been replayed in contemporary experiments that include *The Shrinking
Lover* in Almodóvar's own *Talk to Her*). Allinson sets melodrama alongside
tragedy, that supposedly higher form of representation that is rarely evoked in
studies on Almodóvar. Making a case against the rather simplistic, if historically sedimented, division of high tragedy and popular melodrama, Allinson
adduces the character of Manuela in *All about My Mother* as an example of
"how a melodramatic role can be artistically equal to a tragic one." Yet even
as Allinson discovers a tragic glint in *All about My Mother,* he is more concerned with demonstrating that *Talk to Her,* while retaining many melodramatic features, approaches something more recognizably tragic. Although
Allinson reaffirms the conventions of genre even as he pushes at them, he
points to a critical dynamic between diegesis as "telling" or "relating" and
mimesis as "showing" or "acting out" that raises important questions about
the interplay of the visual and the verbal, enactment and narration, in the
art of cinema.

   Talk to Her is also at play in Linda Williams's meticulously argued "Melancholy Melodrama: Almodovarian Grief and Lost Homosexual Attachments," though it is *High Heels* (1991) or, more accurately and evocatively,
"Distant Heels" that receives the lion's share of critical attention. Whereas
Allinson gestures to the limits of melodrama by way of a genre-oriented
meditation on its relation to tragedy, Williams starts with another sense of
tragedy, one formulated by renowned lesbian-feminist poet Adrienne Rich:
to wit, "the missing female tragedy of 'mother-daughter passion and rapture'" (225). Less convinced than Allinson that tragedy is key, Williams
shifts Rich's observation back to the more familiar Almodovarian territory of
melodrama, which for her is a mode, not a genre. Engaging this long feminized and lately "queered" mode of emotionality and representation from
a psychoanalytic perspective that extends Judith Butler's reading of melancholy and lost or disavowed homosexual attachments, Williams traces
modalities of desire (incest, lesbianism, homosexuality, etc.) that persist

in an array of melodramatic films that seem to adhere to an overtly hetero-normative matrix and that offer, against the grain of established genres or modes, endings that are at once happy and sad. In the process, Williams extracts a less familiar, even uncanny, story about desire and attachment that sheds new light on Almodóvar's work.

Continuing in the vein of melodrama, Despina Kakoudaki, in "Intimate Strangers: Melodrama and Coincidence in *Talk to Her*," explores Almodóvar's narrative craft by focusing on the ethical implications of coincidence and causality. Kakoudaki contends that by tracing Almodóvar's reliance on chance encounters, casual happenings, and fortuitous events, that is to say on the structuring effects of coincidence, one can appreciate the classical echoes of his narrative style, and in the process delve into some of the deeply humanist epistemological and philosophical implications of his representa-tional choices. As seemingly random events and accidents are transformed into satisfying coincidences (satisfying perhaps because they reinforce an underlying sense of order), strangers are revealed to share something, indeed often as not to be intimately interconnected. Accordingly, Kakoudaki also examines Almodóvar's tendency to use coincidence in order to create dense social networks that enfold human beings to the point that the very notion of the stranger often seems devoid of meaning. *Talk to Her*, in many ways one of Almodóvar's most "coincidental" films (with its chance encounters in a theater motivating encounters elsewhere), brings coincidence into play with communication and its limits in silence and nondisclosure. In contrast to the overt imperative to talk in its title, the film in effect uses the narrative logic of melodrama to fuel an eloquent mode of nonexpression.

Almodóvar's ability to create films that are at once expressive and secre-tive, flashy and discreet, informs the third section of the book, "The Limits of Representation," which considers narrative and visual detail with an eye to what cannot be seen and to what cannot be given to identification, at least not fully and finally. Numerous critics have analyzed Almodóvar's films in terms of an excess and an overexposure—a "frenzy of the visible," to bor-row from Linda Williams's borrowing from Jean-Louis Comolli—that are embodied in discernible characters and mobilized in discernible situa-tions. They have celebrated Almodóvar's willingness, even desire, to pre-sent seemingly gritty and bizarre aspects of human sexual life without judg-ment, shame, or fear. And yet, at the heart of these emphatic visibilities lies an uncanny interest in the limits of representation, indeed nonrepresenta-tion. Perhaps the putative overexposure of certain aspects of sex and desire (more than one of Almodóvar's films has been saddled with an NC-17 and even an X rating in the United States) allows for a sort of subtle withholding of others; perhaps the visible, and better still the hypervisible, the frenetically visible, would not be possible without the invisible, without a limit, material and symbolic, that may never be firmly located and, for that reason, never fully overcome.

In "Almodóvar's Girls," Leo Bersani and Ulysse Dutoit, taking *All about My Mother* as their point of departure and of arrival, set their sights on a wide range of films in order to sound out some of the tensions between aesthetics and desire, autobiography and fiction, the repetition and dissolution of identity. Acknowledging the complexity of Almodóvar's plots, and the dauntingly necessary task of summarizing them in and as critical practice, Bersani and Dutoit stress that complexity here obeys a principle of order and, moreover, that "psychic implausibility does not make for narrative chaos." The tales and trajectories of Almodóvar's characters as subjects in the world raise questions about authenticity and inauthenticity—What is a real father, a real mother, a real child? What is a real woman, a real man? What is the real nature of desire?—that push at the divisive force of binary formulations in general. But Bersani and Dutoit are also intrigued by the limits between art and reality, or, more precisely, by the tenuousness of any such distinction. Respectful of difficult questions much more than easy answers, they ask, for instance, how Almodóvar's cinema gestures to a refashioned relationality and a "prospective sociability" that spring not so much from stories *about* women as women as storytellers. In the same complex sweep, they also ask how his cinema gestures to "a solidarity or homo-ness of being," to an intersubjective dynamic that reaches "out toward an *other sameness,*" and that, in so reaching, moves beyond the range of the recorded word and image.

Marsha Kinder's "All about the Brothers: Retroseriality in Almodóvar's Cinema" functions as a nice companion to Bersani and Dutoit's psychoanalytically marked work on "Almodóvar's girls," and boys, for in it Kinder grapples with the fact that, whatever the developmental trajectories of the director or of the country from which he comes, whatever processes of "maturation" and "transition," viewers can enter Almodóvar's work, like anyone's work, from any number of angles and through any number of films. What makes Almodóvar's films especially suited to such different, nonchronological entry points is that they "increasingly perform an evocation of earlier works" in a manner that recalls the structures and mechanisms of soap operas, miniseries, and sequels, modes of representation that

Almodóvar, in his diary on *Volver* here included, explicitly refuses to make. Kinder, who moves agilely between historically informed criticism and theoretically engaged creative ventures of her own, offers the term "retroseriality" to account for an aspect of Almodóvar's films as well as for a method of viewing and reading them that pushes against the director's claim that he "will not do sequels, prequels, or remakes." By "retroseriality," Kinder does not mean to suggest something regressive or nostalgic (the topic of D'Lugo's essay), nor does she signal the recurring theme of a "return" (most evident in the title and cast of *Volver*). Rather, she proposes that Almodóvar's films form retroactive serial bonds with earlier films, reinterpreting, revising, and even revitalizing stories, situations, characters, and actors. The recursive, reticular, and retrospective operations of seriality allow, furthermore, for "predictive" views and expectations. As a way of illustrating an entire, complex way of seeing, Kinder concentrates on the twists and turns of a trio of movies that in one way or another deal with sibling rivalry among boys: *What Have I Done to Deserve This?*, *Law of Desire*, and *Bad Education*. An ambitious and engaging essay, "All about the Brothers" offers an expansive and complex approach to cinematic narrativity.

Brad Epps offers a different take on the limit and what is beyond it in "Blind Shots and Backward Glances: Reviewing *Matador* and *Labyrinth of Passion*," an essay that offers a theoretically inflected interrogation of the play of the visible and the invisible in the cinematic medium itself. Epps attends to the often overlooked fact that, as Mary Ann Doane notes, "the materiality of film is such that almost 40 percent of the running time of any film is effectively invisible," that is to say, "lost in the interstices between frames" (172). Casting the interstices between the frames as well as the divisions and cuts of editing as so many blind shots, Epps explores cinematic viewing as a perpetual process of *reviewing* in which the fantasy of full sight and complete knowledge, of plenitude, is a lure of the most insistent and compelling order. He does so not by turning in ceaseless speculation on the effective invisibility of any film, but by turning to the visual and narrative traces of a breakdown, rupture, or complication of vision and the visible in the male protagonist's desire for reviewing a video on television in *Matador* and in the female protagonist's fear of light in *Labyrinth of Passion*. In both cases, for all the differences between them, a problem of visuality is adumbrated in hysterically histrionic *(Labyrinth of Passion)* and highly stylized *(Matador)* plots and characters.

Complementing Epps's focus on the materiality of the invisible and the impossibility of seeing everything, Steven Marsh discusses the spectral and the subterranean elements of *Volver,* tracking down the ways in which the film prolongs life beyond death and extends death into everyday life. Capitalizing on the polysemy of the "return" that figures as its untranslated title (*Volver* is the only film by Almodóvar so far that has not been distributed internationally in translated form), the film engages ghostly recurrences or revenants (the return of the repressed) as well as self-conscious returns to a cinematic archive that includes Almodóvar's own films, particularly those that feature Carmen Maura, arguably the first and most enduring of Almodóvar's "girls," as they have been called ("chicas Almodóvar"). A multilayered work, *Volver* embodies a number of the challenges of viewing in the light of cinematic and historical tradition, traumatic family legacies, and an (un)knowable past and constantly shifting present.

The limits of historical representation are at issue in Marvin D'Lugo's "Postnostalgia in Almodóvar's *Bad Education:* Written on the Body of Sara Montiel," which takes the Spanish diva as the emblem of an entire fissured past. Drawing on Fredric Jameson's concept of "postnostalgia" as a movement beyond the sentimental ensnarement of nostalgia that impedes rather than facilitates the personal and collective understanding of past events, D'Lugo proposes a hermeneutic activity that wrestles with expressions of "pastness" that insist and return in different, even deceptive, forms ranging from voices to poster art to photographs. Such visual and verbal quotations of the glamorized body of Montiel would be almost immediately recognizable to any Spaniard who lived through those years (that is to say, anyone around Almodóvar's age or older), but they remain considerably more opaque, unrecognizable even, to many other spectators, younger, foreign, and/or less familiar with Spain. While Almodóvar provides references that make the film accessible to international audiences, he also works to disturb, by way of an elaborate, involute plot, the very notions of accessibility and recognizabilty. In so doing, he points to what D'Lugo describes as "the snare of misrecognition of the historical past as it is filtered through the subjective perspective of the individual's present-day circumstance." Through an exquisitely attentive reading of temporal dimensions and pop cultural artifacts, D'Lugo shows how Almodóvar's multilayered film resists the Manichaean moral codes that characterized both Francoism *and* the memory of it. D'Lugo offers, that is, a theoretically insightful and historically nuanced analysis not just of *Bad Education,* whose title in Spanish also means "bad behavior" or "bad conduct," but also of Almodóvar's entire filmography.

"The Auteur in Context" constitutes the final section of the book, one that, even as it brings Almodóvar the man center stage, recognizes that he is not an artist in isolation. Pushing against the well-worn habit of using the director's name to designate work that is, in reality, the result of complex collaborative processes, Ignacio Oliva, in "Inside Almodóvar," and Francisco Zurián, in "Pepi, Patty, and Beyond: Cinema and Literature in Almodóvar," widen our field of vision to acknowledge a welter of other creative people, from publishers, producers, writers, and editors to set designers, costume designers, artistic directors, musicians, and makeup artists: Esther García, Lola García, José Salcedo, José Luis Alcaine, Jorge Herralde, Bernardo Bonezzi, José María de Cossío, Francis Montesinos, Jocomola de Sybila, Jesús Ferrero, Jean-Paul Gaultier, Antxón Gómez, Sigfrido Martín Begué, and, of course, his brother Agustín, among many others. For all the differences between their approaches and objectives, both Oliva and Zurián follow a bio-historical path that is more dominant in Spain than the United States and Great Britain, where broad theoretical and close formal analyses loom large. Resisting the once well-entrenched tendency to dispense with the figure of the author, whether individual or collective, Oliva and Zurián flesh out, with a meticulously attentive appreciation of the value of local history, questions of character, subjectivity, and personhood that run through many of the other articles included in the present volume. Oliva, who is a filmmaker in his own right, takes his documentary *Inside Almodóvar* as a sounding board for his critical reflections, which bring together a sophisticated understanding of cinematic technique with an acute respect for the collaborative logistics of filmmaking. His ear attuned to the voice of others, Oliva gives a place of long overdue privilege to the testimonies of many of the people who have helped make Almodóvar, well, Almodóvar. Judiciously interweaving personal anecdote and cultural history, Oliva provides valuable concrete information and some scintillating theoretical takes on Almodóvar not only as a director but also as a writer and storyteller.

Zurián, for his part, teases out Almodóvar's "other" career as a man of letters. Acknowledged by the Academy of Motion Picture Arts and Sciences in 2003 for his writing of *Talk to Her,* Almodóvar has long been a gifted wordsmith. Indeed, his early career—if "career" at that time it could be called—was arguably as literary and musical as it was visual, as devoted to the letter, both written and sung, as to the image.[21] Zurián, like Oliva, has been privy to the intimate, day-to-day realities of El Deseo and has a profound respect for the director as a diligent and inventive author, and not merely as a more glorified cinematic auteur. In his richly detailed essay, Zurián charts something like a writerly genealogy of the internationally famous filmmaker and revisits many of Almodóvar's numerous publications in newspapers, comics, and alternative magazines as well as his errant alter ego, Patty Diphusa. Attentive to the insistence of the letter, Zurián, like Oliva, provides insights into Almodóvar that few Anglo-American critics have, insights that are the fruit of long-term collaborations and conversations. Together, Oliva and Zurián offer a lovingly grounded, semiprivate glimpse into Almodóvar's public and authorial persona and into some of the people who work with him.

In "*Bad Education*: Fictional Autobiography and Meta–Film Noir," Víctor Fuentes explores what is at stake in Almodóvar's turn to the "dark side" after the success of the deeply humanistic films of love and solidarity that immediately preceded it. Presenting *Bad Education* as a "noir return" to *Law of Desire* that also engages the more horrific elements of *Matador* and *Kika*, Fuentes implicitly validates Kinder's retroseriality. He does so, however, in a way that, as if echoing what Robert Richmond Ellis has called "autobiographical voyeurism" (115), mines the force of the director's return to his personal past and that of his nation. The play of memory, with its embellishments and insufficiencies, its doubts and certitudes, is in *Bad Education* quite serious, implicating as it does a powerful institutional history of religious instruction and sexual repression that outstrips the individual as artist or auteur even as it throws him into the spotlight. As Almodóvar's only extensive depiction of life under Franco (the previous *Live Flesh* contains a very short introductory scene set during a critical moment of the dictatorship), *Bad Education* serves to remind more breezily transnational critics and fans that, years after its integration into a predominantly neoliberal European Union, many Spaniards still struggle with past demons that remain, as the struggle itself indicates, quite present. Seen against the backdrop of a nation that only recently approved a "law of historical memory" (in 2006, to be precise), it is little wonder that Fuentes should attend to the ethical dilemmas—and the beleaguered rhetoric of redemption—contained in such autobiographically and historically fertile material.

The book closes with a coda of sorts: Almodóvar's own account, in the form of a diary, of the shooting of his recent film *Volver*. The film has received praise for the director's ability to recapture the "magic" he once made with

Carmen Maura and, moreover, to make an artist out of its star, Penélope Cruz, or, as an article in *Time* magazine puts it, to "rescue" her from "the lost-property department of blond and bland Hollywood, where she ha[d] lived for the past several years carrying the cross of exoticism" (Keegan 68). In Almodóvar's hands, Cruz has gone from being "exotic" to "motherly"— though admittedly only in the way that Sophia Loren could be "motherly." She was a best actress nominee for the Academy Award in 2007 and won the 2009 award for best supporting actress for Woody Allen's *Vicky Cristina Barcelona*. One of the editors of this volume had the privilege to be on the set of *Volver* for the first days of shooting and to sit elbow-to-elbow beside the director at work. The experience allows him to attest firsthand to the director's gentle rigor and attention to detail and to the actress's willingness to give herself over to her mentor, to "lose herself" in her role. To be sure, Almodóvar, in his diary, does not write of his "gentle rigor," but of his expectations and ambivalences, his passion and search for magic, his fondness for a mode of emotive artifice that has little in common, other than its respect for the avant-garde, with the repudiation of artifice, auteurs, and "unnatural" optical effects advocated by such groups as Dogme 95.

Almodóvar's diary serves as a fitting way to close *All about Almodóvar* because it provides a daily accounting of a work that was then in progress but is now "finished." The present volume was also long in process and is now "finished," even though Almodóvar himself has already finished working on his next film, suggestively titled *Los abrazos rotos (Broken Embraces),* which includes, as a comedy within a melodrama, a remake of *Women on the Verge of a Nervous Breakdown* with Penélope Cruz, dressed to resemble Audrey Hepburn in Billy Wilder's *Sabrina* (1954), reprising the role originally played by Carmen Maura. So, even as we bring our protracted project to an end, Almodóvar returns to his first major internationally commercial hit to reflect on the past and, of course, to continue into the future. The temporal gap that is inevitable when working on the work of someone who is still very much working ensures that our now "finished" volume, even if it *had* attempted some systematic accounting of each and every one of Almodóvar's films, will remain in a profound sense forever *unfinished*— and that we critics, with our hubristic pretensions to produce something "all about Almodóvar," will remain on the verge of a nervous breakdown as we try, impossibly, just to catch up. To make matters even more deliciously complex, even as Almodóvar was fast at work on a new feature, his influence assumed increasingly diverse forms: in April 2008, Antoni Casas Ros, a

French-Catalan writer, published a novel, his first, titled simply *Le théorème d'Almodóvar*. In it, we read that "Almodóvar has no angle. There is a child-like roundness in his body and in his face that contradict the somber gaze, the passionate mobility" (74, translation ours). Even this assessment, focused as it is on the director's physicality, is outdated. Almodóvar is, at least at last viewing (Epps on the set of *Los abrazos rotos*), a trimmer version of himself, a man older, of course, but in many ways closer to the wiriness of his earlier days.[22] Here too there may be a return at play, but whatever the case, and however time alters the body (even unto, and after, death), Casas Ros has, pun intended, a good point: Almodóvar has, strictly speaking, no single angle or, better yet, there is no single angle to be had on Almodóvar.

For whatever it is worth, at the time that we began working on this book, when most of the contributors came together to discuss "all" they knew about Almodóvar at an advanced seminar funded by the Radcliffe Institute of Advanced Study at Harvard University, plans for *Volver* had only just been announced—and we, then as now, had no single angle. Now, as *Broken Embraces* appears on the horizon, the gap between creation and critique impresses itself upon us once again, reminding us to mind it even as we would get beyond it, that is to say, even as we bring the present volume into print. But if time is our steady, stealthy opponent, other people are not. One of the signal features of this volume is its collective and collaborative ethos, its multiangular though still inevitably limited and partial approach, which marked the encounter in Radcliffe as before it had marked an encounter in Cuenca (when Almodóvar was awarded an honorary doctorate) that included Williams, Kinder, Allinson, Smith, D'Lugo, Oliva, Epps, Fuentes, and Zurián. Together, the two encounters offered important parallels to the work of an artist who has a profound respect for collaboration, even "family," and who continues to reinvent himself and to challenge and delight critics and fans alike. As Frédéric Strauss observed many years ago, Almodóvar's work, like the work of the critics that it inspires, is an ongoing experiment. We hope that, taken together, the diverse essays in this volume will contribute to the ongoing appreciation of one of the world's great directors, one with a true passion for cinema.

NOTES

1. The critical work on Almodóvar and postmodernism is, by now, extensive. Among other works, see Víctor Fuentes's "El cine de Almodóvar y la posmodernidad española" and Celestino Deleyto's "Postmodernism and Parody."

2. Camp occupies a place of prominence in Almodóvar's films and in the critical writing on them. See, for instance, Patrick Paul Garlinger and H. Rosi Song's "Camp: What's Spain Got to Do with It," as well as the single-authored essay by Garlinger. Transvestism, often tensely related to camp, is another recurrent subject; see, for instance, Paul Julian Smith's "Un travestismo sin límites" and Alejandro Varderi's publications.

3. Perhaps not surprisingly, Almodóvar's production company is called El Deseo, S.A., or Desire Limited. And yet, as the title of Paul Julian Smith's monograph on the director wittily indicates, Almodóvar repeatedly gestures to desire unlimited, to desire taken to the limit and then pushed, or tripped, or tweaked beyond.

4. Along with the lengthy and informative interviews with Nuria Vidal and Frédéric Strauss, see Almodóvar's "Bordando el borde" (especially page 116, where he discusses his debt to "golden age" Hollywood comedies) and, of course, Marsha Kinder's much-cited 1987 interview in *Film Quarterly*.

5. The literature on Almodóvar and homosexuality has been prolific, to say the least. See, among others, works by Earl Jackson Jr., Hanson, Varderi, Epps, Shaw, Mandrell, and, especially, Paul Julian Smith. For a troublingly earnest psychoanalytic take on queerness as "perversion," see Nancy Blake. For insights on Almodóvar's (re)presentation of women, see, among others, Mendelsohn, Maddison, and Martín.

6. For an earnest—perhaps all too earnest—criticism of the use of drugs in Almodóvar's cinema, see the article by Sánchez-Carbonell and Colomera.

7. A number of very fine articles examine the function of Madrid in Almodóvar's work; see, for instance, essays by Luna-Escudero and Marsh. For a rare treatment of Almodóvar's equally rare treatment of Barcelona, see Amago.

8. The interview is titled "First Film," and was conducted by Juan I. Francia and Julio Pérez Perucha for *Contracampo*, September 1981. See Willoquet-Maricondi 3–8.

9. Attending to the most enduring of critical debates on Almodóvar, namely, the deployment of gender and sexuality and the representation of women, Susan Martin-Márquez goes so far as to speak of "schizophrenia," though she shifts the burden of proof from the director to his critics: "Pedro Almodóvar's films have been reviled as misogynous and celebrated as feminist. In part this schizophrenia may be due to the critic's tendency to focus selectively on particular films: *Kika* (1993), for example, is considerably more challenging to defend from a feminist perspective than is *¿Qué he hecho yo para merecer esto?!* (*What Have I Done to Deserve This?*; 1984)" (498).

10. As Almodóvar says in his essay in the present volume, "*Volver*, which means 'to return,' . . . is about death, though it deals with the subject in a less anguished manner. . . . More than about death itself, the screenplay talks about the rich culture that surrounds death in La Mancha, where I was born. It is about the way (not tragic at all) in which various female characters of different generations deal with this culture."

11. In an open conversation with the public held at Harvard University on October 12, 2004, Almodóvar "joked" that since the Socialists had returned to power after winning general elections in March 2004 (just days after an attack by Islamic terrorists left 191 people dead in Madrid) he was ready to try his hand again at lighter fare. In his contribution to this volume, Marvin D'Lugo examines Almodóvar's polemical relation with the Partido Popular, which had tried to pass off the attacks as the work of the Basque group ETA instead of Al Qaeda.

12. Daniel Kowalsky provides a nice summation of the state of censorship in Spain during the Transition: "Only with Royal Decree 3071, signed on 11 November 1977, did the newly elected government of Adolfo Suárez formally abolish all media censorship. In place of censorship, the Spanish government instituted a four-tiered rating system for film products: (1) all audiences; (2) over 14 years of age; (3) over 18; and (4) S. The S rating was attached to products that 'due to their theme or content might offend the sensibility of the spectator'" (188). Interestingly, the S rating was abolished in 1982 under the Socialist government of Felipe González, which established in turn "regulations for X-rated cinema similar to those existing in Europe and the US. The new standards were codified in Royal Decree 3304 of Dec. 28 1983, a decision largely authored by Pilar Miró, the PSOE's [Spanish Socialist Workers' Party] Minister of Culture [and a noted film-maker in her own right]. The so-called 'Miró Law' granted generous funding to 'serious,' 'quality' and 'artistic' pictures, while ending favourable fiscal subsidies or tax breaks for products considered purely 'commercial'" (Kowalsky 202).

13. The newfound excitement in things Spanish paradoxically spurred a renewed, if more diffuse, form of Spanish nationalism—tensely related to renewed forms of Catalan, Basque, and, to a lesser extent, Galician nationalism—that altered the very notion of Spanish cinema. As Núria Triana-Toribio notes, "an emergent concept of national cinema in the 1980s was unofficially represented by a group of directors which includes Fernando Trueba, Fernando Colomo and, as the highest profile member, Almodóvar, because they renewed Spanish cinema, ethically and aesthetically, its genres, its star system, its locations and its soundtracks (both in terms of music and language)" (134).

14. For more on the perpetual or permanent crisis of Spanish film, see Triana-Toribio (108–11).

15. Although Santiago Segura's 1998 film, *Torrente, the Stupid Arm of the Law (Torrente, el brazo tonto de la ley)*, apparently outdid *Women on the Verge of a Nervous Breakdown* in Spanish box-office returns, it has not enjoyed its international crossover appeal or that of other films by Almodóvar such as *All about My Mother, Talk to Her,* and *Volver*. Then again, as Barry Jordan remarks, "*Torrente* lambastes the very 'eroticised marginalia' which Almodóvar helped to 'normalize' and make visible. Indeed, through the activities of its macho, racist, misogynist cop hero determined to bust a drugs gang, Segura's film is a subversive provocation to the image of a sexually liberated, politically correct Spain which gained hegemony in the Socialist Spain of the 1980s and 1990s, particularly through Almodóvar's camp comedies" (191).

16. As Marsha Kinder noted in 1987: "Almodóvar's films have a curious way of resisting marginalization. Never limiting himself to a single protagonist, he chooses an ensemble of homosexual, bisexual, transsexual, doper, punk, terrorist characters who refuse to be ghettoized into divisive subcultures because they are figured as part of the 'new Spanish mentality'—a fast-paced revolt that relentlessly pursues pleasure rather than power, and a postmodern erasure of all repressive boundaries and taboos associated with Spain's medieval, fascist, and modernist heritage" (34). Although pleasure is never simply opposed to power, as Michel Foucault well knew, its place in the public, political realm had rarely been as vibrantly visible in Spain as in the 1980s, when Almodóvar shot to stardom.

17. Marsh revisits, but does not endorse, criticisms of Almodóvar as being "complicit"

with the Right. He cites one in particular, Antonio Elorza, who in an article in the major Spanish daily *El País,* claims that movies like *All about My Mother* and *Talk to Her* are little more than "local Madrilenian variant[s] of the Spielberg style, in all its astuteness as well as its tricks, applied to the sentiments of a human life taken out of context and which in its excesses confirms order. Transgression has become conservative" (quoted in Marsh 53). As catchy as Elorza's lapidary dictum is, it evinces a gross misunderstanding of both transgression and conservatism. Almodóvar is anything but some unwitting darling of the Right (which is not to say that Rightists universally turn up their nose at his success and at the visibility that he has garnered for Spain), and even received death threats for his criticisms of the conservative Partido Popular in the wake of the terrorist attack of March 11, 2004.

18. Miramax was the distributor for *Tie Me Up! Tie Me Down!.*

19. Almodóvar was born in Calzada de Calatrava, in the province of Ciudad Real, in Castile-La Mancha, and later moved to Extremadura with his family when he was eight. He arrived in Madrid around the age of sixteen or seventeen and has remained there ever since.

20. Almodóvar himself might dispute—and certainly at one time did dispute—some of these assessments. In an article that he published in *El europeo* in 1989, Almodóvar professed himself to be "absolutely ignorant in everything concerning geography and history" (67). If that self-assessment was accepted by many in 1989, two decades later it is not.

21. For more on Almodóvar's love of literature, which is amply on display in his film diary included in this volume, see Harguindey's "El placer de leer."

22. It bears noting that Casas Ros's novel tells the story of a man whose face was disfigured in a traffic accident when he was twenty. The focus on physicality, on the body and the face, is not, in other words, some naive fixation on corporeal presence but a much more profound meditation on art and reality.

WORKS CITED

Acevedo-Muñoz, Ernesto R. *Pedro Almodóvar.* London: British Film Institute, 2008.

Allinson, Mark. *A Spanish Labyrinth: The Films of Pedro Almodóvar.* London: I. B. Tauris, 2001.

Almodóvar, Pedro. "Bordando el borde." *El europeo* 8 (1989): 67–72.

Amago, Samuel. "Todo sobre Barcelona: Refiguring Spanish Identities in Recent European Cinema." *Hispanic Research Journal* 8.1 (2007): 11–25.

Biskind, Peter. *Down and Dirty Pictures: Miramax, Sundance, and the Rise of Independent Film.* New York: Simon & Schuster, 2004.

Blake, Nancy. "Che vou? Jouir du symptôme pervers dans le cinéma de Pedro Almodóvar." *L'évolution psychiatrique* 70 (2005): 613–21.

Burch, Noël. *La Lucarne de l'infini.* Paris: Nathan-Université, 1992.

Casas Ros, Antoni. *Le théorème d'Almodóvar.* Paris: Gallimard, 2008.

Deleyto, Celestino. "Postmodernism and Parody in Pedro Almodóvar's *Mujeres al borde de un ataque de nervios* (1988)." *Forum for Modern Language Studies* 31.1 (1995): 49–63.

Denby, David. "In and Out of Love." *New Yorker* 80.36 (Nov. 22, 2004): 84–88.

D'Lugo, Marvin. "Almodóvar's City of Desire." Vernon and Morris 125–43.

———. *Pedro Almodóvar*. Chicago: University of Illinois Press, 2006.

Doane, Mary Ann. *The Emergence of Cinematic Time: Modernity, Contingency, the Archive.* Cambridge: Harvard University Press, 2002.

Ellis, Robert Richmond. *The Hispanic Homograph: Gay Self-Representation in Contemporary Spanish Autobiography.* Urbana and Chicago: University of Illinois Press, 1997.

Epps, Brad. "Figuring Hysteria: Disorder and Desire in Three Films of Pedro Almodóvar." Vernon and Morris 99–124.

Evans, Peter. *Women on the Verge of a Nervous Breakdown.* London: BFI Film Classics, 1996.

Fuentes, Víctor. "El cine de Almodóvar y la posmodernidad española (Logros y límites)." *Cine-Lit: Essays on Peninsular Film and Fiction.* Eds. George Cabello Castellet, Jaume Martí-Olivella, and Guy Wood. Portland: Portland State University, Oregon State University, Reed College, 1992. 209–18.

Garlinger, Patrick Paul. "All about Agrado, or the Sincerity of Camp in Almodóvar's *Todo sobre mi madre.*" *Journal of Spanish Cultural Studies* 5.1 (2004): 117–34.

Garlinger, Patrick Paul, and H. Rosi Song. "Camp: What's Spain Got to Do with It." *Journal of Spanish Cultural Studies* 5.1 (2004): 3–10.

Hanson, Ellis. "Technology, Paranoia and the Queer Voice." *Screen* 34.2 (1993): 137–61.

Harguindey, Ángel S. "El placer de leer: Pedro Almodóvar, ante el rodaje de su película más literaria." *Babelia. El País* (Jan. 14, 1995): 4–5.

Hirschberg, Lynn. "The Redeemer." *New York Times Magazine* (Sept. 5, 2004): 24–70.

Jackson, Earl, Jr. "Coming in Handy: The J/O Spectacle and the Gay Male Subject in Almodóvar." *Solitary Pleasures: The Historical, Literary, and Artistic Discourses of Autoeroticism.* Eds. Paula Bennett and Vernon A. Rosario II. New York: Routledge, 1995. 251–75.

———. *Strategies of Deviance: Studies in Gay Male Representation.* Bloomington: Indiana University Press, 1995.

Jordan, Barry. "The Spanish Film Industry in the 1980s and 1990s." *Contemporary Spanish Cultural Studies.* Eds. Barry Jordan and Rikki Morgan-Tamosunas. London: Arnold, 2000. 179–92.

Keegan, Rebecca Winters. "How Pedro Rescued Penélope." *Time* (Nov. 20, 2006): 66–68.

Kinder, Marsha. "Pleasure and the New Spanish Mentality: A Conversation with Pedro Almodóvar." *Film Quarterly* 41.1 (1987): 33–44.

Kowalsky, Daniel. "Rated S: Softcore Pornography and the Spanish Transition to Democracy, 1977–82." *Spanish Popular Cinema.* Eds. Antonio Lázaro-Reboll and Andrew Willis. Manchester: Manchester University Press, 2004. 188–208.

Luna-Escudero-Alie, María-Elvira. "La representación de Madrid o la dicotomía del campo y la ciudad en *La flor de mi secreto,* de Pedro Almodóvar." *Espéculo: Revista de Estudios Literarios* 32 (2006): no pagination.

Maddison, Steve. "All about Women: Pedro Almodóvar and the Heterosexual Dynamic." *Textual Practice* 14.2 (2000): 265–84.

Mandrell, James. "Sense and Sensibility, or Latent Heterosexuality and *Labyrinth of Passion.*" Vernon and Morris 41–57.

Marsh, Steven. "Masculinity, Monuments and Movement: Gender and the City of Madrid in Pedro Almodóvar's *Carne trémula* (1997)." *Gender and Spanish Cinema.* Eds. Steven Marsh and Parvati Nair. Oxford: Berg, 2004. 53–70.

Martín, Annabel. "Pedro Almodóvar's *¿Qué he hecho YO para merecer esto?* Realism, Marginality and Women." *Cine-Lit: Essays on Peninsular Film and Fiction.* Eds. George Cabello Castellet, Jaume Martí-Olivella, and Guy Wood. Portland: Portland State University, Oregon State University, Reed College, 1992. 227–31.

Martin-Márquez, Susan. "Pedro Almodóvar's Maternal Transplants: From *Matador* to *All about My Mother.*" *Bulletin of Hispanic Studies* 81 (2004): 497–509.

Mendelsohn, Daniel. "The Women of Pedro Almodóvar." *New York Review of Books* 54.3 (2007): 8–10.

Rich, Adrienne. *Of Woman Born: Motherhood as Experience and Institution.* New York: W. W. Norton, 1976.

Sánchez-Carbonell, X., and P. Colomera. "Consumo de drogas en el cine de Pedro Almodóvar." *Adicciones* 15 (2003): 23–30.

Shaw, Deborah. "Men in High Heels: The Feminine Man and Performances of Femininity in *Tacones lejanos* by Pedro Almodóvar." *Journal of Iberian and Latin American Studies* 6.1 (2000): 55–62.

Smith, Paul Julian. *Desire Unlimited: The Cinema of Pedro Almodóvar.* London: Verso, 1994.

———. "Pornography, Masculinity, Homosexuality: Almodóvar's *Matador* and *La ley del deseo.*" *Refiguring Spain: Cinema/Media/Representation.* Ed. Marsha Kinder. Durham, N.C.: Duke University Press, 1997. 178–95.

———. "Un travestismo sin límites: El cine de Almodóvar." *Antípodas* 11/12 (1999): 15–22.

Strauss, Frédéric. *Almodóvar on Almodóvar.* Trans. Yves Baignères. London: Faber and Faber, 1996.

Triana-Toribio, Núria. *Spanish National Cinema.* London: Routledge, 2003.

Varderi, Alejandro. "Pedro Almodóvar: Escrito sobre un cuerpo." *Alba de América: Revista Literaria* 25.47–48 (2006): 357–67.

———. *Severo Sarduy y Pedro Almodóvar: Del barroco al kitsch en la narrativa y el cine postmodernos.* Madrid: Pliegos, 1996.

Vernon, Kathleen M., and Barbara Morris, eds. *Post-Franco, Postmodern: The Films of Pedro Almodóvar.* Westport, Conn.: Greenwood Press, 1995.

Vidal, Nuria. *El cine de Pedro Almodóvar.* Barcelona: Destino, 1988.

Williams, Linda. *Hard Core: Power, Pleasure, and the "Frenzy of the Visible."* Berkeley: University of California Press, 1989.

Willoquet-Maricondi, Paula, ed. *Pedro Almodóvar: Interviews.* Jackson: University Press of Mississippi, 2004.

I
FORMS AND FIGURES

1 Almodóvar on Television Industry and Thematics

PAUL JULIAN SMITH

Television is vital to an understanding of Pedro Almodóvar's cinema, both because Almodóvar and his independent production company El Deseo have often relied on television for production funding and distribution and because the films themselves engage consistently and substantially with the medium. It is characteristic, then, that Almodóvar's first and fifteenth features are framed by references to television. In the crazy farce that is his first feature, *Pepi, Luci, Bom* (1980), Carmen Maura, who plays the perverse heiress Pepi, at one point sets herself up as an advertising producer. Her first project is a spot for knickers with a twist: they will absorb gas and urine or, when necessary, double as a dildo. In the final titles that bring the recent sober drama *Bad Education* (2004) to a provisional and unsatisfactory close, we read that the mercenary and murderous actor played by Gael García Bernal, known variously as Ignacio, Juan, and Ángel through the course of the complex plot, will spend ten years as a movie star before "now work[ing] exclusively in TV series." While *Pepi, Luci, Bom* gleefully incorporates parodies of pop or mass culture such as television into its defiantly heterogeneous filmic text, *Bad Education* seems to posit television as a radical other to cinema, a fate for an actor—and perhaps a director—that is almost worse than death.

Television is the dark continent of Almodóvar's oeuvre. While references to television are constant in the Spaniard's films (Mark Allinson claims that in the first thirteen features there is only one in which characters fail to watch television, 54), there is almost no criticism, other than Allinson's, that addresses this vital topic at any length. The neglect is no surprise. Spanish critics of film, and indeed of television itself, tend to despise TV, a position that Almodóvar would seem to share in *Bad Education;* foreign critics, even if they are interested in television, tend to lack familiarity with a notoriously domestic medium. What I argue here, however, is that television, however repressed or disavowed by critics, has been central to Almodóvar's work over the course of twenty-five years. Indeed, his later films, which, as I have suggested in *Contemporary Spanish Culture* (144–68), resurrect the distinction of "art cinema," can be profitably reread in the light of TV studies. Although critics have largely failed to discuss this topic, Almodóvar himself has acknowledged the ubiquity of television in his cinema. In an interview that he gave on the U.S. release of *Kika,* the film in which he offers his most savage critique of the medium, he is reported as saying:

> It [TV] is an omnipresent eye in everyone's life. In every country, any place, there is a television. I don't think there is a day in the year in which we don't see an image in that square frame. So if there is an open window, then I thought *[sic]* that someone with a camera could be watching. (Willoquet-Maricondi 102–3)

Almodóvar thus implicitly equates television not only with the space-time matrix of everyday life but also with vision and surveillance, seeing and being seen, in the city: the window that he mentions is indeed quite simply the small screen.

Industry

To address the status of television in Almodóvar's cinema, we would do well to start from an industrial perspective. While Almodóvar's production company, helmed by his faithful brother Agustín, has given the director a wide degree of artistic freedom, it is striking how often El Deseo works in collaboration with TV companies. Even before setting up El Deseo, whose first full production was *Law of Desire* (1987), the Almodóvar brothers had made *Matador* (1986) as a coproduction between a small film producer called Iberoamericana and the then monopoly television broadcaster Televisión Española (TVE). Some ten years later, they made *Live Flesh* (1997) in collaboration with French film producers Ciby 2000 and TV channel France 3; *All about My Mother* (1999) with Pathé's Renn, France 2, and premium cable Canal +, and *Talk to Her* (2002) with minority financial interests from Spanish "free to air" (i.e., nonsubscription) private network Antena 3 and digital platform Vía Digital. More recently, *Bad Education* was partly funded by the public broadcaster Televisión Española, by now locked in bitter competition with the private networks as well as with the Spanish subsidiary of premium channel Canal +, which had long relied on local feature films to attract subscriptions.

It is noticeable, then, that the Almodóvar brothers had substantial recourse to TV production funding even in the case of the recent culturally distinctive films in which Pedro set his sights on the elite status of art or auteur cinema. Interestingly, at the same time, Almodóvar also took to collaborating with actors mainly familiar to Spanish audiences from television, often casting them against their accepted type: for instance, inoffensive romantic lead Toni Cantó played the cruel transsexual father in *All about My Mother;* tubby, buffoonish Javier Cámara played both the troubled nurse in *Talk to Her* and the camp sidekick in *Bad Education.* Even before these recent films, El Deseo had sometimes turned to TV for both funding and distribution. Indeed, Almodóvar's own career was arguably launched by his TV performances in the early 1980s on *La edad de oro* (The Golden Age), a pop music and talk show legendary in Spain for its part in the cultural explosion of the early 1980s that came to be known as the *Movida.* Furthermore, in 1990, soon after the formation of El Deseo and the huge commercial success of *Women on the Verge of a Nervous Breakdown* (1988), he sold his entire back catalog of seven features to TVE for the then unprecedented sum of two hundred million pesetas, and explicit gay melodrama *Law of Desire* was first broadcast on prime time by Televisión Española in April 1991. Given the current wholesale exclusion of foreign-language cinema from British and U.S. network schedules, it comes as something of a surprise to remember that *Women on the Verge of a Nervous Breakdown* played on BBC2 on Christmas Eve 1992.[1] In spring 2004, *Talk to Her* was in rotation on HBO Latino, the Spanish-language channel of the respected and innovative premium U.S. cable channel. Almodóvar, perhaps the only foreign-language filmmaker to achieve theatrical distribution for all of his movies in all major territories, thus also nurtured his audience and increased his cultural profile through screenings on mass television at home and select minority channels abroad. In recent years, El Deseo has expanded its feature production outside Spain and into English. *Mujeres (Women),* the first TV series developed by El Deseo, premiered on TVE1 on September 18, 2006.

Whatever may come of other TV projects said to be in development at El Deseo, two little-known collaborations by Almodóvar with Spanish television are especially significant. *Trailer for Lovers of the Forbidden* (1984) is a promotional, medium-length drama made to tie in with the release of *What Have I Done to Deserve This?* (1984). Inaccessible to the public at large, this work was not shown in theaters and may never be released on DVD owing to El Deseo's inability to clear the music rights. Shot on low-definition video, *Trailer* boasts features that are typical of Almodóvar's film work at the time, but exaggerated and coarsened. The cursory plot centers on a desperate housewife who abandons her home for a young lover, a decision that leads to murder. More interesting than the plot, however, is the form: the story is told almost entirely through stylized sequences of lip-synching to old songs. The mise-en-scène (especially the settings and wardrobe) appears improvised and gaudy, while the cast is relatively unknown, with the exception of longtime collaborator Bibi Anderson, a transgendered Spaniard who had achieved considerable popularity as a TV show hostess and was to reappear in *Kika* (1993). Like the little-seen and extravagantly titled Super-8s such as *The Fall of Sodom* (1975) and *Fuck, Fuck, Fuck Me, Tim!* (1978) that came before *Pepi, Luci, Bom*, *Trailer* seems something of an embarrassment to the Almodóvar brothers, perhaps because its low production values now look incompatible with the director's later perfectionist artistic ambitions. Apparently considering it of interest only to an academic audience, El Deseo screened *Trailer* along with a preview of *Bad Education* for a group of scholars at a symposium held at the Universidad Castilla–La Mancha in 2003 to celebrate the establishment of an archive devoted to Almodóvar's cinema. Most interesting in *Trailer* (whose very title proclaims allegiance to film even in a work made for TV) is the integration of documentary footage of the premiere of *What Have I Done to Deserve This?* into the fictional plot. Marking it from the very outset, television is inseparable from Almodóvar's cinematic history.

Almodóvar's status as an auteur has grown considerably over the last few years in a process that has, ironically enough, been reliant on television, that most maligned of media. In 2000, the state minority channel TVE2 broadcast a show that celebrated the twentieth anniversary of the theatrical release of *Pepi, Luci, Bom*. As Nuria Triana notes (142), the show marked the definitive "canonization" of Almodóvar: *Pepi, Luci, Bom* was the first film to be shown in a series known somewhat paradoxically as "Modern Classics" *(Clásicos modernos)* and, moreover, in a strand called, with gentle irony, *versión española*, or "Spanish version," the name usually given to films dubbed in Spanish. In a format common to Spanish TV but little known in the U.K. or the United States, critical discussion bookends the screening of the feature. The show was promoted as bringing together for the first time in many years the director and his former collaborator Carmen Maura, who would later return to work with Almodóvar in the recent *Volver* (2006). But the show also embodied the intimate connections between cinema and television in the person of its attractive and articulate presenter, Caetana Guillén Cuervo, who had just appeared as the main character's best friend in *All about My Mother* and who is, in real life, the daughter and sister of the two actors who played the father and son detectives in *Law of Desire*. TV, the most domestic of media, is here revealed to be a family business. While the two stars' wardrobe was unexceptional (Almodóvar was clothed in a basic black top and jeans and Maura in a relatively modest wraparound dress), one unusual feature of the studio setup heightened the potential conflict of the reunion: the speakers were confined to an arena-like circle around which the camera crew was shown to be at work. Occasional crane shots even allowed the audience to observe Almodóvar, Maura, and Guillén Cuervo from alarmingly vertiginous high angles.

Within this already charged and suspenseful setting, the somewhat tense studio interviews were interrupted by the presenter's frequent direct addresses to the audience, in short pieces to the camera that introduced brief messages from "survivors" of *Pepi, Luci, Bom* and the *Movida,* some sadly decayed, wishing all involved a "happy birthday," that is to say, a "happy twentieth anniversary." Documentary footage of momentous events of the period completed the historical picture: the passing of Franco, the legalization of the Communist Party, and the death of Enrique Tierno Galván, popular and progressive mayor of Madrid. Interestingly, this public narrative, electronically treated to resemble the gaudy graphics of the *Movida,* was juxtaposed with the personal history of the dramatic relationship between the director and the actress, which was presented with on-screen titles: "A very special union," "Falling out," "Reencounter," and "To be continued." Famous film careers were thus likened to episodes in a TV series.

In the course of the conversation, Maura, who was already an established actress in 1980, stressed how much she had learned about filmmaking from the extended and improvised shoot of *Pepi, Luci, Bom,* while Pedro stated that Carmen was a perfect "instrument" for his direction, although he had received no training for this, his first feature. Maura's wary looks and guarded comments contrasted with Almodóvar's unperturbed fluency. Triana is surely right to stress that this prime-time broadcast marked a definitive change in what is understood by "Spanish national cinema": the shift from an exclusive definition of "quality" or "social-realist" film to an inclusive "discourse of diversity" that permitted a wider range of "generic and aesthetic choices" (142). Be that as it may, what we find here, in the emblematically named *versión española,* are two modes of perception that are typical of the medium. As Palacio has noted (106), television in Spain has served as a "pedagogy" or education in personal and national history; and as Ellis has suggested (9, 72), it functions in many countries as a form of "witnessing" or "working through" of social issues, whether subjective or objective, that can have no definitive conclusion. The legacy of the *Movida* and Almodóvar's earliest works, as well as their significance for recent Spanish history, thus continue to be addressed two decades later on television.

Thematics

Over the last three decades, the post-Franco reform of state broadcaster TVE has witnessed the advent of regional and commercial channels; the controversy over *telebasura* or "trash TV"; and the recent explosion of locally produced quality fiction. If we turn from a consideration of the industrial aspects of Almodóvar's production to look at the content of the films themselves, we see that over the course of the same period Almodóvar has given us a hidden history of TV, or, rather, of the electronic image in Spain.

A brief survey of Almodóvar's creative references to television genres and styles might go as follows: with *Pepi, Luci, Bom* we see not just the commercial for adult panties as diapers mentioned earlier but also a black-and-white TV talk show that plays in the background of a scene in which a policeman rapes Pepi's neighbor, the minor character Charo. In *What Have I Done to Deserve This?* we are treated to a commercial for coffee that "you will never forget" (the coffee is so hot that when it accidentally spills it scars the consumer's face for life) and an idiosyncratic performance of a traditional campy song on the theme of prostitution, "La bien pagá," or "The Well-Paid Woman." Originally performed by Miguel Molina, Almodóvar and musical crony McNamara, who used as a first name Fanny or Fabio interchangeably, reprise the song to comic effect. For its part, *Matador* begins with clips of slasher footage, which a retired bullfighter turned serial killer (Nacho Martínez) enjoys in feverish isolation on his home TV; it also includes a jab at partisan news reporting, which features a strident journalist who denounces the "breathtaking cynicism" of a lawyer (in reality also a serial killer, played by Assumpta Serna) who defends a client accused of murder.

In *Law of Desire*, a more indulgent reporter played by Rossi de Palma conducts a TV interview with the main character, Pablo, a gay film director played by Eusebio Poncela. In *Women on the Verge of a Nervous Breakdown*, Pedro's real-life mother plays a newscaster whose aged appearance and halting delivery make her most comically incongruous in the role. In *Tie Me Up! Time Me Down!* (1990), the director within the film, played by veteran Francisco Rabal, is addicted to the porn videos of his star, Marina, played by Victoria Abril. The latter also plays a newsreader who confesses to a murder live on air in *High Heels* (1991). *Kika*, for its part, is structured entirely around the new genre of reality TV in which Victoria Abril, in yet another role, plays Andrea Scarface (Andrea "Caracortada"), an intrusive reporter who broadcasts footage of the rape of the title character on national television. *The Flower of My Secret* (1995) begins with a training video on closed-circuit

Francisca Caballero, Almodóvar's mother, reading the news in the newscast featured in
Women on the Verge of a Nervous Breakdown *(1988). Photograph by Macusa Cores.*
Copyright Macusa Cores/El Deseo.

Rebeca (Victoria Abril) will soon confess on live television to the murder of her husband, while
her copresenter Isabel (Miriam Díaz Aroca) looks on, in High Heels *(1991). Copyright El Deseo.*

TV for medical personnel specialized in organ transplants and features a song by Chavela Vargas heard by main character Leo (Marisa Paredes) on a TV playing in a bar. *Live Flesh* and *All about My Mother* offer glimpses of classic movies broadcast on TV to very different households: Luis Buñuel's *The Criminal Life of Archibaldo de la Cruz* (1955) plays in the background of the apartment of a junkie (Francesca Neri), and Joseph L. Mankiewicz's *All about Eve* (1950) plays in a loving household headed by a single mother (Cecilia Roth). The otherwise serious *Talk to Her* features a single farcical scene in which a prurient talk-show host (Loles León) literally struggles to hold down her interviewee on set. And *Bad Education,* as we have seen, condemns its antihero, ambitious for a film career, to a postcinematic "living death" in television.

Andrea Scarface (Victoria Abril), the ruthless television reporter in Kika *(1993). Photograph by Jean-Marie Leroy. Copyright Jean-Marie Leroy/El Deseo.*

Although the sheer persistence of Almodóvar's engagement with television is striking, other observations are in order. First, his films cite a wide range of TV genres such as commercials, variety shows, news, reality shows, and feature films, but, perhaps significantly, not made-for-TV drama. Second, they cover several related but distinct electronic media: broadcast television; home-edited videotape played on private VCRs; professionally recorded videotape broadcast live and recorded, and closed-circuit TV used as an instructional tool in the workplace. Finally, the features reveal various modes of reception or consumption: intense solitary voyeurism; sociable family viewing in the home; distracted communal attention in public places, and the hermetic loop of the closed-circuit camera and monitor, at once private and public, as in *All about My Mother,* where the main character's son, a nonprofessional, sits in on a video training session.

It is evident, then, that Almodóvar makes room for TV, in all its variety, even in his last films, which clearly constitute love songs to the medium of cinema. But if we look more closely at the early and later works we see changes in the relationship between elements from television and the films in which they are included. With respect to the earlier films, it is noticeable how often Almodóvar cuts straight into a TV sequence without giving the audience any formal cue in the editing (the equivalent of an establishing shot in a normal cinematic sequence) to orientate us. Thus, with *Pepi, Luci, Bom,* the commercial, which was actually shot before the film itself and thus constitutes a rare precinematic fragment in Almodóvar's oeuvre, simply begins to play in full frame. Although the effect is willfully bizarre, the formal conventions of advertising are observed: omniscient voice-over, direct address to the camera, mood music, and final tagline "Whatever you do, wear PONTE knickers." After the commercial finishes, Almodóvar cuts to a screening room. As the lights come up, the main characters give desultory opinions on what is now revealed as Pepi's debut spot. The cheerful scatology of the advertisement and its fragmentary nature ally it with the rest of the film, composed as it is of barely connected episodes that involve an incontinent minor character, a wide array of genres and styles ranging from musical performances to vérité reportage, and hand-drawn intertitles.

By the time of *What Have I Done to Deserve This?,* televisual material is more integrated into the film proper. Once more, Almodóvar cuts directly to a bizarre musical number in which he and McNamara, dressed as nineteenth-century lovers, lip-synch the aforementioned "La bien pagá." But this time we are given a brief wide shot of the studio that includes the cameras trained on the set, information that would normally be inaccessible to the audience watching at home. The film then cuts to that domestic audience, in this case an enthusiastic grandmother (Chus Lampreave) and her young grandson, nauseous after taking drugs. Another cut follows, to a third location: the bedroom in which Carmen Maura's Gloria pleads with her husband for money as he makes perfunctory love to her. While the lyrics of the song clearly comment on the main action (the poorly paid modern housewife is ironically compared to a "well-paid" prostitute), the entire scene effectively deconstructs the very notion of family viewing by way of a grotesquely implausible variety show (a genre that survived longer in Spain than in the U.K. or the United States) and its variously alienated viewers. Although TV professionals sometimes talk of the "two televisual Spains," the one elderly and rural and the other modern and urban (Palacio and Contreras 187), Almodóvar here posits TV viewing as a kind of ironic communion of social extremes, analogous to other activities that grandmother and grandson perform together: doing homework, forging signatures, and gathering sticks—and lizards—from a dismal urban wasteland.

While the working-class characters of *What Have I Done to Deserve This?* watch television, one of the main characters of *High Heels* works in it. A member of Almodóvar's newly upmarket professional milieu, Victoria Abril's Chanel-suited Rebeca is a news anchor married to the mysteriously murdered CEO of a fictional private network. Rebeca's on-air confession to the murder is pivotal in the film. Although the entire film reveals an increasing interest in the apparatus and industrial practices of recently deregulated Spanish television, for the first time Almodóvar reveals to us the variety of audiences brought together by live national broadcasting and their differing responses to the electronic spectacle. Rebeca's improvised performance is redoubled on-screen by the alarmed sign-language interpreter who regularly accompanies her and framed by cutaways to her professional colleagues (the news-conscious director who instructs his production team not to pull the plug on the unfolding media event) and her private acquaintances (her celebrity mother and the judge who doubles as a transvestite chanteuse). The former, Becky (Marisa Paredes), looks on in horror; the latter, Judge Domínguez (Miguel Bosé), is prompted to take action to arrest Rebeca. The public display of intimacy in this sequence (Rebeca shows family snapshots to the camera) is typical of the (con)fusion of performance and essential being or identity that is held to be characteristic of postmodernism, but it is also oddly familiar in televisual genres and modes, because TV, unlike most film, uses such disparate styles all the time. Among other things, the scene points to a witnessing of a media event that implicates spectators emotionally even as they remain impotent observers: Rebeca's mother, strong-willed Becky, stares dumbfounded at the screen, unable to intervene.

In *High Heels,* then, television is central to the plot and themes of the film. But with *Kika,* which critics, perhaps dismayed by the televisual theme, tend to present as Almodóvar's least successful film, TV dynamics have wholly invaded cinematic space. As I have written elsewhere, in this early scattershot critique of reality shows (made some ten years before the genre was widely programmed in most markets), Almodóvar explores what Paul Virilio called "the vision machine": the confusion of presentation and representation, when an event can no longer be separated from its representation; the passage from vision to visualization, when the act of looking can no longer be separated from those instruments through which we see; and the waning of reality under the onslaught of technology (Virilio 13, 49). More precisely, *Kika* tracks the transition from celluloid, with its sense of dialectical duration (film is never immediate and presupposes some temporal distance from its object), to video, with its stress on the paradoxical incident or accident (the instantaneous character of video makes it ideal for the capturing of unexpected or incongruous events).[2] However, the film's attitude toward such social and technological change is at best ambivalent. Although it is ironic to see Almodóvar, once the champion of popular culture, editorialize against new forms of mass entertainment by mercilessly attacking the sensationalist TV reporter, Andrea, his own cinematic vision comes to be shadowed by the very electronic medium that he critiques. Arguably, the most dynamic scenes of the film occur when Victoria Abril's cyborg reporter tracks down "The Worst of the Day" for her exploitation program of the same name. For example, in one fast-moving sequence she pursues a jealous husband who has just shot his wife dead on camera. In his defense of the notoriously extended scene of the main character Kika's rape, which lasts for some seven minutes, Almodóvar appeals precisely to the confusion of presentation and representation characteristic of the vision machine; the film suggests, unconvincingly, that the real violation of Kika is not her physical rape but the broadcasting of it on television. Moreover, a blurry haze of low-definition video bleeds over into the movie, contaminating the typically glossy big-screen production values that are typical of Almodóvar by the time of *Kika*'s release in 1993.

But even here, in what may well be Almodóvar's most devastating take on TV, the vision of television is not wholly negative: *Kika* also re-creates the unlikely book discussion show "We Must Read More," hosted by Almodó-var's elderly mother, after whom the film itself is titled ("Kika" is the diminu-tive of "Francisca," his mother's name). Greeting the foreign author played by dubbed American actor Peter Coyote, she offers him a "little sausage" *(choricico)*; both the food and its name in the diminutive put the lie to TV's urban sophistication and increase the sense of its local particularity and domesticity. Moreover, Almodóvar's later films indicate that television remains central to his depiction of Spanish forms of sociality. *The Flower of My Secret* begins without editorial warning, with scenes of organ trans-plant donation, which are only later revealed to be closed-circuit training videos. Almodóvar then cuts to his heroine Leo, asleep in the stylish, clut-tered apartment where she is attempting to resurrect her career as a serious author. Here the video performance on "brain death," which precedes the representation of the "real" world, stands as a privileged metaphor for a crea-tive life and a romantic love that are also on life support: Leo's husband—like the romantic fiction she writes but despises—has betrayed her. By con-trast, in *Live Flesh,* junkie Elena's viewing of Buñuel's Mexican melodrama fully exemplifies the distracted attention that TV is often held to embody; desperate for a fix, Elena is heedless of the movie. But once more, the mate-rial shown on television embodies a vital precedent for the cinematic action to come: a fatal bullet rings out both on the screen and in the flat; a look of love will change lives on the film on TV and in Almodóvar's film itself. Elena will become the girlfriend of David, the wounded policeman played by Javier Bardem, who interrupted her listless TV viewing to save her from what he thought was an assailant.

Finally, in *All about My Mother,* Almodóvar suggests a deep bond between mother and teenage son by having them watch TV together. Although the dubbed transmission or *versión española* of *All about Eve* highlights the themes of female community, rivalry, and theatricality that will be developed in the film, the circumstances of *Eve's* consumption are perhaps more important: Manuela (Cecilia Roth) and Esteban (Eloy Azorín) sit together during an extended two shot, sharing the frame as they share the sofa, casually and intimately discussing the movie and their own lives. As we have seen else-where in Almodóvar's work, here television, no less than the theater which is the medium that is more prominently featured and discussed in this film, provides a precious opportunity for working through issues that are at once public and private, social and personal.

The process continues in *Volver* (2006), also the story of the relationship between mothers and children, here daughters. In one important subplot, Agustina, a noble but simpleminded rural woman, goes on a TV talk show in a bid to find her missing mother. The ghoulish presenter asks intrusive questions before announcing to the world that Agustina has cancer and calling for a big round of applause from the studio audience. Almodóvar's condemnation of the horrors of television has rarely been as explicit since *Kika*. However, what is important about this plot strand is that Agustina is played by actress Blanca Portillo, who is best known in Spain from the five years she spent on a TV sitcom, Tele 5's smart and topical *7 Vidas* (which translates literally as "7 Lives," idiomatically as "9 Lives"). Once more, even as he editorializes against the evils of television, Almodóvar appeals to an actor whose skills have been honed in that medium and who is intimately familiar to a mass TV audience.

There is no doubt that Almodóvar is above all a great filmmaker and one who has mastered the technique of his chosen medium. His seventeen feature films to date have come to constitute a national narrative for many Spaniards

Agustina (Blanca Portillo) appears on TV looking for answers about her mother in Volver *(2006). Presenter played by Yolanda Ramos. Copyright El Deseo.*

in a way that only the critically valued medium of cinema can do. Like the best cinema, also, Almodóvar's films serve as potent vehicles for fantasy, a pleasure especially associated with the big screen. I have argued that part of Almodóvar's cinematic achievement is that he has engaged fully with the more domestic and mundane medium of television. Indeed, it is perhaps in that engagement, ambivalent and complex as it is, that Almodóvar's cinema comes closest to connecting with the social reality of post-Franco Spain.

NOTES

1. For more on Almodóvar's films on television, see my *Desire Unlimited* (89, 101–2).

2. For more on *Kika* and the interplays of film, video, and other media, see my *Vision Machines* (38–39).

WORKS CITED

Allinson, Mark. *A Spanish Labyrinth: The Films of Pedro Almodóvar.* London: I. B. Tauris, 2001.

Ellis, John. *Seeing Things: Television in the Age of Uncertainty.* London: I. B. Tauris, 2002.

Palacio, Manuel. *Historia de la televisión en España.* Barcelona: Gedisa, 2001.

Palacio, Manuel, and José Miguel Contreras. *La programación de televisión.* Madrid: Síntesis, 2001.

Smith, Paul Julian. *Contemporary Spanish Culture: TV, Fashion, Art, and Film.* Cambridge: Polity, 2003.

———. *Desire Unlimited: The Cinema of Pedro Almodóvar.* 2d ed. London: Verso, 2000.

———. *Vision Machines: Cinema, Literature, and Sexuality in Spain and Cuba, 1983–93.* London: Verso, 1996.

Triana, Nuria. *Spanish National Cinema.* London: Routledge, 2003.

Virilio, Paul. *The Vision Machine.* Trans. Julie Rose. London: British Film Institute, 1994.

Willoquet-Maricondi, Paula, ed. *Pedro Almodóvar: Interviews.* Jackson: University Press of Mississippi, 2004.

2 Queer Sound
Musical Otherness in Three Films by Pedro Almodóvar

KATHLEEN M. VERNON

Despite its long history of accompanying cinema, music in some sense is always potentially other. Film scholars have written of the classic film score's invisibility; its subordination to story, its submerged role as a guide—or goad—to emotions, and its suturing effects in providing the illusion of continuity against the fragmented character of the motion picture medium, effective to the extent that it remains unacknowledged.[1] Accordingly, music, when it emerges from its conventionally secondary role, shows itself for what it is and contests the presumed dominance of the visual track, represents a disturbing element, a source of possibly overpowering emotion and affective response as well as an opening to "extraneous" cultural or subjective references and associations. Such suspicion of music's nature and effects has an extended history in Western thought. In contrast to the other presumably more cerebral arts, music and especially song were held to be inextricably tied to the bodies that both produce its sounds and register its impact. Both Plato and Aristotle famously warned of music's moral ambiguity, while classical Greek literature thematized the ambivalent power of music vested in the female voice, on the one hand celebrating its beauty and capacity to immortalize heroic deeds, and on the other warning of its seductive charms and magical power to lure men to their destruction as manifest in the songs of the Sirens and Circe in the *Odyssey* (Brett 11; Segal 17–18). In English Renaissance writings, the linkage between women and music served to upbraid both for their "essentially changeable nature, unpredictable and sometime irrational . . . behavior" (Dunn 57). Music's sensuous sounds were said to give it the capacity to "penetrate the ear and so 'ravish' the mind" (ibid.). Theatrical and musical conventions across much of Europe kept women off the stage until well into the seventeenth century, their roles and vocal identities assumed by men and boys. The Roman Catholic Church, even as it sponsored the creation of a repertoire of sacred liturgical music, sought to contain and police the circumstances of performance. Concern over the underlying conflict between music's corporeal versus spiritual natures is expressed early on in Saint Augustine's discomfort at "being moved more by the voice than the words" of liturgical observance (Brett 11). Catholic doctrine banned women from singing in church, with soprano and alto vocal registers served through the use of boy singers and castrati, whose participation received at least tacit clerical approval until banned by the Vatican in 1878.[2]

A similar if differently grounded division over music's origins and effects emerges in psychoanalytic approaches to the role of sound and voice in human development and identity formation. The work of Guy Rosolato and Didier Anzieu privileges the sounds perceived in the "sonorous enve-lope" of the womb as the origin of the subject's emergence into selfhood. For Rosolato, the infant's sustained contact with the soothing and nourish-ing ("nutritive") voice of the mother provides "the first model of auditory pleasure" and the basis for all subsequent musical experience, conceived as the nostalgic fulfillment of an impossible return to a primordial harmony (81–82). Michel Chion articulates a more sinister understanding of that pri-mal scene in which the maternal voice not only enfolds but entraps, siren- or spiderlike, the infant in a web of sound (61). Michael Uebel summarizes a further view within psychoanalytic thinking that regards sound as a poten-tial source of primary trauma to the infant largely unprotected from intru-sive auditory stimuli. This exposure is said to produce "an early close (or 'symbolic') association between sound and the threatening external world" (7). In this conception, the practice of and appreciation for music arise as a defense mechanism born out of a need to process or master sonic chaos into orderly forms.[3]

Almodóvar's cinema has, from the beginning, acknowledged and even solicited this ambiguously charged potential of music, granting song and sound track a foregrounded role in his films. A number of critics have enu-merated the eclectic range of musical sources tapped by the director over the course of his cinema.[4] Where the earliest films largely reflected the punk-pop idioms of the post-Francoist cultural phenomenon known as the *Movida* (including Almodóvar's own compositions and performances with Fanny McNamara), the middle period, beginning with *Matador* (1986), featured a favored role for Latin American music and songs, the bolero in particu-lar, and provided for the deepening emotional resonance of those films. Almodóvar's subsequent collaboration with composer Alberto Iglesias, start-ing with *The Flower of My Secret* (1995) and continuing through his most recent films, suggests a further development in his conception of the role of music in film and arguably a new understanding of the relation between music and narrative and between songs and composed score.[5]

In an earlier article on "the songs of Almodóvar" I analyzed the privileged role accorded the bolero in *Law of Desire* (1987), *High Heels* (1991), and *The Flower of My Secret,* exploring the ways in which those films underscore the emotional expressivity of Latin American love ballads embedded in the unfolding narrative and wielded by characters as instruments of seduction and collective solidarity—a solidarity that includes not only fellow characters but spectators as well.[6] The present study represents a kind of reprise of that work and responds to a number of perceived changes in the emplotment of music, song, and voice in three of Almodóvar's later films, *All about My Mother* (1999), *Talk to Her* (2002), and *Bad Education* (2004). In all three films, the reliance on the affective and cultural associations of Latin American love songs largely drops away. In *All about My Mother* perhaps only Ismaël Lô's "Tajabone" takes on a protagonizing role comparable to the boleros "Lo dudo" (I Doubt It) or "Piensa en mí" (Think of Me) in the earlier films. In *Talk to Her,* songs function within set pieces, specifically, the performances by celebrated German dancer and choreographer Pina Bausch that open and close the film and Caetano Veloso's performance

The young Ignacio (Nacho Pérez), singing in Bad Education *(2004). Photograph by Diego López Calvín. Copyright Diego López Calvín/El Deseo.*

of "Cucurrucucú paloma" before a boundary-crossing cast of friends of Almodóvar and fictional characters. In these two films, song serves the cause of cultural mobility while freezing the advance of the narrative and inviting us to contemplate the transactions between geographic, artistic, sexual, and affective registers and identities. *Bad Education,* in contrast, represents in some respects a return to prior models of more integrated song and story lines, but with important differences. Perhaps more than any other, this film explores the promise and perils of music's alterity and alleged moral and psychic ambiguity, its utopian potential crossed with dystopic drives. I will explore two groups of songs in *Bad Education:* the semisacred repertoire of the boy Ignacio's soprano performances of "Moon River," "Torna a Sorrento"/"Jardinero" (Return to Sorrento/Gardener) and a choral solo in Rossini's *Kyrie;* and the mid-twentieth-century popular numbers recorded by Spanish actress and singer Sara Montiel and performed in lip sync by the adult Ignacio and another Sara imitator.

"Tajabone" and "Cucurrucucú paloma": From the Local to the Global

In his comments on the use of Senegalese musician Ismaël Lô's song in *All about My Mother,* Almodóvar speaks of the way that each element of a film's mise-en-scène must fit the underlying story, just as clothing, styles, or colors fit a given character. He tells of his determination, even before shooting began on location in Barcelona, to use Lô's "Tajabone," whose words he did not understand (they are in Wolof), as "the perfect blanket with which the city of Barcelona covered and protected the broken woman played by Cecilia Roth."[7] The director's remarks underline the nurturing quality attached to the song as the film's protagonist is portrayed as the recipient of the personified city/song's maternal tenderness. The word *manto,* which means "blanket," further evokes the metaphor of an enveloping sonic space that "covers and protects" the grieving woman.

Although long settled in Madrid at the start of the film, Manuela, played by the Argentine actress Cecilia Roth, is a traveler. When her son Esteban (Eloy Azorín) is killed in a car accident, Manuela journeys to northwest Spain following the trail of his donated heart to a recipient in the Galician city, La Coruña. Lô's song presides over a second trip, this time by train to Barcelona to look for her dead son's father. Her voice-over monologue explains the journey as the reverse of one she took eighteen years earlier when she was pregnant with Esteban; as the journey concludes, the first strains of the guitar opening are heard. We shift from the image of Manuela to a train's-eye view that conveys a sensation of hurtling through an unending tunnel that finally emerges into an overhead shot of a green forest, cued by harmonica accompaniment. An advancing panoramic view of Barcelona seen from above cuts, as the words of the song begin, to the side of a city bus that moves to reveal a taxi. The reverse shot shows us the partial facade of the Sagrada Familia, Antoni Gaudí's famous unfinished temple, which reverses again to a blurry image of the church reflected in the taxi window, which then lowers to reveal Manuela. The song continues as Manuela heads to her immediate destination, a cruising ground where transvestite prostitutes display their wares to the motorized prospective clients who circle around them. Australian art critic Robert Hughes's 1992 book *Barcelona* also makes a stop at the site, describing the scene that we later witness in Almodóvar's 1999 film:

> [T]he transvestite hookers stand widely separated, like idealized statues carved from [their] . . . former selves, . . . the older ones stalking and the younger ones teetering slightly in their high heels on the rutted surface. This one looks like Carmen Miranda, that one like the young Anita Ekberg, a third like Veruschka, and a fourth . . . resembles Sonia Braga. . . . The cars drive slowly by, jouncing on the ruts; turn; cruise back. There are battered little Renaults and big Mercedes. Their wheels raise a yellow fog of dust that hangs in the air. . . . Very rarely a vehicle will stop, and one of the apparitions, after a minute's palaver, will get in. But most of the cars keep circulating. Their drivers are there to look not buy. This is street theater of a curiously pure kind, a *tableau vivant* in which the audience moves but the actors do not. (46–47)

Where Hughes reads the scene as an "extreme metaphor" of Barcelona's identification with "cutting-edge design" and the efforts to remake the city in preparation for the Olympic Games (47), its role in Almodóvar's film has both more specific and broader implications.

Manuela's purposeful gaze moves beyond the tourist's vision of two very different "representative" Barcelonan cultural monuments—the Sagrada Familia and the place, according to Hughes, "known by its habitués as the Via Litúrgica"—in her search for her former husband. The Lô song, "Tajabone," with its plaintive harmonica, recurring chorus line, "Tajabone . . . ," and mixture of "exotic" African words and familiar musical gestures, works to grant the sculptural human figures a perhaps unexpected affective content. Lô grew up listening to American soul music and has come to be known as the "Bob Dylan of Senegal."[8] The song's musical hybridization acknowledges the mixed identities and hybrid bodies on display in the film, not just those of the transvestite prostitutes, but also the narrative trajectories and complex lives of the central characters. Within the broadening embrace of the song, as in the film itself, Africa crossed with North America meets Europe and intersects with Argentina just as Madrid connects with Barcelona via La Coruña.

Crossing similar spatial boundaries, the setting of Caetano Veloso's rendition of Tomás Méndez Sosa's 1954 Mexican classic "Cucurrucucú paloma" in *Talk to Her* at first glance presents several parallels to the performances by Pina Bausch's dance company that open and close the film. Both scenes mix reality and fiction, with internationally known performers appearing as themselves before an audience comprised, at least in part, of characters in the film. The close-up shots of the weeping Marco (Dario Grandinetti) return us to the film's opening sequence, in which Marco's tears in response to Bausch's ballet *Café Müller* catch the attention of his fellow spectator, Benigno (Javier Cámara), the male nurse whose care for his comatose patient Alicia (Leonor Watling) includes attending her favorite cultural events so that he might recount them to her the next day. Although the reasons behind Marco's emotional reaction to Bausch's poignant yet abstract work are at first unclear, in the case of "Cucurrucucú paloma," the character's tears might more obviously be prompted by the song's lyrics, the story of a man's inconsolable grief for his lost love.[9]

Despite these thematic and visual links, the syntactical positioning of the song sequence points to a deliberate attempt to cut loose from conventional narrative moorings—whether of geography, chronology, or causality. Marco sits before a laptop computer in the darkened room where his own comatose lover, Lydia (Rosario Flores), lies in a hospital bed down the hall from Benigno's patient. Two successive musical chords sound and the camera dollies in on Marco's expressionless face. The image cuts abruptly to an overhead shot of a submerged male swimmer gliding through glistening blue water as a rhythmic guitar picks up the sound cue.[10] The unknown man, smiling, breaks through the surface of the water as the voice of Caetano Veloso intones the opening phrase. The song and the scene it accompanies thus emerge as a kind of watery memory, a midsummer night's dream interlude characterized by the coming together, in the courtyard of a country house, of attractive, well-dressed friends and acquaintances, grouped before the performers: Veloso and a trio composed of guitar, double bass, and cello. As the camera tracks along the figures of the seated guests, the spectator identifies actors familiar from other Almodóvar films, Marisa Paredes and Cecilia Roth, juxtaposed with Marco positioned against a pillar just behind them and his lover Lydia looking on among a group of women. The festive scene responds to viewers' fantasies not simply of the lives of the rich

and famous but of an imagined community of talented international artists. As such, the sequence challenges the temporal and spatial coherence of
the film's fictional world, expanding its boundaries to embrace the broader
Almodovarian universe.[11] The song, as performed by Veloso and experienced by its on-screen listeners, plays a central role in conjuring up an alternate reality, a moment out of time and narrative action, an intimate space
of melancholy pleasure in which Lydia is miraculously restored to life. Key
to these effects is Veloso's defamiliarizing version of "Cucurrucucú paloma."
The Brazilian singer's lovingly careful articulation of the Spanish lyrics, the
slow tempo and unusual instrumentation—more characteristic of the modern Western art song than Cucurrucucú's original identity as a mariachi-
inflected *huapango*—works to strip away ethnic markers, transforming the
song from folkloric kitsch into an anthem of globalized utopia for spectators
and listeners both within and beyond the diegesis.[12]

The "Tajabone" and "Cucurrucucú paloma" sequences share a number of suggestive similarities, as do the songs themselves. In visual terms,
both scenes deploy a form of birth imagery in their depiction of a transition between geographic spaces (the journey from Madrid to Barcelona in
All about My Mother) and psychotemporal states (between the somber late-
night vigil in Lydia's hospital room and the remembered musical idyll in
Talk to Her). In the first instance, the Lô song acts as bridge over the journey
through a metaphoric birth canal visualized as a long dark tunnel that opens
onto a pastoral "green world" serving as the entry point to the Catalan capital. In the second, the shimmering pool and swimming man figure an emergence from a watery womb. In each case, the symbolic birth is invested with
positive connotations. What is suggested in these scenes is not the shock
of traumatic expulsion from a uterine Eden but rather rebirth or regenera-
tion: the promise of eventual healing for the grieving mother Manuela and
a temporary respite from sorrow and loss in the case of Marco's recovered
memory of Lydia's love.

With respect to the specific role of the songs, both serve to create
moments rich with symbolic resonances and positive affect that stand apart
from their immediate narrative context. Indeed, what is striking about the
function of "Tajabone" and "Cucurrucucú," in contrast to the songs in earlier
Almodóvar films, is their abstraction from the story line. Unlike the boleros, "Encadenados" (Enchained), "Lo dudo," "Piensa en mí," or "Dolor y vida"
(Pain and Life), these songs are not directly implicated in the histories of the
characters. They are no longer instrumentalized as the vehicle of emotional

excess, expressing forbidden desire or unexpected tenderness between lesbian (the Mother Superior and Yolanda in *Dark Habits*) and gay lovers
(Pablo and Antonio in *Law of Desire*) or a mother and daughter (Becky del
Páramo and Rebeca in *High Heels*), or serving as the emblem of a shared life
philosophy (Leo and her editor Ángel in *The Flower of My Secret*). In those
films, Almodóvar appropriated the sentimental content and cultural associations of the Latin American bolero of the 1940s and 1950s for his own and
his characters' ends, at the same time giving new, commercial life to a familiar pan-Hispanic repertoire.[13] The use of the songs in *All about My Mother*
and *Talk to Her* goes further still in detaching the music from its original
cultural context. Freed from their roots in local traditions, "Tajabone" and
"Cucurrucucú paloma" no longer signify solely or primarily within those
borders, but neither do they "belong" to the characters, or even to the director Almodóvar, in the same way as the earlier "songs of Almodóvar." Both
songs propose a horizon of reception that is simultaneously intimate and
expansive. "Tajabone"'s blanket of sound not only soothes the wounded
spirit of Manuela but also softens the artificial contours of what for Hughes
is voyeuristic spectacle, altering and amplifying the spectator's perspective
in the process. As we have seen, the performance of "Cucurrucucú paloma"
enacts a moment of idyllic community and musical enchantment whose
effects and appreciation extend beyond the fictional frame.

Finally, in both their function and their symbolic imagery, the two song
sequences recall the utopian fantasy of music as the vestige of an originary
experience of plenitude and bliss rooted in an intrauterine "memory" of the
mother's voice. Without fully embracing the version of the psychoanalytic
master narrative deployed by Rosolato and Anzieu, one can still appreciate the suggestive power of their model for understanding the affective and
physiological potency of music and song, particularly within a cinematic context. This formulation is also helpful in conveying the special poignancy of
intensely felt musical pleasure, its intimations of separation and loss, experienced as the sense memory of a never-to-be-recovered unity and wholeness.

Voice and Vocality: Sound and Meaning in Bad Education

Caetano Veloso's performance of "Cucurrucucú paloma" does not in fact
mark his first "appearance" in Almodóvar's cinema. The Brazilian singer's
voice, heard in a recording of "Tonada de luna llena" (Song of the Full Moon)
played over the credits of *The Flower of My Secret,* precedes his actual physical presence by several years. The moving effects of that voice on the lis-

tener are explicitly evoked in *Talk to Her* near the conclusion of the song sequence when Marco, having walked away from the group, seeks to explain his response to Lydia, noting, "that Caetano really makes my hair stand on end." The singer's earlier performance of "Tonada," with its eerily beautiful falsetto in the opening phrases and a text that recalls the hypnotic language of Lorca's "Romance de la luna, luna," prefigures Marco's reaction through a particularly vivid demonstration of Veloso's distinctive vocal style and character. Singers are trained to manage the change of registers from lower to higher-pitched sounds so as to mask the existence of corporally differently sourced voices, chest, and head; Veloso does so skillfully, but in a way such that the passage from one to another is thrilling and dangerous.[14] In this he shares with other featured singers in earlier Almodóvar films, Bola de Nieve and Chavela Vargas preeminent among them, a certain hybrid vocal texture and androgynous quality: what Néstor Leal identifies as "voces mulatas" (mulatto voices) (24) and Iris Zavala compares to the voices of castrati (23). The recurring use of such striking vocal types testifies to Almodóvar's fascination with androgynous and uncanny voices, with "feminine" sounds that issue from male bodies (or the reverse) and with the disturbing power over listeners that ensues.

Similarly androgynous and uncanny voices characterize the complex sound world and vocal types of *Bad Education*. In an undated dialogue between Veloso and Almodóvar reproduced on the Club Cultura Web site, the two engage in an explicit discussion of voices, vocal types, and mothers:

> VELOSO: My feminine identification is my voice. I sing like my mother; I learned to sing with her and when I sing—I have a song that says "My mother is my voice"— I feel that she is with me.
> ALMODÓVAR: I had a voice that was sweet like yours. A white or blank voice [voz blanca] as the Salesian brothers called it. It's true; it made me very embarrassed and for that reason I've never included it in one of my films. (Rodríguez 4)[15]

The emotionally charged vocal memories prompted by the exchange between the director and the singer point beyond the utopian vocal meanings expressed in the earlier films to the ambivalence we have already noted attaching to what film theorists Mary Ann Doane and Kaja Silverman further explore in the context of cinema as the "trope of the maternal voice." Marked by "intensely positive or intensely negative affect," such auditory "appearances" cast their shadow over the film experience (Silverman 72). Through the perfect synchronization characteristic of classic cinema practice, characterized by the "subordination of the voice to the screen," the film sound track works to replicate the psychic contours of the womb's sonorous envelope within the theatrical space and thus to "sustain the . . . pleasure derived from the image of certain unity, cohesion, and hence, an identity grounded in the specta-tor's fantasmatic relation to his/her own body" (Doane 45). Any fissures within this seamless fusion of body and voice, such as the kind of excessive and uncanny vocal textures and performances so favored by Almodóvar, threaten to give way to a dystopic obverse, the negative fantasy of difference and destruction of the self (Silverman 73; Doane 45–46).[16]

The conversation between Veloso and Almodóvar cited above clearly took place prior to the filming of *Bad Education,* but it nevertheless reso-nates with many of the issues expressed there, for when Almodóvar turned to certain autobiographical elements from his own school years with the Salesian brothers, he also decided to share his talent as the choir soloist with the character of Ignacio.[17] The special quality of the "voz blanca" or "white voice" projected in the performances of the boy singer, Pedro José Sánchez Martínez, who dubs the two songs and choir solo sung on screen by the young Ignacio (Ignacio Pérez), exercises a defining role in the overall musi-cal character of the film. In the choral repertory for boy soprano voices the primary material is sacred in character, and within the sacred music tradi-tion the most celebrated settings are those for the feast of the Holy Innocents shortly after Christmas.[18] The vocal connotation of innocence, and innocents destroyed, is central to Ignacio's story, but its significance for the whole of the film is arguably more complex.

Strictly speaking, two of the songs that the young Ignacio sings are secu-lar: Henry Mancini's 1961 Oscar-winning hit "Moon River," originally sung by Audrey Hepburn in *Breakfast at Tiffany's,* and the version of the tradi-tional Neapolitan standard "Torna a Sorrento" rewritten for Father Manolo's birthday. However, the sacred associations of vocal type as well as the cul-tural context work to inflect both with a religious accent that stands in ten-sion with other more secular associations. Passing before the now aban-doned Cine Olimpo on their way to a reencounter with Ignacio's former teacher and abuser, Father Manolo (Daniel Giménez-Cacho), Ignacio (Gael García Bernal), dressed as his alter ego, Zahara, and his friend Paquito (Javier Cámara) mention *Breakfast at Tiffany's* along with the movies of Sara Montiel before the spectator is presented with the triply mediated setting of the performance of "Moon River" during Ignacio's riverside picnic with his schoolmates and Father Manolo. The complex chronologies, crossed identi-ties, and story within a story structure that characterize *Bad Education* are particularly on display in this sequence, which comes to us through multiple frames: the director Enrique (Fele Martínez), Ignacio's boyhood friend and schoolmate, reading/imagining Father Manolo reading/hearing Ignacio's short story, "The Visit," as narrated by the boy Ignacio. Guitar chords provide a bridge from Father Manolo's office to the pastoral scene of boys at play. Ignacio remains separated from his peers, next to Father Manolo who accompanies the song on his guitar. The camera alternates between medium shots of the singing boy and the priest and slow-motion segments depicting Ignacio's schoolmates' joyous frolicking in the water. At first, the lyrics seem to celebrate the boys' immersion in the natural splendor of the setting, but as the song advances we come to realize that the words allude to the offscreen seduction. The Spanish lyrics, adapted by Almodóvar, are strikingly different from the English original; they transform the wistful and wishful ode, replete with nature imagery—a nod to Mark Twain—and the prospect of finding happiness or contentment at "rainbow's end," into a much darker consideration of nature as the source of troubling secrets, "murky waters" *(agua turbia),* and a quasi-biblical knowledge of good and evil. In that sense, "Moon River" performs a similar function to the silent film *The Shrinking Lover* in *Talk to Her.* Just as the short film narrates and stands in for a sexual encounter between Benigno and the comatose Alicia, Mancini's song serves at once to allude to and mask, as the altered lyrics note, "what is hidden in darkness" ("qué se esconde/en la oscuridad"): the priest's sexual advances toward the boy.

Padre Manolo (Daniel Giménez Cacho) and Ignacio singing "Moon River." Photograph by Diego López Calvín. Copyright Diego López Calvín/El Deseo.

We never directly see the forced seduction: the music stops; Ignacio screams; the priest scrambles after him, apparently buttoning up his cassock, and the boy falls and strikes his head. Instead, the performance of the song itself conveys the disturbing sense of violation and loss of innocence. Ignacio and Father Manolo may be singing and playing a secular song from a film that the church certainly would not have considered appropriate for schoolboys, but both the context and Almodóvar's words lend it, as noted, a religious cast. In his commentary included on the U.S. DVD release, the director remarks that "Moon River" "is a mythic song that corresponds to a particular historical moment," but that it was not originally composed for boy soprano voices. And yet, this rendition contains echoes of mid- and late-1960s guitar masses and singing nuns that brought folk and even pop songs, as well as guitar accompaniment, into the liturgy. These sacred associations work to heighten the transgressive impact of Father Manolo's actions, while also seeming to intensify and inflame further the priest's desire for the young boy with the beautiful voice.

During each of Ignacio's three vocal performances ("Moon River"; the solo in Rossini's *Kyrie,* first heard during the soccer game celebrating Father Manolo's birthday and naming as school director, then segueing into a scene of the choir at mass; and "Torna a Sorrento"), the camera cuts from the singer to Father Manolo as he watches the boy. In each instance, the priest's expression reveals an impassioned mix of seemingly contradictory emotions, desire mingled with regret and guilt. Music—sacred, secular, or a provocative mixture of both—exercises a familiar role here, as a stimulus and vehicle of outsized emotion that either cannot or dares not find expression in other settings. The *Kyrie* likewise presides over Ignacio's first meaningful encounter with Enrique, in an exchange of prolonged looks, when during the soccer game the former deliberately shoots wide of the goal defended by the latter. In the church scene that follows, Ignacio stares down from the choir loft at Enrique, who turns to receive his gaze. At the same time, as we noted, Father Manolo appears nearly overcome by the sight and sound of the boy, sacred and profane love converging in his celebration of the mass.[19] The priest's "reception" is evocative of the effects that Phillip Brett and others recall from medieval and early-modern discussions of beauty in music as "'ravishing' the sense or the soul" (Brett 11; Dunn 57).

This "sacrilegious" fusion of sacred and secular continues with the third song, Father Manolo's and Father José's reworking—the sound-track album credits Father Manolo—of "Torna a Sorrento" as "Jardinero, Jardinero." Like the writer-director Pablo (Eusebio Poncela) in *Law of Desire,* in several respects the model for the character of the adult Enrique, Father Manolo seeks to script the beloved's expression of love. The clearly allegorical words of the song cast Father Manolo in the role of the "gardener" tending to the "flowers" that are his charges. The gardener is said to nurture the flowers, bringing them to blossom with flaming hues. The figure of the gardener in his garden is, of course, evocative of common liturgical and biblical tropes that identify Christ as the shepherd with his flock or the apostles as fishers of men.[20] Although the on-screen audience of priests seems to miss the song's double entendres, with flowers and blossoming functioning as a reference to sexual experience and sexual maturation, they are not likely to be lost on the offscreen public.

In their collection of essays, *Embodied Voices,* Leslie Dunn and Nancy Jones propose the concept of "vocality" to refer to the function of the voice as a material link and articulation between performance and reception, body and culture, self and other (2). That multidimensional understanding of the role and effects of the singing voice and song seems particularly illuminating for analyzing Almodóvar's film. Vocal music in *Bad Education* enables contradictory drives and opposed identities and desires. If "Moon River" provides the occasion for Ignacio's literal "fall" from innocence in a garden of good and evil, it also carries the cultural reminder of *Breakfast at Tiffany's* and other movie viewings that he shared with Enrique and that function as not-so-coded markers of a precocious gay identity. The boundaries between sacred and secular, the expressions of divine and profane love, are continually breached through song. Father Manolo manipulates his pupil's musical talent, co-opting the boy's ethereal and angelic "voz blanca" for the indulgence of his own darker passions. Ignacio himself makes use of the *Kyrie* to signal his budding love for his friend.

The interarticulation of body and voice, vocality and identity also shapes the complicated adult histories of the characters. Try as he might, Enrique is hard-pressed to recognize his "first love" Ignacio in the young man who presents himself in his production office one day. Father Manolo, subsequently known as Mr. Berenguer (played by a different actor, Lluís Homar), much later tells Enrique that the "real" adult Ignacio (Francisco Boira) "wasn't the Ignacio that you and I loved," but neither, of course, is Juan (Gael García Bernal), Ignacio's younger brother who contrives to assume his role. Both Ignacio's decline and Juan's imposture are figured in their efforts to embody some version of the former's boyhood identity.

Gael García Bernal as Zahara, the femme fatale in **Bad** Education. *Photograph by Diego López Calvín. Copyright Diego López Calvín/El Deseo.*

Ignacio thus appears as a kind of fallen angel, trapped in the way station of a body that is no longer male but not yet fully female. The female impersonator Zahara, the dual creation of both Ignacio and Juan, represents the fullest projection of the film's "lost object," the boy singer's vocal power and pathos now embodied by a femme fatale and siren who would transport men to their destruction.

Enrique too has an investment in the elaboration of Zahara. Her first and only singing performance takes place early in the film and is originally framed as the imagined product of Enrique's reading of Ignacio's semiautobiographical story, "The Visit." The subsequent struggle between the director and Ignacio/Juan over the latter's fitness to play the role is complicated by actor Gael García Bernal's prior appearances in the film: in fact, he plays all three roles, Ignacio, Juan, and Zahara. Introduced onstage by the clownish Paquito, Bernal's Zahara, dressed in a form-fitting Gaultier gown, is a dazzling, if static, fish—or rather mermaid—out of water in a provincial drag revue, "La Bomba."[21] Cued by an insinuating saxophone line, the camera slowly ascends the body of the performer, only to center for the brief duration of the scene on the face of Zahara in three-quarter profile. Borrowing

the voice and mannerisms of Spain's best-known, homegrown diva, Sara
Montiel, the character lip-synchs a single verse from that mid-century clas-
sic of sexual innuendo, Oswaldo Ferrés's "Quizás, quizás, quizás" (Perhaps,
Perhaps, Perhaps).[22]

While the choice of song genre represents a significant shift from Ignacio's boyhood repertoire, the return to the romantic Latin ballad on the part
of Almodóvar signals further changes as well. Zahara directs her musical
seduction toward a young man seated in the front row who will later turn
out to be the fictionalized Enrique, but the calculating and truncated performance leaves us far from the ecstatic release and emotional refuge, characteristic, according to Carlos Monsiváis, of the bolero's utopian address to
its audience (177).[23] Montiel's husky, carnal voice jars with the cool, bottle-
blond perfection of Zahara's features, the diva's familiar persona eclipsed by
the Mexican actor Gael García Bernal's own celebrity aura. If the goal of a
successful female impersonator is to make the spectator aware of the coexistence of contradictory identities, and ultimately of the performative nature
of gender roles while simultaneously embracing the illusion, then Zahara
can be said to fall short. As we later see, Ignacio/Juan approaches the role of
Zahara with drama school diligence, arranging an apprenticeship of sorts
with a Sara imitator, Sandra. Her subsequent performance of Montiel's high-
kitsch number, "Maniquí parisien" (Parisian Mannequin), exudes a physicality and humanity, emblematic of what Eve Kosofsky Sedgwick calls the "generosity" of camp, that are missing from Zahara's act (156).

It is not simply the obvious mismatch between voice and body that renders Juan's identity suspect. In his attempt to lay claim to the moving emotional meaning of the singing voice once wielded by his brother he functions
only as the agent of loss and destruction, leaving a trail of deception and
betrayal of those who would love him: his brother Ignacio, Father Manolo/
Mr. Berenguer, and Enrique. To that extent, his performance achieves the
obverse of the cinematic and musical fantasies of the unified subject and the
utopian fusion of self and other, giving form instead to their dystopic double,
invoked by Mary Ann Doane as the "trauma of dispersal, dismemberment,
difference" (45). As if to reinforce the sense of absence and mourning, an
uncanny prolongation of Ignacio's original voice continues to inhabit the
film, as traces of the sacred repertoire seem to seep from the diegetic song
sequences of Ignacio's boyhood to the composed score, from the short story
within a film imagined by the director Enrique to Enrique's frame narration and Berenguer's own retelling of Ignacio and Juan's history. Two nearly

identical musical cues, one accompanying Enrique's trip to Ignacio's home in Galicia in search of the truth about his friend, and the second arising just before Juan and Berenguer's murder of Ignacio, begin with an instrumental quotation of Schubert's "Ave Maria" and resolve in a wordless chorus. Ultimately, in *Bad Education,* "sound represents precisely what is most disturbing about the other, namely its intrusiveness and power to haunt" (Uebel 2).

With its power to threaten or soothe, unsettle or console, musical sound remains a crucial element in Almodóvar's cinema. The song settings in his films embrace the dual inheritance of music in cultural history, engaging both the promise of utopian release into pleasure outside time or narrative and the dystopian intimations of loss or entrapment. True to its divided nature, music proves both elusive and undeniably material. On the one hand, Almodóvar's cinema insists on the sensuous idiosyncrasies of distinctive vocal textures, grounding musical production and reception in the body, but on the other, and to an increasing degree in the three films studied here, it works to expand and liberate the expressed musical meanings from their cultural origins and performance traditions. Music and song enable mobility and migration, as do the film and recording technology that carries their traces between continents (Latin America and Africa with Europe and the United States), between margin and center, between the sacred and the profane, and between gender and sexual identities. In that respect, music in Almodóvar is always "queer," in the sense of the word as understood by Alexander Doty: inclusive rather than exclusive, oppositional in its resistance to fixed boundaries and stable positionings, and dangerous in its fearless investigations of moral ambiguities at the heart of "culture's erotic center" (72–73).

NOTES

1. Although recent film musical scholarship has offered more nuanced considerations of the relation between musical score and film narrative, Claudia Gorbman's account continues to provide the dominant paradigm.

2. Contemporary musicological scholarship in gender studies and queer theory has sought to dissect the ideological underpinnings of such historical conceptions of music's destabilizing role, often linked to gender dualities. Beyond the goal of debunking such mystifications, the work of many writers and critics is clearly energized by the prospect of claiming music's "irrational" and disruptive force for dissident and previously marginalized identities as women, gays, and lesbians. The consequences of these approaches and the role of queer theory in particular are noted by Mary Ann Smart, who remarks on the new attention devoted to issues of staging and performance, "until recently . . . relegated

to the margins of critical discourse, as if the actual presence of either body or voice could overwhelm analysis with an ungraspable excess of materiality" (9). See also the books and anthologies by Koestenbaum; Brett, Wood, and Thomas; Dunn and Jones; and Solie.

3. Music in this conception is not opposed to noise but is considered as a form of organized or instrumentalized noise, partaking of and channeling the disruptive power of the latter (Uebel 8, 3–4). On the relation between music and noise, see also the work of Jacques Attali.

4. See the works by Allinson, Vidal, Yarza, and Varderi.

5. On Almodóvar's collaboration with Iglesias, see Vernon and Eisen.

6. See Vernon. My title alludes to the song compilation, *The Songs of Almodóvar,* issued by El Deseo and EMI (the U.S. version under license to Metro Blue, a division of Capitol Records), including music from his first eleven films (through *The Flower of My Secret*). Among the issues that I explore in the article is the director's "rebranding" of a number of classic boleros under the label Almodóvar. In December 2007 the director presented an expanded two-CD collection, *BSO Almodóvar,* comprising twenty-nine songs from his films.

7. In the liner notes to "Viva la tristeza" (Long Live Sadness), we find Almodóvar's compilation of the songs to which he listened while writing the script for *Talk to Her* and which he offers as the "secret sound track" of the film.

8. See the Internet biographies listed in the Works Cited.

9. For an insightful reading of the ballet within the film, see Gutiérrez Albilla.

10. In a suggestive reading of this sequence, Brad Epps pointed out to me the allusion to David Hockney's evocative series of paintings of California swimming pools and, with it, the disruptive interjection of a homoerotic subtext in the midst of a heterosexual love story.

11. Almodóvar's DVD commentary reveals the full intersection of fiction and biography in the scene that was filmed at the director's own country house. In the published script of the film, he refers to his first encounter with Veloso's version of "Cucurrucucú paloma" and its effects on him. He had traveled to Rio de Janeiro to promote *The Flower of My Secret*. Tired after much travel, he had to force himself to attend a party at Veloso's home. While there, he writes, the singer "played his version (it is a reinvention more than a version) of 'Cucurrucucú paloma' and all my ills disappeared" (228).

12. It is instructive to compare Veloso's version with the best-known recordings of the song by *ranchera* singer Lola Beltrán. Beltrán herself figures in the Almodóvar discography for her performance of the opening number of *Women on the Verge of a Nervous Breakdown,* "Soy infeliz" (I'm Unhappy).

13. See Vernon 166, 173.

14. Wayne Koestenbaum elaborates on the transgressive properties of the falsetto voice, the head voice as opposed to the "natural" chest voice, when produced by adult male singers. As he notes, "Codified voice production has never been happy with the falsetto, the sound of mystery, unnaturalness, absence. . . . The falsetto is part of the history of effeminacy" (164).

15. The original reads as follows: "VELOSO: Mi identificación femenina es mi voz. Canto como mi madre, aprendí a cantar con ella y cuando canto—tengo una canción

que dice 'Mi madre es mi voz'—siento que está conmigo. ALMODÓVAR: Yo tenía una voz dulce como la tuya. Una voz blanca como la llamaban los Salesianos. Es verdad, me daba mucha vergüenza y por eso no lo he puesto nunca en una película."

16. Almodóvar's play with asynchronous and mismatched voices and bodies extends beyond the strictly musical to numerous instances in which he mocks the conventions of film dubbing *(Women on the Verge of a Nervous Breakdown)* or voice-over (the voice actor Iván in the same film) or has characters engage in forms of ventriloquism, giving voice to sentiments originally expressed by others (in *Law of Desire* where the letter "ghostwritten" by Pablo for Juan is read out loud by Antonio and Ada). See the discussion in Epps, "Figuring Hysteria," especially pages 119–20.

17. Furthermore, the statement in the interview was not strictly true even at that earlier moment. In *Law of Desire,* Tina returns to her school chapel and sings along with the hymn played by the priest seated at the organ. She then identifies herself as a former boy soprano soloist. The scene offers our first clue as to Tina's original identity and contains the germ of what will become *Bad Education.*

18. My thanks to Cliff Eisen for this reference, as well as for overall musical guidance.

19. Almodóvar offers his own eloquently mixed metaphor in characterizing these scenes for the DVD commentary: "[El Padre Manolo] sólo tiene ojos para escuchar la voz de su alumno favorito" (Father Manolo only has eyes to hear the voice of his favorite student).

20. The positioning of the priests seated at a long table with Father Manolo in the center recalls Da Vinci's *The Last Supper,* and perhaps also Buñuel's musical/visual parody of the same in *Viridiana* (1961).

21. In the DVD commentary Almodóvar punningly characterizes the dress as "a miracle in cut and conception" ("un milagro de corte y concepción," a play on words deriving from the Spanish name for the traditional sewing classes to which young women of Almodóvar's generation were consigned, "corte y confección").

22. "Quizás, quizás, quizás" has proved a musical evergreen, recorded by countless performers in Spanish and English. Before Almodóvar's use of the song, another noteworthy recent cinematic appropriation includes the recurring presence of Nat King Cole's Spanish rendition in Hong Kong director Wong Kar Wai's *In the Mood for Love* (2000).

23. "Be inspired, become ecstatic, be moved, let those tears flow, place yourself in the only alternative at your disposal. . . . [The bolero] describes forms of care, tenderness and langour that—generally—exist only in the realm of song" (Monsiváis 177). It is significant that Monsiváis begins his history of the bolero with a "Postmodern Prologue" devoted to Almodóvar's use of the genre (166–67).

WORKS CITED

Allinson, Mark. *A Spanish Labyrinth: The Films of Pedro Almodóvar.* London: I. B. Taurus, 2001.

Almodóvar, Pedro, comp. *The Songs of Almodóvar.* Metro Blue. Capitol Records, 1997.

———. *Viva la tristeza.* Editions Milan Music. Warner Music International, 2002.

Anzieu, Didier. "L'envelope sonore du soi." *Nouvelle Revue de Psychanalyse* 13 (Sept. 1976): 161–79.

Attali, Jacques. *Noise: The Political Economy of Music.* Trans. Brian Massumi. Minneapolis: University of Minnesota Press, 2003.

Brett, Phillip. "Musicality, Essentialism and the Closet." Brett, Wood, and Thomas 9–26.

Brett, Phillip, Elizabeth Wood, and Gary C. Thomas, eds. *Queering the Pitch: The New Gay and Lesbian Musicology.* New York: Routledge, 1994.

Chion, Michel. *The Voice in Cinema.* Trans. Claudia Gorbman. New York: Columbia University Press, 1999.

Doane, Mary Ann. "The Voice in Cinema: The Articulation of Body and Space." *Yale French Studies* 60 (1980): 33–50.

Doty, Alexander. "There's Something Queer Here." *Out in Culture: Gay, Lesbian and Queer Essays on Popular Culture.* Eds. Corey K. Creekmur and Alexander Doty. Durham, N.C.: Duke University Press, 1995. 71–90.

Dunn, Leslie. "Ophelia's Songs in *Hamlet:* Music, Madness and the Feminine." Dunn and Jones 50–64.

Dunn, Leslie C., and Nancy A. Jones, eds. *Embodied Voices: Representing Female Vocality in Western Culture.* Cambridge: Cambridge University Press, 1994.

Epps, Brad. "Figuring Hysteria: Disorder and Desire in Three Films of Pedro Almodóvar." *Post-Franco, Postmodern: The Films of Pedro Almodóvar.* Eds. Kathleen M. Vernon and Barbara Morris. Westport, Conn.: Greenwood Press, 1995. 99–124.

Gorbman, Claudia. *Unheard Melodies: Narrative Film Music.* Bloomington: Indiana University Press, 1987.

Gutiérrez Albilla, Julián Daniel. "Body, Silence and Movement: Pina Bausch's *Café Müller* in Almodóvar's *Hable con ella.*" *Studies in Hispanic Cinemas* 2.1 (2005): 47–58.

Hughes, Robert. *Barcelona.* New York: Knopf, 1992.

"Ismaël Lô." *The African Music Encyclopedia.* Sept. 15, 2005. http://www.Africanmusic .org/artists/lo.html.

———. Sept. 15, 2005. http://www.rfimusique.com/siteEn/biographie_6034.asp.

Koestenbaum, Wayne. *The Queen's Throat: Opera, Homosexuality and the Mystery of Desire.* New York: Poseidon Press, 1993.

Leal, Néstor. *Boleros: La canción romántica del Caribe (1930–1960).* Caracas: Guyalbo, 1992.

Monsiváis, Carlos. "Bolero: A History." *Mexican Postcards.* Ed., trans., and intro. John Kraniauskas. London: Verso, 1997. 166–95.

Rodríguez, Andrés. "Entrevista." March 1, 2005. http://www.clubcultura.com/clubmusicos/ caetanoveloso/entrevistaindex.htm.

Rosolato, Guy. "La voix: entre corps et language." *Revue Française de Psychanalyse* 38.1 (Jan.–Feb. 1974): 75–94.

Sedgwick, Eve Kosofsky. *The Epistemology of the Closet.* Berkeley: University of California Press, 1990.

Segal, Charles. "The Gordon and the Nightingale: The Voice of Female Lament and Pindar's Twelfth *Pythian Ode.*" Dunn and Jones 17–34.

Silverman, Kaja. *The Acoustic Mirror: The Female Voice in Psychoanalysis and the Cinema.* Bloomington: Indiana University Press, 1988.

Smart, Mary Ann, ed. *Siren Songs: Representations of Gender and Sexuality in Opera.* Princeton, N.J.: Princeton University Press, 2000.

Solie, Ruth A. *Musicology and Difference: Gender and Sexuality in Music Scholarship.* Berkeley: University of California Press, 1993.

Uebel, Michael. "Acoustic Alterity." *Exemplaria* 16.2 (autumn 2004): 1–13. Electronic pre-print. http://web.english.ufl.edu/exemplaria/Cohen2003/mu.pdf.

Varderi, Alejandro. *Severo Sarduy y Pedro Almodóvar: Del barroco al kitsch en la narrativa y el cine postmodernos.* Madrid: Pliegos, 1996.

Vernon, Kathleen M. "Las canciones de Almodóvar." *Almodóvar: el cine como pasión.* Eds. Fran A. Zurián and Carmen Vázquez Varela. Cuenca: Ediciones de la Universidad de Castilla-La Mancha, 2005. 161–75.

Vernon, Kathleen M., and Cliff Eisen. "Contemporary Spanish Film Music: Carlos Saura and Pedro Almodóvar." *European Film Music.* Eds. Miguel Mera and David Burnand. London: Ashgate, 2006. 41–59.

Vidal, Nuria. *El cine de Pedro Almodóvar.* Barcelona: Destino, 1988.

Yarza, Alejandro. *Un caníbal en Madrid.* Madrid: Ediciones Libertarias, 1999.

Zavala, Iris. *El bolero. Historia de un amor.* Madrid: Ediciones Celeste, 2000.

3 Performing Identities in the Cinema of Pedro Almodóvar

ISOLINA BALLESTEROS

Performance is a central aspect of Pedro Almodóvar's cinema that at once underscores and outstrips, in its particularities, the general performative condition of cinema itself. Many of Almodóvar's characters are musicians, singers, stage and screen actors, dubbers, television personalities, drag queens, bullfighters, and others whose characterization is closely tied to performance. In many respects, Almodóvar's exposition of the performative nature of culture, particularly as it bears on gender and sexuality, seems to support John Mckenzie's claim that ours is an "age of performance" just as the seventeenth and eighteenth centuries were the "age of reason." With that general proposition in mind, I propose to reflect on the concepts and practices of performance in Almodóvar's films and, more specifically, to argue that it is in the representation of live performance that his characters most acutely (re)define or (de)construct their identities, generally in opposition to established social and sexual norms. As Elin Diamond notes, every performance contains traces of other performances and produces experiences whose interpretation depends on previous experiences (3). Indeed, the omnipresence of the prefix "re-" in discussions of performance—evident in such terms as "re-embody," "reinscribe," "reconfigure," and "re-signify"—signals an ethos of repetition, or rehearsal, that is especially pertinent to situations like the ones staged in Almodóvar's cinema. Prolifically self-referential, Almodóvar's films deploy motifs, situations, and styles whose varied repetition undergirds an authorially based developmental logic whose most common props, dispersed throughout a now extensive body of criticism, include youth and maturity. The tendency to read Almodóvar's production sequentially and to consolidate a chronological trajectory in which characters' emotional acts, especially when performed onstage (or when contemplating others performing onstage), are taken to be expressions of the director's changing perspectives, bears questioning, but it is nonetheless difficult to resist the sense that the reappearance of certain explicitly performative situations has a cumulative effect and, more specifically, that Almodóvar's work becomes "weightier" over time. But if performance, in its rehearsals and repetitions, buttresses notions of identity, authorial and otherwise, it is also prone to duplicity and ambiguity. It is to some of the ethical, political, and social implications of Almodóvar's penchant for performance that I shall attend in what follows.

According to Diamond, performance "may enable new subject positions and new perspectives to emerge, even as [or precisely because] the performative present contests the conventions and assumptions of oppressive cultural habits" (6). As Spaniards worked out a political and cultural transition to democracy, and as social and sexual marginalities achieved greater visibility and legitimacy, Almodóvar and other artists deployed the innovative potential of performance to contest long-standing, often deeply oppressive social and moral conventions. Almodóvar's first two feature films, *Pepi, Luci, Bom* (1980) and *Labyrinth of Passion* (1982), produced at the peak of the *Movida,* the cultural movement that shook Madrid and other parts of Spain out of the controlled lethargy of Francoism, bring the *Movida's* highly performative ethos center stage.[1] The first film showcases the rock-punk-glam scene whose central protagonists, such as singers Alaska (Olvido Gara) and McNamara (Fabio de Miguel), were Almodóvar's friends and nocturnal companions in the Madrid underground. The rehearsal and performance by Bom's punk group, the real-life Alaska and the Pegamoides, coexist alongside the parodic recycling of traditional musical styles like the zarzuela, a Spanish mode of lyric drama. The confrontation and mixing of old and new, tradition and innovation, is in evidence, for instance, when members of Bom's punk group, dressed in folkloric garb and singing the zarzuela "La verbena de la Paloma" (The Festival of the Paloma), avenge Pepi's rape by a fascistic policeman and, in the process, ridicule the remnants of Francoist Spain. Another performative moment exposes the phallic power that the policeman had so violently used as ultimately something of a joke: a contest for the biggest erect penis called "General Erections," for which Almodóvar himself appears on-screen as the master of ceremonies, pokes fun at the seriousness of the recently reinstituted general elections.

In *Labyrinth of Passion,* which centers on the hectic relationship between a photophobic sex addict named Sexilia (Cecilia Roth) and a promiscuous gay exile named Riza (Imanol Arias), Riza performs both onstage and offstage, filling in for an injured singer and hiding his "true" identity as a royal Tiranian—a veiled reference to the family of the deposed Shah of Persia whose fate peppered the pages of gossip magazines. Riza's gift for impersonation, conditioned as it is by external political forces, enables him to enter the inner circle of the *Movida,* epitomized by the appearance of Almodóvar and Fabio McNamara in a diegetic performance of a song, "Suck It to Me," at a crowded nightclub. It is by way of another musical performance, "Gran ganga" (Big Bargain) with the group "Ellos" (Them, in the masculine), that Riza, already living incognito, assumes his new rock-glam-identity. The group benefits from Riza's talents while Riza benefits from "downsizing" his true identity as the son of the king of "Tiran." Interestingly, Riza's entry into Madrid's night-life parallels the real-life entry of actor Imanol Arias into the *Movida.* As Chris Perriam has noted, Arias's "role as Riza . . . immediately associated him . . . with Almodóvar's early role in the process of 'refiguring' Spain his-torically and politically, . . . with the cultural shake-up which was the *Movida* in Madrid in the early 80's, . . . and with questions of gender and alterna-tive sexuality . . . encapsulated by the bringing together of the two real life, straight, close friends, Arias and [Antonio] Banderas, in a gay sex scene" (23). In both of Almodóvar's first feature films, performance in the most obvious and delimited sense of acting onstage is buckled by performance of a more general sort in which "real life" is itself implicated.

Pedro Almodóvar and Fabio McNamara (Fabio de Miguel) singing "Suck It to Me" in Labyrinth of Passion *(1982). Photograph by Pablo Pérez Mínguez. Copyright Pablo Pérez Mínguez/El Deseo.*

Performance and the Mediation of Desire

Along with the interplays between fiction and reality, performance also serves to mediate desire between subjects, be they characters, actors, directors, or spectators. Musical performances, as is well known, can engage, affect, and produce emotive links among the subjects who experience them, on and off the screen. In the aforementioned sequence from *Labyrinth,* the close-ups and shot-reverse-shots between Riza on stage and Sexilia as spectator provide the first evidence of what will quickly become an intense, life-altering relationship. During the performance, Almodóvar introduces the first flashback of many that appear in the film and provides both Sexilia, as spectator within the film, and the spectator of the film itself, with insight into the characters' future relationship: Riza and Sexilia, as the flashback dazzlingly indicates, had a traumatic childhood encounter on a beach, the source of their respective fears and desires (photophobia, erotomania, promiscuity, etc.). The encounter on a sun-drenched beach, there and then, punctuates the encounter on a glaringly lit stage, here and now, and suggests that the beach too is a performative site, one in which a fractured story of heterosexual desire comes to the fore.

The performative plays between past, present, and future, pretense and truth, are in full force in *Dark Habits* (1983) as well, a film that centers on the amorous relationship between a junkie named Yolanda (Cristina Sánchez Pascual) and a lesbian Mother Superior (Julieta Serrano) who oversees an iconoclastic convent of nuns that includes Sor Perdida (Sister Damned; Carmen Maura), Sor Estiércol (Sister Manure; Marisa Paredes), Sor Víbora (Sister Snake; Lina Canalejas), and Sor Rata de Callejón (Sister Alley Rat; Chus Lampreave). In this film, Almodóvar provides two examples of the activation of desire between women through the melodramatic performance of Latin American sentimental music. In the first one, the Mother Superior and Yolanda lip-synch in duet Lucho Gatica's bolero "Encadenados" (Chained), a performance that establishes the Mother Superior's role as would-be seducer and the increasingly libidinal dynamic between her and Yolanda. Later in the film, in anticipation of the melodramatic denouement of their love story, Yolanda celebrates the Mother Superior's birthday by performing I. Curet Alonso's "Salí porque salí" (I Left Because I Left) before an audience comprised of the nuns, a priest, a marquise who is the benefactress of the convent, and one of the nuns' sisters. Inasmuch as both performances suture the spectator through the use of close-up and shot-reverse-shot in what might be called a lesbian gaze, they replay the original heterosexual renditions of the songs in a manner that intensifies the melodramatic—and comic—play of emotion.

Paul Julian Smith has commented on the synchronization of music and image, "each reinforcing the effect of the other," in the performance of Gatica's bolero that effectively positions the spectator in the "unaccustomed place of the desiring woman" (31). *Dark Habits,* with its explicit reworking of the *melos*—or song— of melodrama, is Almodóvar's first serious foray into a genre with which he will come to be tightly associated. As if to underscore the musical power of melodramatic affect, Yolanda refers, after their duet, to the bolero's ability to "speak of the feelings" and to "tell the truth about life," an ability that is merely heightened as the very same bolero is superimposed on the last scenes of the film, thereby underscoring the Mother Superior's heartbreak. For all its similarities to heteronormative renditions, the performance of the bolero here signals something subversive. As Smith so perceptively puts it, *Dark Habits* "lesbianizes the patriarchal Word . . . by suggesting that a certain space for autonomous female desire has already been opened by that Word itself" (40). The subversion of the patriarchal "Word" to which Smith refers is further reinforced by the fact that both songs were composed and originally sung by men. The women, that is, appropriate the masculine voice, symbolically cast as the voice of God the father, and mouth the "Word" anew.

The replay of the word and the voice is neither incidental nor accidental, for, as Almodóvar has explained to Frédéric Strauss, the Spanish treatment— or performance—of religion has always melded idolatry and sensuality (37). Almodóvar clearly has in mind such ceremonies as the Easter processions in Seville and the public and private masses held by the Salesian priests with whom he studied as a boy—and who reappear, darkly, in *Bad Education* (2004). An integral component of the mystical poetry of the Spanish golden age, the melding of spiritualism and eroticism in works by Saint Teresa of Ávila, Saint John of the Cross, and Fray Luis de León established an amorous relationship between the "feminine" soul (*alma* in Spanish) and a masculine God that Almodóvar at once recycles and modifies, extracting, in the process, a transgressive performance from long-sanctified material.

The second sequence, when Yolanda performs at the Mother Superior's party, adds another twist to the replay of tradition and functions as a comic reduplication and camp deconstruction of the previous melodramatic performance. By juxtaposing close-ups of the spectators' grave faces and, more pointedly, the Mother Superior's ecstatic visage with Yolanda's provocative poses and glances (accompanied by the extravagant performances, replete with bongos, of the comedic threesome of Sisters Snake, Damned, and Alley Rat), Almodóvar simultaneously bows to and thumbs his nose at the profane and the sacred. Yolanda, for her part, poorly sings her own "feminized" version of the song, which is a salsa for dancing instead of a ballad. While the lyrics ("I left because I left") speak of forbidden love and foreshadow Yolanda's departure from the convent and her abandonment of the Mother Superior that very night, the song's melodramatic charge lessens as the performance shifts from the lip-synched duet in the Mother Superior's private quarters to the live solo by Yolanda in a more public setting, and as the previously dyadic suturing is diversified through shot-reverse-shots of the audience and the other singing nuns. The result is more absurd than melodramatic, even though Yolanda's voice expresses loss rather than desire, as was the case in the previous sequence.

In *Dark Habits,* the musical numbers function, amid all the transgressive intermixtures, as aural fetishes. In a later film, *Law of Desire* (1987), a similar play signals a rather different excess of affect. In a triangular story of mad love, Pablo (Eusebio Poncela), a successful, openly gay filmmaker, has what he takes to be a one-night stand with a closeted, obsessive, and homophobic gay fan named Antonio (Antonio Banderas) who literally comes to script himself as the replacement of Pablo's lover, Juan (Miguel Molina), who has moved out of Madrid to take a summer job in the south. Unrequited love and a play of interlocking yet conflictive identities move the plot, the action, and the characters' emotions in a manner that highlights the performative ethos that we have been examining. Juan is unable to love Pablo as Pablo would like and Pablo is unable, at least at first, to see Antonio as anything more than a fleeting and inconsequential pickup. Antonio's obsession with Pablo leads him, however, to ensure that the encounter is anything but inconsequential by murdering Juan and seducing Pablo's transsexual sister, Tina (Carmen Maura). Once Pablo realizes that Antonio is behind both the murder and the seduction (and after he recovers from a temporary amnesia caused by a car accident), he sets the police after Antonio, who, having taken Tina hostage, asks for one hour alone with Pablo in exchange for Tina's freedom. What Antonio seeks, as both Pablo and the audience realize, is a last chance to consummate their love—for at this point, in extremis, sex has indeed bled profusely into love. As if to seal the extremity of his act and to prove that he is willing to pay the ultimate price for his otherwise criminal passion, Antonio shoots himself in front of an altar of burning candles that

Tina had erected in the apartment. Even at the conventional moment of truth, that of death, the characters perform their part to the fullest.

As in *Dark Habits,* where two songs—one previously recorded and one performed—frame the articulation of desire between two women, *Law of Desire* combines recorded and performed music to highlight the melodramatic rapport between two queer couples: Pablo and Antonio, but also Tina and her female ex-lover, performed by real-life transgendered diva Bibi Andersen. The two boleros "Lo dudo" (I Doubt It), by Chucho Navarro and sung by the trio Los Panchos, and "Déjame recordar" (Let Me Remember), by J. Sabre Marroquín and sung by Bola de Nieve, enhance the melodramatic import of the love that unfolds between Pablo and Antonio when it is already "too late," the quintessential time of melodrama, as Linda Williams has so compellingly noted. More specifically, Mark Allinson has remarked that the lyrics of "Lo dudo"—"Lo dudo, lo dudo, lo dudo, que halles un amor tan puro, como el que tienes en mí" (I doubt that you will ever find a purer love than the one you have from me)—provide Antonio with an unforgettable vehicle for performing his emotions: the song, after all, henceforth conjures up Pablo's and Antonio's star-crossed relationship for virtually anyone who has seen Almodóvar's film (203).[2] After his suicide, and while Pablo embraces him in a Pietà-like composition in front of Tina's kitschy altar, the music of the other aforementioned song, "Déjame recordar," conveys a grief for a love that springs forth only when it is too late and can thus only be remembered: "pobre amor que nos vio llorar ... hoy que se ha perdido, déjame recordar ... el amor que se va, sé que no volverá este amor, pobre amor" (poor love that saw us cry ... now that it is lost, let me remember it ... that love that is gone and that I know will never return, poor love). Bola de Nieve's heartrending rendition of the lyrics and rhythmic cadence accentuate the excessive, quasi-baroque mise-en-scène of Pablo cradling Antonio's now limp body before the homey altar.

Having surveyed the climax of *Law of Desire,* let us rewind to previous scenes in which the power of music channels another story of grief and lost love, this time in a more obvious theatrical space: the onstage performance of Jean Cocteau's *La voix humaine* (The Human Voice). In Almodóvar's rendition of Cocteau's play, Pablo directs his brother-cum-sister Tina in the leading role, providing her the occasion to act out her personal story of triple abandonment (by her father, her priest, and her ex-lover) in front of an audience that includes her ex-lover and her daughter, Ada (Manuela Velasco). Tina, who has been abandoned not only by a woman but also, and most powerfully, by two "fathers," one biological and the other spiritual, reenacts her suffering onstage as her adopted daughter Ada lip-synchs Jacques Brel's "Ne me quitte pas" (Don't Leave Me) as sung by Maysa Mataraso. Thick with emotion, the song also reactivates Pablo's grief for the loss of Juan—the song is first played during their last night together—and Ada's grief over her abandonment by her mother and her fear that she, who has returned, will take her away from Tina, the "surrogate" mother that she has come to love even more than her "real" mother. The choice of a female rendition of Brel's song reinforces the transformative, and transgendered, nature of desire and loss as embodied and experienced by Tina and Ada. The appearance of Tina's ex-lover and Ada's mother as a spectator revives real feelings in an explicitly theatrical setting, thereby adding to the melodramatic effect and revealing Tina's performance onstage to be virtually indistinguishable from her daily performances offstage. A cinematic device, the dolly, appears onstage as if to underscore the back-and-forth shuttling between the "authentic" and the "acted": the young Ada, mouthing an adult voice, slides across the front of the stage on a dolly twice, the second time shedding ostensibly real tears after having had an argument with her mother backstage. It is clear that, through the inclusion of powerful lyrics and melodies, the ties between reality and performance are as intricate as they are insistent.

Performance and Spectatorship

Live performances in Almodóvar's films function, then, as self-reflexive signposts for the essentially performative condition of cinema—and of life—as well as reminders of the existence and, better yet, constitutive role of the audience. If such explicit onstage performances can have cathartic, autobiographical, and parodic implications for the characters-as-actors' often slippery appreciation of truth and self-identity, they can also provide the means for (re)gaining personal control and for constructing and expressing other modes of identity (Carlson 161). In two of his more recent films, *All about My Mother* (1999) and *Talk to Her* (2002), Almodóvar explores the much-touted therapeutic effects that a performance can have on a spectator.

In *All about My Mother,* a grieving mother named Manuela (Cecilia Roth) embarks on a physical and emotional journey to revisit, if not recapture, her past and, more narrowly, to reencounter the transgendered father of her dead son, Esteban (Eloy Azorín). Manuela's journey is defined by her alternating role as performer in, and spectator of, Tennessee Williams's *A Streetcar Named Desire.* As young students in Barcelona, Manuela and her now long-estranged husband, Esteban (Toni Cantó), had played the roles of Stella and Stanley Kowalski, but offstage Esteban had effected a still more dramatic transformation: from Esteban to Lola, the man-woman who leaves Manuela pregnant with the son whose accidental death spurs Manuela's return to Barcelona. On Esteban's eighteenth birthday, Manuela takes him to see a performance of Williams's play in Madrid staring Huma Rojo (Marisa Paredes) as Blanche DuBois. If theatricality marks Esteban's inception, it also marks his death. When they exit, Esteban is fatally struck by a car as he runs after Huma in pursuit of an autograph.[3] Utterly distraught, Manuela travels to Barcelona in search of Esteban's father, Lola, to tell him about his son; while there, she goes to see the same staging of *Streetcar* that she had seen in Madrid. Through a series of mistaken identities and missing people, Manuela quickly becomes Huma's personal assistant. Another cinematic and theatrical layer accrues, as Manuela comes to play the part of Eve Harrington (Anne Baxter), the upstart understudy in Joseph L. Mankiewicz's *All about Eve* (1950). One night that the actress who normally plays Stella, Huma's drug-addicted lover Nina (Candela Peña), is too high to perform, Manuela steps into her shoes to play, once more, the role that has marked her life. Manuela's rendition of Stella symbolically replays her past abusive relationship with her husband and allows her to work through, however partially, her son's tragic death. In other words, Manuela's recovery hinges on the reenactment of a performative identity of her past, with her appearances as spectator before and after her son's death framing her return to Barcelona and to the stage.

The aesthetic composition of the two sequences in which Manuela is shown as a spectator is virtually identical. In the first one, in Madrid, Manuela sits next to her son and, moved to remember the past, cries during the performance. A second level of spectatorship obtains as she becomes the spectacle of her son's gaze. Her crying prompts her son to ask about his father and triggers her decision to tell him all about his father and, by implication, all about his mother when they arrive home. Her decision, as noted, comes "too late," reinforcing the melodrama. In her second viewing of the play in Barcelona, she sits in exactly the same section of the theater, close to the front, only this time next to an empty seat. Once again she cries, but with even more reason than before. Between mother and son, a variety of emotions ensues: curiosity (on the young Esteban's part), secrecy, confrontation, and grief permeate the spectatorship of Williams's play. By performing once again the role of Stella, Manuela's relatively passive and discreet position as spectator turns into an active and public working through of her personal trauma. By actively reenacting her past through the play, Manuela facilitates the work of mourning and begins to reintegrate herself in the daily realm of the living.

In contrast to the original version of *A Streetcar Named Desire,* in which Stella complies with her husband after Blanche is taken away to a sanatorium, Almodóvar has Stella take her baby and leave Kowalski, swearing never to return to him. A repetition with a twist, the new version of the play unfolds in Manuela's real life, as she takes charge of another baby boy after her mother, a young Sister named Rosa (Penélope Cruz), dies from AIDS-related complications (she contracted the virus through the very same Esteban/Lola who was Manuela's former husband). After finally finding Lola and telling him/her about his/her two sons, she takes Rosa's baby, leaves Lola/Esteban, and returns to Madrid, repeating the trip she took eighteen years earlier. Her real life at once mirrors and is motivated by her fictional performance.

All about My Mother deals, among other things, with the power of live performance to activate agency and to create solidarity among women. The "feminist" version of *Streetcar,* in which Stella leaves her abusive husband in support of her sister Blanche, speaks not only of Manuela's real-life determination but also of the solidarity that springs from her attachment with her figurative sisters Huma (Blanche in the play), sister Rosa (her double inasmuch as she bore a child by the same man), and Agrado (Antonia San Juan), a transgendered ex-prostitute who is an old friend of Manuela and a new assistant to Huma. The rehearsal and performance of the play within the film dictate the interactions of the female characters in their changing roles as spectators and performers.

Live performance, as Catherine Elwes argues, offers possibilities for disrupting the conventional system of spectatorship that are impossible in representations that offer fixed and objectified images of women, most notably in the cinema itself. Almodóvar plays with the ties and tensions between the theater and the cinema, the ephemeral and the permanent, in ways that support Elwes's argument; for the live woman performer can, in Elwes's reading, alter the role of the male spectator by stripping away "his cloak of invisibility" and making his spectatorship "an issue within the work" (172–73). The status of gender is particularly important to melodrama, which posits a "feminine" spectator—passive, vulnerable, and excruciatingly receptive— and which Almodóvar, long considered a women's director making new-fangled women's pictures, has mined to the fullest. In yet another radical twist, Almodóvar follows *All about My Mother* with *Talk to Her* (2002), a melodrama in which men are the ones who "cry too much" while watching a performance. *Talk to Her* explores the emotional bonding between two men, Marco (Dario Grandinetti), a journalist and travel writer, and Benigno (Javier Cámara), a nurse, who meet first at the theater, where Benigno turns his eyes from the stage to look at Marco's tear-filled eyes, and later at the hospital where the women that they love, a bullfighter named Lydia (Rosario Flores) and a dancer named Alicia (Leonor Watling), both lie in a coma. As with *All about My Mother*, spectatorship at live performances frames the film and, more specifically, Marco's emotional journey. The performances revive tragic moments from the past (lost loves, lost lives) but also provide Marco—whose name means "frame" in Spanish—the possibility for a brighter future.

The film begins with a performance of Pina Bausch's *Café Müller*. In it, two women, apparently blind, stumble across the stage as a "very sad" (in Benigno's words) and solicitous man scrambles to clear tables and chairs from their paths. The film's two male protagonists, the tear-prone Marco and the gentle, apparently benign Benigno, are presented to the spectator of the film as spectators of Pina Bausch's dance performance, but one of them, Benigno, is also, as already noted, a spectator of the other's spectatorship. The play across spectator positions, watching and being watched, provides the occasion for the creation of a relationship that, as the film progresses, comes to be intensely homosocial, if not homosexual—a possibility that the film explicitly, and somewhat ironically, explores by way of half-whispered comments among Benigno's coworkers, his psychiatrist (who is also Alicia's father), and later, once it is revealed that the comatose Alicia has become pregnant by Benigno, the staff at the prison where he comes to be confined. Before the sequence of events that leads to the prison and the grave (Benigno, unaware that Alicia has come out of her coma, kills himself while confined), the two men come together briefly but intensely in the space of the theater. Strangers to each other in the audience, their future bonding over the comatose bodies of the women they love will entail the recollection of their different emotional reactions to the dance (Marco weeps; Benigno does not) as they bear on their different emotional reactions to their beloveds' accidents and subsequent vegetative states (like the dancers in the dance, both women "run into" something or something "runs into" them: in the one case a car; in the other, a bull).

As A. O. Scott so elegantly puts it in his review of the film for the *New York Times*:

[the] initial sequence of nonverbal, inadvertent communication contains the film's emotional core; it functions as a cinematic overture, gesturing toward themes and states of feeling that will be elaborated, embroidered and brought together in a work of daunting dramatic scope and breathtaking coherence. Most obviously, Ms. Bausch's blind women prefigure Alicia (played by Leonor Watling) and Lydia (Rosario Flores), shut off from sensory contact with the world. But the emotion that filters from the stage to Marco (Dario Grandinetti), and then to Benigno (Javier Cámara), is also an allegory of both Mr. Almodóvar's message and his method. A work of art speaks to us, and invites us to speak to each other. (163)

Almodóvar's own comments on the film support Scott's reading and invite an interpretation of the scene as a vehicle for the melodramatic involvement of the two men in the performative spectacle of female suffering: "One of the ideas that I wanted to convey was a man who cried for emotional reasons linked to a work of art—from seeing a work of enormous beauty" (cited in Scott 163). The scene undercuts the conventional invisibility of men as impassive—but never simply passive—spectators and forces them to be in some profound sense both *passive* and *complicit* with the injured women.

At the very end of the film, Marco, who is still mourning Benigno's death, returns to the theater, where he encounters the "miraculously" recovered Alicia. A row of empty seats separating them, the two are nonetheless bound together in a mode of spectatorial complicity as they watch another piece by Pina Bausch, *Masurca Fogo,* which provides a form of closure that at the same time opens, in the unseen continuation of their potential relation, a heterosexual romance. The film comes to an end with the names "Alicia and Marco" superimposed on the image, names that signal a new pairing in the way that previous titles, "Marco and Lydia" and "Benigno and Alicia," had signaled previous pairings. Although open-ended, this apparently "happy ending" can only be taken as such in the context of the performance that the two characters are watching. In the first part of *Masurca Fogo,* a group of men raises a woman in their arms, passing her around between them. The woman does not have control over her body, but holds a microphone in her hands and, though sighing heavily, appears to control her voice. While watching it, we, like a teary-eyed Marco, are perhaps reminded of Lydia's body being carried from the bullring after her goring and/or of Alicia's body being partially lifted as Benigno cares for it. Alicia, the once passive and motionless object of the gaze during her coma, has regained consciousness and recuperated her role as spectator.[4] Here too the film suggests a connection between the now revived Alicia and the now dead Benigno. After all, a crucial element in Benigno's devoted caretaking of Alicia was his role as mediator, talking to her about the performances that he had previously seen.[5] The first time we see Benigno and Alicia together, *Café Müller* appears as a narrative flashback as Benigno gives the seemingly unresponsive Alicia the details of the two spectacles that he had seen: one performed by the dancers and the other by Marco, who, as already noted, is visibly moved by what unfolds on stage.

The double layer of spectatorship is reproduced almost identically with *Masurca Fogo,* where Marco's emotional response becomes a spectacle that Alicia, seated a few rows behind him, contemplates as Benigno had before her. After they exchange a few words at intermission, the second dance starts with a line of couples dancing across the stage and ends with one of the couples swaying their hips in what may be the beginning of their courtship. The happy dance scene, which oozes a sensuality in which both dancers seem to share equally, reduplicates the brief interaction between the characters during the intermission and foreshadows their potential future relationship. As Marco turns away from the stage to look back at Alicia in her seat in the audience, the aforementioned superimposition of their names explicitly directs the filmic spectator to this potentially new couple, born of death and grief. Marco's sensitive reaction to the first dance encourages Alicia to initiate the conversation and then to return the gaze and a smile to him during the second dance. The contemplation of a work of art here shifts traditional gender positions and enhances a more truly reciprocal form of communication.[6]

As we have seen, the emotions that issue from watching a live performance, no less than the layers of spectatorship that such an act entails, are transferred in large measure from *All about My Mother* to *Talk to Her.* The continuity between the two films is further reinforced by the election of the same golden stage curtain with which the former ends and with which the latter opens and ends. Superimposed on the curtain in *All about My Mother* is, moreover, a dedication, not just to the "mothers" of the film's title but also to "all the women who perform and all the men who perform as women." The curtain throws into relief the critical nature of performance and spectatorship in these two films and reasserts Almodóvar's belief in the potential transference of female solidarity *(All about My Mother)* to male bonding *(Talk to Her)*—a new take on the transgenderism that characterizes so much of his production. The conviction, or at least the desire, that women and men can—even should—perform their personal dramas before each other resides at the core of *Talk to Her,* expanding on the communicative circuits of *All about My Mother* and gesturing to the ethical potential of performativity in general.

Revelations and Confessions, Performed

In keeping with the conventions of melodrama, the genre so cherished by Almodóvar, revelations and confessions function as especially charged performances of intersubjective identity. According to Linda Williams, melodramatic revelations of secrets and confessions of love alternate between—and sometimes combine—pathos and action, events that occur either "too late" or only "in the nick of time" (69). Almodóvar's melodramas are rich in confessional moments: confessions of love, of crime, of a previous biological self, of the transformation to a new self, and so on. *Law of Desire, All about My Mother,* and *High Heels* (1991) provide perfect examples of confessions performed both to enhance melodrama and to reflect on the constructed and performative nature of gender and identity.

In *Law of Desire,* Pablo has a car accident and wakes up in a hospital with amnesia. His transsexual sister, Tina, who is by his bedside, attempts to spark his memory by telling him stories of their life and showing him photographs of the two siblings before and after the operation. Tina had been Pablo's brother as a child when their father seduced him and convinced him to run away with him to Morocco and undergo a sex change. After the operation, and after her father left her, Tina returned to Madrid and was reunited with Pablo. His amnesia accordingly deprives Tina of the only witness to her past. The bedside story, a veritable confession buttressed by the photographs, the basic element of cinema, constitutes a performative recognition of her former male embodiment and, above all, an affirmation of her present femininity. When asked by Pablo whether she regrets the change, Tina confesses that she is not sorry and that it was a consensual decision. Tina's story shows the power of desire to "redetermine" biology. As with Antonio, who murders and kills himself in order to prove his love to Pablo, Tina also goes to drastic lengths to prove her love for her father. Neither of them regrets their actions and Pablo is, in both cases, the privileged spectator of their performances. By verbally reenacting her transformation, Tina jogs her brother's memory and, in good melodramatic fashion, allows Pablo to arrive "in the nick of time" to save her from Antonio, who has been dating her in order to get closer to Pablo. Antonio's fate, as already noted, is dramatically different, for Pablo, alone with Antonio while the police wait outside, arrives "too late" to snatch the gun from Antonio's hands and save him from himself. The performances and the mise-en-scène cast Pablo and, more explicitly, the police, Tina, and the young Ada, who wait with upturned eyes outside the apartment building where Antonio and Pablo are having what turns out to be their final hour of love, in the role of spectators, like us. What arises is a mode of spectatorial identification that eschews facile moral judgment: in spite of the enormity of his crime, Antonio becomes, by the film's end, a sympathetic character, a "martyr of love," his body laid out in a well-known iconographic position before Tina's kitschy altar.

In *High Heels,* Almodóvar's first maternal melodrama, confessional performances also abound and constitute the core of a conflictive relationship between a television personality named Rebeca (Victoria Abril) and her more famous mother, the great popular singer Becky del Páramo (Marisa Paredes), who has prioritized her career and romantic affairs over her relationship with her daughter. Rebeca, who has spent her entire life trying to emulate Becky, has even gone so far as to marry one of her mother's old lovers, Manuel (Feodor Atkine). Upon her return to Spain after a long absence, Becky restarts her affair with Manuel, prompting Rebeca to kill him and then to confess her guilt on a prime-time newscast. A confession of a crime that is also a confession of love, Rebeca's televised act recasts melodrama as pure spectacle. Almodóvar himself stresses the confessional potential of television:

> For me, . . . the telecamera, more than the cinema, is a great, paradoxical, confessional device. This is all the more true if you think of a woman who works with the television medium. She tells her tragedy to her only witness, the telecamera, which is like telling it to the whole world and to nobody. (Quoted in Cielo 101)

Telling her tragedy "live" on camera, Rebeca introduces a curiously comic element into melodrama. Interspersing her verbal confession with photographs that she has taken of some of her late husband's possessions (his closet and suits, his favorite chair to watch TV, lovely bedsheets they will never use, etc.), Rebeca not only provides evidence of her guilt, but also reveals herself to be pathetically, comically, fetishistic. The comic charge of so many intimate acts and objects put on public display is only heightened by the presence of a woman sitting beside Rebeca who translates into sign language Rebeca's every word.

In response to Rebeca's televised confession, Becky, performing onstage at one of her concerts, dedicates the Agustín Lara song, "Piensa en mí" (Think of Me) to her daughter. Mouthing singer Luz Casal's rendition of the song as if it were her own (in the diegesis, it is), Becky makes public her previously disavowed role as mother. She does so, to be sure, through a ritualized and spectacular performance of the feelings that she imagines that such a role would elicit. Her gestures—she kisses the stage before dedicating the song to her daughter and then weeps, a single tear dropping onto the imprint left by her lipstick—are as studied as they are histrionic and appear to sap her confession's authenticity. After all, at this point in the film, Becky seems to concede greater importance to the grandiloquence of the stage and to the applause that she elicits among her adoring fans than to the subtleties of a direct declaration to her daughter, who listens to her mother from inside the prison in which she has been confined. Both women's performances, one on television and the other on the stage (and broadcast live on the radio), reassert the public, even spectacular, tenor of this mother–daughter relationship and attest to the triumph of mediation that characterizes the age of performance. In the words of Philip Auslander: "whereas mediatized performance derives its authority from its reference to the live or the real, the live now derives its authority from its reference to the mediatized" (202–3). Rebeca's mediatized performance, replete with photographs of the scene of the crime, derives its effectiveness from its improvisation. For the sake of ratings, Rebeca's producers allowed her to continue with her apparently extemporaneous declaration. The illusion of something pro-

Becky del Páramo (Marisa Paredes) singing "Piensa en mí" at the Theater María Guerrero in High Heels *(1991). Copyright El Deseo.*

foundly personal unfolding in "real time" before the viewers' eyes reinforces the authority of the newscast show, which ideally privileges truth and objectivity. Becky's scenario is, of course, different: a musical stage, set for entertainment and emotionality, not for truth and objectivity. Interestingly, however, Becky's artful confession of motherly devotion takes its cues from her daughter's earlier "journalistic" initiative. Amid all of the relays between artifice and truth, the staged and the spontaneous, both characters, accustomed to performing in one way or another, nonetheless communicate their passion to each other.[7] Performance may be shot through with pretense, but that does not prevent it from being "real."

Performing Gender

It is often through performance that Almodóvar's characters—and especially his female characters—affirm or contest their gender identities, whether they are understood in terms of biological essence, social construction, patriarchal imposition, or camp impersonation. It is arguably the transgendered Agrado's onstage confession in *All about My Mother* that serves as the emblematic moment of revelation and confession for women—and for men. In Agrado's words: "It's not easy being genuine. But we mustn't be cheap with anything relating to our image. Because the more a woman resembles what she has dreamed for herself, the more genuine she is." After announcing the suspension of a show, Agrado attempts to assuage the audience's disappointment by telling the tale of her transformation from man to woman. Agrado's act is presented as impromptu, though in effect it is clearly one for which she has long "studied." Given the ignorance and intolerance that still mark popular understandings of transsexualism, the diegetic audience's sympathetic and cheerful response to Agrado's performance is undoubtedly more a manifestation of Almodóvar's own position toward gender ambiguity than a plausible account of spectatorial identification with the trials and tribulations of transformative surgery, but it nonetheless scripts a response for the extradiegetic audience that would be similarly cheerful and sympathetic. Agrado's experientially structured account of the mutability of the body and its availability to (re)construction denaturalizes the terms on which identity and identification "normally" rely—without spelling the end of either identity and identification (if anything, Agrado expands the field of identity). Just as Tina's confession in *Law of Desire* introduces differences into the melodramatic conventions to which it otherwise still largely adheres, Agrado's monologue suspends the scenic illusion to make a compensatory gesture by which an artificially "constructed" woman would be the most authentic extension of the "natural" woman.

But if gender identities are repeatedly brought center stage in Almodóvar's films, sexual identities are rarely performed publicly. Instead, they remain tellingly discreet and ambiguous. The gay male characters who populate Almodóvar's cinema do not engage in acts of "revelation" or "coming out"— perhaps because they are already out. They neither hide nor publicly reveal their sexual preferences, which are assumed in the diegesis and flow liberally between the public and private spheres.[8] Homosexuality here enjoys the same "taken-for-grantedness" as heterosexuality, and coexists easily with transvestism, transsexualism, and pansexualism. The "nonrevelatory" nature of gay identity in Almodóvar's films mirrors the director's own quite public disavowal of normative homosexuality and his reluctance to engage in identity politics and to endorse its often rigid categorizations in favor of ambiguity and queerness. Accordingly, it is not surprising that he confers a special role to drag and cross-dressing in his depiction of the ultimately "authentic" artificiality and instability of gender and sexual identity.

It has become a commonplace in the criticism on Almodóvar to affirm that most performances by characters, and even by the director himself, are in one way or another drag performances. RuPaul's famous aphorism would probably please Almodóvar and suit his cinematic conception of drag: "You're born naked and the rest is drag" (Schacht 228). So too would the following comment by drag queen Gugy (interviewed by Verta Taylor and Leila Rupp as part of their case study of drag queens at the 801 Cabaret in Key West, Florida): "Out of drag, I feel like I am acting. In drag, I feel like myself" (Taylor and Rupp 122). Both quotations underscore the theatrical qualities of drag—experienced as an act rather than as a "lifestyle" or an innate and organic way of being, as a venue for the creation of personae, and as a way of satisfying "inessential" sartorial desires. The use of flamboyant clothing as a sort of masquerade allows Almodóvar's characters to embrace gender fluidity and to perform identities that "they can put on and take off" (Taylor and Rupp 120). Impersonation and drag figure in memorable ways in early films like *Labyrinth of Passion,* where the playful side of the instability and ambiguity that will be modified in later works in more "serious" ways remains prominent.[9]

When Riza disguises himself in order to escape the fundamentalist terrorists who are chasing him in *Labyrinth of Passion,* he asks transvestite *Movida* icon Fanny McNamara for advice. In McNamara's worldview, a change of clothing equals a change of identity; he shows Riza a magazine with samples of women's hairdos from the 1960s, styles that he then revises in a rock-punk-glam register for Riza. In the same film, Queti (Marta Fernández Muro), a devoted fan of Sexilia, the leader of the group *Ellas* (Them, in the feminine), undergoes a fantastic transformation in order to escape from her abusive father and to have a sexual relationship with Sexilia's father. Needless to say, the substitution here requires not just that Queti don Sexilia's clothes but also that she undergo plastic surgery (in arguably one of the most unbelievable turns in all of Almodóvar's cinema) to become the exact replica of Sexilia, who does not, however, reciprocate by becoming an exact replica of Queti. The copying of dress and gesture, bodily parts and personalities, is here invested with libidinal significance that is at once transgressive *and* normative: a surgically altered Queti will live happily ever after with her new father and Sexilia, reborn to monogamy, flies away with a newly heterosexualized Riza.

Almodóvar appears to be most interested, especially in his earlier films, in the camp component of drag, its aesthetics, styles, sensibilities, and entertainment value. But by showcasing drag he points to the inherently performative nature not just of phenomena as ostensibly different as transgenderism and theatricality but also of gender and sexuality in general. Feminist and queer theoretical approaches have abundantly problematized the transgressive—and regressive—potential implicit in "drag," especially to the degree that it hyperbolically imitates heterosexual molds and manners. In keeping with Judith Butler's thought from *Gender Trouble* (1990) to *Bodies That Matter* (1993), drag, as a performance by which gender and other identitarian roles can be questioned, offers alternatives to the male/female dichotomy. And yet, as Butler and others have noted, the performative space of drag does not always challenge, let alone "subvert," prevailing heteronormative values, and can even serve to bolster them. Drag performances, albeit still marginalized, have increasingly entered the public space and have been recuperated by and for capitalist culture and the entertainment industry. Thus, the destabilizing potential of drag is susceptible to institutionalization and thereby loses its much-touted subversive effect.[10] Indeed, this critical trajectory, with all its shifts and turns, runs parallel to Almodóvar's cinematic representation of drag over the years. In Almodóvar's early films, drag, cross-dressing, and sex changes carried an almost unquestionably subversive charge, whereas in later films such as *All about My Mother* and *Bad Education* they seem to have followed the normalizing thrusts that attend, to the eyes of many people, the increasingly organized, complex, and sophisticated questioning of normalcy and normativity.

It is precisely because drag seems to have such specific cultural ties to the *Movida* that a reconsideration of its historical role in that period is appropriate. Critics who discuss the cultural context of post-Francoist Spain often acknowledge that drag performances in the transitional period of the late 1970s and early 1980s were gradually institutionalized as they became an entertainment option for the middle class. Such performers as Ocaña and Pavlovski in Barcelona, Bibi Andersen and Fabio McNamara in Madrid, and Fama in Bilbao began their careers in marginal and alternative nightclubs, but soon became public attractions in clubs and cabarets as well as actors in films, documentaries, and television series.[11] It has also been well documented that gays and drag queens played crucial roles in the sexual openness and freedom of the *Movida*. In *Sólo se vive una vez; esplendor y ruina de la movida madrileña* (1990) (One Only Lives Once: Splendor and Ruin in Madrid's *Movida*), Borja Casani variously describes these nonheteronormative subjects as "dynamic," "avant-garde," "foulmouthed," "brilliant," and "tremendous" (Gallero 20). In his exhaustive study of the cultural history of homosexuality in Spain, *De Sodoma a Chueca* (2004) (From Sodom to Chueca), Alberto Mira documents that the new libertarian era of sexual dissidence that started with the *destape* (literally, the "uncovering," by which the lifting of moralistic bans of erotic materials signified a major shift in Spanish society) provided the occasion for the transvestite to emerge as "a prophet," an exotic object of interest for media eager to "show off" their politically progressive attitudes (435). It is within this context that Almodóvar conceives the drag performances of his early films, in which cross-dressing onstage (and elsewhere) is a way for the characters to express themselves within a heteronormative society and to signal, whether deliberately or not, the performative nature of gender and sexuality.

It is here that the director's own persona, acknowledged at the outset of this essay, proves to be all but unavoidable. Almodóvar's recurrent appearances in drag in his early films, as well as onstage and in magazines, are campy, parodic reappropriations of the folkloric representations of often homophobically constructed gay characters in conventional Spanish cinema and embody the restive mood of the transition to democracy. Almodóvar sings in drag with Fanny McNamara in both *Labyrinth of Passion* and *What Have I Done to Deserve This?* (1984), but he had already appeared in drag in a scene that takes place backstage at the nightclub Bataclán in Pedro

Olea's *Un hombre llamado Flor de Otoño* (A Man Called Autumn Flower; 1978). As Teresa Vilarós argues in *El mono del desencanto* (The Withdrawal of Disenchantment), drag, despite or even because of its marginality, was an integral element in the Spanish transition (194) and provided a space where it was possible to unveil, spectacularly and scandalously, Francoist repression (188). As its name indicates, the *Movida* privileged movement, mobility, and ambiguity, and opposed the territorialization or codification of desire, its primary field of exploration (Mira 514–15). Mobility and ambiguity permeate Almodóvar's early films, in which drag pushes at, if not breaks down, gender, sexual, and political boundaries (Vilarós 189). The drag queens of early post-Franco films played an important social role, ironically recycling cultural forms of the past (Catholic iconography, nationalist folklore, bullfighting) and mocking oppressive orthodoxies (Mira 527).

Almodóvar's own incursion in drag performance is important as well, for it contributes to the construction, and marketing, of his public persona. Leora Lev has observed that on the cover of the director's mock autobiography, *Patty Diphusa,* "Almodóvar is garbed in a 'suit of lights,' a blood red carnation in his hair, draped in the black lace mantilla worn by Spanish *majas* on festive occasion, eyes lined in kohl" (84n2). In 1994, for the May issue of the magazine *Out,* dedicated to the "King of Kink," the Spanish director posed for the cover wearing a giant polka-dot bow on his head, and in publicity pictures for the release of *High Heels* he appeared "appropriately" shod in high heels. On the cover of the *New York Times Magazine* issue that coincided with the North American release of *Bad Education* in November 2004, he posed once more in costume, this time, in keeping with the movie's themes, in priestly attire.[12] Such careful attention to clothing and makeup allows Almodóvar to play with his role of director and the performative condition of cinema, to show the director, even when an auteur, to be a character too.

Almodóvar's cinematic corpus is certainly self-implicating, even "visceral," as Frédéric Strauss has claimed, but it is also a simulated and hyperreal body that lays bare, amid a flurry of costumes, gestures, and poses, the performative aspect of gender. As intimated earlier, Carmen Maura's hyperfeminine performance of Tina in *Law of Desire* is the ultimate joke on femininity as a patriarchal construction. Almodóvar's performative and (de)constructive intentions were clear in the creation of a character whose very nature would be cast primarily as a mode of imitation: "I did not want a real transsexual for the transsexual . . . but an actress who could interpret a transsexual. . . . I was interested in a woman showing the exaggerated, tense and highly exhibitionist femininity of a transsexual" (Strauss 73).

There are, of course, other instances of drag and imitation in Almodóvar's work. Femme Letal's drag performance in *High Heels* deploys imitation to comment on Rebeca's obsession with the glamorous femininity of her mother Becky del Páramo. As Marsha Kinder has noted, the film excels in presenting "a dazzling chain of masquerades":

> the impersonator is really a male pop star (Miguel Bosé) doing an impersonation of an ordinary man (Eduardo) doing an impersonation of a detective (the Judge) doing an impersonation of a female impersonator (Becky), who is there in the audience with her daughter, Rebeca, who has been impersonating her mother all her life. Three anonymous "female" spectators sing along with Letal, imitating his every gesture and taking great pleasure impersonating the impersonator. ("From Matricide to Mother Love" 150–51)

Indeed, by reduplicating Becky del Páramo's performances, Letal's show becomes a drag performance of a performance (pop star) of a performance (femininity). Letal's theatrical embrace of Becky's scenic identity foreshadows, moreover, Zahara's imitation of Sara Montiel's scenic and cinematic persona in *Bad Education*.

Transplants, Implants, and Other Significant Operations

Finally, amid so many transformative acts, organ transplants and implants, comically adumbrated in *Labyrinth of Passion* and dramatically highlighted in *All about My Mother* and *Talk to Her*, assume important symbolic functions in Almodóvar's cinema, extending his problematization of identity to the material body itself. Agrado's onstage monologue is a case in point, but as Almodóvar's cinema evolves over time, the reliance on situations involving the replacement, transplantation, and resuscitation of bodily organs prompts such ethically laden questions as: Do we inherit the identity of the organ donor? Are subjectivity and social identity as interchangeable as organs? Are all means of organ stimulation ethically acceptable for resuscitating life? Are new social and emotional identities mobilized by such operations?

Although the dilemma about organ donations and transplants, introduced in the opening scenes of *The Flower of My Secret* (1995), does not appear to be related to the rest of the film, it will prove to be of crucial importance in the construction of Manuela's character in *All about My Mother*.[13] Manuela's overwhelming need to track down the patient who inherited her son's donated heart, the symbolic site of love, is a melodramatic reference to the visceral but lost authenticity of her son that stands in contrast to the artificiality of his father. No longer the subversive if insubstantial figure of his early films, the transgendered subject has shifted into something tragic. The falsie that Femme Letal (Miguel Bosé) gives Becky in exchange for her earrings in *High Heels* was still a playful reminder of the detachable condition of gender roles, or, as Marsha Kinder has styled it, a "fetish that came from the mother's body, the point of origin of all fetishes" ("From Matricide to Mother Love" 152). Playful in the otherwise somber *High Heels,* the breast assumes a more threatening guise when embodied in Lola in *All about My Mother.* As Manuela confides to Rosa, her ex-husband's attitude after his transformation serves to denounce an act of intolerance and misogyny: "he spent the day in a tiny bikini screwing everything he could and giving [me] a hard time if [I] wore a bikini or a mini-skirt. How could anyone act so macho with a pair of tits like that?" It is as if the liberated and transgressive role that drag and other transitive performances of gender had played in his early films had come, by dint of repetition and celebration, to support rather than subvert heterosexual norms, failing to challenge even so easy a target as machismo. Lola's breast implants, far from ushering in a new subject, merely seem to modify an old one and mark the beginning of a more complex understanding of trans subjectivity that does not stay with a stereotypical frivolity or unjust suffering but that acquires instead some gloomier and more violent traits, most notably in *Bad Education.*

Almodóvar had his reasons for setting *All about My Mother* in Barcelona: it was, after all, the city in Spain that was most fertile in expressions of marginality and dissidence (including that of Catalan nationalists) and had been the capital of the underground before the *Movida* took Madrid by storm (Mira 475). But Almodóvar's camp aesthetic has by now been revised to include more realistic and even moralizing takes on the lived experience, rather than simply the performative exuberance, of transsexuals, drag queens, and other trans subjects. Whereas the campiness of the trans subject is maintained in the character of Agrado and her onstage discussion of her own breast implants, the inclusion of prostitution, violence, drug abuse, and AIDS in the film puts the breaks on the more insouciant and effusive renditions of the past. Rather than being merely a transgressor, the trans subject is both an aggressor and a victim: Lola infects others with HIV, but when she finally makes her appearance at Rosa's funeral, she is weak, decrepit, and forlorn. Agrado is also and mostly a victim: she is robbed by Lola, who was her former roommate, physically abused by a client while working as a prostitute, and taken by a prostitute and asked to perform oral sex on an actor while working as Huma's assistant.

What might be described as the downside of gender bending comes more fully to the fore in *Bad Education,* where Ignacio's implants are presented in close-up to the inattentive gaze of Mr. Berenguer (Lluís Homar), the former pederastic priest who abused Ignacio (Francisco Boira) and conspires with Ignacio's brother to kill him. The explicit reference to, and visual exposition of, Ignacio's breasts while he is preparing a dose of heroin that will prove lethal to him eschews the campiness of previous films. Moreover, by linking Ignacio's sex change to drug addiction and death, Almodóvar appears to punish Ignacio for his/her transgression even as he denounces the repressive climate in which s/he had to live. If even the specter of moral judgment was absent in his early work, here, in *Bad Education,* it seems to return with a vengeance. Alberto Mira's interpretation of Lola in *All about My Mother* as the somber representation of the post-*Movida* body ravaged by years of unbridled hedonism (555) can be extended to the character of Ignacio in *Bad Education* who, like so many in the *Movida* itself, became a victim to heroin. As Marvin D'Lugo has rightly observed, Ignacio himself can be seen as a victim of "the predatory villains of the old Spanish culture," especially when one remembers that the "historical evocation of Francoism and the early years of political transition" in *Bad Education* functions as "a cautionary political tale for Spaniards and an allegory of the persistence of old Spain in its varied disguises" (27). D'Lugo himself cautions his reader, and Almodóvar's audience, against the temptation to idealize the *Movida* years and, more amply and importantly, "the susceptibility to false nostalgia" (ibid.).

Almodóvar's somewhat elliptical re-creation of the *Movida* in *Bad Education* deliberately avoids a nostalgic portrayal of the period by focusing not only on some of the more nefarious effects of Francoism, as D'Lugo states, but also on some of the more unfortunate ramifications of the *Movida.* In so doing, he effectively comments on the impossibility of recapturing the raucous mobility and rampant ambiguity that permeated his early films. Perhaps, as Alberto Mira suggests, the *Movida* faded when institutions appropriated it, when it became a commodity and was recycled in increasingly heteronormative terms (520). Whatever the case, Almodóvar refuses to oversimplify the *Movida.* Instead, he strips it of its glamorous aura and reveals that it was not as liberated as the expressions of the elite, but reduced, group of night birds might suggest. Depictions of the *Movida* in *All about My Mother* and

Bad Education resist, in short, the one-sided codification and institution-alization of a phenomenon whose most definable features are arguably its break with the past and its provisionality.

Performing Identities, Contradictions, and Consequences

By way of conclusion, I want to consider briefly some of the consequences and contradictions of the performative destabilization of identity in Almodóvar's films. Even though Almodóvar has always championed the performativity, instability, and ambiguity of identity, there are signs, even from very early in his career, that the transformation of identity is not as free from contradictions and consequences as many imagine. The imitations and impersonations activated in performance may help characters endure traumas, perhaps even cure them, but they may also support duplicity and (self-)deception. Queti's impersonation of Sexilia in *Labyrinth of Passion* apparently enables her and Sexilia's father to violate the incest taboo within the diegesis but "reassures" the extradiegetic audience, privy to more information than Sexilia's father, that the daughter is not "really" the daughter and, at most, merely deceives the father (in a manner that is curiously consistent with the Freudian notion of the daughter's seduction). The upshot may be comic, but it is certainly not as radical as some may believe, because it ensures that incest remains on the level of appearance while Riza's homosexuality and Sexilia's nymphomania are really "cured." But the performative impersonations and imitations that play as comedy in *Labyrinth of Passion* take some downright tragic turns in many of Almodóvar's later films, in which any number of characters do not simply live out their fantasies but impose them upon others. One of the most notable examples is, as we have already seen, Lola in *All about My Mother,* whose sexual ambiguity generates not liberation but rather desperation and death. An even more negative figure, that exemplifies the vicious potential of impersonation, is Ángel/Juan/Zahara (Gael García Bernal) in *Bad Education.* In many respects a duplication and extension of Tina in *Law of Desire,* the multifarious character played by García Bernal evinces little of Tina's poignancy and loyalty to her brother and is instead a creature who murders his own brother and betrays friends and lovers alike in order to advance his career. Tellingly, Juan/Ángel's dizzying performativity does not so much destabilize identity as secure, however fleetingly, careerist ambitions: Juan, whose stage name is Ángel, appropriates his brother Ignacio's suffering as a sexually abused junkie to star in Enrique's film, *The Visit.* A devious impersonator, Juan/Ángel maintains a sexual relationship with his brother's abuser *and* his brother's childhood love, Enrique (Fele Martínez), enmeshing both men, for all their differences, in a web of deceit and violence.

The playful, parodic, and subversive potential of nonnormative desire, transvestism, and transsexualism that characterized Almodóvar's early films appears to have assumed, in these later films, a more disturbing tenor, almost as if performativity had become a curse and sheer punishment, a painful burden to others, a tragic irony. More sober and somber, Almodóvar has modified his gaze and his camera and has moved from performers and performances that are just meant to be fun, to performers and performances that are deadly serious. I opened this essay by signaling the importance of the interactions between performers and spectators in the cinema

On the set of
Bad Education: *the construction of Zahara. Copyright El Deseo.*

of Almodóvar, especially as they bear on identity, desire, and representation. Although it is true that even in Almodóvar's earlier films, there were interactions between performers and spectators that were not simply "creative" or "liberating," the camera seemed to focus more on the possibilities of the stage than on the constraints of social reality. With time Almodóvar has broadened his field of vision, widened the contexts of his narratives, to include performative agendas and perspectives that engage the private as well as the public, families and friends as well as fans and critics, and that question and even reprove the glamour of the *Movida,* its Francoist and anti-Francoist preconditions and its post-Francoist legacies. This broader, more complex view does not preclude us from arguing that in Almodóvar's cinema, identity, in its incessant performances, is still unstable and provisional, but that it is shot through pleasure as well as pain, liberation as well as constraint, playfulness as well as trouble.

NOTES

I want to thank the editors of this volume, Brad Epps and Despina Kakoudaki, not only for their thorough and rigorous linguistic editing but also for their numerous and pertinent suggestions that unquestionably enriched my interpretative expression.

1. Alberto Mira puts it rightly when he states that the modernity, or postmodernity, of the *Movida* with which Almodóvar is so closely associated "lies in a fragile balance between punk and tonadilla [popular song]" and "entails a camp reappropriation of certain icons associated with Francoism" (87).

2. For the camp function of boleros in the cinema of Almodóvar, see Kathleen Vernon's article "Las canciones de Almodóvar."

3. Huma's name is itself a performance, a feminization of *humo,* meaning "smoke," in honor of yet another actress, the cigarette-wielding Bette Davis.

4. Gutiérrez Albilla has interpreted the scene as a "visual quotation" that allows "the spectator to be affected kinesthetically and to participate in an embodied viewing experience" (52). The sublimation of emotions conveyed in the performance provides both the diegetic and extradiegetic spectators "with a way of understanding the body in its connections with other bodies. The body is understood in terms of the linkages that it establishes, the transformations and becomings that it undergoes, thereby allowing for a transmutation or metamorphosis to occur, for the possibility of becoming something else" (53).

5. Alicia recovers from her coma after Benigno performs sex on her, impregnating her, and she gives birth to a dead baby. His act follows and is triggered by the retelling of another performance: the silent "erotic" film, *The Shrinking Lover.*

6. There is another instance in the film where another live performance by Caetano Veloso induces Marco's crying. Although elicited by a male singer, Marco's crying becomes the spectacle of Lydia and induces an active response in her. Alicia's and Marco's

first interaction at the closing scene introduces another hypothetical pair: "Lydia and Alicia." Although they never met, their reaction to the man who exposes his emotions publicly makes them alike, besides the fact that, at the hospital while in coma, they are often shown as a pair wearing the same gowns, receiving the same treatment, and located next to each other on their rooms' balconies. For an analysis on the "only real couple" of the film, "Benigno and Marco," see Linda Williams's essay in the present volume.

7. According to Marsha Kinder, the two women's aural professions channel their subversion of the patriarchy, which "is achieved primarily by fetishizing the maternal voice, which is amplified through media transmission and hardware as well as through dubbing and impersonation" ("From Matricide to Mother Love in Almodóvar's *High Heels*," 150).

8. For a longer discussion, see the chapter "El despertar homosexual del cine español: identidad y política en transición (Eloy de la Iglesia, Pedro Olea, Imanol Uribe y Pedro Almodóvar)" in my book *Cine (Ins)urgente*.

9. Other, more subtle, forms of drag can be found in such heterosexually centered films as *Women on the Verge of a Nervous Breakdown* (1988) and *Matador* (1986). In the former, Lucía (Julieta Serrano), Iván's first wife, revamps herself after years in a mental hospital by obsessively reclaiming her past with her ex-husband through her campy attachment to her own vintage wardrobe. In *Matador*, María (Assumpta Serna) and Eva (Eva Cobo) wear clothing that mimics that of a bullfighter, which already evokes a complex network of gender-coded transformations. For a contemporary audience, the matador's suit of lights displays a masculine figure that is flamboyantly feminized, even queered. María and Eva's ways of dressing bring both the masculine and the feminine undertones of the torero to the foreground: their red capes recall the colors and forms of the torero's costume, just as their fake (albeit longer) ponytails recall the torero's "rat tail" and María's lethal hairpin recalls his rapier. For more on dress and gender in *Matador*, see Leora Lev's "Tauromachy as a Spectacle of Gender Revision in *Matador*."

10. In the last chapter of *Bodies That Matter*, titled "Critically Queer," Butler goes so far as to say that drag can actually mobilize a return to an idealized bourgeois, white heteronormativity (240). Critics and performers alike can still differ significantly in their interpretations of the social and political effects of drag. One approach contends, as intimated, that drag is a transgressive action that destabilizes gender and sexual categories by making visible the social basis and biases of femininity and masculinity, heterosexuality and homosexuality, and by throwing into relief hybrid and minority genders and sexualities. Another approach, as noted, warns that drag may reinforce dominant assumptions about the dichotomous nature of gender and sexual desire by appropriating gender displays associated with traditional femininity and institutionalized heterosexuality (Taylor and Rupp 115).

11. Filmic examples include Vicente Aranda's *Cambio de Sexo* (*Sex Change*; 1976); Ventura Pons's documentary *Ocaña, retrato intermitente* (*Ocaña, an Intermittent Portrait*; 1978); Pedro Olea's *Un hombre llamado Flor de Otoño* (*A Man Called Autum Flower*; 1978); Antonio Giménez Rico's documentary *Vestida de azul* (*Dressed in Blue*; 1983); Imanol Uribe's *La muerte de Mikel* (*The Death of Mikel*; 1983), as well as Almodóvar's early films.

12. Almodóvar himself establishes the connection between religious iconography and drag in an interview with Gavin Smith for *Film Comment:* "Gavin Smith: Catholicism has its own *mise-en-scene,* decor, and kind of performance. As a connoisseur of performance and design, has Catholicism informed your aesthetic sensibility? Is there perhaps a relationship between the performances of priests and drag queens?" Pedro Almodóvar: "I appreciated the music, the songs, the rituals. I already felt like a director, even then. Given that there was already a director in me, I had a distance that allowed me to see the rituals as performances, rather than feel the fear and guilt that the priests want you to feel. In both cases [the drag queen and the priest] there's the wish for a miracle. For the drag queen, there's the wish to become the icon she's representing; and for the priest there's the wish to represent God" (25).

13. In "Reinventing the Motherland: Almodóvar's Brain-Dead Trilogy," Marsha Kinder points out the "regenerative power of transplants" and interprets them as "a trope for a trans-subjective intertextuality that enables names, plots, words, viruses and other vital organs to pass fluidly from one body or text or nation to another, a process introduced through the recurring figure of the brain-dead youth" (250–51).

WORKS CITED

Allinson, Mark. *A Spanish Labyrinth: The Films of Pedro Almodóvar.* London: I. B. Tauris, 2001.

Altares, Guillermo. "An Act of Love toward Oneself." Willoquet-Maricondi 139–53.

Auslander, Philip. "Liveness: Performance and the Anxiety of Simulation." *Performance and Cultural Politics.* Ed. Elin Diamond. New York: Routledge, 1996. 196–213.

Ballesteros, Isolina. "El despertar homosexual del cine español: identidad y política en transición (Eloy de la Iglesia, Pedro Olea, Imanol Uribe y Pedro Almodóvar)." *Cine (Ins)urgente: Textos fílmicos y contextos culturales de la España postfranquista.* Madrid: Fundamentos, 2001. 91–127.

Butler, Judith. *Bodies That Matter: On the Discursive Limits of "Sex."* New York: Routledge, 1993.

———. *Gender Trouble: Feminism and the Subversion of Identity.* New York: Routledge, 1990.

Carlson, Marvin. *Performance: A Critical Introduction.* New York: Routledge, 2003.

Case, Sue Ellen. *Feminism and Theatre.* New York: Methuen, 1988.

Cielo, Silvana. "Conversation with Pedro Almodóvar." Willoquet-Maricondi 97–101.

Diamond, Elin, ed. *Performance and Cultural Politics.* New York: Routledge, 1996.

D'Lugo, Marvin. "The Politics of Textual Poaching." *Cinematic: The Harvard Annual Film Review* 3 (2005): 25–27.

Elwes, Catherine. "Floating Femininity: A Look at Performance Art by Women." *Women's Images of Men.* Eds. Sarah Kent and Jacqueline Morreau. New York: Writers & Readers Publishing, 1985. 164–93.

Gallero, José Luis. *Sólo se vive una vez. Esplendor y ruina de la movida madrileña.* Madrid: Ardora Ediciones, 1991.

Gutiérrez Albilla, Julián Daniel. "Body, Silence and Movement: Pina Bausch's *Café Müller* in Almodóvar's *Hable con ella.*" *Studies in Hispanic Cinemas* 2.1 (2005): 47–58.

Kinder, Marsha. "From Matricide to Mother Love in Almodóvar's *High Heels*." Vernon and Morris 145–53.

———. "Reinventing the Motherland: Almodóvar's Brain-Dead Trilogy." *Journal of Spanish Cultural Studies* 5.3 (October 2004): 245–60.

Lev, Leora. "Tauromachy as a Spectacle of Gender Revision in *Matador*." Vernon and Morris 73–86.

Mckenzie, John. *Perform or Else: From Discipline to Performance*. New York: Routledge, 2001.

Mira, Alberto. *De Sodoma a Chueca. Una historia cultural de la homosexualidad en España en el siglo XX*. Barcelona: Editorial EGALES, 2004.

Perriam, Chris. *Stars and Masculinities in Spanish Cinema: From Banderas to Bardem*. Oxford: Oxford University Press, 2003.

RuPaul. *Letting It All Hang Out: An Autobiography*. New York: Hyperion, 1995.

Schacht, Steven P. "Beyond the Boundaries of the Classroom: Teaching about Gender and Sexuality at a Drag Show." Schacht and Underwood 225–40.

Schacht, Steven P., and Lisa Underwood, eds. *The Drag Queen Anthology: The Absolutely Fabulous but Flawlessly Customary World of Female Impersonators*. Binghamton, N.Y.: Harrington Park Press, 2004.

Scott, A. O. "The Track of a Teardrop, a Filmmaker's Path." Willoquet-Maricondi 162–67.

Smith, Gavin. "The Curious Catholic." *Film Comment* 40.6 (Nov./Dec. 2004): 25.

Smith, Paul Julian. *Vision Machines: Cinema, Literature and Sexuality in Spain and Cuba, 1983–1993*. London: Verso, 1996.

Strauss, Frédéric. *Almodóvar on Almodóvar*. Trans. Yves Baignères. London: Faber and Faber, 1996.

Taylor, Verta, and Leila J. Rupp. "Chicks with Dicks, Men in Dresses: What It Means to Be a Drag Queen." Schacht and Underwood 113–33.

Vernon, Kathleen. "Las canciones de Almodóvar." *Almodóvar: el cine como pasión*. Eds. Fran A. Zurián and Carmen Vázquez Varela. Cuenca: Ediciones de la Universidad de Castila–La Mancha, 2005. 161–75.

Vernon, Kathleen M., and Barbara Morris, eds. *Post-Franco, Postmodern: The Films of Pedro Almodóvar*. Westport, Conn.: Greenwood Press, 1995.

Vilarós, Teresa. *El mono del desencanto. Una crítica cultural de la transición española (1973–1993)*. Madrid: Siglo XXI, 1998.

Williams, Linda. "Melodrama Revised." *Refiguring American Film Genres: History and Theory*. Ed. Nick Browne. Berkeley: University of California Press, 1998. 42–88.

Willoquet-Maricondi, Paula, ed. *Pedro Almodóvar: Interviews*. Jackson: University Press of Mississippi, 2004.

4   Acts of Violence in Almodóvar

PETER WILLIAM EVANS

From his earliest films, Pedro Almodóvar has maintained an interest in the crosscurrents of sex and violence. One of the posters for *Pepi, Luci, Bom* (1980), a sort of adult cartoon depiction of some scenes from the film, shows a man striking a woman, with the word *Tak* added to emphasize the thump on her face. *Volver* (2006), one of Almodóvar's most recent films, deals explicitly and dramatically with domestic abuse. Indeed, violent sexual practices that deviate from the mainstream abound in his films, showing extremes of behavior that can be shocking to audiences, especially in the context of rising alarm over domestic violence. Often attacked both at home and abroad as pornographic or antifeminist (Smith, *Laws of Desire* 83; Edwards 106–7, 140) and, in the case of *Tie Me Up! Tie Me Down!* (1990), once given an initial X-rating in the United States, Almodóvar's films, not surprisingly, provoke extreme reactions in various levels of audience, since their aim is partly to explore the more difficult areas of human experience.

What Have I Done to Deserve This? (1984), *Matador* (1986), *Live Flesh* (1997), *Tie Me Up! Time Me Down!*, and *Bad Education* (2004), for instance, survey acts of violence between men and women, while *Law of Desire* (1987) and *Bad Education* (2004) explore violence between men, and *Pepi, Luci, Bom* includes violence not only between men and women but also between women. In this, Almodóvar's first feature film, Alaska's character, Bom, is a sadist who becomes involved with the abused wife of a fascist policeman. Characters seem driven to acts of violence in ways that sometimes appear to be an attack not only on the victim but also on the perpetrator's own identity. Even though men are often its most troubled exponents, brutality is often also associated with women.

Consistently drawn to women's lives and melodrama, Almodóvar, like almost no other Spanish director, reflects the lived realities of Spanish women, and responds as much to the residual constraints of traditional Spanish patriarchy as to the realities of postdictatorial society. For instance, *What Have I Done to Deserve This?* has a housewife named Gloria (Carmen

Maura) coping with the demands of an overbearing husband in thrall to
Germanic culture, in a manner that recalls Francoism's affinity with the ideal
of feminine duty known as *Kinder, Küche, Kirche,* or "Children, Kitchen,
Church," that, though perhaps originally formulated by Kaiser Wilhelm II,
came to be linked to Nazi ideology. In Almodóvar's films, reaction by women
to continued stereotyping sometimes takes the form of violence, behavior
given perhaps its most complex treatment in *What Have I Done to Deserve
This?, Matador,* and *Volver.* In a far-reaching discussion of violence, James
Gilligan argues that "violence, like charity, begins at home" (5). He further
comments that violence, affecting as it does both victims and victimizers,
is tragic behavior that is not only individual but also "familial, societal and
institutional" (6–7). These general remarks, though primarily concerned
with conditions in the United States, nevertheless contain, for all their specific relevance to another cultural context, general propositions that help
illuminate films like *What Have I Done to Deserve This?* and *Matador.* Both
films locate violence in domestic spaces, highlighting the family structures
that can drive women—and not just men, as is more commonly the case—to
extreme forms of aggression.

In *What Have I Done to Deserve This?,* Gloria, the haggard, downtrodden housewife, finally snaps and explodes in a fury of revenge. But while
the film raises issues about the traditional dynamic of violator and violated,
as well as the revenge of the violated within a context of traditional gender
roles, other films explore the highly ritualized, fetishistic world of violent
sexuality, characterized above all by *Matador* and, to a less heightened degree,
Live Flesh and *Tie Me Up! Tie Me Down!.* The more naturalistic domestic
violence of *What Have I Done to Deserve This?,* a film often discussed as a sort
of complex homage to Italian neorealism, differs substantially from a film
like *Matador* that inflects social realism with other concerns, especially the
ritualized violence (complete with visionaries, double sights, solar eclipses,
fortune tellers, and references to destiny and fate) of lovers playing out their
own version of a *Liebestod* (love and death), what Roger Scruton, in a discussion of *Tristan und Isolde,* has referred to as death "accepted for love's
sake, . . . the triumph over the empirical world, a final proof of freedom and
personality against the meaningless flow of causes" (193). Whereas *What
Have I Done to Deserve This?* focuses on the all too "classical" imbalance
between the dominant male and the subordinate female, *Matador* concentrates, through the relationship between María Cardenal (Assumpta Serna)

and Diego Montes (Nacho Martínez), on violent sexual reciprocity, and looks ahead to *Tie Me Up! Tie Me Down!*, where Ricky (Antonio Banderas) oscillates between violence and tenderness toward Marina (Victoria Abril), and where kidnapping develops into a romantic resolution in a decidedly less fateful frame. Violence, fantasy, and reality, as well as the codes and conventions of romantic love and passion, are deployed differently in these films.

A criminal lawyer, María Cardenal also metaphorically represents, or enacts, a particularly dire version of the law of desire in her pursuit of Diego and the strangers that she seduces and kills. Diego, though, is not only her prime object of desire (she does not perfunctorily seduce and kill him—though at first she tries—as she does with an unidentified man that she picks up in the opening sequence of the film); he is also her alter ego, her "maestro," the externalization of what might be called her own phallic identity. After watching a Spanish-dubbed version of King Vidor's *Duel in the Sun* (1946) in a movie house, she wanders into not the women's but the men's lavatory, and warns Diego, who questions her presence there, not to trust in appearances: "No te fíes de las apariencias." Her attraction to Diego, therefore, expressed even in such an otherwise humorous detail, seems governed by at least two impulses: a fascination with the power of a once consummate bullfighter who had to abandon his work after being gored, and a desire to appropriate his lame and partly "emasculated" virility. María's cultish worship of Diego, pilfering fetishistic relics and ultimately sacrificing herself for him (and him for her), imbues her devotion with a quasi-religious aura and invites interpretation through René Girard's concept of the mimetic theory of identity, violence, and desire. In the light of Girard's general argument, María might be considered to recognize a lack in herself, and sees in Diego—now, significantly, a teacher, not a practitioner, of bullfighting—the guide to what she considers to be her own "true" identity. As Girard further argues, though, initial esteem often develops into rivalry, envy, and violence.

María's odyssey from adoration to *jouissance* and death, in the couple's act of mutual immolation, carries sacrificial themes, but the fatal climax to her union with Diego may not altogether be free from more localized feminist concerns with male violence toward women. James Gilligan's generalization that "all violence is an attempt to achieve justice, or what the violent person perceives as justice" (11), whatever its limitations, may be to some extent applicable to María Cardenal's obscure attraction to violence and its expression even in pursuit of her obsessional object of desire, Diego Montes.

The film begins with a series of violently pornographic images from snuff movies watched by the macho ex-bullfighter, who masturbates in the privacy of his home as scenes of decapitation, drowning, and dismemberment appear on his television screen. So presented, Diego seems to be the surrogate of a specifically heterosexual male audience, but in view of Almodóvar's frequent moments of self-consciousness (as in *Law of Desire* and *Tie Me Up! Tie Me Down!*), he also seems to stand in more generally for the audience as a whole, at least inasmuch as the entire scene constitutes a *mise en abîme* of the viewing process. Even if perhaps in ways that are not gender neutral, the film's meditation on the pleasure of watching acts of violence implicates the audience, tempting it to experience pleasure in viewing María's attacks on her male victims and/or Diego's against his female victims. Does the film, as Marsha Kinder suggests, in its reliance on a highly stylized mise-en-scène, distance the audience from the depiction of violence, sanitizing and justifying it on aesthetic and other grounds? Questions of audience response require careful handling, because the representation of gender and sexuality obviously signifies differently for different men and different women. Sexual orientation, nationality, class, religion, and age, for instance, constitute yet further differences in the reception of the film and the experience of pleasure.

Complex and important as these considerations are, there is little denying that *Matador* lays great emphasis on aesthetic display. Among other things, the glamour of Assumpta Serna, dressed in José María Cossío's creations, her hair darkened to give her that Ava Gardner look, may well distract us from the horror of her acts. Her glamour functions, moreover, as the self-applied armor that denies her own unhappiness. In associating herself with Ava Gardner and other femmes fatales of the past and, most clearly, with her direct precursor, Pearl Chavez (Jennifer Jones) in *Duel in the Sun,* María effectively presents herself as already dead, or at least as already marked by death.

A comparison with Eva (Eva Cobo), Diego's lover whom María eventually usurps, is instructive. Her ghostly white makeup, along with Nacho's desire that she remain motionless—that is, play dead—during sex, mark Eva as a corpse. In María's case, montage and costume emphasize her fascination with death, even though, in contrast to Eva, her pursuit of this perverse obsession is a mark of agency and not, as in Eva's case, of its abandonment. María's refusal to relinquish such agency may even lie behind Diego's spurning of Eva in favor of her, as in some willfully perverse inversion of the virgin/

whore, Mary/Eve binary. The snuff movie excerpts at the start of the film show the faces of women in close-up in expressions of pain and horror. One of these victims, a woman drowned in a bathtub, resembles María, who, in a following sequence interspersed with shots of Diego with his pupils at his bullfighting school, lures, seduces, and then kills a male pickup. As in, say, a fragment of montage in a film by Eisenstein, the audience seems to be expected to make conceptual links between these shots, and to draw conclusions about their mutual relevance. Costume, too, plays its part. Whereas it is sometimes used, as in the detail of María's delight in wrapping herself in Diego's cape, to emphasize what Paul Julian Smith terms the "abolition of sexual difference" (*Desire Unlimited* 70), the clothes often also reinforce the film's theme of dualities. María's "work clothes," a sort of business ensemble with a black-and-white check pattern, draw attention to the hidden darkness that lurks behind, or beside, the clarity of her desires. In the context of anger and mimicry of which Girard speaks, María's violence toward her nameless male victim and, more intricately and definitively, toward Diego Montes may well include—as we realize that Diego is the killer of women as well as of bulls—elements of something like feminist revenge. The ambiguity of her angry remark, "los hombres como tú" (men like you), after her failed attempt to kill Diego during their first sexual encounter, is sufficiently ambiguous to allow such an additional reading. Watching María attack her victims, the audience, in all its varied constitution, is likely to be governed, however, by a mixed response: on the one hand, seduced by María's (but also Assumpta Serna's) glamour and the strange logic of her actions; on the other, recoiling in horror from the violence of a disordered mind. According to classical psychoanalysis, psychopaths act out the delusions that for mentally balanced individuals are given "life" only in the unconscious and only in the realm of fantasy (Gilligan 61–62).

While women, therefore, provide some of the most provocative instances of violence in Almodóvar's films, his gaze more regularly focuses on violent men who may themselves be, as Vicens Fisas controversially proposes, victims of an ideology vetted by a fear of difference. Male rapists, "raped," as it were, by the symbolic structures of society, commit hostile acts that are readable, as with Ángel's (Antonio Banderas) attempted rape of Eva, in terms of "homosexual panic" (Smith, *Desire Unlimited* 71), part and parcel of mainstream homophobia. A number of Almodóvar's films can indeed be considered explorations of a socially conditioned general crisis of masculinity. *Live Flesh,* where male jealousy and competition take center stage, belongs to this group. Mystery and crime writer Ruth Rendell's account of male psychology in her novel *Live Flesh* (1986) sparked interest in a director whose films have tended to grapple with the ambiguities of male and female identity. Nevertheless, the shift of emphasis in Almodóvar's treatment is revealing. *Live Flesh,* the novel, is concerned with the obsessive, vengeful relationship of a psychopath; *Live Flesh,* the film, avoids perverse psychology, and is more interested in the attempts of a man to recover his own life through relationships with the wives of the two policemen responsible for his wrongful imprisonment.

Live Flesh presents five characters embroiled in two interlocking triangles, with paraplegic ex-policeman David (Javier Bardem) at their center. One triangle adheres to the conventions of adultery—Sancho (Jesús Franco) knows that his wife Clara (Ángela Molina) and his partner David are having an affair—while the other begins as a violently random encounter between the drug-addicted Elena (Francesca Neri), her hapless one-night sexual partner Víctor (Liberto Rabal), and David and Sancho, who burst into Elena's flat after hearing gunshots. In the course of a struggle between Sancho and Víctor, Sancho presses Víctor's finger on the trigger of his gun and shoots David, who as a result becomes permanently paralyzed and forced into early retirement. Víctor, whom the audience assumes is indeed responsible for the shooting, goes to jail, and Elena and David fall in love and marry, apparently in part because of the guilty fascination that they feel about the violence that bound them together. That Sancho does not confront David directly and shoot him outright allows him to elude the law by implicating someone else (here, Víctor). Sancho seems to be caught between conflicting impulses: between the rage against his partner in work and rival in love, David, who has sexually betrayed him, and the refusal to assume responsibility for the act that leaves David paralyzed. Sancho is thus both an upholder and a violator of criminal—and patriarchal—law. The surreal ambience of the scene of the shooting, with its attendant gestures to the power of the unconscious, is reinforced by the presence of a film within the film: *Ensayo de un crimen,* or *The Criminal Life of Archibaldo de la Cruz* (1955), one of Luis Buñuel's masterly analyses of male desire and violence, which has been playing on Elena's television set.

The overriding significance—displaced or not—of Sancho's attempt to kill David bears on the loss of what he considers a possession, his wife, a loss that represents an assault on Sancho's identity. Unable to accept his wife's autonomy, and infidelity, Sancho represents the conformist's failure in post-

Francoist Spain to come to terms with changing attitudes to the relations between the sexes; it is as if he were governed by hegemonic definitions of masculinity, a victim of both psychological and cultural convention. Significantly, Sancho's indirect act of violence against David represents one of the film's most potent instances of an assault on conformist masculinity; after all, it results in the crippling of a character, David, played by one of the icons of Spanish masculinity, Javier Bardem.

Nevertheless, however sympathetically Almodóvar may portray the plight of the embattled male in postmodern times, however much the audience may be pulled emotionally toward Sancho at the end of the film when he reaffirms his love for Clara as they both lie dying on top of each other (as in a replay of *Matador,* and even *Duel in the Sun*), the woman's perspective remains dominant. In casting Ángela Molina in the role of the adulterous wife who becomes the victim of her husband's jealousy and violent refusal to accept her separate identity, Almodóvar makes doubly sure of the audience's sympathies toward her predicament. A far more prominent star than Jesús Sancho in the recent history of the Spanish cinema, Molina appears to embody, with her characteristic look of bitterness, the fate of a woman trapped by the possessive violence of a conformist male. Molina's character, Clara, is at a critical phase in the lifeline of desire: an aging woman brought back to sexual passion, and love, by way of a handsome young lover, Víctor, who learns how to become "el mejor follador del mundo" (the best fucker in the world) only to abandon her for someone younger. Through close-ups of her distraught face, Clara is portrayed as a fading beauty, her fear that Víctor will leave her and her dependence on him providing a contrast to the autonomy that she attempts to claim for herself in her marriage to Sancho.

When Clara's patience with Sancho finally cracks, we are left to wonder in what circumstances individuals cross the border between self-control and loss of control. The most nuanced and sustained portrayal of a male character caught between these two extremes occurs in *Tie Me Up! Tie Me Down!,* where Ricky's actions, speech, and state of mind are marked by intertextual plays with other films and, on a more diegetically discrete level, by his obsessive relationship with Marina, his object of desire and, it would seem, the mirror of his inner self: both are as if lost in alien worlds. Both characters are defined through reference to horror, Marina an actress in horror movies, Ricky, as Gwynne Edwards puts it, a kind of monster (111) who in the outside world, and true to the spirit of the horror genre, reprises Almodóvar's challenge to the taboos of sex and gender. Through reformulation of the

Clara (Ángela Molina) is brought back to sexual passion and love by her young lover Víctor (Liberto Rabal) in Live Flesh *(1997). Photograph by Daniel Martínez. Copyright Daniel Martínez/El Deseo.*

conventions of horror, Almodóvar allows his characters to question the bases on which the rudiments of sex and gender are positioned.

The most direct intertextual, or interfilmic, references are to two well-known science-fiction and horror films: *Invasion of the Body Snatchers* (Siegel, 1956) and *Night of the Living Dead* (Romero, 1968). Marina watches *Night of the Living Dead,* playing on TV in her next-door neighbor's apartment, while Ricky has left in search of dope for her; *Invasion of the Body Snatchers* is invoked by way of a poster that hangs in the house of Máximo (Paco Rabal), the wheelchair-bound director of sleazy movies. Together, the references to the films suggest a link between Ricky's and Marina's behavior and two often overlapping genres that have explored with striking results difficult questions of identity, sexuality, and family life.

The threat to the mainstream in the Siegel and Romero films comes from outside: the aliens in the case of the former and the monsters in the case of the latter destabilize, precisely because they are alien, the certainties of conformist society. The identification of Ricky and Marina, through intertextuality, with horror suggests that their attitudes have been infiltrated and molded by difference. Whereas in 1950s Hollywood horror and science-fiction films, difference is usually regarded as intolerable and ultimately rejected, in Almodóvar difference is welcomed. Although both Máximo and Ricky are "crippled" (in the case of the former physically, in the latter, mentally), they are also both either attracted to elements of difference and/or become its living exponents: Máximo is an old man who desires the young, attractive Marina, star of porno horror thrillers through whom he seeks what must be his longing for otherness; Ricky, young and attractive himself, pursues the same idol as Máximo, though much more aggressively, almost as if he were the active projection of the wheelchair-bound director. Further instances of intertextuality include allusions to *The Collector* (Wyler, 1965), the John Fowles–inspired film about a man's abduction of a young woman, and, through Ennio Moricone's score, to Bernard Herrmann's music for *Psycho* (Hitchcock, 1960).

These allusions are, of course, not mere acts of homage. As Paul Julian Smith has argued, *Tie Me Up! Tie Me Down!* is a detached postmodernist version of horror, playfully deploying, through humor and hyperbole— or, as Rikki Morgan maintains, through a tone of absurdity—the conventions of the genre, as exemplified in *Night of the Living Dead.* The humorous reworking of generic convention bears on its equally conventional ideological content. The oblique reference in *Tie Me Up! Tie Me Down!* to a famous science-fiction film, *Invasion of the Body Snatchers,* is equally significant. In a discussion of the film, David Punter contends that "the invaders represent a possible order based on pure reason, the excision of the messiness of emotion, and there is no doubt that this alternative is held by the director in low esteem, but the psychological conflict is displaced: instead of being between ego and id, between reason and the uncontrolled, it is merely between two different kinds of conventionality" (353). Yet even if one does not attempt to rehabilitate *Invasion of the Body Snatchers*—and, by implication, a genre traditionally held in low esteem by mainstream criticism—as either an expression of queer sexuality (Benshoff) or, following Barbara Creed, a feminist challenge to the patriarchal order, the reference to it in *Tie Me Up! Tie Me Down!* suggests that Almodóvar, as director, endorses the radical potential of the genre. From this view, science-fiction and horror films expose the tyrannies of conventional family life, while celebrating desire—desire often expressed in uncontrollable or transgressive modes.

At one point in *Invasion of the Body Snatchers,* Becky, one of the last characters to be invaded by the aliens, tells her boyfriend: "I want to love and be loved. I want your children. I don't want a world without love. . . . I'd rather die." Given that *Tie Me Up! Tie Me Down!* is, as Robert Stone argues, the story of its main characters' quests for love, the allusion to *Invasion of the Body Snatchers* instead of, say, to a melodrama or romantic comedy, suggests that, beyond a fascination with garish aesthetics, Almodóvar recognizes the previously mentioned potential of horror and science fiction not only to challenge the patriarchal order but also to promote alternative stories of love, allowing for the exploration of taboo areas of sexuality such as sadomasochism, violence, and the wilder shores of desire.

Tie Me Up! Tie Me Down! expands on Almodóvar's interest in the transgressive potential of these films through references to more nuanced horror films like *The Collector* and *Psycho,* two films with strong elements of melodrama. Like *The Collector, Tie Me Up!* relies on abduction narratives and art themes (the artistic talents of the girl in *The Collector* resemble those of Ricky in *Tie Me Up! Tie Me Down!*), and emphasizes primary colors for the mise-en-scène. Bondage and the quest for love similarly connect the two films. But where *The Collector* concentrates almost exclusively on the psychopathic tendencies of Freddie Clegg (Terence Stamp) and grounds the film more firmly in its Gothic heritage (down to the crypt imagery in which Miranda Grey [Samantha Eggar] is imprisoned), *Tie Me Up! Tie Me Down!* avoids the Gothic setting (Marina is trapped in her own and her next-door neighbor's modern flats) and tempers Ricky's psychology with more redeeming tendencies, such as his desire for a "normal family," his care to avoid hurting Marina even as he hurts her. Nevertheless, the evocations of Freddie's childhood, as with Norman Bates in *Psycho,* offer Almodóvar shorthand opportunities for giving the audience access to the mental condition of his own troubled protagonist. Some of the dialogue, too, from *The Collector* seems to look ahead to *Tie Me Up! Tie Me Down!*, especially when Freddie tells his kidnapped victim Miranda: "You know what I want . . . it's what I've always wanted. You could fall in love with me if you tried. I've done everything I could to make it easy."

While intertextuality is one of the strategies adopted by Almodóvar to vary the perspectives on Ricky's pursuit of his object of desire, Marina's gradual enchantment by her captor contradicts the pattern of the film's antecedents—because in *The Collector* Miranda resists all of Freddie's overtures— and allows Almodóvar to explore the difficult terrain of sexual bondage, eventually mitigating Ricky's aggression through his victim's growing pleasurable submission to his will. In *The Collector,* Miranda is never tempted to fall under her captor's spell; in *Tie Me Up! Tie Me Down!,* Marina becomes steadily attracted to Ricky. The pursuit of love also becomes an expression of the submissive/dominant or bottom/top dynamics of sadomasochistic registers of sexual attraction. Almodóvar approaches here the thematic territory of Leopold von Sacher-Masoch's *Venus in Furs* and Pauline Réage's *The Story of O*. As the relationship moves from one between victim and victimizer to one in which Marina apparently becomes a willing partner, Almodóvar gives a glimpse into complex psychological processes, and along the way, as Isolina Ballesteros has argued, subverts the generic codes of mainstream pornography. Beyond the mysteries of sexual fascination, which in Marina's case, as in that of virtually all of Almodóvar's characters, remains unresolved, her eventual willing surrender to Ricky, paradoxically issuing from a restriction of her will, seems to highlight Marina's relief at being forcefully removed from a life of conflict. The film offers no suggestion that Marina's submission to Ricky is an expression of guilt or self-loathing for her life as an addict and porn star. Rather, submission—perhaps, as Stone suggests, in keeping with the so-called Stockholm syndrome—seems to express a release from responsibility, a contentment to allow her *bel homme sans merci* to take charge and to shoulder accountability. The matter is complicated, though, as the dynamics of Ricky and Marina veer between activity and passivity at different moments in their relationship. At first, Ricky seems to be cast as the dominant partner, reversing the Wanda/Severin pattern in Sacher-Masoch's *Venus in Furs*. Marina, seemingly content ultimately to submit to Ricky's authority, is nevertheless portrayed as a strong woman whose submission may be an expression of control. Her unbowed treatment of Máximo; her imperious commands to Ricky even when supposedly under his control; her decision to replace her untied rope and to "play" the part of the bound woman; her desire to be on top during their lovemaking; her pursuit of Ricky in his home village at the end of the film; her role as the killer of the muscular, Masked Avenger in Máximo's film—all are characteristics of a powerful woman. Indeed, her lassoing of the Masked Avenger seems like a prelude to the complex relationship of dominance and submission that she will later have with Ricky. In Máximo's movie, the porno heroine "ties up" the Masked Avenger; later she will not only be tied up by Ricky, but will also tie herself up, as the bonds with her abductor/lover are strengthened. That the role was given to an actress, Victoria Abril, identified with strong women, and not, say, to someone like Veronica Forqué, the raped woman of *Kika* (1993), often cast as a frivolous or incompetent character, is informative. The film's title, after all, is her command: "¡Átame!" (Tie me up!). The interchangeability of positions of submission and dominance in the same individual is ultimately what the film seems intent on demonstrating. The scene where Marina pleasures herself in a bathtub with a toy frogman predicts this outcome inasmuch as the difference in size between the full-grown ecstatic female and the diminutive mechanical male suggests that the eventual power relations between Ricky and Marina as they settle down to their future lives will not conform to conventional gender role patterns.

Nevertheless, for all the extenuating circumstances of Ricky's deprived childhood and mental problems, Almodóvar does not flinch from addressing the more disturbing drives of his personality. Played by Antonio Banderas, who at the time was sufficiently established as a matinee idol to demand audience sympathy whatever the role, Ricky is a character whose complexes are clearly signposted by Almodóvar early on in the mental institution. As Rikki Morgan and others have stressed, the origins of his disturbance have social as well as hereditary dimensions. Ricky is clearly a divided figure, a child-monster and a man-child, an instrument as well as a victim of aggression, a blend of hardness and softness, a narcissist often estranged from reality, yet also capable of great selflessness, such as the beating he takes in order to get Marina a fix. Banderas's soft glamour and vulnerability—noted by

Marina (Victoria Abril) trapped by Ricky (Antonio Banderas) in the cradle of violence in Tie Me Up! Tie Me Down! *(1990). Copyright El Deseo.*

Perriam and Stone, who refer to the actor's "suitability" for explorations of the ambiguous underside of machismo—are further nuanced through facial scars, visible signs of past beatings. The upshot is that this "monster" is not only the living affirmation of a femininity presumably accommodated in a male body, but also the expression of a subjectivity shaped and wounded by external pressures. Not perhaps a psychopath, then, but a character capable of psychopathic acts, Ricky comes across as a damaged individual whose obsession says as much about his own past as about the future he envisages with Marina.

Although not expressed as a simplistic psychoanalytic explanation for the causes of his troubled personality, Ricky's description of his life as a sort of metro map offers important clues to his condition. Significantly, he offers this graphic account of his life following the first act of mutual sexual longing and expression. A cut from the previous scene of lovemaking shows us Ricky at a drawing board; Marina approaches, and Ricky shows her his drawing, explaining its significance. Chris Perriam reads in the drawing's "goal-oriented dominance" a statement about male narcissism. The choice of an *underground* guide to his personal history is, of course, not incidental, and serves as an expression of previously buried desires. Orphaned at three, an escapee from the orphanage at eight, interned at a reform school and then, at sixteen, at a mental hospital from which he repeatedly absconds, but to which he always returns until he meets Marina at the Lulú club, Ricky is clearly someone whose final destination—the metro stop named Marina—has been determined by a history of adversity. But what draws Ricky to Marina? Why is Marina Ricky's magnificent obsession? His passion—at a moment in her life where she is still a druggie porn star—is a form of self-knowledge, a route map to the self. It not only illustrates Linda Williams's point about the shared predicaments of monsters and victims in the horror genre, but also plays out a drama of primary narcissism in childhood, that form of self-love present at birth and distinguishable from secondary narcissism that follows on from object-love. Ricky's failure to break free from the mental institution—repeatedly leaving but returning—as well as his obsession with Marina, are readable as examples of a repetition compulsion, Freud's "manifestation of the power of the repressed," a deeply ingrained tendency to "revert to earlier conditions," in short, a death drive. Although at an important level there is clearly a difference between Ricky's involvement with Marina and his relationships with other women (most notably, the director of the mental institution, played by Lola Cardona), there is also an interesting set of underlying determinants that point toward unconscious overlaps. Ricky sees Marina as his journey's end on his figurative metro station itinerary. She is his sexual *and* emotional destination, and his night of passion after their meeting at the Lulú club is the prelude to the long-term relationship and conventional family bliss that he has craved ever since. Ricky's loss of his mother has apparently led to a search for her in the women with whom he has relationships in adult life, a search that culminates in a hybrid object of desire, Marina, whom he can simultaneously worship as the nubile wife and potential ideal mother and denigrate as porn star. The director of the mental institution is clearly a mother substitute, but Ricky's relationship with her and other women plays out a classic pattern of a man who, deserted—whether by accident or design—by his mother, seeks to punish women by seducing and abandoning them. Ricky's passion for Marina, as well as his craving through her of "normality," is coupled with feelings of loss, anger, and revenge.

On returning from the Chueca neighborhood in Madrid, where he is beaten up by dope peddlers for failing to pay for drugs on a previous occasion, Ricky sits in front of a mirror back at the next-door neighbor's apartment where he has imprisoned Marina. As Marina joins him and begins to tend to his wounds, he comments that the scene reminds him of how, during his childhood, his mother used to shave his father. Ricky and Marina become for an instant, in the mirror of time present, reflections of his parents in time past. Marina hears his words, and seems perfectly content to play out her implicit Oedipal role. In this and other scenes, the gentleness and even respect with which he treats Marina represent conventionally positive feelings of a son for his mother. The scene before the mirror is followed by their prolonged lovemaking in the bedroom: Marina's desire, kissing Ricky for the first time, is prompted not only by domestic nostalgia but also by interrelated sensations of pain and pleasure; Ricky's passion is fired by complicated memories of his parents, at once sweetly nostalgic and full of anger, that seem to play themselves out in Marina. Giving themselves over to an intense session of lovemaking, Ricky winces in pleasure as Marina caresses his battle-scarred body, while Marina, for her part, both suffers and delights in the painful pleasures of her physically and emotionally wounded lover. Now a dominatrix, now a mother figure, Marina is a double-sided character: an active participant in the narrative, with her own drives and ambitions, as well as the projection of Ricky's obsessions and traumas.

The Madonna imagery that marks the relationship between Ricky and Marina—brought to the viewer's attention above all through pictures of the

Virgin Mother and Christ in the neighbor's flat, where, significantly, Ricky and Marina begin to grow closer—suggestively highlights a problematic mother–child dynamic from which Ricky has apparently yet to recover and which continues to define his relations with women. The fragmented nature of these and other visual reflections of Ricky's Oedipal trauma provides spatial equivalents of the repetition compulsion, because the images are not only multiplied but also repeated.

In the very last scene of the film, as Ricky, Marina, and her sister Lola (Loles León) head for Ricky's home village of Granadilla, Lola and Ricky begin to sing a cheery song: "Resistiré" ("I will resist" or, perhaps, "I will survive"). As ever in an Almodóvar film, music is highly significant. For instance, Lola's song to the company assembled at a party celebrating the end of shooting Máximo's movie provides, as Mark Allinson has suggested, a break in the dramatic tension (203). At the end of the movie, as Lola and Ricky sing, Marina remains silent, but responds to the lyrics, a little tearfully, as if in recognition of their relevance to her own lately discovered happiness, the satisfaction of the sadomasochistic heroine who has found her love's desire: "Cuando pierda todas las partidas/Cuando duerma con la soledad/Cuando se me pierda la salida/Y la noche no me deja en paz . . . Resistiré" (When I lose at all the games/When I sleep in solitude/When I find no more ways out/And the night does not bring me peace . . . I shall survive). This hymn to resistance and survival appears to be, from Marina's point of view, a perfectly apt summary of her redemption from unhappiness through her love for Ricky.

But the irony of the lyrics as Ricky and Marina head for the conventional bliss that they have so erratically and violently sought is not lost on Lola, who looks away, the expression on her face offering a coda on the complicated future that may well await the now happy couple. The optimism of the lyrics and the melody, and their jaunty delivery by Lola and Ricky, do not obliterate the memory of the earlier nondiegetic music that accompanied Ricky in his first visit to Marina's flat. The horror-genre score comprised of relentless string and horn instruments, at once reinforcing and reinforced by Ricky's look of dementia as he tracks his "beloved" down, no less than the blow to Marina's face that Ricky delivers in an early scene at her flat, suggest, for all their comic, campy expressiveness, a displaced anger toward the absent mother. Ambiguity and saving graces are characteristic features of Almodóvar's films, poised between comedy and melodrama, between light-hearted romance and drama, even tragedy, and, here, between horror and science fiction as well. *Tie Me Up! Tie Me Down!* deals, as ever in Almodóvar, with provocative themes. Its treatment of violence avoids patterns found in recent Spanish films with more social-realist agendas such as Icíar Bollaín's *Take My Eyes* (2003), an approach that Almodóvar comes closer to taking in *Volver*. At the other end of the spectrum of Almodóvar's exploration of violence are films like *Pepi, Luci, Bom; Law of Desire; Kika; Matador;* and, as I have here been insisting, *Tie Me Up! Tie Me Down!,* where sadomasochism, pain, and aggression are elements of complex forms of sexual pleasure. In *Tie Me Up! Tie Me Down!,* as in *Matador,* Almodóvar's treatment of violence is not confined to a reflection of social patterns of abuse involving real-life violators and victims. Instead, in these films, the complicity of the characters in changing roles of domination and submission shows Almodóvar to be the heir to Sacher-Masoch and Pauline Réage, a cinematic poet of fantasy—and of the pain and pleasure of sexual desire.

WORKS CITED

Allinson, Mark. *A Spanish Labyrinth: The Films of Pedro Almodóvar.* London: I. B. Tauris, 2001.

Ballesteros, Isolina. *Cine (Ins)urgente: Textos fílmicos y contextos culturales de la España post-franquista.* Madrid: Fundamentos, 2001.

Benshoff, H. M. *Monsters in the Closet: Homosexuality and the Horror Film.* Manchester: Manchester University Press, 1997.

Creed, Barbara. *The Monstrous Feminine: Film, Feminism and Psychoanalysis.* London: Routledge, 1993.

Edwards, Gwynne. *Almodóvar: Labyrinths of Passion.* London and Chester Springs: Peter Owen, 2001.

Fisas, Vicens, ed. *El sexo de la violencia: Género y cultura de la violencia.* Barcelona: Icaria, 1998.

Freud, Sigmund. "Beyond the Pleasure Principle." *On Metapsychology: The Theory of Psychoanalysis.* Harmondsworth: Pelican Books, 1984 [1920]. 269–338.

Gilligan, James. *Violence: Reflections on a National Epidemic.* New York: Vintage, 1997.

Girard, René. *Desire, Deceit and the Novel: Self and Other in Literary Structure.* Trans. Yvonne Freccero. Baltimore and London: Johns Hopkins University Press, 1969.

———. *Violence and the Sacred.* Trans. Patrick Gregory. Baltimore and London: Johns Hopkins University Press, 1997.

Kinder, Marsha. *Blood Cinema: The Reconstruction of National Identity in Spain.* Los Angeles: University of California Press, 1993.

Morgan, Rikki. "Dressed to Kill." *Sight and Sound* 1.12 (1992): 28–29.

Perriam, Chris. *Stars and Masculinities in Spanish Cinema: From Banderas to Bardem.* Oxford: Oxford University Press, 2003.

Punter, David. *The Literature of Terror.* London: Longman, 1980.

Rendell, Ruth. *Live Flesh.* London: Arrow, 1986.

Scruton, Roger. *Death-Devoted Heart: Sex and the Sacred in Wagner's* Tristan and Isolde. Oxford: Oxford University Press, 2004.

Smith, Paul Julian. *Desire Unlimited: The Cinema of Pedro Almodóvar.* London: Verso, 1994.

——. *Laws of Desire: Questions of Homosexuality in Spanish Writing and Film 1960–1990.* Oxford: Clarendon Press, 1992.

Stone, Robert. *Spanish Cinema.* London: Longman, 2002.

Williams, Linda. "When the Woman Looks." *Re-Vision: Essays in Feminist Film Criticism.* Eds. Mary Ann Doane, Patricia Mellencamp, and Linda Williams. Los Angeles: University Publications of America, 1984. 83–99.

5 Heart of Farce Almodóvar's Comic Complexities

ANDY MEDHURST

The moment when a daughter discovers that her mother has not died but is in fact still alive should, one might reasonably expect, be a moment of intense emotional depth. Yet what happens to that emotional depth if the daughter makes this discovery while she is urinating, her knickers pulled down to her knees, and bases her conclusion on the lingering smell of her mother's farts? This is what happens at a pivotal point in Pedro Almodóvar's *Volver* (2006), which, in the collision that it mischievously engineers between a profound thematic seriousness and a robust delight in what is quite literally "toilet humor," neatly crystallizes both the director's continuing determination to use comedy, even in the unlikeliest of contexts, and the implications that such a determination has for the reception and reputation of his work. In what follows, I will trace two of the ways in which Almodóvar's comedy is critical to a fuller, more complex understanding of his films: first, by considering how his commitment to comedy troubles his standing as a director increasingly placed in the venerated tradition of the European art film, and second, by exploring whether the specifically Spanish contexts of his comedy are lost on, or overlooked by, those international admirers (myself included) who revere Almodóvar as a totemic figure in queer culture.

Value, Seriousness, and Ennui: Almodóvar and Art Cinema

According to one British account of his work, Almodóvar is "the only remaining European *auteur*" (Maddison 271). This sweeping claim might not be entirely accurate, but it does indicate something about how Almodóvar has come to be perceived outside Spain. As Paul Julian Smith has pointed out, the consolidation of Almodóvar's international critical reputation from the late 1980s onward made his films "a regular source of high-profile new product" for art-house cinemas (5), one of the few venues designed, under the promotional banner of the director's name, to attract audiences looking for cinematic stimulation beyond the confines of Hollywood. Yet the location of Almodóvar in the art-house tradition is not, to my mind, an entirely comfortable one, and the chief source of the discomfort that attends attempts to place him in that pantheon is his devotion to comedy. The grand tradition of European art cinema has never been an environment in which comedy could breathe easily; indeed, it might be fair to say that one of the qualities that unite the very disparate films and filmmakers shoehorned into the art-house tradition is their humorlessness.

For those middle-class audiences seeking cultural uplift from cinema, comedy is always problematic, because it so often trades in the undermining of dignity and the mockery of pretension. Comedy is part of mass culture, aimed at large audiences instead of at that self-selecting minority who populated those cinemas that, in James Monaco's sly formulation, "served espresso and pastries rather than popcorn and coca-cola" (7).[1] Comedy courts the vulgar; art cinema yearns for the refined. A book like Penelope Houston's *The Contemporary Cinema,* published in 1963 as an explicit beginner's guide for the middle-class viewer eager to understand the art film and its practitioners, drew a cinematic map whose key topographical features were individual creativity, internationalism, and freedom from the supposed constraints of popular genres and large audiences. The first four directors named by Houston were Antonioni, Bergman, Resnais, and Truffaut, all benchmark figures in the discourse of art cinema that books like Houston's were helping to forge and disseminate, and all, to varying degrees, filmmakers for whom comedy was hardly a high priority. In later decades, as film became institutionalized as an academic subject respectable enough for university degrees, textbooks emerged that further strengthened the links between high cinematic reputation, the cult of the director as unchallenged source of meaning, and an overriding sensibility of seriousness. A 1970s collection edited by Braudy and Dickstein, called with what now seems like an almost endearing pompousness *Great Film Directors,* deigns to include a few makers of comedies among its elite platoon of artists, but any threat that they may have posed to high cinematic seriousness was contained and neutralized. Chaplin and Keaton are included, but made safe by the relative antiquity of their best work. Hawks and Capra are there as well, but their comedies are only one thread in the wider generic repertoire required by the Hollywood studio system. Buñuel is also covered, but his is a comedy made intellectually respectable through its placement in the unimpeachably high-cultural zone of surrealism.[2]

One of the first attempts to offer a systematic account of what the term "art cinema" actually signified came from David Bordwell in "The Art Cinema as a Mode of Film Practice." Written in the late 1970s, but still anthologized as a key critical piece in the early twenty-first century, Bordwell's article proposed a systematic, itemized account of art cinema's distinguishing features. In it, he noted that films routinely placed in the art-house category tended to be made outside the United States; were looser, less cause-and-effect–driven narratives than those of Hollywood; stressed the psychological complexity of their characters; favored dialogue over external action, and offered an abiding tone of ambiguity and uncertainty. Art cinema, claimed Bordwell, diminished the role of genres and stars as focal points of audience appeal while elevating the director as the governing framework through which each film should be understood, a move predicated on the perception or assumption that directors making such films had a creative freedom that was simply unavailable in production contexts more concerned with maximizing audiences. Films acclaimed as art cinema often, he argued, played games with formal and temporal norms and frequently returned to a thematic trope centered on "the realization of the anguish of ordinary living" (777). Once again, the implication here, unstated but hovering throughout, is that art cinema is a site of seriousness, broadly existential in tone, and dedicated to encouraging its audiences to recognize and empathize with angst and ennui. (The linguistic internationalism of such terms is a telling index of the self-flattering cosmopolitanism of the art-cinema audience in Britain and North America.)

For witty confirmation of the umbilical cord that links art cinema and high seriousness, consider an article written in 1983 by John Waters, the director whose exaggerated and scandalous bad-taste comedies (*Multiple Maniacs* [1971] is the best, *Pink Flamingos* [1972] the best known) have been acknowledged by Almodóvar as an influence on his early films (Strauss 13). In the 1980s, the American journal *Film Comment* ran a series of articles called "Guilty Pleasures" in which critically acclaimed filmmakers lightheartedly confessed their secret love of gory horror films, or tacky teen musicals, or some other allegedly disreputable genre. It was a space where those sanctioned as emblematic of good taste could humanize themselves a little by revealing their penchant for particular strands of bad taste. Asking Waters to contribute a piece to this series immediately inverted the premise of the enterprise, as his whole career was founded on producing trash-saturated, queer-inflected, carnivalesque assaults on conventional codes and hierarchies of taste. The surprise element of the series would be lost if Waters disclosed his obvious fondness for kitsch and schlock, so his scandalous admission was his hidden desire for the high citadels of European art cinema. "Give me black and white, subtitles and a tiny budget, and I'm impressed. I really like snotty, elitist theatres . . . where if you ask for popcorn they look at you as if you're a leper asking for heroin" (108).[3] Being Waters, he cannot resist sending up the characteristic traits of art cinema and suggests that posters for such films should include faux-sensationalist lines like: "Watch as Bresson directs an entire film where nothing happens" (109). Nevertheless, his genuine admiration of these films is clear. For the purposes of my argument, what matters here is the way that Waters's jokes, and the jokey premise of his whole piece, underline the point that solemnity, existential gloom, and a lack of humor are intrinsic, constituent parts of the general perception of art cinema. Yet Almodóvar's films, for all their artful turns, are full of humor, ranging across the comedic palette from the outlandish punky camp of *Labyrinth of Passion* (1982) to the swishy boulevard farce of *Women on the Verge of a Nervous Breakdown* (1988) and the consoling humorous warmth that alleviates the tragedies of *All about My Mother* (1999).

Given all of this, it is apparent that Almodóvar does not fit easily into the art-film mold and that comedy is where much of the awkwardness of the fit resides. Not all of Almodóvar's films merit the straightforward generic designation of comedy, but with the possible exception of *Live Flesh* (1997), they all use comedy as part of their tonal armory, and they often switch rapidly from the serious to the comic or parachute comedy into the unlikeliest of contexts: the aforementioned toilet scene in *Volver* exemplifies this. Almodóvar's fondness for farcical plots full of outrageous coincidences and dramatic conclusions contradicts the classic art-film preference for loose ends and ambiguity, and even though he is, following art-cinema models, undoubtedly touted as the key creative force behind his films, his fondness for constructing and capitalizing on the star personae of his lead performers aligns him firmly with tendencies more associated with the popular genre film. He plays the games of celebrity culture just as deftly as he consolidates his reputation with intellectual criticism, and in that sense he is not so much antagonistic toward the art-film tradition as engaged in an enterprise of cross-referencing it with less elite approaches. Revealingly, when interviewed about the films that most excited and influenced him early in his life, he names paradigmatic art films by Antonioni, Godard, and Truffaut—all feted by both Houston and the *Great Film Directors* collection—directly alongside Hollywood melodramas and comedies (Strauss 2–5). Such cross-referencing mirrors the generic flexibility of his own films, in particular their continued refusal to relinquish the comic.

Kathleen Rowe has made the interesting claim that "comedy is . . . often confined to the realm of amusement [rather] than art because of its popular accessibility and its connections with gossip, intrigue and the everyday, areas of culture tied to the feminine" (43). Rowe's insight seems particularly resonant with Almodóvar's ambiguous placement between the comic and the serious. It would be risky to venture any absolute statement, but there might well be a correlation between comedy and femininity in his films. Certainly, if *Live Flesh* is the least comic, it is also the least feminine, while *Matador* (1986) and *Talk to Her* (2002) might also be tentatively placed at the same end of the spectrum. *Bad Education* (2004) is a film similarly centered on male characters and relationships and similarly imbued with a dark seriousness, though in early scenes it is notable that it is the cross-dressing figure of Paquita (Javier Cámara) who provides an injection of both humor and femininity. The relevance of these points to the discourse of art cinema is not difficult to deduce, for another of the characteristics shared by most of the films given that label tends to be their masculine sensibility, both in terms of the gender of the directors central in forming the canon and in the preponderance of narratives of masculine angst. Almodóvar's films repeatedly connect femininity and comedy, not in the sense of that ignoble tradition of sexist humor in which men make fun of women, but in the sense that women embody the humor of survival, the laughter that gets people through difficult times, what Rowe has called "a laughter that expresses anger, resistance, solidarity and joy" (41). Rowe makes this assessment in an analysis of Hollywood comedy, but to me it seems richly evocative of the uses of laughter and humor in recent films by Almodóvar. There is a scene in *All about My Mother* where the characters of Huma, Manuela, Rosa, and Agrado share cava, ice cream, and raucous laughter about their friendships, rivalries, and the terminology of the male anatomy, which is almost a textbook evocation of Rowe's formulation. Almodóvar's "return" to both the feminine and the comedic in *Volver* after the relatively masculinized dramas of *Talk to Her* and *Bad Education* might thus be seen as supporting Rowe's claim about laughter as a mode of female empowerment and resistance. Such a return might even be another meaning of the film's title.

The centrality of comedy to Almodóvar seems evident enough, yet this very centrality poses a problem for any critic who wants to place Almodóvar

Javier Cámara performing as Paquita onstage in Bad Education *(2004). Copyright El Deseo.*

squarely in the art-cinema lineage. To put it crudely, putting him there means "rescuing" him from comedy: his serious dimensions must be stressed, his humor pushed to the side. Maddison has noted how much of the critical praise bestowed upon *All about My Mother* strove to separate the "maturity and emotional gravitas" of the film from its "less appealing camp histrionics" (276). A similar dichotomy sometimes emerges cloaked in the mantle of maturity, suggesting that Almodóvar's films have become less comic as his career has unfolded. "Accustomed as we are to Almodóvar's heady hedonism and crazy comedy, are we adult enough for a Pedro who has well and truly grown up?" asked Paul Julian Smith in an account of *Live Flesh* (182). The suggestion here—and it comes from a critic who has otherwise shown an assured awareness of how important comedy is for Almodóvar—is that the comedic equals the immature, something to be left behind before full cinematic adulthood is attained. Echoes of the same critical narrative also surface in Bersani and Dutoit's account of Almodóvar's trajectory, according to which his more recent films explore areas of "difficulty" that the earlier films could only represent "light-heartedly" (119). As an alternative strategy, certain components of Almodóvar's comedy can apparently be accepted, while others continue to be placed at a distance. Mark Allinson, for instance, has written of Almodóvar's use of "satire, irony, the sardonic, parody, the absurd, even slapstick" (127), where the giveaway word is *even,* placed so as to demarcate five rather respectable comedic forms from the tainted low-ness of slapstick (Carmen Maura's farting self-exposure in *Volver* would, I presume, prove even more troubling).

On one level, these critical moves are entirely understandable. There is a commonsense journalistic perception in Britain, the United States, and else-where of Almodóvar as a filmmaker of kitsch surfaces and shock-tactic sexu-alities, hence the profusion of newspaper articles that call him "the schlocky king of Spanish sex comedy" (Glaister 10) or that are headlined "Ooh, Pedro, You Are Awful" (Griffiths 3), adapting a catchphrase from the lowbrow Brit-ish television comedian Dick Emery. Even a travel guide to Spain feels enti-tled to present, and dismiss, Almodóvar as having "a trademark obsession with transsexuals" (Baskett et al. 1116). Faced with such misrepresentative simplifications, the urge felt by Smith and Allinson, two key champions of the director in the British academy, to insist on Almodóvar's seriousness makes sense, but the risk incurred by such moves is to overlook one of the most compelling aspects of what Almodóvar does: namely, his skill in hold-ing together the serious and the ludicrous, interpersonal profundity and the fart joke, in order to insist on the indivisibility of comedy and tragedy (and all points in between) in the lives that he represents.

Cultural Kidnapping: Is Almodóvar Internationally Queer?

Sitting in a cinema in a provincial English city in 1989, I had my first encoun-ter with Pedro Almodóvar. As *Women on the Verge of a Nervous Breakdown* unfolded, I was mesmerized, but I also became increasingly annoyed by a couple in the seats in front of me. They were annoying me because they laughed at the film in different ways to how I laughed. They laughed more often than I did, slightly before I did, and sometimes when I did not laugh at all. The reason became clear as the film ended and they began to talk to each other in perfect Spanish. Their laughter was different from mine because they heard the verbal jokes before the subtitles could translate them for me and because they grasped the cultural reference points that I only recognized in a limited way or not at all. My annoyance with them was frustration, or envy, or embarrassment at my ignorance, and this anecdote has stayed with me because it crystallizes the cultural specificity of comedy. More than any other cultural mode, comedy requires an inside knowledge of the culture that produces it, because so much of comedy's raw material is deeply rooted in the locale from which it is generated. As much as I value Almodóvar, and as much as that value centers on his use of the comedic, I am still concerned that I do not get all the jokes. My Spanish is much better than it was in 1989, and frequent visits to Spain have introduced me to the camp wonders of Carmen Sevilla's epics of diva excess on *Cine de Barrio* as well as to the apparent indestructibility and particular fashion sense of the Duquesa de Alba, but my enjoyment of such phenomena can only ever be from the outside—from an increasingly well-informed outside, I would like to think, but an outside nonetheless, still sitting somewhere in the cinema behind that Spanish couple.[4]

The issues of belonging, location, and cultural knowledge also relate to another aspect of Almodóvar's international standing. In a cross-cultural framework that runs parallel to, but remains differently inflected from, his relationship to art cinema, Almodóvar is acclaimed as a figurehead for queer cinema, and rightly so, because the images and themes found in his films are saturated with the issues and concerns that occupy the minds of those interested in analyzing the interrelationships of sexuality and culture. There are moments in Almodóvar films which seem predesigned to set queer analytic pulses racing, not least the sequence early in *High Heels* (1991) when the drag-act character of Femme Letal mimes to the song "Un Año de Amor" (A Year of Love). In its fusion of masquerade, seduction, excess, glamour, parody, intrigue, sexual complexity, sexual politics, comedy, melodrama, performativity, style, outrage, kitsch, and camp, the sequence summarizes, in one brief efflorescence of cinematic bravura, everything that makes Almodóvar such a queer visionary. Yet the word *queer* is far from unproblematic in a discussion of Almodóvar's work, not least because it is rooted in a particular critical vocabulary developed to suit the needs of the Anglo-American academy (and was in any case smuggled into that academy from the more confrontational sphere of street activism). I cannot shake off a concern that I, and other Anglophone queers like me, have somehow "stolen" Almodóvar. Perhaps *stolen* is not exactly the right verb; perhaps it is not so much a matter of stealing as of kidnapping. At any rate, in my fervent determination to elect Almodóvar the preeminent queer artist of contemporary times (which is still, despite the contortions of this article, what I believe him to be), I have had to steal him away from home. Worse still, I have encouraged others to commit the same act. Every year, I teach an MA course that examines the intersections between popular culture and sexual minorities, and every year at least one student chooses to make Almodóvar the focus of his or her term paper. Yet, in almost all of these term papers, both the excellent ones and those that are less successful, one aspect of Almodóvar is routinely sidelined or even ignored: his Spanishness. Again, there is a process of cultural kidnapping going on here, in the sense that Almodóvar has become such a benchmark figure for a certain internationalized version of queer culture that the precise, rooted core of his cultural belonging is as often as not elided or played down. His films offer such rich pickings for those eager to write about camp or gender performativity that they are routinely excised from their Hispanic contextual specificity and placed in a grid of intellectual reference points that are overwhelmingly Anglo-American.[5]

The discourse of camp is probably the best ground on which to look more closely at these issues. Nobody with even the slenderest understanding of that slippery term could fail to acknowledge that Almodóvar's films are drenched in camp, yet there are huge risks in simply assuming that the term and/or the concept mean identical things in different cultural contexts. Although there are clearly international dimensions to camp, in the sense that iconic Hollywood stars like Bette Davis and Marilyn Monroe signify as camp to gay subcultures in North America, Britain, and Spain (two of the other drag queens savoring Letal's performance in *Tacones lejanos* are dressed as Davis and Monroe), this may say more about the all-pervasive twin hegemonies of Hollywood cinema and Anglophone gay subcultures than it does about any rashly presumed consonances between sexual subjectivities across cultural boundaries. Then again, there do seem to be intriguing transborder parallels in how gay men respond to the star systems of their national cinemas as well as to the icons delivered through internationally marketed products. It is doubtful, to say the least, that the young Almodóvar, growing up in rural La Mancha in the 1950s and 1960s, was at all conversant with the homosexual subcultures of San Francisco, New York, or London, yet his enraptured, youthful devotion to both Spanish stars (such as Sara Montiel) and Hollywood ones (Davis, Monroe, Elizabeth Taylor) seems strikingly reminiscent of how queers in more modern, urban centers responded to their divas of choice. Almodóvar's subsequent gathering and nurturing of his own divas takes that adolescent starstruck queer consumption to its dazzling conclusions. Yet, for all the compulsively seductive overlaps, Carmen Maura is still *not* Bette Davis; Marisa Paredes is still *not* Greta Garbo, because to reduce the Spanish stars to their Hollywood approximations would diminish the specifically Hispanic camp of Almodóvar's approach.

Once again, Almodóvar is engaged in cultural cross-stitching: just as he plays out a fruitful tension between art cinema and popular genres, he also meshes and contrasts Anglophone traditions of camp with more specifically Spanish applications of that sensibility. The interplays he manages between camp and Catholicism seem especially relevant in Spain (only a lapsed Spanish Catholic and a particular kind of homosexual could have made *Dark Habits* [1983]), as are the complex and often troubled currents between camp and the traditional Spanish vision of the family. Chris Perriam has noted how Almodóvar uses the codes of camp to stage a critique of Francoist culture, not through a head-on attack but more subversively, by exposing the limitations of its moral certainties and proscriptive propensities and by reimagining its most cherished cultural codes as camp. Even an outside eye like mine cannot help but notice how popular culture of the late Franco era is ripe for camp appropriation. The impossibly heartfelt trilling of Joselito, for example, or Rocío Dúrcal leading well-scrubbed teenagers and kindly nuns in a musical march through the woods in *Canción de juventud* (Song of Youth) (Lucia, 1962), are images of such overdetermined normativity that they cry out for queer ridicule.[6] Even so, the way I might go about undertaking such a comedic critique could never be the same as those that issue from a more direct, inside experience of Spanish constructions of culture and identity.[7] It is that dimension of cultural specificity that too many non-Hispanic queer celebrations of Almodóvar neglect—a particularly regrettable neglect given that so much of the aesthetic power and political daring in his work is so intimately connected to the cultural context in which it is made.

Laughter at the Limits

I want to return now to the question of Almodóvar's ability to blur boundaries. One of the most dangerous of those boundaries is the line, always wavy and anxiously policed, between topics that we should and should not find funny. As a number of critics have argued, many of Almodóvar's films meld comedy and melodrama, often to the point where the two become hard to distinguish. Topics that in other hands would be rendered representable through the emotional extremities of the melodramatic mode (sexual obsession, infidelity, jealousy, revenge) sometimes emerge in Almodóvar's world as comic—or, more often than not, they are caught oscillating between comedic and melodramatic poles. The film historian Gerald Mast once formulated the useful idea of the "comic climate," by which he meant "the signs by which we recognise that we are in the presence of a comic work" (9). Such signs might include the title of a work, its typology of characters, the casting of performers who bring with them particular expectations, the use of particular stylizations of speech or dialogue, tonal paradoxes where usually trivial matters are handled with the utmost gravity and vice versa, certain deployments of costume and decor, all of which, and more, can function as indices of levity, reassuring audiences that laughter is not only permitted but encouraged.

Almodóvar's uses of the comic climate are many, varied, and densely packed. He asks us to laugh through his love of flagrantly contrived and infamously intricate plots, or through the strategic deployment of regional accents (this, I now know, is one of the things that amused that Spanish couple whose laughter so eclipsed mine). In his earliest films, made in the febrile context of the *Movida,* the liberalizing and liberating cultural upheaval that followed the death of Franco, interpolations and reworkings of English phrases—"¡Qué overdose!" shrieks Fanny McNamara at the beginning of *Labyrinth of Passion*—work to cue laughter through their establishment-baiting disregard for official Spanish cultural norms. Almodóvar's extravagant and stylized use of costume often signals the arrival of a comic climate, as does the physical appearance of some of his favored performers; Peter William Evans, for one, has perceptively observed how Rossy de Palma's "exotic bird features, especially her toucan beak, belong to comedy's traditional disrespect for the body" (23). Furthermore, the decor of houses, apartments, and public spaces is rarely naturalistic in Almodóvar's films, and often works to signify that they are sites in which the comedic can occur. In these and other ways, Almodóvar equips himself, and prepares us, for the flirting with cultural danger that occurs when the boundaries of the comic climate are pushed to their limits.

A particularly spectacular example of such boundary crossings occurs in *What Have I Done to Deserve This?* (1984), when Gloria (Carmen Maura) undertakes a transaction in which she agrees to send her son to live as the sexual companion of a middle-aged male dentist. How can such a scene be funny and not shockingly offensive? Putting to the side the idea that it is perfectly plausible for a text be both funny *and* shockingly offensive, I would nonetheless suggest that there are three aspects of the scene that keep it (just) within the confines of the comic climate. The first hinges on the question of authorship. If, as Mast suggests, the casting of a recognizably comic actor can be a key cue for invoking the comedic, then in the realm of director-centered European cinema, this could also be the case when a director with a reputation for comedy is making the film. Furthermore, the fact that it is Almodóvar, and that Almodóvar's use of comedy is specifically skewed in a queer direction, enables me to welcome and relish the scene in a way that I would not be able to if it were part of a film directed by a conservative and/ or homophobic filmmaker like, say, Mel Gibson. This is, of course, an embarrassingly crass and naive deployment of the concept of film authorship, but nevertheless it is one that I suspect a majority of queer spectators relies on regularly.

Second, the comic climate is signaled by the performance codes of the actors themselves.[8] The scene in *What Have I Done to Deserve This?* is taken into the realms of the absurd by the performative excess of the dentist—his flickering tongue, his over-lascivious pouting, his rocking on his heels as he scents the proximity of prey, his lowering of the chair just a bit too far, all of these actions highlighted in their comedic extravagance by the contrasted underplaying of the mother and son. Casting and the cultural specificity of its significance are also notable here, as the dentist is played by Javier Gurruchaga, singer and front man of the Movida-era group Orquestra Mondragón, well known to Spanish audiences for their subversive humor and dedication to excess.[9]

Third, and perhaps most contentiously, the scene is rendered comic by its sense of morality, by which I mean its absolute lack of moral hypocrisy or panic. Everyone involved in the negotiation is fully aware of their own and everyone else's motives, with the clearest index of this being the unemotionally pragmatic materialism of Miguel, the son who is the object of both the dentist's affection and his mother's transaction. Miguel is the antithesis of the stereotyped "passive prey" victim of adult predation; he is fully aware of his needs, desires, and the rewards they can sometimes help to unlock. The scene is shocking, if one is easily shocked, because nobody within the film is shocked at all. Indeed, it is precisely in the contrast between unshocked characters and a (supposedly) shocked audience that the comedic core of the scene resides. When Miguel's older brother hears what has happened, his response is simply one of rueful envy that Miguel will be enjoying a better standard of living. Earlier in the film we have learned that Miguel has a taste for older men (he regularly sleeps with a classmate's father), so any sense of moral panic or righteous indignation on the spectator's part becomes strained, to say the least. Responses to this scene will probably be shaped by how old one imagines Miguel to be (I would say about thirteen or fourteen) and whether the relationship with the dentist is consequently a cross-generational relationship between two self-aware homosexuals or a predatory pedophile exploitation of a child by an adult. The performative dimension of the scene suggests, if anything, that Miguel is the more mature of the two, a suggestion that is borne out in the last scene of the film, in which Miguel returns home and tells his mother that he has ended his relationship with the dentist in order to take care of her. As he so wryly puts it, "Well, it was fun at first but I'm too young to settle down."

The scene leaves me in no doubt that its drift is comic, but it is also a scene that shows just how complex Almodóvar's use of comedy can be, for it pushes at boundaries and crosses categories in ways that typify his work as a filmmaker who makes easy cultural demarcations almost impossible to sustain. One of the reasons that I have titled this article "Heart of Farce" is that it is concerned with Almodóvar's ability to keep two apparently different elements in play at one and the same time: heart and farce, the serious and the comedic, intensity and irreverence. By eluding the neat and lazily polarized labels of "art-house director" and "popular entertainer," he has been able to produce work of almost unrivaled richness. Yet, a wholehearted understanding of that richness is not possible until those of us watching Almodóvar from outside Spain abandon our fondness for cultural kidnap, peer beyond the subtitles, and put in the spadework of grasping his Hispanic specificities. When the women (one of whom has a penis, of course; after all, this *is* an Almodóvar film) gather for cava and laughter in *All about My Mother;* when Paquita hurtles gleefully through the early scenes of *Bad Education;* when Raimunda (Penélope Cruz) tracks down her mother (Carmen Maura) in *Volver* for a devastatingly moving reunion predicated on a trail of farts, it is clear that we are looking at the work of a director whose greatest achievement may well be the refusal to take the easy option of *either* outright seriousness *or* undiluted comedy. Almodóvar works in a sphere of blurred genres and meshed modes, insisting that the comic must always remain in his repertoire of meticulously calibrated emotional messiness.

Tragedy and the Bedroom Farce

In a February 2008 episode of *Coronation Street,* one of British television's most popular soap operas, a young couple about to move home are looking through their shared belongings, deciding whether or not certain items are worth packing up and taking with them. A brief, jokey discussion arises when they reach a heap of DVDs: Violet cannot fathom why her boyfriend

Jamie wants to take his copy of *Rush Hour 3* with them, while he is equally baffled by her insistence that she cannot leave behind her collection of Almodóvar films. She tells him they are "art-house classics," and therefore, we are left to infer, immeasurably more significant than any Jackie Chan vehicle (most readers of this book would, I imagine, side with Violet here). The relevance of this reference is to reinforce two points that are central to this essay. First, the invocation of Almodóvar's name in the everyday conversational weave of this hugely popular soap shows just how deeply embedded he has become—in Britain at least—as a shorthand sign for cultural worth. Within the soap's wider narrative, one of the many hurdles Violet and Jamie's partnership had needed to negotiate was their differing relationship to cultural capital, and in this scene that difference is crisply summarized by her awareness of Almodóvar: to know him is to know cinematic quality and thereby to be more cultured. Second, if, with equal crispness, you wished to name a kind of cinema that represented Almodóvar's polar opposite, there could be no better example to cite than the type of lowbrow, mass-market, slapstick-heavy comedy inhabited by Jackie Chan. So here, in soap opera just as in academic discourse, the enduring notion that cinematic value and widely accessible comedy are mutually exclusive and irreconcilable is summoned up yet again. That false but tenacious binary does Almodóvar's work a recurring disservice, so in order to revisit its limitations one final time, I would like to consider how the comedic operates in the film with which I began: *Volver*.

Like all of Almodóvar's recent films, *Volver* is not, strictly speaking, a comedy. After all, it begins in a graveyard, tells a story in which rape, sexual abuse, terminal illness, and three murders are pivotal, and juggles a thematic dialectic between betrayal and redemption. The film's poised sensitivity would hardly be sustainable if, to return briefly to the specter of *Rush Hour 3,* some Spanish equivalents of Chris Tucker and Jackie Chan came careening into the street between Raimunda's house and Emilio's restaurant. Yet there is another, more pressing specter in *Volver* in the form of Irene, the ghost-who-is-not-a-ghost around whom the film's comedic threads cohere. In a film that draws sumptuously from the well of melodrama, a well the audience is invited to refill with its tears, there are also moments where out-loud laughter is sought and rewarded. Forty minutes into the film, after a violent death, an attempted sexual assault on a teenage girl, the sad passing away of an elderly relative, and the manifestation of what might be a spirit from the afterlife, comedy makes its spectacular entrance, or "return," when Sole (Lola

Dueñas) opens the trunk of her car, a space we have last seen filled with the tools used for the hardly comic task of cleaning gravestones, only to find the body of her supposedly dead mother, very much alive in the ragged, shabby person of Carmen Maura. Maura's portrayal of Irene, no small part of which includes her apparent willingness to be deglamorized to an extent virtually unthinkable for any major Hollywood star, shifts the film's mood so that alongside its wrenching emotionality runs a more slender, but utterly vital, skein of farce. Bedraggled, unkempt, and wearing remarkably unfortunate stockings, Maura's Irene invites laughter, but never "just" or "only" laughter, and so the film shifts gear to allow room for the comedic without relocating itself entirely inside the comedy genre.

Daringly, however, the comic mode introduced here is not subtle or restrained, but broad and bold; in other words, what is at play here is not so much wit or irony as farce. Mistaken identity is a core device of farce, and a bedroom full of unexpected arrivals and games of hide-and-seek are others, and all are ushered into *Volver* as Irene surreptitiously takes up residence in Sole's apartment. Maura's performance strikes a sublimely paradoxical note of underplayed excess, especially in the conspiratorial games that she, Sole, and, a bit later, the young Paula play around her masquerade as "la rusa," the Russian. (Note the broad farcical touch of Sole shouting Raimunda's name at great volume to warn Irene, "la rusa," that her other daughter, who is at this point still unaware that her mother has "returned from the dead," is arriving.) The humor that can be mined from differing levels of knowledge and awareness between characters is likewise a staple trope of farce, and the sequences focused on the comic misunderstandings of who does and does not know the real identity of "the Russian" work this seam with gusto. Maura's penchant for hiding under the bed intensifies the significance of the ridiculous in the film, a ridiculousness that is not the chief ingredient in the generic recipe of the film, but that nonetheless adds a particular, peculiar, and memorable flavor without which the dish could grow stale. The crowning moment of the film's devotion to the unsophisticated and irresistible joys of bedroom farce occurs when Raimunda first sees her mother, whom she has long taken to be dead. It is a reunion on which the entire film's emotional charge is pinioned, yet which is rendered indelibly ludicrous by Irene sliding out from under the bed with a clownish grin plastered across her face. This critical scene is delivered with the childish glee of a flung-open jack-in-the-box, yet the film's more somber dimensions are not dismantled by this excursion into the toy shop. If anything, the complexity of the women's relationship is strengthened by the acknowledgment that foolishness and tragedy are rarely far apart.

The moment of discovery and reunion is preceded, tellingly enough, by the toilet humor of a smelly maternal fart, a smell that prompts childhood reminiscences between Raimunda and Sole that bring them to laugh more loudly together than at any other point in the film. Loud, the laughter is also infectious and inclusive, and brings to mind Rowe's comedy of female solidarity as both the young Paula and, secreted beneath the bed, the matriarch Irene join in, three generations of women toughened by adversity using laughter to cement their bonds and sideline the many troubles they face. Yet neither the toilet humor nor the bedroom farce, which fuse together here, prevent the redemptive conversation between Irene and Raimunda that subsequently ensues from being one of the most moving scenes in the whole of the director's work.

That conversation is anything but comic, yet for the aficionado of Almodóvar, it does echo an outlandishly comic scene that I examined earlier. In *Volver,* we watch a mother played by Carmen Maura acknowledge the

Emerging from her hiding place under the bed, Irene (Carmen Maura) finally meets her granddaughter Paula (Yohana Cobo) in Volver *(2006). Photograph by Emilio Pereda and Paola Ardizzoni. Copyright Emilio Pereda and Paola Ardizzoni/El Deseo.*

damage done to her daughter by childhood sexual abuse; twenty-two years earlier, in *What Have I Done to Deserve This?*, another mother played by Carmen Maura made, as noted, a financially determined arrangement in which her teenage son was brought into a sexual relationship with a much older man. It would be reckless to make too much of the comparison, yet a brief reflection on the two scenes may prove enlightening. In the 1980s film, Almodóvar is still very much engaged in a comedy of shock, daring the audience to follow him into zones of risk and outrage, as if he were determined to show that every facet of social life, and especially every corner of sexual identity, is open to comedic inflection. By the time of *Volver*, that point has long been made, and there is apparently no need to implant comedy into a scene in which Raimunda and Irene finally reach back into the past to acknowledge a terribly painful truth. Yet, if the film's spectators share an in-depth knowledge of the director's work, they may note here the distant echo of the cross-generational sexual transaction that Carmen Maura brokered in *What Have I Done to Deserve This?*. Consequently, the cathartic tone of the mother–daughter reconciliation in *Volver* is made all the more envelopingly affective because of the simultaneous presence and absence of comedy.

Irene eavesdropping under the bed in Volver. *Photograph by Emilio Pereda and Paola Ardizzoni. Copyright Emilio Pereda and Paola Ardizzoni/El Deseo.*

Given his track record in demonstrating that the comic can crop up in any context (most contentiously, a rape scene in *Kika* [1993] was played largely for laughs), Almodóvar could still have injected comedy into this redemptive conversation. Accordingly, the omission of comedy here seems very much to be a conscious choice, rather than, as would be the case with the work of more generically or emotionally constricted filmmakers, some sort of wary backing off from a subject matter understood as inhospitable to the comic mode. In this way, Almodóvar's insistence on retaining (though not always utilizing) a comedic option places him as an influential figure on later directors who share his notion that comedy somehow refuses to be evicted even from the most troubling recesses of lived experience. Within Spain, Alex de la Iglesia has learned this lesson better than most, while in North America Todd Solondz would seem to know his Almodóvar very well indeed.[10]

So, when mother and daughter finally talk and bond in *Volver*, making peace after years of distrust and guilt, the scene that we witness is not

Irene and Raimunda (Penélope Cruz) after their emotional reconciliation in the park. Photograph by Emilio Pereda and Paola Ardizzoni. Copyright Emilio Pereda and Paola Ardizzoni/El Deseo.

in itself comic; indeed, it seems highly improbable that any film that contains such a scene could ever be simply labeled a comedy. Yet, without its comic moments, its farcical farts, and its infectious laughter, *Volver* would be a lesser film, denuded of something crucial. Without its farce, it would be less tragic. Without its lacerating pain, its laughter would not be as consoling as it is here. Without their ability to laugh, these and all the other women in the film might suggest that men can destroy them—and destroy them from beyond the grave; without its belief in comedy's power to protect both those in the story and those in the audience from an irretrievable surrender to heartbreak, *Volver* would not be a film by Almodóvar.

NOTES

Considerable thanks are due to Thomas Austin, Martin Dines, Brad Epps, Maria Eugenia Greco, Ian Huffer, Paul Johnson, Despina Kakoudaki, John Mercer, Sharif Mowlabocus, Silvia Taylor, Dolores Tierney, and Garth Twa for helpful comments on earlier manifestations of this paper and for cultural and practical assistance without which it could never have existed.

1. Perhaps not all comedy is concerned with the broadest public reach, since there are some subgenres of comedy, such as satire, which have often sought primarily to amuse minority, or even elite, audiences.

2. The possibility of correlations between Buñuel and Almodóvar suggests itself here in terms of a shared Spanishness, a shared commitment to humor, and a shared ambiguousness with relation to the art-cinema bracket, but the limitations of space prevent exploring it further in this article.

3. It is interesting to note that Waters, like Monaco, uses food as a reference point for how cinemas position themselves in terms of class.

4. *Cine de Barrio* (Neighborhood Cinema) is a weekly show on Spanish television that broadcasts a vintage Spanish popular film (very often a comedy), prefaced and followed by a conversation between its presenter and the veteran actress Carmen Sevilla. The Duquesa de Alba is an indomitable Spanish aristocrat of remarkable longevity who features in almost every issue of every Spanish celebrity gossip magazine. Both the actress and the duchess exude an overwhelming aroma of the ripest camp.

5. Maddison provides an instructive example of this—the cultural shortcomings of his work's conceptual map is indicated by the fact that of its thirty-one footnotes only the smallest handful come from sources concerned with Almodóvar as a Spanish figure working in a Spanish context. Honesty compels me to admit that many of my own sources are similarly non-Hispanic, but at least I am aware that this might be a limitation.

6. Joselito was a child star whose films flourished at the Spanish box office in the 1950s and 1960s. *Canción de juventud* (Song of Youth) was the first film to star the teen-

age actress and singer Rocío Dúrcal. A huge success on its release, it has been screened many times in the *Cine de Barrio* slot (see note 4), underlining its emblematic status.

7. For more on the complex issues of the translatability of Anglophone understandings of sexuality into other cultural contexts, see Altman and Sinfield.

8. Paul Julian Smith has also commented on this (60).

9. Thanks to Brad Epps for illuminating this point to me.

10. See especially Alex de la Iglesia's *Acción mutante* (Mutant Action) (1993), which was produced by Almodóvar's company El Deseo, as well as *La comunidad* (Common Wealth) (2000) and *Crimen Ferpecto* (Ferpect Crime) (2004); see also Todd Solondz's *Welcome to the Dollhouse* (1995), *Happiness* (1998), and *Palindromes* (2004).

WORKS CITED

Allinson, Mark. *A Spanish Labyrinth: The Films of Pedro Almodóvar.* London: I. B. Tauris, 2001.

Altman, Dennis. "The Internationalisation of Gay and Lesbian Identities." *A Dangerous Knowing: Sexuality, Pedagogy and Popular Culture.* Eds. D. Epstein and J. T. Sears. London: Cassell, 1999. 135–49.

Baskett, Simon, et al. *The Rough Guide to Spain.* 12th ed. London: Rough Guides, 2007.

Bersani, Leo, and Ulysse Dutoit. *Forms of Being: Cinema, Aesthetics, Subjectivity.* London: British Film Institute, 2004.

Bordwell, David. "The Art Cinema as a Mode of Film Practice." *Film Theory and Criticism.* 6th ed. Eds. L. Braudy and M. Cohen. New York: Oxford University Press, 2004. 774–82.

Braudy, Leo, and Morris Dickstein, eds. *Great Film Directors: A Critical Anthology.* New York: Oxford University Press, 1978.

Evans, Peter William. *Women on the Verge of a Nervous Breakdown.* London: British Film Institute, 1996.

Glaister, Dan. "Why Is the Schlocky King of Spanish Sex Comedy Tackling Fascism?" *Guardian,* May 8, 1998, 10.

Griffiths, Glyn. "Ooh, Pedro, You Are Awful." *Independent,* Jan. 20, 1996, 3.

Houston, Penelope. *The Contemporary Cinema.* Harmondsworth: Penguin, 1963.

Maddison, Stephen. "All about Women: Pedro Almodóvar and the Heterosocial Dynamic." *Textual Practice* 14.2 (2000): 265–84.

Mast, Gerald. *The Comic Mind; Comedy and the Movies.* 2d ed. Chicago: University of Chicago Press, 1979.

Monaco, James. *The Connoisseur's Guide to the Movies.* New York: Facts on File, 1985.

Perriam, Chris. "Gay and Lesbian Culture." *Spanish Cultural Studies: An Introduction.* Eds. Helen Graham and Jo Labanyi. Oxford: Oxford University Press, 1995. 393–95.

Rowe, Kathleen. "Comedy, Melodrama and Gender: Theorising the Genres of Laughter." *Classical Hollywood Comedy.* Eds. K. Brunovska Karnick and H. Jenkins. London: Routledge, 1995. 39–59.

Sinfield, Alan. *Gay and After.* London: Serpent's Tail, 1998.

———. "Identity and Subculture." *Lesbian and Gay Studies: A Critical Introduction*. Eds. A. Medhurst and S. R. Munt. London: Cassell, 1997. 201–14.

Smith, Paul Julian. *Desire Unlimited: The Cinema of Pedro Almodóvar*. 2d ed. London: Verso, 2000.

Strauss, Frédéric. *Almodóvar on Almodóvar*. Trans. Yves Baignères. London: Faber and Faber, 1996.

Waters, John. *Crackpot: The Obsessions of John Waters*. London: Fourth Estate, 1988.

II
MELODRAMA AND ITS DISCONTENTS

6 Mimesis and Diegesis
Almodóvar and the Limits of Melodrama

MARK ALLINSON

Tragedy is clean, it is restful, it is flawless.
It has nothing to do with melodrama.
—Jean Anouilh, *Antigone*[1]

One of the key features that mark out Almodóvar as an auteur is his consistent borrowing from genre movies, in particular his acknowledged debt to Hollywood melodrama. This constitutes something of a paradox, for genre films are usually defined in opposition to auteurist attributes based on the assumption that genres—as industry-driven products—tend to work against authorial originality. Almodóvar's melodrama is, however, self-conscious, aware of its existence in a world where film melodramas already exist. The Oscar-winning and critically acclaimed 1999 film *All about My Mother* is the culmination of Almodóvar's exploration of melodrama. But toward the end of the 1990s and into the new century, Almodóvar's intertextual citations are as likely to be of literary works as they are of other films. Indeed, his next film, *Talk to Her* (2002), was awarded an Oscar for best original screenplay. In this essay, I argue that while *All about My Mother* focuses on dramatic performance in a traditionally melodramatic fashion, *Talk to Her* prioritizes reporting or telling stories, and in doing so has something in common with tragedy. Much has been written about the distinction between melodramatic and tragic modes, but it has been largely confined to literary studies.[2] Here, I will consider *All about My Mother* and *Talk to Her* in an attempt to locate the limits between melodrama and tragedy in cinematic texts.

"Melodrama" means drama with musical accompaniment and, as Christine Gledhill reminds us, owes its existence to the eighteenth-century prohibition of dialogue in all but a few official theaters (*Home Is Where the Heart Is* 14–15). Alongside music, a wide and sometimes complex range of visual effects tried to compensate for the lack of dialogue. Given the moral and often Manichaean conflicts that marked much drama, the theater developed a form of "pictorial sensationalism" (ibid., 27). For his part, Peter Brooks has characterized melodrama as the "theatrical impulse itself: the impulse towards dramatization, heightening, expression, acting out" (xv). At the beginning of the twentieth century, melodramatic style proved perfectly suited to the cinema, also deprived of speech for its first thirty years. Once again according to Gledhill, silent film adopted the nonverbal sign systems of melodrama, but many of them survived into the sound era (*Home Is Where the Heart Is* 27–28). With the advent of sound technology, the gestural, theatrical conventions of mime and stage melodrama that had informed film acting were superseded by an emphasis on verbal exposition, narration, and dialogue, on telling as well as showing. From its origins in the popular theater, and despite being saddled with a legacy of critical scorn by the majority of scholars until the 1970s, melodrama in the cinema developed in the first half of the twentieth century into what Thomas Elsaesser has called "the most highly elaborated, complex mode of cinematic signification . . . ever produced" (52). While other mainstream genres, such as westerns and gangster films, concentrated on external conflicts and mostly male characters, melodrama became the vehicle for the exploration of internal, often moral conflicts, frequently involving female protagonists, often in the role of victim. Melodramatic plots involve omniscient narration,[3] twists and reversals, chance events and encounters, and secrets. Flashbacks are another common feature, a result of the need for dramatic action without the sense of progression that characterizes other more dynamic genres (Gledhill, "Genre" 80).

While the focus of studies in melodrama shifted through the twentieth century from stage to screen with a concomitant recuperation of critical value thanks to critics such as Elsaesser and Gledhill, studies in tragedy remain firmly focused on literary genres and have rarely been applied to film texts. Analysis of tragedy tends to depart from Plato's question: "Why does a painful event produce a pleasurable response?" (Palmer 13). Most definitions of tragedy start with Aristotle's answer, an attempt to describe a very specific group of dramas some 2,500 years ago. Aristotle described tragic heroes of some standing, who suffer because of some error of judgment, leading to the arousal of pity and fear, "wherewith to accomplish its catharsis of such emotions" (*Poetics*, ch. VI). According to Aristotle (ch. XIII), the trajectory of the hero must be "from happiness to misery." Although Aristotle was descriptive, rather than prescriptive in the *Poetics* (Leech 14), the formal restrictiveness of such definitions, reinforced during the neoclassical period, was only lifted in the twentieth century when critical debates about tragedy were played out with special intensity. Richard H. Palmer summa-

rizes Dorothea Krook's usefully comprehensive definition of the genre in
Elements of Tragedy (32–33):

> 1. an act of shame or horror that produces 2. suffering, out of which is generated
> 3. knowledge, in the sense of "insight into, understanding of man's fundamental
> nature or the fundamental human condition," but with 4. an affirmation, or reaffir-
> mation, of the dignity of the human spirit and the worthiness of human life.

The aforementioned elements combine into a broad dimension that Krook
sees as a moral "order of values" (15). Although the protagonist may experience these elements directly, he is primarily the catalyst for the audience's
knowledge (13). The tragic hero is essentially a good man but with a flaw
(*hamartia,* or an error of judgment), who experiences *peripeteia,* a change
from one state to the opposite, often a sudden reversal or change of fortune,
followed by *anagnorisis,* the change from ignorance to knowledge.

The twentieth century sees a widening of the social standing of the
tragic hero from kings and princes to more ordinary people, which Geoffrey
Nowell-Smith sees as a reflection of an increasingly hegemonic bourgeois
culture (71). Some critics see tragedy as being reborn in modern times.[4]
Such is the case of George Steiner in his evaluation of the "silent scream"
of Bertolt Brecht's *Mother Courage* (354), or of Leech, who holds that Federico García Lorca's plays "indicate supremely that tragedy belongs to the
twentieth-century theatre as surely as it has belonged to any other" (29).
Others reject any tragic status for the twentieth century's heroes, frequently
locating them in a melodramatic, rather than a tragic, tradition. For Robert
Heilman, a lowly hero such as Arthur Miller's Willy Loman "is so consistently blind that *Death of a Salesman* becomes pathetic rather than tragic"
(15). Heilman's full-length study, *Tragedy and Melodrama,* further distinguishes between tragedy and disaster: while tragedy is the consequence of
a decision (a wrong or bad decision), disaster is a misfortune afflicted upon
someone. Tragedy, he argues, is not "victimhood" (25). He further differentiates the "monopathic" characters of melodrama (one-sided, unified, with
unchanging psychological attributes, and whose problems come from the
outside), and the "divided" or "polypathic" characters of tragedy whose
problems originate within themselves (89). Heilman's distinction reflects
the widespread elitist position that assigns a much higher cultural value
to tragic characters than to melodramatic ones. Frequently, the distinction
leads to a simplistic division between tragic theater as high art and melodramatic cinema as popular art.

Against such a simplistic division of high tragedy and popular melodrama, we might adduce the character of Manuela (Cecilia Roth) in *All about My Mother,* who amply shows how a melodramatic role can be artistically equal to a tragic one. I aim to demonstrate that while much of *All about My Mother* can be explained by the legacy of melodrama, *Talk to Her,* while retaining many melodramatic features, goes beyond the limits of melodrama to something approaching the tragic.[5] What differentiates the two, for me, is their relative use of diegesis (telling) and mimesis (showing). In the third book of Plato's *Republic,* Socrates explains the difference (392c–394d). In diegesis the poet is clearly the speaker, while in mimesis the poet attempts to create the illusion that it is not he or she who is speaking. The preference for telling stories or performing them ("acting out") has changed over history, and some cultures have tended to prefer one to the other. However, there seems to be a gradual and general shift toward performance as cultures move increasingly away from orality and toward the visual arts. During the modern period, storytelling has tended to edge further toward mimesis. One of the reasons is the establishment, over time, of a series of conventions accepted in representational media, whereby artificially produced effects contingent on technological advances, such as stage lighting in theater or continuity editing in cinema, are read by audiences as "realistic" or "believable" (the concept of verisimilitude). The tendency toward mimesis or performance has tended to favor, in short, the melodramatic mode, which is based, as Brooks says, on "acting out" (xv).

In *All about My Mother,* classic screen melodrama entails a self-reflexive investigation of performance. This self-consciousness goes further than the great theater-based melodramas of Hollywood. In *All about Eve* (Joseph L. Mankiewicz, 1950), *All I Desire* (Douglas Sirk, 1953), and *Imitation of Life* (Douglas Sirk, 1959), the theater is both a dramatic context for the action and a metaphor for life as a stage. In *All about My Mother,* however, the traffic between onstage and offstage worlds is two-way: characters extend their stage dramas into their offstage lives, and turn their personal dramas into performance. Almodóvar has stated that his first idea was "to make a film about the acting abilities of certain people who aren't actors." "As a child," he continues, "I remember seeing this quality among the women in my family. They pretended much better than the men. Through these lies they were able to avoid more than one tragedy."[6] Almodóvar thus sees performance— and in particular female performance—as a preventative medicine. The idea of acting to avoid tragedy—understood by Almodóvar here in the wider, less formalist sense—could be compared with the classic, Aristotelian concept of catharsis that necessitates the suffering of tragedy. In *All about My Mother,* the performances of Manuela and Agrado (Antonia San Juan) do avert tragedy, by virtue of their stoicism in the face of loss and struggle. I refer here not to the performances of actresses Cecilia Roth and Antonia San Juan, but rather to the stage performances of these two characters within the story, and to their sustained performances of strength. A good example of the performance of strength is Agrado's humorous and optimistic response on stage to the indisposition of Huma Rojo (Marisa Paredes) and Nina (Candela Peña). Such displays of strength and optimism lead to a hopeful ending for the main characters.

Yet in Almodóvar's next film, *Talk to Her,* one of the main characters has a trajectory that is clearly "from happiness to misery" (Aristotle ch. XIII). A tragic ending is not avoided by "acting out." While *Talk to Her* retains many of the melodramatic features of its predecessor, it prioritizes diegesis over mimesis. By depriving its characters of the chance to act out their dramas, and thus by depriving them of the outlet of a melodramatic ending, *Talk to Her* condemns them to telling and retelling stories. But retelling, far from being simply a problem, is also a solution, one that is close to the conclusions of Breuer and Freud in their early case studies on hysteria: the now fundamental notion that the verbalization of problems is important in therapy.[7] This therapeutic concept is, of course, a modern application of the notion of catharsis as applied originally to tragic drama. *Talk to Her,* in its emphasis on noncommunication and in its more acute ethical dilemmas, moves beyond melodrama, as I have been arguing, to something closer to tragedy.

All about My Mother: *The Limits of Melodrama*

All about My Mother is melodramatic in theme and in construction. An intense exploration of motherhood, grief, and personal fulfillment, its drama involves moral conflicts and themes of sacrifice, renunciation, and tolerance typical of melodrama, and its structure depends on the omniscient narration that characterizes the genre, though in this case with few flashbacks.[8] But while it is almost classically melodramatic in theme, style, and register, *All about My Mother* is also quite aware of its own status as melodrama. Almodóvar clearly participates in the more recent critical recuperation of melodrama by feminists and neo-Marxists searching for ideological fissures in the genre's content and in its construction.

Feminist theorists from the 1970s onward have seen melodrama as an antidote to what Laura Mulvey refers to as the "overvaluation of virility under patriarchy" (40). For Mulvey, melodrama is a genre whose simultaneous aims were to allow the exploration of female-orientated issues and to "soften" sexual difference, making the domestic sphere "acceptable" to men (ibid.). What interested Mulvey and other feminist critics was the extent to which melodrama might be understood as conservative, as educating women to accept the constraints of the patriarchal order, or conversely, the extent to which it might be understood as more subversive, as exposing and exploding the myths of patriarchy (Kaplan 25). Almodóvar's world, partly a reflection of a postfeminist reality and partly an idealization or fantasy, represents a disavowal of patriarchy. The domestic sphere in *All about My Mother* is entirely female, even to the extent that the biologically male father, Esteban (Toni Cantó), has become a partial transsexual. Male characters remain tangential to the dramatic action, and they determine neither the suffering of the females nor the resolution of their suffering. Consequently, unlike classic melodramas in which, according to E. Ann Kaplan, "events are never reconciled at the end in a way which is beneficial to women" (26), *All about My Mother* offers a happy ending, in which single motherhood and female friendship have replaced the conventional patriarchal family unit.

The reassessment of gender representations in melodrama paralleled the reevaluation of its formal styles. Working at the same time, albeit independently, in literary and cinematic circles, academics questioned why melodrama had been considered not just less important than tragedy in the theater, but also less important than westerns or gangster films in cinema. The way in which melodrama tends to be constrained by the dictates of realism or verisimilitude is crucial to understanding both its previous undervaluation and its subsequent recuperation. Gledhill explains:

> Whereas the realist-humanist tradition had privileged aesthetic coherence as the embodiment of authorial vision, the neo-Marxist perspective looked to stylistic "excess" and narrative disjuncture for their exposure of contradictions between a mainstream film's aesthetic and ideological programmes. Formal contradiction became a new source of critical value because it allowed apparently ideologically complicit films to be read "against the grain" for their overt critique of the represented status quo. (*Home Is Where the Heart Is* 6)

Geoffrey Nowell-Smith defines the concept of melodramatic "excess" as "undischarged emotion which cannot be accommodated within the action" and which therefore has to be expressed in the music and the mise-en-scène (73). Nowell-Smith also points out that music and mise-en-scène do not merely heighten the emotionality of melodrama, but "to some extent they substitute for it." His remarks are particularly relevant to Almodóvar.

Whereas in *High Heels* (1991) characters frequently resort to the histrionic, in *All about My Mother* the emotions are conveyed as much through mise-en-scène and music as through dialogue. Almodóvar is not subject to the institutional constraints of a defensively patriarchal and socially conservative Hollywood that characterized the industry at the height of cinematic melodrama from the 1930s to the 1950s, and consequently he is not constrained in terms of what he can depict—hence the presence of self-sufficient women, transsexuality, lesbianism, drugs, AIDS, and so on. And yet, though not constrained, he nevertheless does not abandon the compensatory use of classic melodramatic mise-en-scène.

In a pioneering article, Thomas Elsaesser attributes melodrama's (often unacknowledged) sophistication to the restricted scope for external action, because everything, as Douglas Sirk said, happens "inside" (52). Critics regard Sirk, a European working in the United States, as the master of this metaphorical mise-en-scène.[9] His 1950s melodramas are rich in examples of what Elsaesser refers to as "the contrasting emotional qualities of textures and materials" (53). Surfaces, furniture, and, above all, objects take on metaphorical significance, enhancing or even carrying the full weight of the emotional dynamics of the drama. Extreme close-ups of objects in the mise-en-scène are used as a kind of shorthand, quickly expressing the relationships of characters to the world around them. Almodóvar engages the mise-en-scène in a similarly dynamic way. When the young Esteban (Eloy Azorín) asks to see a photograph of his mother Manuela as an amateur actress, she presents him with only half a photograph. Esteban runs his finger along the rough edge of the photo, its very texture indicating an untidy rupture rather than a clean break. Esteban subsequently writes in his notebook that the photograph symbolizes the half of his existence that he feels is always missing—his father.

Such examples of directorial economy (making the mise-en-scène speak) in *All about My Mother* are to some extent made possible by the "siphoning off"—to use a phrase from Nowell-Smith (73)—of excess emotionality into the stage performances included in the film. Performing Tennessee Williams's melodrama provides an escape valve for Manuela, and rehearsing García Lorca's grieving mother has the same function for Huma.[10] The diversion of theatricality into the safely theatrical space of the stage also contributes to a general thematization of performance itself. Even at its most "excessive," narrative cinema tends to stay within certain limits dictated by verisimilitude, in other words, by what is "realistic" or "believable" for audiences. To escape such constraints, a director can turn to distancing devices, which foreground the constructed nature of cinema itself. In many of his earlier films, Almodóvar uses self-reflexive or *mise en abîme* techniques, including films within films, theatrical or even camp performances, clearly meant to emphasize how *unrealistic* they are. Parodies, such as the TV spoofs in early films like *Pepi, Luci, Bom* (1980) and *What Have I Done to Deserve This?* (1984), make for good comedy, but in his dramas, Almodóvar often finds a more metaphorical mode of address (less restricted by cinematic notions of verisimilitude), by using the theater.[11] As well as offering Almodóvar a more abstract, metaphorical mise-en-scène, the world of the theater enables the introduction of a further thematic element, that of acting, performance, and, by extension, the "performativity" of life itself.

The idea for *All about My Mother* is prefigured in a performance at the start of Almodóvar's eleventh film, *The Flower of My Secret* (1995). In the earlier film, a secondary character, a nurse named Manuela, volunteers to play the part of a grieving mother in a video simulation designed to train doctors how to approach newly bereaved relatives for their consent for organ donations. The character reappears with the same profession and the same name as the protagonist of *All about My Mother;* life dramatically imitates the simulation when Manuela's own son is killed and she is forced to enact the grieving mother for real.

If the idea for *All about My Mother* is prefigured in *The Flower of My Secret,* its title pays homage to Joseph Mankiewicz's 1950 classic *All about Eve.* At the beginning of Almodóvar's film, the impressionable young writer Esteban and his mother Manuela watch Mankiewicz's film, which inspires the young man to wait outside the theater for his idol, the actress, Huma Rojo, just as Eve Harrington (Anne Baxter) waited for actress Margo Channing (Bette Davis) in *All about Eve.* Esteban dies while running after Huma in search of an autograph after her performance in *A Streetcar Named Desire.* Manuela's obsession with the play, which in her words "has marked her life," is twofold: she met her husband in a production of the play years before, and now she loses her son after another production. Drawn to the play, Manuela encounters the actresses who play Blanche and Stella, and eventually plays the role of Stella for the second time in her life. Just as in *All about Eve,* Manuela first becomes an assistant to the diva and then an understudy, though in her case without calculation. Manuela also "performs" the role of surrogate mother twice in the film, and maintains the pretense of strength despite overwhelming grief for her lost son.[12] By making Manuela both a stand-in actress and a stand-in mother, Almodóvar indicates how much the roles have in common. So, when he dedicates the film to all those actresses who have played actresses on the stage or in films, it is a dedication that colors the entirety of *All about My Mother*. Moreover, the line between professional actresses and women who simply act is deliberately blurred in the second part of the dedication. Manuela thus represents the actress in all women, as Almodóvar makes clear in the press book of the film. Here, motherhood and, more amply, gender are equated with performance. Almodóvar's long list of types of actresses on the stage and in life, in the dedication that concludes the film, includes men who "perform" as women. Performing gender is, in short, a theme that runs throughout Almodóvar's work.

In many of Almodóvar's films, gender role-playing reflects the play of femininity that Jean Baudrillard sees in male transvestism:

> What transvestites love is this game of signs, what excites them is to seduce the signs themselves. With them everything is makeup, theater, and seduction. They appear obsessed with games of sex, but they are obsessed, first of all, with play itself. (13)

The frequently ludic qualities of Almodóvar's transvestite and transsexual characters stem from such "plays" of femininity. But biological women are also implicated, as Joan Riviere's early psychoanalytic study of "womanliness as masquerade" makes clear; for Riviere, women play the role of the feminine so as "to avert anxiety and the retribution feared from men" by those women who aspire to masculinity (35). In the case of men masquerading as women, humor can also be engaged as a defense against hostility.

While play and humor tend to characterize Almodóvar's drag, transvestite, or transsexual characters, their appearances in more recent films do much more than provide comic relief. A predominately comic line runs from *Labyrinth of Passion* (1982), in which Almodóvar himself appears in grotesque drag, to *Bad Education* (2004), in which the character of Paquito (Javier Cámara) camps it up. Though twenty years apart, both roles are legacies of the highly performative, almost carnivalesque *Movida,* during which willful gender ambiguity was part of a reaction against a hitherto intransigent structuring of social identities and a virulent application of the norms of patriarchy under the Francoist dictatorship. By the time of *High Heels,* a fully developed transvestite character appears in the guise of Letal, played "straight" in both senses of the word by pop star Miguel Bosé. For Paul Julian Smith, Letal represents "the primacy of voluntarism, the freedom of the subject to place him/herself on either side of the sexual divide" (125).

Carmen Maura's memorable interpretation of the transsexual Tina in *Law of Desire* (1987) is a good example of a much more complex performativity. Not only does a well-known female actor incarnate Tina's male-to-female transgender character, but she also at times comes close, in her performance, to parodying the melodramatic genre itself. For example, Tina claims on three separate occasions that three different things are all she has left, apparently unaware of contradicting herself. And when her brother Pablo (Eusebio Poncela) questions her about what she plans to do, she responds, "cry until I am too tired to cry anymore." Almost two decades later, in *Bad Education* (which is set in the same period of post-Franco Madrid as *Law of Desire*), the transsexual character of Ignacio, played by male actor Francisco Boira, and his film incarnation Zahara, played by another male actor, Gael García Bernal, are far from providing a reassuring, comic shield from the potentially hostile reactions of a newly (and precariously) democratic Spain. Rather, they are a function of a complex metacinematic structure of performances that disturbs both the audience's framing of the narrative and any comfortable identification with the transsexual as "victim."

As variously powerful as *Law of Desire* and *Bad Education* are, it is in *All about My Mother* that the notion of gender as performance is most explicitly investigated, embodied as it is in the character of Agrado. Agrado spends all her time performing womanhood. She is a prostitute and a half-operated transsexual: she has breasts but has not had her penis removed because her male clients like their women "well hung." She abandons prostitution when she reencounters Manuela, and begins to work for Huma in the equally performative world of the stage. Agrado's entry into the world of the theater culminates in a veritable—indeed, quite literal—*coup de théâtre* that is the film's most humorous sequence. When Huma and Nina have come to blows and are unable to act, Agrado takes to the stage to explain why the play has been canceled. In an episode that Almodóvar based on a real event involving famous Spanish theater actress Lola Membrives, Agrado tells the audience the story of her life. What she actually tells is the story of her body and its relationship to plastic surgery and silicone. She explains how much her body has cost her, part by part. Agrado's theatrical price list culminates in a brief lesson of philosophy: "The more you become like what you have dreamed for yourself, the more authentic you are."[13] Agrado's impromptu performance onstage asserts that authenticity—in her case, womanhood—is achieved as much through desire as through nature.

Antonia San Juan as Agrado performing her monologue of body transformations in All about my Mother *(1999). Photograph by Teresa Isasi. Copyright Teresa Isasi/El Deseo.*

In describing her body and her gender as a narrative or a process, Agrado seems to literalize Judith Butler's argument about the performative basis of gender. Butler, of course, asserts that all gender is "performatively enacted signification" (44) and so includes not just transsexuals and transvestites but also, and importantly, women acting "naturally" as women. Although Almodóvar has here chosen the exception—a consciously nonnormative gendered body—to demonstrate the rule, Agrado's speech is an eloquent, self-conscious staging of how drag can subvert the very idea of true gender (Butler 174).[14] And though it is not expressed in such self-conscious terms, Manuela's self-determined motherhood can also be seen as an example of performance: "doing" motherhood rather than "being" a mother. In Almodóvar, the self-conscious foregrounding of gender and other signs of identity forms part of a more generally self-conscious mode of representation that lays bare the constructed or performative nature of all art and all identity. The falling stage curtain at the end of the film, as well as Almodóvar's dedication to actresses and woman/mother-performers, are reminders of the timeless adage that "the world is a stage."

Talk to Her: *Beyond the Limits of Melodrama*

As if continuing on the same train of thought, one that includes performances, stages, and sets, the stage curtain that falls at the end of *All about My Mother* is echoed in the stage curtain that rises at the start of *Talk to Her*. But despite this gesture of connection, *Talk to Her* significantly redirects questions of performance; for, despite the plea to communication in the words "Talk to Her" superimposed onto the faded red curtain, in the ballet that follows, both the female dancers and their male caretaker are mute and make no verbal or bodily contact with one another. Unlike *All about My Mother*, where the characters have no problem showing or talking about emotion, here communication itself is an issue. The film alternates between silence and speech; for much of the duration of the film, both female protagonists Lydia (Rosario Flores) and Alicia (Leonor Watling) are deprived of speech owing to physical trauma. Their silence paradoxically gives voice to their male partners, imposing on the men the need to retell and review their stories. While Benigno (Javier Cámara) lives his life merely so that he can retell it to his beloved Alicia, Marco (Dario Grandinetti) finds himself obliged to recall (and thus retell) the story of his relationship with Lydia. Almodóvar creates a complex narrative that is also about the complex and therapeutic act of narrating, and a lesson in communication that is also about the eloquence of silence.

Talk to Her commences and closes with staged dance performances. Although diegetically motivated (the protagonists of the story are in the audience), the performances also function on both structural and thematic levels, framing the dramatic action with a formal prologue and epilogue and commenting on the theme of communication and noncommunication. Ballet is, of course, communication through the body rather than words, which is significant in this film, where the main female characters are performers with highly trained, specialized bodies, for whom speech is not required in their professions. As Julián Gutiérrez Albilla has noted, Marco reacts to the silent dance that begins the film with silent tears in a way that cannot be matched by verbal communication, in spite of his trade as a journalist (52).

The opening ballet, *Café Müller* by Pina Bausch, presents a dystopian world of illness and obstacles. Given the narrative development of the film, the ballet functions as an allegory of the trauma that the subsequent narrative has to work through and heal. The sequence is replete with metaphorical allusions to the film's principal story and characters. The two dancers, who

Benigno (Javier Cámara) notices Marco (Dario Grandinetti) weeping openly in the theater during a performance of Café Müller, *the ballet that opens* Talk to Her *(2002). Photograph by Miguel Bracho. Copyright Miguel Bracho/El Deseo.*

stumble blindly and in isolation through a forest of tables and chairs across a bare stage, are metaphorical representations of the two comatose women in the main plot of the film. The sad-faced man who scrambles to remove each of these obstacles so that the women do not collide with them is the poetic incarnation of the male figures Benigno and Marco who, in their different ways, care for the comatose women. Despite their protector, the dancers collide with the walls of the stage, a relatively open space that nonetheless is made to feel like a prison. Prisons—both literal and metaphorical—are another feature of *Talk to Her*. And as the dancers fall to the ground, their limbs become stiff, a further link to the immobility of the bedridden Alicia and Lydia. Even their costumes are the same: simple white nightdresses.

With satisfying symmetry, the film also ends with a ballet performance in a theater, a spectacle divided into two parts. The setting for both is in stark contrast to the bare, almost black-and-white staging of the opening ballet. The background is comprised of lush greenery, a picture of health and growth in contrast to the signs of pain and infirmity of the earlier performance.[15] And where the two dancers in the opening ballet are dressed in white, hospital-like gowns, here we see a solitary female dancer, wearing a colorful, flower-patterned dress. The obstacles that the women in *Café*

Müller faced give way here to a line of male dancers who, prostrate on the stage, support the female dancer on their outstretched arms, a human bridge across which her movement is effected.[16] The metaphorical representation of care and support is continued, but with a more positive outcome. The dancer is offered a microphone into which she merely sighs, a wordless expression of emotion. After the intermission comes the piece *Masurca Fogo,* again by Pina Bausch's company, in which a line of couples enters the stage dancing "to the rhythm of a bucolic Cape Verde song," as Almodóvar puts it in the script (209). The perfect synchronization of male and female dancers, in contrast to the opening ballet, is a utopian model of human reciprocity, accompanied—again without words—by the soothing diegetic sound track of Bau's "Raquel" (which is seamlessly mixed into the final titles music composed by Iglesias). The harmony is enhanced by the water that is now gently cascading from the wall of greenery in the background.

Framed by the two ballet performances, allegories of silence, noncommunication, and reconciliation, the main story of the film revolves around models for bridging the communicative gap across four relationships: Benigno and Alicia, Marco and Lydia, Marco and Benigno, and Marco and Alicia (though this last relationship remains unexplored at the end of the film). The focus on couples also provides for a new take on gender relations, an old favorite in Almodóvar films—and Almodóvar studies, which have provided so much material for scholars of gender and sexuality (Allinson 72–92). Although many of Almodóvar's films focus on female characters, here the focus is on the men, and although many of his other films see gender relationships almost exclusively in terms of power structures, here the focus is on communication between the sexes, or, more accurately, on the consequences of a breakdown in communication.

Talk to Her presents two alternative models of male communicative behavior. Both Marco and Benigno are in love with women who do not and cannot reciprocate. Marco, with all his experience of desperate women, as he boasts to Lydia on their first meeting, is dependent on the effeminate and virginal Benigno to give him valuable lessons on communication between the sexes. And Benigno, a passionate believer in talking and sharing, eventually abandons his chaste attentiveness, and, ironically, after years of one-way verbal communication, finally "gets through" to Alicia by physically penetrating her. Gender stereotypes are ruptured in the two men. Contrary to expectations, and counter to Benigno's characterization of him, Marco is not the strong, silent type. And in spite of a series of overt (if stereotypical) sig-nals of homosexuality, Benigno is apparently heterosexual.

The two men are much more similar than they first appear. Their com-mon problem is not their inability to talk, but rather their incapacity to hear. Marco is not out of touch with his feelings. He cries on three occasions in the film, and he is perfectly able to relate to Lydia his broken relationship. He begins to tell Lydia about his past romantic life on their first meeting, but when Lydia desperately needs to talk to him (to end their relationship), he fails to hear her, assuming her anxiety is about *his* past. Marco's inabil-ity to see beyond himself is reinforced by a sequence that—uniquely in Almodóvar—is actually repeated unchanged in a later flashback:

> LYDIA: Marco, after the bullfight we have to talk.
> MARCO: We've been talking for an hour.
> LYDIA: You have. I haven't.

This proves to be Marco's last opportunity for dialogue with Lydia, who never wakes up from her coma. The truncation of their conversation after Lydia's goring in the bullring imposes silence on both of them.

On the other hand, Benigno, whose opportunity for dialogue with his love object Alicia is minimal, is convinced of the effectiveness of his strategy of monologue. "Talk to her" is his answer for everything. Armed with a few fragments of Alicia's life that he has garnered from one brief conversation and from snooping in her room, he sets out to construct a relationship—ostensibly for her benefit—based on his continuous monologue. Benigno's mistake is to equate absolute but unsolicited devotion with a reciprocal rela-tionship. Subjugating his own life to the needs of Alicia is not, in fact, a sac-rifice on his part. He lives, vicariously, a much happier life than he could on his own. He tells Marco, "These last four years have been the richest of my life." It is hard to see his selfless attentiveness and his feminine-coded care-taking skills (hairdressing, manicure) as entirely positive, as they are a direct result of a deprived childhood spent caring for his mother. Benigno's naïveté is at once comic and disturbing. When he remarks, "Alicia and I get on bet-ter than most married couples," the humor inherent in his misconception does not diminish the dangerous self-deception, which leads him to rape Alicia and eventually to commit suicide.[17] What is ironic—and, in the light of Benigno's subsequent actions, troubling—is that "talk to her" remains good advice for Marco as well as for a certain type of reconstructed male that Almodóvar appears to endorse in this film and elsewhere.[18]

But these two relationships, both cases of unrequited love further curtailed by accidents that render them even more one-sided, are perhaps not the central relationship of *Talk to Her*. The relationship that works through and resolves communicational problems is that of Marco and Benigno. Theirs is also the relationship that develops most in the film, passing through three phases of indifference, conflict, and finally reciprocity. Although their pairing is not designated by one of the "chapter headings" afforded to the other pairings, Marco and Benigno are the first characters introduced to us in the film, framed together in the theater. Although they do not know each other, and do not actually communicate, Benigno notices Marco's tears, recalling them later. When they meet again, in the context of a hospital in which Marco is in a predicament similar to Benigno, they hold conflicting opinions about (their) relationships. Benigno tells Marco, "Talk to her. Tell her about it," but Marco knows that Lydia is unable to hear. Benigno, undeterred, replies that "A woman's brain is a mystery, and in this state even more so." His advice on how to treat women comes from experience, he claims. When Marco asks Benigno what kind of experience he has had with women, Benigno replies, "Every kind. I've spent twenty years day and night with one woman and four years with this one." Notwithstanding Benigno's subsequent rape of Alicia, there is a profoundly woman-centered (I dare not quite say "feminist") attitude here: for Benigno, to know women is not to "possess" them sexually but to tend to their needs. The trajectories of the two male characters are thus inverse: Marco moves from an arrogant, egocentric, and failed attitude toward women to a potentially healthy relationship with Alicia at the film's close; Benigno begins with an innocent and nurturing attitude to women but destroys it, in the eyes of society, through rape.

After Lydia's death, Marco returns to Madrid, where his new priority is to help his friend Benigno, now in prison for raping Alicia. Marco rushes to the jail in Segovia, but is told by the receptionist that "today is not a communication day," a literalization of the obstacles that constantly block their communication. The mise-en-scène henceforth will emphasize separation between the two men while, paradoxically, they come closer in emotional terms. A glass screen divides them during their two meetings in prison, though their reflections in the glass are superimposed on each other's faces, highlighting their mutual empathy. Benigno tells Marco that the hospital staff has been prohibited from talking to him. The hopelessness of Benigno's situation and the tragic missed opportunity to give Benigno the news that would have saved him (i.e., the news of Alicia's awakening) are reinforced by the lack of synchronization in their final exchanges. The gap or delay between enunciation and reception (Benigno's speaking and Marco's hearing) provides a good illustration of the difference between direct speech and indirect or reported speech to which I will return later. First, Benigno sends Marco a voice message that Marco only hears the next day, when it is too late. Then Benigno writes a farewell note that we hear in a voice-over in Benigno's own voice, but which Marco, once again, only reads when it is too late. Benigno's last advice to Marco is "Talk to me. Tell me everything. Don't bottle things up." Only here does Marco finally accept Benigno's advice: despite Benigno's inability to hear him, Marco, at his grave, is able to talk to *him*—in a way that he was not able to "talk to *her*."

With its profusion of relationships, moral conflicts, secrets, and chance encounters, *Talk to Her* is in many regards a classic melodrama. The emphasis on communication and noncommunication in romantic, sexual relationships confirms the sphere of action as the domestic, also in keeping with the conventions of melodrama. The hospital setting, with its victims, coping with trauma and loss, and with the moral consequences of unequal patient–carer relationships, further consolidates this generic focus. The narrative is omniscient as the audience witnesses all the various trajectories of the characters; there are a number of twists and reversals, such as Marco's chance meeting with Alicia at the end. Thomas Elsaesser defines melodrama as "a dramatic narrative in which musical accompaniment marks the emotional effects" (50). And he continues, "[t]his is still perhaps the most useful definition, because it allows melodramatic elements to be seen as constituents of a system of punctuation, giving expressive colour and chromatic contrast to the story line, by orchestrating the emotional ups and downs of the intrigue." Elsaesser's definition is appropriate to *Talk to Her,* whose musical score by Alberto Iglesias carries much of the film's emotional weight. Similarly, objects in the mise-en-scène take on meaning as visual metaphors. In the case of Alicia, a ballet student, we learn as much about her through the objects in her bedroom as through her speech (she spends most of the duration of the film in a coma). We glean from her possessions that she likes silent movies, lava lamps, ballet, and travel. And when Benigno introduces the comatose Alicia to Marco, instead of a response, the camera takes Marco's point of view as he scans the room taking in Alicia's possessions—mostly the same ones we have seen earlier. Indeed, some of the most emotive moments in the film are silent ones in which dialogue is replaced by images and musical accompaniment. When Marco surveys Benigno's empty flat, we see from his point of view first a photo of Alicia, then Alicia's ballet school from the window, and finally Alicia herself. Marco's discovery of Alicia, now awake, through the same ballet school windows that had been the obsessive object of Benigno's attention, is like a silent film in which music and gestures are sufficient to make a dramatic revelation. Such is the power of mise-en-scène and music in conveying a significant dramatic turning point in the narrative that the two minutes of screen time are free of dialogue and virtually empty of diegetic sound. Moreover, the music is the same that is used in an earlier sequence in which Benigno first views Alicia's room, making even more explicit the extent to which Benigno has tried to re-create Alicia's world for his own benefit.

Much of the critical work on film melodrama can be applied to *Talk to Her,* but some of it can also enlighten us as to the extent to which the film departs from classic melodrama in some interesting aspects. Whereas *All about My Mother* is consistently performance-orientated, with much of the action taking place in theatrical contexts with parallels in the performative mode of characters even when not on the stage, *Talk to Her* mitigates the power of the stage and performance (ballet and bullfighting) and the tendency toward melodramatic acting out more generally through the insistent recourse to reported speech. If the basis of melodrama is performance itself ("acting out," showing, or mimesis) which, to return to Plato, involves creating an illusion of reality, then the device of repeatedly interrupting the illusion, with speakers directly reporting events, marks a clear shift away from the mimetic (showing) and toward the diegetic (telling). The preference for the diegetic can be traced back to the origins of the tragic form in fifth-century Greece as an "alternation between a single actor's speech and the chorus" (Leech 12), where most of the action takes place off stage and is reported.

The use of characters to narrate, often in first-person voice-overs, the events of a story in flashback, is a common enough narrative strategy in film melodrama.[19] Flashbacks are often introduced by one character telling another about something that has already happened. This type of storytelling is frequent in Almodóvar, but becomes a thematic concern in itself in *Talk to Her,* where characters retell their stories to people who apparently cannot hear, comprehend, or reply. When we first meet Benigno, he is reliving the experience of *Café Müller* as he relates it to Alicia, the retelling more important to him than the experience itself. Benigno narrates a large part of his story—and all of his contact with the conscious Alicia—to Marco, which provides the audience with images of a backstory. Benigno's penchant for telling stories (much the way we all do when recounting a film) culminates in his more physical retelling of the silent film *Shrinking Lover,* which motivates a cut to the film itself. The most celebrated sequence in *Talk to Her,* the re-creation of a black-and-white silent movie in which a miniature male lover literally enters his female love object, functions as a "cover" for Benigno's rape of Alicia. In its affectionate parody of silent melodrama, this metacinematic interlude signals a final flourish of the melodramatic mode before it gives way to something more tragic in the last quarter of the film. And it is also, crucially, the moment when Benigno fatally confuses fiction with reality: his recounting of an extended, literalized metaphor (reentering the womb) leads to rape. As the Prince of Denmark discovers when he sets up his metatheatrical mischief in *Hamlet,* telling stories can be dangerous.

But it can also be necessary. The story told in *Talk to Her* unfolds via a narrative that is far from linear. The spectator can only reconstruct the story's chronology with the help of voice-over narrations, recollections, letters, and messages. Such voice-overs also serve as a reminder that the audience is party to a subjective point of view in the retelling of past events. For example,

Telling and retelling in the silent film: Alfredo (Fele Martínez) and Amparo (Paz Vega) in a scene from The Shrinking Lover. *Copyright El Deseo.*

Benigno on his way to the silent film **Amante Menguante (Shrinking Lover).** *Copyright El Deseo.*

we witness the story of the meeting of Alicia and Benigno as a simple flash-back that is cued not by Benigno's words but by a close-up of Alicia's tranquil face (suggesting *her* past rather than Benigno's). After three minutes, the sequence is suddenly interrupted by a voice-over from Benigno, reminding us that what we are watching is his reconstruction of the events and not some omniscient narrator's perspective on them. There are five flashbacks in the film, which account for eleven of the seventy-one sequences. One flash-back even contains a further flashback. The reporting of events thus covers a range of tenses and modes, to the extent that it constitutes an exercise in reported speech or "indirect style" worthy of any undergraduate grammar class. Benigno reports the *Café Müller* ballet in the dramatic present tense, excitedly bringing it to life for Alicia. But he narrates his meeting with Alicia in the imperfect and past historic as he brings Marco up to date on his pre-history. In his retelling of *Shrinking Lover,* he wavers ominously between the past and the present tenses, indicating his confusion of fiction and action. The range of tenses is even extended to the conditional (strictly speaking, a mode rather than a tense). At one point, Benigno and Marco stand behind their women, and discuss what they would be talking about if they could.

Marco's response, "She *would tell her* that it's been two months since the goring by the bull" (emphasis added) cues another flashback to an extended sequence set on the day of the bullfight. And when Marco dreams of a beautiful summer evening party that he once attended with Lydia, this cues another of the film's artistic performances: a song performed by Caetano Veloso. The well-known song amounts to a reported story:

> *Dicen* que por las noches nomás se le iba en puro llorar
> *Dicen* que no comía nomás se le iba en puro tomar
> *Juran* que el mismo cielo se estremecía al oír su llanto
> Cómo sufría por ella que hasta en su muerte la fue llamando
> Ay ay ay ay ay *cantaba*. Ay ay ay ay ay *gemía*
> Ay ay ay ay ay *cantaba*. De pasión mortal *moría*

> *They say* that his nights were spent just crying
> *They say* that he never ate but only drank
> *They swear* that the very sky shivered to hear his wailing
> So great was his suffering that even in death he continued to call to her
> Ay ay ay ay ay *he sang*. Ay ay ay ay ay *he moaned*
> Ay ay ay ay ay *he sang*. Of a mortal passion he was dying. (Emphasis added)

Thus, the chosen song consolidates the thematization of reporting events and narrating stories. Scholars of Shakespeare have regarded such songs as the equivalent of the chorus that reports events (Lenson 10). In the final exchange of the film, ballet teacher Katerina (Geraldine Chaplin) tells Marco: "One day you and I should talk," again using the conditional, "should talk." Marco's calm response—"Yes, and it will be much more simple than you think"—suggests that he has learned Benigno's basic lesson: "talk to her."

That in *Talk to Her* so much of the action is conveyed in reported speech provides a contrast to the much more consistently performative (mimetic) *All about My Mother*. Where that film takes the performative aspect of melodrama and turns it into a theme, *Talk to Her* thematizes storytelling. The insistence on narrating, on speech, and on self-imposed silence recalls Shakespeare's greatest tragedy, *King Lear*. There too, the failure to speak, to articulate affection in Lear's youngest, Cordelia, sparks tragedy.

But what of the film's main candidate for the status of tragic hero? Benigno is clearly a "divided" character, at once comically innocent in his assumptions and gravely mistaken in his actions. His error raises moral questions. His death is thus due to *hamartia* (some error of judgment), and even, it could be argued, hubris (his belief that his love for Alicia justifies a sexual act to which she has not consented). Benigno suffers in excess of his crime and, like the characters in Shakespearean tragedy, dies without learning the good news that would have kept him alive (in Benigno's case, his beloved Alicia's awakening from her coma).[20] And although Benigno is deprived of the opportunity for *anagnorisis,* the moment of recognition is transferred to his friend Marco, who has also demonstrated hubris (in his arrogance about his experience with women) and *hamartia* (his belief that loving communication could not rescue Lydia or Alicia). Krook's five tragic "elements," listed at the outset of this essay, are all applicable to *Talk to Her.* Benigno's rape of Alicia is an act of shame or horror that produces suffering, and, arguably, generates insight into something fundamental about the human condition: what constitutes a relationship, what constitutes love, or even, what is worth dying for. With Alicia's awakening there is, moreover, something like what Palmer calls "an affirmation, or reaffirmation, of the dignity of the human spirit and the worthiness of human life" (32). Of all these features, only the last one could be applied to *All about My Mother.* Our heroine Manuela is not divided; she makes no shameful or horrific errors of judgment, but is rather a victim of "outrageous fortune" entirely within the mold of melodrama.

If we approach *Talk to Her* as a tragedy, and Benigno as a contemporary tragic hero, where do we find the film's cathartic value? Just as in the endings of the great Shakespearean tragedies, *Talk to Her* does not end, despairingly, with Benigno's death. Rather, lessons have been learned and the remaining characters, Alicia and Marco, appear unlikely to make the same mistakes. Marco's words at Benigno's grave, followed by his reencounter with the reawakened Alicia, recall Northrop Frye's association of tragedy with the scapegoat: "a vision of death which draws the survivors into a new unity" (215). As is often the case with the endings of Shakespearean tragedies, the words of those left behind confirm for the audience the lasting positive effects of the suffering just experienced. Partly as a result of Benigno's sacrifice, communication has prevailed over noncommunication. Despite (or because of) its traumatic content, *Talk to Her* stimulates a cathartic response typical of tragedy. Given the thematization of diegesis—of dialogue, conversation, communication—in this film, talking is not only the mechanism by which the problem of the narrative is resolved, but it is also, in and of itself, the solution to the problem. On the one occasion when this potential is demonstrated—Benigno's visit to the psychiatrist Dr. Roncero—it is, ironically, not realized. The satirization of this psychomedical relationship does not negate the therapeutic value of talking. Rather, Benigno already subscribes to this method and has only come to the consultancy for a chance to see Alicia, the doctor's daughter. Much earlier, a chat-show hostess played by Loles León tells a reluctant Lydia: "But talking is good for you, dear. And talking about your problems is the first step toward solving them." If the mimetic *All about My Mother* amounts to drama therapy, the more diegetic *Talk to Her* is a cinematic talking cure.

NOTES

1. The comparison—made by the chorus (a single actor in this twentieth-century play)—follows the established hierarchy of tragedy over melodrama (34–35). The melodrama to which Anouilh's single chorus refers is that of "wicked villains, persecuted maidens, avengers, sudden revelations and eleventh-hour repentances." Interestingly, a few lines earlier, the work presents silent film as a metaphor for the silent reaction, "mouths agape," of the audience of tragedy.

2. Heilman's monograph is a good example of a book on tragedy and melodrama that ignores cinema.

3. Omniscient narration in cinema is whenever the viewer has privileged access to the perspectives of all the characters rather than being limited to that of just one (called "restricted narration").

4. Raymond Williams's *Modern Tragedy* provides the most comprehensive evaluation of tragedy in the modern period, but concentrates exclusively on literature.

5. Part of my analysis of melodrama in *All about My Mother* is adapted from a chapter of *A Spanish Labyrinth: The Films of Pedro Almodóvar* (Allinson 138–40 and 212).

6. From the press book of *All about My Mother;* all translations, unless otherwise stated, are mine.

7. The practice of the "talking cure" derives largely from Breuer and Freud's co-authored case study on hysteria, first published in 1895.

8. Only two short flashbacks are used in *All about My Mother,* in contrast with more hybrid genre films such as *High Heels* and with more structurally complex films such as *Talk to Her* and *Bad Education* (2004), both of which use nonlinear narratives.

9. Gledhill (*Home Is Where the Heart Is* 7) argues that Sirk's European origins and flight from Nazi Germany prompted critics to reassess him as a Brechtian director of distantiation, working at once within and against a reactionary Hollywood studio system.

10. The same holds for the hypermelodramatic stage performance of Tina (Carmen Maura) in Jean Cocteau's *La voix humaine* in *Law of Desire* (1986).

11. The stage environment, though it also features in earlier films like *Labyrinth of Passion, Dark Habits* (1983), *Law of Desire,* and *High Heels,* is most prominent in *All about My Mother* and *Talk to Her.* On the question of performance in other films by Almodóvar, see Allinson 209–16.

12. Manuela's performance of the role of the heavily pregnant Stella in Williams's play is intuitive and unrehearsed, in contrast with the performance by professional actor Nina (Candela Peña).

13. Almodóvar borrowed the phrase from his own discussion about women, color, and literature in the press book of *The Flower of My Secret.*

14. Butler refers to Divine in the early films of John Waters as an example of gender performativity, one "whose impersonation of women implicitly suggests that gender is a kind of persistent impersonation that passes for the real" (xxviii). Almodóvar's early drag characters have much in common with Divine, but where Waters is consistently comic and grotesque, Almodóvar's films are more hybrid and his gender bending more complex.

15. The verdant background has been prefigured in an earlier shot of Alicia and Benigno on the balcony of the hospital, filmed from behind with the trees and greenery in the background. The potential reciprocity of their relationship is only in fact realized in the allegorical form of the ballet at the end of the film.

16. As Almodóvar writes in the script of *Talk to Her*: "The 'sigher' floats on a sea of hands" (205).

17. Benigno's naive attitude to relationships is not unlike that of Ricky (Antonio Banderas) in *Tie Me Up! Tie Me Down!* (1990). Ricky is a young love-obsessed man who kidnaps the object of his obsession, Marina (Victoria Abril), in a bid to make her fall in love with him. Of course, where Ricky's irrepressible pursuit pays off, Benigno's more subtle pursuit does not.

18. A number of Almodóvar's male characters express their feelings in ways not traditionally associated with male film characters and thus fit the profile of the "new man." Both David (Javier Bardem) and Víctor (Liberto Rabal) in *Live Flesh* (1997) are sensitive and articulate.

19. Almodóvar's own Hollywood reference within *All about My Mother, All about Eve,* is a good example of this first-person flashback narrative.

20. In particular, Benigno's needless death recalls those of Romeo and Juliet and of Cordelia in the final scene of *King Lear.*

WORKS CITED

Allinson, Mark. *A Spanish Labyrinth: The Films of Pedro Almodóvar.* London: I. B. Tauris, 2001.

Almodóvar, Pedro. *Hable con ella: El guión.* Madrid: Ocho y Medio/El Deseo, 2002.

Anouilh, Jean. *Antigone* and *Eurydice.* Trans. Lewis Galantière. London: Methuen, 1951.

Aristotle. *Rhetoric and Poetics.* Trans. W. Rhys Roberts and Ingram Bywater. New York: Random House, 1954.

Baudrillard, Jean. *Seduction.* Trans. Brian Singer. London: Macmillan, 1990.

Breuer, Josef, and Sigmund Freud. *Studies in Hysteria.* Trans. A. A Brill. Boston: Beacon Press, 1958.

Brooks, Peter. *The Melodramatic Imagination.* New Haven: Yale University Press, 1976.

Butler, Judith. *Gender Trouble.* London: Routledge, 1999.

Cook, Pam. *The Cinema Book.* London: British Film Institute, 1985.

Elsaesser, Thomas. "Tales of Sound and Fury: Observations on the Family Melodrama." *Home Is Where the Heart Is: Studies in Melodrama and the Woman's Film.* Ed. Christine Gledhill. London: British Film Institute, 1987. 43–69.

Frye, Northrop. *Anatomy of Criticism.* Princeton, N.J.: Princeton University Press, 1957.

Gledhill, Christine. "Genre." *The Cinema Book.* London: British Film Institute, 1985. 58–112.

———, ed. *Home Is Where the Heart Is: Studies in Melodrama and the Woman's Film.* London: British Film Institute, 1987.

Gutiérrez Albilla, Julián. "Body, Silence and Movement: Pina Bausch's *Café Müller* in Almodóvar's *Hable con ella.*" *Studies in Hispanic Cinemas* 2.1 (2005): 47–58.

Heilman, Robert B. *Tragedy and Melodrama; Versions of Experience.* Seattle: University of Washington Press, 1968.

Kaplan, E. Ann. *Women and Film: Both Sides of the Camera.* London: Routledge, 1983.

Krook, Dorothea. *Elements of Tragedy.* New Haven: Yale University Press, 1969.

Leech, Clifford. *Tragedy.* London: Methuen, 1969.

Lenson, David. *Achilles' Choice: Examples of Modern Tragedy.* Princeton, N.J.: Princeton University Press, 1975.

Mulvey, Laura. *Visual and Other Pleasures.* London: Macmillan, 1989.

Nowell-Smith, Geoffrey. "Minelli and Melodrama." Gledhill 70–74.

Palmer, Richard H. *Tragedy and Tragic Theory.* Westport, Conn.: Greenwood Press, 1992.

Plato. *The Republic.* Trans. Desmond Lee. Harmondsworth: Penguin, 1974.

Riviere, Joan. "Womanliness as Masquerade." *Formations of Fantasy.* Eds. Victor Burgin, James Donald, and Cora Kaplan. London: Methuen, 1986.

Smith, Paul Julian. *Desire Unlimited: The Cinema of Pedro Almodóvar.* London: Verso, 2000.

Steiner, George. *The Death of Tragedy.* London: Faber and Faber, 1961.

Williams, Raymond. *Modern Tragedy.* London: Verso, 1979.

7 Melancholy Melodrama
Almodovarian Grief and Lost Homosexual Attachments
LINDA WILLIAMS

The loss of the daughter to the mother, mother to the daughter, is the essential female tragedy. We acknowledge Lear (father–daughter split), Hamlet (son and mother), and Oedipus (son and mother) as great embodiments of the human tragedy but there is no presently enduring recognition of mother–daughter passion and rapture.
—Adrienne Rich, Of Woman Born

Adrienne Rich's words celebrating the missing female tragedy of "mother–daughter passion and rapture" have always haunted me. Her claim that the "cathexis between mother and daughter—essential, distorted, misused—is the great unwritten story" (225) strikes me as both terribly true, in the sense that there *is* no powerfully acknowledged high cultural valuation of the loss of mother to daughter and daughter to mother, but also as terribly false. For if there is no essential female tragedy of mother–daughter, there is certainly plenty of melodrama. In the form of maternal melodrama (whether popular novels, film, radio, television), the cathexis of mother–daughter has become a familiar, if culturally underrated, story.[1]

I shall argue here that we do not have to reach back, as Rich does, to such lost female rituals as the Eleusinian mysteries from which men were excluded to find the missing mother–daughter story. The great restorative mother–daughter melodrama, the maternal melodrama to end all maternal melodrama, has already been "written" by Pedro Almodóvar in the form of a 1991 film titled *Tacones lejanos*. Literally translated, the title means "Distant Heels," but has been rendered into English as *High Heels*, which misses some important nuances that I will explain later. Accordingly, I will continue to call the film *Tacones lejanos*. I want to make a case for the importance of this film as one of the world's great film melodramas, one that, with a few notable exceptions, has not received the respect I believe it is due.[2]

Thanks to critics like Marsha Kinder and Paul Julian Smith, the queering of melodrama is now a well-recognized phenomenon in Almodóvar's films. What is less recognized, and what I hope to explain through the primary example of *Tacones lejanos* and the less fully developed example of

Talk to Her (2002) is the way the melodramas that may seem less queer, more about heterosexual romance, are especially suffused with the grief of lost homosexual attachments, or what Judith Butler, in *The Psychic Life of Power,* has called the unresolved grief, the melancholia, of heterosexual gender identification.

Melodrama and Melancholia

Let me first be clear about these two primary terms, melodrama and melancholia. Melodrama, as I have frequently argued, is a broad mode, not a genre. It describes a perpetually modernizing form that is neither opposed to the norms of the "classical" nor to the norms of "realism" but which adapts both. It emerges from primal sentiments of love and loss. It is a protean "leaping fish" that flies from one spectacular manifestation to the next in popular culture, generating novel objects of sympathy. In mid-nineteenth-century United States, the radically novel object of sympathy was a black slave who missed his old Kentucky home when sold downriver. His beating death at white hands inaugurated a new mode of feeling, unprecedented among white Americans, for the suffering of slaves (Williams, *Playing the Race Card* 10–44). In contemporary Spain, the cinema of Almodóvar offers novel objects of sympathy: sadomasochists, drag queens, male whores, pregnant nuns, a daughter hopelessly in love with her mother, an ambiguously sexed male nurse hopelessly in love with a comatose patient, and much, much more.

The happy-ending dramatic outcome often derided as the most unrealistic element of melodrama—the reward of virtue—is only a secondary manifestation of the much more important recognition of virtue in a world in which virtue has been "occulted," as Peter Brooks puts it in his classic study of melodrama (56–80). The melodramatic climax can then tend in one of two directions, each of which is conventionally gendered: it can either consist of a paroxysm of (often feminized) pathos in which suffering becomes the very coin of virtue, or it can consist of a pathos that can be channeled into the typically masculine action of flight, rescue, chase, or fight. In this latter case the action of deeds becomes the coin of virtue. Melodrama usually involves a give-and-take between the pathos of the recognition that it is too late to save virtue and the rescue or escape that takes place "in the nick of time" (Williams, *Playing the Race Card* 30–44).

Many of Pedro Almodóvar's films are, in all these senses, obviously melodramas. In particular, they tend toward the sad-ending paroxysm of feminine pathos rather than toward the masculine culmination in adventurous action. It would be a mistake, however, to say that Almodóvar's unique queering of melodrama "subverts" it, for to subvert would be to undo the very important feelings of the form. Nor do I want to argue that this queering is only a matter of bringing sexual minorities to the forefront of the drama as novel objects of feeling, the way Harriet Beecher Stowe once brought African slaves to the forefront in the mid-nineteenth century. Rather, I want to argue that in some films—to my mind some of the most powerful ones—a more fundamental process of integrating what Judith Butler calls the "unresolved grief" (*The Psychic Life of Power* 133) of the object choices of compulsory heterosexuality is woven into the fabric of the melodrama. Paradoxically, then, it is sometimes those "Almodramas"—a felicitous term used to describe Almodóvar's unique twist on the overblown Hollywood aesthetics of melodrama[3]—that end with the formation of heterosexual couples that also tend to be the most suffused with the melancholia of gender—what Judith Butler calls the grief for the homosexual attachments that have been lost in the process of heterosexual identity formation.

Melancholia is an excessive, pathological form of mourning that fails to get over the loss of a love object or of an ideal that functions as such. Mourning, according to Freud, is a form of dejection, a cessation of interest in the outside world and a general attempt to prolong one's cathexis to the lost object. Little by little, however, the work of mourning allows the mourner to let go of grief. As Freud puts it, "the ego becomes free and uninhibited again" (245). Melancholia is like mourning in that it also prolongs cathexis to a lost object, but with the difference that grief remains perpetual and may even be displayed when there is no obvious object loss to cause it. The melancholic also differs from the mourner in that he or she suffers from what Freud describes as an "extraordinary diminution in his self-regard, an impoverishment of his ego on a grand scale" (246). Where mourners find the world poor and empty, melancholics seem to find *themselves* poor and empty.

There are two great melancholic figures in Almodóvar's films: Rebeca (Victoria Abril) in *Tacones lejanos* and Marco (Dario Grandinetti) in the later and more "mature" *Talk to Her*. Both characters display an unaccountable sadness long before they have suffered the actual physical losses of loved ones. Both are successful journalists (Rebeca is a TV anchorwoman and Marco is a travel writer) who are profoundly and inexplicably melancholic. Rebeca would seem at first to have the more "explainable" cause. Numerous flashbacks in *Tacones lejanos* explain Rebeca's status as an abandoned daughter of her glamorous pop-star mother, Becky (Marisa Paredes), who left her as a child to pursue her career. At the beginning of the film, Rebeca is a sad, thin, pale imitation of her mother, who awaits their reunion at the airport after fifteen years of separation. One flashback strongly suggests that as a child Rebeca had switched her stepfather's pep pills with sleeping pills, thus causing his death in a car crash. As a crime committed in order to have her mother to herself, Rebeca's act backfires, freeing Becky to pursue a career far from her daughter in Mexico. It is thus a crushed, dejected, "poor and empty" daughter who greets her glamorous mother at the airport.

We first meet Marco, Almodóvar's other great melancholic, in *Talk to Her* at a dance performance of Pina Bausch's *Café Müller*. Marco is in the audience seated next to Benigno, a male nurse. The first image we see after the curtain rises is the grief-stricken face of an older woman dancer (Bausch herself) on the stage. With closed eyes she hurtles herself back and forth across a space littered with chairs and tables, occasionally running into walls. A thin man with a sad face (Benigno will later describe him as having "the saddest face in the world") makes it his job to move the chairs and tables out of the way of first this woman and then another's blind, chaotic hurtling. We see Benigno sneak a sympathetic, interested glance at Marco, who weeps openly during the performance. The dance's sad man who cares for the physical well-being of vulnerable women in harm's way is an apt metaphor for a film about men who care for women accident victims in comas. One woman, Lydia (Rosario Flores), Marco's lover, is a female bullfighter in the very business of putting herself in harm's way who has been horribly gored. The other, Alicia (Leonor Watling), Benigno's patient, is a dancer who has been hit by a car.

Marco weeps in most of the film's important scenes. But he does not weep only for the loss of Lydia, who eventually dies in her coma. We see him weep in several flashbacks, both before and after Lydia is gored by a bull. For example, he weeps the night he meets Lydia, after killing a snake in her apartment and, in one of the films most affective moments, he weeps in Lydia's presence at yet another concert performance: a poolside party where the great Brazilian singer Caetano Veloso performs a heart-wrenching version of the *ranchera* classic, "Cucurrucucú paloma" (music and lyrics: Tomás Méndez Sosa). The song describes the wasting-away misery of a man whose beloved has "flown" from home, leaving only a dove to symbolize her lost soul. Veloso's haunting, slow rendition to cello and guitar accompaniment transforms a traditional song into precisely the sort of inconsolable, despairing portrayal of loss that is characteristic of melancholia.

Each of the primary characters in both films has an official reason to be sad: Rebeca is sad owing to her past abandonment by her mother; Marco is sad owing to his loss of Lydia. But each of them also expresses a melancholia that goes beyond normal sadness, even—or perhaps especially—when they find themselves in the presence of those they love. Rebeca is sad even when in the presence of her mother and Marco is sad long before Lydia is gored. One of the ways that Freud describes the psychic mechanism of melancholia is as an "object-loss" (as in normal mourning) that in melancholia becomes incorporated as an "ego-loss" (249). The ego incorporates the lost object into itself, thus "regressing" from object choice to an ambivalent narcissism that feels perpetually "slighted, neglected, or disappointed" (251).

This melancholia is not the same as the often quite extravagant neuroses and psychoses of the typical Almodovarian cast of characters. Rather, it is a specific instance of what Judith Butler has called gender melancholia—the process by which the heterosexual ego assumes normative gender by giving

Marco (Dario Grandinetti) weeping during the performance of Caetano Veloso's "Cucurrucucú paloma" *in* Talk to Her *(2002). Copyright El Deseo.*

up its forbidden homosexual attachments. As we have seen, unlike the normal mourning process that ultimately learns to let go of the object for which it grieves, melancholia holds on to the object and incorporates it as part of the ego. Following this model, Butler extends Freud's analysis of melancholia into the realm of gender (*The Psychic Life of Power* 134). She argues that heterosexual gender identifications—the process by which one identifies as "masculine" or "feminine"—entail the ungrieved loss of these incorporated, homosexual attachments.[4]

Masculine and feminine gender identities are thus not so much "natural" dispositions as they are accomplishments. In the words of Judith Butler, "the girl becomes a girl through being subject to a prohibition which bars the mother as an object of desire and installs that barred object as part of the ego, indeed, as a melancholic identification" (*The Psychic Life of Power* 136). Long before the girl transfers her love from her father to a father substitute, she must first "renounce love for her mother, and renounce it in such a way that both the aim and the object are foreclosed" (137). Butler adds that when there is no public discourse through which such a loss might be named and mourned, then melancholia acquires important cultural dimensions. Indeed, heterosexual identity is purchased through a melancholic incorporation of the love that it disavows. Almodovarian melancholy melodrama, I will argue, manages to grieve these losses. Let's first consider the case of the Rebeca in *Tacones lejanos* and then turn at the end to Marco in *Talk to Her*.

Becky and Rebeca

Adrienne Rich's great book *Of Woman Born* is a paean to the lost story of the mother–daughter bond and is one of the works of 1970s feminism most in need of revival. Rich writes: "Probably there is nothing in human nature more resonant with charges than the flow of energy between two biologically alike bodies, one of which has lain in amniotic bliss inside the other, one of which has labored to give birth to the other" (225–26). The feminist interpretation of a pre-Oedipal, "amniotic bliss" underlying the daughter's connection to a perpetually undervalued mother is quite familiar. What is less familiar, especially for the time when it is written, is the undercurrent of post-Oedipal—as opposed to pre-Oedipal—incestuous lesbian desire. Rich writes: "I . . . remember lying in bed next to my husband, half-dreaming, half-believing, that the body close against mine was my mother's."[5] Rich's text anticipates Judith Butler's argument that gender itself is acquired, at least in part, through a melancholic repudiation of homosexual attachments:

"the girl becomes a girl through being subject to a prohibition which bars the mother as an object of desire." The heterosexually "normal" identification with the mother thus "embodies the ungrieved loss of the homosexual cathexis" (*The Psychic Life of Power* 136).

Western culture's familiar way of thinking about intergenerational rivalry is so entirely determined by the Oedipally structured tragedies of father–son rivalry over the mother that we often forget about other structural possibilities. Yet, in an astute discussion of *Tacones lejanos,* Marsha Kinder has provocatively cited René Girard's thesis that the Oedipal myth's deepest desire is actually homosexual: "homoerotic desire to love/imitate the parent of the same sex . . . drives the oedipal narrative" (40). Film theorist Kaja Silverman borrows Freud's infrequently used term "negative Oedipus complex" to avoid the pitfall of thinking of mother–daughter union as a pre-Oedipal dyad of merger and nondifferentiation. The mother–daughter pre-Oedipal dyad familiar to feminist theorists preexists awareness of sexual difference, fear of castration, and everything that, in the Freudian schema, makes desire possible. Yet, as Rich's own substitution of her mother for her husband suggests, the desire for the mother is not merely nostalgia for, or regression to, nondifferentiation, it is also a post-Oedipal, postseparated longing that is both incestuous and, unlike Oedipal desire, homosexual. In this negative Oedipal complex, the little girl, in parallel to Oedipus, wants to "conquer" the mother for herself and get rid of the father. There are certainly good feminist reasons to resist a theory of castration and fetishism that depends on a perception of the female body as absence or "lack." However, there are some equally good feminist reasons to think through these issues of "loss" and "lack" from the perspective of the girl's ungrieved abandonment of the desire for her mother.[6]

Pedro Almodóvar's *Tacones lejanos* is a maternal melodrama that flirts radically—Almodramatically—with the taboo against mother–daughter incest. It explores a negative Oedipal passion from the daughter's perspective and twice over enacts the daughter's murder of her mother's husband/lover. Rebeca, the mother-obsessed daughter, is the murderous "Oedipa" who has already been responsible for her father's death. But once liberated from her obligations as wife in "old," patriarchal Spain, this mother, Becky, seized the opportunity to be liberated from motherhood as well.

Explored from the side of the daughter's transgressive "negative Oedipal" passion, the main action of *Tacones lejanos* tells of the reunion of the now grown daughter and her diva mother, returned to Spain for a triumphal concert. This reconciliation affords a remarkable opportunity for melodramatic expressions of "mother–daughter passion and rapture." The passion and rapture will take place on Becky's deathbed thus making up, just in the nick of time, for years of maternal neglect.

The film opens at the airport as Rebeca eagerly awaits the arrival of her long-lost mother. Their reunion is flawed by a number of discordant notes: first their earrings entangle and they cannot pull apart, embarrassingly prolonging their first embrace. Second, flamboyant Becky is disappointed that a crowd of fans is not waiting to greet her. Third, possessive Rebeca is disappointed that her mother will not be staying with her; she is also jealous of the female secretary who watches Becky's every move (we will later discover that this is because of a dangerous heart condition). Finally, a much larger problem arises when Becky learns that Rebeca has married her mother's former lover, Manuel. When all three go to a nightclub to watch—and hear—female impersonator Femme Letal (Miguel Bosé) lip-synch one of Becky's early pop songs, the air is thick with crosscurrents of illicit desire.

Although all eyes are on Letal's highly fetishized imitation of Becky, all at the table—mother, daughter, present and past husband—find the imitation a way of mediating their own desirous relation to Becky. Even Becky herself mediates her own pleasurable relation to her younger self through the imitation. And even Manuel, who packs a gun that he lets be seen later by Letal, and who actively resists Letal's seductions, preferring to give his attention to Becky herself, finds himself drawn into conflict with this Becky imitator who also happens to be a judge. In the subsequent scene when Letal joins the party at their table, Manuel will look directly at Letal's crotch as if to interrogate his/her phallic credentials. As Rachel Swan has noted, Letal returns the gaze and from this perspective we see the gun peeking out from Manuel's belt—the gun that Rebeca will soon use to murder Manuel (28–29). In the wonderful way of Almodovarian "desires unlimited" (to use Smith's apt phrase), the aforementioned illicit desires, including the deployment of the gun first as weapon and later as fetish, will all be realized. The most illicit of them, however—the incestuous, homosexual desire of Rebeca for her mother—becomes the melodramatic centerpiece, and "mad love," of the film.

The first instance of this mad, melodramatic love is enacted right there in the nightclub through Rebeca's brief fling with Femme Letal. After the six-foot-tall impersonator of her mother lip-synchs her mother's torch song, "Un año de amor" (A Year of Love) in the Club Villarosa, Rebeca and Letal have acrobatic sex backstage in his dressing room. The fact that sex occurs when Letal is only halfway out of his Becky drag makes it clear that Rebeca's attraction is directed much less toward the handsome hunk underneath the blond wig, padded hips, falsies, platform heels, and pink lipstick and much more toward these very fetishes for her mother.

This wonderfully comic-erotic scene offers a perverse enactment, in drag, of exactly the incestuous relation that Rebeca so clearly desires, and whose loss she grieves throughout the film. Although Eduardo-Letal asserts his desire to be more than a mother to her, Rebeca does not desire "something else besides a mother."[7] She desires *this* mother, the much-imitated but ultimately inimitable Becky. It becomes even clearer that it is the imitation of her mother, not Eduardo himself, that Rebeca desires when, later in the film, Eduardo again attempts to seduce her, this time without his Becky-drag accoutrements. Although he is shirtless, handsome, and virile, Rebeca does not give him a second look.

The film's plot would seem to clear the way for the formation of a heterosexual couple, concluding, as it does, with Rebeca impregnated by her deluded and infatuated female-and-mother-impersonating, yet heterosexual, judge. I would argue, however, that the formation of the heterosexual family that has occurred by the film's end is both informed and upstaged by the much more central passion of incestuous mother love. Critics who have described Victoria Abril's performance as Rebeca as "grave, even glum," might consider that the reason for this extreme melancholia has less to do with what Paul Julian Smith calls the "drama of sexual rivalry between mother and daughter" (*Desire Unlimited* 121) and more to do with a fatal desire for a much more taboo object than her mother's husband or lover.[8] Sexual possession of Manuel, like possession of Letal, is simply a way for Rebeca to get closer to her elusive mother. The melodrama of mother–daughter Oedipal rivalry thus masks a deeper, negative Oedipal, incestuous, and homosexual melancholy of a love that dare not speak its name. This mad love informs every fiber of Victoria Abril's brilliant performance, and finds its expression not only through the murder of the Oedipal "father" figure, which is significantly never shown, but much more importantly through the guilty complicity and closeness with her mother that the murder enables. Rebeca's crime will also make it possible for diva Becky—the most unlikely of figures to perform a sacrificial maternal gesture—to give up her own good name for the "good" of her daughter.

Much has been made of the connections between *Tacones lejanos* and Douglas Sirk's *Imitation of Life* (1959) or, more to the point, the real-life triangle and murder involving Lana Turner, Cheryl Crane, and Johnny Stompanato.[9] But an equally important thematic comparison can be found in Michael Curtiz's *Mildred Pierce* (1945), in which Mildred's daughter steals her mother's lover and, like Rebeca, kills him, giving rise to the criminal investigation that drives the narrative. In many ways, Almodóvar's film is a melancholic revision of *Mildred Pierce* that acts out the queer incestuous romance that the heteronormative Hollywood classic violently represses at its end. As in *Mildred Pierce,* mother–daughter passion (this time originating from the daughter) runs amok and the lover of both is murdered by the daughter. Also as in *Mildred Pierce,* the mother assumes the guilt for a crime her daughter committed. Unlike it, however, this mother will get away with taking the blame, effectively fooling the patriarchal law that so violently puts things "straight" and restores the rule of the father at the end of Curtiz's film.[10]

In Almodóvar's maternal melodrama recast as taboo queer romance, mother and daughter will get away with the crime of "negative Oedipal desire," although this desire will only become expressible at the melodramatic moment at which its enactment is "too late." Thus, unlike *Mildred Pierce,* the law of patriarchal heterosexuality will not solve the crime and expose the guilt of that film's venal daughter; nor will it effect the conventional separation of mother and daughter and allay a dangerous fusion. Instead, the daughter's crime(s) will be forgiven by the mother and their love will be able, through the primal but "mute" gestures of a melodrama that is both parodied and played straight, to "speak its name" (Brooks 73).

To consider the precise ways that this negative Oedipal transgression is enacted we will look first at the "torch songs" that serve as fascinating aural fetishes of the body of the mother, and second at the melodramatic tour de force of that greatest cliché of all melodrama, the deathbed farewell—all three of them—that climax the film's last half hour. In looking closely at the melancholic queer romance of these songs and the escalating climax of the three final deathbed scenes I do not mean to imply that Rebeca finally succeeds in achieving the desire of her negative Oedipal complex. Rather, I want to claim that her constantly out-of-phase desire for her mother is enacted as escalating signs of the grief of her lost homosexual attachment, first in the *melos* of the songs, then in the pathos of a melodramatic ending.

Kathleen Vernon has written eloquently of the melodramatic compo-nent of the "canciones de Almodóvar" and the importance of the voice of the mother as an archaic, pre-individualistic memory of unity and bliss (168–69). However, it would be a mistake to attribute the *melos* of the particular songs in the film only to pre-Oedipal fantasies of union and merger. I would argue, rather, that the songs in *Tacones lejanos* are crucial aural fetishes linked to the body of the mother and to the daughter's decidedly post-Oedipal desire to reclaim that body. The most overt *melos* of *Tacones lejanos* is expressed in two songs (actually sung by Luz Casal) associated with the mother's body. The first song, "Un año de amor," performed by Eduardo-Letal in drag, is taken from Becky's early "pop phase." As Marsha Kinder has aptly noted, this first song forms part of an endless chain of substitutions distanced from the "real thing"—the flesh and blood body and voice of the mother, present to her daughter (43–44). "Un año de amor" is the torch song of an abandoned lover asserting that the beloved will one day be sorry to have ended "a year of love." As the film's first refashioning of an ostensibly heterosexual love song to queer and incestuous ends, the beauty of the piece is that it speaks as much to Rebeca's spurned passion for her mother as it does to Manuel's and Becky's former attachment.

The second song is "Piensa en mí" (Think of Me), an Agustín Lara bolero sung by Becky (again, lip-synching to Luz Casal) in a live concert celebrat-ing her triumphant return to Madrid. Like "Un año de amor," it is another love song whose lyrics express the feelings of an abandoned lover: "Piensa en mí/cuando sufras"—"Think of me when you suffer." This time, however, a love song is refashioned somewhat more pointedly as perverse maternal "passion and rapture" in the context of its dedication by Becky to Rebeca, who is indeed suffering in prison. As Kathleen Vernon has pointed out, the original feeling of the song is a familiar expression of masochism, in which a lover pleads with a lost love to think of him/her whenever he/she too is in pain, and becomes here the expression of a bereft and passionate mother (168). Lyrics such as "tu párvula boca/siendo tan niña/que me enseñó a pecar" (your childlike mouth that taught me to sin), which originally treat the lover's mouth figuratively as that of a child, take on a more literal sense when Becky sings them to her actual daughter. As Vernon points out, the morose Rebeca, seen in prison for the first time without makeup and in an oversized sweater, is suddenly rendered childish herself (169). Rebeca, who is both her mother's child and her impossible, mad lover, does, as the song instructs, think of her mother, and does indeed "suffer," as the words drift to her on the radio in the prison dormitory. So too, for the first time, does Becky think of her daughter, so much so that Becky also suffers, albeit more publicly, as is indicated by way of a single supremely theatrical tear that drops upon the lipstick traces of a kiss that Becky had planted on the stage at the beginning of her concert. But if Becky kisses the stage, in a grand gesture of homecoming, and drops a tear on the marks of that kiss, she still does not kiss the daughter who so craves her affection. Unlike the song's other avid listeners—the entwined lesbian couple in possession of the radio that Rebeca attempts to purchase in order to silence the sound that makes her cry—she and her mother are perpetually out of phase; they cannot bring voice and body together in the same present space of desire.

Not until the next melodramatic set pieces—the three "deathbed" scenes in which Becky, ever the diva, milks every ounce of pathos from her impending demise—do mother and daughter physically converge as whole bodies present to one another in reciprocal love. But first they have a showdown. Rebeca is released from prison when she recants her confession. In an empty courtroom, the daughter effectively puts her mother on trial, accusing her of never returning her love. Becky is hurt by the accusation, but Rebeca, ever the dutiful daughter, cannot remain angry and writes her a conciliatory note: "I'd love to see you and hug you and kiss you if it's not too late." In the very next scene, however, "too late" rears its ugly head: Becky, suffering from a preexisting heart condition, collapses onstage in mid-performance, and Rebeca rushes to her bedside. From this point on, the film obeys the demands of the temporal question raised by all melodrama: will the recognition of virtue—in this case, perversely, virtue equals the transgressive love between mother and daughter—come pathetically "too late," or will it be achieved, actively and happily, "in the nick of time?" (Williams, *Playing the Race Card* 30–38).

I want to argue that the achievement of *Tacones lejanos* is to sustain brilliantly the suspense of a prolonged ending in which it is, almost, *not* too late. There is no particular narrative necessity for the final reconciliation of mother and daughter to be suspended over three separate locales and three beds, in each of which Becky is about to die. Like Rebeca's three different confessions to the murder of Manuel, however, repetition allows each scene to be played out in a very different emotional register in an obsessive repetition compulsion that constantly reenacts the crime. In this case, the first two "deathbed" scenes function as affectionate parody, while the final one is played "straight," but in a way that is also consummately queer. Repetition permits, moreover, a gradual process by which Rebeca takes over and incorporates the colorful vividness of her mother's first screen incarnation.

The first "deathbed" scene takes place in the hospital to which Rebeca has been rushed. Becky plays the scene apparently naked under a white sheet, her white hair offering a bright crown to the lesser shades of white. She will be in variations of white in each of the subsequent scenes, later wearing white silk pajamas. Becky thus moves from the vivid red suit and hat that she wore at the airport to a bloodless white; Rebeca, in turn, moves from her original pale white at the airport to red via an intermediate pink, the color she wears in this scene. The figuratively lifeless daughter will thus come alive through the incorporation of her dying mother in a melancholic enactment of passion and loss.[11] This first deathbed scene efficiently dispatches the two patriarchal institutions to which individuals are asked to confess: the law and the church. First Becky, like the judge (who does double duty as Femme Letal), demands the truth from Rebeca: Did she kill Manuel? When Rebeca confesses, Becky immediately constructs her own system of maternal justice as a means of making up to Rebeca her own failures as a mother. In quick order, Becky falsely confesses to the judge and then immediately afterward confesses to a bewildered priest that she has lied to the judge. When the priest asks if she is sorry to have lied, she apologizes, vaguely, for all the unhappiness she has caused. With these two major forces of patriarchal power now either deluded or hamstrung by Becky's Mildred Pierce–like assumption of her daughter's guilt, we move on to the second deathbed scene.

This scene takes place in the back of an ambulance as Becky is rushed home. Rebeca, still in her pink suit and big earrings, sits beside her pale mother. Still deferring the big mother–daughter expression of love and forgiveness (yet indirectly enabling it), Becky insists that Rebeca tell her the details of the murder, so that she can more convincingly confess her false guilt to the judge. In conspiratorial whispers, with Becky occasionally retreating for breath to her oxygen mask, Rebeca again recounts, and gesturally reenacts, the crime. These first two deathbed scenes, as if playful rehearsals for the final real one, have some terrific moments of deadpan humor. In this one, for instance, Becky, avid for more details, reacts to her daughter's "news" that Manuel had been asleep when she arrived home by exclaiming: "How could he sleep after our argument!" Rebeca had intended to commit suicide, but when she abjectly asked Manuel whether she should take pills or shoot herself, his uncaring answer caused her to turn the gun spontaneously on him instead. Still breathing with difficulty, Becky asks in a whisper for more detail. How did Manuel fall? Rebeca's deadpan answers are duplicated by hand gestures that indicate that he fell faceup, but that she could not bear to see his astonished look and so rolled him over. The conclusion to the scene is Becky's first and last piece of motherly advice: "you need to find a better way to solve your problems with men." "Yes, Mama, you will teach me," answers Rebeca solemnly, alluding to a future they will not have, but basking for the moment in the love she has so craved.

These first and second "deathbed" scenes contain comic touches that affectionately parody the conventions of maternal melodrama while creating a bond over the grisly details of what amounts to a kind of patricide. In contrast, the third and final scene, as mentioned, plays straight both the melodrama and the melancholia. Having "incorporated" in a red top and red shoes the color originally associated with her mother, Rebeca arrives at her mother's basement apartment with a red suitcase to announce that she has brought her things for a permanent stay. "At last we are together," she begins. And indeed, Rebeca has finally attained her mother's inner sanctum of bedroom, finally with no men—priests, judges, lovers, or husbands—around. This is what she has dreamed of attaining, her mother to herself. Once again, however, their bond is played out over an Oedipal crime. To comply with the judge's need for hard evidence, Rebeca will again act out the crime at her mother's bedside. Only this time she will do it with a prop: the actual murder weapon. Rebeca pulls the weapon, wrapped in a red silk scarf and accessorized with her red jacket, out of her handbag. She places it in her mother's hand and helps an extremely weak Becky mime the shooting so as to imprint her fingers on the gun. This gesture seals the bond of mother and daughter as an act of transgression against patriarchal law.[12]

When Rebeca says "thank you," we understand that the exchange—that of maternal sacrifice for daughterly forgiveness—has been completed. Even though the "big moment" in which each woman would speak of her love or perform it in an embrace has been perpetually deferred, the actions that take place around the gun and subsequently around the aural fetish of "distant heels" are themselves revealed as poignant expressions of love. In the first instance, their love has been enacted, as we have seen, not so much through words of love and touch as through the fondling of the phallic weapon, which Rebeca reverently wraps up again in a red silk scarf and puts back in her red handbag. Becky then sends Rebeca across the room to open the basement window. Even before she opens it, we hear a clicking sound and see a pair of low red heels on the pavement. The image then cuts back to Becky at the precise moment of her death. Rebeca's final speech to her mother will thus begin with our knowledge (but not yet Rebeca's) that Becky is already dead and that it is now, finally, too late to possess her.

Rebeca's speech is, as Marsha Kinder has noted, an appropriation of her mother's memory of watching the well-heeled feet of bourgeois passersby from the window of the basement apartment in which she grew up (41). The three clicks of the heels replace the music that one might expect—in a more conventional melodrama—to swell at this point. Like the convention of soaring *melos,* these three clicks, emblematic of the aural fetish of Rebeca's memory of her mother, constitute the emotional climax of the film. They cue Rebeca's speech about the sound of distant heels: "When I was little and we still lived together, I couldn't sleep until I heard your heels clicking." At this point she throws the window fully open and we hear more clicking heels, this time louder and mixed with street noise. Rebeca continues: "I heard your heels clicking down the hall after you'd looked in on me." Rebeca then turns away from the window and now recognizes that Becky is dead. She completes her story, now speaking directly to her mother's body: "No matter how late you came back, I stayed awake until I heard your heels." Merging the past story now with the present, "No matter how late" refers to then as well as now. No matter how late, but indeed very late, Becky *has* come back.

These sounds of the mother are the elusive signs of her "fugitive" presence.[13] But the "lack" that this aural fetish disavows is not that of the phallus but of the ability, in a heteronormative world, to express fully the deep longing Rebeca feels for the felt presence of her mother's body. Climbing onto the bed, Rebeca performs the full body embrace she could never have performed when her mother was alive: she stretches out alongside Becky, first laying her head on her breast, then lowering it to rest on her stomach. With nothing but the sound of Rebeca's soft sobs, turning at one point into a low wail, the light slowly fades.

This third of the three deathbed scenes is thus finally played straight as melodrama and, as such, it finally comes to the heart of the incestuous queer romance that lies at the film's center. The fetishes of gun and the (sight and sound of) high heels give way to the embrace of the forbidden, yet now incorporated, lost object. Marsha Kinder has argued that in this final scene Rebeca describes her aural memory to her mother, "like a lover confessing her love," in a fetching "familial fusion of fetishistic fantasies" (41)—fantasies,

Returning to her mother's womb, too late: Rebeca (Victoria Abril) and Becky (Marisa Paredes) in the climactic ending of **High Heels** *(1991). Copyright El Deseo.*

we might add, that foil the force of phallic law. Feminist critic Lucy Fischer has insisted, to the contrary, that these fetishes are not so fetching, that they buy into a point of view that sees the female body as the threat of castration and lack. To Fischer, Rebeca's gesture of "forcing the gun on Becky" "turns the latter into the archetypal Phallic Mother—a classic figment of the male child's imagination" (210), and the entire film into a Tootsie-like triumph of masculine law through Letal's fetishized imitation of the Phallic Mother.

The problem with such a reading is that it misunderstands the queered refunctioning of aural and physical fetishes and the melodramatic and melancholic power of the prolonged deathbed scenes, which use these erotic fetish-objects *to foil* masculine law. Fischer, for example, refers to Rebeca as a "repressed lesbian—a woman who can only want a man who appears to be a woman" (208). I both question this definition of lesbian and argue that Rebeca's passion has never been for anyone but her mother, nowhere more so than in these three deathbed scenes. It would be more accurate to say that Rebeca can only love a man who also loves her mother, as is the case with both Eduardo-Letal and Manuel. Her desire is both incestuous and, in the too-late moment that Rebeca climbs into bed with her mother, overtly homosexual.

Tacones lejanos is not about Oedipal desire and the myth of the Maternal Phallus. Nor is it about regression to pre-Oedipal nondifferentiation and fusion. It is a remarkable instance of Silverman's "negative Oedipus," enacting Adrienne Rich's "flow of energy between two biologically alike bodies, one of which has lain in amniotic bliss inside the other." In this light, the gun that Fischer sees Rebeca "forcing" on her mother is not a conventional phallus and does not turn Becky into a phallic, and thus pre-Oedipal, Mother. Rather, it functions much more like the phallus that Judith Butler argues is "no longer determined by the logical relation of mutual exclusion entailed by a heterosexist version of sexual difference in which men are said to 'have' and women to 'be' the phallus" (*Bodies That Matter* 88). This phallus operates, rather, as a signifier whose privilege is contested, and whose structure is more various and revisable than any Lacanian or Freudian scheme can affirm.

Open to variation, the lesbian phallus can be reiterated, resignified, and refunctioned, much the way *Tacones lejanos* resignifies Manuel's gun.[14] However, when mother and daughter fondle the phallic weapon, they are not repeating heterosexual archetypes. Detached from the "father," used as weapon against him, and re-eroticized to act out the daughter's impossible passion, this fetish, like that of the clicking heels, speaks of an impossible and "too-late" love—a love that has no official recognition as erotic attachment. The beauty of Almodóvar's film is not to have acted out, as lesbian porno might do, the erotic possibilities of this lesbian phallus. Nor is it to have acted out possession of the mother. As we have seen, if the now-pregnant Rebeca cannot *have* the mother, she must now *be* the mother—she must incorporate her. But in the process of showing the trajectory from daughter to mother, *Tacones lejanos* has made us feel, if for only an instant, the full sense of what Rebeca has lost and what we as a heteronormative culture have lost: a "presently enduring recognition of mother–daughter passion and rapture," to cite Rich once more. This is what Almodóvar has given us in the final image of a daughter who lies down to embrace her dead mother: the melodrama and the melancholia of lost homosexual attachments.

Marco and Benigno

Many critics have described Almodóvar's exquisitely melodramatic and melancholic *Talk to Her* as a departure from the director's usual focus on female relations. José Arroyo, for example, states: "*Talk to Her* is a melodrama through and through except here it is the men who desire and suffer; who hide what they are; who live in a world where things are more than they seem; who cannot say what they feel; and whose very muteness leads to chaos. What the characters repress, the film-making must express" (76).[15] Of course, *Talk to Her* is hardly a maternal melodrama; indeed, it is a film whose immobilization and silencing of its two primary female characters (not to mention the ingeniously staged "curative" rape of one of them) would seem to be Adrienne Rich's worst nightmare.[16] Yet it too is a melodrama, and it too revolves around the melancholia of putatively heterosexual characters who, hovering about the bodies of the women they love, develop an unlikely, close relation with one another. The homosexual possibilities of this relation will only be spoken at the point at which they become impossible to realize. Like *Tacones lejanos,* then, this is a film about the grief of lost homosexual attachments whose expression comes melodramatically "too late."

Paul Julian Smith has suggested that *Talk to Her*—"apparently so straight in its premise of twin heterosexual couples"—nevertheless continues Almodóvar's investigation of queer sexualities, only this time obliquely ("Only Connect" 2). For Smith, this obliqueness resides in the way characters, sexually coded in one particular way, turn out to be ambiguous: Benigno, the mama's boy nurse and beautician, seems at first to be a "stereotypical queen." Yet he is obsessed with Alicia and turns out to be her "benign" rapist; Lydia, the female bullfighter who defies bulls and who, as Arroyo puts it, is her bullfighter father's best "son," has passionate affairs with two men— her bullfighter lover and Marco. Smith also astutely notes that Marco and Benigno bond over "a common melancholia" (ibid.). I would add, however, that this common melancholia is never only about the loss of the women they love but that it also, by the end of the film, registers as the loss of each to the other.

Almodóvar introduces his two male leads sitting side by side at the Pina Bausch dance concert. He then shows each of them in his relationship with the woman he believes to be "his." We see Benigno bathe the already comatose Alicia, and "talk to her" about the dance concert, as if she could understand him. In the meantime, Marco watches Lydia on television, resolves to do a story about her, watches her fight a bull, and then meets her in a bar. After these introductions, Almodóvar structures the rest of his film as two intersecting love stories, each introduced symmetrically in the form of superimposed vivid red titles—first "Lydia y Marco," then "Alicia y Benigno," and finally, at the very end, with no ensuing story, "Marco y Alicia." The fact that both of these "love stories" lead to the hospital where both women are in comas, and thus incapable of any real relationship with the men who hover over them, already gently mocks the substance of these ostensible "love stories." In the case of "Alicia y Benigno" there is no "real" relationship at all—only an obsessed lonely man who has watched, and even stalked, Alicia and who now, in his capacity as nurse, has the pleasure of caring for her comatose body. In the case of "Lydia y Marco," a love story that seems, for a while at least, actually to exist between two sentient beings, we eventually learn that Lydia had reconciled with her former bullfighter lover and would have informed Marco had she not been gored and fallen into a coma. Thus Marco recognizes, as Benigno does not, that he has been living a fantasy and that it was Lydia's fellow bullfighter lover who was really entitled to attend to Lydia's comatose body. But Marco too is an obsessed, lonely man. He determines to leave the hospital and to resume his career as a solitary travel writer at the precise moment that the hospital staff becomes aware of Alicia's pregnancy and Benigno's fantasy of himself as harmless would-be husband comes crashing down.

The film will end on the red superimposed titles of yet a third heterosexual couple: Marco and a miraculously revived Alicia, who meet at a yet another Pina Bausch dance concert, *Masurca Fogo*. The sad but funny K. D. Lang song "Hain't It Funny" accompanies a first dance in which a group of supine men pass around a melancholic woman who occasionally emits profound sighs into a microphone she carries in her hands. Lang sings: "We made love last night/Wasn't good, wasn't bad/Intimate strangers made me kinda sad/Now when I woke up this morning/Coffee wasn't on/It slowly dawned on me that my baby is gone/My baby's gone." Although this is all of the song we hear, those who know the rest may be aware of how ambivalent its ending is—much the way Almodóvar's film is ambivalent—about the loss it laments.[17] Marco cries and Alicia, sitting a few rows behind him, notices, just as Benigno once did.

Ambivalence about the possibility of the couple in the song accompanies the very real melancholia of the loss of the couple in the film. During the dance's intermission, Marco makes Alicia's acquaintance. A final shot shows Marco and Alicia back in the theater—not side by side as Benigno and Marco were at the film's beginning, but aware of each other nevertheless. They watch the film's last dance: exquisitely beautiful, simple movements of barefoot male and female couples dancing in a line, two by two, hips swaying, across a stage. In the last shot, the red letters "Marco y Alicia" superimpose over a view of the two of them in the audience, watching the dance and watching each other from their separate places in the audience. The seductiveness of the dance lures us into hope for this final permutation of the heterosexual couple—a permutation that is left only as potential. But what do we know about this potential and, most important, how does the film ask us to *feel* about it?

In this "happy ending," we might regard Alicia's sleeping beauty to have been awakened by Benigno's "kiss." In the wake of Benigno's suicide in prison, Marco is positioned as the new prince and Alicia's more appropriate lover. He now lives in Benigno's apartment across from the dance studio—the home that Benigno had decorated for himself and Alicia—and has already taken over as the obsessive onlooker (and sometime stalker) of Alicia. But how do we account for the melancholia that we may feel at this potential happy ending and the dance of apparent heterosexuality with which it closes? I do not want to argue that the "real" couple of the film has been the one permutation that has been so studiously avoided: "Marco y Benigno." For Almodóvar there is no proper couple, there are only impossible ones. However, it is painfully obvious that the only couple that has actually been in an actual relation throughout the film, the only couple to have had the kind of melodramatic love scene with the emotional valence of the grand melodramas of old is indeed "Marco y Benigno."

Just as the faux silent film within the film both reveals and hides what is really going on the night Benigno impregnates the insentient Alicia, so the ostensible concentration on heterosexual couples in *Talk to Her* both reveals and hides the relationship that is actually happening between the two men. The point is not that either Marco or Benigno can be said to desire one another while they are spending their days attending the women they believe they love. It is to say, however, that in the great melodramatic scenes of the film, the scenes that occupy a position equivalent to the deathbed scenes in *Tacones lejanos* in which Becky and Rebeca act out their forbidden love through the details of the murder of Manuel, we and they recognize "too late" how much they have meant to one another.

When Marco reads about Lydia's death in a newspaper on a beach in Jordan, he rings the hospital to talk to Benigno and learns that he is in prison. He rushes back to Spain and to Benigno's surprisingly calm, sterile prison in Segovia in which all direct communication is impeded by intercoms and loudspeakers. They will have three meetings, just as there were three deathbed meetings between Becky and Rebeca, although one of these meetings will be beyond the tomb. As in the earlier film, Almodóvar protracts the

drama of the climax of union or separation. In the first of Marco's interviews with Benigno, Almodóvar's camera glides back and forth between the
two men as they speak to each other from their respective glass booths and
through necessary microphones. Benigno is in agony over the fate of Alicia,
but over the course of their conversation he relaxes and tells Marco that
he thinks of him often, "especially at night." Although this phrase raises the
specter of a friendship that is also something more, it is ostensibly defused
by the explanation that Benigno is reading Marco's travel books at night and
feels as if he is traveling with him. Early in the interview, the reflections off
the glass that separates the two men cause Marco's face to be superimposed
on Benigno's face. Toward the end of the interview, as Benigno expresses his
closeness to Marco through the travel books and, more particularly, through
a portrait in one of them of a Cuban woman who had nothing and thus,
like Benigno, had to "invent everything," the superimposition of Benigno's
and Marco's faces becomes more prominent, especially at the moment when
Benigno says: "I thought that woman was me."

The superimposition and mirroring of the two men function much as
Becky's and Rebeca's exchange of colors does in *Tacones lejanos;* merging
one body into the other, they render visible the incorporation of the lost

Marco and Benigno (Javier Cámara) divided and reflected on the glass prison walls in Talk
to Her. *Photograph by Miguel Bracho. Copyright Miguel Bracho/El Deseo.*

object into the ego—precisely what Freud tells us is the process of melancholia. Freud describes the psychic mechanism of melancholia as an "object-loss" that becomes incorporated as an "ego-loss" (249). Where normal mourning lets go of the bereaved object, melancholia, as noted earlier, holds on to it and incorporates it as part of the ego.

We have seen that Judith Butler argues that heterosexual identity is purchased through a melancholic incorporation of the love that it disavows. In the case of love between persons of the same gender there is no acknowledged public discourse through which this love can be named—and mourned. Incorporated into the ego as gender melancholy, it can become a diffuse sadness of the sort that we see played out in the exquisite melodrama of the three prison scenes that occupy most of the end of *Talk to Her*. The prison scenes, followed by the ultimate melodramatic topos of the graveside conversation with the deceased, function Almodramatically much the way the deathbed scenes do at the end of *Tacones lejanos.*

In the second prison scene, Marco and Benigno are again encased in their glass booths. Benigno has been told that Alicia's baby was born dead, which is the truth, and that Alicia is still in a coma, which is a lie, for the experience of giving birth brought her out of her coma. Benigno is thus distracted by grief, a grief that we assume to be caused by his realization that he will have a long prison sentence and never again be close to Alicia (he is even denied the fetish of the hair clip that he once stole from her bedroom). But when Marco, who worries that Benigno may kill himself, asks him if he is all right, Benigno at first rotely answers "yes" but then corrects himself: no, things are not all right, "I would like to be able to hug you." To do so he would have to request a "vis-à-vis"—an interview unmediated by glass windows and apparently restricted to close kin: "They asked if you were my boyfriend. I didn't dare say yes in case it bothered you." Marco, holding back tears, says that it would not. Benigno continues: "I've hugged very few people in my life." In response, Marco puts his hand up against the glass as a token of the embrace he cannot give. Benigno pauses, registers the importance of the gesture with his own tears, kisses his fingers and puts his hand up to meet Marco's.

In the third prison scene, Marco receives a call from Benigno announcing his decision to "escape" from prison by suicide. Marco hurries by taxi to the prison. In a relatively quiet film with little overt action, this muted, slightly lugubrious rush to the rescue awakens us to the familiar formulas of melodrama. Will Marco arrive in time to save Benigno? We know he won't.

Still, we hope against hope, as with Becky and Rebeca, that it will not be "too late." Once at the prison, all that awaits Marco is a letter from Benigno explaining his hope that the pills he has taken will issue in a coma in which he will be reunited with Alicia. Standing in the middle of the warden's office, Marco reads and weeps as Benigno's voice-over implores Marco to come and see him "wherever they take me." He also orders Marco, as he once did with respect to Lydia, to "talk to me, tell me everything. Don't be so secretive." The next scene shows Marco with a bouquet of red roses doing just that at Benigno's grave. In the ultimate melodramatic cliché of the graveside conversation with the dead, Marco tells Benigno what he should have told him before: that Alicia lives, "you woke her up. . . . When I got your message, I raced back to the jail but it was too late."

Marco had never taken Benigno's advice to "talk to her" when Lydia was in her coma. He could not believe that she could hear him, and he would later chastise Benigno for his belief that he and Alicia were in a relationship just because he "talked" to her. Marco's point was that when Alicia was sentient, Benigno had no real relation with her and would not again were she to revive. But Marco and Benigno, unlikely as it may seem, have had a sentient relation with one another and this "talking" to Benigno now attests to a love that has been recognized "too late." Marco's tears, for the first time, seem to have a focused object. For much of the film, before "falling" for Lydia, Marco had been melancholically attached to a previous love, a beautiful woman frightened by snakes. Now this focus on an object (which is, of course, another subject, Benigno) appears to produce a cathartic release. According to literary theorist Franco Moretti, tears are not so much triggered by the sheer pathos of death and loss as by a cessation of tension at the moment that desire must be given up and that one recognizes that it really is too late to reverse time (180). Tears are, according to this schema, a sign of relief as one is reconciled with the irreversibility of time. Marco experiences this relief at the very moment he recognizes that he has been "too late" to help Benigno really connect with life. But of course a connection *has* been forged between Benigno and Marco throughout the film. But by what name should we refer to it? In a note to an essay on *All about My Mother,* Leo Bersani and Ulysse Dutoit argue that Almodóvar has offered an "extraordinary reimagining" of the intimacies referred to by the words *love* and *friendship.* He adds that it is a "relation so strong, so inclusive and so new that it would be inexcusably reductive to describe it as homoerotic and, perhaps, even to appropriate it for the familiar category of friendship" (Bersani and

Dutoit 122). It might be reductive to call it homoerotic, and yet it is precisely a reimagining of same-sex relations under the sign of melancholy that gives this reimagining its power.

Open hands "touching" another across the separation of glass, tearful conversations between prisoner and loved one, recognitions of love "too late" on deathbeds and at gravesides—these are the clichés of melodrama into which Almodóvar, like any good melodramatist, breathes new life, making an old form seem new. We do not come away from these two films saying, "if only Becky had lived," "if only Benigno had been released from prison." We know that these grieving expressions of love and longing are possible because death and prison glass separate these beings who would love in new ways. Because it is too late to overcome the obstacles to same-sex—and in Becky and Rebeca's case also incestuous—love, the "passion and rapture" that Adrienne Rich signaled can melodramatically flourish in a flood of emotion. Judith Butler's suggestion that gender melancholy exists because there are no culturally accepted forms for the mourning of the loss of same-sex "passion and rapture" seems absolutely true. And yet the melancholic, melodramatic beauty of Almodóvar's two most ostensibly heterosexual films comes close to forging a new acceptability in the celebration of these sad "happy endings."

NOTES

Thanks to Rachel Swan for showing me Almodóvar. And thanks to Marsha Kinder for inviting me to the Congreso Internacional Pedro Almodóvar, where this essay first took shape.

1. Obvious examples include *Stella Dallas* (novel, radio serial, three films), *Mildred Pierce* (novel, film), *Imitation of Life* (novel, two films: John Stahl, 1936 and Douglas Sirk, 1959), *Autumn Sonata* (Ingmar Bergman, 1978), *Terms of Endearment* (James Brooks, 1983), and *Steel Magnolias* (Herbert Ross, 1989).

2. *Tacones lejanos* has been popular in some venues, especially Spain, without, however, being much of a critical success anywhere. Almodóvar cites the poor reception of the film in both the United States and Germany, attributing the latter to the ill effects of dubbing and the former to reviews in the conservative national press, of which Terrence Rafferty and Janet Maslin can be taken as the most prestigious examples. Among English-speaking scholars the film has not fared any better, with the single exception of Marsha Kinder. See, for example, Paul Julian Smith's *Desire Unlimited* and Lucy Fischer.

3. Paul Julian Smith cites this term in *Desire Unlimited* in two different places; one attributes it to a review by Spanish writer and critic Vicente Molina Foix (127), the other to the Cuban writer and critic Cabrera Infante (190). Whoever deserves credit, the term is

a handy way of describing the luxurious Hollywoodian aesthetic of this and many other of Almodóvar's films. Referring to the melodramatic style of *Tacones lejanos,* Almodóvar himself describes the film as a conscious search for qualities of Sirkian artifice: "an artifice which belongs essentially to Hollywood, most of all to the melodramas of the Forties and Fifties, made during the birth of colour. To use the Hollywood aesthetic seemed logical—especially since the mother is a singer, a show business character" (Strauss 120).

4. According to Butler, "[t]his heterosexuality is produced not only through implementing the prohibition on incest but, prior to that, by enforcing the prohibition on homosexuality" (*The Psychic Life of Power* 135).

5. Rich goes on to cite a dream of Simone de Beauvoir in which her mother, otherwise rather unimportant in her conscious life, "blended with Sartre, and we were happy together. And then the dream would turn into a nightmare: why was I living with her once more? How had I come to be in her power again? So our former relationship lived on in me in its double aspect—a subjection that I loved and hated" (quoted in Rich 243). Rich also recalls her own "Black mother" as a child raised in Baltimore: "For years she had drifted out of reach . . . as the double silence of sexism and racism intended her to do. She was meant to be utterly annihilated" (255). Rich notes that we withdraw from our natural mothers similarly. In adolescence it "is toward men that our sensual and emotional energies are intended to flow. . . . Women are made taboo to women—not just sexually, but as comrades, cocreators, coinspiritors. In breaking this taboo, we are reuniting with our mothers; in reuniting with our mothers, we are breaking this taboo" (ibid.).

6. As Silverman puts it, "Within the present symbolic order, desire for the mother can never be anything but a contradiction of the daughter's much more normative and normalizing desire for the father" (123).

7. "Something more than a mother" is a well-remembered line from King Vidor's version of the great maternal melodrama *Stella Dallas.* See Williams, "Something Else besides a Mother" (2).

8. Smith informs us that the script describes Rebeca's passion for her mother as "inexorable, fatal" (*Desire Unlimited* 124).

9. Almodóvar himself notes the connection to Sirk, without citing *Imitation of Life,* as well as to the life of Lana Turner and the films of Joan Crawford (Strauss 120). Lucy Fischer notes the similarities between all three films, calling the references to *Mildred Pierce* "extensive" and citing Roger Ebert's notion that Marisa Paredes's performance as Becky is inspired by Joan Crawford. However, Fischer reserves most of her discussion for the similarities between *High Heels* and *Imitation of Life,* calling the former a "remake," a "copy of a copy, an imitation of an *Imitation,*" and arguing for the shortcomings of the gender politics of Almodóvar's film and the usurpation of the maternal function by Judge Domínguez (201).

10. See the extensive commentaries on the famous last shot of *Mildred Pierce* by Pam Cook, Joyce Nelson, Janet Walker, and myself ("Feminist Film Theory").

11. Another sign of Rebeca's growing resemblance to her mother is her oversized earrings worn in these first two scenes.

12. In one of his interviews with Frédéric Strauss, Almodóvar explains that he had Victoria Abril play this scene very tentatively, making sure that the decision to put the

prints on the revolver is her mother's alone: "She is partly manipulating her mother's guilt and pain, but she will respect her decision whatever it might be and, in the end, it is the mother who decides." Her fingerprints on the gun thus become "her most precious heirloom" (108).

13. Almodóvar uses the word *fugitive* to describe Becky's relation to Rebeca; "she is always leaving her" (Strauss 109).

14. For more on the lesbian phallus, see Judith Butler's article of the same name.

15. Arroyo adds: "if men were the structuring absence of *All about My Mother* . . . male friendship and desire are the very subject matter of *Talk to Her*" (76).

16. I am also aware that to compare *Tacones lejanos* and *Talk to Her* as melancholy melodramas is to link one of Almodóvar's least critically acclaimed films to one of his most critically acclaimed films.

17. In the song, it turns out that the missing lover, the "intimate stranger" who suddenly is "gone," has only gone out for smokes while the abandoned lover in the meantime had all too easily reconciled herself to the loss; "Maybe I'm a little bit relieved/Maybe even a little bit glad/Now that you're gone maybe I won't feel so sad." It is also worth noting that both this song and Caetano Veloso's heart-wrenchingly melancholic rendition of "Cucurrucucú paloma," both about the loss of lovers, are sung by performers known to be gay. Thus, here too, songs and stories that might seem, on the surface, to be heterosexual are "bent" into something else.

WORKS CITED

Arroyo, José. "*Talk to Her.*" *Sight and Sound* 12.9 (Sept. 2002): 76–77.

Bersani, Leo, and Ulysse Dutoit. *Forms of Being: Cinema, Aesthetics, Subjectivity.* London: British Film Institute, 2004.

Brooks, Peter. *The Melodramatic Imagination: Balzac, Henry James, Melodrama, and the Mode of Excess.* New Haven: Yale University Press, 1976/1995.

Butler, Judith. *Bodies That Matter: On the Discursive Limits of "Sex."* New York: Routledge, 1993.

———. "The Lesbian Phallus and the Morphological Imaginary." *Differences* 4.1 (spring 1992): 133–71.

———. *The Psychic Life of Power.* Stanford, Calif.: Stanford University Press, 1997.

Cook, Pam. "Duplicity in Mildred Pierce." *Women in Film Noir.* Ed. E. Ann Kaplan. London: British Film Institute, 1978. 68–82.

Fischer, Lucy. "Modernity and Postmaternity: *High Heels* and *Imitation of Life.*" *Play It Again, Sam.* Eds. Andrew Horton and Stuart Y. McDougal. Berkeley: University of California Press, 1998. 200–216.

Freud, Sigmund. "Mourning and Melancholia." *The Standard Edition of the Complete Psychological Works.* Vol. 14. Trans. James Strachey. London: Hogarth Press, 1957. 239–58.

Kinder, Marsha. "*High Heels.*" *Film Quarterly* 45.3 (spring 1992): 39–44.

Maslin, Janet. "Mother Love and a Murder: Review of *High Heels.*" *New York Times,* Dec. 20, 1991.

Nelson, Joyce. "*Mildred Pierce* Reconsidered." *Film Reader* 2 (Jan. 1977): 65–70.

Rafferty, Terrence. "Unnatural Acts." *New Yorker* 67.51 (Feb. 10, 1992): 81–85.

Rich, Adrienne. *Of Woman Born: Motherhood as Experience and Institution.* New York: W. W. Norton, 1976.

Silverman, Kaja. *The Acoustic Mirror: The Female Voice in Psychoanalysis and the Cinema.* Bloomington: Indiana University Press, 1988.

Smith, Paul Julian. *Desire Unlimited: The Cinema of Pedro Almodóvar.* London: Verso, 1994.

———. "Only Connect." *Sight and Sound* 12.7 (July 2002): 25–27.

Strauss, Frédéric. *Almodóvar on Almodóvar.* Trans. Yves Baignères. London: Faber and Faber, 1996.

Swan, Rachel. "Perversions in the Limelight: Weird Sex and Spanishness in the Films of Pedro Almodóvar." Honors thesis, Department of Rhetoric, University of California, Berkeley, 2002.

Vernon, Kathleen. "Las Canciones de Almodóvar." *Almodóvar: el cine como pasión.* Eds. Fran Zurián and Carmen Vázquez Varela. Cuenca: Ediciones de la Universidad de Castilla–La Mancha, 2005. 161–75.

Walker, Janet. "Feminist Critical Practice: Female Discourse in *Mildred Pierce.*" *Film Reader* 5 (1982): 164–71.

Williams, Linda. "Feminist Film Theory, the Female Spectator and *Mildred Pierce.*" *Female Spectators: Looking at Film and Television.* Ed. E. Deidre Pribram. London: Verso, 1988. 12–30.

———. *Playing the Race Card: Melodramas of Black and White from Uncle Tom to O. J. Simpson.* Princeton, N.J.: Princeton University Press, 2001.

———. "'Something Else besides a Mother': *Stella Dallas* and the Maternal Melodrama." *Cinema Journal* 24 (fall 1984): 2–27.

8 Intimate Strangers
Melodrama and Coincidence in *Talk to Her*

DESPINA KAKOUDAKI

I know very little about Alicia. Only what is seen in the film. At times, the writer knows the characters' past and their future, far beyond the ending of the film. In this case, I have the same information as the spectator. Alicia's real film begins at the end, in the theater, when she meets Marco who has been so moved by the sighs in Masurca Fogo. *Perhaps, at some other time, I'll tell the story of the two of them, Marco and Alicia, but first I'd have to write it.*
—Pedro Almodóvar

Marco and Alicia seem to meet for the first time during the intermission of Pina Bausch's *Masurca Fogo*, the performance that concludes *Talk to Her* (2002). Although this is not in fact their first meeting, it marks the first time that they are both conscious and aware of the other's presence: Alicia (Leonor Watling) was in a coma when Marco (Dario Grandinetti) first saw her in the hospital, and she could not see him when he spotted her in the ballet studio across the street after her recovery. In this first mutual meeting, and in a subtle reversal of how much they know about each other, it is Alicia who notices Marco first, recognizing the man seated just a row ahead of her in the theater, the man who cried during the ballet. As the conscious Alicia's emerging story intersects here with Marco's story, the brief encounter between the characters both concludes the film's original plotlines and opens new narrative possibilities for the future. This poignant moment warrants close attention for its handling of narrative closure and fantasmatic opening, as well as of the topics that will be my focus in this essay: narrative, intimacy, and coincidence.

Marco enters the lobby lighting a cigarette, and clearly still inhabiting a private emotional space. In a luminous close-up of Alicia's face we see her looking at him: her eyes seem steady and intrigued, but also dreamy and intense, as if she is trying to see through him or to reach him, in Pedro Almodóvar's own commentary on the sequence, from "a remote place."[1] This is not a gaze of casual curiosity for the plight of a stranger, as when Benigno (Javier Cámara) noticed Marco crying during a Pina Bausch piece in the first scenes of the film, but one that seems to involve the subtle demand for a corresponding or reciprocating gaze. She is trying to catch his eye, to be looked at in return, perhaps even to register that she was also moved by the ballet or that she noticed him crying. In a film that constantly references dialogue and communication, Alicia is actively trying to communicate with Marco.

The reaction she receives from him is appropriately intense: in what functions as a signature element by this point in the film, the sight of Alicia takes his breath away, startling him into palpable if momentary shock. She holds his gaze as he calms himself and sits on a couch across the room, then initiates a short conversation that Almodóvar reports rewriting eight hundred times. "Are you all right?" Alicia asks. "Yes," Marco replies, but then adds, "I don't know." Although they are in the theater lobby, their voices are low, as if they are alone in the space, an intimacy accentuated by their visual presentation as they sit on matching red couches depicted in corresponding long shots. Clearly evoking a mirror-image effect, with Alicia seated on her couch on the right edge of the frame and Marco on the left of his, their visual arrangement also brings them perceptually closer to each other and to the

Coincidence and art: Katerina (Geraldine Chaplin) and Alicia (Leonor Watling) at the same theater where Marco and Benigno first met in Talk to Her *(2002). Photograph by Miguel Bracho. Copyright Miguel Bracho/El Deseo.*

invisible gutter between the frames of the film. In the next shot, a close-up
of her face, she smiles; we cut to a close-up of his face as he smiles back and
replies, "I am much better now," so softly that she cannot hear it. "What?" she
asks, still smiling. At this point Alicia's ballet teacher Katerina (Geraldine
Chaplin) notices Alicia speaking to someone, motivating a camera pan to
the right that follows her point of view and delivers Marco's answer, a self-
conscious dismissive gesture that may be interpreted as "Never mind," or
"Oh, it is not important."[2] But Katerina's face registers the fact that indeed
this *is* important. She hurries to enter the space between them and helps
Alicia back to her theater seat.

Alicia's presence and agency at the end of the film, summarized here in
the intensity of her gaze and her short exchange with Marco, activate a sense
of wonder, both for him in the diegesis and for the audience. The very fact
that this young woman moves, walks, and talks seems like a miracle, because
Alicia has spent four years in a coma and most of the film in the confines of
her hospital room. That she and Marco occupy the same space is similarly
amazing, a magnificent coincidence that promises to deliver a satisfying and
melodramatic sense of closure. One of the few conscious and willed actions

*Coincidence and closure: Alicia seeks out Marco at the theater lobby. Photograph by Miguel
Bracho. Copyright Miguel Bracho/El Deseo.*

we see her perform in the film, Alicia's gaze and desire to communicate with Marco also seem designed to activate a set of impossible expectations for the audience, as Almodóvar proposes in his commentary: "She doesn't know who that man is. She doesn't have a memory of her previous state, but she looks at him from a place where she feels she knows him." The provocative and illogical reading that Almodóvar's visual treatment of her gaze invites is that Alicia may be unconsciously recognizing the already dense web of connections between them. Perhaps she recognizes or catches a glimmer of what everyone else, including the audience, knows: that they are not really strangers to each other.

In this essay I will explore the ways in which Almodóvar's subtle narrative and visual strategies construct immediate and dense relationships between strangers, to such a degree that true strangers rarely exist in his films. I propose that this stylistic tendency, which has narrative, political, and philosophical implications, pivots on Almodóvar's deft handling of coincidence, which in itself can be considered a signature element in the work of this constantly evolving and increasingly self-assured auteur. Although coincidental plot developments characterize many of Almodóvar's films, *Talk to Her* in particular provides us with an extensive and multivalent deployment of coincidence as a narrative feature, and one that connects Almodóvar's style to classical narrative patterns. Always a storyteller, and an accomplished cinematic narrator as well, Almodóvar has become a master of classical film modalities and indeed seems intent on mining classical forms for their expressive potential in contemporary film. Combining theatricality and melodramatic intensity with narrative and dramatic concepts from other media, Almodóvar's use of coincidence has epistemological and political ramifications: it presents the desire for the formation and retention of common histories among strangers, in effect revealing a utopian desire for a sense of community that is both political and emotional.

A coincidence is a special kind of event, more open-ended than fate and less random than accident. The word *coincidence* itself points to questions of sociality, because it can refer to agreement or correspondence of opinion, as well as temporal or spatial concurrence and coexistence. Describing events as coincidental paradoxically means that they share no apparent or inherent causal connection (as when we say "This doesn't mean anything, it's *just* a coincidence"), but also reflects the speaker's sense of surprise or recognition that events may actually be related (as when we say "I can't believe it, this is *such* a coincidence"). Notably for my discussion of *Talk to Her,* coincidence carries an implicit sense of agreement or harmony of opinion between people, a state that, as I will discuss, is easy to idealize and difficult to attain. And for stories and films, coincidence is that fundamental building block that structures narrative unfolding, even as it may be experienced as both too random and too deterministic, both accidental and forced.

Almodóvar's particularly coincidental narrative style and his fluid and exuberant storytelling posed a challenge for his early viewers and critics. While often resorting to analyses of postmodern experimentation, early reviewers also described Almodóvar's convoluted structures, coincidence-filled stories, and fine mix of unpredictability, randomness, and propensity for high melodrama as "zany," a term that rightly annoys film critics. Paul Julian Smith, for example, alerts us to the fact that despite its "conspicuous frivolity," Almodóvar's cinema approaches serious contemporary issues with unparalleled nuance and sensitivity. For Smith, the use of terms such as "zany" or "kitsch" diminishes the import of Almodóvar's thematic and visual choices and enacts a widespread if implicit disrespect for cultural productions coded as "feminine" (Smith, *Desire Unlimited* 2). While the plots of Almodóvar's films have remained characteristically complex, in recent years critics have began to notice his supreme control of stylistic and narrative structure. *Bad Education* (2004), for example, has been described as a tour de force, and noted both for its visual handling of trauma and temporality and for the fluid execution of the text-within-a-text narrative structure. In his essay on the autobiographical tone of the film, Garrett Stewart notes that the film's plot is actually "its own imagery in the making" (163). Few, if any, would describe Almodóvar's style in recent years as a "dizzy free-for-all" (Vineberg 31), or as a loony and random collision of frenzied character "particles" (Maslin).

In addition to their visual and thematic energy, unconventional character types, and unflinching critique of middle-class morality, in my view it is the plotlines and narrative handling of Almodóvar's early films that partly inspired such epithets.[3] Forcing critics to revise or give up on the very notion of plot summary, Almodóvar's early comedic plots discard essential elements of cinematic narration, such as carefully crafted suspense, gradual character development, and space–time continuity.[4] Films such as *Pepi, Luci, Bom* (1980) and *Labyrinth of Passion* (1982) revel instead in turns and surprises, unexpected flashbacks, coincidental meetings, radical changes of pace, and an apparent disregard for generic conventions. Almodóvar's treatments of motivation and causality in his early films, as in the flashback sequence that reveals Rizo and Sexilia's childhood acquaintance and emotional connection in *Labyrinth of Passion,* for example, gravitate toward associating co-incidence with surprise, and it is this eruptive and unforeshadowed quality that renders his early coincidences excessive. As Alfred Hitchcock famously declared in his 1963 interview with Peter Bogdanovich, powerful story-telling pivots on handling the difference between surprise and suspense. The first is sudden and shocking, but does not contribute to narrative tension, while the second can motivate and propel the narrative, endowing seemingly mundane scenes with resonance and emotional force.[5] Following this line of reasoning allows us to account for the particularities of Almodóvar's early narrative styles. Rizo and Sexilia's attraction to each other appears random, inexplicable, or open-ended for most of the film, only to be suddenly revealed as preordained and inevitable, fated even, after the flashback to the childhood encounter that proved formative for their identities and sexualities, his homosexuality and her nymphomania. By violating the prioritization of suspense that characterizes classical cinematic form, Almodóvar thwarts or frustrates viewers' expectations, hitting them with what might have been experienced as an onslaught of surprises followed by overwrought or excessive retroactive formations of meaning and order.

If Almodóvar's early films display an association of coincidence with surprise, his experiments with forms borrowed from melodrama and film noir, and his constant return to Hitchcock's own films for inspiration, soon turned his use of coincidence toward more suspenseful treatments. Although Almodóvar consistently deploys coincidence in his films, his handling varies from one film to another, partly because his treatment of coincidence flows from the overall emotional, epistemological, and stylistic experiments of each project. Also surprisingly consistent is the fact that Almodóvar's characters never merely meet for the first time. As we see with the prefigured meeting between Marco and Alicia in *Talk to Her,* Almodóvar's characters have always already met as children (*Labyrinth of Passion, Bad Education*), seen each other in a public space, on TV, or onstage (*Matador* [1986], *High Heels* [1991], *Talk to Her*), heard each other's voice in public media (*Women on the Verge of a Nervous Breakdown* [1988]), read something in a news-paper or magazine about each other's lives or deaths (*High Heels, Kika* [1993]), or picked each other up for a one-night stand they no longer want to remember (*Tie Me Up! Tie Me Down!* [1990], *Live Flesh* [1997]). Further escalating the overall effects of coincidental plotlines, Almodóvar's visual treatments provide additional opportunities for recognition—this time for the benefit of the audience. In *Women on the Verge of a Nervous Breakdown*, for example, it seems that each time Pepa (Carmen Maura) exits a building in her quest for the ever-elusive Iván (Fernando Guillén), he enters seconds later from another direction. Each time she walks into a phone booth to call him, he walks past it behind her back. Each time she takes the stairs, he is in the elevator. Although these missed connections exacerbate the pace of Pepa's frustrated rush around town, it is the relative stability of the camera, its reluctance to follow the characters as they dash about, that delivers their import. In one scene, for example, we see the entrance to Pepa's building from across the street, where the camera is presumably located; from that point of view we observe Pepa come out, hail a taxi, and leave, frame left. Only seconds later, and without the audience experiencing any cuts or other discernible changes in focus or point of view, Iván appears from frame right, and enters her building. For the audience, the fact that for most of the film the two lovers have occupied the same space and time, but not quite, registers as a new kind of visual and spatial coincidence.

As Almodóvar himself points out, creating the tight rhythm of a screwball comedy is a rather disciplined affair.[6] Almodóvar's stylistic preferences indeed highlight his innovative sense of timing, the result of breaking some classical narrative conventions and retaining others, but also reveal his underlying textual and social investments. In *Women on the Verge of a Nervous Breakdown,* for example, with the characters constantly moving and the camera remaining stable in order to deliver the visual punch line of their missed meetings, other objects emerge to propel and motivate the narrative: Carlos's and Iván's suitcases, both thrown away at random only to hit their proverbial marks and bring the characters together,[7] and the beloved "Mambo Taxi" that appears designed according to a logic of repetition and visual pleasure. It is as if the audience's own enjoyment of the "Mambo Taxi" serves to bring it back: why have many separate uninteresting taxis when we can have one absolutely fascinating one?[8] In a different sense, however, the reappearance of the taxi has both structural and epistemological implications, as it accentuates the importance of mediating spaces in a film that is so constantly on the go, and so much about mediation. The usually anonymous and merely transitional space-time of the taxi ride acquires density and weight in this story. It becomes an episode rather than a transition between episodes. The return of the increasingly familiar and intimate taxi driver also subscribes to a consistent Almodovarian approach to people and characters, an approach that ensures that no one is merely a prop in his narrative world.

The concierge, the telephone operator, the street cleaner, the taxi driver, the passerby may have only a momentary presence in the diegesis of the film, but for that moment they are deep characters whose concerns, personality, and conflicts become immediately felt and quickly familiar to the audience. As I will explain in more detail in the case of *Talk to Her*, the construction of familiarity, of shared histories and immediate connections, between strangers is one of Almodóvar's most fundamental narrative tendencies.

While developmental narratives focus on Almodóvar's maturation as a writer and director and on the increasingly professional modes of production that have disciplined the improvised and loose rhythm of his earlier films,[9] the recent appreciation of Almodóvar's narrative craft, ranging from critical work on *Bad Education* to the numerous nominations he has received for screenwriting awards, is also clearly the effect of generic factors. Comedy can be lauded for being loony, random, irreverent, and seemingly lawless, even when its execution and design demand detailed attention to characterization and motivation as well as the requisite expert sense of timing. Comedy specifically addresses its audiences by presenting a spectacle of its own presumed unruliness, by showcasing the possibility that one can ignore or overturn the laws of physics, the thresholds of the body, and, in Almodóvar's case, many accepted notions of propriety, morality, sexuality, and gender. Melodrama, on the other hand, while requiring similar care in terms of timing and character, seems to draw attention to its own ordering principles by connecting the timing of events with important emotional and narrative implications, by extending the import and impact of an event rather than abbreviating or minimizing it. Clearly, I am oversimplifying these structures here in an effort to highlight the difference between the two modes. Although I will only be able to deal with only one example of Almodóvar's narrative handling in this essay, it seems to me that the coincidence plot remains consistently central to his work in both comic and melodramatic modalities, and therefore could function as precisely the kind of entry point we need in order to study his narrative propensities as an auteur.

What fascinates me about Almodóvar's treatment of coincidence is the way he uses it as a narrative gesture that enacts closure and openness simultaneously. The traditional coincidence plot, presented by Aristotle in the *Poetics* and still considered relevant to narrative theories today, revolves around an interaction between recognition *(anagnorisis)* and reversal of intention or circumstance *(peripeteia)*. As in the case of Sophocles' *Oedipus the King*,

Aristotle's frequent example, recognition "is a change from ignorance to knowledge" and has the best dramatic results "when it occurs simultaneously with a reversal" (*Poetics* 52a30–52b6). Reversal and recognition indeed coincide in that play, both triggered by the messenger's news to Oedipus that the people he thought were his parents were not really his parents, a message that activates a series of further recognitions of the meaning of Oedipus's past actions and present relationships. Traditional coincidence plots often produce the recognition of kinship ties, and in *Oedipus* these ties have been complicated by the long delay in recognition that led to the murder of his father and his marriage to his mother. Kinship reunion in this sense is a *catastrophe*, Aristotle's word for a radical change of fortune.[10]

These ancient narrative concepts prove to be apt descriptors of the last scenes of *Talk to Her*: Marco and Alicia seem to recognize each other, though each on different grounds, and this recognition has the potential to change the future for both of them. And yet this is a recognition that is enacted in an intriguingly unclassical way. They know little about each other, and their momentary spark does not explain or disclose their true connection. The text ends soon after staging this coincidental encounter, and therefore its open-ended structure partly allows for an expansive fairy-tale–like fantasy in which Marco and Alicia may be imagined as "living happily ever after." Such a fantasy is satisfying precisely because it remains potential, untested against the realities of human communication that the film otherwise presents with significant nuance. Surely this is not a full Aristotelian recognition then, because it lacks stability on all temporal sides: it reveals nothing critically important about the identity of the self or the other, it creates no binding structure for any future outcomes, and it is rather haphazardly motivated by a random event, their attendance at the same dance performance. It also fails to qualify as a classical coincidence in cinematic terms, because it arrives at the very end of the film to tie up loose ends, a fundamental liability for a classical structure. In effect, the encounter between Marco and Alicia shares the textual placement of the flashback in *Labyrinth of Passion,* and poses comparable dangers to the structure and balance of the film. As David Bordwell observes in his work on classical Hollywood cinema, "the later in the film a coincidence occurs, the weaker it is; and it is very unlikely that the story [in classical Hollywood films] will be resolved by coincidence" (*Classical Hollywood Cinema* 13). Indeed, early screenwriting manuals of the 1910s and 1920s recommended restraint in the use of coincidence, and advised reserving it primarily for initial situations. Bordwell remarks: "Boy and girl may meet by accident, but they cannot rely upon chance to keep their acquaintance alive" (ibid.). Classic cinematic narrative demands a certain kind of realism, which in turn prioritizes psychological causality and obscures its own modes of construction. Because it can radically undermine this fragile realism, coincidence has to be deployed very carefully.

Contemporary cinema offers examples of numerous narrative innovations that both adhere to and revise classical patterns, in mainstream Hollywood as well as in independent film and international and art-house cinema. What I call the "coincidence plot" in Almodóvar's work partly corresponds to what Bordwell elsewhere describes as "network narratives" or "converging-fates plots." For Bordwell, such experiments are the result of a productive cross-pollination of storytelling modes, as classical story lines are infused with the excitement of new conventions from alternative traditions, comic books, independent cinema, television, serial narratives, chaos theory, and so on.[11] In addition to Robert Altman and Quentin Tarantino, who exemplify the basics of this mode in contemporary Hollywood, Krzysztof Kieślowski and Wong Kar-wai loom large in the art-house and international festival circuit that prominently includes Almodóvar. The circuit also includes younger directors with a propensity for coincidence plots such as Alejandro González Iñárritu (*Amores perros* [2000]; *21 Grams* [2003]; and *Babel* [2006]), and Paul Haggis (*Crash* [2006]). Although these directors use variations of network or coincidence plots, such stylistic conventions compete with a personal and distinctly auteurist approach to narrative structure, partly instigated by larger cinematic, epistemological, or political concerns and filtered through cultural expectations that often differ from the Anglo-American assumptions we can presume structure the classical mode.[12]

How does Almodóvar handle coincidence in narrative terms? Although most of the narrative structure of *Talk to Her* adheres to the norms of classical narration, coincidental events are naturalized and acceptable in this story, while it is willed and causally motivated events that paradoxically carry the weight of surprise and unexpectedness. The film also repeatedly returns to a contrast between real and fantasmatic narrative expectations, to the projective potential of self-narration and the problems that ensue from narrative itself. Almodóvar's capacity for facilitating an audience's projections, a feature of melodramas and soap operas that he has exploited consistently in his work, is literally thematized in *Talk to Her,* in the character of Benigno, who has written his own story with Alicia and happily inhabits it. Indeed,

Almodóvar's willingness to stage events of such emotional import in epis-
temologically ungrounded territory is characteristic of his handling of the
characters in *Talk to Her*, who are depicted as floating, unmoored, and somewhat fluid throughout the film. In contrast to the palpable sense of limits
and the effort to push against these limits that characterize the emotional
and representational landscape of *Bad Education*, the setting and action of
Talk to Her revolve around nonknowledge, uncertainty, and ambiguity, both
for the characters and for the audience.

Narrative, Melodrama, and Coincidence

To explore the dynamic structure of this film, I return to its coincidental
ending. Despite the fact that it occurs between relative strangers, the scene
of mutual recognition between Marco and Alicia in the theater lobby has
heightened stakes. We know very little about Alicia, as Almodóvar himself
points out,[13] and what we do know is reported by other characters, especially her devoted attendant Benigno, who provides all we do know in
his flashback: she loves dancing, traveling, and watching silent films. But
there is much that Alicia herself doesn't know as well. For example, she is
unaware of the fact that Marco knows *her* or that they have "met" before. Is
it indeed pure chance that they both attend this performance? Given the
information provided by the film, theirs seems a somewhat fated meeting.
We know that Marco is interested in Pina Bausch, and that he attended a
performance of *Café Müller* a few months back, where Benigno noticed
him crying. We know that Alicia loves modern dance. Was she inspired to
attend this particular show because she found the framed autograph of Pina
Bausch in her hospital room, the one that Benigno acquired for her after
Café Müller?

And what does she know now about that time in her life? In a way,
Marco holds a key to crucial elements of her memory and history, having
witnessed her everyday life at the hospital and the events that ensued: her
rape by Benigno and her subsequent awakening from the coma after the
baby she conceived died at birth. Marco is also the witness of Benigno's
emotional attachment to Alicia and his earnest, if misguided, devotion to
her. As Katerina's intervention reveals, with Benigno now dead this aspect of
the story has been submerged or erased for Alicia by those around her.

The fact that a stranger could have access to such an important personal
history is an obvious melodramatic topos: because he knows what happened

Benigno (Javier Cámara) with the autograph of Pina Bausch from Café Müller. *Photograph by Miguel Bracho. Copyright Miguel Bracho/El Deseo.*

to her, Marco has the potential to fill in the gaps in Alicia's personal story. At the end of a film that stages multiple scenes of narration, and that Almodóvar has described as being about narration,[14] Marco is "loaded" with a story he can narrate to her, the story of the missing years of her own life. And yet it is Alicia who is the active partner in this potential tale that begins at the end of the film. Although she does not really recognize him, not knowing the role he has played in her life, she recognizes certain things about him, his sadness at the performance and his intense reaction to *her,* and it is these qualities that seem to draw her attention and her gaze.

Of course, given that the preceding scenes involved Benigno's suicide and Marco's visit to Benigno's grave, the audience knows why Marco reacts so intensely to her gaze in the theater lobby. Alicia facilitates or embodies Marco's personal and continuous contact with the uncanny, in the way she opened her unseeing eyes when he first saw her while she was still in a coma—reclining like Francisco Goya's *Nude Maja* on her hospital bed—and the way she now seems to have come back from the dead as if by a miracle and reemerge in his everyday life when he least expects it. In addition to the coincidence that brings both of them to the same performance, and the coincidence that they are seated only one row away from each other, the possibility that he is crying because he is thinking of her story with Benigno adds another kind of coincidence, this one more fantasmatic in its implications. Although as viewers we should know better, it is difficult to resist the impulse to supply a specific emotional background to Marco's tears, to imagine that we know why he cries and to seek our reward for this projection in Alicia's reactions. This kind of projection is, after all, what all melodramatic structures facilitate: they provide the necessary information and emotional background that allow us to imagine that we know, or understand, or feel the effect of the events on the screen. As a type of animation or projection, the viewer's ability to fill in emotional content has distinct similarities with Benigno's own projection onto Alicia, his sense that he knows what she wants. "Why does this man cry?" Alicia seems to be asking. "Because he is thinking of a story that involves *you*" may be the answer mentally supplied by the audience. The film barely retains a realist register under the pressure of this romantic fantasy of absolute and circular connection, in which lovers-to-be have always been destined for each other, in which a first look may carry all the density and depth of a shared history, and in which a lover already knows something intimate about the beloved, something that the beloved does not know. The narrative coincidence of their presence at the theater is thus built into a sublime and layered fantasy of recognition, one that proposes that strangers are already related and know more about each other than anyone could reasonably imagine. Regardless of their motives and reactions, Marco and Alicia can never be strangers in this film; they can never meet for the first time.

Among their many pleasures, narrative and representational media often replace the randomness of everyday life with order, sometimes even a sense of fate, as if in our cultural productions we constructed the kinds of closure and meaningfulness that everyday life rarely provides. Meaning itself may be regarded as an effect of narration, of the stories we create in order to make significant arrangements from the arbitrary elements of personal and social events. Coincidence, as I mentioned earlier, adds a complex note to this desire for causal and narrative meaningfulness, both in life and in representation. As a narrative choice, coincidence has the capacity to overturn or redirect the narrative, bringing narrative strands together, or fulfilling narrative aims in satisfying ways. But coincidence can also undermine narrative pleasure if it is experienced as forced or overdone. Although we often recognize coincidence in everyday life, narrative decorum limits its use, because coincidence has routinely been associated with forced causality. This is because coincidence, in the novel, for example, has a "transcendental-izing effect": it makes readers aware of the structuring principles of the fic-tion, and specifically of the author's hand, the author's choice in arranging the chain of depicted events (Goldknopf 43).

Coincidental events in fiction have the potential to present an omnipo-tent author, and certain authors, such as Charles Dickens and Thomas Hardy, have often been faulted for their frequent use of them. According to Neil Forsyth, Dickens struggled with balancing the delight in the unexpected that coincidence engages with the need to thoroughly structure his complex novels. Spontaneity, openness, and freedom, the emotional effects of coinci-dental events, can easily give way to more somber feelings, to the sense that events conform to "an overriding pattern of significance," that they are fated or preordained (152). As a result, while a novel must be designed so that events and characters fit together coherently, this overall design should be obscured for much of the fiction. Narrative exposition thus oscillates between the reader's naive delight at the discovery of connections, espe-cially when such discoveries predate those of the characters, and an autho-rial perspective that already knows all (Forsyth 158). The paradox, then, is that while coincidence in everyday life may precipitate a feeling of the pre-ciousness and importance of human relations in the context of a rather ran-dom universe, in fiction it can quickly become a proxy for forces that fore-close possibility and enforce certain outcomes. When the outcomes seem forced or unnatural, they reveal the author's presence and maneuverings, and although such authorial presence can be experienced as omniscient and powerful, it is also somewhat oppressive.

Dickens describes his sense of plotting in a letter to Wilkie Collins, him-self famous for his elaborate plots, through a distinction between fate and Providence:

> I think the business of art is to lay all that ground carefully, but with the care that conceals itself—to show, by a backward light, what everything has been working to—but only to suggest, until the fulfillment comes. These are the ways of Provi-dence, of which all art is but a little imitation. (Ibid. 163)

If the author's hand were to become palpable in the fiction, it would be aligned with the workings of fate, foreclosing the pleasure of discovery and the feeling of suspense that comes from guessing but not fully knowing what will happen next. Dickens proposes that a better method for channeling the expectations of readers comes from treating authorial design as equivalent to that of providence. Events are not ever truly random in this mode, as the reader anticipates that plotlines will cohere and eventually make sense; but the overall design and outcomes are not obvious, nor do they conform to a fixed and preexisting order. Providential readings are hopeful for specific future outcomes (there must be some hidden reason for this) but are also often retroactive (new event y makes sense because it fits with previous event x).

Whereas a classic tragic narrative restores a certain human and divine order and safeguards the limits between them, a providential narrative, despite the religious echo of the term, allows for more potentiality, because the unfolding of the fiction may surprise or challenge the preexisting orders we recognize in the world. Dickens exploits this possibility in the many reversals of status and social standing featured in his books. The business of fiction in Dickens's texts is not to enforce the social order but to subtly undermine it, presenting alternatives or hidden possibilities even in the categories of the real that readers too complacently accept. Melodrama also enables this transgressive possibility. If fate is associated with tragedy in Dickens's schema, the connection of providence with the "rescue plot" confirms the link between narrative, suspense, meaning, and the possibility of melodramatic reversal. Rescue plots are, of course, a major feature of melodrama, a mode that operates, as Linda Williams has suggested, with the tension of important events occurring "too late" or "in the nick of time" (35).

Dickens provides an interesting reference point for exploring Almodóvar's work. Both design their fictions in temporal and spatial connection to their own milieu; both use character types that have become thoroughly identified with their work; both thrive on the connectivity of the cosmopolitan modern city; and both create intimate connections among characters that at first do not seem related. Dickens's narrative styles also structure the study of cinematic melodrama, informing major approaches to melodramatic narrativity, such as Sergei Eisenstein's "Dickens, Griffith, and the Film Today" (1942), and Rick Altman's influential essay "Dickens, Griffith, and Film Theory Today" (1989). Partly because of these essays, much of what we recognize as the classic modes and critical methods for understanding cinematic melodrama has at some point or other been inspired by Dickens's literary style, and so it is fitting for me to bring him up in relation to Almodóvar, whose narrative modes in *Talk to Her* most approximate classical narration. Whether melodramatic structures conform to popular desire and wish fulfillment or can be used to radicalize a complacent public has also been the main question in Bertolt Brecht's writings on the political potential of melodrama, which have influenced my own approach here.[15] In a wider philosophical sense, melodrama fundamentally engages the desire for reversibility and change, enabling alternative endings where tragedy presents causal inevitability.

Even this brief discussion of the narrative treatment of coincidence should alert us to its epistemological and philosophical potential, its navigation of problems of determinism and freedom. In his later novels Dickens establishes a dialectic between fate and coincidence, and often uses coincidence as a way to bring to light familial relationships that have themselves been ruptured by chance, malice, or oppressive social structures. Characters that seem to move in completely different social realms are revealed to be intimately related: lost children and parents are reunited, beggars are discovered to have been of noble birth, and the seemingly absolute difference between social classes turns out to be a fiction itself. Dickens's biographer writes that "the coincidences, resemblances and surprises of life" were some of his recurrent delights: "The world, he would say, was so much smaller than we thought it; we were all so connected by fate without knowing it; people supposed to be far apart were so constantly elbowing each other."[16] We see this fascination with the modern connectivity of strangers in Almodóvar's films as well, where it similarly seems to signal an epistemological and philosophical concern rather than a mere mannerism.

There are a number of characteristic elements in Almodóvar's treatment of coincidence as a stylistic feature. Some are distinctive of his narrative style, while others belong to the causal vocabulary of classic cinematic narration itself. *Talk to Her*, for example, provides numerous examples of classic cinema's unwritten "rule of three," which proposes that an event becomes important if it is mentioned three times (Bordwell, *Classical Hollywood Cinema* 31). Almodóvar seems to be enacting that rule when he presents objects in the mise-en-scène and goes to great lengths in order to provide them with their own history and emotional density. Take Alicia's hair clip, for example. We never see Alicia wear it, but we see it at least three times in the film: first, when Benigno steals it from her room and puts it in his pocket; second, when he is playing with it while awaiting her arrival at the ballet studio across the street; and finally, when Marco retrieves it along with Benigno's other belongings from the prison after Benigno's suicide. Although it is a mundane object on its first appearance on-screen, the hair clip becomes increasingly more significant. Almodóvar uses close-ups to highlight the actual design of the object, the way it resembles a set of jaws and can thus be imagined as representing Benigno's own proprietary desire toward Alicia. The voice-over that concludes his long flashback by explaining Alicia's accident indeed comes on as Benigno gazes out the window, holding her hair clip and pressing it to clench and unclench its little jaws. The hair clip in that instance becomes instrumental in representing a desire and an unvoiced plea that the universe is about to answer: as he will later say to Marco, Benigno considers Alicia's accident as a kind of gift given personally to him by the rain and the accident. But in its third appearance the object carries an entirely different feeling: the fact that Benigno always had this object in his pocket, the fact that the prison authorities did not let him keep it, and the fact that Marco now discovers it incongruously stuffed in a paper envelope convey all the sadness of the preceding events, of unspoken love and missed connections. The emotional content of the hair clip is thus created both by its recurrence in the film and by Marco's grief in the final scene. Always eager to push the emotional envelope, Almodóvar brings up the hair clip one more time, during Marco's visit to Benigno's grave: Marco made sure that Benigno was buried with the hair clip in his pocket, thus circling back to the first instance of the object's presence. The sexual analogies invited by this line of reasoning are obvious in retrospect, with Benigno's desire to have something belonging to Alicia in his pocket standing for his action of entering her metaphorical "pocket" and eventually leaving something of himself there. As with other events in this film, meaning and causality are affected by the small things one cannot see, by secret feelings and secret objects in secret pockets.

The story of the hair clip offers the kind of iconic repetition and narrative density that accrues around objects in classical melodrama, as in the action of lighting two cigarettes that punctuates the bittersweet relationship between Charlotte (Bette Davis) and Jerry (Paul Henreid) in *Now, Voyager* (Irving Rapper, 1942). Almodóvar constructs emotional meaning by carefully placing bits of information about an object throughout the film, clues he allows the audience to slowly gather and connect as the film progresses. This is a classical utilization of suspense structures, as it involves the audience in a satisfying detective story that is not necessarily overtly thematized by the film. The interior of Benigno's apartment provides another such opportunity. We see paint swatches on the wall behind Benigno's bed at the beginning of the film; then cut to a magazine on the floor turned to an earmarked page displaying a modern bedroom set. In the makeover narrative that unfolds over the course of the film, we also see the "before" pictures in Benigno's flashback, which features the apartment decorated, we imagine, according to his mother's taste. Benigno shows the magazine with the modern bedroom to Alicia and describes his intention to re-create this look in his apartment. Marco's visit to the apartment after Benigno's arrest reveals the completed renovation, bringing the makeover subplot to a satisfying conclusion and ratifying the clues dispersed throughout the film for the detecting audience. The operative classical text here for me is *Mildred Pierce* (Michael Curtiz, 1945)—a film that Almodóvar returns to frequently in his work. Before and after pictures of the renovations both of the beach house and of the family mansion are dispersed throughout that film and provide visual cues for the film's complex treatment of temporality. But the final apartment sequence in *Talk to Her* includes another poignant summation: when Marco wakes up in the renovated bedroom, he receives Benigno's phone message announcing his intention to commit suicide. As with the hair clip, we experience the allegorical or symbolic dimension associated with the object after all the important actions have already taken place, here on the day of Benigno's death: Benigno has literally brought the magazine image to life, an evocative counterpart of his other enlivening actions that culminate in Alicia's pregnancy and awakening.

But while the film overtly provides these opportunities for discovery and detective work, and rewards audiences for retaining these clues and putting them together, some of the most important events in the film remain secret. Benigno's sexual relationship with the comatose Alicia and Lydia's return to her old boyfriend El Niño are surprising events, because they are unheralded by the hints and gradual developments that characterize other events in the film. When it comes to these absolutely important events, and in contrast to the treatment of the hair clip and apartment, the film is more withholding, and does not provide access to details and background for the audience. These surprising events, so absolutely pivotal for the action of the film, are allowed to remain inaccessible, belonging to the domain of the characters' own private sphere and the author's realm of influence. In technical terms, these are causally motivated events, the personal and chosen actions of specific characters, and according to classic narration, should feel like they follow fluidly from melodramatic conventions of characterization and psychological motivation. Almodóvar, however, reverses the surprise quotient of these willed actions: they are more unexpected, for example, than the true coincidences of the film, which the director has taken great care to contextualize and naturalize. Their surprising nature is also augmented by their strange temporality: although we find out about them suddenly, they seem to have had a much longer diegetic duration. As we find out from El Niño, he and Lydia had been together for a month before her injury; and it seems that Benigno was having sex with Alicia for a while before being caught—indeed, it seems that Alicia became pregnant sometime during the diegetic span of the film. In contrast to the many other instances of sharing complete causal trajectories with viewers, as with the "before," "during," and "after" stages of Benigno's apartment renovation, these absolutely important reversals occur without prefiguration. We find out about them too late.

Almodóvar provides only subtle clues about Lydia's and Benigno's actions, in effect also making it difficult for the audience to use principles of psychological motivation to understand these characters. Lydia conceals her intentions and decisions from Marco, and the film also conceals the complete subplot of her actions from the viewer. As a result, her secret reconciliation with El Niño and her secret phone call to him during the wedding she attends, feel sudden, surprising, and even unmotivated in narrative terms. It is only in retrospect that we can figure out the sequence of events, the fact that Lydia's phone call has already or just occurred by the time we see her crying and by the time Marco enters the church. Her tears may even eventually strike Marco as a cruel and ironic coincidence: talking to Lydia after the wedding of his ex-girlfriend, Marco reveals that he used to cry when he saw something that moved him because he could not tell her about it. Little does he know that this is precisely why Lydia was crying too, and in her own way she did what he could not do, she called El Niño. Lydia and Marco share a certain emotional experience, but at different times and places and in relation to different people. Although such experiences are the kinds of events that may bring people closer together, these missed clues and connections imply a realm of privacy and secrecy that remains inaccessible both to the characters and to the viewers of the film.

In contrast to the imperative of its title and its overt encouragement of communication, the film's action actually pivots on nondisclosure, privacy, and secrecy, even when the beloved is not comatose. Communication, knowing someone's actions or intentions, and sharing someone's personal and emotional life are thematized as consistent problems between people, as, in fact, somewhat unsolvable or inescapable problems. The interiority of other people remains a boundary, one that verbal communication is supposed to, but cannot always, traverse. It is this boundary that Benigno ignores in his own extreme approach to communication. The secret subplot here shares

with Lydia's deception the same narrative emphasis on a retroactive reordering of important events, the same obsessive treatment of timing and manipulation of screen time. A second viewing of the film, for example, reveals that
we might have guessed the truth about Alicia's pregnancy given that her
period is such a recurring theme in the diegesis. She is menstruating at the
very beginning of the film, a fact that her nurses notice and mention publicly while they bathe her. As we discover during the hospital investigation
scenes, Alicia has missed two periods by the end of the film. Benigno falsi-
fies the charts to cover her first missed period, which he adds in the week
that the other nurse is out with the flu, the week that also includes the night
of Benigno's attendance at *The Shrinking Lover*. Her second missed period
alerts the hospital staff and leads to the discovery of her pregnancy. Benigno's
narration of *The Shrinking Lover* provides the first clues of the real situation between Benigno and Alicia for the audience, a situation that is delivered through the themes and visual images of the silent film, followed by the
close-up of the lava lamp on Alicia's bedside table that further discloses the
sexual nature of their relationship. But when we scrutinize the film's internal
timelines, and realize that Alicia is already pregnant when Benigno's indirect
confession takes place, it becomes clear that these important visual clues
(sexual imagery in *The Shrinking Lover*, the lava lamp) occur at a temporal
disjunction from the events they symbolize (the initiation of sexual contact between Benigno and Alicia). Benigno may have been having sex with
Alicia already by then, during the film's insistently innocuous representation
of the relationship.

The Shrinking Lover thus enables three allegorical readings, all retroactive: in the first, the short film constitutes Benigno's indirect confession
of what he is about to do to Alicia, as the tenor and quality of his body language when he narrates the story to her seem ominous for the first time in
Talk to Her. First viewings of the film thus invite a partial temporal coincidence between the narration of *The Shrinking Lover* and Benigno's rape of
Alicia. In the second allegorical reading, *The Shrinking Lover* provides viewers with imagery and sexual connotations for what Benigno has already
been doing to Alicia: because she may already be pregnant that evening,
Benigno's rape of Alicia precedes the scenes of his newly sexualized body
language and coincides with the screen time of the first part of *Talk to
Her* (when Benigno was the exemplary devoted attendant). By overtly locating Alicia's first period, Almodóvar has cruelly implicated screen time with
rape, as Alicia has been raped and impregnated as if "in front of our eyes."
And although her pregnancy proves that she has been raped at least once,

it does not preclude the possibility of Alicia's repeated violation—a possibility that results in my own choice of tenses (Benigno has been raping Alicia) and registers the feeling of ambient guilt that renders subsequent viewings of the film increasingly painful. Finally, the third allegorical reading of *The Shrinking Lover* depends on how literally or liberally we are willing to read the imagery of the silent film and on how willing we are to register its implicit disclosures in language. At the end of *The Shrinking Lover*, for example, we follow the minuscule man's decision to fully merge with his gigantic beloved by taking off all his clothes and disappearing fully inside her body. Considered allegorically as another of Benigno's retroactive confessions, this aspect of the short film's narrative indeed presents not just the basic facts of the case but also hints at a change in Benigno's secret actions, perhaps from a stage in which Benigno is careful to cover his tracks to less guarded sexual behavior (the lover's removal of his clothes standing for perhaps removing a condom, his decision to remain inside the body of his beloved standing for a decision not to withdraw before ejaculation). In addition to exposing the sexual interaction between Benigno and Alicia to the audience, then, the silent film enacts an additional confession designed to remain secret. Because he is the one falsifying the charts that week, Benigno must both know and not be able to acknowledge that Alicia is pregnant—and perhaps his narration of the plot of *The Shrinking Lover* enacts his first and only acknowledgment of what he has done and how.

By showing and not telling, the film traffics in a mode of presentation that both enables and negates knowledge, and this contradiction allows Benigno to remain sympathetic and likable to an audience that can both criticize his actions and partly (and implicitly) exonerate him. Utilizing the melodramatic potential of secrets and their slow or partial disclosure, Almodóvar ensures that the audience remains ignorant of Benigno's sexual relations with Alicia and that when the secret is revealed, it is already "too late" because Alicia is already pregnant. While we have been complimented by the film for being good detectives, we have remained clueless to this most important set of events. For viewers, Benigno's representation thus produces a pattern of initial discomfort, when Alicia's nudity and Benigno's extraordinary attentions to her feel strange to us at first, followed by a stage of familiarization and normalization, as Benigno's persona and good humor lull us into a sense of trust, and culminating in a disorienting phase, when discomfort and trust give way to a sense of being betrayed. Now in retrospect we may imagine, as the hospital personnel also does, that we share some responsibility in the film's events, that our first sense was right and that

Benigno's intimacy was inappropriate. I will return to this complicated ethical situation and its epistemological implications later.

How Strangers Meet

Almodóvar thus tends to transform one kind of event into another: willed events become unmotivated surprises for the viewer, as we saw with Benigno's sexual relationship to Alicia and Lydia's call to El Niño, while accidents or events we could consider random become coincidences, or narratively meaningful events, through the gradual accretion of important details and the revelation of past histories. Almodóvar's handling of coincidence is subtle and complex. For example, the fact that both Marco and Alicia attend the Pina Bausch performance feels at the same time coincidental, accidental, *and* fated. If we were to imagine a future conversation in which they compare notes about why they were both there, they might consider that they each had their own motives and reasons, some of which the audience can easily supply, for attending the show. The real coincidence of their meeting would pivot on how and why they decided to attend on that same night (assuming, of course, that there were other evenings they could have chosen), and how they happened to sit just one row apart. From the point of view of the audience, of course, this purely coincidental aspect of their meeting, the aspect that is closest to revealing authorial intervention and design, is elided or irrelevant: there is nothing more fitting than their meeting at the end of the film. Indeed, this kind of coincidence, which in other texts or other textual circumstances would have seemed heavy-handed or forced, is here fluidly integrated into the film's structure, and emotionally satisfying, perhaps precisely because it is also thoroughly prefigured. These are masterful strokes and Almodóvar shows them off brilliantly in this film: the fundamental coincidences, the ones specifically designed by the author to bring characters together and connect the narrative threads of the film, appear to be either random or fated events, and the evidence of the power of the author is subtly transformed until it becomes something altogether different.

This transformation of authorial intervention is nowhere more visible than in the representation of Alicia and Lydia's accidents, which the narrative indeed transforms into something akin to acts of nature. Both events are also specifically prefigured in the narration. The first bullfight we see Lydia perform includes cuts to the observant El Niño and his manager, fearful that Lydia is endangering herself that day because El Niño is there. The slow-motion visual treatment of the bullfight adds a palpable sense of foreboding to the scene, which is exacerbated by the fact that at the end Lydia seems to turn her back to the bull before the kill. By contrast, her goring is all too quick, a head-on collision without suspense or temporal extension, and a rather unexpected turn of events, particularly after the ritualistic buildup of her dressing and preparation scene. Narrative conventions have not accustomed us to expect such rapid reversals, especially after scenes that seem designed to heighten the visual pleasure of what is to ensue. The bull, featured in a close-up profile after the accident, acts as a force of nature, uncontained by narrative parameters and expectations. Similarly, Alicia's accident is prefigured in the scene in which she jaywalks after talking to Benigno, a scene filmed as if to provoke a sense of danger for the audience when she breezily threads through the busy street. As Benigno will mention more than once later in the film, it was raining on the day of her accident, and he thus associates the rain with a kind of benign and generous force— the force that gave Alicia to him. The bull and the rain thus act as diegetic stand-ins for the decisions made by the author, and as agents of a naturalized and inescapable causality. By being associated with natural forces, both events belie or hide the very sources of narrative causality: the events that the author specifically chooses are transformed into the kinds of events that in everyday life people usually *do not* choose.

Prefiguring accident: Alicia walking away from Benigno through the busy street in Talk to Her. *Photograph by Miguel Bracho. Copyright Miguel Bracho/El Deseo.*

A related use of prefiguration structures the most characteristic of Almodóvar's tendencies in the handling of strangers and of coincidence: his tendency to consistently transform first meetings among strangers into second or subsequent meetings. In a clear parallel to his treatment of objects,
this feature infuses casual events, such as the short conversation between
Marco and Alicia in the theater lobby, with the kind of intimacy, prefigured
poignancy, and emotional intensity we experience in his films. The meeting
of two complete strangers may be the effect of chance or accident, but it is
not a coincidence. In order for a meeting to be a coincidence, one of the two
people, or at least another person, or the audience, has to recognize that
this meeting is surprising or unexpected. Coincidence is thus crafted out of
the partial knowledge second meetings stage, an effect of recognition and
not surprise.

In describing a narrative event as a coincidence we may refer to the
author's action, the ways in which he or she sets the characters in a particular way so that they can meet and propel the narrative further; or describe
the experience of the characters and their impression as to whether their
meeting is surprising or not. We may also use the term to express the audience's sense of the event. For example, Benigno and Marco's meeting in the
first dance performance in *Talk to Her* can be described as a coincidence
in technical narrative terms: this is how Almodóvar chose to bring these
two characters together and start the film. Authorial intention in this case
is related to randomness: unless we are told otherwise, we assume no inten-
tionality or causality in how people who buy one ticket are seated in a public
event. Although the film will gradually transform precisely this randomness
of everyday life into something akin to fate or destiny, its beginning alerts us
to the ways in which public culture connects strangers, in settings that allow
very intimate private experiences to occur in public.

Within the world of the film, the two men cannot describe the same
meeting as a coincidence because they had no expectation of meeting or not
meeting, they just happened to be seated next to each other. They also have
no sense of the future connections the film will thrust upon them. Everyone
who attended the same performance has "met" in this general way, but their
meeting is by no means important unless other events render it important
somehow, in the past or the future. When Benigno and Marco meet again
in the hospital, their brief previous meeting changes the dynamic of their
current encounter. Benigno remembers that Marco was the man who cried
next to him at the theater, and he mentions it. Marco had only seconds ear-

lier, and almost at the same time, noticed the autograph of Pina Bausch that Benigno framed for Alicia hanging on the wall over her bed. In technical terms, this is partly a motivated meeting because the text has established a causal chain of facts and events that explain the men's presence at the same place: Benigno works in a hospital in the coma ward, the injured Lydia is in a coma, it makes sense that she might be brought to the same hospital and that Marco would follow. For the characters, the event is not causal but coincidental because both Benigno and Marco recognize it as their second meeting. First meetings cannot be experienced as coincidental, but second meetings usually are.

The audience's sense of when a coincidence occurs differs dramatically as well, because in a cinematic text the filmmaker can easily provide the impression of second meetings through visual and spatial continuity. Careful viewers may have anticipated Marco and Benigno's meeting at the hospital at many points earlier in the film, as when we see Lydia's family and Marco walking down the hospital hallway after taking Lydia there, or when Marco peeks into Alicia's room on his way to the doctor's office. Viewers may recognize the hospital, or recognize the similarity of circumstances, or recognize Alicia, or even recognize the narrative drive toward a hospital or coma ward when Lydia is injured. The recognition of the coincidence of Marco and Benigno's meeting at the hospital thus occurs earlier for the viewers than for the characters. If we were to include the audience's cultural or media experience of the film before they actually arrive in the theater, we would have to extend this recognition even further: if a viewer has read a review or seen images of the film beforehand, he or she may be able to appreciate the coincidental nature of Marco and Benigno's *first* meeting at the theater, on the grounds that these two men are *about to* become more intimately related in the future. Although somewhat closer to the authorial perspective of the meeting, this forward-looking sense of its coincidental nature is again different from both the author's and the characters' perspective.

In general, then, we can summarize that the reading of a scene or event as a coincidence depends on the divergence of authorial, spectatorial, and character points of view, as these different points of view apply radically different rules for such an assignation. Because cinematic representation manipulates both spatial and temporal dimensions, the recognition of coincidence is fundamentally shaped by visual representational choices and by the narrative order or unfolding of the film, its discursive dimension. I am referring here to the narratological distinction between story and discourse: the story of the film (what happened and when) can follow a real-life order of events as they occur earlier and later, much in the same way that we may describe the film's plot in a linear fashion. Its discourse, however (how things are depicted on-screen and in what order), follows a logic of exposition that is independent of the reality and order of the actual events.[17] Almodóvar manipulates the distinction brilliantly in this film, using it to exacerbate the problem of knowing and not knowing, to hide from audience and characters any means of knowing when events occur, and to constantly modulate the distances between the points of view of the audience, the characters, and the author.

Cinematic coincidence is more than a plot device. Arranging elements in the visual and aural planes in order to facilitate recognition is a fundamental feature of cinematic narration; indeed, it is a major element in the genres that Almodóvar frequently references, such as melodrama and film noir. This is because visual coincidence heightens suspense by precisely exploiting the divergence of spectatorial and character points of view. Almodóvar's visual treatments often manipulate this divergence by constructing the coincidence specifically for the benefit of the audience. For example, in the last theater scene of *Talk to Her*, the audience is the first to recognize the coincidence when we see Marco crying through Alicia's point of view—clearly, they are both in the same theater and only feet from each other. Then there is a sequential parceling out of this same coincidence, a repetition that treats it like a slowly turning prism: first, the audience realizes that this is a coincidence but the characters don't know yet; then Marco realizes this is a coincidence when Alicia catches his eye in the lobby, but she doesn't know yet; then Katerina realizes that this is a coincidence when she sees them talking, and Alicia still doesn't know.

A classic melodramatic resolution might push forward to the climactic moment when Alicia herself finds out, as that moment would finally merge all the dispersed points of view that the scene presents, staging the kind of fantasy of unification and "central plenitude" that Peter Brooks describes as one of the fundamental functions of melodrama in modernity (200). This the film refrains from doing, a withholding that, in my view, generates a sense of relief for the audience. Although such a final recognition would be the stuff that high melodrama is made of (painful, unimaginable, excruciating, delicious), explaining the story to Alicia on-screen would resemble a spiral and self-conscious return to all the traumatic events of the diegesis, events that were tolerable in their subtle and veiled first run and that would be difficult to watch again in full knowledge of the circumstances. Here Almodóvar self-consciously deploys a Hitchcockian narrative structure, revised to allow for the introduction of potentiality and a certain decorum. We can imagine *Vertigo* (1958) as the operative reference, with some editions and reconfigurations to its narrative unfolding that aim to avoid, for example, Scottie's (James Stewart) recognition that Madeleine and Judy are the same woman (Kim Novak), or to rewrite Judy's final fall at the Mission that returns the film to its initial trauma (Scottie's chase and fall from the rooftops) *and* its midpoint trauma (Madeleine's fall). Although some of that sense of vertigo caused by recognition and repetition is clearly experienced by Marco in this scene (and motivates my own description of the spiral-like sequence of recognitions), Alicia's realization is deferred. Almodóvar revises or avoids in *Talk to Her* the cruel doubling over the film's traumatic territory that Hitchcock deploys in *Vertigo*. To engage in my own genre-appropriate metaphor here, Hitchcock stabs the audience and then twists the knife, more than once. Almodóvar stabs but doesn't twist, and we are relieved he doesn't because we know he could have. Marco's gesture in the lobby, which can also be described as signaling something like "Let's not get into that," is precisely Almodóvar's narrative and textual gesture. This is the moment when with one or two phrases Marco could have stepped over the boundary of Alicia's ignorance with a simple line like, "I am sorry I seem so startled, I just realized that I know who you are," and so on. Marco's gesture marks a character's decision coinciding with the author's decision not to talk more—or at least not now—about the events of the film.

Countering the film's overt endorsement of talking, verbal description is insistently deferred on other grounds as well. A situation in which the events of the film would have to be recast in language, spoken or read, or summarized, paraphrased, and generally externalized, would undermine the subtlety and visual care with which Almodóvar has actually presented them. Discourse would have to turn into story, in other words, in the process dispatching the film's brilliant deployment of the distinctions between the two modes. Almodóvar has created a situation in which a kind of knowledge is transmitted through seeing long before it arrives into actual words, or sometimes without arriving into words at all. What difference would the words make? They would probably register the speaker's own evaluation of the moral and ethical status of the events reported, adding moral content to the ambiguity that allows the audience to deal with the numerous questions that arise out of Benigno's actions: what happened, when did it happen, did we see it, did we know it, when did we see it, how could we have not known it, and so on. What has been verbalized by the hospital staff is the official story, which the nurse quickly reports to Marco: *they claim* that he *raped* Alicia. The very choice of tenses and words presumes that this was a one-time event. But while the fact of Alicia's pregnancy proves sexual contact, her nonpregnancy (or the audience's ignorance of her pregnancy) does not prove the absence of sexual contact. Based on the timeline I proposed earlier, my own verbalized version of Benigno's acts would be more sinister than the nurse's: Benigno was having sex with Alicia, and probably for a while before getting caught.

The unverbalized story, on the other hand, follows Marco and Benigno's emotional connection, Benigno's continued reverence of Alicia, and the moral ambiguity that his love creates for the audience. Although we know what has happened, Almodóvar's emotional treatment of Benigno in the last part of the film does not confer judgment onto him, nor does it activate the Manichaean tendencies of melodrama that could so easily apply here. Instead, the film largely operates by careful manipulation of silence, silent viewing, and a kind of visual cognition that may or may not be verbalized. In a way, the film's presentational mode is designed to leave certain things unspoken, and because this treatment revolves around the most provocative and potentially disrupting feature of the film, I will need to return to Benigno's actions and their implications later.

What emerges from Almodóvar's deployment of first and second meetings is a subtle distinction between seeing and meeting. Marco saw Alicia often in the hospital, but is only meeting her at the end of the film—and even this meeting leaves room for further "not-quite-first" meetings because of its brevity. Alicia noticed Marco during the performance, so their lobby encounter is a second meeting for her too, however incomplete. Many aspects of a real meeting are deferred here for both of them, especially for Alicia: they are not properly introduced, she does not know his name, he does not know how she feels or who she really is, they don't shake hands or touch, they don't find out more about each other, and so on.

So, while Marco and Alicia have already met in some way, their relationship still belongs in the wide realm of sociality that lies between strangers and family. Although Almodóvar has presented numerous family narratives in other films, important familial relationships are mostly absent in *Talk to Her,* replaced by a focus on the interactions among the peer group of the four main characters and the professional or specialized teams that populate their immediate social realms (the bullfighting arena, the hospital, the ballet school, the prison). We hear of the formative influence of Benigno's mother and Lydia's father, both dead by the diegetic real time of the film and present only through photographs, and we see the helplessness of Lydia's sister and Alicia's father when they visit the hospital. But the important debates and concerns of this film do not revolve around the family but around strangers: the connectedness that emerges between strangers, the ways in which lovers may remain relative strangers to each other, the estrangement that befalls some lovers in the film (Lydia and El Niño, Marco and Lydia), and the complete absence of estrangement that is projected in the representation of other potential lovers (Benigno and Alicia, according to Benigno, of course, Marco and Benigno in the fusion of their faces over the prison glass, Marco and Alicia at the end of the film). The tension between realism and fantasy that I emphasized in the lobby scene, that is, between the causal explanation as to why Alicia looks at Marco and the transcendental explanation of prefigured connection between them, extends to these figurations of intimacy as well. As even this preliminary listing implies, it is only the potential relationships, the fantasy relationships, that sustain the possibility of total fusion and absolute nonestrangement between lovers. The real relationships in the film have to grapple with the realities of communication and of difference, with the fact that we need to talk and listen to each other because we cannot guess and should not project what the other feels or thinks. I will return to this didactic dimension of the film's depictions of communication and intimacy later.

In a nutshell, Almodóvar's general narrative tendencies combine prefigured relationships among strangers with the constant deferral of a full and final meeting. This signals an insistence that even strangers are already connected, in the way Dickens also describes, and that meeting someone is an unfolding process, not a single event. By presenting his characters as nonstrangers who have, however, not fully met, Almodóvar produces a continual process of recognition and return whose familiarizing and socializing effects are palpable both in the diegetic worlds of his films and in the experience reported by his audiences. As many critics and reviewers have noted throughout his career, Almodóvar consistently achieves a fine balance between the joys of artifice and constructedness and the intensity of emotional investment. In contrast to directors such as Douglas Sirk, who may use melodrama to produce distantiation or estrangement, Almodóvar's melodramatic style often has the opposite result, a kind of enfolding of characters, audience, and even critics into a familiar circle of shared references and experiences. Even when Almodóvar self-consciously imitates a Sirkean

Boundaries, reflections, and Almodóvar's enfolding of Douglas Sirk: Benigno and Katerina with the comatose Alicia on the hospital veranda. Photograph by Miguel Bracho. Copyright Miguel Bracho/El Deseo.

style, as in his use of reflective surfaces and saturated colors, estrangement in the film is reserved for the kinds of events that even fiction cannot correct, those caused by natural forces and by the difficulties of human emotion.

In terms of its epistemological implications, then, this film operates in a mode both influenced by and precisely converse to the family drama: we imagine that our immediate family members are familiar and intimate, known or knowable; yet, in melodramas they are often revealed to be more complex than we imagine, sometimes even threatening or alien. *Talk to Her* instead revolves around the possibility of compassion, friendship, and intimacy among strangers, continuing an emotional and intellectual exploration that was already under way in *All about My Mother* (1999). The enduring relationships in that film revolve around characters that are not related by blood, while both Sister Rosa (Penélope Cruz) and her baby are repeatedly abandoned by her indifferent parents. As if in counterpoint, the performances of *A Streetcar Named Desire* punctuating that film constantly remind viewers of Blanche DuBois's famous line "I have always depended on the kindness of strangers," a line that reverberates subtly at the end of *Talk to Her* and further connects the two films. The song by K. D. Lang that accompanies one of the movements of *Masurca Fogo* includes the phrase "intimate strangers."[18] "Intimate strangers" can indeed describe many relationships in this film and is an especially apt interpretation of the secretive and mysterious relationship between Benigno and Alicia. Intimate strangers may always be what people remain to each other—our struggle for communication and understanding, for emotional and sexual sharing, and for joint political and aesthetic projects can be imagined as responses to the fact of difference, as efforts to overcome or counteract our distance from each other. The desires that the film thematizes, to understand and to be understood, to communicate and to create communal meanings, thus elicit the full range of problems associated with the existence of others, their difference and distance from the self, the inaccessibility of their minds and thoughts, and the incomprehensibility of their motives. Melodrama in this setting functions as a translation device, one that externalizes and distributes all that is private and secret, even as it preserves the facts of distance and difference.

Art and Life

Almodóvar's tendency to highlight the formation of social relationships extends to his references to and quotations of other art forms, which thus acquire an allegorical dimension that signals the intimate enfolding of one text into another. In *Talk to Her* we have a number of such textual references, both overt and covert. Some performances are situated as set pieces or distinct episodes in the film. The two Pina Bausch ballets and the performance of Caetano Veloso's "Cucurrucucú paloma" are depicted as "live" events (they are filmed for the film's viewers but live for the characters). Along with the two bullfights we see Lydia perform, these events present the characters' direct involvement in live cultural and musical events, events that are different from watching a televised ballet performance because they occasion participation in the public sphere. Indeed, the first meetings of many of the characters in the film occur in such events, and it is their participation in art and culture that brings them into contact with one another. Marco sees Lydia for the first time on TV and then in the bullfight; Marco and Benigno see each other for the first time when they attend the dance performance, as do Marco and Alicia. In an interesting variation of this connecting structure of public culture, Benigno "meets" a version of himself and his actions on-screen in the plot of *The Shrinking Lover,* and, unbeknownst to him, Marco is looking at what will happen to Lydia when he looks at a black-and-white photograph of bullfighter Manolito at the bar. As if in an effort to further extend the life of the Pina Bausch autograph, which functions as a motivating object on a number of occasions in the film, in his commentary Almodóvar reveals that he has his own autograph of Pina Bausch from *Café Müller,* and had it for numerous years before beginning work on *Talk to Her.* Is the film, then, directly inspired by some element of this particular dance piece? This would explain why the dances fit so beautifully in *Talk to Her,* and it would also provocatively reveal the film's inspiration and origins to have occurred in the same public culture that we find thematized in the diegesis—a new kind of coincidence between idea and product, as the director could be said to have "met" his film for the first time in the same context where his characters meet for the first time.[19]

As always with Almodóvar's stylistic techniques, specific references to other art forms and literary and filmic texts abound in the visual plane and the mise-en-scène. In *Talk to Her* these references further expand both the emotional logic of the film and its insistence that we are bound to each other through our participation in culture. Recognizing Almodóvar's referential gestures in this case engages the audience in a different kind of textual expansion, because the film provides for us, brought to life as it were, art pieces from very different media. For example, Alicia's visual representation in the hospital, her reclining posture and aesthetic treatment, often resemble famous paintings of nudes, from Goya's *Nude Maja* (1800) to Edward Manet's *Olympia* (1863). When Lydia is carried away after her accident, the visual representation and spiritual aura of the scene bring to mind paintings of Christ's descent from the cross, a major and much-dispersed religious theme. Something about her posture while being carried, the angle of her bent knee, and the gorgeous colors of her suit of lights, mark this scene as an aesthetic object in general. The fact that the camera snaps a picture of her from above contributes to the aestheticization of the moment: the photograph functions as an invasion of a painful and important moment in her life, a sign of our collective lack of privacy in contemporary media culture. Yet, if imagined as an artifact, the ensuing image would be quite painterly in composition, and its style might directly resemble a painting of Christ's descent. Along with such general references that bring the aura of painting into the film or quote particular paintings, Almodóvar clearly brings to life David Hockney's swimming paintings, such as *Portrait of an Artist (Pool with Two Figures)* (1971), and his numerous lithographs and "camera works" involving pool scenes.[20] Almodóvar's visual treatment similarly transforms the conversation between Marco and Benigno in the prison through the glass partitions into a video art piece (I think of Tony Oursler's work, but other references are possible as well), as the face of one man becomes the sculptural surface on which the emotions of the other are projected.[21]

In addition to dance, painting, video art, religious iconography, photography, and bullfighting, this process of enfolding other art forms into *Talk to Her*—and I use enfolding as the opposite of the concept of distantiation here—includes innumerable cinematic references. *The Shrinking Lover* obviously and lovingly echoes the visual, narrative, and acting styles of silent films of the 1920s, but also 1950s science-fiction films such as *The Incredible Shrinking Man* (Jack Arnold, 1957), and contemporary revisions of these styles in experimental films such as Guy Maddin's *The Heart of the World* (Canada, 2000). Because Almodóvar is conscious of both Sirk and Buñuel as his personal ancestors in terms of melodramatic and artistic heritage, *Talk to Her* includes many Sirkean frames that combine reflections and projections, especially revolving around Benigno (for example, when he sits with Alicia on the hospital's balcony, or when he talks to Marco during the prison visit). Using the most overt stylistic vocabulary of distantiation, Almodóvar dares or warns us to keep our distance from Benigno, even as he makes it virtually impossible to actually do so through other means. *Talk to Her* also includes a sustained textual and visual homage to Buñuel's *Belle de Jour* (1967). The restrained upper-class elegance of Benigno's apartment before the remodeling resembles Séverine's (Catherine Deneuve) apartment in that film, while Benigno's devotion to the unresponsive Alicia also echoes Séverine's happiness at the end of the film, when she settles in to care for her blind and paralyzed husband. Perhaps Almodóvar's treatment of classical narrative structure constitutes a similar homage. I have already mentioned *Vertigo,* but Hitchcock's *Psycho* (1960) resonates even more closely with the structure of *Talk to Her.* Benigno's portrayal as the shy and endearing young man dominated by the presence of his mother (a mother we never see) and eventually revealed as a psychopath, clearly has parallels to Norman Bates's (Anthony Perkins) portrayal of a similar character, while Lydia's goring occurs as early in the film and in as unexpected a way as Marion's (Janet Leigh) murder. Again, in *Talk to Her* Almodóvar refrains from the psychological exposition that dominates the ending of *Psycho* just as he refrains from the traumatic repetitions of *Vertigo.* The classical Hollywood film, partly exemplified by Hitchcock, is thus one of the many kinds of texts and aesthetic models Almodóvar quotes, references, incorporates, and transforms in *Talk to Her.*

If at the heart of the Aristotelian coincidence we find the revelation of kinship and familial ties, and at the heart of the Dickensian coincidence the revelation that kinship ties undermine class divisions, at the very heart of the Almodovarian coincidence in *Talk to Her* we find the intricate workings of art and mass culture as they create potential ties among strangers. As part of his exploration of audience and reception, of the intimacy of popular culture and the effect popular culture can have on a personal level, Almodóvar's inclusion of other films, texts, plays, art pieces, dance performances, and songs creates a realm of sociality and relationship among texts, as among characters. Almodóvar's extended and careful handling of prominent and emotionally resonant references to other art forms is more than quotation and certainly more complex than pastiche, and it makes a claim for the film's own participation in an art scene that it both absorbs and transforms. The emotional treatment of these art pieces, some of which become resonant for the characters on a very intimate personal level, seems to also imply that popular culture is personally made, and made by particular people in order to communicate with others and be understood. It is also personally consumed and appropriated, incorporated into the self and into the narrative structures we employ in everyday life. Neither production nor reception is impersonal, alienated, glib, or estranged in this film. Despite the well-known complaints about the abuse of televisual culture and the onslaught of mere spectacle and *telebasura* in the public sphere, as discussed by Paul Julian Smith in this volume, Almodóvar thus presents a utopian vision of participation and interpretation, one that confirms his overall humanist presentation of connected strangers.

Although primarily utopian in my view, Almodóvar's approach to the desire for modern connectivity is neither naive nor simplistic. Indeed, isn't Benigno's sexual use of Alicia one of the worst things a stranger might do? How can the utopian vision presented by the film coexist with the ethical difficulties that arise from Benigno's actions, especially when Benigno himself cannot recognize them as questionable or unethical when Marco confronts him? As I mentioned earlier, by representing Benigno as a fundamentally likable and understandable character, and by refusing to confer moral judgment on him in the last part of the film, Almodóvar resists the Manichaean tendencies of melodrama. Indeed, the film not only resists positing a dichotomy between good and evil but also actively frustrates or impedes such characterizations. Just as many of the film's coincidences feel motivated because they flow from a desire for connection that viewers and characters share, at the base of the film's causal spirals we find not intention but a kind of indescribable inevitability. In addition to thwarting viewer efforts to truly see *what* Benigno did, the film also thwarts any clear method for understanding *why* he did what he did. The possible answers to this second question are contradictory: because he is a sociopath (an explanation made possible by Benigno's short description of his childhood during a visit to the psychologist); because he loves Alicia and thinks she loves him (the explanation Benigno himself might provide); because people are unpredictable (an open-ended response implicit in the film's handling of ethical responsibility); because people are driven by passion and desire (another possible Almodovarian explanation based on his treatment of sexual desire in other films); and, of course, the final answer, "nobody knows." In his DVD commentary Almodóvar adds another indirect possibility when he states that "nature is amoral in itself," thus connecting Benigno's actions to natural forces, as he does with Lydia's and Alicia's accidents. Almodóvar thus partly absolves Benigno, ascribing his willed actions to the workings not of will, nor of Providence, but of human nature, or even just "nature," the agent that is closest to fate in Almodóvar's nondeterministic secular structures. As if equated to the other natural forces that have been the causes of important events (the rain that caused Alicia's accident, the bull that gored Lydia), Benigno's passion counters all moral and social limits, acting as a causal agent and a redeeming agent at the same time. Almodóvar's transformational treatment of events becomes visible here as well, in the association of authorial perspective with nature: the three events that fundamentally carry out the author's intentions belie their origin and design, instead appearing to be as inevitable and unquestionable as natural forces.

But although it does not conform to Manichaean binaries, the melodramatic treatment of Benigno produces a deep and, again, unspoken moral complexity that is only exacerbated by his suicide. In the alternative moral universe of melodrama, Benigno's suicide is both fitting and severe as a self-punishment. Since Spain abolished the death penalty for all crimes in 1995, no judge could have punished Benigno in the way that he punishes himself. His suicide adds a fantasmatic dimension of fairness to the film: whereas in everyday life rape often goes unpunished or is inadequately punished, the film engages the imaginary possibility that the wages of rape should be death, even as it allows viewers to avoid making a choice about Benigno's proper punishment. Almodóvar's insistence that much of the story has to remain unspoken operates in this instance too, because a court case would verbalize Benigno's actions and reasons, and would require deciding among the mutually exclusive answers I just presented. By not providing the context for such a choice, the film allows viewers to sustain completely contradictory emotions about Benigno without feeling such contradiction as a problem: Benigno can thus be both a man driven by love and a sociopath, both a predator who took advantage of his professional position and a childlike romantic.

I am not sure what punishment Benigno would have received if the case had ever been tried in court, but the real punishment has already been conferred: Alicia is awake. By coming back to conscious life, Alicia is "dead" to him now: they could not continue as before; his role as her surrogate has ended. Because he has not truly considered Alicia as a separate person during the four years of taking care of her—an altogether different "crime"— Benigno is also unequipped to deal with what she may say, do, or decide now that she emerges from her coma. With Alicia awake, any relationship between them would have to start from a different sort of mutuality, but allowing Alicia to agree to this kind of connection would also allow her to disagree, to reject him if that were her wish, no matter how much he loved her. Could Benigno enter into this fundamental and challenging element of living in the company of others? Could he understand the fact that other people, or the person he loves, have their own minds and may see things differently? Alternatively, can we imagine Benigno banished from Alicia's life? Although Marco feels guilty that he never told Benigno about Alicia's recovery, Benigno's fate is sealed in either case, because he seems unable to understand the balance between familiarity and strangeness that living with others entails. A relationship that depends on a beloved's absolute silence cannot be real; it is a fantasy, and cannot last for long.

Along with overt fairy-tale connections, in the film's representation of a vulnerable "sleeping beauty" lying in a new kind of forest (the name of the clinic is "El Bosque" [The Forest]) and awakened with a (sexual) kiss,[22] in Almodóvar's treatment of Alicia and Benigno's relationship we also discover what I would argue functions as the most extended and structural intertextual relationship in *Talk to Her*: the film's association with Ovid's *Metamorphoses*. Clearly, Benigno's devotion to an inaccessible and silent beloved parallels Pygmalion's love for the statue. Alicia's malleability and silence evoke many Pygmalion-like stories and films in which women are valued for their silent beauty, here literally objectified by the narrative of the film and the cinematic apparatus. The connection between the film and the ancient story goes even deeper, however. Pygmalion's story is set in motion by problems with human sociality, as Pygmalion decides to shun

love and live alone after he is shocked by the cold-heartedness and immorality of women (women that Venus turns to stone in the preceding story).
Apparently having lived alone with his mother for most of his life, Benigno
is released from her demands and in turn devotes himself to a differently
cold woman, one, however, who seems to have no desire and no need he
cannot fulfill, partly because she has no desire or need that does not originate in him. He treats Alicia as his artifact, a doll he can play with, dressing
and undressing her, polishing her nails, and fixing her hair. In Pygmalion's
story, the goddess animates the statue to prove her power and exact her
revenge: while originally imagining that he could resist her power, after falling in love with the statue, Pygmalion reenters the realm of erotic passion
that Venus reigns over. By animating the statue, she proves her sovereignty,
her dominion over Pygmalion, complete since he has fallen in love with a
woman who is first stone and then flesh in the same tale. Alicia's awakening is similarly a punishment for Benigno in the film, not a reward. He
has been forgetting the rules of human communication, misunderstanding silence for agreement, and imagining his own desires and wishes to be
reflected and returned in Alicia's comatose face. Narcissus's story, also from
the *Metamorphoses,* easily comes to mind.[23]

In contrast to Benigno, Almodóvar goes to some length to show Alicia
as a separate person, in the process developing a subtle discourse on the
perils of projection and narcissism, but also on the ethics of looking. He
uses Alicia's representation to ensure that the audience is guilty of looking at
her nude form, as are Benigno, Marco, and the other characters that observe
her in the hospital and witness Benigno and Alicia's interactions. But, over
the course of the film Almodóvar also insists on providing subtle clues in
order to create a distinction between the comatose Alicia and the awakened
Alicia—a necessary gesture, in my view, and one that ensures that at the end
of the film the real, live woman could be recognized as a person outside of
Benigno's projective point of view.

If we trace the visual presence of Alicia through the film, in addition to
the luminosity of her gaze when she is awake, we notice a couple of subtle
gestures that highlight the difference between her two states. Alicia appears
nude from the very beginning of the film, with a close-up of her breasts
among the first images we see of her body. The medical setting, artistic references to famous nude paintings, and Benigno's own performance of profes-
sionalism allow us to sustain this presentation of nudity as if it were dis-
connected from structures of shame and propriety, as well as from structures

of cinematic objectification. Here it seems that Almodóvar courts a reading of objectification, and even thematizes this interpretation by presenting a woman who is unaware of being looked at; her lack of awareness renders both camera and viewers inevitably voyeuristic, perhaps even unapologetically so.[24] In Benigno's flashback, however, Alicia immediately covers herself when she runs into Benigno in the hallway of her apartment; her shock at being caught in the nude is palpably the opposite of the aesthetic and visual accessibility the film has imposed on her body up to that point. Does the audience keep this difference in mind when the film returns to its diegetic time frame? In a way, Almodóvar alerts us that perhaps the film's representation of nudity and the constant handling of Alicia may have a problematic or troublesome side. Similarly, while Benigno insists on maintaining Alicia's hair exactly as it used to be before her accident, certain that this is what she would have wanted, Alicia changes her hairstyle when she awakens, replacing her utilitarian (but also romantic) pulled-back style before the accident, and Benigno's various girlish pigtails and braids for her in the hospital, with lighter highlights and an angular cut that frames her face.[25] When the real woman can, she intervenes in the construction of her image, and the accord that Benigno imagines in their relationship proves to be a fantasy even in

Alicia covering herself after discovering Benigno in her apartment. Photograph by Miguel Bracho. Copyright Miguel Bracho/El Deseo.

the case of such a mundane thing as a haircut. But is the audience's easy assumption of Benigno's point of view challenged and undermined by these small gestures? What do we learn from the clues given to us by the film?

In tracing the coincidences that structure the narrative of *Talk to Her* and Almodóvar's general diegetic style, I have tried to identify the significance of the different kinds of causalities reserved for different kinds of events in the film. In Alicia's gesture of covering up and her change of hairstyle we witness her willed actions, actions that are portrayed as intentional and motivated, and confluent with her insistent gaze at Marco, her effort to communicate with him at the theater lobby. Despite the brevity of her time as an agent in the film, Alicia is given a certain amount of visibly personal action, significant because so many important actions in this film do not have such overtly willed personal and causal content. I think that these small clues alert us to the self-consciousness of Almodóvar's style, and have interesting implications for the film's treatment of objectification. This again returns us to an interrogation of Benigno's, and the audience's, fantasy space. Benigno clearly loves and might even prefer a comatose Alicia. Do we? How do we escape Benigno's fantasy of complete and total agreement between idealized lovers, a fantasy that we actually might share in everyday life despite knowing better? How can the film train us to value the difficulty of reciprocity, reaction, and difference that an awake Alicia embodies, the kinds of qualities I argue would have challenged Benigno? If we have seen, and perhaps loved, Alicia through Benigno's eyes, how can we see her differently?

Part of the effect of the romantic treatment of the last scenes of the film, of the promise or possibility of a relationship between Marco and Alicia, is to ensure that we accept the value of the real woman as a person with choice and complexity, after being perhaps accustomed to the complete narcissism of Benigno's love for a pliable and convenient "perfect" woman. By presenting Alicia in the act of inviting a connection with Marco, the act of saying "yes," the film dispels the imaginary scenes that have been withheld from us and from her, scenes that would include her in acts of self-preservation. Alicia says "yes" (to Marco) rather than saying "no" (to Benigno). This is how the film ensures that we can forgive her for waking up: in the emotional logic of melodrama (which here replicates a logic that is unfortunately endemic in rape cases as well), the audience may have already forgiven Benigno. The only "crime" that remains is hers, because her life has taken away his. It is this illogical crime that we have to forgive, and indeed forgive implicitly and silently, and without being aware of the process. The fact that we know her story is a liability for Alicia because it might actually cause the audience's disengagement from her. In a film with no strangers this would be a unique estrangement, a distantiation that would threaten Almodóvar's overall aim.

As with all texts that include references to Pygmalion and his statue, the work of *Talk to Her* revolves around mourning and loss, and seems indeed to be most intimately and pervasively informed by Book X of Ovid's *Metamorphoses* where the Pygmalion story occurs. Pygmalion's story is among the series of songs that Orpheus sings in great sadness after he has irretrievably lost Eurydice, songs of other lost or impossible loves. Orpheus's desire for a dead beloved, symbolically transposed onto lovers turned into trees, flowers, statues, and animals in the poem, saturates the film's representation of Benigno's love for Alicia, the film's loving representation of almost animate objects, as well as the audience's allegiance to Benigno as a lost object in the film's emotional landscape after his suicide. Through his masterful handling of classical narrative and cinematic codes and conventions, Almodóvar transforms characters, objects, and story elements into important emotional nodes, all similarly saturated with the fundamental representation of cinematic storytelling as an enlivening act. Characters, stories, and objects thus become detailed explorations of the transformation of mourning into art, symbolic of the participation of art in the ebb and flow of human life, and of its capacity to enfold and surround us. This, in a way, is the punch line of Almodóvar's staging of so many of his characters' first meetings in this film in artistic and cultural events: art becomes one of the originating points of the expansive web that connects us to one another. Our participation enlivens the events, and they enliven us in return.

Talk to Her portrays the necessity and depth of social connections, whether shared, imagined, lived, narrated, or projected. As I hope to have shown, there seems to be very little that is strange in human nature for Almodóvar, and there are hardly any strangers in the film. Even rape, an act of violence, results from intimacy and familiarity, as Benigno seems to completely forget that other people have boundaries and thresholds, private spaces and inaccessible thoughts. It is the fact that he is *not* a stranger to her that allows Benigno to use Alicia's body without concern for her will or desire, for her difference and separateness. In contrast to Lydia, who remains distinct as an individual in the film and whose desires and actions as a result remain inaccessible both to Marco and to the audience, the availability of Alicia's body and thoughts, mediated through Benigno's point of view, both facilitates the utopian visions of the film—for lovers who have met before, for the perfect merger of points of view, for absolute intimacy—and warns us about the deceptive nature of these fantasies. Although initially it seems that Benigno's actions would undermine the utopian vision of connected strangers of the film, his actions are an appropriate symptom of this cinematic world, an exaggerated and pathological version of the constant enfolding that the film enacts on its strangers.

The only things that remain strange in *Talk to Her* are precisely the things that we cannot alter but seem intent to transform somehow through art: the inevitable and unforeseeable death of a beloved, exemplified in the suddenness of accident and the natural forces that provide causation for the main events in the film, and the emotional force of all the tangible and intangible things that linger after such a death, the emotional force of stories and objects. Although, as I have proposed, the film's invitation to talk to each other is countered by the numerous withholdings of meaning and knowledge enacted in the diegesis, the ideal sociality of the film includes shared experience, especially as this includes public art forms, and the creation of shared meaning even in the case of mundane objects, such as hair clips and paint colors. It is in these narrative treatments that Almodóvar's melodramatic credentials, as well as his Ovidean and Orphic aspirations, become most visible. Perhaps acting as a powerful antidote to the true randomness of the universe, art provides both origin and final destination for Almodóvar in this film. Beginning and ending *Talk to Her* in the same place, and with the same palpable quality of a meeting between people that is about to become important, Almodóvar seems to both explain and represent the usually unseen coincidence of beginnings and endings in narrative forms.

By utilizing the workings of coincidence as a narrative force, Almodóvar engages in a sustained exploration of a kind of causation that lies between accidental and willed actions, a hybridity in the representation of causality that leads to the complex moral landscape of the film. When we recognize coincidences in everyday life, we are recognizing the effect of our sustained contact with others, the fact that we have already met people elsewhere or before, that we are not strangers. Coincidence can thus function as an alternative to the structures of alienation that affect contemporary life, and, in Almodóvar's emotionally saturated narrative style, also as an alternative to the insistence on ironic distantiation that affects our critical approaches to melodrama. But desiring a merger of points of view is a dangerous dream, as Benigno's actions remind us. Almodóvar's artistic and political allegory here manages to represent the need for utopian desires while respecting the fact that social and political unifications can only occur when we also recognize the difference of other people, their distance and separateness. Inevitably connected by the forces of accident and change that surround us, and inevitably separated by the very fact of difference, we remain both intimate and strange to each other. And that, I think Almodóvar proposes, is how it should be.

NOTES

1. In his commentary on the DVD of *Talk to Her*, Almodóvar says: "I asked the actress, Leonor, to look as if she were somewhere remote. Her eyes don't seem to be two meters from here. Her eyes seem to have the memory of being in a very remote place." Unless otherwise noted, all quotations from Almodóvar are from the Director's commentary on the US DVD release of *Talk to Her*.

2. Almodóvar is very aware of the physicality of the film medium, as we see here: the long shots of Marco and Alicia connect them to the actual space between frames, the gutter in the film stock. The camera pan that follows Katerina's gaze bridges that gutter, creating the sensation of continuous space that constitutes one of the fundamental epistemological implications of film. While Katerina's actions delay a real meeting or recognition between Marco and Alicia, by looking from one to the other she has already united them in space and time.

3. Roger Ebert begins his review of *Bad Education* with this sentiment: "I was attempting to describe the plot of *Bad Education*. It was quicksand, and I was sinking fast. You and I have less than 1,000 words to spend together discussing this fascinating film, and not only would the plot take up half of that, but if I were by some miracle to succeed in making it clear, that would only diminish your pleasure."

4. In their analysis of *All about My Mother*, Leo Bersani and Ulysse Dutoit marvel at the difficulty of avoiding plot summaries when discussing Almodóvar's films, even when such summaries could easily become "a nightmarish chore" (83).

5. This is how Hitchcock describes it to Peter Bogdanovich: "Here we are, back in our old situation: surprise or suspense. And we come to our old analogy of the bomb: you and I sit talking and there's a bomb in the room. We're having a very innocuous conversation about nothing. Boring. Doesn't mean a thing. Suddenly, boom! the bomb goes off and they're shocked—for fifteen seconds. Now you change it. Play the same scene, insert the bomb, show that the bomb is placed there, establish that it's going to go off at one o'clock—it's now a quarter of one, ten of one—show a clock on the wall, back to the same scene. Now our conversation becomes very vital, by its sheer nonsense. "'Look under the table! You fool!' Now they're working for ten minutes, instead of being surprised for fifteen seconds."

6. Almodóvar himself recognizes this in an early interview: "Making a screwball comedy such as *Labyrinth of Passion* wasn't easy. One needs great technical mastery to make an illogical, headlong, 'disparatada' comedy" (Strauss 23).

7. Iván's ex-wife Lucía (Julieta Serrano) throws the suitcase that their son Carlos (Antonio Banderas) has packed out the window, and it falls on the phone booth Pepa is using to call Iván. As the contents of the suitcase spill in the street she sees Carlos's photographs and realizes who he is. Later in the film, Pepa herself exasperatedly throws Iván's suitcase away, and it miraculously, coincidentally, and absolutely perfectly lands on the car that Iván and Paulina Morales (Kiti Manver) drive on their way to the airport. The suitcases thus both open a new cycle of connection and relationships between the characters and close the spinning circle that Pepa and Iván trace in the film.

8. We find a similar treatment to Almodóvar's "Mambo Taxi" (and in my view actually inspired by it) in Wes Anderson's *The Royal Tenenbaums* (2001), in which the characters always seem to hail the same "Gypsy Cab." Almodóvar's impact on a younger generation of American directors has not been critically examined.

9. Paul Julian Smith discusses these transformations in terms of distinct phases in Almodóvar's work. For his analysis of Almodóvar in an "art-cinema" tradition, see Smith's "Resurrecting the Art Movie? Almodóvar's Blue Period" (*Contemporary Spanish Culture*, 144–68).

10. For an analysis of the coincidence plot in fiction, see Dannenberg, who also distinguishes between nineteenth- and twentieth-century modes of coincidence.

11. See Bordwell's *The Way Hollywood Tells It,* especially 98–103. Bordwell does not mention Almodóvar's work in this book, although he briefly discusses directors who have, in my view, been directly influenced by him, such as González Iñárritu, whose *21 Grams* can be imagined as taking off from the abandoned organ transplant plotline of *All about My Mother.*

12. Accounting for cultural as well as auteurist differences in these narrative treatments is, in my view, essential, because the treatment of strangers depends on a culture's assumptions and definitions of space, family, privacy, interpersonal boundaries, individuality, and so on. Anglo-American narratives often begin with the baseline assumption of privacy or individualism, an assumption that does not necessarily structure the expectations of other cultures. In this respect, the use of classical Hollywood narrative codes may already entail a process of cultural translation. Contemporary narratives should thus be investigated not only for their overt patterning of modern experiences and desires but also for the alternative or additional nuances that reveal the resilience of cultural difference in the midst of a desire for connectivity. In an essay titled "The Chinese Side of the Mountain," Chris Berry traces such an interaction in Ang Lee's work on *Brokeback Mountain* (2005).

13. The quotation that begins this essay is from Almodóvar's own writings on the characters of *Talk to Her* on the film's official Web site.

14. Here is the conclusion of the film's synopsis, from the official Web site: "*Talk to Her* is a film about the joy of narration and about words as a weapon against solitude, disease, death and madness. It is also a film about madness, about a type of madness so close to tenderness and common sense that it does not diverge from normality."

15. In "A Short Organum for the Theater," Brecht proposes that melodrama and other popular forms can be deployed to educate and sensitize the public if they remain active texts, that is, if they use their style and allure to pose questions to viewers rather than lulling them into fantasies or facilitating escapism.

16. John Foster, *The Life of Charles Dickens* (London, 1876). Quoted in Forsyth 151.

17. For a careful and influential discussion of this distinction, see Seymour Chatman's *Story and Discourse*.

18. The song by K. D. Lang is titled "Hain't It Funny," and we hear this first stanza during the first part of *Masurca Fogo*: "We made love last night/Wasn't good, wasn't bad/Intimate strangers made me kinda sad/Now when I woke up this morning/Coffee wasn't on/It slowly dawned on me that my baby is gone/My baby's gone."

19. In his commentary, Almodóvar also states that his own autograph of *Café Müller* was used for the set decoration of Huma Rojo's dressing room for the last scenes of *All about My Mother*, information that could be used to expand my approach for first and subsequent meetings to a wider intertextual and extradiegetic rubric.

20. In *Talk to Her*, the swimming scene seems independent from the diegesis, while Almodóvar's expansion of a similar Hockney reference in *Bad Education* is narratively and visually integrated in the diegesis. For images of Hockney's cameraworks and composite photographs, see Weschler.

21. Relevant pieces include *Timestop* (1997) and *Man She She* (1997).

22. For an analysis of fairy-tale motifs in *Talk to Her*, see Novoa.

23. The power of passion is even more pronounced in the next tale of the *Metamorphoses*, the story of Pygmalion's grandson, Cinyras, and his daughter Myrrha. Myrrha falls in love with her father and tricks him into having a sexual relationship. After she is discovered, she runs away and is eventually turned into a tree by Venus, who delivers her baby from the pregnant trunk. The baby is Adonis, who grows up into such a beautiful man that Venus herself falls in love with him—as if to complete the discourse on the absolute power of love that motivates this series of stories, because even the goddess of love is not immune to the power of love. When Adonis is gored by a wild boar while hunting, Venus flies to him, tearing out her hair and reproaching Fate. She turns him into a flower, "anemone," or the windflower, because its frail, easily shaken petals resemble the brevity and frailty of human life.

24. As with other elements in the film, the viewers' later recognition of Benigno's sexual use of Alicia retroactively questions this early comfort. For the notion of objectification and the woman's passive position as "being looked at," see Mulvey.

25. We actually do not know what Alicia's hair used to be like because all scenes of her before the accident, and the covering-up gesture I described, occur in a flashback. The flashback is attributed to Benigno in a somewhat unorthodox way, announced through a close-up of Alicia's face as if it were *her* memory. We can even describe it as an impossibly coinciding flashback, shared between Alicia (whose face we see right before) and Benigno (whose voice at some point takes over the visual narration of the past). Significantly, this flashback includes our clues about Benigno's mental status, his stalking and possessive tendencies toward Alicia, and the sneaky and devious sides of his personality.

WORKS CITED

Altman, Rick. "Dickens, Griffith, and Film Theory Today." *South Atlantic Quarterly* 88.2 (1989): 321–59.

Aristotle. *Poetics*. Trans. Malcolm Heath. London: Penguin, 1997.

Berry, Chris. "The Chinese Side of the Mountain." *Film Quarterly* 60 (2007): 32–37.

Bersani, Leo, and Ulysse Dutoit. *Forms of Being: Cinema, Aesthetics, Subjectivity*. London: British Film Institute, 2004.

Bordwell, David. *The Way Hollywood Tells It: Story and Style in Modern Movies*. Berkeley: University of California Press, 2006.

Bordwell, David, Janet Staiger, and Kristin Thompson. *The Classical Hollywood Cinema: Film Style and Mode of Production to 1960*. New York: Columbia University Press, 1985.

Bogdanovich, Peter. "Interview with Alfred Hitchcock." Originally published in *The Cinema of Alfred Hitchcock*. New York: Museum of Modern Art, 1963. May 5, 2008. http://www.moma.org/exhibitions/1999/hitchcock/interview/index.html.

Brecht, Bertolt. "A Short Organum for the Theater." Willett 179–205.

Brooks, Peter. *The Melodramatic Imagination: Balzac, Henry James, Melodrama, and the Mode of Excess*. New Haven: Yale University Press, 1995.

Chatman, Seymour. *Story and Discourse: Narrative Structure in Fiction and Film*. Ithaca, N.Y.: Cornell University Press, 1980.

Dannenberg, Hilary P. "A Poetics of Coincidence in Narrative Fiction." *Poetics Today* 25.3 (2004): 399–436.

Ebert, Roger. "Bad Education." *Chicago Sun-Times,* Dec. 22, 2004.

Eisenstein, Sergei. "Dickens, Griffith, and the Film Today." *Film Form: Essays in Film Theory*. Trans. Jay Leyda. New York: Harcourt Brace and Company, 1949. 195–256.

Forsyth, Neil. "Wonderful Chains: Dickens and Coincidence." *Modern Philology* 83.2 (Nov. 1985): 151–65.

Freud, Sigmund. "Fetishism." *The Standard Edition of the Complete Psychological Works*. Vol. 5. Trans. James Strachey. London: Hogarth Press, 1957. 152–57.

Goldknopf, David. "Coincidence in the Victorian Novel: The Trajectory of a Narrative Device." *College English* 31.1 (Oct. 1969): 41–50.

Mannoni, Octave. "Je sais bien, mais quand même." *Clefs pour l'imaginaire ou l'Autre Scène*. Paris: Éditions du Seuil, 1969. 9–33.

Maslin, Janet. "Sex and So Many Characters in a Comedy by Almodóvar." *New York Times,* Jan. 19, 1990, C6.

Mulvey, Laura. "Visual Pleasure and Narrative Cinema." *Screen* 16.3 (1975): 6–18.

Novoa, Adriana. "Whose Talk Is It? Almodóvar and the Fairy Tale in *Talk to Her.*" *Marvels and Tales* 19.2 (2005): 224–48.

Official Web site, Club Cultura. Sept. 13, 2006: http://www.clubcultura.com/clubcine/clubcineastas/almodovar/hableconella.

Smith, Paul Julian. *Contemporary Spanish Culture: Television, Fashion, Art and Film*. Cambridge: Polity Press, 2002.

———. *Desire Unlimited: The Cinema of Pedro Almodóvar*. London: Verso, 1994.

Stewart, Garrett. "Vitagraphic Time." *Biography* 29.1 (2006): 159-92.

Strauss, Frédéric. *Almodóvar on Almodóvar.* Trans. Yves Baignères. London: Faber and Faber, 1996.

Vineberg, Steve. "Upholding the Law of Desire." *Threepenny Review* 37 (spring 1989): 31–33.

Weschler, Lawrence. *David Hockney Cameraworks.* New York: Knopf, 1984.

Willett, John. *Brecht on Theater: The Development of an Aesthetic.* New York: Hill and Wang, 1994.

Williams, Linda. *Playing the Race Card: Melodramas of Black and White from Uncle Tom to O. J. Simpson.* Princeton, N.J.: Princeton University Press, 2002.

III
THE LIMITS OF
REPRESENTATION

9 Almodóvar's Girls

LEO BERSANI AND ULYSSE DUTOIT

The title of Pedro Almodóvar's *All about My Mother* (1999) makes promises that can be neither easily defined nor easily fulfilled. The title in Spanish—*Todo sobre mi madre*—proposes, overambitiously we may suspect, to tell us everything there is to know about "my mother," although we may also wonder if what we are being promised is a film entirely *about* "my mother," one in which everything—*todo*—has her as its subject. And, of course, the second promise is not necessarily identical to the first: I could speak exclusively about my mother without telling you everything there is to tell about her. It is nonetheless possible that the two promises will overlap: in speaking only about my mother, I could also be telling you everything about her. The title in English is somewhat less assertive in what it promises. It does suggest that "my mother" will be the film's subject, but it is much more casual about the exact amount of information it will give us about her. The "all" here is less emphatic, less independent; it is part of the colloquialism "all about," and as such it signifies totality less seriously, even somewhat carelessly. When we say "Tell me all about your day," or "Tell me all about your trip," we are expressing our (real or feigned) eagerness to hear about these subjects, but not at all necessarily a hunger for an exhaustive account of either "your day" or "your trip." Indeed, depending both on the subject and on the tone with which the request is made, "all about" can even be ruthlessly selective. Anxious to be let in on some secret, to learn something scandalous, we demand, "Tell me all about him!" which, far from being a request for biographical or psychic totality, is a demand for particulars, for the nitty-gritty, the very particular dirt.

But why speak at all about the English title of Almodóvar's film—a title that could simply be a faulty translation? We do so because the film suggests that something very close to the English translation may have been the original title, and that the translated title may be the Spanish title. Early in the film, Esteban (Eloy Azorín) and his mother Manuela (Cecilia Roth) are sitting on a couch having dinner and watching a dubbed version of Joseph

Mankiewicz's 1950 film *All about Eve*. Esteban, whose ambition is to be a writer, and who has begun writing about his mother for a competition, complains to Manuela that the Spanish version of Mankiewicz's title—*Eva al desnudo*—is all wrong: the proper title, he claims, is *Todo sobre Eva*. Immediately after this, we see Esteban beginning to write in his notebook what will presumably be the title of the piece he has just referred to. He forms the word *Todo,* and then the title of Almodóvar's film appears on the screen for the first time, in red and white block letters, in the space between the seated Esteban and his mother.

A lot is going on here. First of all, it is not at all certain that Esteban's—and Almodóvar's?—version of the American film's title is closer to "all about Eve" than the official Spanish translation is. Mankiewicz's title has its own share of perverseness. It suggests, casually but unambiguously, that the film's principal subject is Eve Harrington (Anne Baxter), whereas *All about Eve* is at least as much about Margo Channing (the true star role, played by Bette Davis). Insofar as the film is about Eve, *Eva al desnudo* captures very well the more sinister connotations of the English title. The trouble with the Spanish title is not exactly that it is wrong, but rather that it gets those connotations too quickly. Ideally, we would go into the film taking "all about Eve" in its neutral, or benign sense (the "Tell-me-all-about-your-day" sense), and then the film would teach us to read the title as a more portentous promise: the sweet adoring fan is unmasked as a monster of envy and unscrupulous ambition. What is interesting about Esteban's not too accurate correction is that it is picked up, as it were, by Almodóvar. More exactly, Almodóvar has chosen to present his choice of his own film's title (and its possible source in the title of Mankiewicz's film) as his copying of his character's choice. The film has been without a title for its first few minutes; it is only when Esteban writes *Todo* as the first word of his own composition that *Todo sobre mi madre* appears on the screen as the title for Almodóvar's finished film. The effect of this juxtaposition is to encourage us to identify Almodóvar with Esteban—or rather, to identify the boy with a younger Almodóvar, an Almodóvar without accomplishments, with, for example, only a project for a piece of writing to be called *Todo sobre mi madre* (and not a work finished more than thirty years later in his—whose?—life, a film this time, with the same title).

The serious problem with this identification is that Almodóvar the writer and filmmaker does away with Esteban a few minutes after the scene we have been discussing. The boy is run over by a car on his seventeenth birthday (after attending, with his mother, a performance of *A Streetcar Named Desire*), and what will interest us most about his mother will take place after his death. Almodóvar and Esteban have important things in common: their artistic vocation and their devotion to their mothers. (Almodóvar's mother, about whom he has spoken with great affection, appears in four of his films; she died shortly after the completion of *All about My Mother*.) To say that is to suggest, according to popular psychoanalytic wisdom, that they have something else in common: homosexuality. Remember also that, at least in English, a gay man might refer, perhaps ironically, to that psychoanalytic "wisdom" by saying about the "origins" of his homosexuality: "Of course, it's all about my mother. . . ." Esteban, it is true, is not portrayed as a homosexual; he is coded as one. As if his artistic sensibility, his father's absence, and his great love for his mother were not enough, his aesthetic tastes leave no doubt—for a public even minimally trained in such codes—about his gay sensibility: Bette Davis, Truman Capote, and Blanche DuBois. We may begin to suspect that in plotting the death of his young double, Almodóvar is also doing away, at least aesthetically, with his—with their—homosexuality. The presumed gay sensibility does not, however, disappear. *A Streetcar Named Desire* will play a major role in the rest of the film, and Almodóvar appears to be at least as devoted to the great campy actresses, and to his mother, as Esteban is (among those to whom Almodóvar dedicates his film are actresses who play actresses—Bette Davis is one of those mentioned—and Almodóvar's mother).

There is also a dedication to men who act and become women, which could be taken as a tender joke on poor Esteban. It (more or less) describes his father, about whom the boy knows nothing. He does, however, very much want to know about his father, and Manuela promises—a moment before Esteban is struck down running after a taxi to get an autograph from the actress he has just seen in the role of Blanche DuBois—to tell him all when they return home later that evening. Curiously, Esteban's "homosexuality" is neither established nor denied; it is heavily coded, and ignored. The identification between Almodóvar and Esteban has been subtly made, the gay sensibility has been, and will be, subtly embraced, but homosexuality as a sexual preference is irrelevant to both Esteban as a character in the film and, correlatively, Almodóvar's identification with him. What is relevant to Esteban's character is his obsessive curiosity about his father. It is as if the gay coding were put into place as the perhaps secret logic of that curiosity and, primarily, in order to be separated, liberated, from that curiosity. Esteban is insistently anguished about the paternal gap in his life, a gap that has been just as insistently maintained by Manuela. He begs her to talk to him about his father and when, much later, she finds Esteban's father in Barcelona, she shows him passages from their son's notebook in which Esteban had expressed his grief at finding photos from Manuela's youth from which half of the image had been torn away. It was, he wrote, as if half of his own life had been taken from him; to be whole, he needs that missing image, which would mean knowing about his father. Almodóvar's film may be "all about my mother," but the story his surrogate self wants to hear would be, and he says exactly these words, "todo sobre mi padre."

Almodóvar at once tells and refuses to tell that story. In a sense, the entire film is a search for the father, at first on the part of Esteban, and then on the part of Manuela, who leaves Madrid for Barcelona after Esteban's death in order to find his father and tell him about his son. But the story Almodóvar has to tell about the father is a startling subversion of paternal identity. It is a story that might have seriously compromised, even while satisfying, Esteban's longing for a father, and it ultimately dismisses whatever attributes—of power, of justice, of legality—we might "normally" associate with the paternal function. It turns out that half of the missing half in Esteban's life is the same as the half he already knows. The young lovers Manuela and Esteban had come from Argentina to Spain. Esteban left to work in Paris, and returned to Barcelona as Lola two years later. He returned, more precisely, half-transsexualized, with his male genitals intact and with breasts larger than his wife's. It is with this partial copy of herself that Manuela conceived her son. Unhappy with her more or less newly gendered mate (not, as far as we can tell, because of his new anatomical makeup but rather because of a persistent machismo that led him/her to run after other women while forbidding Manuela to wear a miniskirt or a bikini on the beach), Manuela had fled to Madrid early in her pregnancy without telling Lola that he/she was soon to be a mother/father.

Back in Barcelona, Manuela eventually finds Lola, although she really has not spent much time searching for him/her. The Barcelona sequences are about Manuela's friendships with three other women. Soon after her arrival, she takes a cab to a remote pickup area where, in a Felliniesque scene, the cars and motorcycles of male clients circle around, and inspect, variously gendered prostitutes (women, drag queens, and transsexuals). Apparently hoping to find Lola at work here, Manuela instead runs into Agrado, a former truck driver and friend from many years ago who, like the elder Esteban, had had a partial sex change in Paris that had allowed her to return to Barcelona as a prostitute specialized in oral sex. The warm, funny, generous Agrado is magnificently played by Antonia San Juan, while the role of the more somber Lola (drug user, thief, dying of AIDS) is taken by Toni Cantó—casting decisions that schematize and reflect these characters' anatomical allegiances to both sexes (Agrado has also kept his/her penis). Agrado and Esteban are gender transitions without normative end points. Somewhat less sexually ambiguous is the great actress Huma Rojo (Marisa Paredes), whose autograph Esteban had been pursuing when he was killed and who is now playing Blanche DuBois in Barcelona. Huma, who is having a troubled affair with the actress who plays Stella (Candela Peña) in *Streetcar,* hires Manuela as her personal assistant, and they become friends. Finally, Manuela takes in Rosa (Penélope Cruz), a nun who, in the course of her social work with prostitutes, has been seduced by Lola and is now carrying their child. Rosa dies giving birth to Esteban Number Three who, like his parents, is HIV-positive. Manuela returns to Madrid with the baby and comes back with him two years later to Barcelona. Esteban has negativized the virus, and scientists at an AIDS conference in Barcelona will study his case. In the film's final scene, Manuela happily tells all this to Agrado and Huma (the former took over Manuela's job with Huma). Huma's drug-addicted lover-colleague Nina has married a man, returned to her native village, and given birth, as Agrado reports with some satisfaction, to an exceptionally ugly child. Thus the friends are reunited, and Esteban lives again.

"My films," Almodóvar has said, "always told a story. That was my strongest desire from the first moment I held a camera" (Strauss 14).[1] The plots of Almodóvar's films can be extraordinarily intricate—and improbable. His films are about much more than his stories, but it will be difficult to avoid plot summaries when speaking of them. So many wild plotlines are being simultaneously developed in an Almodóvar film that to summarize his stories could become a nightmarish chore. The filmography of the valuable *Conversations with Almodóvar* includes a plot summary of each film, but by the eleventh of the thirteen films covered the person responsible for the summaries seems to have given in to his or her exasperation and, for *The Flower of My Secret* (1995) and *All about My Mother,* stops the summary, without explanation, before getting halfway through the narratives. Almodóvar moves comfortably among various sorts of narrative wildness: the campy, improbable comedy of *Pepi, Luci, Bom* (1980) and *Labyrinth of*

Passion (1982), the melodramatic violence of *Matador* (1986), in which two lovers kill each other just as they reach the most ecstatic orgasms of their lives, the murderous jealousies of *Live Flesh* (1997), the protracted conversational rape scene *and* the serial killer protagonist of *Kika* (1993)—(*Matador, Live Flesh,* and *Kika* all have climaxes in which a man and a woman kill each other), and the somewhat unusual spirituality of *Dark Habits* (1983), with its convent run by a lesbian, coke-sniffing Mother Superior surrounded by nuns who are called Sister Manure, Sister Rat, Sister Damned, and Sister Snake. The most extravagant roles are played with neither melodramatic intensity nor ironic self-consciousness, but rather with the sort of casual seriousness perhaps best exemplified by Chus Lampreave as, for example, the sensationalist novelist Sister Rat in *Dark Habits*. Almodóvar, like Jean-Luc Godard and Alain Resnais, has "his" actors (in Almodóvar's case, mainly actresses, referred to in Spain as "Almodóvar's girls") who appear in several of his films. It is as if he recognized and cultivated, most notably in Lampreave, Carmen Maura, Victoria Abril, Marisa Paredes, Cecilia Roth, Rossy de Palma, and Antonio Banderas, a remarkable talent for playing extravagance as if it were wholly natural, without, however, in any way attempting to make it appear psychically plausible.

In Almodóvar's work, psychic implausibility does not make for narrative chaos. Part of the fun in making up these wild stories may well have been in not allowing for any loose narrative threads, in making compatible the multidirectional story with compositional tightness. And yet this exceptional talent for imaginative play—for a seemingly undisciplined indulgence in, and control of, that play—would have a somewhat limited formal interest if it were not at once motivated and countered by another register of the imaginary, one that is neither plausible nor implausible and that can, as it were, lend its pressure to either realistic or fantastic narrative. This other imaginary gives to Almodóvar's work a psychic consistency and a psychic depth, although it is also, as we shall see, inherently antagonistic to the aesthetic. This is the consistency of desire—more specifically, of sexual desire. At first, sexuality is presented as nothing more serious, and nothing more interesting, than a funny psychic anomaly. In *Labyrinth of Passion,* Sexilia (Cecilia Roth) consults a psychoanalyst in order to be cured of her nymphomania and her phobic avoidance of the sun. Intentionally or unintentionally, Almodóvar rewrites a similar coupling of sexuality and a terror of the light in Racine's *Phèdre*. When Phèdre flees the sun, she gives a great, if monstrous, dignity to her sexual passion for Hippolyte: it pollutes the universe, and in fleeing the unforgiving gaze of her solar ancestor, Phèdre's guilty desire proclaims its cosmic importance. Sexilia's phobia, on the other hand, is not the consequence of her uncontrollable desires. They are equal, both on the same level of psychic pathology, both merely weird symptoms of dysfunctional being. The other sexually obsessed figure in the film is similarly trivialized and pathologized. Sadec (Antonio Banderas in his first Almodóvar role), having had sex and fallen madly in love with Riza (Imanol Arias), son of the emperor of Tiran, follows Riza's traces around Madrid after Riza leaves him and almost catches up with him, thanks to his (Sadec's) exceptionally developed sense of smell. Thus desire performs itself as passionately sniffing nostrils, and Almodóvar once again (intentionally or unintentionally?) comically refers us to another illustrious cultural precedent: that of Freud asserting, in *Civilization and Its Discontents,* that "the whole of [man's] sexuality" has suffered from the depreciation, in the course of human evolution, of his sense of smell (62).

Sexual obsession will soon become more central—and less comical—in Almodóvar's cinematic narratives. Violent death brings together the heterosexual couple of *Matador.* Both María Cardenal (Assumpta Serna) and the retired matador Diego Montes (Nacho Martínez) kill their sexual partners during sex; the perfect sexual act, and the perfect act of violence, will be killing each other as they reach orgasm together. *Law of Desire* (1987) homosexualizes this fantasy of sex and violence. Antonio (Antonio Banderas) becomes obsessively attached to the film director Pablo Quintero (Eusebio Poncela) after having with Pablo his first homosexual experience. Antonio kills the young man Pablo loves and, after keeping the police at bay long enough to make love once more with Pablo, shoots himself. *Law of Desire* at once centers this obsessive sexuality and distances itself from it. The film opens with a young man acting in a sequence from a porno film. He masturbates with his back turned to us, his buttocks raised, repeating: "Fuck me!" The words are instructions given by a man who remains offscreen and are dubbed by two middle-aged men who seem more turned on than the actor, who refuses to cry "Fuck me!" until he is assured that no one will take up the invitation. Once the scene is over, he picks up his money, with a more authentic expression of pleasure, on the table next to the bed where the pseudo-action has taken place. Soon after this we see Antonio alone in a toilet stall in the movie theater, voicing the same request, but turned on by the prospect of its being satisfied. Pablo accommodates him shortly thereafter in a scene whose nonpornographic realism is emphasized by Antonio's obvious discomfort as he is being penetrated for the first time. The film *moves toward* sexual seriousness; it is as if that seriousness were anticipated, and put into question, in a version of sex as pure construction. We see it both as an unexciting construction for the porno actor and as an exciting one for Antonio in the toilet stall before sexual demand becomes the film's deadly serious subject. The suggestion of desire as artifact is made even stronger by the solipsistic nature of Pablo's love for Juan (Miguel Molina): as if he were writing a scenario for one of his films, Pablo sends himself letters in which "Juan" tells him how much he loves him. Desire is construction, and law. The porno sequence makes the connection very clear: the two older men dub the dictated scenario of mounting desire to the compliant (and indifferent) actor. Antonio's subsequent real excitement is just as constructed. His excited demand to be fucked, delivered to no one, and inspired by the porno sequence he has just seen, can only be addressed to his own desire; it formulates the laws of a desire he will then actualize with Pablo.

Unhappy obsessive desire returns as a dominant motif in several of Almodóvar's films subsequent to *Law of Desire*. Women suffer from their lover's, or husband's, indifference to them in *Women on the Verge of a Nervous Breakdown* (1988), *High Heels* (1991), in which the wife kills her womanizing husband, and *The Flower of My Secret*. In *Live Flesh,* it is men who desire obsessively and, this time, heterosexually. The three principal male characters all suffer from an unhappy passion. The film does end with a happy marriage and the birth of a child (it began with the birth of the child's father), although this is made possible by the violent deaths of one unhappy couple and the self-imposed exile of the man indirectly responsible for those deaths. Interestingly, the narrative is a model of intricate construction. Early in the film, a young policeman is crippled by a shot from a gun pointed in his direction by an older colleague whose wife has been his lover. The gun was held by a young man who had made his way into the apartment of a woman with whom he had recently had his first sexual experience, but who now rejects him. The young man is sent to prison, and the woman marries the crippled policeman, who becomes the star of a team of wheelchair-bound basketball players. When Víctor, the young man (Liberto Rabal), is released from prison, he pursues Elena (Francesca Neri), the young policeman's wife, and has a casual affair with Clara (Ángela Molina), the older policeman's wife. He promises to leave Elena alone if she will have sex once with him. Until now, she has had only oral sex with the disabled David (Javier Bardem), and the night of genital sex proves to be unforgettable. Furious upon learning all this, David threatens Víctor, who reveals to him that his jealous colleague Sancho (José Sancho) had been responsible for his having been shot several years earlier. Anxious to get rid of both Víctor and Sancho, David tells Sancho that his wife has been having an affair with Víctor. But Clara saves Víctor, and it is she who is killed by her jealous husband, who is also killed by her. The price David pays for his role in this double murder is exile to Miami, and Víctor and Elena can live happily together.

The relational knot of *Live Flesh* is a paroxysm of both obsessive desire and narrative construction. Interestingly, all this concentrated passion seems to explode itself out of the frame of Almodóvar's cinematic world (at least temporarily),[2] and *All about My Mother,* made two years later, is purified of desire. The mode of purification had in fact begun to be visible several years earlier. Already in *Matador* and *Law of Desire* we find characters outside the circuit of desire. Ángel (Antonio Banderas) in *Matador* makes explicit the imperative of desire in his inability to obey it. In attempting to be as virile as the master matador who teaches him the art of bullfighting, Ángel unsuccessfully tries to rape his young neighbor Eva (Eva Cobo). He suffers from his undeveloped sexuality (and wants to be punished for his failed rape), but his failure to conform to any recognizable sexual identity—radically unlike Diego and María, who live and die within the melodramatic cliché that links sex and death—also seems to be the precondition for his very special sensitivity. He can somehow see and hear all the murders being committed in the city (and this allows him to bring the police to the house where Diego and María are making their deadly love), and he also seems to have a connection to extrahuman, cosmic phenomena. His body responds with the suggestion of a mysterious, somehow knowledgeable sympathy to the eclipse of the sun that takes place just as Diego and María consummate their love in death. This is, however, exceptional in Almodóvar's work; it is an alternative mode of coupling that plays a much more prominent role in Jean-Luc Godard's *Contempt* (1963) and—spectacularly so—in Terrence Malick's *The Thin Red Line* (1998).

More in line with possibilities that will be fully developed in *All about My Mother* is the Carmen Maura figure in *Law of Desire.* As with Antonia San Juan in the later film, Almodóvar asked Maura to play a man "playing" a woman. Tina, Pablo's sister, was once Tino, Pablo's brother; he had a sex change in order to please his father, with whom he was in love (and who later abandoned her). Both actresses are, we might say, asked to be women for the second time, to test what it might be like to be a woman differently, a woman who was originally a man. It is as if Almodóvar were telling them to think female identities and desires "interrupted" by male identities and desires—a request complicated by the fact that Tina's male antecedent had a sexual passion for his father, and she, Tina, has had a "lesbian" affair with the mother (played by the transsexual actress Bibi Andersen) of the young girl Tina now takes care of. In Agrado's case, does she—did he—have any sexual desires at all? In both cases, constructed female identity emerges as an excessive femininity that simultaneously hides and theatrically exposes the construction. Most interestingly, Tina is a dissonant presence in *Law of Desire*'s plot of willfully violent homosexual passion. Or rather, she renounced *that* identity in trying to satisfy her incestuous version of it, a move that has left her in an identificatory and sexual limbo where, however (at least until she falls into the trap of desire Antonio sets for her in order to have Pablo once again), she circulates—her excessive body circulates—as a deeply appealing and undefined promise.

A somewhat different version of neutralized desire is enacted in *Women on the Verge of a Nervous Breakdown*. Very early in the film we are given what might be called a technical dilution, or dispersion, of passion's intensity. Pepa (Carmen Maura) and Iván (Fernando Guillén) are dubbing actors; we see them—separately—sitting in front of microphones dubbing a scene between Joan Crawford and Sterling Hayden from Nicholas Ray's *Johnny Guitar* (1954). Iván, much to Pepa's distress, does not simply stand in for the passionate utterances of others; he is Pepa's unfaithful lover. If Pepa is on the verge of a breakdown, it is because he has told her that he wants to leave her, and during much of the film she frantically tries to get in touch with him. Iván, we also learn, is the father of another woman's son: he and Lucía (Julieta Serrano) had been lovers many years ago, and she has been confined to a psychiatric hospital since Iván abandoned her. She regains her memory when she hears, in a film on TV, Iván's voice saying the same words of love he had said to her twenty years earlier. What she hears, in all likelihood, is Iván speaking someone else's role of passion. The dubbed voice replaces a voice belonging to someone else, to an actor who is himself playing passion. What brings back Lucía's memory is, then, the expression of Iván's wholly constructed, wholly inauthentic passionate desire. Lucía can now act sane enough to be released from the hospital; she is determined to find Iván and to kill him. In other words, she, unlike Pepa, fails to profit from the film's demonstration of passion's theatricality, its reiteratively scripted nature.

We are not explicitly told how Pepa manages to come back from the verge of *her* breakdown. After saving Iván from being killed by Lucía, she simply says good-bye to him, refusing his invitation to have a talk over a drink. What has happened? Nothing like a direct critique of desire; instead, the experience of a more joyful theatricality. The mood of *Women on the Verge of a Nervous Breakdown* changes with the arrival of an improbable number of visitors in Pepa's apartment: her friend Candela (María Barranco), pursued by the police as a result of her having taken in, without knowing it, Shiite terrorists; Lucía; Lucía's son Carlos (Antonio Banderas) and his nagging fiancée Marisa (Rossy de Palma); the two policemen on Candela's trace, and a telephone repairman. Pepa serves them gazpacho spiked with sleeping pills, and in a few moments all her guests (except Lucía, who has left to find Iván) are asleep. We have moved into farce: Pepa's apartment—which, Almodóvar has said, respects the aesthetic code of a type of comedy in which "spaces are vast and artificial even if the people living in them are penniless" (Strauss 81)—has become the stage for a production that, improvised by Pepa, is very different from the productions of canned passion that Pepa and Iván the dubbing artists are asked to put on. What goes on in Pepa's apartment is gratuitous, and without "serious" consequences. Pepa leaves just long enough to go to the airport (in the same taxi that has shown up, with wonderful improbability, every time she hails one on the street) to save and to dismiss Iván. The film ends with her return to her apartment. The unpleasant Marisa has been sleeping on a chair on the terrace; Pepa joins her and Marisa, marvelously transformed into a relaxed and charming woman, tells Pepa that she has lost her virginity in a dream. This Immaculate Deflowering—and the magical gazpacho potion—have worked marvels on her temperament; she has, Pepa tells her, lost the unpleasant hardness of virgins. (A certain misogynistic wisdom, at once repeated and mocked here, of course attributes any such transformation to the wondrous real thing.) The unfaithful lover has been dismissed; Marisa's fiancé is asleep on the couch next to Candela, and the film ends with the camera moving away to a long shot of Pepa and Marisa sitting together on the terrace, the city behind them, continuing a conversation we can no longer hear.

In one of his conversations with Frédéric Strauss, Almodóvar remembers with affection an at once ordinary and highly suggestive scene from his childhood: that of women in his provincial village sitting together and talking. He has also said: "This vagueness, this walking about, of the female characters [in his first feature film, *Pepi, Luci, Bom*] interests me very much. Someone who is alone, who does not have any particular goal, and who is always close to a state of crisis is exceptionally *available,* anything can happen to her, and she is therefore an ideal character for telling a story [c'est donc un personnage idéal pour raconter une histoire]" (Strauss 29). The phrasing is somewhat ambiguous: ideal as the author of a story or as someone to tell stories about? Let us read the remark both ways; the essential point is that such women *originate stories.* Interestingly, Almodóvar has a very non-Proustian reaction to the spectacle of people speaking together, perhaps just far enough away so that he cannot hear them. In Proust, such spectacles tend to set off paranoid mistrust: they must be saying something unflattering about him, or at the very least something they want to keep from him, a perhaps sinister secret. In Almodóvar's response to his ideal female character, the key word is *availability* (the person he describes is "dans une situation de grande disponibilité"). Like that character, the women sitting together in his hometown (in *The Flower of My Secret,* Leo [Marisa Paredes] participates in such a scene when she returns to her native village) are evoked as a promise. They are remembered not exactly for the experience they have already shared, but rather for the impression they give him of experience yet to be, of a prospective sociability.

What might that sociability be like? *All about My Mother* comes as close as any of Almodóvar's films to answering that question, although it does so within a motivational structure that might have stifled any such project. Manuela returns to Barcelona in order to make the torn photographs that her son had found whole again, in order, that is, to put the father back in the picture in the only way now possible: by giving him a photo of his son. In other words, Manuela returns in order to make the *family* whole. To find the first Esteban implies closing a circle, returning her dead son to his point of origin, and thus ending his—their—story. But of course the "point of origin" had already made a trip outside the family circle—to Paris—and had returned bearing the signs of a more radical crossing: transsexualized, Esteban/Lola has traveled from one sex to the other, although continuing to seduce women. Lola makes an at least temporary return to the Esteban still appended to her body. Long before we know all that, the film has trained us to expect and to enjoy more diversified forms of traveling, of moving from one point to another. The first credits, which appear juxtaposed to medical instruments in a hospital room, are accompanied by a multidirectional feast of camera work. We move in a tracking shot from left to right along an unidentified background of light-colored rectangles (probably the room's windows); the shot continues in a downward vertical movement along an IV apparatus. Tanks of oxygen fade in as a new horizontal tracking shot from left to right begins. This movement ends on an objectless gray background against which UN FILM DE ALMODÓVAR appears in white and red letters. The camera pauses with the appearance of each credit. A third tracking shoot repeats the first one in reverse directions: at first in an upward vertical movement along a panel of brightly colored controls, and then from right to left, and ending finally and up to a close-up of Manuela's face. She is an organ-transplant coordinator, and we are watching the first of three organ-transplant sequences (all of which take place in the first fifteen minutes of the film). A patient has just died; his liver will be given to someone else. Manuela also acts in simulations designed to train medical personnel in transplant procedures and psychology. Esteban comes to the hospital to watch his mother play the role of a woman who has just lost her husband; two male doctors attempt to get her permission to use one of his organs for a transplant. Finally, the same two doctors will, soon after, sit in front of Manuela no longer playing a role; they confirm Esteban's death to her and she signs a document authorizing the use of his heart for a transplant. Almodóvar had used almost exactly the same transplant-motif sequence at the beginning of *The Flower of My Secret,* but it seems to have been only with *All about My Mother* that he was able to account for its appeal. The sequence is narratively gratuitous in the earlier film; in *All about My Mother* it is the first of numerous transports or crossings over, the first variation on multiple cases of mobile or shifting identities. Manuela reacts to the transplant as if it gave her one more chance to see Esteban, as if he were alive in a new body. She goes to La Coruña to see the man who has received Esteban's heart leave the hospital—that is, as she explains it, to follow her son's heart.

Not only will there be all sorts of movements or crossings throughout the film (from country to country, from city to city, from one sex to another, between different sons, among different mothers); the repetition of the trans motif takes place within its first appearance. Rather than prefiguring the importance of the motif with just one version of it (the donation of Esteban's heart), Almodóvar juxtaposes three cases of the organ-transplant example, and the second of the three is a theatrical rehearsal of an aspect of organ-transplant procedures. Movement in *All about My Mother* will be inseparable from repetition. The points of arrest along lines or circuits of movement between places, psychic functions, or identities are not wholly heterogeneous; there is also a certain persistence or continuity within the trajectories of mobility. But it will be difficult to define both the content and mode of continuity. What exactly is repeated when a theatrical character or situation reoccurs, differently, in reality—a reality that is, of course, itself the aesthetic construction of Almodóvar's film? We are beginning to suspect that there may be a type of construction very different from the constructed imperatives of desire. The laws of desire conceal its imaginary nature; they can perhaps be undone only if the being of the subjects to whom they are applied becomes uncertain. The laws of desire will collapse with the disappearance of the subjects of desire. In Almodóvar's work, repetition, far from certifying the reality of what is repeated, undermines the very category of the real (at the very least, as a category to which the imaginary might be confidently opposed). The relation between the imaginary and the real will be one of exchange, not of opposition. The remarkable beginning of *All about My Mother* announces the dissipation of the real and of the identities that the real at once shelters and constrains. That dissipation is, as it were, decoratively performed by the liquefied script of the credits. Names and functions appear on the screen like inflated bubbles, and they disappear by slowly collapsing into themselves. Liquefaction can be contained, but it is inherently a loss of boundaries, a flowing out of frames. The first image we see is that of a plastic bag of intravenous fluid; we follow it flowing drop by drop through the IV tubing. The containment of falling drops is, a few moments later, more humorously exemplified by the diaper ad on TV that precedes the showing of *All about Eve:* as numerous dry, diapered infants are shown exercising and jumping around, children's voices sing the reassuring message: "Not a single drop! With Dodotis you won't feel a drop." Names as droplets, intravenous drops, drops of urine: *All about My Mother* begins with appealingly light reminders of the beauty of liquidity, its life-saving virtues, and the relative ease with which an undisciplined flowing can nonetheless be contained and absorbed.

Identities in *All about My Mother* are dissipated *as* they are being repeated. Manuela's return to Barcelona leads us to ask yet another question about the film's title: to whom does the "my" refer, whose mother is she? She begins by taking care of Agrado, who has been beaten up by one of her tricks; she will take in Rosa and care for her during her pregnancy; her job with Huma seems to consist mainly in watching over the drug-addicted Nina; and she will become the new Esteban's mother after Rosa's death. Manuela more or less becomes everyone's mother (including other mothers: Rosa, and to a certain extent even Rosa's mother), although it seems somewhat reductive of the richness of those relations to fit them all into a familiar maternal mold. Furthermore, the original family model is kept intact—we might even say protected—at the same time that Manuela is continuously stepping outside that model. By insisting on the first son's uniqueness, Almodóvar reveals a reluctance merely to repeat the category of "the mother" with different figures filling in for "my." Manuela's grief persists. And it persists not only because young Esteban can never be simply replaced by anyone else, but also because Manuela's move into new relational modes requires a certain mourning for the relationality left behind. Lola had already wreaked havoc with the myth of unambiguous family identities, but in fleeing from him/her and in destroying his/her image on her photographs, Manuela has worked to preserve that myth. Eliminated as a presence, paternal identity and paternal prestige might be, and nearly were, permanently secured. The security is, however, threatened by the same move designed to reconfirm it: the search for the person who might fill the gap. In sobbing over the loss of her son, Manuela also grieves over the loss of the principal guardian of the paternal myth. And it is undoubtedly right that she should do so: to lose the father's absence, or the paternal function at once dependent upon and incommensurable with any real father, is to lose the Law that governs and stabilizes the attributing of identities. Manuela's move outside the family circle is, most profoundly, a dismissal of legitimating symbolic systems, an implicit claim that social presence and social viability do not necessarily depend on symbolic authorizations.[3]

The symbolic cannot be *seriously* contested. The film does not, so to speak, take on the paternal phallus directly; instead, it dismisses that constitutively unlocatable fantasy product with numerous lighthearted evocations of the penis. During their dinner in front of the TV screen, Esteban, responding to his mother's joke that he should eat more because he might have to keep her up one day, shocks her slightly by saying: "You don't need pounds for that, you need a big dick." His point is confirmed by Agrado, whose credentials in this matter are impeccable: she informs Nina that "clients like us to be pneumatic [with, she explains, 'a pair of tits as hard as newly inflated tires'] and well hung." It was apparently a wise move on

Agrado's part, given his/her intention of returning to Barcelona as a female prostitute, to keep his/her penis. In fact, nearly everyone is turned on by her male appendage, not exactly as an object of solemn desire, but as—what? Huma's lover Nina tries to feel Agrado's breasts and, not seeming to expect much of a response, presses her behind against Agrado's crotch. When the good-looking and rather dim-witted Mario (Carlos Lozano), who is playing Stanley Kowalski in *Streetcar,* tells her that he has been feeling tense and sweetly asks for oral sex, he also shows an interest in her penis. Agrado, somewhat exasperated by all this highly focused attention, asks Mario if men ask *him* to suck their cocks because *he* also has one. And, during the wonderful sequence in Manuela's apartment when she, Rosa, Agrado, and Huma improvise a party of drinks, ice cream, and talk, the general good humor builds up to hilarity on the subject of the penis. Agrado describes herself as "a model of discretion, even when I suck a cock," to which Huma responds: "It's been ages since I sucked one." Rosa the pregnant nun, to the laughter of the others, cries out with mock naughtiness: "I love the word cock—and prick!" as she joyfully bounces on the sofa. The penis does, then, get a great deal of attention, which, far from highlighting its sexual appeal, makes it an occasion for fun. Not exactly something to be made fun of, but rather something to have fun with. Not quite neutralized, the penis is, we would prefer to say, naturalized. Unlike the absent father and the phantasmal phallus, the Almodovarian penis is present even where, in principle, it should not be: on the bodies of such (at least self-proclaimed) women as Agrado and Lola. The many reoccurrences of the penis help to dephallicize it. Lola's penis, it is true, is at once an anomaly and a menace (she is, as Manuela says, not a person but an epidemic), but she can scarcely be said to represent phallic power and authority. And Agrado is anything but a phallic woman; she rather embodies the agreeable (as her name suggests) perspective on the penis as an attractive object of sensual and social interest, detaching it from fixed ideas of male and female identities. And it is perhaps this possibility of the penis lending itself to a noncastrating detachment that accounts for its presence as an enlivening, civilized, and nonobsessive topic of interest—a passing topic of interest—at the little party Almodóvar's four women throw for themselves in Manuela's apartment.

All about My Mother invites and dismisses several serious attempts to get an identification right. Who is the real mother? Who is the real child? Who is the real woman? We are seduced into these questions mainly to be educated in the techniques by which they may be ignored. Crucial to this double enterprise are Agrado's play with the motif of authenticity and, most important, the movement within the film between "reality" and art, and between stage and film. "All I have that's real," Agrado tells Manuela, "are my feelings and the pints of silicone" that constitute her made-in-Paris body. Authenticity is the principal motif of the monologue that, standing in front of the closed curtains, Agrado delivers to a charmed audience on the evening when, with both Nina and Huma in the hospital after a fight, the performance of *Streetcar* is called off. "I'm very authentic," Agrado starts by announcing, as if in deliberate contrast to the make-believe drama that will not be shown this evening. Good actors disappear within the characters they play (it is most often meant as a criticism to say that an actor always plays himself). Agrado makes herself the subject of her performance, drawing the audience's attention to nearly every part of her body. The complication is, of course, that this body is almost entirely surgical artifice; the part that Agrado conspicuously fails to mention, perhaps out of *pudeur,* is also the only real, or original, part: her penis. As for all the rest, it was made to order, and for a price: almond-shaped eyes, 80,000 pesetas; two tits, 70,000 pese-tas each; jaw reduction, 75,000 pesetas; and so on. "It costs a lot," Agrado concludes, "to be authentic," adding, with a not entirely transparent logic, "the more authentic you are, the more you resemble what you dreamed you are." If anything is being made fun of here, it is not the wholly sympathetic Agrado's claim to authenticity, but rather the notion of authenticity itself. Agrado the construction is Agrado's dreams materialized, but her body does not become "real" because it expresses those dreams. To ask if she is real or false is itself a false alternative; she is perhaps best described as intensely performative.

Agrado's monologue is a set piece; it isolates a mode of being that also circu-lates throughout the film. We have spoken of Manuela's grief as her mourn-ing for a form of relationality that she, and the film, will leave behind. But she does not always sob "for real." On the evening she substitutes for Nina in the role of Stella in *Streetcar,* the scene we are shown is the one in which Stella begins to have labor pains as she argues with Stanley over Blanche. She sobs loudly as Stanley carries her out of the house. (We continue to hear her anguished sobbing after she and Stanley leave the frame—a reminder that in a play actors do not have to produce tears; their crying is communicated by gesture, and especially by sound.) Manuela-Stella's sobs are not unlike Manuela's wail of grief when she realizes that Esteban is dead. One of the two doctors who have just left her son says "Unfortunately," and Manuela, in a gesture whose exaggerated visibility would have been especially appropriate on a stage (where distance from the audience requires larger gestures), flings the entire upper half of her body forward and down, and breaks out crying. Film actors can, of course, be moved by the roles they are playing and produce their own tears, but, as we know, there are techniques for the production of cinematic tears. One of the most trustworthy signs of real emotion is, in film and in the theater, yet another artifice. Almodóvar encourages us to remember this not only by means of the scene chosen from Tennessee Williams's play, but also by the positioning of tears within a structural design: it belongs to the droplet motif initiated by the IV bottle in the film's first sequence. In more ways than one, Manuela's tears are an aesthetic construction, and yet, perhaps because it is impossible to dissociate tears from authentic feelings, we cannot but be moved by them. This double pull—at once inward, toward a grieving subject, and away from the subject, toward the producers of filmic structures and effects—is also at work (and working on us) in the brilliantly arranged close-up of Lola-Esteban crying as (s)he reads the passages from his/her son's notebook in which the boy had expressed his longing to know all about his father. It is a moving scene, but while (s)he cries (s)he lifts her hands to his/her face, and in doing so gives us a close-up of long painted fingernails. Thus it is the constructed Lola who moves us with the real tears of the father grieving for his lost son. Everything is real, and everything is false—which may mean that we are being asked, here and in the entire film, to construct and to accommodate a "place" where the choice between the two, and the very formulation of such an alternative, would no longer be necessary.

Almost everything happens more than once, and happens not exactly as the same, in *All about My Mother*. We have mentioned the three versions of organ-transplant procedures at the beginning of the film, as well as the reappearance, when Manuela is asked to authorize the use of Esteban's heart for a transplant, of the two doctors who played (with Manuela as the bereaved wife) in the simulated version of a similar request. Doubling is at least as important in *All about My Mother* as it is in *Contempt*; indeed, in Almodóvar, it is deliriously omnipresent. Rosa, like Manuela eighteen years earlier, gives birth to a son (Esteban), fathered by Lola-Esteban. Manuela leaves Barcelona pregnant with Esteban and returns after his death; she will leave Barcelona again with Esteban (Rosa's son) and return, this time with Esteban, two years later. Agrado and Esteban the First double each other, although in Agrado's case the new female seems to be dominant (she will be a prostitute for male clients), while Esteban-Lola, far from sharing Agrado's impatience with other people's interest in his/her retained penis, has clearly profited from that interest to continue seducing women. Anatomically, they both have dual identities: they announce themselves as women with their clothes, their breasts, and their makeup, and, with their genitals, they repeat themselves as men.

Most interesting are the numerous communications among different art forms. One of the film's several dedications is to actresses who play actresses, and this includes not only the actresses that Almodóvar mentions but also figures from his own film. Marisa Paredes, Cecilia Roth, and Candela Peña all play actresses in *All about My Mother;* Paredes repeats herself, differently, as Huma, who repeats herself as Blanche. Such repetitions place the imaginary at the heart of the film's realism: Huma playing Blanche reminds us that Huma herself is a role, that she is both the actress playing such roles as Blanche *and* a role being played by Paredes. Curiously, the scenes chosen from *All about Eve* and especially *A Streetcar Named Desire,* as well as the sequence of Huma rehearsing lines from Federico García Lorca's *Blood Wedding,* assume the status of the film's narrative raw material, the already given texts that "life" in *All about My Mother* mysteriously imitates. But it is, of course, not quite a question of life imitating art, but rather of art (this film) imitating, or repeating, art—although, because the film does distinguish what is meant to be real from the film, the play, and the poem it inaccurately replicates, Almodóvar is in fact constructing a much more interesting comment about the tenuous nature of any such distinctions. He constructs not derivations (such as life from art) but rather exchanges within a vast realm of possibility. Long after Manuela goes to La Coruña in pursuit of her son's heart, a scene from *Streetcar* is performed in which a distraught Blanche searches for what she calls her heart (which, Stella explains, is the heart-shaped case in which she keeps her jewelry). It is a curious repetition: occurring long after the episode it revives (although as part of a play written long before that episode, at once preceding it and, as a text, contemporaneous with it), and vastly different in its terms of reference (a jewel box rather than a son's transplanted organ), it nonetheless confirms the finitude and the formal unity of a linguistically designated world—a world made familiar not by inherent attributes of being but by inevitable reoccurrences within our descriptions of it.

Mostly, however, the film's terms of repetition correspond more closely. The brief sequence from *All about Eve* that we see on Manuela and Esteban's TV screen is of Eve coming into Margo's dressing room and being introduced to her; later on, Manuela, also with a concealed if very different purpose, will go backstage to Huma's dressing room. The scene from *Streetcar* in which Manuela performs the evening she replaces Nina is the play's final moments: Stella, carrying her child, walks out of her home, leaving Stanley and vowing never to return. It is a role Manuela had played long before, in Argentina, with Esteban as Kowalski; and, between these performances, she had left Lola-Esteban carrying the son she would give birth to and raise in Madrid. The lines from Lorca that Manuela watches Huma rehearse near the end of the film connect—almost as if they were a deferred inspiration for the earlier scene—to Esteban's death: a mother speaks of finding her son lying dead in the street, his blood flowing to the ground. The fictive doubling of the real also takes place within the real, without reference to other dramatic or filmic texts. When Manuela tells Rosa the story of her marriage to Esteban, she tells it as a story not about herself, but about a friend. With the doctor whom Rosa consults about her pregnancy, Manuela also momentarily doubles herself as Rosa's sister. Finally, repetition is figured more physically—as specularity—with the shots of Manuela and Huma speaking to each other in front of a mirror in the actress's dressing room.

In Godard's *Contempt*, *The Odyssey* serves as a means of derealizing the story of *Contempt* itself. The film's realistic narrative deceptively presents Paul (Michel Piccoli) and Camille (Brigitte Bardot), and Odysseus and Penelope, as alternative versions of the conjugal couple. Lang (Fritz Lang) and Paul speak of Homer's couple not as an imaginary construct, but as a historically real precedent to the modern couple exemplified by Paul and Camille. They disagree not about the mode of being that should be attributed to Odysseus and Penelope, but rather about whether they were like or unlike Paul and Camille. We have argued that the film proposes an alternative reading: Odysseus and Penelope are neither ancient nor modern; rather, they *persist in time* as a permanently unsettled and unrealized possibility of coupling. They are like Paul and Camille not because they are as real as they are, but because Paul and Camille are, in an important sense, as imaginary as the ancient couple. The realism of *Contempt* is indispensable to this demonstration. It is only by at first affirming the distinction between the real and the imaginary that Godard can effectively represent his modern couple's failure to profit from the porosity of the boundaries separating the two. The film implicitly argues for the imaginary status of the so-called real—not by reducing the real (absurdly) to pure immateriality, but by making a claim for the potentiality that persists in and beyond all realized being. (Thus, in a consequence fraught with political implications, pastness is only one attribute of past events. The horrors of Nazism, for example, cannot be historically "explained" and thereby conveniently sequestered.) The couple that Paul and Camille fail to be is, precisely, a couple that *fails to be,* one that would persist as a timeless, imaginary relation whose sense is permanently deferred. The aesthetic is the ontological drawing back, the potentializing, of Paul and Camille's unhappily realized passion.

In a curious reversal, the illusion of completed or settled being is projected onto the art incorporated into *All about My Mother.* The principal realistic narrative of the film unseriously repeats the art it quotes. The fascination of such works as *All about Eve* and *A Streetcar Named Desire* most probably derives from the skill with which they, like so many other unselfconsciously realistic plays and films, reformulate psychological fantasy as a given, irrevocably realized world. Lacan has spoken of the defensive function of desire. The fantasy scenarios of desire are imperative constructions, made imperative by the drives that must at all costs remain hidden. Desire's scenarios are phantasmal fortresses, and their strength depends on the finality of their plots, the strength with which they resist being potentialized. Desire presents itself not only as a law, but also as a fatality. Because desire constitutively mistakes its object for its cause (this is the truth desiring fantasy hides from us), the failure of those objects to satisfy desire is interpreted as a gap or hole in the objects themselves. Lack is judged to be omnipresent: what desire lacks is also missing in the world, not as something lost but, more tragically, as something that was never, that never could be, in the world. This does not mean that objects that might satisfy the repressed drives could ever be found in the world. *Those* objects (the partial body-objects aggressively incorporated and expelled by infantile fantasies?) constitute by their very nature a rejection of the real world. To satisfy the drives, we must die to the world; the "death instinct" pursues a fantasy-ecstasy given by fantasy-objects, and in so doing it removes us from life itself. The death drive can be satisfied only by the violence that annihilates it.

If these psychic depths have entered our discourse, it is thanks, most

notably, to Freud's metapsychological speculations, the identification by
Melanie Klein of the very being of the human subject with fantasy-objects,
and the line of reflection in Lacan that would lead him to assert not only
that "there is no sexual relation," but also, perhaps even more radically, that
object-investment is something of a miracle. These are the great moments
of psychoanalysis, and, as Lacan never tired of proclaiming, they have nothing to do with a supposed cure presumed to help us adapt more happily
to reality. The failure to adapt—which Freud traced in *Civilization and Its
Discontents* to the incomparable *jouissance* of a self-destructive and world-
destructive aggressiveness—constitutes the *psychoanalytic subject*. And it
accounts for, among other things, the perennially unsatisfied (and therefore productive) nature of desire and the melancholy attached to what can
only be the secondary, derived, and always misaimed scenarios of desire. If
A Streetcar Named Desire is such an important foil in *All about My Mother*
against which the Almodovarian world will be constructed, it is perhaps
because Almodóvar recognized in Williams's play an ideally transparent version of the failures and the melancholy inherent in desire. Blanche DuBois
is a glamorously pathetic caricature of the psychoanalytic subject's absence
from the world.

To say this, however, is also to say that the psychoanalytic subject and
psychoanalysis itself have little to say to us about possible exchanges with the
world, exchanges that would be neither projections nor incorporations nor
adaptive techniques. *All about My Mother* shows us such exchanges working out of, and against, desire and its fantasies. More precisely, it implicitly
makes an argument for an aesthetic subject, one for whom a relationality
that includes the real world (and not merely our fantasy inscriptions on the
world) is born not from a dismissal of the real, but rather from an elaboration of the real as always in the process of being realized. By inaccurately
replicating them in his own film, Almodóvar appears to be suggesting that
the characters from *Streetcar* and *All about Eve* are *insufficiently aestheticized*. His many repetitions—both intertextual and intratextual—are a way
of reinitiating identities and situations rather than emphatically reconfirm-
ing them. As a result, the film becomes a massive deconstruction of its title.
"All about" is mere epistemological fantasy. There is no single (or proprietary) subject to support "My" (Esteban? which one? Rosa? Almodóvar?), and
"Mother" has no clearly identifiable referent (Almodóvar's mother? what is
the relation between the mother of the title and the mother of the dedication? can "mother" include all the ways Manuela cares for others?). "Mother"

is both present and already lost everywhere; its presence *is* its lostness, the unlocatable and unsettled nature of its referent and its attributes. Repeatable being—being that continuously fails to be unique—creates a hospitable world of correspondences, one in which relations, no longer blocked by difference, multiply as networks of similitudes. It is as if the reappearance of identities were antecedent to their realization; we could even say that nothing is ever even about to be because imminence is always preempted by the power to persist inherent in purely potential being.

Unlike the Homeric references in Godard's *Contempt,* Almodóvar's aesthetic references in *All about My Mother* are to works that are phantasmally heavy and deficient in the imaginary. The movement in the film between these works and the diegetically defined real is nonetheless crucial to Almodóvar's elaboration of the imaginary. They serve, on the one hand, to make the important point that the imaginary as a mode of potentialized being is not to be restricted, and sequestered, within the category of "art." The retreat from being is not a particularity of the aesthetic narrowly conceived; it is an ethical duty coextensive with life itself. On the other hand, the continuous visiting of works of art provides us with a perhaps necessary renewed contact with an activity consecrated, so to speak, as the most specialized manifestation of the imaginary. The inherent immateriality of all works of art subverts the melancholy gravity of even the most phantasmally weighted indulgence. The astonishing final shot of *All about My Mother* reasserts the necessity of this movement to and from the work of art. Manuela, Agrado, and Huma have been reunited in Huma's dressing room. The actress has to leave to go onstage; the film ends with a close-up of her face as she stands in the doorway of the dressing room looking at her friends (and directly into the camera), and she asserts, solemnly, "I will return [Me vuelvo]." We may at first find the solemnity disconcerting, strangely inappropriate (is she not simply saying "I'll see you after the performance"?). And yet this remarkable moment condenses, and very nearly sacralizes, the movement that has sustained the entire film. Huma, looking like a priestess in her long wig, seems to be carrying us with her to an unidentified performance which, however, we will never see, at the same time as she announces, with oracular authority, her return to the diversions of ordinary sociability.

All about My Mother is a performative reflection on the possibility of a nonphantasmal imaginary. It proposes an answer to a question of great consequence: how might the imaginary be separated from the defensive functions of fantasy? Almodóvar's very early films lightheartedly answer this question without, as it were, taking the trouble to acknowledge its difficulty. *All about My Mother* is of necessity less exuberantly wild than *Pepi, Luci, Bom* and *Labyrinth of Passion*: the exhilarating lightness of the imaginary is, in *All about My Mother,* in frictional and possibly dangerous contact with the seriousness of settled identities and established being. The threat comes from two directions: from the rigid fantasy structures of the very works that seem to inspire Almodóvar's version, in this film, of a nonphantasmal imaginary, and from the family structure that unravels even as Manuela awaits the meeting that might consolidate it. Much earlier in this discussion we noted the persistence of a gay sensibility in the film long after the son coded as gay has died. This was, it now seems, too rapid an identification of what remains of a homosexuality that was never, after all, entirely present. The death of the son, the transsexualizing of the father, and the ironic repetitions of the icons of a gay sensibility create a psychic climate in which gayness is nearly unrecognizable. And yet, having been so emphatically posited in the film's early sequences, it continues to operate in important ways. But we should perhaps no longer speak of a cultural sensibility. Our entire analysis has anatomized a more fundamental relation between the subject and the world. The dispersal and repetition of identities in the film point to a solidarity or homo-ness of being, the partial reoccurrences of all subjects *elsewhere.* Identities are never individual; homosexual desire would be the erotic expression of a homo-ness that vastly exceeds it, a reaching out toward an *other sameness.*

Almodóvar's nonphantasmal imaginary in *All about My Mother* seems to depend on the extinction of desire, an extinction signaled by the absence of the father as the legislator of desire and the death of the (author-)son as the possible subject of desire. Homosexual desire is, however, obliquely referred to by nearly everyone's very unsolemn interest in the penis. The male organ, we have suggested, is naturalized. It is by no means excluded as an erotic object, but it has become an erotic object dephallicized and depsychologized, thereby at least raising the possibility of a gay (and straight) desire for the male body that would no longer be burdened by fantasy illusions of power and castration. More important, the erasure of any relations at all between men in *All about My Mother* clears the field for an extraordinary reworking of the absence of desire for women. Far from being the more or less willing participants in a nonerotic gay sociability, women are given the space not only to reinvent themselves, but, more radically, to refashion relationality itself. Almodóvar's women, unlike those in the work of Tennessee Williams, are not fantasy constructions of a repressed, distorted, and vengeful heterosexual desire. Such elaborations are undoubtedly—however reluctant many of us may be to agree with this—*one* fate of heterosexual desire when, at least as far as conscious sexual preferences go, it has been completely occluded by homosexual desire. It is perhaps Almodóvar's desexualizing and his depsychologizing of homosexuality that make possible a very different version of sexual indifference toward women. In a discussion of *All about My Mother* with Frédéric Strauss, Almodóvar has said: "the fact that a group of women are speaking together constitutes the basis of fiction, the origin of all stories" (Strauss 164). But what stories will they tell? We take it as a sign of Almodóvar's generosity that he does not simply identify those fictions with his own stories *about* women. If his work suggests that he is not quite sure what those stories will be, what forms the talk will take, it may be because his talk, like everyone's talk, cannot help being inspired and nourished by our culture's richly significant narratives of desire and psychic complexity. In a new relational regime, what will there be to talk about? Almodovarian sociability is remarkably less constrained by that richness than sociability usually is, but perhaps because Almodóvar has come very close to escaping from "the laws of desire," he is all the more anxious (eager, and a little worried?) about what exceeds them. There is, at any rate, the exhilarating freshness of that modest party in Manuela's apartment, and there is the great and touching modesty of Almodóvar himself moving his camera out of hearing range as Pepa and Marisa converse on Pepa's terrace at the end of *Women on the Verge of a Nervous Breakdown.* As if his characters were about to speak of things that he, Almodóvar, has not yet been able to imagine.

NOTES

1. All translations from Frédéric Strauss's *Conversations avec Almodóvar* are ours.

2. It would be not quite accurate to say that "passion" returns in Almodóvar's film *Talk to Her* (2002), because what would ordinarily qualify as "love" and "friendship" (the two men's attachment to the two women in a coma, and their developing attachment to each other) is, we feel, Almodóvar's extraordinary reimagining of the intimacies referred to by those words. The women, unable to speak, somehow "speak" so powerfully in being spoken to that they create between the two men—as a kind of innovative refraction of the feelings directed toward them—a relation that includes them, a relation so strong, so inclusive, and so new that it would be inexcusable and reductive to describe it as homoerotic and, perhaps, even to appropriate it for the familiar category of friendship.

3. The possibility of *un*authorized community is extravagantly explored in Jean Genet's fiction, especially *Our Lady of the Flowers.*

WORKS CITED

Freud, Sigmund. *Civilization and Its Discontents.* Trans. James Strachey. New York: W. W. Norton, 1961.

Strauss, Frédéric. *Conversations avec Almodóvar.* Paris: Cahiers du Cinéma, 2000.

10 All about the Brothers
Retroseriality in Almodóvar's Cinema
MARSHA KINDER

Looking for Blood Brothers

In **1987,** when I interviewed Pedro Almodóvar shortly after the release
of *Law of Desire,* he told me that the most important thing about the
movie was that it was a story of two brothers ("Pleasure and the New
Spanish Mentality" 33–44). Although I did not find the comment illuminating at the time, I do now as I look back at *Law of Desire* through *Bad
Education* (2004) and the comments that Almodóvar has made about fraternity in its wake: "Fraternity is the result of two great feelings, love and
friendship, bound together by something as unfathomable as consanguinity" ("Self-Interview"). In narrative terms, it is *consanguinity* that is the rub,
for it means that the characters derive from the same source, which not only
heightens the love and rivalry they feel for each other but also facilitates
fluid identifications between them and their proliferating doubles across
borders of bodies and texts.

In a "Self-Interview" posted on his official Web site, Almodóvar acknowledges that *Bad Education* and *Law of Desire* are "blood brothers," two texts
based on the same source. Although he admits that *Bad Education* derives
from the scene in *Law of Desire* in which a transsexual played by Carmen
Maura confronts the priest who molested her when she was a boy, he claims
that both films were based on an earlier story and set of events:

> Long before *[Law of Desire]* I wrote a story about this transvestite going back to
> the school he attended in order to blackmail the priests who harassed him as a kid.
> During the making of *Law of Desire,* I remembered that story and found the inspi-
> ration for the sequence where Carmen enters the school chapel and comes across
> the priest who loved her when she was a boy. At that time I was already thinking
> about working further this story. In this sense, Carmen is the premonitory shadow
> of Zahara [the transvestite played by Gael García Bernal's character Juan/Ángel in
> *Bad Education*]. ("Self-Interview")

According to his own explanation, Almodóvar replicates the structure of *Bad
Education,* which he describes as consisting of "three stories, three concentric

triangles that end up in one single story" (ibid.), a compulsive repetition reminiscent, as several critics have noted, of the spiral structure of Hitchcock's
Vertigo (1958). But in Almodóvar's personal myth, this strategic repetition
threatens to draw his entire filmography into a spiraling *mise en abîme*, generating new versions while keeping the point of origin out of reach.

As René Girard reminds us about the original crime of the father against
the son (which generated the Oedipal narrative and its homoerotic variations that play such a key role in film noir), the original act must remain
hidden if a myth is to retain its structuring power (190). Yet, according to
Claude Lévi-Strauss, repetition can be used to reveal a myth's underlying
structure:

> A myth exhibits a "slated" structure, which comes to the surface . . . through repeti-
> tion. However, the slates are not absolutely identical. And since the purpose of myth
> is to provide a logical model capable of overcoming a contradiction (an impos-
> sible achievement if, as it happens, the contradiction is real), a theoretically infi-
> nite number of slates will be generated, each one slightly different from the others.
> Thus, myth grows spiral-wise until the intellectual impulse which has produced it
> is exhausted. (229)

Although we do not have access to the first version of Almodóvar's story or
its point of origin, we do have an earlier film by him featuring two brothers,
What Have I Done to Deserve This? (1984), which he presents as a neorealist
portrait of his own family. Although it may not be a "blood brother" in the
strict sense, I hope to show that this film is at least a close cousin and that all
three are "consanguineous" variations of the same genetic material. In performing what I will be calling a "retroserial reading" of these three films as
a trilogy about brothers, I will use repetitions to reveal the films' structuring
contradictions about fraternity and to explore the following questions:

1. What are the contradictions about fraternity that *Bad Education,* like its predecessors, tries to overcome? In other words, how does it address the contradictory desire for fusion and the fear of interchangeability? Can fraternal love, a love
   ostensibly between equals or doubles, dispel a murderous sibling rivalry over the
   love of the father? Can it prevent a domestic civil war?
2. Why does a compulsive retelling of the fratricidal story of Cain and Abel replace,
   as appears to be the case, Oedipus as the primary myth of homoerotic desire for
   Almodóvar? Does the father's favoring of one brother over the other (or some
   other variant of the prodigal son) strengthen or weaken the favorite, especially if
   the father's desire is inflamed by absence and his favor expressed through seduction? Is it possible to tell a story about a violated child without his remaining a
   stunted victim or becoming a violent abuser himself?

Despite his teasing disavowals about the alleged autobiographical dimensions of *Bad Education,* I am not interested in speculating on Almodóvar's relations with his own priests or siblings—not even with his brother Agustín, who appears as an extra in many of his films.[1] Rather, I want to explore how *Bad Education* enables us to *reread* two of his earlier films featuring a pair of brothers, which also involve murder and molestation and which marked important steps in Almodóvar's emergence as a world class auteur: *Law of Desire,* the first film produced by his fraternal production company, El Deseo, that he and his brother Agustín control; and *What Have I Done to Deserve This?,* his first film to win recognition from international critics. Conversely, I want to see how these two earlier films affect our reading of *Bad Education.*

I recently traced a similar dynamic of retroseriality through what I have called Almodóvar's "brain-dead trilogy": *The Flower of My Secret* (1995), *All about My Mother* (1999), and *Talk to Her* (2002), each of which contains an episode in which a young person is rendered brain dead. I claimed that this recurrence leads us to follow Almodóvar's development of the trope from a symbolic image in *The Flower of My Secret,* to a major pivot in the plot of *All about My Mother,* to the central narrative situation of *Talk to Her.*[2] In some ways, this paper is that earlier essay's spectatorial sibling—a sequel that shows how Almodóvar again leads us to choose two earlier works from his canon to illuminate what a later film is doing and to redefine them as a trilogy through this act of retroserial rereading.

Defining Retroseriality: Four Models

I am using the term "retroseriality" to describe both an aspect of Almodóvar's films and a method of reading them. I am not suggesting that his work is regressive or nostalgic; nor am I referring to his recurring thematic of a "return," which can be found in many of his films, as well as in the title of the recent *Volver* (2006). Rather, I am arguing that his films increasingly perform an evocation of earlier works (both his own and intertexts of others) that leads us to read them as an ongoing saga and to regroup them into networked clusters. Thus, like T. S. Eliot's classic essay "Tradition and the Individual Talent" and Mikhail Bakhtin's concept of dialogism, his films remind us that new works influence old works just as old works influence new ones, for new variations lead us to reread older works in new ways.[3]

Although this "retroserial" rereading can be applied to many artworks, it takes on new meaning in the postmodernist era of television, where intertextuality becomes deliberate and pervasive. Retroseriality acquires special irony in the case of Almodóvar, because in the 1980s he disavowed the past and pretended that the Francoist era had never existed. But retroseriality also acquires special resonance inasmuch as his hyperplotted, multithreaded narratives create a supple form of sexually mobile melodrama with an extraordinary tonal range, what he himself, in his "Self-Interview," has called "a labyrinth of passions." This unique combination enables Almodóvar to create his own alternative universe, a personal mythology in which memories of earlier movies are frequently more important than historical events. Nowhere is this more evident than in *Bad Education,* which he calls "a sort of anthology of all the themes that have interested me up until now, with a sort of more pessimistic and serene look" ("Bad Education" 5). To experience fully the reverberating pleasures of his texts, we need to remember the earlier movies in detail and recognize their variations. "All I want is to see people going to the theatre and watch the film so they can't get it out of their heads afterwards" ("Self-Interview").

There are at least four basic models for retroseriality, which Almodóvar combines in uniquely productive ways: (1) auteurist cinema; (2) serial television; (3) the transformational trilogy; and (4) open-ended database narrative. The first model comes from auteurist cinema, where filmmakers become obsessed with certain issues that they compulsively rework in film after film. Because of the total control that Almodóvar exercises over his own movies, this model is usually applied to him—particularly in the wake of earlier auteurs like Buñuel, Bergman, Fellini, Wenders, and Hitchcock. His own comments about *Bad Education* in his "Self-Interview" encourage us to apply this model, for he claims that this film grew out of a compulsion to revisit the fraternal family romance:

> I definitely had to make *Bad Education.* I had to get rid of it before it turned into an obsession. The story had been in my hands for over ten years already, and I knew I could still wait another ten years. Due to the multiple combinations possible, putting the writing of *Bad Education* to an end was only realizable once the film was shot, edited and mixed.

Despite the association of this kind of auteurist obsession with the European art film, Almodóvar made his debut with "low" popular forms—the serial memoirs of porn star Patty Diphusa and early sex farces like *Pepi, Luci, Bom* (1980) and *Labyrinth of Passion* (1982), works that established his reputation as "the Spanish Andy Warhol." As an artist who unraveled the boundary between high art and pop culture, Warhol provided Almodóvar with a brilliant model for how marginality could be transformed into mainstream success. Yet Almodóvar treated this Warholian entitlement with mixed emotions—at first leveraging it as he was rising to global stardom, but then discarding it once he had arrived. No matter how successful he became and how sophisticated his cinematic mastery grew, Almodóvar never lost touch with these lower popular forms, which provide the second model for retroseriality: serial television.

Serial television is the most familiar model, one that applies not only to production and reception, but also to transnational marketing. In serial television, an episodic narrative is launched by a pilot, but usually takes several episodes to captivate its viewers. If the series proves successful, it generates a more complex structure in syndication or foreign sales, which provides a nonlinear entry into the overarching story and a haunting afterlife that survives cancellation, even after the narrative possibilities of the basic premise have supposedly been exhausted. By entering a TV series in medias res or picking up back episodes in syndication while simultaneously watching the new season unfold (possibilities enhanced by VCRs, TiVo, and DVD releases of past seasons), viewers experience a slated, multitiered structure that enriches the narrative reverberations of any individual episode.

Although Almodóvar tends to treat television disparagingly as cinema's evil twin, he has steadily used it as a source not only for humor but also as a model of narrative rupture. As with a television series, we viewers can enter his serial myth with any specific film and then can wait for the next film (or episode) to be released. Or, we can go back to earlier works on film, video, or DVD in any order we choose. Even his earliest references to television evoke issues of nonlinear structure. For example, in his serial memoirs of Patty Diphusa published "sometimes without continuity," Almodóvar claims: "If she were in America, she'd have her own TV show" (*Patty Diphusa* 7). In his debut feature, *Pepi, Luci, Bom,* the entangled plots are interrupted by a series of hilarious television commercials for miraculous Ponte panties that turn farts into perfume, urine stains into new spring colors, and—when used as a dildo—commodity fetishism into pleasures of the flesh. If this mundane medium could make such miraculous transformations convincing, then it was ideally suited to promote those cultural changes celebrated by the *Movida,* the irreverent cultural movement of the giddy early post-Franco era.[4] With its growing regionality and expansion of global sales, television increasingly proves effective in violating spatial borders, enabling series with distinctive urban and suburban locales (like *Sex and the City* and *Desperate Housewives,* whose Almodovarian traces are blatant) to reimagine a transnational community of loyal fans.

The third model, the transformational trilogy, is rarer and more challenging: the expansion of a story across a number of sequels that demand an ideological shift in understanding the underlying contradictions, which were only implicit in the original episode. Like the TV pilot, the first episode is designed to capture and prepare an audience for the more threatening segments that follow, and the connections between them may be strengthened by the use of flashbacks, particularly to scenes of victimized youths. The best-known examples are Sergei Eisenstein's *Ivan the Terrible* (1943–48) and Francis Ford Coppola's *Godfather* saga (1972, 1974, 1990). Although the Communist Party interpreted Eisenstein's sympathetic portrayal of Ivan in Part I as a defense of Stalin and his cult status as hero, the more critical Part II, despite its flashbacks to Ivan's perilous childhood, was read as an attack, thereby preventing Part III from being finished. In the case of the *Godfather* saga, Part I was originally read as an exciting work in the gangster genre that defended the Corleone family and its use of violence in its rise to power, but Part II emphasized the family's mirror relationship with the corrupt establishment it had initially challenged. Although Almodóvar does not claim either of these trilogies as an intertext, he does praise *The Godfather* for having "left us with wonderful sequences with brothers and sisters loving, beating, protecting and killing one another" ("Self-Interview"), thereby linking this transformational trilogy structure to his own personal obsession with siblings.

In contrast with these two trilogies and the more typical series of sequels whose episodes are blatantly linked by titles—from Robert Zemeckis's *Back to the Future* (1985, 1989, 1990) to Krzysztof Kieslowski's *Three Colors: Blue* (1993), *White* (1993), and *Red* (1994)—Almodóvar's films are more fluid in their relations with each other. They can always be reconfigured into a new cluster whenever a new film comes along. Yet, they share with *Ivan* and *The Godfather* trilogies the kind of ideological shift that is rarely found in the more popular ongoing series of sequels. For example, when we compare *Bad Education* to earlier films like *What Have I Done to Deserve This?* and *Law of Desire,* we find a darker reading of sexual mobility and authorial power; they no longer perform a radical sex change on Spain's national stereotype (as I argued in the past), but seem to avenge his own victimization as a child. As Almodóvar acknowledges: "The good thing about cinema, among many other things, is its capacity to convert into spectacle and entertainment the worst of our nature" ("Self-Interview"). In *Bad Education,* the worst seems to be a priest molesting a child, the notorious patriarchal crime, which, despite its recent prominence in the press, still remains largely hidden in the bushes. This crime is rivaled by the fratricidal betrayal of a brother, an act dramatized on-screen. No matter which crime is deemed worse, they are both inflicted on the same victim, the "favored" prodigal brother, Ignacio, who dared to leave home.

The fourth and most recent model of retroseriality is the open-ended database narrative that has emerged within digital culture—a form of narrative experimentation that has been the focus of my own research and multimedia production for the past decade. By database narrative, I mean those structures that reveal the underlying database of possibilities out of which any particular tale or story element—character, event, object, setting—is chosen, by either author or spectator. By suggesting that all of these elements can easily be reshuffled, and by demanding an active mode of reading that searches for new connections, this structure weakens the ideological hold of any master narrative and thereby encourages transformation and mobility. Although this structure has been fostered and fetishized by digital culture, it also can be found in earlier nondigital narrative forms (including experimental theater, fictional cinema, and television) and is therefore compatible with the other three models of retroseriality. Database narrative is especially well suited to a personal *mythos* like Almodóvar's that celebrates sexual and social mobility and that constantly gives his open-ended "laberinto de pasiones" new life. As he put it in *Patty Diphusa:* "My life, like my stories, has only foundations, but lacks a beginning and an end" (66).[5]

The Way In: An Overview of Bad Education

In order to show the connections among this trilogy of films on fraternity, I need to provide a brief plot summary of *Bad Education,* which, given its intricately slated structure, is not so easy to compress; for the film is both "three concentric triangles" and "one single story" divided into seven episodes.

Part I introduces the narrative frame, set in 1980, that begins with a visit. A young actor named Ángel (Gael García Bernal) visits the office of filmmaker Enrique Goded (Fele Martínez), claiming to be his old schoolmate Ignacio and showing him a fictional story he has written about their relationship. Although Enrique does not believe that the visitor is really Ignacio, he is eager to read the story, for he desperately needs new material.

The inset story, "The Visit," contains Parts II and III. It is divided into two time periods, which were shot in different styles and were presumably written by different authors. Set in 1980 (like the frame), Part II is pure fiction and played primarily for laughs. It was written by Ángel, who plays the starring role of Zahara, Ignacio's female persona inspired by real-life Spanish movie diva Sara Montiel. After a dazzling onstage performance, Zahara goes home with a handsome drunken biker, who turns out to be a fictional version of Enrique (played by beefy Alberto Ferreiro rather than wiry Fele Martínez). Before Zahara can rob him, she discovers Enrique's identity and the fact that he is now married and has a son. After giving the sleeping Enrique a flamboyant farewell fuck (the only sex scene García Bernal seems to relish), she leads her friend Paca/Paquito (another transvestite played by Javier Cámara) to an alternative source of funding: they go to her religious school where Zahara/Ignacio tries to blackmail Father Manolo (Daniel Giménez Cacho), the impassioned priest who molested him as a child. These acts of revenge lead into a flashback to the 1960s when Ignacio and Enrique were innocent boys at Catholic school.

Part III is devoted to a series of poignant childhood memories from the inset story, which has a range of tones not found in the rest of the movie. Allegedly written by the real Ignacio, it includes scenes of the young Ignacio (Nacho Pérez) sweetly singing a Spanish version of "Moon River" for the smitten Father Manolo and his fellow lecherous priests at the annual picnic, where the "hidden" molestation presumably takes place; of Ignacio and his little friend Enrique (Raúl García Forneiro) tenderly groping each other in a movie theater as they watch Sara Montiel on-screen; of Ignacio and Enrique later being caught together in the toilet by the outraged Father Manolo; of Ignacio losing his faith when he succumbs to the priest's advances; and of the jealous priest separating the young lovers by forcing Enrique to leave the school.

Part IV returns to the more cynical contemporary frame, which focuses on a melodramatic power struggle between Ángel and Enrique. Their interaction turns erotic in a poolside sequence where the sexual dynamics are played out primarily through gestures and movements rather than words, evoking the mysterious scene in *Talk to Her* in which the graceful gliding of an anonymous male body through a swimming pool is set to music as if he were performing an erotic dance. Significantly, this is the sequence in *Bad Education* where Almodóvar's brother Agustín makes a brief appearance, playing the pool man who is linked to the erotic site. Although Enrique distrusts Ángel as an actor, he still wants to conquer him sexually but refuses to cast him as Zahara. Enrique traces Ángel to his family home in Galicia, where his mother reveals that Ignacio died four years earlier (in 1976, shortly after the death of Franco) and that Ángel is in fact Ignacio's younger brother Juan. She gives Enrique the letter that Ignacio left for him, and tells him about a publisher named Berenguer, who turns out to be the former Father Manolo. Like the fictional Enrique in Part III, Berenguer is now married and has a son.

Part V presents the finale of Enrique's film adaptation of "The Visit," which is being shot on the set with Juan/Ángel in the role of Zahara. Instead of accepting Juan's happy ending of revenge (depicted in Part II) Enrique writes a new ending that lets him vent his own hostility toward the actor. Meanwhile, Mr. Berenguer (the former Father Manolo, now played by older, heftier Lluís Homar) has been there on the set, watching the action from the shadows; he promises to tell Enrique what really happened to Ignacio.

Part VI presents Berenguer's film noir version of the ending, which is set in 1976 and is much darker in tone than the two earlier versions. Berenguer admits that he refused to publish Ignacio's story and then was threatened with blackmail. When he went to Valencia to negotiate with Ignacio, who was by then a transsexual junkie, he fell passionately in love with his younger brother Juan, who looked innocent and boyish. While Ignacio is in rehab, Berenguer manages to spend a week alone with Juan, seducing him with the blackmail money promised to his brother. After attending a film noir movie (where the characters "are just like them"), Berenguer and Juan plot to kill Ignacio, who dies of tainted smack while typing the final letter to Enrique.

Part VII depicts the final segment of the frame: the final bitter encounter between Enrique and Juan, which is followed by a postscript from ten years later (the 1990s) that summarizes the fates of the three surviving homoerotic male characters. Despite all these explanations, at the end of the film, we are still left wondering: why did Juan kill his brother? One way of answering this question is to turn back to the two earlier films in Almodóvar's fraternal trilogy.

The Esperpento Family Romance in What Have I Done to Deserve This?

When Wim Wenders decided to win the heart of the Americans and the general audience, he made a story about the family; a melodrama with an absent mother and a redeeming brother, plus a straight-haired boy. The family never fails. I found that out when I shot ¿Qué he hecho yo para merecer esto?. People began looking at me with different eyes, sort of like "he's modern, but sensible." The family is always first-rate dramatic material. (Almodóvar, "Law of Desire")

The Wenders film to which Almodóvar refers is *Paris, Texas,* which was made in 1984, the same year that his own *What Have I Done to Deserve This?* was released and close to the time when the narrative frame of *Bad Education* is set. In contrast to Wenders's melancholy melodrama about a runaway mother, Almodóvar's film is an absurdist comedy about a downtrodden housewife and cleaning woman named Gloria (Carmen Maura), who is addicted to a Spanish version of NoDoz. When her husband Antonio smacks her in one of their spats, she kills him with a ham bone. Her two sons pair off with the surviving matriarchs: the older brother Toni, a drug dealer, goes back to the family village with his paternal Granny (Chus Lampreave) so that he can "work the land." The younger, sexually precocious Miguel (who, with a spin of a Zoetrope, defines himself as a future filmmaker like Almodóvar) returns home to mother Gloria, even though she had loaned him to their pedophiliac dentist to pay off their bills.

Although I am treating this film as the first episode in Almodóvar's fraternal trilogy, its genre—comic melodrama—keeps the focus on the women rather than the brothers: not only on Gloria and Granny, but also on Cristal (Verónica Forqué), the friendly whore next door who dreams of going to Vegas. Yet, there are blatant connections between the young brothers (the drug dealer and molested child) and the grown-up siblings in *Bad Education.* By reading this earlier film with hindsight, we can find the potential rivalry between these two brothers, even though it is displaced onto the rival matriarchs.

Before leaving for their home village, Toni tries to get Cristal to seduce Miguel, hoping to "cure" his brother's homosexuality—a sentiment that prefigures Juan/Ángel's lame excuse for killing Ignacio at the end of *Bad Education:* "You don't know how hard it is to have a brother like that in a small village." Like Juan/Ángel, Toni's gay sexuality is more ambiguous and closeted than his brother's; not surprisingly, he also turns down Cristal's sexual favors. The person the brothers compete for is their father, who, like Granny, clearly prefers the older son Toni, who has inherited his name as well as his talents for forgery. When the younger son Miguel returns home, he poignantly asks, "Did Dad miss me?" His mother candidly responds, "He was so busy he didn't realize you were gone, but I missed you." This exchange helps explain why Miguel is attracted to older men, such as his friend Raúl's father, and why he willingly goes home with the dentist.

By sending Miguel to live with the dentist and taking Toni back to the village, the competing matriarchs succeed in keeping the brothers apart and holding their rivalry in check. According to Almodóvar, as soon as two brothers encounter someone they both desire, jealousy erupts into violence: in *Bad Education,* "the presence of F. Manolo blasts the existence of the two brothers [and] 'fraternity' turns into 'murderous rivalry'" (Almodóvar, "Bad Education" 5). Like the two artistic brothers molested by the same priest in *Bad Education,* the two abused children in *What Have I Done to Deserve This?*—Miguel and his neighbor Vanesa—have special powers that keep them from being seen merely as pathetic victims. But here those powers are pushed to comic extremes. Miguel has a superadult sophistication on matters of sexuality, art, and familial love. Like Almodóvar, Miguel is "modern but sensible": he cheerfully goes with the dentist so long as he can get free art lessons. The other victimized child is the little redhead Vanessa, who relies on her telekinetic powers to retaliate against her abusive mother, a situation that parodies such Hollywood horror films as Brian De Palma's *Carrie* (1976).

The film's primary Hollywood intertext is, however, Elia Kazan's *Splendor in the Grass* (1961), which belongs to Almodóvar's eclectic list of fraternal classics, for, as he explains in his "Self-Interview," like *Paris, Texas,* it features a supportive relationship between two suffering siblings:

> I love the sense of fraternity, and I have always enjoyed movies with siblings: Warren Beatty being beaten up in the parking lot for watching his sister's loss of honour . . . in *Splendor in the Grass* . . . Thrilling Harry Dean Stanton in *Paris, Texas* and his silent visit to brother Dean Stockwell.

These intertextual connections and allusions help counteract the potentially dehumanizing effects of Almodóvar's grotesque humor, which masks the movie's emotional core.

In *What Have I Done to Deserve This?,* the puppetlike characters and absurd situations evoke the tradition of *esperpento,* a distinctively Spanish version of the grotesque that can be traced back to Goya and to the puppet theater of modernist Ramón María del Valle-Inclán (1866–1936), who described it as a reflection in a concave mirror. Yet, Almodóvar sets his story in a realistic low-rent apartment complex on the outskirts of Madrid. As his "most social picture," it revealed his own "most unmodern roots, the small town" (*Patty Diphusa* 91). Such statements connect *What Have I Done to Deserve This?* to the Spanish adaptations of Italian neorealism that helped launch Spain's "modern cinema" of the 1950s. As Almodóvar puts it in *Patty Diphusa:*

The theme is a classic one: a rural family moving to the metropolis and their fight for survival—*Rocco and His Brothers* [Luchino Visconti, 1960] and *Surcos* [José Antonio Nieves Conde, 1951]. I tried to adopt a sort of revamped neorealism with a central character that's always interested me: the housewife . . . and victim of consumer society. (126)

This "revamping" led Almodóvar to reject the "Falangist neorealism" of *Surcos* (literally, "Furrows"), which turned Valle-Inclán's puppet theater into a right-wing moralizing, misogynist form that "saves" the younger brother from urban corruption and sends the family back home to their conservative village.

For a more politically compatible model, Almodóvar turned instead to the black humor of "absurdist neorealism," which was associated with the leftist opposition and which made a more corrosive use of *esperpento*. In the words of John Hopewell:

In the 50s and 60s Spain experienced a kind of neorealism which was far less sentimental than the Italian brand and far more ferocious and amusing. I'm talking about the films of Fernán Gómez *(La vida por delante, El mundo sigue)* and *El cochecito* and *El pisito* [by Rafael Azcona and Marco Ferreri]. It is a pity that the line has not been continued. (238–39)[6]

By continuing that line in *What Have I Done to Deserve This?*, Almodóvar demonstrated that, despite its grotesquerie, the unique Spanish tradition of *esperpento* could provide access to emotional truth.

Ricardo Gullón's description of the emotional ruptures in the puppet melodramas of Valle-Inclán also apply to these early films:

Now and then buffoonery comes to a halt, and in the sudden stillness of the moment, brought about by the intrusion of something unexpected and tragic . . . there is a change of atmosphere. And the reader, like the characters in the story, suddenly discovers he is in the presence of true drama. The puppets take on a human aspect. (133)

This is precisely what happens at the end of *What Have I Done to Deserve This?*, when Gloria says good-bye to her elder son Toni and is reunited with her younger son Miguel. Despite the comic grotesquerie of its puppetlike characters, the movie still ends with a moving emotional climax. When Gloria goes home to her empty apartment, she walks out onto the balcony and looks down at the many similar tenement buildings, as if recognizing the neorealist setting. We know she is thinking of jumping. When describing "the desolation of these housing projects," Almodóvar observes:

In Madrid life was not all fun and games. Cities have suburbs and pollution, noise and poverty. . . . When I went to work at a telephone company warehouse near the suburb of Fuencarral, every day I drove along the M-30 highway [which effectively circles Madrid]. The enormous buildings shaped like beehives that sprout up along the highway have always made an impression on me. That impression and a certain feeling found their outlet years later in *What Have I Done to Deserve This?*. (*Patty Diphusa* 91–92)

Gloria's suicidal feelings are interrupted, however, by another sudden switch in tone when she spots her son Miguel trudging "home from the hill"—the title of a 1960 Hollywood fraternal classic by Vincente Minnelli. The music swells—the same music that we will hear again later in *Law of Desire*—for the melodramatic reunion, as Miguel rushes into his mother's arms and says, with a precocious heroism: "I know about Dad. . . . I'm here to stay. This house needs a man." In case we wonder where the *esperpento* went, Miguel sensibly adds, "At first it was fun with the dentist, but I'm too young to get tied down."

The emotional intensity of this scene depends heavily on Carmen Maura's superb performance, but also on Almodóvar's masterful manipulation of *esperpento,* which becomes central to his unique tonal range. This fusion of neorealism and grotesque melodrama might lead us to recall the earlier sequence in which Granny helped Toni with his homework assignment by labeling a series of writers either Romantic or Realistic. Consistently (and comically) making the wrong choices, she labels Goethe and Byron realists; and Balzac, a romantic. The exercise calls attention to Almodóvar's own ability to manipulate the tone of this familial melodrama that slides so fluidly between neorealism and hyperromance.

Reading Bad Education *through* What Have I Done to Deserve This?

When read with retroseriality in mind, we realize that the loving mother Gloria and her sensitive gay son Miguel from *What Have I Done to Deserve This?* are later conflated into the nurturing transsexual Tina, played by Carmen Maura, in *Law of Desire,* an erotic thriller with many scenes that achieve the same kind of emotional intensity, but without using *esperpento* for contrast. This is not the case in *Bad Education,* despite the fact that it also contains a loving mother and sensitive gay son, for its only scenes of comparable emotional intensity occur within the childhood flashbacks to the 1960s, when the primary molestation occurs. Yet, *Bad Education* features an alternative form of puppetry, which is tailored to the generic conventions and coldhearted manipulations of film noir.

The puppet image occurs in the very first sequence of *Bad Education*, which takes place in Enrique's production office. On the wall there is a painting by Sigfrido Martín Begué that reflexively captures the dehumanized puppet-show dynamics in this multitiered story. The painting depicts a tall tower-shaped toy box full of open drawers, on top of which sits a square theatrical stage framed by a clapboard, with a director (like Enrique) precariously perched on a platform. The director is pictured as a yellow, long-tailed, horned devil with red-and-blue wings, who stands behind the camera shouting directions through a megaphone to a Pinocchio-like puppet with a long nose (like the lying Juan/Ángel), whom he looks at through the clapboard. Like an archive or database, the open drawers reveal what mate-

The picture on the wall of Enrique Goded's production office, a painting by Sigfrido Martín Begué.

rial goods go into the production: wooden mannequins ready to serve as extras or doubles; fabrics, hairbrush, and cosmetics for costuming, makeup, and drag; lenses, light meters, and other visual equipment for the stunning mise-en-scène; film stock and scissors for editing; and, at the base or bottom line, stacks of money and a pile of books or intertexts, including Almodóvar's breakthrough mainstream success, *Women on the Verge of a Nervous Breakdown*.

The puppet image recurs later in the film, in the crucial noir sequence where Juan/Ángel and Berenguer plot Ignacio's murder. They are standing in a Valencia museum that is lined with a number of grotesque icons whose smiling faces all wear frozen expressions and whose mouths remain open as if waiting to speak whatever lines they are given to read. Like the wooden mannequins in the Begué painting, this database of extras seem ready to be cast as doubles in a noir plot. In his "Self-Interview," Almodóvar compares the scene to the supermarket sequence in *Double Indemnity*, identifying Juan, who here sports dark sunglasses, with Barbara Stanwyck's femme fatale and insisting that it is the moment when Juan's manipulation of Berenguer becomes blatant: "Juan tells his lover that, after doing it, they shall not meet

Gael García Bernal as Juan and Lluís Homar as Sr. Manuel Berenguer facing the puppets. Photograph by Diego López Calvín. Copyright Diego López Calvín/El Deseo.

for a while. With the naiveté particular of manipulated lovers, Mr. Berenguer thought the killing would bind them together forever, but it is too late now to avoid the separation." All of the characters in these self-reflexive movies about brothers are easily manipulated puppets, especially the interchangeable siblings and lovers who are repeatedly split and doubled, as if such doubling allowed the victimized child to regain control of his destiny.

Like the Begué painting, these puppets underscore the reflexive dimensions of these three movies, which explore the tyranny and power dynamics of authorship. In *What Have I Done to Deserve This?*, the most resonant reflexive dimension resides in the publishing crimes of the murdered father Antonio, a cabdriver who forged Hitler's love letters to Ingrid Müller, a suicidal German singer who managed to lose the originals; now he resists another plot to forge Hitler's memoirs. This noirish subplot links corrupt publishing practices both to fascism (and the kind of censorship that was operative under Franco and Hitler) and to the venal commercialism and piracy that were rampant in Spain during the 1980s. Although Antonio is killed off in the film, he prefigures the paternal publisher Mr. Berenguer from *Bad Education,* who rejects Ignacio's story for telling the truth and who kills him to avoid scandal and save money. Once the priest becomes a publisher, he performs a more secular version of the same censorship and exploitation that he exercised as principal of Ignacio's religious school: for, the tyrannical publisher quite literally fucks the author, whose story undergoes a chain of appropriations and accommodations.

Brotherhood in Law of Desire

Despite the great leap in genre, story, and tone, Almodóvar recognized that the move from *What Have I Done to Deserve This?* to *Law of Desire* was essentially a return to his obsession with fraternity. Only now, the rival brothers and their relations moved into the central spotlight and the reflexive emphasis on showbiz became more pronounced. As Almodóvar himself put it:

> I focused *What Have I Done to Deserve This?* on the Mother figure. I'm focusing on the Brothers now. I didn't know what type of fraternity to opt for when I started writing the screenplay: . . . Given my temper, I turned for reference to Warren Beatty and Barbara Loden in *Splendor in the Grass*. . . . I've always been sensitive to stories of siblings; even in those with a good main love story, my interest was always on the siblings. . . . Pablo and Tina are the type of siblings working [in] show business. Like Vivien Leigh and Kim Hunter, they are attracted to the same man. And like Harry Dean Stanton and Dean Stockwell, they support one another when necessary. ("Law of Desire")

The generic move from comic melodrama (*What Have I Done to Deserve This?*) to erotic thriller *(Law of Desire)* entails a shift of dramatic focus onto the male characters and the erotic encounters between them. As Almodóvar puts it, "This is a movie about guys; from now on nobody can accuse me of only directing women" (*Patty Diphusa* 82–83). Yet, whereas women virtually vanish from *Bad Education, Law of Desire* recasts Carmen Maura as the transsexual brother, a move that strengthens the bond between it and the earlier *What Have I Done to Deserve This?*. While retaining Gloria's maternal nurturing and humor from *What Have I Done to Deserve This?*, Maura's Tina acquires a more flamboyant sexuality and, as a child molested both by her father and a priest, a doubly victimized past. The combination turns her into a diva rivaling Sara Montiel and "the premonitory shadow of Zahara."

Like *What Have I Done to Deserve This?*, *Law of Desire* contains two abused children, a boy and a girl. Although we never see Tina as the sexually abused little boy (except for a brief glimpse of his family snapshot), we do see her adoptive daughter Ada repeatedly abandoned by her lesbian birth mother, played by real-life transsexual Bibi Anderson. The doubling relationship between Tina and Ada is featured in their collaborative performance in Jean Cocteau's play *The Human Voice,* in which the Jacques Brel song "Ne me quitte pas" is addressed both to Tina's incestuous father, who abandoned her after her sex-change operation, and to Ada's mother, who is backstage. As if following in Tina's footsteps, Ada falls in love with an older man—Tina's older brother Pablo (Eusebio Poncela), who directs the play and who serves as surrogate father. In fact, all of the sex scenes in *Law of Desire* are transgenerational: between an older man and the young lover he controls, seduces, and abandons. On the one hand, the film celebrates a libertarian sexual mobility by suggesting that issues of age, gender, and biological sex do not matter, insofar as anyone, regardless of past sexual history, is capable of being sexually attracted to anyone else—especially while watching an Almodóvar movie. On the other hand, some limits do seem to hold, for a sexual love between brothers, or even between males of the same age, is avoided. As Almodóvar puts it in his press book for the film, "I also discarded the incestuous thing for being too obvious. Fraternity doesn't need sex to be manifest, and sex simplifies the stories that deal with it. *[Law of Desire]* had to be something else" ("Law of Desire").

In the light of Girard, we cannot help wondering whether this deliberate omission of fraternal incest indicates its structuring power. Be that as it may, what we see dramatized is, instead, the more traditional model of father–son

seduction. Nowhere is the paradox of Oedipal sexual mobility more striking than in the opening self-reflexive sequence—an erotic excerpt from an
inset film by Pablo, in which an older man directs a sexy young hustler as if
he were a puppet, dictating precisely how to masturbate in front of a mirror and camera—though, as it turns out, two middle-aged men have been
dubbing the voices and sex sounds to go with the action. The scene has a
powerful impact on Antonio (Antonio Banderas), a young right-wing man
in the audience whose heterosexuality is instantly destabilized and whose
homoerotic imagination is inflamed. As the inset film ends, Antonio runs
to the men's room to replicate the sex moves and spends the rest of his life,
and the movie, gaining control over the dictatorial director, even though
it makes him become equally manipulative and eventually drives him to
murder and suicide. The power struggle between the young puppetlike performer and the older manipulative director becomes more corrosive in *Bad
Education*—whether played out in church or in cinema.

As in *What Have I Done to Deserve This?*, the emotional peak of *Law of
Desire* occurs in a climactic embrace, but this time between the two men—
Pablo and his young lover Antonio. Once again, the embrace involves redemption and forgiveness: just as Miguel had to forgive his mother for sending
him away and, as if he had intuited the truth, for killing his father, Pablo
must forgive Antonio for murdering his boyfriend, and Antonio's rival, Juan
(Miguel Molina). But here, Antonio is redeemed by the sheer intensity of his
passion, for which he gladly sacrifices his life. It is this intensity, musically
amplified by the Mexican bolero "Lo dudo" (I Doubt It), that replaces religion and that is so urgently sought by all of the other characters. It arouses
envy in all of us spectators who witness (or imagine) their final embrace—
including Tina and Ada who wait below with upturned, tear-streaked faces.

Unlike the other two films in the trilogy, *Law of Desire* has no publisher;
but it does have a powerful, manipulative auteur, Pablo Quintero, the sensitive writer/director who stands in for Almodóvar and who prefigures both
Enrique and the demonic figure in Begué's painting from *Bad Education*. As is
apparent from the self-reflexive soft-core sequence that opens the film, Pablo's
authorship is a matter of control rather than criminality. He ghostwrites love
letters from Juan to himself, which Antonio intercepts and misinterprets
with murderous consequences; exploits his sibling's pain to empower his
own writing; invents the fictional Laura P., who later becomes a prime suspect in Juan's murder; and displaces his own guilt onto the typewriter as an
infernal machine. Yet this man who might otherwise appear to be an autho-

rial tyrant is rehumanized by the intensity of Antonio's love, which shifts the balance of power—even though his brother, or rather sister, Tina is still left out in the cold. As Almodóvar remarks in his "Self-Interview": "They are heads and tails of the same coin; Tina had to pay a price too high for being herself, and Pablo suffered the unbearable load of his own conscience and talent."

In the light of *What Have I Done to Deserve This?, Law of Desire* seems radical and exhilarating—particularly the aforementioned sexual mobility, which is liberating, dangerous, and edgy. The emotional range is more comprehensive; the humor more supple; the colors more vibrant; the costuming more expressive, and the music more engaging. There are moments of zaniness, but they do not detract from the grand sweep of emotions, which are kept at full force by the vibrant performances of Maura and Banderas, the two courageous changelings who are willing to take risks and be controlled by their feelings. They are the ones who bring Pablo's stories and Pedro's movie to life.

But when we look back at *Law of Desire* through *Bad Education,* the film seems darker and the sexual mobility more dangerous. As Almodóvar writes in *Patty Diphusa*: "[i]n a tone very different from the tabloids, *Law of Desire* . . . deals with brotherhood. It tells the story of brothers, who, in addition to a dark family past, share a lover, a crime and a secret" (82). In many respects, Pablo is a manipulative puppeteer who tethers Tina and Ada to a telephone in his production of Cocteau's *The Human Voice*. Antonio is more pathetic, and his relationship with Pablo more repressive. Despite the ostensible centrality of the relationship between Pablo and Antonio, Tina emerges as the central character, one who combines many of the strands from the later film, *Bad Education,* and who overcomes her serial victimization through bravado, warmth, and humor, qualities she passes on to little Ada. Not only is "Carmen's physical mimicry . . . incredible," but "Maura proves herself to be in possession of so many registers that her performance becomes an actual festival. This woman enlarges in front of the camera. She was so generous, intuitive, sincere, that for her sake alone I'm happy to have made the film" (*Patty Diphusa* 83). Although Almodóvar claims that Tina prefigures Zahara in *Bad Education,* there she is split into two transvestites played by male buddies; indeed, the legacy of Maura's performance is stronger in Zahara's friend Paca, played with brilliant comic resilience by Javier Cámara, than in the coldhearted changeling embodied by García Bernal.

Reading Bad Education *and Gael García Bernal*
through Law of Desire

What does the preceding reading of *Law of Desire* tell us about *Bad Education*? It might make us question Almodóvar's own "tyranny of authorship" and his apparent penchant for "conquering" heterosexual hunks like Banderas and Bernal, by casting them as homosexuals who perform graphic sexual acts on-screen. Almodóvar seems to have turned against Banderas, whose fame he helped orchestrate but who abandoned both the Spanish auteur and his nation. Although Banderas also plays key roles in *Women on the Verge of a Nervous Breakdown* and *Tie Me Up! Tie Me Down!* (1990), *Law of Desire* was the last Almodóvar movie in which he played an explicitly homosexual role. Once Banderas "crossed over" to Hollywood, he soon was playing straight Latin lovers and macho action heroes, whereas Almodóvar, like Enrique, kept making films of passion, at home in Spain.

While Banderas's character Antonio is redeemed by his passion, the actor Juan/Ángel, played by Gael García Bernal, in *Bad Education* remains a cold, calculating killer who is sodomized and humiliated in every version of the story. Although I am not suggesting that sodomy is inherently humiliating and recognize that this sex act can be pleasurable for both partners, in the sex scenes with García Bernal (except for the first comic encounter with the "hunky" Enrique already mentioned), the Mexican actor always has a pained expression on his face, whether or not he is in drag. Like Enrique's attempts to possess and humiliate Juan/Ángel, Almodóvar seems to enjoy transforming the young Mexican heartthrob into an opportunist who claims: "I'm capable of doing anything. I'm an actor!" Then he turns this mobility into a turnoff by having Enrique say: "There's nothing less erotic than an actor seeking a role." In this noir thriller, García Bernal's character turns sexual mobility, previously a progressive political force in Almodóvar movies, into a venal form of opportunism, stripping away its political edge and glamour.

These power dynamics take on a more complex transnational dimension with Bernal, for Almodóvar also has the Mexican actor pose as a Spaniard and adopt a "lisping" Castilian accent. Almodóvar acknowledges the connection between these two forms of masquerade: "To the difficulty of having to change sex, without looking grotesque, you have to add the phonetic issue; I wanted him to speak Castilian." Whereas I have written before on how Almodóvar frequently uses Mexican and Brazilian music and casts Latin

American actors in his films to strengthen their connection to a broader Spanish-language culture, here something else seems to be occurring.[7] The director's treatment of Bernal could be read intertextually alongside a group of venturesome films from Latin America—Alejandro González Iñárritu's *Amores perros* (2000), Alfonso Cuarón's *Y tu mamá también* (2001), and Walter Salles's *The Motorcycle Diaries* (2004)—that established the young actor's global stardom in Spanish-language works that rival Almodóvar's unique success in the transnational market. All three films feature homosocial characters in plots that are explicitly political beyond the registers of sexuality and gender, where Almodóvar has reigned supreme.

García Bernal's resentment has been widely reported in the press. According to Lynn Hirschberg in the *New York Times*:

> Bernal . . . clashed with Almodóvar during the filming of *Bad Education*: in particular, he had difficulty with some of the explicit homosexual love scenes. Neither Bernal nor Almodóvar would talk about it, but Bernal did tell me, several weeks after Cannes: "Everyone has their inner transvestite, but my inner transvestite is Mexican-Caribbean, and that's a very different way of putting on a show than Pedro's. Making this film was very hard." (4)

The Director and the Actor: Pedro Almodóvar and Gael García Bernal on the set of Bad Education. *Photograph by Diego López Calvín. Copyright Diego López Calvín/El Deseo.*

Despite, or possibly because of García Bernal's own growing stardom, Almodóvar seems to take pleasure in making the power dynamics of their collaboration very clear, even while mocking his own tyranny. Here's how he describes their interaction in his "Self-Interview":

> Q: Poor Gael!
> A: Not at all. Gael is going to work a lot and make lots of money.
> Q: How and why did you choose him after dressing up every Spanish brat?
> A: After two or three casting sessions, just like everybody else.

Even when praising Bernal for his hard work, Almodóvar claims that he gave him the most challenging role that he had ever had, as if his earlier parts were easy.

Yet Almodóvar has also stated in his "Self-Interview" that he chose the actor for his looks rather than his acting abilities: "As a transvestite Gael definitely reminds me of Julia Roberts—the same huge smiling ship-shaped mouth floating on her face"—a remark that teeters on the border of ridicule. Although Almodóvar claims that he never judges his characters, "however atrocious their behavior might be," he never denies that he judges his actors. In this case, he seems to fuse the actor Gael García Bernal with the opportunistic actor and femme fatale that he plays in the movie, finally asking himself, "Is Gael the evil one in this story?" The question of Gael as the evil one brings us back to the question we left hanging earlier: why does Juan kill his brother Ignacio?

The Question of Fratricide in Bad Education

With respect to the trope of puppets, Almodóvar has the following to say in his "Self-Interview":

> *Whatever Happened to Baby Jane?* . . . [is] a wonderful puppet show with two sisters, both former child stars, who live together despite their hatred. One of them (Bette Davis) ends up killing the other (Joan Crawford). There's a bit of this in *[Bad Education]*, although not so explicit. As kids, Juan (Ángel Andrade) envies his elder brother Ignacio for doing everything better than him. Jealousy among brothers is very common when they are young, but Juan's grows [over] time. Both want to become artists, and Ignacio is able to do everything so naturally: sing, dance, write, read, transform and act. Everything Juan would like to do, Ignacio did better. And Juan hated him in silence until Ignacio gave him reason to hate him openly when he began taking drugs and dressing up as a woman, in their hometown. Family life was like hell due to Ignacio's behavior. The mother, with a heart condition, lived an eternal unbearable situation. The father could not take the shame and began to drink, . . . until he was found dead on a frozen puddle one winter day.

As Almodóvar moves from the Hollywood intertext to the plot of his own film, he reveals the fratricidal rivalry that lies at the heart of this neorealist portrait of his family. The father's death and Juan's desire to imitate Ignacio (despite the risk of humiliation) emerge as primary motives. According to Girard, what is central to the Oedipal myth is mimetism—the son's desire to imitate his father (or, in this case, the older brother)—rather than his erotic attraction to the mother. Girard claims: "By making one man's desire into a replica of another man's desire, it invariably leads to rivalry; and rivalry in turn transforms desire into violence" (169). Mimetic doubling is thus the source of the murderous impulse, and doubling relies on splitting, the way Ignacio felt "split into two" (male and female, victim and killer) after he was molested by Father Manolo. In Almodóvar's first feature, *Pepi, Luci, Bom,* the act of rape and the resulting desire for revenge trigger a similar splitting (but of the rapist rather than the victim) into a pair of identical twins. Thus, paradoxically, Almodóvar presents fratricide as expressing a desire to be whole again—regardless of the consequences.

Almodóvar's splitting of characters in *Bad Education* is more extreme than in any of his previous films. One actor (Gael García Bernal) has four avatars: Juan, Ángel, Zahara, and Ignacio. Another character, Enrique, is split into three avatars: the child, the filmmaker, and the biker, each played by a different actor, all using the same name. A third character is split into two avatars, Father Manolo and Mr. Berenguer, who are renamed and recast so as to bear little similarity to each other, except for their desire for boys and young men. These variations become a dizzying database of doubling worthy of Buñuel.

Evil Twins and Movie Queens

At the end of *Bad Education,* Juan/Ángel is sentenced to a life in television as punishment for his fratricide, apparently a fate worse than death. In the earlier two films, it is the Almodóvar figure who is held captive in that realm: the film director Pablo Quintero appears in a TV interview, which clinches his seduction of Antonio and teaches his captive how to seduce him in return; and Almodóvar himself appears in a parodic TV sequence in *What Have I Done to Deserve This?*. But these parodic television excerpts are always offset by cinematic intertexts from melodrama that feature sympathetic siblings.

The inset film at the heart of *Bad Education,* the Francoist tearjerker *Esa mujer* (That Woman) (1968), may be the most revealing, for this is the film that the young Enrique and Ignacio see at their local movie theater, the kind that was historically displaced by television. This Mario Camus melodrama has several parallels to the plot of *Bad Education* and provides Ignacio a strong basis for identification. Sara Montiel plays Soledad Romero, a woman accused of murder who finally tells her sad story in flashback. Formerly a nun who was raped when her convent was attacked, like Ignacio, this sister lost her faith and fled the religious life. Becoming a sexy singer like Zahara, she had many lovers but then met Carlos, her one true love. Unfortunately, he turned out to be the husband of her daughter. When Carlos died, she was falsely accused of his murder, a familial turn in the plot that evokes Almodóvar's *High Heels* (1991).

Even more important than the parallels in plot are the circumstances in which the film is experienced, for Soledad's flashback is embedded within Ignacio's own flashback to his childhood. This tale of love and violation accompanies Ignacio's first sexual encounter with his young friend Enrique. It is this "primal scene," this fusion of forbidden sex and cinema, that forever makes film viewing the ultimate erotic experience in Almodóvar's world. We have seen its erotic power dramatized in earlier Almodóvar movies, but here the boys not only desire Montiel across barriers of gender and sexuality, they also want to *be* her. One becomes a transsexual and the other a filmmaker—like the two brothers in *Law of Desire*.

Montiel also provides a fantasy of transnational mobility, for the Spanish-born actress succeeded in the Mexican film industry and in Hollywood, where she married American director Anthony Mann and played in Robert Aldrich's *Veracruz* (1954) and Samuel Fuller's *Yuma* (1957), before returning to a successful movie career in Spain in the late 1950s. Thus, even when playing a victim, she still carried an aura of triumph for Spanish spectators. Like the young Ignacio and Enrique, Spanish moviegoers could embrace this empowering identification with Montiel as part of a libertarian cinematic spectatorship, one associated with sexual transgression and other forms of rebellion, especially during the repressive Francoist period of the 1950s and 1960s when censorship codes were still strictly enforced. As I have argued elsewhere,[8] one of Almodóvar's major achievements was to carry this libertarian cinematic spectatorship into the global sphere, where it became linked to subversive pleasures and to a sexual mobility that performed a sex change on Spain's national stereotype.

But whereas in *Law of Desire* these pleasures were still associated with the father–son axis of Oedipal desire, in *Bad Education* they become more directly identified with fraternity, a term whose underlying tensions will always have special resonance in the national context of Spain. Given its history of civil war and recurring conflicts between the "two Spains," fraternity connotes rivalry and violent opposition as much as it does solidarity and identification. The very closeness and consanguinity of brothers raises both an incestuous desire for fusion and a fear of interchangeability—with an accompanying guilt for wanting to be unique, favored, or superior. This paradoxical combination can unleash violence in either sibling—no matter whether he longs for unity, differentiation, or both. Perhaps that is the contradiction that lies at the heart of the "trilogy" and that helps explain why Juan murdered Ignacio: to deny his brother's superiority or difference by becoming him.

Nacho Pérez as the young Ignacio and Raúl García Forneiro as the young Enrique near a poster of "That Woman," Sara Montiel. Photograph by Diego López Calvín. Copyright Diego López Calvín/El Deseo.

In the recent discourse on nationalism, "fraternity" has proved to be a problematic term, especially in Benedict Anderson's influential definition of the nation, which has been widely applied to national cinemas; for Anderson's use of the term "fraternity" exposes his overall lack of attention to issues of gender, sexuality, and cultural specificity:

> It [nationality] is imagined as a *community*, because, regardless of the actual inequality and exploitation that may prevail in each, the nation is always conceived as a deep, horizontal comradeship. Ultimately it is this *fraternity* that makes it possible, over the past two centuries, for so many millions of people, not so much to kill, as willingly to die for such limited imaginings. (7, emphasis added)

Despite Almodóvar's earlier disavowal of the Spanish civil war and the recurring conflicts between the "two Spains," he still dramatizes the masochistic and murderous dimensions of a culturally specific fraternity: not across the grand sweep of Spanish national history, but within the cloistered halls of lecherous priests and nuns and within the hothouse atmosphere of fraternal family melodrama and dark noir romance. His movies successfully expand the term "fraternity," by "queering" it for gay and straight spectators of all genders (including transsexuals and other sisters), and by using a pervasive transnational intertextuality to extend these lines of bonding, identification, and murderous rivalry beyond borders of every kind; for, even within his domestic settings we find traces of transnational conflicts of power, particularly in *Bad Education*.

Almodóvar's treatment of Mexican actor García Bernal and of Spanish diva Montiel poses opposite extremes, which might help explain why Enrique was so resistant to the idea of Juan playing Zahara, even though he had studied with a Montiel impersonator. With García Bernal, Almodóvar uses his supreme authorial power to reassert Spanish identity by "colonizing" a younger Spanish-speaking Mexican and by casting him as the false younger brother or evil twin in a personal drama of fratricidal revenge. With Montiel, he embraces an elder Spanish straying sister—not unlike the sister in *Splendor in the Grass*—with the ardor of an adoring younger brother or transnational fan, using her wayward moves to weaken the boundaries between nation and region, victim and victimizer, the sacred and the profane.

While Almodóvar's reliance on transnational intertextuality runs throughout his entire body of films like "a deep, horizontal comradeship" (to redeploy Anderson's phrase), his retroseriality enables us both to perceive and to preserve the distinctive identity and evolving meanings of each film more clearly—even as they form new networked relations with each other. There is no danger of their becoming interchangeable—not even those "blood brothers" in the fraternal trilogy that was defined by *Bad Education.*

NOTES

1. In his "Self-Interview," Almodóvar says that "[t]he film is autobiographic in the deeper sense—I'm telling [the story of] the characters, but not [of] my life." And also: "*Bad Education* is a very intimate film. It's not exactly autobiographic—i.e., it's not the story of my life in school or my education in the early years of the *Movida,* even though these are the two backgrounds in which the argument is set (1964 and 1980, with a stop in 1977). My memories have definitely paid a heavy burden in writing the story—after all, I've lived those times and scenarios."

2. See my "Reinventing the Motherland."

3. See T. S. Eliot's *Selected Essays* and Mikhail Bakhtin's *The Dialogic Imagination.*

4. For a fuller account of Almodóvar's use of television as well as the industrial history of the medium in Spain, see Paul Julian Smith's essay in this volume.

5. I am not claiming that the association with database narrative is unique to Almodóvar. Indeed, I have made a similar argument regarding Luis Buñuel; see my "Hot Spots, Avatars and Narrative Fields Forever."

6. For an analysis of *Surcos* and a fuller discussion of the use of *esperpento* in these films, see my *Blood Cinema* (40–53, 113–26); for a discussion of its pertinence to Almodóvar, see D'Lugo (287–300).

7. See my "Pleasure and the New Spanish Mentality" and "Reinventing the Motherland."

8. See my "High Heels," *Blood Cinema,* and "Refiguring Socialist Spain."

WORKS CITED

Almodóvar, Pedro. "Bad Education." *Film Magazine* (fall 2004): 4–5.
———. "Law of Desire." [Press book.] *Pedro Almodóvar, página oficial.* ClubCultura.com. Aug. 21, 2006. http://www.clubcultura.com/clubcine/clubcineastas/almodovar/eng/engpeli_ley.htm.
———. *Patty Diphusa and Other Writings.* Trans. Kirk Anderson. Boston and London: Faber and Faber, 1992.
———. "Self-Interview." *Pedro Almodóvar, página oficial.* ClubCultura.com. Aug. 21, 2006. http://www.clubcultura.com/clubcine/clubcineastas/almodovar/eng/engsustextos.htm.
Anderson, Benedict. *Imagined Communities: Reflections on the Origin and Spread of Nationalism.* London and New York: Verso, 1983.
Bakhtin, Mikhail. *The Dialogic Imagination.* Trans. Caryl Emerson and Michael Holquist. Austin: University of Texas Press, 1981.
D'Lugo, Marvin. "El extraño viaje alrededor del cine de Almodóvar." *Journal of Spanish Cultural Studies* 5.3 (October 2004): 287–300.

Eliot, T. S. *Selected Essays, 1917–1932.* New York: Harcourt Brace Jovanovich, 1932.

Girard, René. *Violence and the Sacred.* Trans. Patrick Gregory. Baltimore and London: Johns Hopkins University Press, 1977.

Gullón, Ricardo. "Reality of the *Esperpento.*" *Valle-Inclán: Centennial Studies.* Ed. Ricardo Gullón. Trans. Miguel González-Guth. Austin: Department of Spanish and Portuguese, University of Texas, 1968. 125–31.

Hirschberg, Lynn. "The Redeemer." *New York Times,* Sept. 5, 2004, 26–27, 38–45, 70.

Hopewell, John. *Out of the Past: Spanish Cinema after Franco.* London: BFI Books, 1986.

Kinder, Marsha. *Blood Cinema.* Berkeley and Los Angeles: University of California Press, 1993.

———. "High Heels." *Film Quarterly* 45.3 (spring 1992): 39–44.

———. "Hot Spots, Avatars and Narrative Fields Forever: Buñuel's Legacy for New Digital Media and Interactive Database Narrative." *Film Quarterly* 55.4 (summer 2002): 2–15.

———. "Pleasure and the New Spanish Mentality: A Conversation with Pedro Almodóvar." *Film Quarterly* 41.1 (autumn 1987): 33–44.

———. "Refiguring Socialist Spain: An Introduction." *Refiguring Spain: Cinema/Media/Representation.* Ed. Marsha Kinder. Durham, N.C., and London: Duke University Press, 1997. 1–32.

———. "Reinventing the Motherland: Almodóvar's Brain-Dead Trilogy." *Journal of Spanish Cultural Studies* 5.3 (October 2004): 247–62. *Film Quarterly* 58.2 (winter 2004–5): 9–25.

Lévi-Strauss, Claude. *Structural Anthropology.* Trans. Claire Jacobson and Brooke Grundfest Schoepf. New York: Basic Books, 1963.

11 Blind Shots and Backward Glances
Reviewing *Matador* and *Labyrinth of Passion*
BRAD EPPS

Para Lola García y Paz Sufrategui

Whatever I photograph, I always lose.
—Mark Lewis (Karlheinz Böhm) in *Peeping Tom* (Michael Powell, 1960)

Ruptures overlooked: that's film for you.
—Garret Stewart, *Between Film and Screen* (9)

Stopping to See Again: A Theoretical Rehearsal

When I watch a film, I am struck by how much I do not see, cannot see, no matter how much I reverse and review, no matter how much I reflect on the images that, moving mechanically before me, I bring to a quasi-photographic stop.[1] Seeing a film critically entails, of course, seeing it over and again, as if the breakage or separation that is at the root of "critique" could be overcome by dint of repetition and the elusive fullness of meaning could finally be captured.[2] Yet this critically oriented repetition, compellingly close to obsession, entails an arrestation that is itself subject to repetition and, hence, to movement anew. The repeated interplay of movement and arrestation, of starting, stopping, reversing, stopping again, and restarting, resembles in some alluringly deceptive respects the critical reading of written texts. Of writing, Roland Barthes famously declared that "those who fail to reread are obliged to read the same story everywhere" (*S/Z* 16). Of cinema, one might say that those who fail to review are obliged to view the same story everywhere—though in the light of the fast-moving photogram that is, or rather once was, the fundament of film, one might also say that even those who do review are obliged to *fail to view* something as well.

Overblown as both story-bound statements are, the relation between them is by no means smooth. As Raymond Bellour notes in a reading of cinematic textuality that draws explicitly on Barthes's more literary articulation of textuality, the forward-driven movement that is arrested and altered in rereading and reviewing is fraught with difference: in rereading a passage, sentence, phrase, or word in a book, "[c]ontinuity is suspended, meaning fragmented; but the material specificity of a means of expression is not interfered with in the same way" (26). The interference of which Bellour speaks in relation to reviewing involves stilling, and hence *losing,* the motion of the motion picture. It is an interference that is at once volun-taristic and mechanistic, typically involving the play not of the reader's eyes across the printed or written pages of a book or other documents (there are, of course, written documents that appear in films), but of the spectator's eyes on a screen or monitor and, increasingly, the spectator's hands on some sort of control panel. The tactile qualities of reading (holding a book, turn-ing a page, running a finger underneath a line of words) may well be more significant than is often recognized (the "feelings" that one may experience while reading must surely include that of hands on paper), but the tactile qualities of viewing a film or, more commonly, a video or DVD, entail the willful manipulation of an interconnected yet discrete series of mechanical functions whose simplest unit is a stop, start, rewind, fast forward, or freeze button. Such mechanical manipulation, shot through with the desire to see and to know (more closely, more completely), distinguishes filmic from lit-erary critique, at least as commonly practiced.[3]

Of course, the distinction between filmic and literary critique obtains from the outset, before the critic wills, desires, or manipulates anything, in the variegated materiality of verbal and visual signs themselves. Prone to exaggerated and dogmatic deployments, usually in the name of some media-specific notion of autonomy or purity (film as film, literature as litera-ture), the distinction, not surprisingly, informs even the most sophisticated attempts to read *across* media and to find similarities between them. Garrett Stewart's insistence on literature, amply understood, and cinema as "equally differential mode[s] of representation" (2) is a case in point. For Stewart, whose interest in the relations between film and screen leads him to inter-rogate the relations between film, photography, and writing, the "shared tex-tuality" (3) of literature and cinema issues from, and points back to, the fact that "[f]ilmic frames flickeringly disappear into cinematic image rather as the fluctuations of alphabetic language congeal into units of meaning on the page, in each case awaiting normative reception at a level other than the medium's material base" (2–3). To Stewart's discerning eye and demand-ing pen, both cinema and literature, and more precisely spectatorship and readership, rely on the suppression of a material base (the filmic frame or photogram, the alphabet or phoneme) and a corresponding release, if not inflation, of symbolic meaning.

Accordingly, Stewart, even more than Bellour, "advances" a recurrent, reverse approach to cinema that strives to retrieve the fixity of the frame—which is like, but not quite like, the stillness of script—from the rush of moving pictures. As he rather heroically styles it: "in working back to an often forgotten and almost always ignored distinction in the experience of cinema—between the material base that must be dematerialized in projection and the screen effect that results—I am working uphill against a different tendency in media studies" (3); or, less dramatically: "film studies . . . does not have a material object in the strict sense until the attention of such study is drawn back to the track" (ibid.). Stewart's emphasis on the backward glance and on the return to a material object in the form of the track, strip, and photogram—part and parcel of what he calls "the specular unconscious" (1)—takes, tellingly enough, not so much the triumphant cast of a recuperation as the rather uncanny cast of a meditation on death: "whereas photography engraves the death it resembles, cinema [as the symbolic suppression of the filmic materiality that is its base] defers the death whose escape it simulates. The isolated photo or photogram is the still work of death; cinema is death always still at work" (xi).

In an age of seemingly irrepressible digitalization, Stewart's backward glance, which brings him face-to-face with something deathlike in the very materiality that he "tracks" down, is in many respects profoundly nostalgic, even melancholy. After all, his express desire to return to—and, in returning, to hold on to—something "often forgotten and almost always ignored" would seem to place him among those for whom, in D. N. Rodowick's elegant summation, "the photographic basis of cinema is coded as 'real,' the locus of a truthful representation and the authentic aesthetic experience of cinema" (5). From this perspective, Rodowick goes on to write: "[p]hotography becomes the sign of the vanishing referent, which is a way of camouflaging its own imaginary status" (ibid.). The vanishing referent, no less than the vanishing material (the filmstrip, the photo-impression of the desiring and desired body), imposes itself on the viewer perhaps most acutely when what the viewer views is *another* viewing (the ambiguity of "another viewing" is deliberate) and brings us, once again, impossibly face-to-face with the passing of time, the passing of materiality, that is to say, with death.

The oft-repeated relation between death and photography, obsessively reinforced in Barthes's much-cited work on the medium, hinges on the stilling or freezing of movement and implicates the cinema, the art of motion pictures, in a manner most paradoxical. Although Stewart and Laura Mulvey, among many others, address it, Bellour articulates the "paradox of the moving image" most suggestively:

> On the one hand it spreads in space like a picture; on the other it plunges into time, like a story which its serialization into units approximates more or less to the musical work. In this it is peculiarly unquotable, since the written text cannot restore to it what only the projector can produce: a movement, the illusion of which guarantees the reality. That is why the reproduction of many stills is only ever able to reveal a kind of radical inability to assume the textuality of film. However, stills are essential. Indeed they represent an equivalent, arranged each time according to the needs of the reading, to freeze-frames on the editing table, with the absolutely contradictory function of opening up the textuality of the film just at the moment they interrupt its unfolding. (25–26)

Amid all of the similarities and distinctions between literature, photography, and even music (Bellour also considers theater and other art forms), what imposes itself in the reversals, arrestations, and presumptive retrievals that constitute a critical review of a motion picture is the loss of a sense of movement, progression, continuity, and plenitude by which an illusion of life is maintained. If cinema, in its projected movement, does indeed defer the death whose escape it simulates (to return to Stewart's formulation), to draw attention back to the track and to contemplate the quasi-photographic fixity of the frame, to attempt to see cinema *as* film (and film *as* film), is to engage in an interruptive encounter with something that seems uncannily like the specter of death.

The material or physical acts of stopping and returning, in viewing as well as in reading, have, in short, profoundly symbolic implications. But if the mechanics of writing, as a symbolic system, are such that the reader—and, for that matter, the writer—can be swept along without attending to the meaning that lies often devilishly in the details, the mechanics of cinema, more literal in their dependence on chemical, electronic, and optical processes, are such that the spectator can be swept along in what Gilles Deleuze, glossing Henri Bergson's formulation, critiques as "a movement or time which is impersonal, uniform, abstract, invisible, or imperceptible, which is 'in' the apparatus, and 'with' which the images are made to unfurl" (1). Long understood as the effects of instantaneous and immobile sections or cuts (which is how Stewart, for all his contrarian claims, seems to perceive them), the images can also be understood, Deleuze argues, as "image-movements" and the sections or "cuts," from their very inception, as mobile (2). These "mobile cuts" are mobilized anew by mechanisms that paradoxically naturalize them in a seemingly unbroken visual flow, typically between sixteen and twenty-four frames per second—the very flow that Stewart, working "uphill" and against the grain, would reverse and resist.[4]

Now, for those films or shots that are not materially cut and for which the speed of the camera and the speed of the projector coincide, the process of naturalization is accordingly smoother and can issue in the sensation of "real time" and "real life."[5] According to Mary Ann Doane, in a reading that includes a critical gloss of Deleuze's critical gloss of Bergson:

> the movement on the screen [unfolds] in a time that is isomorphic with profilmic time, or what is generally thought to be our everyday lived experience of time— hence the term *real*. The time of the apparatus matches, is married to, the time of the action for the scene. This "real time" is marked by an apparent plenitude. No lack or loss of time is visible to the eye or accessible to the spectator. (172)

Plenitude is only apparent because it is in fact, as Doane so beautifully puts it, "haunted by absence, by the lost time represented by the division between frames" (ibid.). The division, absence, and "lost time" that are fundamental to a certain critical view of the cinema—one that, like Stewart's, does not depend on a "denial of discontinuity" (Doane 177) or on a counterintuitive assertion that all cuts are already mobile—come to the fore only by way of a recognition that no "marriage" or "match" of the time of the apparatus to the time of the action or the scene is as smooth as it may appear. In fact, even in those rare films that are physically uncut and that seem to capture things as they "really are," the interstices of the photogram and the fixity of the frame constitute what may well be the cinema's most uncanny feature: the unseen and unseeable of the act of cinematic seeing.[6]

Seeing a film critically entails, in sum, not merely seeing it over and again and, at times, bringing it to a quasi-photographic stop, but also attending to the cuts, divisions, and separations, the absences, losses, and blind spots, within the material, mechanical, yet ever so symbolic flow of images. Writing about a film critically, even with the support of a select number of stills, entails, of course, deepening the cuts, proliferating the losses, and replaying, as Bellour knows only all too well, the impossibility of restoring to the moving image the illusion of life that only the projector can produce. It is under the sign of loss and impossibility, then, that I now turn, or rather return, my sights to two films by Pedro Almodóvar.

Reviewing Desire: Division, Loss, and
the Specter of Materiality in Matador

If cuts, divisions, and separations, absence and loss, mark even the most realistic of films, they mark with still greater incisiveness those films that push
at the conventions of realist representation and that thematize, whether consciously or unconsciously, the cuts and divisions of the cinematic apparatus
itself. With respect to Pedro Almodóvar, a filmmaker whose accomplishments as a storyteller have tended to overshadow his achievements as a technician and whose penchant for vibrant visual design and flashy characters
has tended to overshadow his more nuanced interrogation of the limits of
representation, a particularly telling example of the importance of reversing
and reviewing the image as something *seen and not seen* occurs in *Matador*
(1986), when a retired bullfighter-turned-teacher-turned-murderer, Diego
Montes (Nacho Martínez), watches a video of the moment when he was brutally gored and carried—pale, limp, bleeding, and unconscious—out of the
ring. It is not the first time, but rather, as his girlfriend Eva Soler (Eva Cobo)
impatiently reminds him, the nth time that he has contemplated his own
wounding. His eyes fixed on the screen of a television set that sits raised
slightly before him, Diego plays the part of the spectator, but one who has
been so intent on reviewing his past pain, on wallowing in a melancholy and
masochistic self-sighting, that he has apparently failed to see, until "now,"
that among the spectators to his wounding one in particular, the would-
be woman of his life (and death), shared his pain with special intensity. So
intense is this spectatorial sharing that the woman continues the matador's
craft in the diegetic present, at once replaying and reliving it, duplicating
and displacing it, in the highly stylized deaths of the men that she all but
bullies into bed.[7]

The woman in question is María Cardenal (Assumpta Serna), a beautiful raven-haired lawyer who, apparently under the spell of the injured matador, engages in the ritualized erotic murder of anonymous male pickups
(their names are only given postmortem by reporters and the police), and
who, though already known to Diego, does not truly impress herself on him
until he *re-cognizes* her in his video as a witness to the traumatic event that
left a gimp in his gait and put an end to his career.[8] Interestingly, Almodóvar
resorts to a video playing on a television set in order to gesture to a more
interactive way of watching a movie, one that surely more than a few critics
have employed (lately, more likely than not in digital form), for it is in the

The victim on the floor in Matador *(1986). Photograph by Jorge Aparicio. Copyright Jorge Aparicio/El Deseo.*

privacy of his own dwelling that Diego attempts to control the image, stop its flow, back it up, train his eye on it, and try to make sense of something and someone that had heretofore escaped him.[9] Diego may have seen the video for the nth time, but in an important respect it is as if he were seeing it for the first, as if he had been blind to what he had seen before. Seated in the center of a room that he uses for his bullfighting classes and for at least one of the murders that he commits (a room with an intricately patterned design on the floor that recalls certain configurations of the solar system), Diego engages in an act of seeing that is as critical as it is common, at least since the advent of so-called home entertainment centers, but that is also as compulsive and uncommon as his and María's seemingly literal fusion of sex and death.

Critical as this instance of (re)viewing is, it is not, however, the first time that we spectators see Diego as spectator. After the titles that announce the subsidized support of Spain's Ministry of Culture and Spanish Television (TVE), the film begins with Diego furiously masturbating as he watches, on a television in the privacy of his home, a spliced-together series of slasher films that graphically depict the murders of a jumble of unidentified women.[10] As Paul Julian Smith remarks, "Diego would [thus] appear to be set up as the male gaze par excellence: voyeuristic, fetishistic, and sadistic" ("Pornography" 184). The melancholy, masochistic self-sighting of Diego's own wounding is preceded, in other words, by the sadistic sighting of the annihilation of others, all women, and the frenetic manipulation not just of a mechanical device but of his sexual organ (another "tactile" mode of viewing). "Taking pleasure in women's victimhood," Smith goes on to write, Diego "might also however (and this is confirmed by the subsequent narrative) identify with those victims and crave a similar fate for himself" (ibid.). Right as Smith is to invoke psychic functions in a film so thick with psychic fantasy, there is nonetheless something more material at issue.[11] For whatever identities and identifications are here at play, and however much a male/female divide may be both maintained or dismantled, what is also at play is, as Earl Jackson Jr. suggests, a matter of cutting, of editing: "In *Matador* the masturbating man is simply viewing excerpts of already made films, lacerated segments of films metaphorizing the dismemberments depicted therein" (168–69). Although Jackson does not tease out the material implications of his observation, he helps us to recognize that the lacerated segments of the slasher films in which Diego takes such troubling pleasure also metaphorize the cinematic cuts and the interstices of the photogram, absented, suppressed, or sutured in most films, *Matador* included, by way of the "invisible art" of editing and the mechanical movement of the filmstrip along its track.

These two instances of mediated spectatorship, both located in the proverbial privacy of the home and both marked by bodily violence, are accompanied by a third, located, as we will see, in a movie theater and also marked by bodily violence. But before turning to the scene in the movie theater, and before *re*turning to the scene with which we began (the masochistic self-sighting that is also a resighting of María), it is important to note that all of these instances of spectatorship lead, as if *inevitably*, to a climactic scene of Diego and María dying while making love during a solar eclipse, itself a darkly refulgent "coming together" of celestial bodies.[12] It is precisely the semblance of thanato-erotic plenitude which lies at the end of *Matador*, and which has led many perceptive critics to speak a bit too surely of simultaneity and reciprocity (dying together, coming together), that I shall be querying by acknowledging or attending to the cuts, divisions, and discontinuities that fleck the film both materially (i.e., the interstices between the frames and the cuts that are part and parcel of editing in general) and symbolically (i.e., the lag between the orgasmic deaths of the two protagonists and the cuts, slashes, and piercings that punctuate the narrative as a whole).[13]

Fatalistic in tone and teleological in thrust, *Matador*—which Paul Julian Smith has called Almodóvar's "most abstract melodrama" (*Desire Unlimited* 66)—dangles before the spectator the appearance, then, of an ecstatic melding of a man and a woman in love.[14] However "perverse" in its execution, the psychosymbolic force of this melding is so compelling, so embedded in the dominant heterosexual imaginary, that the aforementioned material divisions and discontinuities, already bound to loss, risk being lost entirely, swept up and away in a narrative whose somberly consolatory end point (of lovers melded in death) seems as familiar as it does ineluctable.[15] And yet, as Smith has argued, "[t]he moral of *Matador* is that there is no sexual relation: heterosexuals can achieve reciprocity only when sexual difference itself is suspended in fantasy or death" ("Pornography" 187). The observation, which is drawn from Lacanian psychoanalysis, might well be modified and extended to *all* sexual subjects regardless of their orientation, but inasmuch as homosexual, bisexual, and other sexual relations are *already* posited by the dominant heterosexual order as "impossible" (in the sense of "unnatural," "abominable," "intolerable," "outrageous," and so on), Smith has good reason to cite heterosexual relations explicitly.[16] Another good reason, perhaps indeed the best of all, is that the dominant mode of heterosexuality relies on a fantastically essentialist gender divide whose reiterative maintenance in daily life nourishes the counterfantasy of its overcoming in a simultaneous, reciprocal orgasmic coming together.

Accordingly, *Matador* points to what Smith has variously styled as "the *fantastic* dissolution of sexual difference, the pleasures and perils of an intersubjective fusion that is both desired and feared" (*Desire Unlimited* 70, emphasis added) and "an *impossible*, utopian bisexuality (in which we can, for a moment, be both sexes)" ("Pornography" 187, emphasis added). Like the more normatively configured fantasy of a heterosexual union (by which the difference between two is dissolved in the service of the one), the fantasy of a dissolution of the markers of sexual difference comes at the expense of the divisions, discontinuities, gaps, and lags that haunt the materiality of film and that, on the level of narrative, keep Diego and María apart and different even as they would come together.[17] My aim in "reviewing" such divisions and discontinuities—some general to the cinema, some specific to Almodóvar's film—is not to account for loss and make it good, but to signal instead the constitutive irrevocability of loss and, in so doing, to insist on the fantasy of plenitude that inflects cinematic continuity, romantic love, the "conservative" maintenance as well as the "progressive" abolition of sexual difference, and so on as just that: a fantasy that insists.

Long before the climactic moment of thanato-erotic plenitude with which *Matador* closes and which prompts the police detective (Eusebio Poncela) to declare the two dead lovers to be the happiest people that he has ever seen, divisions and discontinuities are already subtly in evidence: most densely in the aforementioned scene in which Diego "first" sees that he had been blind to María's spectatorial presence when he had come close to dying in the ring. Significantly, Diego's home viewing, or reviewing, does not proceed without a hitch; for, as Eva Soler berates him during what is clearly the breakdown of their relationship, Diego struggles to stay focused on the scene that unfolds before him on the small screen. First kneeling, then standing, beside him, Eva remains peripheral to Diego's field of vision and, in what threatens to become a crescendo of violent glances, gazes, and gestures, strives desperately to take center stage by grabbing his face with her hand and forcibly turning him toward her. Visibly vexed at having his attention so aggressively divided, Diego spurns Eva's desire for eye contact and the mutual recognition that it might entail, and responds by jerking his head away from her and turning back to the video, his eyes glued on images darker than Eva, part of whose last name, "Sol," spells something a little too sunny for the melancholy matador. Indeed, by this point in their relationship, Diego seems to see Eva as little more than an annoying distraction, a woman whose artificially deathly attributes—Eva repeatedly appears wearing white cake makeup and a flowing black cape and even plays dead during sex—are no match for another woman's artfully deadly acts.[18]

The other woman is, as noted, María Cardenal, whose silent scream at the sight of Diego's goring is forever captured on video.[19] María's scream is silent, in contrast with Eva's distracting chatter, perhaps because Diego has turned down the sound, or perhaps because the video is itself silent, or perhaps, more realistically, because María's voice is lost in the roar of the crowd. Then again, realism is hardly dominant in *Matador*, where seeing is buckled by a total eclipse of the sun—or, in keeping with the film's melancholy dynamics, by the advent of a "black sun"—that coincides, as already amply remarked, with the ecstatically consensual death of the two star-crossed lovers. Seeing is further buckled, and denaturalized, by the total insight of Diego's pupil Ángel (Antonio Banderas), the film's privileged spectator, a telepathic voyeur, as Smith has rightly noted (*Desire Unlimited* 67), who is also a darkly angelic visionary that sees and takes on the "sins" of others.[20] Privileged as Ángel may be, Diego is also a perceptive and passionate spectator as well as an amateur director who makes videos of aspiring bullfighters like Ángel so that he can later review and critique, with them, the finer points of what he, in keeping with tradition, calls the "art of killing." So inspiring is the maestro's instruction that Ángel attempts to follow in his footsteps by raping and murdering Eva, who, in one of the many instances of Almodóvar's fondness for fatefully marked coincidences, "just happens" to be his neighbor. Ángel's essay at criminality fails miserably, for he ejaculates between Eva's legs without penetrating her (as Eva later informs the police) and faints at the sight of a rivulet of blood that oozes from a cut that she accidentally inflicts on herself when she slips in the mud while leaving her assailant.

The dark cut on Eva's pale face—which spectrally evokes other cuts and divisions—will later be exaggerated with red makeup when she participates in a fashion show titled "Divided Spain" run by a designer named Francisco Montesinos, played by none other than Almodóvar himself. A bizarrely modish detail made to sell garish blood-red wedding gowns (marriages and matches are here divisive and bloody), the facial cut will also prove to be a source of erotic stimulation to Diego, who, after contemplating it while Eva is asleep, commands her to play dead as he mounts her. However instructive the videos of Diego's students may be, however fashionable the cut on Eva's face, the video in which Diego sees María seeing him being gored, and which includes a brief shot of a gory red hole in a man's rump, is wrenchingly amorous, for in it Diego encounters evidence of a love of which he had been unaware, a love uttered, amid the roar of a crowd, at the very moment when he came close to dying. Later, as the film's climax, Diego does indeed die, and does so apparently while coming in María, who apparently comes *just a bit later,* long enough to put a gun in her mouth and blow herself away.[21] But in once again invoking the climactic scene of *Matador,* and the temporal lag that gives the lie to the fantasy of orgasmic simultaneity (coming together, dying together, at *absolutely* the same time), I am getting ahead of myself and would do well to linger with the moment when Diego first sees María as an image emanating electromagnetically from his television set.

That Diego would set his sights on María and lose sight of Eva, who has been hovering insistently at his side, is only one of many aspects of a complex circuit of seeing in which concentration contends with interference, interruption, and distraction. The fact that interference, interruption, and distraction are here the effects of bodily presence only underscores the *magical* appeal of the mediated image: the full-bodied Eva, fluttering beside Diego, is simply no match for the blurry, partially obscured image of María on the TV screen. Part of the magic in this film that makes much of the pro-verbial mystery of love and death is conveyed in Diego's off-the-cuff expres-sion of astonishment, "no puede ser ella" (it can't be her), as he realizes that María witnessed his wounding, that she, here forever saved on video and film, was there when his life, which came so close to being cut short, was for-ever altered. His life, and her life: for it is only after his accident that Diego turns to murdering women and that María, bereft of the maestro's socially acceptable displays of tauromachian prowess, turns to murdering men. As if in recognition of the power of absence, loss, displacement, and substitu-tion in the play of desire, the sight of María's presence *then and there* all but eclipses the sight of Eva's presence *here and now* and reinforces the sense that "reality" is never as banal as when its is confronted with representation or, alternatively, that "reality" is never as magical and moving as when it is reworked and reviewed as representation. An implicit tribute to the hyp-notic, revelatory power of the cinema as a whole, the particularities of this act of viewing merit, however, another, even closer look.

On a general level, the act of stilling the moving image invokes, albeit negatively, the passing of time. As Laura Mulvey has remarked in relation to Dziga Vertov's *Man with a Movie Camera*, "[w]hile movement tends to assert the presence of a continuous 'now,' stillness brings a resonance of 'then' to the surface" (*Death 24x* 13). The relation between the "then" and the "now" is not, however, merely oppositional, but dialectical, for the "then" resonates, in its very stillness, in the "now," and in so resonating per-turbs the presumed fullness and continuity of presence, here most visibly and vocally embodied in the touchy, garrulous person of Eva. The question of the voice is not incidental. Indeed, although Mulvey does not sound it out, the "resonance of 'then'" that is supposedly brought to the surface (of what? the screen? the monitor? the film? the spectator's consciousness?) in the activation of stillness and the deactivation of movement is rife with silence. Put more laconically, muteness accompanies stillness. The sense of temporality that Mulvey underscores "is not simply a matter of movement and stillness, but of the single image as opposed to the filmstrip, the instant rather than the continuum" (ibid.), true enough, but it is also a matter of silence rather than sound, and so much so that one may speak of a resonant, resounding silence, one that is articulated only through the "pointedly foolish" trope of oxymoron (from *oxus,* "sharp," + *mōros,* "foolish"). For it is only by rewinding and pausing the video, a "vulgar" and "faster" translation of film (normally thirty frames per second instead of twenty-four), that Diego *sees* María's silent scream and is pierced by a play of passion that he had missed in so many repetitive and apparently rote viewings before.

And yet, to say that Diego comes to see María by retracing a path from something like a motion picture to something like a still photograph (the video, of course, is neither) is too simple. Diego had, we can speculate, *already* seen María flash across the screen, an indiscriminate face in the crowd. He had already seen her, but, then again, he had clearly *not* seen her, not seen her clearly. Here clarity, and the emotional intensity to which it is bound, shines through as a blurry effect of mediated hindsight, of reviewing, for although Diego is shown as first seeing María on a TV news show, where she is being interviewed as Ángel's defense lawyer, and as first seeing her "in person" in front of Eva's house, where she promptly vanishes like a genie in a cloud of smoke, it is in the reviewing of the video that he first *sees her* as the woman for him, that is to say, as his destiny. Watching the video playing on the television in his home and waving Eva away, Diego experiences a veritable *coup de foudre,* but one in which the surprise of a "love at first sight" is, in fact, and still quite surprisingly, "love at another sight." The diegetically prior sightings of María (on television and in front of Ángel's house) are thus also imaginatively posterior (Diego has, as Eva remarks, watched the video many times before), and the ephemeral "now" is thus shot through with an eternal "then"—all of which is in keeping, by the way, with the temporally involute workings of fate.

For her part, María first sees Diego—in the diegetic present, that is— after a meeting with Ángel's ultra-Catholic mother in the house into which Diego had seen her, or rather had not seen her, vanish shortly before. Although less mechanically mediated, María's sighting of Diego—which is, as we learn, a (re)sighting—is also involute: after leaving Ángel's house, María gets into her car, takes out her compact mirror, and carefully applies a new coat of bright red lipstick—the same shade of lipstick with which she stamped a kiss on the neck of her male victim at the beginning of the film before stabbing him with her hairpin. Sensing that she is being observed, María moves her eyes away from her compact mirror to the rearview mirror (*retrovisor,* in Spanish) on the side of her car, where she spots Diego watching her from his car, stationed just behind hers. Startled, María drops her lipstick, which leaves a bright red spot on her black-and-white checkered skirt (Eva, by the way, sports a black and red checkered outfit when she harangues Diego before the video). The detail, an apparently insignificant accident (but, then again, Diego's goring was also an accident), will provide a chromatic link to the video that Diego reviews later on in the film and that has been at the fissured center of the present reflections, but for the moment suffice it to say that what the spectator notices on first viewing *Matador* is, at most, a relay between the eye, the mirror, and the camera, which seems to be invisibly located behind María and in front of Diego, that is to say between the two. Visibly linked in a specular play, María and Diego are also invisibly divided, a linkage and division subtly reinforced by the fact that the spectator is offered María's naked eyes while Diego's remain concealed behind a pair of dark sunglasses—the same sunglasses that he later gives María (and that would be needed to view a total eclipse of the sun). The side-to-side and back-and-forth direction of vision is rife with reflections, refractions, and retrospections and sets things in motion for a brief but teasingly seductive trip through the streets of Madrid—each of the two characters in his or her respective automobile—that ends, momentarily, with both entering a movie theater, that third instance of mediated spectatorship which I had invoked earlier and to which I now return for a closer look.

The movie on which María and Diego are brought to stumble is none other than *Duel in the Sun* (1946), King Vidor's film of racial tension, sibling rivalry, and bad-blood love whose climactic gun battle is crosscut with shots of Diego and María partially enveloped in darkness and framed by the lush red curtains of the theater.[22] It is the first time in the diegesis that Diego and María are positioned in the same physical space—and a theatrical, metadiegetic one at that—and the first time that they are both presented as *spectators* of the *same* mediated performance. The famous "lust-in-the-dust" scene with which *Duel in the Sun* ends, and which Diego, María, and we see (again) in the space of the movie theater, is shot through with a sort of fatal foreshadowing, for in it Lewt (Gregory Peck) and Pearl (Jennifer Jones) engage in a shoot-out that leaves both of them mortally wounded, crawling through the dirt for one final, bloody, sweat-drenched embrace. A "deviant doomed couple," as Laura Mulvey styles them (*Death 24x* 77), Lewt and Pearl anticipate, in the potentially endless replays of a now classic piece of cinema, the final thanato-erotic paroxysm of Diego and María, itself now given to potentially endless replays. As Almodóvar himself put it in an early interview with Marsha Kinder, "when the ex-matador and lawyer come to the cinema, they look at the screen and see their future. It's like when you look into a magic crystal ball. When you go to the cinema, the cinema reflects not your life but your end" (41).

In both films, moreover, the foreshadowing by which a doomed sense of the future is "magically" conveyed is intensified through the figure of the sun—that source of heat and light that is also a source of shadows—that is explicitly signaled in the title of King Vidor's film and in the repeated announcements of a solar eclipse in Almodóvar's. *Duel in the Sun* is notable for its fusion of two prominent modes of cinematic ending, kissing and dying; as Mulvey puts it, "the sexual drive of desire and the death drive are woven together in the 'dying together' ending" (*Death 24x* 77). And yet, this "dying together" that is so redolent of orgasmic simultaneity is not as tight as it may seem. After all, the "dying together" is sliced by a temporal gap, with Lewt expiring a few seconds, a few frames, before Pearl. A similar gap holds for the "dying together" ending of *Matador,* rending the consolatory illusion of full reciprocity and simultaneity, of love-in-death, with the disturbing reality that, even when "together," we die, each of us, alone.[23]

We will return to the rupture of reciprocity at the end of *Matador,* but for the moment let us linger in the space of the movie theater within the movie. Pearl and Lewt dead, *Duel in the Sun* over, Diego follows María to the men's room (she has clearly no patience for what Lacan called a principle of "urinary segregation" ["L'instance" 257]), where she has gone to wash the aforementioned red spot from her skirt and where he, evidently as interested in her as she is in him, goes through the motions of urinating. This is the first time that Diego and María come *face-to-face,* but here too their encounter is caught in a specular circuit: the camera concealed naturalistically behind them, they speak to each other as they stand before a mirror, he washing his hands and she, as noted, scrubbing her skirt (echoes of Lady Macbeth?). What follows is a trip to Diego's house, where María notices that a video of Ángel is playing on Diego's television set, and where Diego gives María his sunglasses as a sort of consolation prize for the cape that she had requested. These visually charged clues in place (the video, the sunglasses, the cape), the two proceed to kiss passionately and she, in a gesture more faltering than the one we had seen at the beginning of the film, takes out her hairpin and makes as if to murder him. Wresting her decorative weapon from her (every act and instrument of violence is stylized in this film), Diego solemnly proclaims that one should never hesitate at the moment of killing. María responds by saying that she was only defending herself from sexual assault (a reasonable, legally defensible argument that would gainsay the irrational passion that binds them) and the pair separate, their lust giving way to anger. All told, the would-be erotic encounter, replete with significant exchanges (not merely a kiss, but also Diego's sunglasses for María's hairpin, which Diego wrests from her hand), has morphed into an impromptu class on the art of killing that sets the stage for Diego's video review—to which we, armed with more details, again return.

Diego's review of his wounding in the bullring is preceded, then, by a violent face-to-face encounter with María that functions as a sort of mock bullfight. Interestingly, before trying her hand at the more passionate and deadly act already described (the attempted murder of Diego), María turns on the video player, which "just happens" to have been stopped at a moment that shows Ángel practicing "the art of killing." In so doing, she subtly sets the stage for the scene in which Diego reviews his wounding. Deeply traumatic and located at the outer limits of the narrative (where it functions as its generative moment), it is a scene whose structural centrality I have been implicitly acknowledging by coyly circling it, now focusing on it, now drawing away to something else, now returning to it. The back-and-forth movement is critical here, for the various modes of prior visual interaction between Diego and María—her appearance on television; her disappearance in a cloud of smoke; the relay of reflected and refracted glances in their cars; their mutual yet separate viewing of *Duel in the Sun;* their stance before the restroom mirror—all lead, together with the moment of attempted murder, to Diego's review of the video of his wounding in the privacy of his home, a review that lifts his fitful relationship with María out of the diegetic present and back into a different, more "magical" temporality in which María's body, which Diego has already groped, is buttressed by the image of her body as it silently mouths his name. The flickering image of María, which we first see as Diego pronounces its impossibility—"no puede ser ella"—is momentarily stabilized only after Diego frees himself from Eva and stops, rewinds, and stops the video again. The source of physical distraction now eliminated, Diego is able to concentrate on what he has deemed impossible: evidence of a passionate prehistory in which María had set her sights, her desire, on him. Diego's seeing is thus a return to seeing, a seeing again, a re-vision, perhaps indeed a sort of second sight, not unlike Ángel's.

But so, it would seem, is ours, and perhaps to an even greater degree. For once Diego has rewound and stilled the video (yet another lust-in-the-dust "movie" within the movie), we can see what we, already fleetingly aware of María's obsession with Diego, could only have imagined that we saw in the grainy video flitting across the TV screen in Diego's home. Seated amid a crowd of spectators at the bullfight, María captures our attention as the camera draws close to the television screen, captures our attention not only because of the intensity of emotion that seems to rack her body but also, albeit more subtly, because she is dressed in a black-and-white outfit with a red flower in her hair, a combination that recalls, as if in a flash, the black-and-white outfit that María had pricked with a spot of red lipstick. Like the lipstick stain, the red rose is a detail that, as Roland Barthes might put it, pierces our sight, a *punctum* whose third and most lethal version is the dot that María's hairpin leaves in the hollow of the neck of her victims.[24] But if wounds and cuts punctuate the film from start to finish, the red rose—whose displaced, more active counterpart is the silver hairpin—is a detail so brief and blurry that it can only be discerned by way of a review.

And yet, review alone is not enough to *capture* the image, which proves decidedly more restive than we might expect. As the movie camera draws in on the television screen, and as María comes to the center of our attention, Diego springs into action. Rising from his chair, and approaching the camera, the camera then shifts to show him coming as close as humanly possible to the television screen, pressing his face against it and forming a kiss in response to María's mouthing of his name. María's mouthing of "Di-e-go," though silent, has the force of a siren's call, and breaks, as noted, the documentary-like realism of the scene: Diego has, after all, paused the video (we see him pressing the remote control, arm outstretched as if wielding the sword whose proper handling has been the subject of one of his classes), and yet María's stilled image springs back into movement, impossibly, or rather *magically,* as soon as Diego utters her name in response to her silent mouthing of his. Passion and mystery here trump reason and mechanics, as the two lovers appear to communicate beyond the bounds of time and space. This is perhaps the most surreal and poignant of the violations of realistic representation that mark this critical scene (the video itself, which shows the bullfight from a wide array of angles and which opens with a nonsequential shot of the wound, appears to be edited, spliced together like the slasher films at the opening of the film), and it underscores the magic that suffuses the second sights, crossed destinies, and symbolically laden solar eclipses of the film as a whole.

Live flesh made machine: Diego (Nacho Martínez) scanning the crowd as he obsessively re-watches the videotape of his accident in Matador. *Photograph by Jorge Aparicio. Copyright Jorge Aparicio/El Deseo.*

One person's magic is, however, another person's mechanical manipulation, and if the spectator shares Diego's enchantment it is because the director, along with his cinematographer, Ángel Luis Fernández, and editor, José Salcedo, has managed to convey something seemingly beyond mere mechanical manipulation. *Seemingly* beyond, for this ostensible moment of cinematic magic constitutes what Garret Stewart calls a "mimetic breach" that points the way back to the materiality of a filmic machine. For Stewart, *"mimesis may at any time be breached by a stylistic extremity clueing the viewer in to the constructedness not just of the story but of the image itself"* (17, emphasis in the original). María's image, springing "by itself" into movement after having been visibly arrested by Diego's hand, is one such stylistic extremity or, as Stewart also puts it, one of "those exceedings of narration that plunge the viewer from stylistic inflection back to mechanical process, from hypertrophic screen effect to the normative action of the track" (16). In the case of a director like Almodóvar, whom critics have so persistently associated with stylization and excess, it is rather surprising how little critical attention has been paid to what occupies Stewart's, and my, attention: to wit, "the photogrammatic moment in film textuality, the regress from cinematic narration to its animating track" (ibid.), and, more laconically, "the textuality beneath style" (17)—a textuality whose materiality is punctuated, at least in its classic celluloid modality, by the interstitial absences between the photograms. Beneath and beside all the stylized stories and narrative excesses there is, in other words, an acute and wily reflection on the technical processes of filmmaking and spectatorship alike.

While the "mimetic breach" that we have been examining in *Matador* can take us back to the material basis of film in general, it can also take us to specific films in which materiality of another sort, human embodiment, is at the center of speculation. In its interactive approach to the video player, the television screen, the camera, and the human body, *Matador* recalls, if only for one brief scene, David Cronenberg's *Videodrome* (1983), a film in which the boundaries between the real and the virtual, live flesh and machines, are disturbingly blurred and in which media prophet Professor Brian O'Blivion so memorably proclaims: "the television screen has become the retina of the mind's eye." Despite the visionary fantasies that inflect *Matador* and that are conveyed most intensely in the interplay at the end of the film between shots of a solar eclipse, close-ups of Ángel's face as he "sees," "hears," and "communicates" Diego and María's lovemaking, and medium shots of the two lovers spread out on the blood red and golden yellow matador's cape (the colors, by the way, of the Spanish flag), Almodóvar does not go as far as Cronenberg or, closer to home, as far as his friend Iván Zulueta in *Arrebato* (Rapture), an extraordinary work from 1979 in which the camera functions as a vampire that devours human images and leaves a red stain in their place. Instead, as if signaling a path that he does not quite want to follow, Almodóvar pulls Diego back into a diegetic reality of concrete objects and subjects. And yet, even as he pulls Diego back, he pushes the close-up to a contradictory paroxysm: a mechanical pause "magically" broken by a silent scream. Yet, even before María's stilled image springs "magically" into action, something mechanical continues to move: María's image is cut, that is, by a black line that rolls regularly across the entire visual field of the video. Such movement is, of course, typical of the technical difficulties involved in stabilizing a televised image on film: the differences in the number of frames per second, the contrast in ambient lighting (it is usually darker in a movie theater than in one's home), and the fact that there is a full screen refresh in film while in video each frame is drawn horizontally line by line (sixty refreshes per second, thirty frames per second). The material disjunctions between video and film, television screens and movie screens, are not without symbolic effects, and here serve to underscore the separation or disjunction between María, her image, and Diego, who is himself, of course, an image, one whose greater clarity—the effect, again, of material differences between the media—nonetheless belies the dark divisions, gaps, and absences that, inherent in cinematic representation, are typically naturalized out of sight.

"Cinema works," writes Doane, "by obliterating the photogram, annihilating that which is static. It appears to extract a magical continuity from what is acknowledged to be discontinuous. The moment of fascination in the early cinema is the moment when the still image projected on the screen bursts into movement" (176).[25] Doane's historical precision—"the early cinema"—does not mean that the moment of fascination when the still image bursts into movement has had no afterlife, that it no longer obtains, merely that it no longer saturates a film to the degree that it did in cinema's origins. Indeed, one might even argue that the moment when the still image bursts into movement is fascinating today because it reactivates an earlier fascination, one that is neither fully conscious nor fully visible, and returns the spectator to a more unabashedly magical view of cinema. Magic and fascination can be of many stripes, however, and what Almodóvar—who is fond of speaking of cinematic magic—casts in the register of unyielding passion and love, Zulueta, in *Arrebato,* casts in the register of voracious horror. In *Arrebato,* the still image that bursts into movement, reanimated without any realistic stimulus, is that of an amateur filmmaker (Will More) who has been consumed by celluloid. Zulueta, an erratic genius who did the poster art for such Almodóvar films as *Labyrinth of Passion* (1982) and *Dark Habits* (1983), mined both the material and the magical qualities of the cinema by opening *Arrebato* with a close-up of editorial cuts of a dark strip of film and by endowing the photograms with the standard power of obliterating not just themselves (in the whirl of the track) but also, and more uncannily, the human bodies they ever so discontinuously capture. Human bodies, but more strikingly, human faces: for in *Arrebato* as well as in *Matador,* for all the differences between them, the moment of fascination when the still image bursts into movement is concentrated in a close-up of the face.

In *Matador,* as noted, the face that bursts magically into movement is María's and its site of (de)materialization is a television screen, the very screen into which Diego seems desirous to fuse his own face. The face as a screen: the idea, or rather the image, although complicated here in an abyssal interplay between film, video, and television, is by no means new. As early as 1929, Jean Epstein waxed ecstatic about the force of the face, particularly when it fills the screen in the close-up. Professing to be "hypnotized" by the drama with which the spectator comes "face-to-face," Epstein called the close-up "the soul of the cinema" (9), but a soul whose photogenic revelation is "measured in seconds" (ibid.). Brief and intense, "the photogenic," which for Epstein constitutes the primary value of the close-up, "is like a spark that appears in fits and starts. It imposes a *découpage* a thousand times more detailed than that of most films, even American ones" (ibid.). The "cut" that the close-up supposes is, in its fits and starts, rife with movement, so much so that "[t]he photogenic is conjugated in the future and in the imperative. It does not allow for stasis" (ibid.). Or rather, inasmuch as it *can* allow for stasis, for stops amid the fits and starts, the close-up, "the keystone of the cinema" and "the maximum expression of this photogeny of movement," as Epstein would have it, "[w]hen static, . . . verges on contradiction" (10).

The contradiction that attends the stasis of something whose "essence" (9) is movement resembles, albeit in inverted form, the contradiction that is implicit in Deleuze's understanding of the instantaneous and immobile cut as essentially mobile. But it also resembles the contradiction that attends the very fantasy of thanato-erotic plenitude that Diego and María, like many a spectator, find so compelling. The movement whose aim is the release *from* movement (and not just a release *of* movement) and whose trajectory entails an impossible *return* to a sort of prenatal, even preconceptual, stasis (the Freudian death drive), is, in *Matador,* linked to a return to mobile images, or image-movements, whose *momentary* resolution, so to speak, depends on a stoppage or freezing, on a critical "cut" that, external to the material and symbolic cuts of film and video alike, would nonetheless accede to the images: static *and* mobile at the same impossible time.

I have been insisting on gaps and divisions, the unseen and the unseeable, the static and the mobile, because even as it is easy to be dazzled by the passionate intercourse that marks the film's climax, it seems to be even easier to turn a blind eye to the gaps and divisions that mark both the story of the deadly love affair and the material conditions of film in general. For the fact remains that, in the end, María masters the master, piercing him with her hairpin as she had pierced other men before him, and then, as noted, shooting herself in the mouth with a gun. The charge of such a symbolically violent fellatio notwithstanding, María kills herself *after* killing Diego and kills herself, moreover, in a way that removes her from an arena of highly stylized gestures in which the sword is the extension of the arm and the hollow of the neck the bodily site opened up to death, as Diego tells his students at the beginning of the film. If anything, María's recourse to a firearm likens her not only to Pearl in *Duel in the Sun* but also to the protagonist of *Videodrome* (James Woods), whose hand is literally fused to a gun, an instrument that typically allows for a greater space of bodily separation between killer and victim (even when the killer is her own victim, as here, it is not the gun that pierces the flesh but rather the bullet that is expelled from it). María's fascination with the accoutrements of "the art of killing" is at least as long-standing as her fascination with Diego's prowess *and* with Diego's loss of prowess—his wounding—in the bullring. For Diego's disastrous exit from the arena of such highly ritualized violence marks both María's and Diego's entry into the more nebulous arena of homicide. It is as if this trajectory, replete with substitutions and displacements, were conveyed to Diego in María's silent scream—a silent scream that he "sees," in review, only after María has tried her hand at killing him.

With the evidence of María's anguish at the sight of his undoing and the insight that her murderous intentions toward him were modeled on his work in the ring, Diego is now all but sure of what he wants. What he lacks, but soon finds, is material proof that María's formerly compassionate attitude—which he has seen, "then and there," in the video—is maintained in the here and now of the diegesis. After ridding himself of Eva and reviewing the video, Diego seeks María out, bestowing on her the cape that she had previously requested, and, after another verbal skirmish or two, accompanies her to her home, which she has transformed into a shrine to Diego, filled with a welter of seemingly disparate objects that function as the fetishized fragments of his life. Pilfered and sold by Diego's cleaning woman to María, for whom she "just happens" to work as well, Diego's possessions, which range from a suit of lights to a drinking glass to his sunglasses, provide Diego the final material proof that María is, for him, still in the here and now, the woman to end all women.

Although the material possessions are proof of María's devotion, it is, I repeat, the image of María, and more specifically of María watching Diego at the moment of his public undoing, that elicits the strongest response in him and that has steeled him in his resolve to be, or rather to cease to be, with her. Alone before the image of María, Diego is not moved to masturbation as in the opening scene of the film; instead, he is moved to a sort of mystified adoration that mimics María's for him. In this film that takes its cues from an amalgamation of two modes of ritualized sacrifice that have been deeply enshrined and stereotyped in Spanish culture, namely, bullfighting and Christianity, it is not surprising that Diego, the matador, renounces Eva to adore María, Eve to adore Mary.[26] What is surprising, I suppose, is that the renunciation does not announce so much a sunny redemption as a somber annihilation, or, if you will, that the renunciation announces redemption only by way of annihilation. I say that I suppose that this is surprising, because in many respects redemption in the Catholic tradition—and perhaps especially in its mortally charged Spanish stereotype—is nothing without annihilation, salvation nothing without sacrifice, eternal life nothing without historical death.[27]

It is here that I would like to draw on Jean-François Lyotard's understanding in "Acinema" of the *value* of return and repetition, the sense that sense, in cinema, involves, as one of its fundamental conditions, a back-and-forth movement, forward and reverse (reenacted, as should by now be more than evident, in my own critical writing on the film). There is, of course, a not so implicit semblance of the erotic in this back-and-forth, which Lyotard adumbrates in his reading of a nonintegrative, disruptive, even "perverse" series of starts and stops in which pleasure is most decidedly *not* the effect of a neat, straightaway ordering. As Lyotard notes, "every movement put forward *sends back* to something else, is inscribed as a plus or minus on the ledger book which is the film, *is valuable* because it *returns* to something else, because it is thus potential return and profit" (170, emphasis in the original). Relating cinematic and aesthetic value to a post-Marxian notion of exchange value, Lyotard goes on to remark that "to be valuable the object must move, proceed from other objects (production . . .) and disappear, but on the condition that its disappearance makes room for still other objects (consumption)" (ibid.). Alongside the interplay of returns, reviews, and reiterations, of appearances, disappearances, and reappearances by which a certain notion of narrativity is intricately reinvigorated, I would argue for the importance of attending to the interplays between seeing, not seeing, and seeing otherwise.

In *Matador,* these interplays are condensed in the scene of the video (re)viewing with which I have been rather fitfully tarrying, but they include, in a more or less scattered fashion, any number of other images, most powerfully that of the solar eclipse, with all its negative luminosity and its golden yellow and blood red radiance. The eclipse, which I have repeatedly invoked without looking at closely, looms large in *Matador,* where, to borrow from

Melville's "Benito Cereno," what the spectator sees, perhaps without ever see-ing fully (solar eclipses can lay waste to the naked eye) are "[s]hadows present, foreshadowing deeper shadows to come" (239). *Matador's* greatest insight, campy and overwrought as it may be, may well be that darkness is not only the other side of light, absence the other side of presence, stillness the other side of movement, but that both can appear to coincide and, in appearing to coincide, can open up onto something that paradoxically resists resolution, union, and fusion, something that divides, disrupts, or cuts a plenitude pre-sumably purchased in some ecstatic coming together.

As happy as the two dead lovers may seem to the detective and, by specu-lative implication, the director, the cinematographer, the editor, and the spectator, the final words of María, frantically clasping the man of her life that she has just killed, sound a decidedly less happy note: "Look at me; look at how I die." Diego cannot, strictly speaking, look at María, see her, cannot rewind, review, and revive something magical and mysterious between them. His dead eyes, realistically speaking, can return nothing but the desperation in María's own eyes, nothing but an agitated sense of solitude that breaks against the fantasy of fusion and plenitude. Of course, to speak realistically about such a highly stylized scene and such a highly stylized film, to speak as if reel time were here real time, is itself profoundly unrealistic. But realis-tic, unrealistic, or otherwise, it is no doubt significant that seeing is here so tightly bound not just to knowing but also to dying; that María's reiterated demand for recognition must go unsatisfied at the very moment of a satis-faction presumably to end all satisfaction; that hers, like his, is a *jouissance* whose measure is not plenitude but the sundering of plenitude, its division, breakage, and cut. In the critical reviewing of *Matador*, our eyes trained like Diego's on the unstable freeze-frame by which Diego sees María as already bound to him, we may see, just possibly, not simply a familiar fantasy but also an uncannily material process, not simply the prefiguration of the fate-ful fulfillment of love in death but also the ghostly trace of the editing table, that all-too-real site of broken, repatched dreams.[28]

Photophobia and Nymphomania: Labyrinth of Passion

The interplays of light and darkness, sight, insight, and blindness, continu-ity and discontinuity, plenitude and lack, are rich in *Matador*, but they are also, as I have been insisting, a fundamental part of cinema in its frac-tured entirety. As Doane notes, the materiality of film is such that almost 40 percent of the running time of any film is effectively invisible (172).

Accordingly, "much of the movement or the time allegedly recorded by the camera is simply not there, lost in the interstices between frames" (ibid.). This materially constitutive loss inflects or, better yet, haunts the symbolically charged encounters and misencounters of *Matador*, but it also haunts the symbolically charged plays of lights and shadows in *Dark Habits*, where Sor Estiércol's (Sister Manure's) (Marisa Paredes) mystical visions are linked to the consumption of psychedelic drugs; and the plays of an impossibly limitless visualization in *Kika* (1993), where Andrea "Caracortada" (Victoria Abril) sports a video camera atop her head so as to capture usually violent events in "real time"; and the plays between rehearsal and reality in *All about My Mother* (1999), where Manuela (Cecilia Roth) reviews educational videos for transplants that foreshadow, and then replay, her own tragedy; and the plays of showing and telling in *Talk to Her* (2002), where Alicia's (Leonor Watling) intermittently open eyes that "see nothing" are linked, narratively, to Benigno's (Javier Cámara) passion for putting pictures and performances into words; and, finally, for the moment, the symbolically charged plays of seeing and (not) believing in *Volver* (2006), where the "return" that is the title of the film is at once the return of Carmen Maura, arguably the iconic actress of Almodóvar's oeuvre, and the return of a supposedly dead mother, Irene (Maura), one of whose daughters, Sole (Lola Dueñas), cannot believe her eyes when she sees her (the returning mother as revenant) while her other daughter, Raimunda (Penélope Cruz), does not, for a long time, see her as much as smell her.

Rich as all of these films are, I would like to return to one of Almodóvar's earliest films, ostensibly far removed from the more somber, meditative plays of so-called mature works like *Talk to Her* and *Bad Education* and, for that matter, from the melodramatic abstraction of *Matador*: the raucous *Labyrinth of Passion*, perhaps the quintessential film of the *Movida*, that deliciously loose movement which, not long after the death of the dictator Francisco Franco, seemed to sweep Spain into postmodernity. Campy, cheap, and crazy as *Labyrinth of Passion* is, its "failed seriousness"—to cite only one of Susan Sontag's famous definitions of camp (115)—involves a play of blindness and vision in which, as we shall see, the main female character's sexual excess is bound to her visual shortcomings, her nymphomania to her photophobia, and her heteronormative "cure" to a review or revision of a dazzling past trauma. Here too, a rather flighty and frivolous narrative film contains some delicious insights into some fundamental processes of the art of cinema in general.

Labyrinth of Passion gets going in the Rastro, Madrid's flea market, where goods and bodies compete for the attention of consumers. And of consumers, two—Cecilia Roth as Sexilia and Imanol Arias as Riza Niro—impose themselves, from start to finish, on our attention. As the camera moves from the eyes of the protagonists to the crotches of unidentified pass-ersby, the phallus, duly veiled in denim, assumes a telling protagonism.[29] The object of both the male and the female gaze, it imposes itself as the object of speculation and consumer desire, the ultimate sexual package. But if the object of the gaze is powerfully veiled, so is the gaze itself. Sexi and Riza both sport sunglasses, which, as a close-up shot of a row of dangling sunglasses makes clear, are themselves on sale in the market (there is no solar eclipse here, no deadly "duel in the sun," only, as we shall see, the daz-zlingly hot "sol de España" or sun of Spain). Vision, desire, movement, and commerce are thus bound together from the very outset. Sexi and Riza are similarly bound, not just through their perceived and imagined desire for dick, but also through the material guises and disguises of their gaze, hid-den under sunglasses. The montage is as subtle as it is effective, because even as Sexi and Riza are bound together, they do not at first see, let alone desire, each other. Indeed, it is as if the very same glasses that conceal and enable their desire for the phallus concealed and disabled their desire for one another. This is a significant point, for the plot of this rambunctious film hinges on the movement, or better yet transference, of desire from a register of wildly errant phallic objectivity to a decidedly more normative register of homey intersubjectivity (as with *Matador, Labyrinth* ends with an orgasm, though here it announces not death but a happy, monogamous future). For Riza and Sexi only begin to renounce their fixation on the ram-bling phallus when they see each other at a nightclub, a classic site of urban debauchery, and realize that what they *truly* desire, in and out of the market, is heterosexual monogamy and something uncannily akin to the stability of the home. In the quirkily psychoanalytic language that the film engages, Riza's and Sexilia's fitful relationship is thus a case, as James Mandrell has wittily remarked, of "latent heterosexuality."

Yet while their desire may seem reciprocal, their renunciation is not. In other words, while Sexilia renounces the ostensible *variety* of the phallus (as penis), Riza renounces it, or appears to renounce it, altogether. I qualify this renunciation as "apparent" for the not so simple reason that it may also be read as a condensation, metaphorically speaking, of phallic power: Riza renounces the phallus (as penis) in order to have it (as phallus) all the better;

Sexilia (Cecilia Roth) on the prowl in Labyrinth of Passion *(1982). Photograph by Pablo Pérez Mínguez. Copyright Pablo Pérez Mínguez/El Deseo.*

Riza Niro (Imanol Arias) on the make in Labyrinth of Passion. *Photograph by Pablo Pérez Mínguez. Copyright Pablo Pérez Mínguez/El Deseo.*

and Sexilia renounces it (or at least its metonymic displacements) in order
to have it in the more constant and concentrated form of Riza or, in accor-
dance with the Lacanian distinction between having and being, in order *to
be* the phallus for Riza. Now, if the couple's renunciations are different, so are
their losses and their gains (the economic metaphors, long part and parcel
of psychoanalytic theory, are motivated and buttressed by the opening in
the flea market, a largely unregulated site of exchange). Curiously enough,
the queer Riza, renouncing more, gains more, at least insofar as power continues to be tied to normative heterosexuality: as the film's denouement
indicates, it is Sexi who follows Riza out of the darkness and into the light,
and not the other way around. Uneven as their trajectories are, Sexilia and
Riza are both passionate in the truest sense, the sense of suffering.[30]

Sexilia and Riza are passionate sufferers not just because desire, fraught
with absence and loss, can be painful, but also because they have experienced a particularly dazzling instance of it. That is to say, like the bullfighter
in *Matador*, both Sexilia and Riza have had a traumatic experience, but
unlike him, their trauma is a symbolic cut or tear in vision, not in the flesh of
the body. And yet, even though both Sexilia and Riza have had a traumatic
experience, it is she, Sexilia, who appears to have experienced the trauma
more intensely than he. Sexilia suffers, as already noted, from a debilitat-
ing fear of the sun known as photophobia, a condition that Leo Bersani and
Ulysse Dutoit, in a high cultural gesture that would surely delight the director, relate to Racine's *Phèdre* (85). An exile from the sun, Sexilia is by psychic
necessity a creature of the night. Whenever she does venture out in the daylight, she wears sunglasses and tends to wears a large, billowing cape, *à la
Vampira*—a costume that resembles, interestingly enough, the one that Eva
Soler dons in her last visit to Diego's house in *Matador*.

In the Rastro, the most visible locus of the labyrinth of desire, Sexilia
does not see Riza, nor he her. Instead, she "first" sees him when he is singing
in a nightclub where Almodóvar himself is performing ("first" is in quotations because, as with *Matador*, it is later revealed that they had seen each
other at a much earlier point in time). Riza also performs, prancing onstage
for all to see, yet masked in makeup and going by an assumed name. As
the song "Gran ganga," or "Big Bargain," plays, Sexilia watches and listens.
The song is replete with economic and psychosexual references (sales, deals,
and steals, yet also "sex, luxury, and paranoia"), but its refrain is considerably more ponderous: "¿Quién soy yo y adónde voy? ¿De dónde vengo y qué
planes tengo?" (Who am I and where am I going? Where am I from and

what are my plans?). Mesmerized by a man who is not quite himself (he is incognito throughout most of the film), Sexilia is in many respects the ideal (feminine) spectator: fascinated, oblivious, indifferent to the truth, and all aglow with desire.

Feminist film theorists since Laura Mulvey have grappled with the perils and pleasures of female spectatorship. One of the perils and pleasures involves the presumed passivity of women watching men (it is not a presumption that I share), but another, arguably less marked by gender, involves distraction, diversion, and a disturbingly entertaining displacement. As Sexilia sways to the music, she turns her head slightly and is suddenly blinded by a stage spotlight. She staggers and puts her hand before her eyes, unable to bear the intensity not just of the light, but of the sight that has cut quickly across the screen and, apparently, across her mind's eye: a seemingly incongruous image of a young girl walking along a sunlit beach. The cut is important, because Sexilia's photophobia is motivated, as the film later reveals, by an adolescent misrecognition of Riza. But here, in this explicitly staged scene, Sexilia, like the spectator, does not yet see the connection; she does not yet see that what flashes forth as love at first sight and blinds her to all other men is actually love at another sight, as in *Matador*. This "other sight" is, tellingly enough, a delayed, retrospective event, a *flashback*.[31]

As adolescents, Sexilia and Riza once found themselves on the same beach; they were playmates whose games had, as even the silliest Freudian knows, serious erotic implications. In a more extended flashback, Sexilia is buried up to her neck in the sand (the raw material of the glass that, once tinted, makes sunglasses and that, once tained, makes a mirror), and asks Riza to make a hole for her to breathe through. He obliges by screwing one of his fingers into a spot just above her genitals. Left alone, these early erotic games might well have issued into a normative sexual partnering, into a presumptively monogamous heterosexuality. Such, at any rate, is what the film so slyly suggests. And yet, these games, and their players, are *not* left alone, but are interrupted, diverted, and altered. The agent of interruption and alteration is Toraya, the ex-empress of the imaginary nation of Tiran and the ex-wife of Riza's father, the deposed emperor whose unstable situation supposedly motivates Riza's incognito status and assumed name (the saga of the Shah of Iran is clearly at play here). As performed by the heavily accented and fabulously campy Helga Liné, Toraya is the quintessentially nasty stepmother, bent on seducing her stepson in compensation for the loss of his father. As the two children play, Toraya bursts onto the beach, throws sand in Sexilia's eyes, and drags Riza off into the bushes to play "hide-and-seek." Riza struggles to get away, but Sexilia mistakes his movements for those of passion. Believing that Riza has rejected her for Toraya, Sexilia rushes to her father, an eminent gynecologist and pioneer in artificial insemination named Doctor de la Peña (Fernando Vivanco), who, eager to speak to the emperor, shakes her off. She falls to the ground, looks up, and is blinded by the summer sun. Dazed for a moment, she gets up and turns to a group of boys who ask her to play house, to be "la mujer de todos," everyone's wife. Riza, finally freeing himself from Toraya, rushes back to Sexilia, only to find her surrounded by the boys. Believing that Sexilia has rejected him, Riza, in yet another compensatory gesture, turns to a boy who has left the group, walks off with him arm in arm, and the scene ends.

Silly as it is, there is clearly more here than meets the eye. The two basic mechanisms of this scene, a flashback, are misperception or misrecognition (méconnaissance) and displacement, mechanisms that resonate on both psychoanalytic and cinematic registers. Both Sexilia and, to a different degree, Riza see things as other than they are, and both, in so seeing them, turn to something, or someone, else. To complicate matters, both the image and the movement of and from the image are laden with violence, be it Riza's struggle to free himself from Toraya or Sexilia's struggle to hold on to her father. Violence, both physical and symbolic, is thus at the root of both Riza's and Sexilia's promiscuity, their continuous turning from one sexual sight (and site) to another.[32] Violence, and the pain, frustration, and aversion it entails, spawns, it would seem, Riza's homosexuality as well. Interestingly, the very promiscuity and homosexuality that led Kinder to declare that the film "positively bristles with vibrant color and a wildly comic sexual energy" (34) are plotted as pathological and hence as problems to be overcome. Passion may be labyrinthine, but it apparently needs to be set straight. Whether or not the story of such straightening should itself be taken straight is, however, another question.

Structure is here, as it is so often elsewhere, thick with morality, for straightness is not only a characteristic of classic narrative cinema (or at least an idealized abstraction of it) but is also a virtual synonym for sober, upright, reproductive heterosexuality. In both instances, straightness stands in contrast to the nonintegrative, disruptive, and perverse series of starts and stops that, as we have noted earlier, Lyotard examines. The problem with straightness is not, or not only, that it is "deceptive" (inasmuch as it denies the labyrinthine processes of subjectivity and, moreover, the discontinuities and divisions, cuts and returns, of the cinema itself) or even that it is "immoral" (inasmuch as it denies difference and diversity), but rather that it goes against what Almodóvar is *apparently* all about. Almodóvar, or rather his work, seems here to shy away from a wildly irreverent queerness at the very moment at which he and his work were, to many a spectator's eye, most vigorously associated with it. For those fond of reading backwards— or of reviewing—in order to extract a narrative of development and destiny, one might go so far as to venture that the wild *Labyrinth* anticipates more sober endeavors like *The Flower of My Secret* and *Talk to Her,* but it is undoubtedly "safer" to venture only that *Labyrinth of Passion* advances a portrait of Sexilia and, less visibly, of Riza as traumatized subjects in need of a cure that takes the form of their loving coupling, the *reconstitution* of a loving coupling that was earlier missed.

And yet, to see *Labyrinth of Passion* or, for that matter, any number of the "mature" films of Almodóvar as following, let alone endorsing, a straight-and-narrow mind-set is to impose a teleological reading on both the individual films and the director as auteur. Indeed, the very dynamic of trauma and cure is not so much straightforward as recursive, caught in a back-and-forth movement that, attentive to cuts and wounds, understands the cure as the *memorialization of trauma* whose most notable emblem may well be a psychic and/or physical scar. Presumably removed when remembered, trauma is here a brilliantly banal moment: banal, because it adheres to a well-established Freudian script (desire is frustrated, disavowed, and displaced), and brilliant, because it plays with a wounding of vision itself.[33] "Trauma" derives, after all, from the Greek for "wound," itself from a form of the verb meaning "to pierce" (we might also recall, at this juncture, the stilettos, swords, cuts, and wounds of *Matador*). Sexilia's trauma, strikingly suited to the cinema, is hence a psychological wounding of the eye, a violently symbolic piercing of vision. This wounding centers on the rays of the sun, but is adumbrated in the scene where Toraya flings sand into Sexi's eyes. Specters of Oedipus and the Sandman are no doubt tempting, but given the gender of the players, it is the spectacle of hysteria that is arguably more imposing.[34] I have explored what I call the hysterical histrionics elsewhere,[35] and so here I would note only that while Freud describes hysteria as a "psychic trauma, a conflict of affects," and "a disturbance in the field of sexuality" (*Dora* 39), hysteria is also, as Freud makes clear in his reading of Jean-Marie Charcot, a disturbance in the field of vision.[36] Disturbance is itself a loaded concept. It is the enemy of straight development, whether of cinematic realism or sexual convention; and yet it is its ally, legitimating straight development by qualifying whatever disturbs it as a disorder, deviation, or deviance.

The disturbance of sex and sight is, in *Labyrinth of Passion,* only fully recognized and reversed through an act of remembrance. The retrospective, reflective, specifically cinematic nature of this act of visual disturbance entails a review and reordering by which the pieces of Sexilia's and Riza's lives fall into place. Not surprisingly, the act of remembrance occurs toward the close of the film, and functions as its most visible climax; the *invisible* climax is the sexual union of Riza and Sexilia, conveyed by an orgasmic voice-over of the freeze-framed image of an airplane shortly after takeoff, something like Almodóvar's spin on the train in the tunnel with which Hitchcock ends *North by Northwest* (1959). What follows this act of remembrance (which I shall describe directly) is an act of communication in which Sexilia tells her story to Queti (Marta Fernández Muro), the daughter of a dry cleaner who, in order to escape her father's drug-induced advances toward her (incestuous rape, that is), agrees to trade places with Sexilia by cosmetically altering herself so as to become Sexilia's mirror image (a fact that the film underscores by placing the "original" Sexi and her "copy" side by side before a mirror). What precedes the act of remembrance (which, I repeat, I shall describe directly) is a two-tiered stimulation of memory, first with Toraya and then with Susana (Ofelia Angélica), the Argentine Lacanian analyst, who is obsessed with bedding Sexilia's father.

The act of remembrance, whose content I have been skirting in an attempt to replicate in words the labyrinthine nature of Almodóvar's presentation of desire, goes as follows: Sexilia, gleeful about her newfound love (as opposed to sex), returns to Riza's room and finds Toraya dressing. Startled by such a classically postcoital scene, Sexilia confronts Toraya, who promptly informs her that she has just become Riza's "first woman," in other words, that before Toraya Riza had been a virgin to heterosexuality. In the course of their argument over Riza, Toraya opens her compact, whose tiny mirror catches the filtered light of the sun. Aware of Sexilia's photophobia, Toraya turns the cosmetic mirror aggressively toward her rival's face. As Riza enters to explain, Sexilia collapses into a corner of the room, blinded by Toraya's game of little mirrors. Dazed, almost hypnotized, her eyes staring blankly out before her, Sexilia asks if all the sex and lies can possibly have anything to do with love, pulls herself up, brushes Riza off, and runs out into the street.[37] We next see her—out of breath and muttering "el sol de España" (the Spanish sun)—at the office-home of her Lacanian analyst. Well schooled in such crises, the analyst does not miss the significance of Sexilia's words, and quickly opens the shutters of a window, as if replaying in a broader yet more controlled manner the shutter of the camera and, more pointedly, the *compact,* cosmetically marked scene of blinding light that preceded it. With the shutters pulled open and the Lacanian analyst babbling in excitement, the bright light streams in, but this time it is direct and natural instead of indirect and artificial (reflected and refracted in a cosmetic mirror). This time, moreover, Sexilia does not put her hand before her face as she did when she watched Riza perform onstage and was dazzled by yet another artificial light. This time, sitting before Susana, Sexilia does not screen her sight, her memory. Rather, she gives herself over to her analyst, heeds her call to talk, and proceeds to review and remember the scene of childhood trauma.

As is the case with so much of *Labyrinth of Passion,* Sexilia's analytically framed act of remembrance is farcical yet strangely painful. "The hysteric suffers mostly from reminiscences," Breuer and Freud said (4), and yet the "cure" is reminiscence as well. Susana stimulates in Sexilia a secondary vision, or re-vision, that is part of a visually aided talking cure. She redirects, that is, Toraya's insightful discovery in order not to harm, but to help Sexilia, specifically to help her to love. Sexilia's fear of light is bound to her love of sex, her photophobia bound to her pornophilia (or, as her name suggests, her sexophilia). What blinds her, binds her, however, for the sun that blots out both her father and Riza exposes Sexilia to a series of surrogate attachments—the myriad men that she picks up in the Rastro and elsewhere. For their part, these other attachments blind her to the fact that she remains bound, as Susana herself suggests, to both Riza and her father.[38] And lest these bonds appear hopelessly incompatible, Almodóvar comes up with an absurdly effective solution: as if from some photographic negative, Sexilia is duplicated, as noted, over and onto the body of her newly found friend Queti. Cosmetically altered to look *exactly* like Sexilia (Cecilia Roth takes over both roles), Queti-cum-Sexilia promptly seduces Sexilia's father as the now "original" Sexilia runs off with Riza. If what traumatizes Sexilia is her apparent rejection by Riza *and* her father, she overcomes this trauma, sees it and sets it right, by apparently attaching herself, *completely,* to both.

Appearances can be deceiving, as María tells Diego in the men's room of the movie house in *Matador,* especially when, as in *Labyrinth,* what is disturbing (incest is real) is reassuringly asserted as merely an appearance and when what is reassuring (incest is a simulacrum) is disturbingly asserted as real. The movement of reality and appearance is dizzying, but it bears an uncanny resemblance to the history of hysteria. This history, at least in its modern versions, views hysterical symptoms as arising from either suggestion and simulation or actual events. Freud, going further, linked hysteria to seduction, particularly the incestuous seduction of daughters and fathers; his notorious abandonment of the real basis of seduction in favor of a constellation of psychic fantasies, wishes, and desires remains, as is well known, a subject of much debate. As Laplanche and Pontalis note (via P. Janet), Freud largely subscribed to the view of hysteria as a "malady through representation" (195). The stakes of representation are of a different order for Almodóvar, needless to say. There, on the screen, the audience sees—and yet does not see—incestuous seduction as the resolution of disorder: Sexilia's father overcomes his fear of sex; Sexilia can be with Riza without, in a sense, leaving her father; and Queti can leave *her* father without relinquishing an incestuous image of *the* father. This last point is especially problematic: Queti leaves her father because he forces her to have sex with him, rapes her. And yet, inasmuch as she immediately takes up (with) another father, she suggests a disturbing convertibility, or complicity, between rape and seduction.[39] At one moment Sexilia even suggests that Queti may actually enjoy rape, and though Queti immediately rejects such a suggestion, Almodóvar's film does not. Its playfully subversive tone not withstanding, *Labyrinth of Passion* is here, it appears, complicit with an extensive masculinist tradition that, slyly strategic, converts seduction into rape and rape into seduction. The fact that it replays this tradition as high farce is, however, one of its most subversive moves, hollow as it may ultimately be.

So convoluted are these family romances that the apparent moment of resolution is in many respects what is most disturbing, though resolution in the form of the daughter's seduction (Queti as Sexilia with Sexilia's father) and in the form of heterosexual monogamy (Sexilia with Riza) are disturbing in considerably different ways. The former is obviously not an accepted sign of the status quo, while the latter obviously is. This does not mean that incest (whether seduction, rape, or both) is a sign of resistance to the status quo, far from it. In fact, it is my contention that *both* the (apparently) incestuous relationship and the heterosexually monogamous relationship may be seen as powerful abdications of resistance and critique. Seen in this light, Almodóvar's film, for all its farcical fancy, is not without some rather labyrinthine troubles of its own. Opening with the vagaries of vision and continuing with a procession of wild and crazy images, it closes with the image of father–daughter incest and monogamous heterosexual love. This trajectory may well be ironic, quite probably is, but part of the irony may also be that the trajectory ensures the film's integration into a wider market (especially after the success of *Women on the Verge of a Nervous Breakdown*), enabling the general public to see it, titillated with the image of something subversive, without being challenged too strongly. In saying this, I do not mean that the film is comfortably complicit with the status quo, or that it is complicit in all scenes and to the same degree, or even that its value must be measured in terms of social resistance. What I am saying is simply that the restive and rebellious are often restrictive, the silly often quite socially serious, and vice versa.

The flipping, which is ethico-political as well as structural, is also evident in the depiction and narration of Sexilia's trauma. On the one hand, the film, through the traumatic flashback, shows homosexual and nonmonogamous sex to be detours or deviations, the "tragic" effects of an original misperception and displacement; on the other hand, it shows monogamous heterosexuality to be a re-vision, a re-cognition, or an afterthought, that closes (down) the comedy. Such flipping can make for some rather flip responses, the most insistent being an aversion to ethics and politics in the name of "pure" comedy. Almodóvar himself has asserted that the film is amoral, a parody of romantic comedy, and that the biggest error has been to take it seriously (Vidal 64, 43). Scandal, so often associated with Almodóvar, is accordingly diffused in such a statement—all too neatly. In such an easy amoral context, taking Almodóvar seriously may thus be the only scandal left.[40] Then again, if his latest films are any indication, he has long come to take himself, and his craft, seriously—and to have fun while doing so.

Fun and seriousness: any review of Almodóvar's work, particularly his earlier work, must grapple with the sense and suspicion of taking *too* seriously not just the melodramatic abstraction of a film like *Matador* but also the lighthearted, tongue-in-cheek post-Freudianism of *Labyrinth of Passion*. It must grapple, more pointedly, with the retrospective shadow, so to speak, of more acclaimed and "accomplished" recent films that alternatively lift (into the light) and submerge (into the shadows) earlier films such as *Labyrinth of Passion*. Along with the rewindings, reviewings, and revisions that are variously at play in *Matador* and *Labyrinth of Passion,* there are more overarching returns and revisions that bear on Almodóvar's work as a fissured whole. But this, as I come to an inconclusive conclusion written under the sign of loss and impossibility (including, of course, the much-trumpeted loss of celluloid itself), is something to which we will have to return, something which we will have to review, over and again, amid all the unseen and unseeable gaps and divisions, all the dark shots and bright spots, as time goes by.

NOTES

1. Pausing a movie, stilling an image, is perilous if not impossible when the movie and the image are in the form of a 35 mm or 16 mm film and when a projector is involved. The projector not only moves and produces motion (and the illusion of motion), but it also produces heat, so much so that a stilled image in its grip can melt or burn, thus damaging the film and provoking even more gaps, divisions, and losses than those already contained in the filmstrip. Studies of film stills typically entail a transference, or translation, to slides and slide projectors, a recuperation of the photographic status of the photogram, and/or a return to the dispositions of the filmstrip. I want to thank my colleague, coeditor, and friend Despina Kakoudaki for her insightful reminders about the materiality of film and, by extension, the materiality of the act of viewing.

2. As Garrett Stewart notes, "[t]he photogram is the individuated photographic unit on the transparent strip that conduces in motion to screen movement. Shot past the projector's gate, the photogram propagates itself as film only in order to vanish on-screen. By definition, then, the photogram has no ordinary place in the movies, no prevalent role in the cinematic institution. It is mostly on film alone—though with exceptions that test and prove the rule of its suppression" (5).

3. In the words of Laura Mulvey, "[c]inema, as it ages, has become more and more the object of 'I desire to know,' most obviously in the expansion of film and related studies over the last 25 years [Mulvey's text is from 2006], but also through the new availability of old cinema through new technology. At the same time, cinema's aesthetic polarities, debated throughout its critical history, seem to become less important in their differences and more important in their dialectical relations with each other. Rather than diverging into an either/or, for instance, specificity of the filmstrip versus illusion of movement, fiction versus document, grounding in reality versus potential for fantasy, these aspects of the celluloid-based medium move closer together" (*Death 24x* 12). It is just this interplay between the material and the symbolic, the filmstrip and the illusion of movement, that I will be exploring in the present essay. The "desire to know" that Mulvey deploys, via Christian Metz, points, moreover, to the fetishistic and libidinal charge of watching a movie and to the variegated "feelings" that the act of (re)viewing elicits.

4. The idea of film as arising from photographic images is as widespread as it is contested. V. F. Perkins, in his now classic *Film as Film*, observes that "Bazin and Kracauer share the view that film is 'essentially an extension of photography' [Kracauer] and that as a result 'the nature of photography survives in that of film'. The position is taken for granted, not argued; it is both theoretically misleading and historically false. Movies owe their existence to a peculiarly mixed marriage between the camera, the magic lantern and the optical toys of the nineteenth century. . . . Magic lantern shows provided the ear-

liest approximation to cinema: the use of superimposed slides provided an illusion of movement as, for example, a night scene dissolved into a daylight one" (41). Interestingly, Rudolph Arnheim, in an essay titled "The Thoughts That Made the Picture Move" written in 1933 and included in his *Film as Art,* also stressed continuity, albeit without recourse to philosophy, Bergsonian or otherwise: "the motion picture is not a synthetic agglomeration of individual images but based on a recording process that is as continuous and unitary as the movement of the photographed objects. The dividing of the movement into single 'frames' (just as their subsequent unification in the projection) is nothing but a technical detail, which does not concern the nature of the procedure. There is, then, a difference in principle between the recording of visual motion and the immobile images of photography, painting, or sculpture. Film is more than a variation of the immobile image, obtained by multiplication: it is fundamentally new and different" (179–80). Although what is "new and different" in 1933 is not so in 1986, when *Matador* appeared, let alone in 2007, when this essay was written, it is nonetheless intriguing that Arnheim, after having rehearsed the technical history of film, discounts the division and subsequent unification of movement into single frames as a mere technical detail. Indeed, it is almost as if newness and difference depended on the suppression of any "fundamental" similarity between film and photography. And yet, as Stewart, Doane, and others remark, the similarity persists, returning, somewhat uncannily, to disrupt the continuous and unitary process on which Arnheim here implicitly makes the art of film hinge.

5. Even those rare films that are comprised of a single shot are "cut" inasmuch as they take the material form of a strip of framed and segmented images.

6. Compelling as Deleuze is, Doane argues that he "has a stake in the idea that the cinema gives us real movement, for he allies himself with Bergson's claim [in *Matter and Memory,* not in the later, more cinematically engaged *Creative Evolution*] that both movement and time constitute irreducible continuities. The investment in plenitude and consequent rejection of any underlying lack or absence are clear" (177). Doane stresses instead "that a belief in the cinema's alliance with real movement rests on a denial of discontinuity, or of the significance of the distance separating the photograms and incarnated in the frameline" (ibid.). Stewart, for his part, designates Deleuze as "at once a magisterial signpost and a massive roadblock. He [Deleuze] theorizes the photogram, in relation (via Bergson) to the mind's photographic sense of emplaced matter, at a philosophical depth unapproached in previous commentary. But he then fends off its implications in his subsequent work on movement and temporality in cinema *as it appears to view.* The photogram gets lost, as in viewing it must, at what Deleuze everywhere calls, borrowing Bergson's terminology, 'the plane of immanence'" (85–86, emphasis in the original).

7. A deadly principle of symmetry, and of heterosexual desire, seems to inform the murderous activity of the two protagonists: she kills two men; he kills two women, all fleeting sexual partners. Only one of the murders that María commits is depicted on-screen and it is crosscut with Diego's class on "the art of killing" and, more particularly, with close-ups of his fainthearted student Ángel as he seems to see, along with the audience, what María *is doing.* As with María, only one of the murders that Diego commits is depicted on-screen, and it too is crosscut with close-ups of Ángel as he "sees," again along

with the audience, what Diego *had done*. The difference is not merely one of gender but also of time: in the first case, the murder is presented as occurring at the same time that Ángel "sees" it, whereas in the second case, the murder is presented as having occurred before Ángel "sees" it. In the first case, vision is (impossibly) simultaneous, and in the second case it is (impossibly) retrospective.

8. As the physical reminder of his having been violently penetrated by a bull's horn, the bullfighter's gimp suggests castration and even homosexuality (as in the Spanish phrase "más maricón que un palomo cojo" [queerer than a lame pigeon]). Although Diego appears to be an object of Ángel's polymorphous desire, it is the police detective played by Eusebio Poncela who most densely embodies the linkage of limping and homosexuality. Indeed, whereas Diego's gimp is the effect of a real physical event, the detective's gimp is explicitly articulated as the effect of a psychic problem.

9. As Mulvey notes: "The year 1997 saw the first marketing of film on digital format. The resonance of ageing, and of death, associated with the cinema's centenary coincided with the arrival of a technology that created a divide between the 'old' and the 'new' media. However significant the development of video had been for film, the fact that all forms of information and communication can now be translated into binary coding with a single system signals more precisely the end of an era. The specificity of cinema, the relation between its material base and its poetics, dissolves while other relations, intertextual and cross-media, begin to emerge" (*Death 24x* 18).

10. As Marvin D'Lugo notes, Almodóvar availed himself of "special subsidies from the Ministry of Culture's Miró law (named for the director of the socialist government's Film Office who spearheaded the policy of energetic government film subventions)" (45). Pilar Miró was herself, by the way, a filmmaker.

11. Claiming that "cinema was founded on the male castration trauma" and an accompanying fetishistic disavowal and displacement, Smith reads Diego's accident and María's replay of his craft in terms of castration and fetishism, where cuts, disavowed or not, are of a more phallic order ("Pornography" 180). As illuminating as I find Smith's psychoanalytic reading, the cinema is founded on cuts of a more material order than "the male castration trauma."

12. Nothing, or at least very little, "just happens" in *Matador*, whose original title was "Lo inevitable" (The Inevitable). Whatever choices the characters appear to make in the film, they are shadowed by fate—as when a flower vendor (Bibi Anderson) "reads" Diego's hand and quickly steps away from him. Diego, for his part, responds with a knowing wink: he is, after all, about to give himself over to the ecstatic death that is his destiny.

13. Marvin D'Lugo, undoubtedly one of Almodóvar's most discerning viewers, is one of a number of critics who sees the eroticized death of Diego and María as simultaneous and reciprocal: "Aided by Ángel's powers of foresight, Inspector Del Valle tracks Diego to María's cottage, only to arrive just as they reach simultaneous orgasm and kill each other at the exact moment of a solar eclipse" (48). However, as we shall see, Diego and María do *not* kill each other (she kills him and then herself) and, as in the first and only of María's murders depicted in the film, María seems to come, or to continue to come, a little later.

14. Abstractly melodramatic, the film effects what Smith calls "a certain banalization of the perverse . . . : it is Ángel's neurotic mother who is stigmatized for her unacceptable behavior in rejecting her son" ("Pornography" 185).

15. By invoking a heterosexual imaginary, I do not mean to discount the homoerotic plays that run throughout the film. Two examples will have to suffice: Ángel is explicitly cast and questioned as "potentially" homosexual, and the detective who investigates the case is shown through subjective camera work to be especially interested in the crotches and rumps of the male students who practice their bullfighting passes.

16. In *Le Séminaire XX,* Lacan makes one of the most celebrated and polemical of his many aphoristic claims: "il n'y a pas de rapport sexuel" (17).

17. Smith follows his assertion that *Matador* points to a dissolution of sexual differ-ence by saying that "María marks the place of her penetration with a lipstick trace on the male neck; and it is to the men's toilet that she retreats in a cinema to wash off a red lipstick stain on her black and white business suit. If sexual difference is, as María sarcasti-cally claims to Diego in this sequence, merely a matter of appearances, then subjects may choose to place themselves on whichever side of the phallic divide they wish. It is symp-tomatic the whole of this exchange is shot in a mirror" (*Desire* 70). Alluring as the idea of the abolition of sexual difference is, it is also true that the film, even as it dangles before us the image of a masculinized woman and a feminized man, lingers on the *differences* between the female body (offered up almost entirely to the camera in a close-up, full frontal nude) and the male body (more discreetly couched in the shadows or clothes) and subordinates choice—as in "subjects may choose to place themselves on whichever side of the phallic divide they wish"—to instinct or destiny. The attention to differences is critical, of course, to the fantasized dissolution of differences in what Smith calls "a unique moment of reciprocity" (ibid. 76). According to Smith, "[a]s Diego penetrates María, she plunges a hairpin into the nape of his neck and, entreating him to look at her, fires a gun into her mouth" (ibid.). The word *entreat* is well chosen, for it effectively troubles the assertion of any reciprocity that is not limited to a unique, fleeting moment: María "entreats" Diego to look at her, but he cannot, because he is already dead—hence the passion and poignancy of her entreaty. If there is reciprocity of desire and intention, there is not, strictly speaking, reciprocity of act, for the look in a dead man's eyes cannot reciprocate the look in a live woman's eyes, even when the live woman is about to blow her head off. In other words, it is easier to imagine or even to intend reciprocity than it is to achieve it, let alone secure it, hence Smith's use of such qualifiers as "fantastic" and "impossible." After all, Smith ends his reading by reiterating a division: "*Matador* speaks in spite of itself of a crisis of division which is as much national as it is libidinal, which must also find its place in the frenzy of cinematic visibility" (ibid. 77)—and, I might add, invisibility.

18. Eva's attempt to secure Diego's attention is not without motivation: she is trying to tell him that she has been offered a modeling job in Japan. The passing reference to Japan is at once reinforced and slipped into something altogether more artificial by Eva's deathly white cake makeup in other scenes, a detail that conjures up an image of Kabuki theater. Almodóvar himself, who wrote the screenplay for *Matador* with Jesús Ferrero (a writer who rose to fame around the time of the *Movida* for "exotic" novels like *Bélver Yin* [1981] and *Opium* [1986]), has referred to the Japanese qualities of this otherwise very Spanish film. For Alejandro Varderi, Almodóvar's cinematic presentation of death and beauty recalls the works of Yukio Mishima (360).

19. I had long wondered what, if any, relation there might be between Almodóvar's and

Ferrero's María Cardenal and French feminist writer Marie Cardinal. Fortunately, Susan Martin-Márquez has brilliantly sounded out the connection, noting how Marie Cardinal's theoretical reflections on menstrual blood and feminine abjection dovetail María Cardenal's penchant for letting the blood of men. Rejecting the rather facile feminist rejection of the character of María Cardenal (already parodied in the film itself, when a TV announcer denounces Cardenal for "making a show of her cynicism" by defending a man who has confessed to attempted rape and murder), Martin-Márquez, following Peter Evans, argues instead for seeing Cardenal as something of a radical feminist avenger whose violent actions "emphasize the horror of a patriarchally-defined femininity" (500). For more, see Martin-Márquez (especially 498–501) and Evans (332).

20. Ángel is the product of a suffocatingly austere, ultra-Catholic upbringing. His mother, who is played "over the top" by Julieta Serrano, is a fervent member of the Opus Dei and comports herself as if she were an inquisitorial demon. The film clearly presents Ángel's "guilt complex" as an effect of his "bad education." The provenance of Ángel's second sight, his visionary powers, is less clear, but it suggests nonetheless a mystical protest against the authoritarianism of his mother and the priest who so unctuously accompanies her.

21. For Martin-Márquez, "María is shown to be the only 'real man' by the end of the film, for Diego is unable to comply with their mutual assassination pact: he fails to kill his lover with the phallic hairpin, which remains clutched, impotently, in his lifeless hands as it grazes María's still inviolate back, and María is then forced to insert a pistol into her own mouth and commit suicide" (499). The necrophilia that had previously been signaled in Diego's command to Eva that she "play dead" is here extended and inverted: Diego, the former agent of necrophilic desire, is "really dead" and provides the material for María's slightly delayed final pleasure.

22. As Earl Jackson reminds us, *Duel in the Sun* "is the very film which prompted Laura Mulvey to reconsider the possibilities for the female spectator she had formulated in 'Visual Pleasure'" (172).

23. Indeed, the sexually sublimated duel between Lewt and Pearl is, if anything, slightly more reciprocal than the sexually explicit union of Diego and María at the end of *Matador*, for Lewt and Pearl use the same kind of weapon, a gun.

24. I refer, of course, to Barthes's *Camera Lucida*, where he develops his notion of the penetrating, poignant visual detail, or *punctum*.

25. As I see it, it is not so much that cinema "appears to extract a magical continuity from what is acknowledged to be discontinuous" as that it appears to extract a magical continuity from what is frequently *disavowed* as being discontinuous.

26. The figure of the bullfighter, alone before the bull and the crowd, harks back in Spanish cinema at least to Vicente Blasco Ibáñez's *Blood and Sand* from 1916. For an interesting reading of tauromachy and Spanish cultural markers in *Matador*, see Leora Lev.

27. As María Donapetry rightly notes, "some of the names and all of the personalities of the main female characters—María (the matadora), Eva (the quintessential embodiment of femininity) and Berta (the Opus Dei mother)—and the name and personality of Ángel (Berta's son and Diego's follower), have unequivocal religious resonances," reinforced, as Donapetry goes on to note, by María's surname, "Cardenal" (70). "God may

very well be dead or may not 'be' at all for Almodóvar personally," Donapetry declares, "but the ethics and emotions, particularly the pathos of his characters, come through loud and clear" (74–75).

28. "Throughout the history of cinema," Mulvey writes, "the stilled image has been contained within the creative preserve of the film-maker, always accessible on the editing table and always transferable into a freeze frame on the screen. It was video, arriving in the late 1970s and gaining ground during the 1980s, that first extended the power to manipulate the existing speed of cinema. Although the instability of the electronic image undercut the exhilaration that these experiments brought with them, the accumulated experience of the last video-dominated decades can be carried into the digital age" (*Death 24x* 22).

29. Drawing from the Lacanian distinction between phallus and penis, Luce Irigaray curiously deflates the power, and the problematic nature of the power, of male homosexual desire: "Once the penis itself becomes merely a means to pleasure, pleasure among men, *the phallus loses its power*" (193, emphasis in the original). I dispute the notion of the penis as ever being a "simple means of (or to) pleasure," as if pleasure and symbolic power, even between men, were inimical.

30. On the score of suffering, Almodóvar contrasts his comic work with that of Richard Lester, noted mainly for his collaborations with the Beatles, and says that a certain sadness subtends the light tone of *Labyrinth of Passion,* something typical of comedy but also very dramatic (Vidal 44).

31. Put rather flatly, *Matador* is marked by foreshadowing, while *Labyrinth of Passion* is marked by flashbacks.

32. Sexilia's pursuit of Riza entails her flight from her father. This father–daughter relationship is marked by specular inversions: she is addicted to food, gambling, and sex, while he is addicted to work, research, and thought; he is disgusted by bodily pleasure and dedicates himself to the study of asexual reproduction, while she is obsessed with the pleasures of the body and dedicates herself to promiscuous, nonreproductive sex. She is "cured" of her nymphomania by finding a soul mate in the equally promiscuous and male-oriented Riza; he is "cured" by finding a partner who is, to his eyes, his biological daughter.

33. The script is not only Freudian but also, as Almodóvar tells Nuria Vidal, Hitchcockian and, as such, inflected by irony and dark humor. Almodóvar goes on to clarify that his use of trauma tends, in fact, toward the burlesque: "I've always taken traumas as something of a joke, but they comprise a separate genre in film. In life you can't explain everything with traumas, but in a comedy you can; they justify everything" (Vidal 59).

34. According to Almodóvar, the "Oedipus complex was something I was thinking about a lot [when filming *Labyrinth*]. I was looking for a father in everyone around me. The fact is that, given my personality, the father I would have liked to have had was one that I could have adopted, a type of son-father" (ibid.). It is thus not surprising that Almodóvar claims that he identified with Queti more than with any other character in the film.

35. For a fuller account on Almodóvar's "hysterical histrionics," see my "Figuring Hysteria."

36. As *Labyrinth of Passion* rushes to its close, Sexilia exclaims at least three times that she is "histérica" (hysterical). The fact that the expression is so widespread in present-day Spain as to designate virtually any feeling of exasperation, confusion, or impatience does not so much empty it of content as point to a curious success. Hysteria spills over into popular discourse, becomes trivial, banal, and common, so common that it can characterize anyone and everyone, women as well as men.

37. I do not agree with Smith's assertion that "at no point in the film does Cecilia Roth's Sexi appear disabled by her condition" (*Desire Unlimited* 25). In fact, the film makes dazzlingly clear that Sexilia is, at least in the scene of confrontation with Toraya, "disabled" and, furthermore, that Toraya understands and can thus manipulate Sexilia's "disability," her fear of light.

38. Although she calls herself a Lacanian, Susana gives a rather Freudian rendition of Sexilia's nymphomania: "It's all your father's fault. You hate the sun because you identify it with him, because you are in love with him and you fuck everything that moves to see if he will react. But your father is blind; he doesn't realize that your happiness depends on him."

39. According to Marsha Kinder, Queti is a "two-faced incestuous daughter [who] feeds both daddies powerful potions that render one impotent, the other horny" (34–35).

40. In the words of Paul Julian Smith, "[o]ne problem with approaching Almodóvar's work is the difficulty of finding a tone appropriate to discuss his very particular comic sensibility" (*Desire Unlimited* 167). Smith resolves this difficulty by declaring "respectful academicism" to be "inappropriate" (167–68). I myself am curious about what is at stake in articulating the problem of tone in terms of appropriateness and inappropriateness, especially inasmuch as it suggests a dynamic of propriety and impropriety. Indeed, I am more intrigued by Smith's assertion that Almodóvar turns Sontag's notion of camp as failed seriousness on its head. As Smith puts it, many of Almodóvar's films "suggest rather a seriousness that is fully achieved, but which remains articulated none the less within a comic context" (169). Then again, comedy takes itself seriously whenever it defends its own integrity, whenever it attempts to stave off serious, let alone tragic, encroachments. If this implies that comedy, in the strictest sense, borders on the impossible, it is obviously not because the only thing possible is straight seriousness; rather, comedy is possible to the very extent that it can slip into something serious, in other words, that it matters.

WORKS CITED

Arnheim, Rudolf. *Film as Art.* Berkeley and Los Angeles: University of California Press, 1957.

Barthes, Roland. *Camera Lucida: Reflections on Photography.* Trans. Richard Howard. New York: Farrar, Straus and Giroux, 1981.

———. *S/Z: An Essay.* Trans. Richard Miller. New York: Hill and Wang, 1975.

Bellour, Raymond. "The Unattainable Text." Trans. Ben Brewster. *The Analysis of Film.* Bloomington: Indiana University Press, 2000.

Bersani, Leo, and Ulysse Dutoit. *Forms of Being: Cinema, Aesthetics, Subjectivity.* London: British Film Institute, 2004.

Breuer, Joseph, and Sigmund Freud. *Studies in Hysteria.* Trans. A. A. Brill. Boston: Beacon Press, 1937.

Deleuze, Gilles. *Cinema 1: The Movement-Image.* Trans. Hugh Tomlinson and Barbara Habberjam. Minneapolis: University of Minnesota Press, 1986.

D'Lugo, Marvin. *Pedro Almodóvar.* Urbana: University of Illinois Press, 2006.

Doane, Mary Ann. *The Emergence of Cinematic Time: Modernity, Contingency, the Archive.* Cambridge: Harvard University Press, 2002.

Donapetry, María. "Once a Catholic . . . : Almodóvar's Religious Reflections." *Bulletin of Hispanic Studies* 76 (1999): 67–75.

Epps, Brad. "Figuring Hysteria: Disorder and Desire in Three Films of Pedro Almodóvar." Vernon and Morris 99–124.

Epstein, Jean. "Grossissement." *Bonjour Cinéma.* Paris: Éditions de la Sirène, 1929. 93–108.

Evans, Peter. "Almodóvar's *Matador*: Genre, Subjectivity and Desire." *Bulletin of Hispanic Studies* 70 (1993): 497–509.

Freud, Sigmund. "Charcot." *Early Psychoanalytic Writings.* Ed. Philip Rieff. New York: Macmillan, 1963.

———. *Dora: An Analysis of a Case of Hysteria.* Ed. Philip Rieff. New York: Macmillan, 1963.

Irigaray, Luce. *This Sex Which Is Not One.* Trans. Catherine Porter. Ithaca, N.Y.: Cornell University Press, 1985.

Jackson, Earl, Jr. *Strategies of Deviance: Studies in Gay Male Representation.* Bloomington: Indiana University Press, 1995.

Kinder, Marsha. "Pleasure and the New Spanish Mentality: A Conversation with Pedro Almodóvar." *Film Quarterly* 41.1 (1987): 33–44.

Lacan, Jacques. "L'instance de la lettre dans l'inconscient, ou la raison depuis Freud." *Écrits 1.* Paris: Seuil, 1966. 249–89.

———. *Le Séminaire, livre XX. Encore.* Paris: Seuil, 1975.

Laplanche, Jean, and J.-B. Pontalis. *The Language of Psycho-Analysis.* Trans. Donald Nicholson-Smith. New York: W. W. Norton, 1973.

Lev, Leora. "Tauromachy as a Spectacle of Gender Revision in *Matador*." Vernon and Morris 73–86.

Lyotard, Jean-François. "Acinema." *The Lyotard Reader.* Trans. Paisley N. Livingston. Ed. Andrew Benjamin. Oxford: Blackwell, 1989. 169–80.

Mandrell, James. "Sense and Sensibility, or Latent Heterosexuality and *Labyrinth of Passion*." Vernon and Morris 41–57.

Martin-Márquez, Susan. "Pedro Almodóvar's Maternal Transplants: From *Matador* to *All about My Mother*." *Bulletin of Hispanic Studies* 81 (2004): 497–509.

Melville, Herman. "Benito Cereno." *Great Short Works of Herman Melville.* Ed. Warner Berthoff. New York: Harper & Row, 1969. 238–315.

Mulvey, Laura. *Death 24x a Second: Stillness and the Moving Image.* London: Reaktion Books, 2006.

———. *Visual and Other Pleasures.* London: Macmillan, 1989.

Perkins, V. F. *Film as Film*. Middlesex: Penguin, 1972.

Rodowick, D. N. *The Virtual Life of Film*. Cambridge: Harvard University Press, 2007.

Sontag, Susan. "Notes on Camp." *A Susan Sontag Reader*. New York: Vintage, 1983. 105–19.

Smith, Paul Julian. *Desire Unlimited: The Cinema of Pedro Almodóvar*. London: Verso, 1994.

———. "Pornography, Masculinity, Homosexuality: Almodóvar's *Matador* and *La ley del deseo*." *Refiguring Spain: Cinema/Media/Representation*. Ed. Marsha Kinder. Durham, N.C.: Duke University Press, 1997. 178–95.

Stewart, Garret. *Between Film and Screen: Modernism's Photo Synthesis*. Chicago: University of Chicago Press, 1999.

Varderi, Alejandro. "Pedro Almodóvar: Escrito sobre un cuerpo." *Alba de América: Revista Literaria* 25.47–48 (2006): 357–67.

Vernon, Kathleen M., and Barbara Morris, eds. *Post-Franco, Postmodern: The Films of Pedro Almodóvar*. Westport, Conn.: Greenwood Press, 1995.

Vidal, Nuria. *El cine de Pedro Almodóvar*. Barcelona: Ediciones Destino, 1989.

12 Missing a Beat
Syncopated Rhythms and Subterranean Subjects in the Spectral Economy of *Volver*

STEVEN MARSH

"It is the wind,** this damn *Solano* wind that makes people lose their minds," says Raimunda (Penélope Cruz) as she sits at the wheel of her car somewhere between her Manchegan village and Madrid in an early scene from *Volver* (2006).[1] She makes the comment while driving beneath the huge luminous skies and among the towering modern wind turbines that "populate" the landscape of southern-central Spain. It is the wind, racing among the graves being cleaned by the women in a ritual act of remembrance, that provides an impalpable protagonist for the film's opening sequence, one that occasions what Jacques Derrida, in a different context, has called a "whirling dance of ghosts" (129) that disorients and dislocates.

Disorientation and displacement can assume, however, more palpable forms. Throughout Almodóvar's oeuvre, bodily metamorphosis plays a central role, as is evident in the many depictions of organ transplants, sex changes, test-tube babies, cyborgs, and plastic surgery. Bringing fluid conceptions of bodily identity into play with more fixed conceptions of the body in medical discourse and practice, Almodóvar grapples with the possibilities and limits of transforming, remaking, or restyling the human. He does so, moreover, in a manner that often brings to the fore the uncanny doublings that have become part of his signature as auteur. The doublings of *Volver,* in which the return of the repressed and the defamiliarization of the familiar loom large, are once more connected to the human body, but arguably in a more subtle and integrated way than in previous ventures, for they provide the film with a dramatic tautness in which spectral returns and (un)familiar sights—including the "reappearance" of a haggard Carmen Maura at a far remove from her glamorous, if harried, appearance in *Women on the Verge of a Nervous Breakdown* (1988)—are critical. *Volver,* after all, is—or at least appears to be—a ghost story, but one in which ghosts, far from remaining immaterial spirits, are materialized in palpable, even odoriferous, bodily form.

The return of the dead—or of someone presumed to be dead—stands in tense contrast with the dying of the living, here specifically that of Raimunda's longtime family friend Agustina (Blanca Portillo), whose cancer-ridden body is a reminder of the inevitable transformation of life into death. Lest this transformation be taken as definitive and unidirectional, the measure of death here is not the cadaver, the exterior husk of an extinguished psychic interiority, but rather the emotionally charged expectations and remembrances that the specter of death elicits among those still living. *Volver*, in sum, plays on the twists and turns of the material and the immaterial, the palpable and the impalpable, the corporeal and the psychospiritual, the buried and the unburied. Little wonder, then, that its most insistent and intricate concern is with spectrality.

Trauma and Temporality

The present essay seeks to analyze the implications of spectrality by exploring how the physical bodies of the characters and the symbolic body politic of the Spanish nation converge in the film's presentation of such diverse yet interrelated questions as temporality, reconciliation, and inheritance. Opening as it does with a depiction of mortuary customs of rural La Mancha that are either lost or out of place in the urban sprawl of Madrid, *Volver* implicitly questions a transnational critical approach that would limit itself to registering generic modes of syncretism instead of examining more locally inflected relations of power. Drawing on Derrida's *Specters of Marx,* I suggest that although *Volver*, with all of its spirits and superstitions, is arguably Almodóvar's most "provincial" film, it is also perhaps his most universal. The film is not only a ghost story in terms of its generic themes and codes, but also, and most importantly, in its uncanny exploration—and exploitation—of the residues of its cinematic heritage, be they in the form of Italian and North American antecedents or of Almodóvar's own previous endeavors. Indeed, it is my contention that *Volver*'s densely combined precedents function as a palimpsest and generate a countertradition, a means by which supposedly sedimented elements, whether texts or beliefs, can be reactivated as both countervailing and counter*veil*ing figures to and of dominant culture— both global and local—that range from established religion to populist "tabloid" television. By employing the neologism *counterveiling* here, I aim to suggest the veiling and unveiling of the hidden and the sought, the buried and the unburied, that lie at the heart of *Volver*.[2]

Along with *The Flower of My Secret* (1995) and *Talk to Her* (2002), *Volver* is, at first sight, one of Almodóvar's more low-key films. Restrained in tone and linear in narrative development, it nonetheless includes many of this filmmaker's habitual motifs, yet under more muted, at times even comic, control—in stark contrast with, for instance, the dark, convoluted diegesis of his previous film, *Bad Education* (2004).[3] A number of the more thorny emblems of Almodóvar's cinema—rape, incest, conflictive mother–daughter relations, superstition, and even scatology—all emerge once again, but in ways that point to the value of popular wisdom, a wisdom as hauntingly understated as the bodies that inhabit the tombs of the cemetery—or the "ghosts" that hide beneath the beds of the homes.

Such spectral linkage applies to the living but also extends to the dead and the *apparently* dead. *Volver* is structured around a series of inherited traumas, from betrayal to murder, that link three generations of women from the same family. Fourteen-year-old Paula (Yohana Cobo) kills Paco (Antonio de la Torre), the man she believes to be her father, in an act of self-defense after he attempts to rape her. Her mother, Raimunda, in a corresponding act of self-sacrifice and self-implication, refuses to notify the authorities and proceeds instead to conceal the body—a proposition that proves to be more easily said than done. In the last section of the film, after having transported Paco's cadaver from her apartment to the freezer of the neighboring restaurant to a final resting place in the country, Raimunda reveals (to the spectators, though not to Paula herself) that she too was abused by her own father, and that Paula is the incestuous issue of the abusive relationship. By taking matters into her own hands rather than going to the police with a reasonable, and truthful, story of murder in self-defense, Raimunda "returns" to her own highly charged past—or rather, Raimunda's past returns to her—and attempts to set right, as it were, her prior inaction as a young woman by acting decisively on behalf of her daughter. Of course, Raimunda's own mother, Irene (Carmen Maura), now presumed dead, is even more powerfully implicated in the failure to act. Raimunda herself was estranged from Irene, whom she blames for not having defended her and whom she believes to have died in the arms of her husband (Raimunda's abusive father) in a fire that destroyed an outhouse in the fields adjacent to the family home in their village in La Mancha. So sketched, this story is the material of such film noir masterpieces as Michael Curtiz's *Mildred Pierce* (1945), and also recalls Frank Capra's black comedy *Arsenic and Old Lace* (1944), with its hidden corpses in the basement. It is likewise indebted to postwar Italian cinema, most explicitly to Luchino Visconti's *Bellissima* (1951), but also, as Marsha Kinder has indicated, to Vittorio De Sica's *Two Women* (1960) (8). Indeed, along with such thematic similarities as a mother and daughter alliance forged in the face of rape, what *Volver* shares with *Two Women* is the physical presence of Sophia Loren, whose body—a neorealist body—the Spanish director takes as a model for Penélope Cruz in *Volver*.[4] Such intertextual turns and returns prove important, as we will see, throughout *Volver* and, indeed, to its resolution.

Interestingly, in a film whose on-screen narrative progression is linear rather than retrospective and circular as in *Mildred Pierce,* an otherwise straightforward female genealogical chain, marked not just by emotional and bodily violation but also by murder and ghostly returns, *disturbs* rather than reinforces any neat unfolding of chronological time.[5] A sense of this disturbance, close to madness, is rendered explicit when Raimunda, her sister Sole (Lola Dueñas), and Paula visit their Aunt Paula (Chus Lampreave) at the end of the day that they spent cleaning tombstones. Aunt Paula, who will die soon after the visit, greets Raimunda warmly, asking her if she has given birth yet. When Raimunda, amusedly taken aback, responds by saying, "Fourteen years ago," Aunt Paula comments, "Ooh, how time flies!" The moment is symptomatic of the temporal hiccups and gaps in memory that pervade the film; for Aunt Paula, surprised that Raimunda has given birth so many years earlier, is also surprised to discover that her grandniece is her namesake. Despite the possibility of taking her niece as her nominal double, as the differential replay and extension of herself over time, Aunt Paula is seemingly incapable of making, let alone sustaining, an affective connection with her grandniece. What is initially depicted as senility or dementia in a realistic context comes to be a sign of a more widespread disorientation and disruption that distinguishes the history of this family. The linearity and sequentiality that structure *Volver*'s narrative are belied by this and other gaps in memory. Disjointed time is, in short, intimately linked to this women-centered family's persistent if fractured generational trauma.

Almodóvar's previous films have often used strikingly incongruous juxtapositions, improbable conceits, and outlandish characterization, frequently to comic effect. However, as with so much else in *Volver,* comedy is here far from direct and is instead partially submerged, embedded in the variegated intertexts (film noir, the supernatural or ghost story, and neorealism) that crowd its subterranean strata.[6] Indeed, in its deployment of comic, tragic, farcical, and other generic conventions, the film seems incongruous despite the *appearance* of a chronological narrative. Tellingly, the most exemplary representative of this incongruity or disjointedness comes from just outside the family. Agustina, Aunt Paula's neighbor and friend, is in some ways at

Returning to the village in Volver *(2006): Sole (Lola Dueñas), Raimunda (Penélope Cruz), and Paula (Yohana Cobo) visiting Aunt Paula (Chus Lampreave) in La Mancha. Copyright El Deseo.*

once the most comic and the most tragic of the film's female chorus. Kinder offers an insightful observation when she describes Agustina as sporting a Falconetti hairstyle, like that of Renée Marie Falconetti in Carl Dreyer's *La Passion de Jeanne d'Arc* (1928), that marks her as a martyr (6). However farfetched it may seem, the reference to Joan of Arc invokes the specter of someone whose popular provenance and communitarian status disturb the authoritarian certitude of the church. Though hardly a national religious icon, Agustina is clearly not someone who docilely follows the dictates of established, institutionalized morality; among other things, she thumbs her nose at juridical prohibitions regarding marijuana, which she smokes in order to alleviate the pain that cancer occasions her. In fact, it is just her desire to seek relief from pain and suffering that troubles high-sounding comparisons to martyrs and that prevents us from seeing Agustina, or the other women in the film, as being easily "at home" with the abstemious and self-suffering understanding of life, dying, and death that both the established church *and* the (once) recalcitrant Joan of Arc champion. Faced with her impending death, Agustina urgently wants to know the fate of her own mother, who vanished inexplicably three years previously, when Raimunda's parents died. In what comes to be a crucial subtext of the central plot, Agustina's filial narrative offers less a parallel than what might be called a means of inoculation, or structure of defense, for the principal drama involving Raimunda, her mother, and her daughter Paula. Agustina's cancer is, of course, within her, a toxic stranger or foreign body that gnaws at her insides and renders any erstwhile bodily familiarity uncanny. But in another sense, Agustina's cancer, so deeply inside her, motivates a movement outside her in the form of a quest for knowledge about her mother, a quest that implicates in intimate and uncanny ways Raimunda and her family as well.

Almodóvar's much-touted fondness for irony and paradox holds for Agustina, who is at once the most localized of the film's characters and, in a sense, the most cosmopolitan, the most traditional, and the most modern. She lives across the street from Aunt Paula and checks on her each night; she is a source of sustenance who brings the older woman a daily loaf of bread and who believes her when she insists that it is the ghost of her dead sister, Irene (Raimunda's mother), who takes care of her. Agustina also adopts more fashionably modern methods to assuage the physical suffering she experiences from her cancer as well as the psychic pain from not knowing

The almost saintly image of Agustina (Blanca Portillo) on a stark background of empty village streets in Volver. *Copyright El Deseo.*

the true fate of her mother: for the former, as mentioned, she smokes marijuana; for the latter (but also perhaps for the former), she appears on one of the gruesome talk shows so typical of prime-time television in a desperate appeal for help. Contradictory and consistent, Agustina sits in the homely confines of her interior patio with Raimunda, Sole, and the young Paula, where she recalls how her own mother, that traditional emblem of stability and care, was nomadic and given to frequent disappearances. "She was the only hippie in the village," says Agustina of her mother, adding that "she was so modern." Although Agustina might seem something of a hippie herself, neither her pot smoking nor her TV appearance is a simple matter of choice. If she resorts to marijuana in extremis, it is her sister Brígida, yearning for cheap fame, who sells the story of the family mystery to trash television. In a moment of desperation, as the film approaches its denouement, Agustina finally agrees to appear on one of these programs to appeal for news of her missing mother in exchange for a promise of treatment at the Houston Cancer Center.[7] Out of place in the sensationalist world of the media and unmoved by televised promises of miracles in the United States, Agustina returns to the village, where she prepares to die in the same bed in which she was born, her mother's bed. And yet, Agustina's inability to fight the cancerous cells in her own body might be read as providing a symbolic form of "immunity"—an engagement with susceptibility and defenselessness—for the female community with which she is allied.

Immunity is a medical and legal notion signifying both a resistance to disease or poison and an exemption from liability and prosecution, that is to say, the capacity to defend as if from within. Although inoculation against, and immunity from, cancer do not appear to be tenable (Agustina dies, after all, from a disease that is not, strictly speaking, "contagious" or "communicable"), immunity from the law is another matter, more of the order of the social body than its physiological counterpart. Acute as the presence of disease may be in *Volver,* the presence of criminality is much more pressing— and more likely to implicate others. A great deal of the activity in which the women in this film engage is illegal, both before and after the murder. Raimunda, for instance, occupies a restaurant and sets up a catering business without informing its owner; her sister Sole runs a clandestine beauty salon; Raimunda's neighbor, Regina, is an undocumented immigrant who earns her living as a prostitute. All three women work, that is, in what is known in Spain as the "submerged" economy. Untaxed and unlicensed, the submerged economy fosters underground or subterranean strategies for survival that function as uncanny doubles of the *supposedly* more transparent strategies of the "real economy" and of the official, administrative world of statistics and figures.

Agustina, on the other hand, is noticeably less tactically ingenious than her friends and—owing apparently to her illness—more vulnerable and susceptible. While Raimunda, Sole, and Regina have been in different ways uprooted and displaced from their locational origins, Agustina is particularly connected to a sense of home. Unlike her peripatetic mother, prone to impromptu disappearances, or her ambitious sister, Agustina is linked to the village, to her street, and to her family residence, where she was born and plans to die.[8] She first appears among the women busily at work in the village cemetery, where she tends her own tomb. When the teenage Paula comments on the strangeness of the practice, her mother replies: "Here it is the custom. People buy their plot of land and look after it as if it were a chalet." In keeping with local tradition, Agustina cares for her tomb as the anticipated home of her body after death, but in her case, the traditional act is shot through with something more particular, more personal. She knows, without of course quite knowing, that her body "houses" the lurking alien, the intimate enemy, of cancer. Her body a home to cancer, the tomb a home to her body, Agustina is enmeshed in a circuit in which discrete time lines and stories are twisted into an almost indistinguishable mass. Writing on Derrida's texts on terror and autoimmunity, W. J. T. Mitchell has explained that "cancer cells are the body's *own* cells; their DNA lineage is indistinguishable from the host body. So the immune system sleeps through the attack by the body's own cells" (283). The sacrificial, suffering figure of Agustina, whose body has been invaded by something at once intimate and alien, provides a link, by means of her diseased interior, to the illicit activities of her friends in the body politic of a society governed by law; physical evidence is critical, after all, to a criminal investigation. Raimunda, her daughter who kills in "self-defense," and their accomplices "get away" with murder by disposing of Paco's body in a remote location where it is unlikely to be discovered. Put slightly differently, they strive to immunize themselves from prosecution by binding themselves together as accomplices and by burying Paco *under* the ground.

Offstage and Incomplete

Agustina's dignified departure from the glitzy prurience of the television studio—she walks off the stage in disgust—is both a profoundly moving and a structurally symptomatic moment in the film. In an earlier sequence, Agustina visits Raimunda in the restaurant that she has taken over during its owner's absence and begs her for news of her own mother. "I only want to know if she is alive or dead," Agustina pleads, drawing attention to *Volver*'s repeated play on knowledge and ignorance; a lack of knowledge, in this case, makes her mother—for Agustina, at least—"undead." At this critical point she alleges that, unbeknownst to Raimunda, Agustina's mother and Raimunda's father were lovers. Raimunda has hitherto attributed her own mother's blindness to the abuse that she (Raimunda) experienced at the hands of her own father to Irene's unconditional love for her husband. Rejecting Agustina's suggestion, Raimunda retorts with contempt, "I understand that between the wind and the cancer you've lost your mind, but that doesn't give you the right to complicate the lives of the rest of us."

Agustina reveals the affair between her mother and Raimunda's father in a sequence that takes place in the storage room where Paco's cadaver lies concealed in the freezer, on ice as it were, pending burial. Once more we are privy to a narratological game of hide-and-seek. The storage room is haunted by Paco's immaterial presence, as well as by the original text-within-a-text of *The Flower of My Secret,* entitled *Cold Storage.* It is a spectral site into which Raimunda ushers Agustina; away from the focal point of Raimunda's success—her illegal restaurant—that later serves as a platform for her rendition of the song "Volver." There are also echoes here of Alfred Hitchcock's *Rope* (1948). As in *Rope,* an eating place—in this instance, the restaurant—stands in ghoulish proximity to a cadaver in a trunk. The Hitchcock film also serves as a pertinent reminder of the uncanny effect—as much on the spectator as on the on-screen characters—of the unseen presence of a body, of not seeing who "looks" at us, a "spectral asymmetry" described by Derrida as the *"visor effect"* (6–7).[9] Paco's lingering spirit in the storeroom recalls, once more, Irene's status as "undead." As far as Raimunda is concerned, Irene died more than three years previously, but we, the spectators, know otherwise.

Although Irene first appears on-screen when she pops from the trunk of Sole's car, traces of her impress themselves on Raimunda and Sole from the very beginning of the film. Both sisters sense Irene, in sentient form, at Aunt Paula's house long before they actually see their mother. "This house still smells of Mamá," says Raimunda as she marches into Aunt Paula's abode. The more timid Sole sniffs tentatively, before a fleeting oneiric vision of her mother snoozing in an armchair. A palpable uncertainty reigns. The smell and the sniff become more insistent later in the film, when, at Sole's home that doubles as her clandestine beauty salon, Raimunda, in the bathroom, gets a whiff of what she remembers, rightly, to be her mother's farts. Meanwhile, Irene hides beneath the bed, privy to her unsuspecting daughter's presence—Raimunda, as always, talks incessantly—just as earlier she has listened to Raimunda's singing from the cover of Sole's car. In all of these instances, the sentient traces of the body are offered up. A partial body is brought to the floor, as it were—now heard, now smelled, now sensed. Irene's body, moreover, is unseen by those over whom it "keeps watch." Among other things, *Volver* is also a film about bodies and spirits in incongruent movement, bodies that, unseen, accompany the film's characters; Paco's corpse, stored in the restaurant's freezer before being transported for burial on the banks of the River Júcar; Irene's ghostly body stowed away in the trunk of her daughter Sole's car. Convinced that her mother is a phantom, Sole realizes that Irene has come back for a reason. "Do you have something you want to tell me?" she asks Irene. She knows that, like all revenants, Irene has returned to complete unfinished business.

The image of a woman urinating is a favorite of Almodóvar's, one that goes back to his very first feature film, twenty-five years earlier, when the image was employed to scandalously comic effect with two of the same actresses who appear in *Volver* (Chus Lampreave and Carmen Maura). In his later films, however, he has used the image to suggest the kind of decentered or fractured intimacy discussed earlier. Almodóvar has always been fond of bathrooms, dressing rooms, and offstage spaces, locations on the sidelines of the conventional main action. These are threshold locations, intermediary sites, and zones of transit that often work to accentuate the flexibility of identificatory processes. In *Volver,* they are not merely the aforementioned storage room at the restaurant but also, more generally, the highway, the airport, the cemetery, and the riverbank. It is perhaps not incidental, for example, that Paula, after killing Paco, should anxiously await her mother at a bus stop.

The constant comings and goings between the working-class neighborhood in Madrid where Raimunda lives and the Manchegan village that she periodically visits emphasize a spectral sense of uncertainty—of knowing and not knowing. The highway is a site of transit between two places; in a sense, it is neither here nor there, an indeterminate space that corresponds to the temporal disturbances that emerge and reemerge throughout *Volver* and that establish a rhythm that, in turn, reflects *Volver*'s taut intertextual framework. One of the pivotal moments of the film is when Penélope Cruz lip-synchs the eponymous title song "Volver." Sung in this instance by one of the recent stars of flamenco, Estrella Morente, "Volver" was originally recorded by the greatest of the Argentine tango singers, Carlos Gardel, and performed by him in John Reinhardt's *El día que me quieras* (1935).[10] Behind Cruz's Raimunda lie, then, the ghosts of more than her mother. Furthermore, as in tango or flamenco, the film's rhythm, of which *Volver*'s highway is symbolic, is syncopated; its syntax is irregular and incomplete, full of skipped beats and surprises, disturbed as in *Volver*'s deceptive narrative claims to chronological exposition, or in the gaps in Aunt Paula's faulty memory, or, in fact, in the unfinished business that Irene—an unseen witness to her daughter's performance—has returned to finish, which in turn reflects the repeated game of concealment and revelation, of veiling and unveiling, that the film plays upon the spectator.[11]

The principal female characters in *Volver* are all in search of a home or, as Derrida puts it, "a hospitable memory" (175). As we will see, although *Bellissima* is quoted diegetically in one of the final sequences of *Volver,* there is another less direct citation from Visconti's film. It is the occasion for Irene's confession, for her reconciliation with Raimunda, and it takes place on a street bench. In *Bellissima,* Maddalena (Anna Magnani) and her daughter

Raimunda sings at the restaurant in Volver. *Photograph by Emilio Pereda and Paola Ardizzoni. Copyright Emilio Pereda and Paola Ardizzoni/El Deseo.*

Maria (Tina Apicella) similarly wander through the streets of Rome late at night after Maria's disastrous screen test at Cinecittà and, like Irene and Raimunda, sit on a bench in the street. Although there is no verbal confession as such, the Visconti film transmits the same sense of maternal regret. In *Volver,* the sequence provides an explanation of the film's enigmas and leads to the resolution of the mother–daughter conflict while subtly underscoring the association between the two actresses, Magnani and Maura.

It is important that the confession should take place in public, after Irene's prolonged seclusion first in her sister's and then in her daughter's house. But it is also important that the public scenario should be as anonymous and transient a place as a bench, a point between different homes, neither here nor there, like the journeys on the highway between Madrid and the village. While the sequence recalls *Bellissima,* it also provides a missing link between generations. Irene's confession hinges on her realization that she failed to defend Raimunda from her father (Irene's husband), that she failed to provide the immunity that her daughter expected of her. In the six minutes of almost entirely uninterrupted monologue, Irene refers to eyes on at least three occasions. Of her husband's abuse of Raimunda, Irene says, "I was blind. I found out on the day of the fire." Later, she adds, "How could such a monstrosity take place in front of my very eyes without my knowing." And then she adds, "I went to the outhouse prepared to rip his eyes out." The image of the scorned wife and mother as a blinding avenger is compelling. In his analysis of E. T. A. Hoffmann's "Sand-Man" story, in his much-cited 1919 essay "The Uncanny," Freud repeatedly refers to the fear of having one's eyes stolen. In addition, on consulting the 1877 Grimm's dictionary for definitions of the words *heimlich* and *unheimlich,* Freud focuses on their meanings principally as "homey" and "un-homey," but he also refers, unsurprisingly, to their sexual significance: "Secret places on the human body, the pudenda" (133).

Seeing and blindness, knowing and not knowing, concealing and revealing, veiling and unveiling, acknowledging and not acknowledging: *Volver's* key themes all emerge in condensed form in this key sequence. What is at stake, of course, is physical evidence: the body or bodies of Paco, of Agustina's mother, of Raimunda's father and whoever it was who died with him (Agustina's mother, as it turns out). Irene's physical presence refutes her own daughter's firmly held belief, her knowledge. Raimunda's response to Irene's confession, which is for the younger woman nothing less than a "revelation," directly concerns corporeal evidence. "So you are saying that the ashes in the cemetery are those of Agustina's mother?" she asks. Ashes are the lingering traces of the past, charred incorporeal remains. They are, of course, richly symbolic—ashes to ashes, dust to dust—and provide a sense of a return that is borne out in the film's structure: opening at a "public" cemetery, it moves to a more "private" burial place beside the river where the women of the family are reunited. It is a structure, incidentally, that stands in counterpoint to the syncopated rhythm of the film. The sense of an organic cycle is furthered, subtly, in Raimunda's peasant earthiness and the brightly colored fresh food she prepares in her restaurant. Such elemental connections also enable, it seems, a restoration of origins, the curing process of reconciliation and forgiveness, a genuine return (radical, in its etymological sense) beyond the glare of television (as with Agustina) and new technology (Paula's cyborg-like attachment to her cell phone, which from this moment on she ceases to use).

However, even Almodóvar's much-heralded return to his Manchegan roots in the earthy characterization of Raimunda is not as straightforward as it seems. Raimunda's apparent closeness to nature is also just that, *apparent*. We have already seen that the director had Penélope Cruz fitted with a prosthetic posterior for this film, an artificial rump that ironically links her to a filmic tradition that purports to be naturalistic and that Almodóvar had previously engaged in *What Have I Done to Deserve This?* (1984), which also starred Carmen Maura: Italian neorealism. The connection is emphasized stylistically in *Volver*'s most neorealist sequence, when Raimunda returns from the market after the morning shop, having been contracted to cater for a film crew. In a long take, she drags her shopping trolley uphill, her false butt swaying from side to side. The street is lined by small low-lying houses built in the 1950s and typical of Madrid's working-class neighborhoods. First she meets Regina, her close friend and neighbor, from whom she asks to borrow money and from whom she purchases a hunk of pork. Then she talks to Inés, who has recently returned from her village with sweets and sausages that Raimunda cheerfully asks to purchase. In both instances, the requests are mixed with affectionate observations on the physical condition of the two neighbors. "In any case, you need to slim," Raimunda says to Regina. To Inés she says, "With your levels of glucose and cholesterol, what do you think you are doing eating stuff like that?" In keeping with neorealist technique, the sequence is shot in deep focus with no cuts. Here the intertexts that underlie *Volver* are brought to bear on the real "submerged" economy that sustains Raimunda and her friends and that is most forcefully expressed through the body. Penélope Cruz's artificial butt extension is thus a spectral supplement

Raimunda returns from the market. Photograph by Emilio Pereda and Paola Ardizzoni. Copyright Emilio Pereda and Paola Ardizzoni/El Deseo.

to her own "natural" body, one that links the physical body to *Volver*'s filmic legacy, to the submerged economy, and to the film's network of spectrality. Regina, the Cuban prostitute who works with bodies, and whose own body is voluminous, voluptuous, and prosthetically enhanced, is, crucially, also Raimunda's ally in disposing of Paco's cadaver. Regina's presence in the film, moreover, as an undocumented immigrant, an "illegal alien" uncannily placed within the national body, recalls the situation of the new immigrants to Spain and the changing body politic of Spanish demographics.

Conclusion: Almodóvar and the Zeitgeist

Volver was made in the traumatic aftermath of the March 11, 2004, bombings of the Madrid commuter trains in which 191 people died. Indeed, the premiere of Almodóvar's previous film, *Bad Education* (2004), scheduled for the same week, was postponed out of respect for the national mourning that ensued. The trains had departed from Alcalá de Henares, the city where Cervantes once lived.[12] What has been described as a "sleeper cell" of Islamic fundamentalists claimed responsibility. Many of those subsequently convicted were residents of the popular and central Madrid district of Lavapiés;

some were Spanish nationals; others were long-term residents. A video was issued in which a spokesman for the terrorist group attributed the attacks to Spain's involvement in the previous year's invasion of Iraq. He referred explicitly to Spain's Arab heritage, Al-Andalus, and called for a return of the Caliphate.[13]

Such a historic conjuncture, or disruption, provides a violently unexpected context for *Volver*. Throughout his career, Almodóvar has had to contend with charges that his work is frivolous and gratuitous, and indeed it appears that virtually everything from Shiite terrorism (in *Labyrinth of Passion*, 1982) to the genocidal war in the former Yugoslavia (in *The Flower of My Secret* and *Live Flesh*, 1997) has been fodder for entertainment. The tone of restraint that distinguishes *Volver* is, however, at a far remove from such extravagance and excess. Nonetheless, the film is highly sensitive to the spirit of the times of its production, the zeitgeist. The strength of *Volver* lies in its muted tone, its concern with, and its respect for, the particularities of local cultures and popular wisdom, that field of residual philosophy that Antonio Gramsci called "common sense" (328). For Agustina, Irene is a real ghost. Her faith in the supernatural is pharmaceutical, like the marijuana that she smokes, and casts fresh light on the Marxist injunction that religion is the "opium of the people."[14] Almodóvar's playfulness is also deadly serious. His parodies and criticisms of institutionalized religion have always been accompanied—I am tempted to say "haunted"—by a respect for popular customs and inherited belief.

The final sequences of *Volver* offer two uncanny moments, both involving the "ghost" Irene. Reconciled with Raimunda and back in Alcalfor de las Infantas, Irene slips out of the family home late at night and crosses the street to accompany Agustina in death. The sequence commences with garbage containers rolling out of control down the street, blown through the night by the unruly wind, the same *Solano* wind of the film's introductory sequence, as if possessed, in an uncanny, poltergeist-like moment. Garbage containers are, of course, also the depositories of things that have been cast away—like Paco's body, which the women nonetheless decide to bury more properly. The second uncanny moment of this "terminal" chapter is the encounter, as it were, between Irene and Maddalena, the central character of *Bellisima*. Irene has administered the injection that Agustina needs in order to die in hospitable circumstances, to be reconciled with her body in her bed in her own home, and to be "returned," finally, to the grave that she has long and lovingly prepared for herself. Irene, who has seemingly come back to life and who has been keeping watch over her daughters in life, now accompanies Agustina in a vigil in death. Here, though, other roles are reversed.

Having seen and known the truth of *Volver*'s ghosts and spirits, at this point in the film, we, the spectators, are for once kept in the dark. We do not know if Agustina has died, if she will wake up the next day, or if Irene has, in fact, assisted her friend in an act of euthanasia. Agustina's final words—which implicitly refer to Agustina's mother and Irene's husband's affair—before losing consciousness are pointed: "That's our business," she says. "That's right," Irene replies, "and nobody else's." Alone and in peace, Irene sits in front of the TV to watch *Bellissima*. Maddalena, while combing her hair and preparing for bed, looks around slightly alarmed, as if she senses that she is being watched, recalling once more Derrida's *visor effect,* by which "we do not see who looks at us" (7). For a moment—and it is an extraordinarily brief one—Maddalena/Magnani looks straight at the camera and her eyes meet Irene's and, of course, Maura's. Irene/Maura smiles in recognition of the shared identification that crosses the artifice of national frontiers and bridges a time difference of forty-five years.[15]

NOTES

I am grateful to the students of my Film 598 class ("The Cinema of Pedro Almodóvar," fall 2007) at the University of South Carolina for their enthusiasm and insight, which helped me clarify my own ideas regarding this film. I thank Tatjana Gajic for her perspicacious comments on a preliminary draft of this text. I am wholeheartedly indebted to the editors of this volume for their rigor and their very useful suggestions.

1. The Spanish word *volver* is open to various translations. It means "to return," "to come home," "to go back," and "to repeat."

2. The English word *veil* has an aptly double translation in Spanish. The Spanish verb *velar* has two meanings: first, "to enshroud or veil," and second, it refers to the custom (in La Mancha, among other places) of "keeping watch over the bodies of the dead until they are buried" (Derrida 183).

3. Kinder has pointed to the relationship between *Volver* and *The Flower of My Secret* as exemplary of what she suggestively calls Almodóvar's "retroseriality" (for more, see Kinder's essay in this volume). As Kinder observes, Leo (Marisa Paredes), a depressed writer of popular romances, delivers a manuscript titled *Cold Storage,* which had been rejected by her publishers for not having the optimistic tone of her other titles, all more conventionally within the limits of the Romance genre. *Cold Storage* is important in the present context for it contains, in embryonic form, the plot that Almodóvar takes for *Volver.* Kinder might have added that the manuscript in the earlier film is also marked by something ghostly: Leo is befriended and willingly supplanted by a *ghostwriter,* tellingly

named Ángel (Juan Echanove), who functions both as a figure of salvation and as the most "down-to-earth" character in the film.

4. In an interesting variant on the palimpsest, Penélope Cruz was fitted with a prosthetic rump to play this role—an extra layer was added to her body—in order to enhance the resemblance to the great actresses of 1950s and 1960s Italian cinema such as Loren, Anna Magnani, Gina Lollobrigida, or Claudia Cardinale.

5. *Mildred Pierce* is narrated by its eponymous heroine, played by Joan Crawford, in the form of a series of flashbacks that constitute the false confession of an innocent mother who takes on the guilt of her murderous daughter (though in *Mildred Pierce* the murder is *not* justifiable in terms of self-defense). Almodóvar has used flashbacks in many previous films, most notably in *Bad Education,* but not in *Volver.*

6. The "subterranean" element in this analysis has three objectives, the first two of which relate to the notion of the palimpsest. "Subterranean" thus refers, in the first place, to the array of intertexts (Spanish, Italian, French, and North American, literary, theatrical, and filmic) that underlie the text of *Volver.* The second element refers to the disposal, usually by burial or entombment, of a cadaver (as in *Arsenic and Old Lace*). The third subterranean element is that of the "clandestine economy" that I discuss later.

7. Shortly before the *Volver* shoot commenced, one of Spain's best-known folkloric singers, Rocío Jurado, was treated for pancreatic cancer at the Houston Cancer Center. The subject was thus indeed a regular item on Spanish TV programs at the time the film was being made. Jurado died on June 1, 2006, shortly after *Volver* was released.

8. The only time we hear the village named is, ironically enough, during the live TV show when the presenter says that Alcalfor de las Infantas has the country's "highest rate of madness per inhabitant."

9. Earlier in the film, Raimunda subtly reinforces the connection to Hitchcock's *Rope* when she buys rope at the hardware store with which to bind shut the freezer containing Paco's corpse. In another Hitchcockian touch of retroseriality, the shop assistant in the hardware store is played by Almodóvar's brother, Agustín, who has had similar Hitchcockian cameos in all of the director's previous feature films.

10. *El día que me quieras* was Gardel's final film, made shortly before his tragic death in an airplane crash in 1935 in Colombia. It was shot on Long Island and directed by the North American John Reinhardt for Paramount. In a further ghostlike twist, a recent remake of the same film, starring Lindsay Lohan and titled *Dare to Love Me,* is scheduled for release in 2010.

11. The relation between narrative subjectivity and linear time seems relevant here. The flashback technique in *Mildred Pierce* emphasizes its subjective quality. It is precisely owing to the lack of flashbacks in *Volver* that subjectivity is disturbed.

12. Alcalá de Henares is today formally in the province of Madrid, but historically it has been considered a city of La Mancha.

13. Al-Andalus refers to those parts of the Iberian Peninsula ruled by the Arabs at various times between 711 and 1492.

14. The quote from Marx has been much abused and decontextualized. It has often been regarded as a sign of Marx's contempt for religious belief. In fact, it is a remarkably sympathetic approach not dissimilar to that of Almodóvar himself. The more representative

citation is as follows: "*Religious* suffering is, at one and the same time, the *expression* of real suffering and a protest against real suffering. Religion is the sigh of the oppressed creature, the heart of a heartless world, and the soul of soulless conditions. It is the *opium* of the people. The abolition of religion as the *illusory* happiness of the people is the demand for their *real* happiness. To call on them to give up their illusions about their condition is to *call on them to give up a condition that requires illusions.* The criticism of religion is, therefore, in *embryo,* the *criticism of that vale of tears* of which religion is the *halo*" (244, emphasis in the original).

15. Clearly relevant to *Volver's* diegesis and to Almodóvar's preoccupation with current affairs are two news items that coincide with the making of the film. On July 17, 2005, eleven firefighters were killed in a forest fire in the province of Guadalajara, in the region of La Mancha. This item is diegetically included in the film during the televised news broadcast overheard during Raimunda, Paula, and Sole's visit to Aunt Paula's house. Second, in October 2007, the Spanish parliament finally passed the "Law of Historical Memory," which acknowledges the victims of the civil war and pledged to open mass graves of Spain's "disappeared" from the war and the postwar period.

WORKS CITED

Derrida, Jacques. *Specters of Marx: The State of the Debt, the Work of Mourning, and the New International.* Trans. Peggy Kamuf. London: Routledge, 1994.

Freud, Sigmund. *The Uncanny.* Trans. David McLintock. London: Penguin Classics, 2003.

García, Rocío. "Tengo el mismo miedo de siempre." Interview with Penélope Cruz. *El País,* Feb. 18, 2007. May 11, 2008. http://www.elpais.com.

Gramsci, Antonio. *Selections from the Prison Notebooks.* Trans. Quintin Hoare and Geoffrey Nowell-Smith. London: Lawrence and Wishart, 1971.

Guerrero, Jacinto. *La rosa de azafrán.* Jan. 28, 2008. http://www.zarzuela.net.

Kinder, Marsha. "*Volver* [Review]." *Film Quarterly* 60.3 (2007): 4–9.

Marx, Karl. *Early Writings.* Trans. Rodney Livingstone and Gregor Benton. Harmondsworth, England: Pelican, 1975.

Mitchell, W. J. T. "Picturing Terror: Derrida's Autoimmunity." *Critical Inquiry* 33 (2007): 277–90.

Smith, Paul Julian. "Women, Windmills and Wedge Heels." *Sight and Sound* 16.6 (2006): 16–19.

13 Postnostalgia in *Bad Education*
Written on the Body of Sara Montiel
MARVIN D'LUGO

Unlike any of Pedro Almodóvar's previous films, *Bad Education* (2004) is deeply rooted in the historical specificity of the Francoist period. The rubbish of Spanish popular culture, relegated to oblivion but recycled in images, sounds, and cultural associations from the past, has usually appeared as incidental comic details in Almodóvar's cinema (Yarza 17). Not until *Bad Education,* however, have these artifacts, many of them kitsch, assumed so central a position in the formulation of his cinematic narratives. In this new turn of his auteurist style, Almodóvar gives special privilege to the figure of Sara Montiel, the legendary Spanish star of the early 1950s who became the embodiment of the Spanish cult of nostalgia in the 1960s (Vázquez Montalbán 193) only to reemerge in the 1970s as a popular Spanish gay icon (Mira 144). The recycled image of Montiel, an emblematic expression of gender demarginalization in the post-Franco years, mirrors the social and political dynamics through which the broader plot intrigues of *Bad Education* take shape.

Rather than giving in to a facile nostalgic impulse, fairly common in the retro style of Spanish films of recent decades, Almodóvar undercuts what might have been merely a sentimental narrative by enticing the spectator to decipher a hermeneutical mystery involving the multiple representations of the past bound up with the figure of Montiel. The objective of such a process is to forge for the film's audience a critical distance from, and a postnostalgic lucidity about, personal and collective history. Derived from a term originally coined by Fredric Jameson (279–96), "postnostalgia" suggests a movement beyond readers' and spectators' sentimental ensnarement in memories. It implies the recognition of nostalgic affect as an emotional blockage in the understanding of personal and social collective experience of past events. Consequently, to achieve postnostalgic lucidity is to recognize the past not as a fixed and immutable "then" but as a malleable substance open to conscious remaking and, inevitably, distortion. The things one thought buried in the past return, or are made to return, but in different, even deceptive forms. The

Posters of Sara Montiel in front of the Cine Olympo in Bad Education *(2004). Photograph by Diego López Calvín. Copyright Diego López Calvín/El Deseo.*

"post" of postnostalgia, in this light, signals the hermeneutic activity of inter-rogating these protean expressions of "pastness." A seemingly broad category, with applications to a wide range of literary and cinematic works, postnos-talgia, as Almodóvar develops it in *Bad Education,* is intimately rooted in the conjunction of Spanish cultural and political history with his own auto-biographical narrative.

Questions of history per se are never openly addressed in *Bad Education.* Instead, they are part of an intricate narrative structure marked by striking shifts among specific moments from the past that have particular histori-cal and social resonance for Spanish audiences. The spectator's task is to piece together these fragmented episodes into a coherent "story," one that, while it makes sense as fiction, also holds a recognizable symbolic value as collective history. Initially set in Madrid in 1980, the complex plot focuses on Enrique Goded (Fele Martínez), a filmmaker who receives a visit from a young man (Gael García Bernal) who claims to be Ignacio Rodríguez, a childhood friend. From the start, something about Ignacio seems wrong to Enrique. The young man does not look at all like the Ignacio he remembers as his first childhood love. Further perplexing Enrique is Ignacio's insistence that he be called by the name he uses as a professional actor, Ángel. Ignacio/ Ángel offers Enrique a short story he has written as a potential script, "La visita" (The Visit), which is set in a town in the province of Valencia in 1977 but also contains a flashback involving intimate details of their childhood experiences at school in this same town in 1964. As Enrique reads the story that night, we view his mental projection of the film he would make from his friend's narrative. Much of the first half of *Bad Education* consists of this film-within-the-film, a flashback to a fictionalized past that, ironically, is also the projection into the future of Enrique's next film.

The three pivotal historical dates of the action mark specific phases of popular Spanish cultural history. As noted, the early scenes in Enrique's production office are set in the Madrid of 1980, the beginning of Spain's prodigious

Paca (Javier Cámara) and Zahara (Gael García Bernal) in front of the shreds of political history, with "Vote Centro" visible among the torn posters behind them. Photograph by Diego López Calvín. Copyright Diego López Calvín/El Deseo.

political and cultural transformation. The year 1977 saw the first
orship general elections. Although Almodóvar explains the cine
atic significance of 1964 for his own creative formation,[1] the year has
a broad political resonance as well, as it recalls the Franco regime's self-
congratulatory celebration of "twenty-five years of peace." Notably, 1977
and 1980, both resonant dates in modern Spanish history, become "present-
tense" frames from which the 1964 story of childhood love between Enrique
Goded and Ignacio Rodríguez is narrated.

Built into this intricate interplay of personal and collective memories
lies the snare of misrecognition of the historical past as it is filtered through
the subjective perspective of the individual's present-day circumstance. We
note this, for instance, in the manner in which Enrique first projects in his
mind's eye the ideal film he will make as he reads Ignacio's story. Although
still skeptical about Ignacio's identity, he nonetheless imagines the latter's
voice as the story's voice-over narrator and even projects Ignacio as its protagonist. The action of that imagined film is set on a fateful night in 1977
in the same rural town that housed the religious school where, years earlier,
the two boys had studied. The Ignacio of 1977 is a member of "La Bomba," a
traveling troupe of female impersonators; he appears under the stage name
Zahara, dressed as Sara Montiel. Just as that name is a play on Sara Montiel's
name, his performance consists of lip-synching Montiel's songs. During one
performance, Zahara flirts with a young man who turns out to be the Enrique
of Ignacio's first schoolboy crush, though at this point he does not yet realize it. After the show, Ignacio seduces Enrique. The next day, still in drag,
Ignacio visits the religious school in the town to settle an old score with his
former teacher, Father Manolo (Daniel Giménez Cacho). Years earlier, this
same priest had seduced him and, out of jealousy, expelled Enrique, his rival
for Ignacio's affections. Confronting Father Manolo, Ignacio hands him a
copy of the narrative of their sordid relations, which he threatens to sell to
the newspapers if Father Manolo does not give him one million pesetas.

Throughout these early sequences, all foregrounding the imposture of
the body of Sara Montiel, the famed movie star becomes indirectly the arbiter
of melodramatic meaning for each of the protagonists. First, she is a proxy
object of gay seduction in the musical review, then, through Zahara's continued impersonation of her when he visits Father Manolo, she is transformed
into the agent of retribution for the crime of pedophilia. Perpetually remade
by the storyteller Ignacio and the filmmaker Enrique to suit their own purposes, the version of Montiel that Almodóvar gives us is also the persistent

mark of an alluring and yet irretrievable past. In this essay, I will examine the ways in which Almodóvar channels the complex dynamics of nostalgia built around the figure of Montiel as a strategy through which to engage his audience in a critical interrogation of personal and collective manipulations of history and memory.

Autobiography, History, Cinema

Bad Education's historicist project is transacted through a narrative that highlights self-references to Almodóvar's personal and professional auto-biography, the most prominent of which is the choice of Madrid in 1980—the year and place of the premiere of his first commercial feature *Pepi, Luci, Bom*—as the framing site from which nearly all other actions are presented as flashbacks. The Madrid of Almodóvar's early career is refigured within the recognizable genre of the thriller, emphasized through Alberto Iglesias's score, which recalls Bernard Herrmann's music for Hitchcock films during the 1950s and 1960s. A noir plot further underscores genre associations in which the "dirty little secrets" of the characters' past are paramount. The evocation of Hollywood-period filmmaking introduces a critical tension between the depiction of the past and the viewing present of 2004, the year *Bad Education* was released. More than merely the filmmaker's incidental homage to his own professional origins, 1980 is transformed into the starting point of a mystery plot involving both individual memory and cultural history. Cinematic autobiography is further emphasized through the device of a filmmaker's making a film that dramatizes moments in his childhood.

The connection between these highly personal memories and what is commonly understood as collective memory is an important one. Susan Suleiman explains this correspondence as she speaks of what she calls the "crisis of memory" in reference to the French experience of the Second World War: "there is an interplay between certain individual memories and a group memory, so that the expression of one is in symbiotic relation to the other" (4). For Suleiman, particular depictions of individual experience evoked through personal memoirs, novels, documentaries, and fictional films pose images that are locked into the minds of larger audiences, thereby bridging the gap between personal and collective memory. She goes on to argue that "[i]ndividual memories may become an object of public debate or conflict; they may help establish a consensus or an 'official memory' about the collective past; they may figure as representative of the experience of a particular group and, finally, they may crystallize the difficulties of remembrance itself,

self-reflexively" (5). Suleiman sees a challenge to the monolithic sense of the collective past in the emergence of countermemories voiced through the agency of individual reminiscences, testimonies, and recollections posed in a variety of texts: memoirs, novels, documentaries, stories. Contested memories are what Suleiman calls the "crises of memory" because they represent conflict for the individuals recalling them just as they challenge the broader societal acceptance of official memory.

The theme of such contested memories as they relate to Spanish society of the Franco period has been aptly characterized by Joan Ramón Resina as "disremembering the dictatorship" and has, in fact, become a topic of extensive cultural debate in Spain.[2] Almodóvar joins that debate by embedding into the plot of Bad Education two such "crises of memory," both rooted in his own autobiography, that will have an inevitable resonance for the contemporary audiences of 2004: the characterization of the Francoist past as the "bad education" to which the film's title refers, and the focus on the Madrid of 1980 as the symbolic site of origin of cultural and political attitudes destined to reshape Spanish social and political life for the next quarter century. The specificity of these two clusters of allusions reinforces the deeper historicist project of Bad Education, which is to engage the Spanish audience in a rethinking of its own place within the flow of contemporary Spanish culture. Because this narrow "local" history is less accessible for international audiences, Almodóvar provides links between these and more universally legible cinematic references.

The "bad education" of the film's title, for instance, has a double meaning of a literal bad education depicted in the plot and also of bad behavior or conduct. It thereby suggests the continuum from childhood to adult behavior as it has affected Spain's contemporary social life and politics. International audiences may relate the scenes of the literal bad education suffered by Ignacio and Enrique at the religious school to a recognizable film genre involving young boys and their traumatic experience at the hands of teachers. These include films as diverse as Jean Vigo's Zéro de conduite (1933), Federico Fellini's 8½ (1963), François Truffaut's The Four Hundred Blows (1959), and Louis Malle's Au revoir les enfants (1987). Closer to home, Carlos Saura's La prima Angélica (Cousin Angélica) (1973) was widely distributed internationally during the final years of the Franco dictatorship and bears a highly suggestive connection to Almodóvar's film. In Saura's work, aspects of repressive schooling during the civil war are pointedly represented as a bridge to attitudes and a mind-set that pervaded later Francoist culture in the 1970s.

Representing oppressive structures: Padre Manolo (Daniel Giménez Cacho) patrols the dormitory in Bad Education. *Photograph by Diego López Calvín. Copyright Diego López Calvín/El Deseo.*

The association with Saura's film may also mark an important revision of Almodóvar's attitude toward Francoist culture within his own film work. Famously deriding the Spanish auteurist obsession with the Francoist past, he had often denied any causality between the cultural politics of Francoism and his own formation and outlook. Thus, the alignment of certain details of his childhood with the repressive social praxis of the dictatorship is significant in that it mirrors images and treatments of the cultural formation of earlier generations of Spanish writers as expressed in widely disseminated nonfiction writing of the 1970s and 1980s.

Perhaps the most prominent of these is Manuel Vázquez Montalbán's nonfictional essay *Crónica sentimental de España* (Sentimental Chronicle of Spain) (1970), which describes the phenomenon of "popular education" to which Spaniards were subjected after the civil war: the mass-mediated indoctrination of Spanish youth to the cultural norms and moral attitudes of the regime. Of particular note in the Catalan writer's notion of popular education is how materials that were at the time called "subcultural," such as songs, myths, and symbols, circulated through the mass media in an effort "to promote the falsification of our recognition of what constituted reality and where we as individuals fit into that reality" (20–21). Vázquez Montalbán emphasizes the cult of social conformism as a form of brain-washing whose true aim was pedagogical, that is, to teach Spaniards how to fit into the triumphant social order of the victors of the civil war.

Resistance to that form of "bad education" begins to emerge in several Spanish films in the late 1960s, but only in cautious—or wily—ways that receive the approval of the Francoist censorship boards. We see instances of resistance in Jaime Camino's *España otra vez* (Spain Again) (1968) and Basilio Martín Patino's *Canciones para después de una Guerra* (Songs for after a War) (1971), two films that rely heavily on documentary film footage to evoke the historical past of the defeated population. More boldly, Saura's brilliant *Cousin Angélica* dramatizes the painful psychological indoctrina-tion of a child of a Republican-sympathizing family trapped in the Francoist zone during the war as a traumatizing experience that deftly conflates Spanish memories of growing up under the regime with the international stereotype of Spanish fascism. Similar to Saura's depiction of a grown man in 1973 imagining himself in his adult body reliving the experiences of his childhood in a provincial school, *Bad Education* develops the theme of the ghosts of Francoism as luring the adult Enrique back to the past.

Fifteen years after Vázquez Montalbán's essay, famed novelist Carmen Martín Gaite published her celebrated recollections of growing up in Spain in the decade of the forties, *Usos amorosos de la postguerra española* (Court-ship Customs in Postwar Spain) (1987), which focuses on the construction of female identity during the Franco regime. Martín Gaite, who was born in 1929, and whose recollections center on social life in the 1940s, might seem unrelated to the generational focus of Almodóvar's more historically recent material. Yet part of Martín Gaite's theme is the impact of National Catholic Education on the cultural and social formation of various generations of Spaniards, both male and female. In particular, her essay provides a useful bridge to Almodóvar's own treatment of the relation between sexual iden-tity and the bad education of the Franco years.[3]

A second pivotal "crisis of memory" that structures the historicist proj-ect of *Bad Education* is rooted in the "present-tense" frame of the film, the mise-en-scène of Madrid in 1980. Almodóvar gives special prominence to the visual style of film noir, suggesting that Madrid is also the locus of moral ambiguity: "the great bad place" so often depicted in Hollywood noir films. Rather than being the ebullient site of sexual liberation as in *Pepi, Luci Bom,* or of a culture of drugs and sexual cruising in the Rastro, the Sunday-morning Madrid flea market, as showcased in the opening scene of *Labyrinth of Passion* (1982), the period now seems emblematized by the shadowy interiors of Enrique's production office and a subdued sound track that contrast sharply with the raucous street sounds of the early *Movida* films.

The noir milieu of *Bad Education* rewrites the post-Franco years of the *"Cambio"* (literally "change," but usually loosely translated as "The Transition") as a troubling continuity with the Francoist past.[4] Following the opening credit sequence, the intertitle "Madrid, 1980" appears, promptly giving way to the interior of the production office of El Azar, which means "chance," the fictional equivalent of Almodóvar's own production company, El Deseo, which means "desire." Working with his assistant Martín, Enrique Goded peruses newspaper clippings in search of inspiration for his next project. The sunlight streaming through Venetian blinds produces a striking visual effect in which the lines of shadow and light traverse the faces of the characters in a recognizable homage to one of the hallmark features of classic American noir cinema. As the two men work, they are interrupted by a knock on the office door. When Martín answers, the caller refuses to be turned away and insists on speaking to Enrique, claiming to be an old friend from his childhood. Enrique is brought face-to-face with what he believes to be an updated image from his past, his childhood friend and first love, Ignacio Rodríguez. With a notable economy of cinematic expression, the principal themes of the film—a remembered past aligned with the cinematic markers of film noir and conflated with nostalgic desire—are introduced around the simple diegetic gesture of the opening of a door.[5]

The door-opening image may appear to be merely a way to put the plot in motion, but it is important to recognize how, in the process of evoking a recognizable cinematic style of "pastness," Almodóvar uses this simple device in order to suggest the symbolic eruption of the ghosts of the past at the moment in his own professional career when his creativity was built upon the *denial* of recent Spanish history. The gesture poses a suggestive linkage to the writings of various contemporary cultural critics who have similarly proposed the depiction of Spain's recent embrace of modernity as a break with the past. This is, in fact, as Resina puts it, a form of "induced amnesia" (88–93). Indeed, the eccentric, somber depiction of Madrid in *Bad Education* seems consistent with what Eduardo Subirats has described as Spain's "rigorously ambiguous process of modernization" (39).

Although Almodóvar boasted throughout the 1980s that he made films as though Franco had never existed, as critics have noted, cultural history, and eventually political history, intruded at various points in his films of the early and mid-1990s (Yarza 124; Vilarós 218; Smith, *Desire Unlimited* 185). The connections between a nationally marked personal past and contemporary Spain are depicted in an elaborate scene from *High Heels* (1991). As Teresa Vilarós points out, the return of Becky del Páramo (Marisa Paredes) to Madrid after the dismantlement of Francoism is the occasion for characters and audience to acknowledge their distance from the recent past. We observe the brilliant staging of drag queen Femme Letal's (Miguel Bosé) impersonation of Becky on the stage of the Villarosa nightclub, with Becky and her daughter Rebeca (Victoria Abril) in the audience. Not only is Letal's performance a fossilized appearance of the period before Becky left Spain in the 1970s, but, as Vilarós points out, the musical number she performs, "Recordarás" (You Will Remember), mouthing the voice of Luz Casal, invokes personal and collective memory (218–19). The background against which Letal performs is an incongruous tableau of traditional Andalusian models of femininity. With her daughter at her side, the real Becky becomes a spectator of herself, one who is offered a view of her future as well as of her past. The folkloric images of nineteenth-century Spanish Romanticism that serve as a backdrop to Letal's performance serve a parallel function in showing the out-of-date icons of Spanishness that were cultivated during the Franco years. As in these earlier films, *Bad Education* depicts the conjoining of personal and historical past. At the same time, it makes explicit the connection of autobiography to a broader collective retelling of aspects of modern Spanish history.

A Geography of Nostalgia

Bad Education might be appropriately described as the dramatization of the snare of nostalgia, a theme that Almodóvar has insinuated into nearly all of his films since *Tie Me Up! Tie Me Down!* (1990). After the broad international success of *Women on the Verge of a Nervous Breakdown* (1988), which represents for Paul Julian Smith the achievement of a utopian space unfettered by the specifics of a recognizable national communal space (*Desire Unlimited* 93), Almodóvar's films gave increasing prominence to narratives of geographic dislocation in which his characters are disoriented within menacing urban spaces.[6] As early as *Dark Habits* (1983) and *What Have I Done to Deserve This?* (1984), such dislocations had depicted more positive backstories as women who had migrated to the city eventually recognize Madrid as the site of their personal liberation from confining patriarchy. By contrast,

Almodóvar's protagonists, from Ricky (Antonio Banderas) in *Tie Me Up! Tie Me Down!* to Leo (Marisa Paredes) in *The Flower of My Secret* (1995), actively engage in the pursuit of a sense of rootedness through emotional and physical returns to their past. In *Tie Me Up! Tie Me Down!,* Ricky goes back to his Andalusian village to view the remains of his childhood home. In *High Heels,* Becky del Páramo moves back to the basement apartment in Madrid in which she had grown up. In *Kika,* Ramón (Alex Casanova) chooses to remain just outside Madrid in his mother's cottage, which is named "Casa Youcalli," after a lyric from a Kurt Weill song, and which means "the place of happiness." In *The Flower of My Secret,* Leo returns to her mother's house in La Mancha in an effort to recover from an emotional collapse. Such references insistently suggest nostalgia for a lost maternal presence.

The provincial village, feminized through the characters' association of it with their mothers and symbolized as a place of origins, seems to allude to some collective historical scenario (Mazierska and Rascaroli 37). *Live Flesh* (1997) makes explicit the associations between individual and collective scenarios by establishing an affective linkage between Víctor's (Liberto Rabal) birth on a public bus on a January night in 1970 as a state of emergency is declared and his mother's and Spain's political past. The birth on the bus serves as a historical prologue and includes a recording of Franco's minister of information, Manuel Fraga Iribarne, announcing on the radio the official suspension of civil liberties. The prologue introduces a contemporary story set in the 1990s and rhymes with the film's epilogue, set in 1996, which returns us to an analogous situation. The setting is once again downtown Madrid during the Christmas season and the scene evokes the impending birth of Víctor's son. Earlier images of empty streets have now given way to a festive holiday air with Christmas lights and throngs of shoppers. In the final words of the film, Víctor says to his soon-to-be-born son: "You're lucky, you are, little kid! You don't know how things have changed. Spain lost its fear a long time ago."

Shot on the eve of the 1996 Spanish general elections, the film's ending proposes a new genealogy for Víctor's family that moves him from the shadows of the dying dictatorship in 1970 to an optimistic view of a future very different from Spain's political past. Historically, however, in a kind of "return of the repressed," the political monsters of that era, emotionally linked to Víctor's birth through Fraga's voice, reemerge with the election results that bring to power the Partido Popular, founded by Fraga and led to electoral victory by his more youthful disciple, José María Aznar. This narrative of return of the monsters of the political past that fills the years between Almodóvar's completion of *Live Flesh* and his production of *Bad Education* will become the backstory of the latter film in which the Father Manolo of 1964 is transformed into the Mr. Berenguer of 1977. This metamorphosis of the priest of the Francoist past into the businessman of the post-Franco period reminds the audience of the persistence of a repressive political past emotionally bound up with sentimental associations.

Related to this sentimental and political "return of the repressed," Noël Valis has examined the historical roots of the use of the concept of nostalgia in nineteenth-century Spanish culture and literature. She suggests a broad scenario for nostalgia as a "cultural practice, not a given content" (254–55). "Romantic thought," according to Valis, "made nostalgia incurable, that is, a permanent condition of loss and exile, childhood as a lost paradise serving as its central metaphor" (207). She further associates the psychological features of nostalgia with an unresolved historical shift in Spanish culture by which the migration from the provinces precipitated a spatialized exilic scenario that continues to haunt the Spanish cultural imaginary throughout the twentieth century and beyond. Nostalgia begins as a geographic longing and becomes interiorized within the human psyche. As Valis writes:

> Nostalgia intensified when more and more people moved from their villages to the cities, losing that topographical, sense-oriented identification with the particular landscapes of their lives. . . . As a side effect of historical processes, nostalgia is imbued with the historical. . . . [It] has always been associated as well with absence and loss, that is, with what has already moved or been removed from the experiential present. Nostalgia means a form of deprivation, whether felt on a cultural or a psychological level. (Ibid.)

The importance of Valis's argument lies in its repositioning of what we usually understand as an individual memory in relation to collective history. Her discussion suggestively proposes a genealogy of the trope of nostalgia that mirrors in an uncanny way the processes of Almodóvar's films.

Moving through nearly all of Almodóvar's films of the 1990s, we can discern a similar nostalgic dimension in the cinematic presentation of geocultural artifacts from the past: photographs, letters, even sounds that punctuate the films. In *Bad Education*, these personal and collective migrations remit to the provincial spaces of Valencia and Galicia, once again invoking the historical backstory of geographic dislocations. The connection between the past and the present as dramatized in the film is, however, more than a simple matter of the characters' recollections and mementos. Memory is continually fueled by a melodramatic desire that is most notable in Enrique's efforts to reconstitute his sentimentalized past through the agency of certain artifacts now transformed into fetish objects. The history of "bad taste, kitsch, and social marginality" of which Valis speaks is concretized in the extravagant body of Sara Montiel, the Spanish actress and singer of the 1940s and 1950s, who, by the final decade of the Franco dictatorship, had become a kind of Spanish Mae West, a gay icon whose image had been replicated through the performances of female impersonators and further reinforced through her own self-parody later in her career. Evoked through the words of Ignacio's story, then linked to the recordings of her singing voice in Enrique's projection of the film he plans to make, Montiel becomes a fetish, gaining force precisely because she is not reduced to a material object but pervades the subject's aural imagination and memory. Aligned with dated popular tastes in the protagonists' memories, Sara Montiel thus comes to define the conceptual core of the film.

The Historical Fetish

With respect to Almodóvar's reconfigurations of the marks of Spanish national identity, Paul Julian Smith singles out *Matador* for its recycling of stereotypical Andalusian elements—bullfights, folkloric music, flowers—as "fetishized allusions to a threatening history" (*Desire Unlimited* 76). According to Smith, "[j]ust as the sexual fetish is a defence against female lack and a disavowal against that lack, so the historical fetish protects the subject from the wounds of history, while abolishing that history, confining it to the hermetic, aestheticized space of the cinematic mise-en-scène" (ibid.). Philip Rosen expands the conception of the historical fetish in a manner that helps to clarify the two protagonists' emotional investment in the figure of Montiel in *Bad Education*:

> Suppose we consider the authentic, preserved historical object in analogy with a fetish object. . . . First the fetish object is "part" of the woman's body that, in the fantastic logic of the symptom, restores it as a "whole" body (one not subject to castration). This is a structure of metonymy-as-synecdoche: a bordering "part" the fetish object replaces the missing "part" (the penis), so as to symbolize a complete "whole." Similarly, if one fixates on an authenticated, preserved object as a trace of a vanished past that brings one into contact with it, that object is just one fragment or part of a postulated total past. (73)

Far from being a random icon brought into the service of the plot as a mere narrative embellishment, Sara Montiel's presence in *Bad Education* is given prominence through repeated references to her in film clips, movie posters, songs, and female impersonations that dramatize the protagonists' highly personalized emotional investment in an important episode of their shared past.

Unlike any of the other "fictional" characters, Montiel bears a historical trace, her image continually alluding to, confirming, and yet disavowing the presence of the historical field outside the filmic fiction. The "historical" Montiel is presented in the film through Enrique's remembrance of his time in the religious school when he and Ignacio went to a movie theater in the town to see Mario Camus's film *Esa mujer* (That Woman) (1969).[7] The scene is introduced by an extended sequence in which Ignacio has been brought to perform a version of "Torno a Sorrento" (Return to Sorrento) on the occasion of Father Manolo's birthday. As though escaping the clutches of the pedophile priest, Ignacio runs off with Enrique to see the Montiel film. In the dark interior of the theater, away from the vigilance of the priests and under the flickering lights of the screen, the two boys masturbate each other.

Although Almodóvar has used the device of the film-within-the-film over the years, the interpolation of a scene from *That Woman* is the first instance in which a cinematic-historical figure breaks out of the movie frame and is dispersed, through impersonation, throughout the fictional narrative. That dispersion process is, in fact, reaffirmed in Almodóvar's choice of *That Woman,* inasmuch as it mirrors much of the story line of the first part of *Bad Education.* The plot, which involves the return to a religious cloister by a former nun in search of forgiveness from her Mother Superior, bears an obvious parallel to Zahara's return to the religious school. At the same time, however, Almodóvar may have found *That Woman* appealing for its dramatization of moral ambiguity at the root of Montiel's star persona and hence for its ability to illuminate one of the underlying historical questions of *Bad Education.* In the figure of Montiel, both in her films and in her off-screen life, we find someone "able to transgress the morality that Francoism imposed on the nation while simultaneously retaining all of the clichéd virtues associated with Spanishness" (Borau 696).

As Annabel Martín cogently observes, "Francoism finds its kindred spirit in the hyperbolic language of melodrama, its moral Manichaeism" (17). "Melodrama is a language drawn from the emotions by various generations of Spaniards and an otherwise incomprehensible aesthetic form if we do not recognize it as a 'second skin' inseparable from the political framework of each historical moment" (ibid. 28). In the convergence of popular cultural styles and inflexible social definitions of propriety and sin, Montiel becomes an ambivalent icon, embodying both the disavowal and the reaffirmation of the inflexible moral dichotomy of good and evil so closely tied to the regime's ideology. That moral ambiguity folds back on Almodóvar's characters when both Enrique and Ignacio condemn Father Manolo's immorality within the same Manichaean value system that had so tortured them as children.

Historians of Spanish film, however, have treated Montiel in a much less complicated manner, simply seeing in her an actress of striking beauty and passable singing talent who achieved a broad and spontaneous popular triumph in 1957 in the role of María Luján, the music-hall singer in Juan de Orduña's *El último cuplé* (The Last Torch Song) (1957). Her success in the film not only rekindled her floundering movie career but also situated Montiel on the level of a national myth. As Vázquez Montalbán observed, Montiel's ascendancy as a Spanish superstar coincided with a specific historical moment and broader cultural tendencies: "It is not strange that, at the start of the age of the 'American Way,' adults of that period should experience for the first time in Spain an irruption of the culture of nostalgia. The height of that symptom was *The Last Torch Song,* its face, its voice: Sara Montiel. The commercialization of nostalgia had as much importance then as the intellectualization of nostalgia is beginning to have now" (193). Kathleen Vernon sees Montiel in a similar light, as "personif[ying] the ambivalence of a society caught between moralizing and modernizing impulses and reflecting back to spectators the face of Spain as shaped by their own beliefs and desires" (195).

The simulations of Montiel within *Bad Education* are symptomatic expressions of the historical fetishization of a particular kind of collective yet personalized "pastness" associated with the "culture" of female impersonators in the entertainment scene of Spain in the 1970s (Mira 439–40). From the 1940s on, the *travesti* or female impersonator had been a staple of the Spanish music-hall circuit, whose formula for success was the imitation of stars, especially those identified with popular folkloric music, such as the bolero and the *cuplé* or torch song. As Alberto Mira contends, the essence of that music-hall tradition was a form of cultural recycling of artists whose work was already perceived as so stagy as to constitute "an imitation of an imitation" (439). By the later decades of the dictatorship, the audiences for such performances in the relatively more tolerant cosmopolitan centers of Madrid and Barcelona were, according to Mira, a mixture of both straights and gays (440).

The first evocation in *Bad Education* of Sara Montiel underscores the complex historical and personal trajectories that converge around the figure of the *travesti*. Montiel enters the narrative as total artifice, a figure visualized by Enrique as he reads the opening pages of "The Visit" and imagines a provincial theater in which a *travesti* show is in progress. In this way, Enrique's imaginative recycling of Montiel assumes the literal and figurative center stage of the film. Sporting an outrageous Jean-Paul Gaultier body suit that emphasizes the constructedness of femininity (highlighting buttocks, nipples, and pubic hair), Gael García Bernal, in the role of the female impersonator Zahara, evokes Montiel by lip-synching a recording of her singing "Quizás, quizás, quizás" (Perhaps, Perhaps, Perhaps), composed by Cuban Osvaldo Farrés and made famous in the United States by Nat King Cole. Although imaged by Enrique, this version of Montiel as scripted in the short story is also the product of Ignacio's twin desires: to become Sara Montiel and to be sexually possessed by Enrique. Thus, the figure of Zahara is in a pointed way the product of the creative collaboration of both Enrique and Ignacio, and prefigures their sexual union later that evening.

Unlike the "fictional" characters, Montiel bears, as already amply noted, a historical trace, her image continually alluding to and confirming the presence of the historical field outside the filmic fiction. The simulations of Montiel are symptomatic expressions of the historical fetishization of a particular kind of collective yet personalized past. Through her performance in *El último cuplé*, Montiel became identified in the popular imagination as inhabiting a slip zone between proper social conduct and proscribed sexual behavior embodied in the liminal space of Spain's musical theater tradition. Even the *cuplé*, the song with which Montiel becomes identified, derives from a tradition of risqué musical numbers filled with sexual innuendo performed by women. Vernon cites various contemporary cultural commentators, including Catalan writer Terenci Moix, in order to underscore the metonymic links between the figure of Montiel in her on- and offscreen roles and the theater and cinema as "space[s] of liberty and creativity for homosexuals" (195).

At some point in the late 1960s, as Almodóvar has observed, Montiel was transformed into a gay pop icon: "She is, and above all, she was a pop icon of the 'homos' and of the transvestites. She was a star in the style of Mae West or of Marlene Dietrich, a personality, a form of being in front of the camera that made her different. . . . I like the way she sings, the 'kitsch' of her films. These are very important elements for those trying to understand our sensibility. It doesn't surprise me at all that certain individuals found themselves captivated by her. She was a character, an icon, a genre unto herself" (Rioyo 34).[8] Almodóvar's description underscores the subversive implications of the dual processes of textual and sexual poaching that are embodied in the kitsch iconography of Montiel. Following Michel de Certeau, Rosemary Coombe describes "poaching" as a creative act by "marginal social groups [that] are continually engaged in nascent constructions of alternative identities" (112), a social bricolage that resignifies cultural texts in order to adapt them to one's own interests. In the social environment of extreme repression of openly gay culture described by Alberto Mira and others, cultural critics read the historical moment of Sara as an incipient form of the gender politics that will come to the surface in the gay culture of the immediate post-Franco period. It is precisely by privileging anachronism as camp, with all the implied history of gay marginalization under Francoism, that Montiel's condition of "pastness" becomes a cipher for the film's historicizing project.[9] The emphasis on Montiel's recorded voice further underscores the power of what Marsha Kinder identifies as an "audio fetish," itself part of the broader historical fetishization of the singer. On the subject of fetishization, Kinder reminds us that *High Heels,* in its original Spanish version as *Tacones lejanos,* or "Distant Heels," builds the audio fetish into the very title of the film (148) and reinforces it in Becky's career as famous torch singer and her daughter's career as a television newsreader. As Kinder notes, Almodóvar gave his female protagonists "oracular professions that rely on their voice . . . implying that their speech is connected to their status as sexual subjects" (149). The evocation of Montiel derives from that earlier audio fetish even as it at once evokes and subversively refigures the repressive patriarchal culture identified with Francoism.

The Visits

As he details the thirty-year gestation of *Bad Education* (*Bad Education* 11–14), Almodóvar notes that the final version of the script was built around three different *visitas,* a word that ambiguously means in Spanish both the act of the visit and the visitor himself or herself. The first of these *visits* is Juan's to Enrique's film production company in 1980 when he offers Enrique "The Visit" as a potential film script. The second visit, recounted in Ignacio's story, is made by Zahara to Father Manolo. This episode was, in fact, the original source story that Almodóvar wrote in 1973 as a passionate revenge against his own religious education. The third visit is that of a stranger,

Mr. Berenguer (Lluís Homar), who turns up at the studio where Enrique is shooting the final sequence of his film. Berenguer is the former Father Manolo and his appearance on the film set enables him to witness a fictionalized version of Ignacio/Zahara's death in which he, the priest, is cast as an accomplice to murder. This final visit, according to Almodóvar's structuring of the film, is the crucial motivation that triggers Berenguer to tell the "true story" of Ignacio's death. Almodóvar was so focused on the centrality of these visits that at one point he tentatively titled the script in progress "Las visitas," *The Visits* (U.S. DVD commentary).

The three visits appear guided from beginning to end by an inexorable narrative and visual logic. The opening credits start with the production company name, "El Deseo," and introduce a series of radically juxtaposed images of characters from the story that has yet to unfold. The chain of images leads to the door of the Madrid offices of "El Azar" through which Juan will intrude on Enrique's life. Therein begins a complex weaving of narrative threads that eventually moves to the film's final scene, Enrique's closing of another door on which is emblazoned the word *Pasión,* as the director throws Juan out of his house and, presumably, his life. Each of the visits is in some way connected to the image of Montiel's body and mediated through expressions of desire and passion, ironically underscoring through words the genre of melodrama against which the film's postnostalgic project works.

The first of these visits, the encounter between the fictionalized Ignacio and the fictionalized Enrique, rechristened Enrique Serrano, is followed by Ignacio's staged performance as Zahara. As he reads Ignacio's story and visualizes it as a film, Enrique casts Juan (impersonating Ignacio) in the role of Zahara impersonating Montiel. Ironically, within the story, Enrique's fictional double misrecognizes Ignacio in drag in ways that parallel his own real-life difficulty in recognizing his old lover Ignacio in the imposter Juan. Misrecognition, an integral aspect of the noir world evoked in the plot, is also an integral part of the fetishizing process that surrounds the multiple imaginings of Montiel.

Although not included in Almodóvar's enumeration, two other scenes involving Montiel might also appropriately be titled "visits." The first is the one in which, in the darkness of the provincial movie theater, the young Ignacio and Enrique watch the Montiel film as they seek respite from the torment of the religious school. In the clip of *Esa mujer,* Montiel plays the role of Sor Soledad (Sister Solitude), now a woman of the world, who returns to the convent many years after she had been raped. The Mother Superior does not recognize her at first, which prompts Sister Solitude to say: "Don't you recognize me, Mother. Has the world changed me that much?" As evoked in this film-within-the-film, Montiel's body is located in an emotional slip zone for the two impressionable boys. It is at this moment that Ignacio and Enrique look at the face of Montiel on the screen and seem to see their own futures: one as a drag queen, the other as a filmmaker. The staging of this scene—technically, a film-within-a-film-within-a-film—reaffirms the notion of the theatrical as constituting a privileged space of sexual freedom and artistic creativity.

The second scene takes place in 1980 in another theatrical space, the nightclub where Juan, in preparation for his audition for the role of Zahara, pays a visit to a drag show in order to observe Sandra, who is performing as Sara Montiel. Here again, the voice of Montiel is heard as Sandra lip-synchs "Maniquí" (Mannequin), a song that self-consciously underscores the condition of the fetishized female body. The sequence recalls the scene in *High Heels* in which Femme Letal performs the previously mentioned "Recordarás." In *Bad Education,* as in *High Heels,* the impersonator chooses a version of his subject from the past. Almodóvar notes, for instance, that the Sara of Sandra's performance is already from a bygone time (U.S. DVD commentary). In an ironic doubling of what his brother Ignacio did when he viewed the scene from *Esa mujer* as a young boy sitting alongside Enrique, Juan/Ángel projects onto Sandra's performance of Montiel the desire to forge his own future career in movies. As it circulates among the characters, the image of the fetishized body of Montiel thus comes to connote the fluidity of both history and identity. Precisely because the version of Montiel that is the object of the characters' attention in each of these visits is really the imitation of an imitation, her figure provides the occasion for a breaking down of the borders between illusion and reality.

We see this "breakdown" most pointedly in the final representation of Montiel's body in the film, which coincides with Mr. Berenguer's visit to the movie set where Enrique is completing the filming of the final scene of his movie adaptation of "The Visit." It is perhaps the most complex moment in the entire film: the point at which Juan, having poached his older brother's identity, stolen his story, inhabited his fictional alter ego (Zahara), and occupied the place of Enrique's lover as fantasized by Ignacio, finally meets his fictional end in a plot twist written by Enrique to replace the "happy ending" that Ignacio had originally imagined. Enrique's ending lays the blame squarely on the Catholic church, which he depicts as being capable

of anything, including murder. The final scene in which Enrique kills off
Juan exacts a perverse form of poetic justice on the man who is impersonating his first love, as it signals the end of his infatuation with the memory
of Ignacio and also his infatuation with the very present body of Juan. With
the return of Father Manolo, however, now transformed into Mr. Berenguer,
Enrique and the contemporary audience are thrust beyond a merely artistic or fictional closure. After the shooting is complete, Enrique submits to
Berenguer's retelling of the real-life murder of Ignacio. At this point, the
filmmaker is forced to face the past beyond the fetishized nostalgia that
he has reworked as melodrama, opening up the audience to confront the
perplexing world that is not so easily ordered by genre and Manichaean
moral codes.

Postnostalgia

If *Bad Education* were merely an evocation of the past as cinematic camp,
the film would be little more than an elaborate exercise in visual and narrative stylistics. Cinematic and cultural retro styles are, however, at the service
of a more serious conceptual project built on a structure of what Fredric
Jameson has described in *Postmodernism, or, The Cultural Logic of Late
Capitalism* as "postnostalgia," the reconfiguration of narrative as a hermeneutical mystery about the representations of the past and its political and
personal meaning in the present. According to Jameson, "postnostalgia" is a
formal visual-narrative strategy that seeks to free its audience from the pull
of "pastness" by developing a form of narration that works as a diagnostic
apparatus through which to view and question one's relation to the representations of the past (287–88, 296). Describing the narrative strategies that
evoke postnostalgic consciousness, Jameson observes:

> Only by means of a violent formal and narrative dislocation could a narrative apparatus come into being capable of restoring life and feeling to this only intermittently
> functioning organ that is our capacity to organize and live time historically. . . .
> [W]hat is at stake is essentially a process of reification whereby we draw back from
> our immersion in the here and now (not yet identified as a "present") and grasp it as
> a kind of thing—not merely a "present" but a present that can be dated. (284)

In a postnostalgic narrative, the text freezes the representation of the past,
transforming it into an object of analysis that will enable the reading subject to scrutinize critically the distortions and contradictions inherent in
historical representation. What we find in *Bad Education* is a pattern of historicized address developed around a series of aural and visual allusions to

popular culture of the Franco period as a way of prompting critical reflection on the ways the past has been "used," that is to say, manipulated.

One of the most pointed demonstrations of this mode of address is the early scene of class recess in which the young boys and their teachers, the priests, play soccer. The image of a priest serving as goaltender, shot from behind the net, is presented in freeze-frame to give the impression of the priest levitating. The frozen image recalls a widely circulated photograph by the famed Spanish photographer Ramon Masats, "Partit de Fútbol" (Soccer Match) (1960).[10] The brief pause works as a fissure in the filmic text, momentarily breaking the cinematic illusion of characters in movement. As such, it invites the critical contemplation of a Spanish audience old enough to recall that famous media image in which the photographer took a commonplace moment from a schoolboys' soccer match and mockingly transfigured it into a religious miracle. In remembering that iconic photograph from the Franco years, the audience of 2004 may also come to appreciate how far Spaniards have come from that time when the Catholic church, as the surrogate of the Francoist state, pervaded much of everyday life.

Almodóvar re-creates Ramon Masats's famous photograph "Partit de Fútbol" (Soccer Match, 1960) in Bad Education. *Copyright El Deseo.*

Bad Education is, in fact, punctuated with other images, not all so self-referentially presented, that form a metaphoric picture album of the innocent past shared by the two young protagonists that holds collective meanings for generations of Spaniards as well. The image track of the soccer match is rather incongruously accompanied by the haunting musical refrains of Gioacchino Rossini's "Kyrie," from "Petite Messe Solennelle." The "Kyrie" is "naturalized" in the next scene, which depicts the mass in which Ignacio performs in the choir. Yet the same musical motif recurs during the scene of Enrique's expulsion from the school, Ignacio's death from a heroin overdose, and the final coda of the film ending with the enlarged word *passion*. This insistent musical strain works to recompose these scenes in a way that challenges the broader line of the plot. They may be bound together as a separate narrative album, one that traces moments in the story of Ignacio's and Enrique's love, thwarted, as the religious music reminds us, by the menacing figure of Father Manolo as the incarnation of the church.

As a more generalized postnostalgic strategy of address, music and song become a means through which the film freezes a moment in the ear and mind's eye of the audience. Perhaps the most striking moment comes at the end of the sequence detailed in Ignacio's story about Father Manolo's trips with his favorite boys to a rustic campsite. While the other boys swim, Manolo plays a guitar as Ignacio sings a Spanish version of "Moon River." The lyrics, as Kathleen Vernon points out, are significantly darker than the original English-language version. In the middle of the open-air performance, we do not see the priest's attempt to molest Ignacio, but we do hear the child's protesting voice and then see Ignacio jump away from a thicket of bushes and trees near the place where he and Father Manolo had been seated and singing. In his effort to flee from the priest, Ignacio falls to the ground. A close-up of the boy's stunned face reveals that he has cut his forehead in the fall. A crimson line of blood trickles down, abruptly splitting the screen and dividing Ignacio's face into two half-images in freeze-frame. The image next cuts to a close-up of Father Manolo in 1977 as he reads Ignacio's story, followed by a cut to a parallel image of Enrique completely absorbed in the story of Zahara's visit to the priest from the vantage of 1980. The extradiegetic splitting of the image of Ignacio's face is obviously motivated by the attempted sexual attack; that rupture is then recuperated textually by the child Ignacio's words from the story that Enrique is reading: "A thread of blood split my face in two. I had a sense of foreboding that the same thing would happen to my life: it would always be split in two and there would be no way to avoid that."

As the most complex of all the staged memories in *Bad Education,* Ignacio's split face underscores how multiple voices work to destabilize simplistic conceptions of the alignment of personal memories and collective history. The contrasting emotional perspectives of the three protagonists— Ignacio as teller of the tale, and Father Manolo and Enrique as readers-in-the-text—produce what is at times a disorienting labyrinth of stories within stories. At moments such as this one, the past is conflated with the present for the film's audience, who must inevitably read the scene through the contemporary filter of newspaper headlines about pedophile priests. At the same time, Manolo's attempted sexual attack on his young ward is equated in the minds of contemporary spectators with the abuses of the Catholic church and its historical collusion with the Franco regime.

Such readings, while appropriately satisfying as an expression of poetic justice, are still rooted in melodrama's hoary Manichaean structures, which, like Francoist culture itself, leads the audience to reframe the narrative world into unproblematic categories of good and evil (Martín 28–29). The image of the broken pedophile priest whose story ends pathetically as he is run down by one of his victims seems to offer a conscience-soothing albeit "easy" solution to the crises of memory. Juxtaposed against these conventions of cinematic narrative closure, Berenguer's final "visit" to Enrique's movie set proves especially disruptive, upstaging Enrique's ending to the story of Zahara and disrupting the certitude of the moral categories of good and evil built into Enrique's assumptions about the true relation between Juan and Ignacio.

The story Berenguer tells during his visit opens new figurative doors for Enrique, doors that ultimately prove impossible to keep closed. We see the opening of doors prefigured in the dismantlement of the movie-set construction of the church school setting that coincides with Berenguer's arrival. At the end of the film-within-the-film, in which Zahara's neck has been broken by Father Manolo's accomplice, Enrique calls "cut," and all of the actors except Juan step out of character and begin to take off their costumes. Juan remains seated and breaks down in uncontrollable tears. What we had previously viewed as the claustrophobic scenery of the provincial school of Ignacio's story is revealed, as workmen begin to strike the sets, to be a movie. Against the back wall of the set we see the actors' dressing rooms. Berenguer's appearance serves to expose to the audience the contrivance of the cinematic ending that Enrique has imposed on Ignacio's story.

Before he begins his narrative, the former priest and present businessman Mr. Berenguer presents himself to Enrique as "el malo de tu película" (the bad man of your movie), his words implicitly challenging Enrique's melodramatic way of reading the world and of giving false closure to insoluble problems. Through his telling, therefore, we begin to discern the post-nostalgic revision of Enrique's sentimental past, the inevitable end of his infatuation with the memory of Ignacio. Indeed, the story that the former priest recounts to Enrique is a radical updating of the two earlier versions that were set in the provincial town of the religious school, now reframed as the story of the two brothers in the city. In Berenguer's account, the adult Ignacio (Francisco Boira) reentered the ex-priest's life in 1977—when the ex-choirboy was already a transvestite junkie in the process of having a sex change—and proceeded to blackmail Berenguer by threatening to expose his past identity as a pedophile priest. Through his renewed contact with his former victim, Berenguer met and became infatuated with Ignacio's younger brother Juan, who led the older man on for money and gifts in exchange for sexual favors. Meanwhile, Ignacio's desperation for money reached such a point that Berenguer felt he had no choice but to kill him. Juan participated in the murder by giving his brother a fatal dose of pure heroin. After hearing Berenguer's story, Enrique throws Juan out of his house, literally closing the door on him.

In updating the plot, Berenguer also reimagines a very different Sara Montiel, one that reflects the radically different position of the former priest as storyteller. In Ignacio's story and Enrique's visualization of it, the body of Montiel signified freedom from the constraints of a repressive social and sexual order. However, in Berenguer's version, focused on events from 1977, the Montiel that comes to the fore is cast onto the devastated body and face of the drug-addicted Ignacio. The death of Ignacio thus symbolically marks the death of an illusion as well.

Almodóvar has described the plot of *Bad Education* as a variation on Scheherazade and *The Arabian Nights* (Strauss 196), within which, as in the original, the framing situation is reflected in the stories narrated. At the center is Enrique Goded, the storyteller as filmmaker, who willfully vampirizes the events surrounding his first childhood love for the sake of making a movie. For his part, Ignacio has vampirized his own life by writing "The Visit." As Almodóvar observes, each creator's motivation always exceeds the simple desire to create: Ignacio has written the story to blackmail Father Manolo; Enrique agrees to make the film spurred by the desire to understand Ignacio's death and to know the real identity of Ángel (who presents himself as Ignacio, but is actually Juan) (ibid.).

Enrique's motivation in knowingly submitting himself to Juan's deception—once he discovers part of the truth in his visit to the home of Ignacio's mother in Galicia—is explained in a scene in which, while cutting out curious *faits divers* from the newspapers in search of material for his script, he comes across a macabre news item about a woman who jumped into a crocodile pit at a Taiwanese zoo. As the crocodiles devoured her, she embraced one of them without ever screaming. Enrique's perverse motivation in knowingly accepting the situation, in which he is manipulated by Juan, thus appears to be an almost suicidal desire to know the source of Juan's enigmatic being and the true circumstances of Ignacio's death. Read as the allegorical reflection of the contemporary audience's interrogation, Enrique's pursuit of the truth behind the mask resembles the deeply felt need of contemporary Spaniards to break through the deceptive surface of the democratic Transition and modernization. The interrogation of the past leads inexorably, for Enrique and his audience, to the reappearance of Father Manolo, as though his return reaffirmed the possibility that the central theme of *Bad Education* revolves around the denunciation of the excesses of the Catholic church. Although that is indeed an important theme, at the same time, the figure of Mr. Berenguer is fraught with another unpleasant recognition by Enrique and his audience: the fraudulent basis of the past beyond which they thought they had moved.

Like Benigno, the rapist in *Talk to Her* (2002), Berenguer is, from a moral position, a despicable character. Yet, also like Benigno, he evokes a certain pathos by virtue of being doomed by his own uncontrollable desires. Having altered his appearance and name, he seems after all these years still unable to control his sexual desire for young boys. Precisely through Berenguer's reappearance, the old Manichaean structure of good and evil that seemed to rule Francoist morality has been replaced by a more compassionate understanding of what Almodóvar had famously called "the law of desire." It may well be for that reason that the director tells an interviewer, "the priest is probably my favorite character in *Bad Education*" (Hirschberg 27). Although at first sounding like a provocative authorial metacommentary, perhaps intended to further disconcert critics and audiences, Almodóvar's comment points to the underlying personal and collective structure of *Bad Education* within which characters are no longer perceived as being simply good or bad but as occupying the shifting middle ground of moral and political ambiguity. Such recognition may finally be the guiding objective of the film's postnostalgic turn.

On the eve of the Spanish debut of *Bad Education,* Almodóvar found himself again confronting the demons of the old regime in a real political skirmish with the Partido Popular, the conservative political party founded by Fraga Iribarne that had held governmental power since 1996. The film had already achieved a unique historical status by being the first Spanish film ever invited to inaugurate the Cannes Film Festival, and it was scheduled to open in Spain two days after the general elections. Three days before the elections, on March 11, 2004, a series of terrible bombings shook Madrid's Atocha train station and two nearby suburban stations, killing 191 people. Spokesmen for the conservative government of José María Aznar claimed that the bombings were the work of the Basque terrorist group ETA in an attempt to downplay the evidence that the attack was in fact the work of Al Qaeda to avenge Aznar's support of George W. Bush's invasion of Iraq. There were massive street demonstrations in Madrid and other Spanish cities as Spaniards demanded information from the government before they went to vote. Rumors spread that the government was planning to postpone the elections. At a press conference for the film, Almodóvar echoed these rumors. His televised statements were taken by the Aznar administration as a direct accusation against them as plotters of a presumed preelection coup. They threatened to have Almodóvar jailed. He spent the next month receiving threats from far-right extremists.

The political firestorm that accompanied the Spanish release of *Bad Education* seemed to vindicate the film's political themes. The "bad education" of the title, Vázquez Montalbán's notion of the pervasive cultural processes of the old regime, also has come to mean the whitewashing of the past for present-day expediency. That unexamined past, never fully repudiated within the culture of the Transition, seemed presciently embodied in the very ambiguous figure of Berenguer, saved by Almodóvar's script from the fate of mere melodramatic stereotype as the evil priest. Almodóvar's script reaffirms the destructive attraction of the past in a manner that is pointedly dramatized in Enrique's double bind: his effort to recuperate his memory of Ignacio— an irretrievable, first love—and his involuntary engagement with Juan, the imposter Ignacio, who embodies the falsification and exploitation of that past. What is at stake here is more than merely a questioning of nostalgia, but a recognition that the "cast of characters" from a memory of the past, even an artistically embellished memory, are also the protagonists of contemporary life, be they larger-than-life political figures like Fraga Iribarne's heir and ideological double Aznar or seemingly anonymous members of a postdictatorial society like Berenguer.

The "post" of postnostalgia, therefore, can be understood as an internalized perceptual distance that enables the individual to see beyond the trap of memory, to look beyond the ideological structures that mask the recollections of the past in recognizable but distorted forms. In constructing this, his most complex script, Almodóvar has recycled his and Spain's obsession with a repressed and fetishized past into a self-conscious acknowledgment of where he was in 1980 and how, through the evolution of a style and a conception of filmmaking, he has moved to a critique of his own past and the culture out of which his cinema has taken shape. With no small irony, therefore, he has, as mentioned, situated the center of the plot in the suggestively autobiographical Madrid of 1980, the very year and place of the premiere of his first commercial feature.

NOTES

1. Almodóvar explains that the year 1964 underscores the moment of a coming to awareness of the young Enrique and Ignacio and, more symbolically, of Spanish cinema itself. He reads his artistic origins as a filmmaker in what he has called "sordid neo-surrealist comedies," which he closely identifies with a critical moment in Spanish film history. As he explains in an interview: "The year of the film is 1964, the year of [Fernando] Fernán-Gómez's *The Strange Journey,* and the same year as *Aunt Tula* (Miguel Picazo). I know that closed world very well, it was a world filled with mourning clothes, of a religiosity that kept one from living. It's not the same now since they can't possess our life anymore to the point of keeping us from living it" (Rioyo 30).

2. See in particular Resina's anthology of critical essays under this same title, especially those that contextualize some of the principal themes of Almodóvar's treatment of the Spanish crises of memory: Salvador Cardús Ros, "Politics and the Invention of Memory: For a Sociology of the Transition to Democracy in Spain" (17–28); Jo Labanyi, "History and Hauntology; or, What Does One Do with the Ghosts of the Past? Reflections on Spanish Fiction of the Post-Franco Period" (65–82); and Dieter Ingenschay, "Identidad homosexual y procesamiento del franquismo en el discurso literario de España desde la transición" (157–89).

3. In *La grámatica de la felicidad,* Annabel Martín has explored the affinities between Almodóvar and both Martín Gaite and Vázquez Montalbán in her rereadings of melodrama in the Francoist and post-Franco periods (241–80).

4. Writing in the late 1990s, Teresa Vilarós observes the logic of disavowal that attends Francoism in the artistic production of the immediate post-Franco years. The defiant apoliticism of Almodóvar's films of the early 1980s mirrors that broader cultural position and thus becomes the basis of the return of the repressed. Vilarós observes: "In the early post-Franco period, just as in the immediate post–Civil War period, the past became transformed into an impenetrable 'thing' because it was the only way in which Spain could rewrite its new identity. Both the social purges of the dictatorship and the political

reforms of the Transition inevitably hid a fissure written in the deepest corner, the habitat of the monster into which our historical past has been converted" (253–54).

5. The motif of the opening and closing of doors that recurs throughout the film comes to signify for various characters the intrusion and rejection of an unwanted past. Indeed, in the final image of the film, Enrique closes the door of his house and throws Ángel out of his life.

6. Smith describes the utopian setting of Madrid in *Women on the Verge of a Nervous Breakdown* as the juxtaposition of an aging lover and "'an aggressively modern' architectural project" (*Desire Unlimited* 94). According to Smith, by the time Almodóvar makes *Kika,* that utopian milieu will become the non-place: "territorial space . . . devalued" (*Vision Machines* 44).

7. The film that the two boys go to see in 1964, Camus's *Esa mujer,* was not made until 1969. The premise of the evoked past is not necessarily based on faulty history, but on faulty memory, further suggesting that the historical fetish operates on multiple planes in Almodóvar cinema.

8. Alberto Mira notes Sara Montiel's camp status in popular Spanish entertainment in the Franco era: "The Cross-Dressing Review was a well-established tradition throughout the Franco years and it continued the formula of imitating the stars. The most imitated celebrities were Lola Flores . . . Rocío Jurado or Sara Montiel among the Spanish stars and Liza Minnelli . . . and singers like Mina or Dova among the foreign ones. The folkloric divas were well aware of being the object of imitation by the transvestites. Montiel repeatedly acknowledged this fact" (441).

9. Here again the historical and the autobiographical merge as we recall that Almodóvar's earliest sustained dramatic appearance on-screen is that of a drag queen named Lola Nicaragua, "la reina de la banana" (the Banana Queen) in Pedro Olea's *Un hombre llamado Flor de Otoño* (A Man Called Autumn Flower) (1978).

10. In her discussion of the writings of the prominent journalist Eduardo Haro Tecglen on the phenomenon of soccer, Teresa Vilarós reminds us that soccer was one of the favorite instruments for the apoliticization of the masses used by the Francoist state apparatus (44).

WORKS CITED

Almodóvar, Pedro. *La mala educación.* Madrid: Ocho y medio, El Deseo, 2004.

———. "Una sórdida comedia neosurrealista." *Conversaciones con Pedro Almodóvar.* Ed. Frédéric Strauss. Madrid: Akal, 2001. 55.

Borau, José Luis, ed. *Diccionario del cine español.* Madrid: Alianza Editorial, 1998.

Coombe, Rosemary. "Author/izing the Celebrity: Publicity Rights, Postmodern Politics and Unauthorized Genders." *The Construction of Authorship: Textual Appropriations in Law and Literature.* Eds. Martha Woodmansee and Peter Jasi. Durham, N.C.: Duke University Press, 1994. 101–31.

Hirschberg, Lynn. "The Redeemer." *New York Times Magazine* (Sept. 5, 2004): 24–27, 38–45, 70.

Jameson, Fredric. *Postmodernism, or, the Cultural Logic of Late Capitalism.* Durham, N.C.: Duke University Press, 1991.

Kinder, Marsha. "From Matricide to Mother Love in Almodóvar's *High Heels.*" *Post-Franco, Postmodern: The Films of Pedro Almodóvar.* Eds. Kathleen M. Vernon and Barbara Morris. Westport, Conn.: Greenwood Press, 1995. 145–53.

Martín, Annabel. *La gramática de la felicidad: Relecturas franquistas y posmodernas del melodrama.* Madrid: Libertarias, 2005.

Martín Gaite, Carmen. *Usos amorosos de la postguerra española.* Barcelona: Editorial Anagrama, 1987.

Mazierska, Ewa, and Laura Rascaroli. *From Moscow to Madrid: Postmodern Cities, European Cinema.* London: I. B. Tauris, 2003.

Mira, Alberto. *De Sodoma a Chueca: Una historia cultural de la homosexualidad en España en el siglo XX.* Barcelona: Editorial Egales, 2004.

Resina, Joan Ramón. "Short on Memory: The Reclamation of the Past since the Spanish Transition to Democracy." *Disremembering the Dictatorship: The Politics of Memory in the Spanish Transition to Democracy.* Ed. Joan Ramón Resina. Amsterdam: Editions Rodopi, 2000. 83–95.

Rioyo, Javier. "Todo sobre mi escuela." *El Periódico Dominical* 78 (March 14, 2004): 28–41.

Rosen, Philip. *Change Mummified: Cinema, Historicity, Theory.* Minneapolis: University of Minnesota Press, 2001.

Smith, Paul Julian. *Desire Unlimited: The Cinema of Pedro Almodóvar.* London: Verso, 2000.

———. *Vision Machines: Cinema, Literature and Sexuality in Spain and Cuba, 1983–1993.* London: Verso, 1996.

Strauss, Frédéric. *Pedro Almodóvar: Entretiens.* Paris: Cahiers du Cinéma, 2004.

Subirats, Eduardo. *Después de la lluvia: sobre la ambigua modernidad española.* Madrid: Ediciones Temas de Hoy, 1993.

Suleiman, Susan Rubin. *Crises of Memory and the Second World War.* Cambridge: Harvard University Press, 2006.

Vázquez Montalbán, Manuel. *Crónica sentimental de España.* Barcelona: De Bosillo, 2003.

Vilarós, Teresa M. *El mono del desencanto: Crítica cultural de la transición española (1973–1993).* Madrid: Siglo XXI Editores, 1998.

Valis, Noël. *The Culture of Cursilería: Bad Taste, Kitsch, and Class in Modern Spain.* Durham, N.C.: Duke University Press, 2002.

Vernon, Kathleen M. "Theatricality, Melodrama, and Stardom in *El último cuplé.*" *Gender and Spanish Cinema.* Eds. Steven Marsha and Pavarti Nair. Oxford: Berg, 2004. 183–99.

Yarza, Alejandro. *Un caníbal en Madrid: La sensibilidad camp y el reciclaje de la historia en el cine de Pedro Almodóvar.* Madrid: Ediciones Libertarias, 1999.

IV
THE AUTEUR IN CONTEXT

14 Inside Almodóvar

IGNACIO OLIVA

TRANSLATED BY SUSANA SARTARELLI AND BRAD EPPS

Knowledge and technique, *logos* and *technē,* go hand in hand in the work of art, that of the cinema most definitely included. Even though *technē* is most commonly associated with a practical ability, in the area of art it is associated, as Heidegger reminds us, not merely with a practical task but also, and more importantly, with "a mode of knowing," which means, among other things, "to have seen, in the widest sense of seeing, which means to apprehend what is present, as such" (57). Endowed with such perceptual qualities, art not only re-presents reality but also, as was said in the nineteenth century, captivates the spirit or, less ponderously, *names* an era. The notion of epochal nomination, certainly more than some vague invocation of "spirit," is germane, I believe, to a consideration of Almodóvar's cinema, especially to the degree that it is taken, over and again, as representative of an entire sociocultural era known as the *Movida* and, more broadly, as postmodernism and post-Francoism, as signaled in the title of a 1995 collection of essays on Almodóvar edited by Kathleen Vernon and Barbara Morris. Although Almodóvar's cinematic production outstrips both the *Movida,* which is now a historically delimited movement, and, increasingly, post-Francoism, which no longer accounts for a consolidated democratic order, it is interesting to note how the director's cinema continues to be *seen,* perhaps especially internationally, as particularly attuned to the unfolding present of Spain.[1]

Pedro Almodóvar is an artist with an acute capacity to see, even to *foresee.* From the very beginning of his career, Almodóvar has evinced a special ability to see *beyond* the limitations of the filmic medium in his home country—indeed, beyond the social and economic limitations of his home country—and has forged a body of work from a position of uncompromising expressive freedom that many have effectively read as testing the limits of Spain's newly regained democratic freedoms in general. Saddled with such a heavy epochal burden—Almodóvar as a spectacular representative of postmodern, post-Francoist Spanish freedom or, from a slightly different perspective, of what Marsha Kinder called "pleasure and the new Spanish mentality"—Almodóvar's cinema risks being seen in terms of social and sexual symbolism rather than (also) in terms of artistic technique. And yet, the symbolic ritualization of basic aspects of narrative cinema, notably among them interplay of space and time, has always been for Almodóvar part and parcel of a deeply personal conception of what we might call, in allusion to Walter Benjamin's reflections on translation, the task of the filmmaker.

In order to address Almodóvar's technique more thoroughly, it is important to examine such critical aspects as the writing process, set and costume design, shooting, and editing. To do so, however, it is also important to advance a more grounded, interpersonally inflected appreciation of the filmic process by way of substantial citations from many of the people who have worked most closely with the director. José Salcedo, the editor of Almodóvar's films, provides a privileged perspective into the director's first full-length feature, *Pepi, Luci, Bom* (1980). Although it is commonplace to say that Almodóvar lacks formal cinematic training and appears to work, at least in his first ventures, in an "intuitive" and/or "visceral" way that conditions the content of his films, Salcedo offers a more nuanced take that emphasizes the director's grasp of narrative technique. As he puts it in the documentary *Inside Almodóvar:* "I learned a lot with Pedro in this first film because he would always tell me that it was about telling a story and that I should not worry about the rest."[2] We shall return to Salcedo and his role in Almodóvar's cinema, but for the moment suffice it to say that editing is here typically in the service of narrative—no matter how complex and convoluted the narrative may be.

Almodóvar's *lack* of preparation quickly proved itself to be, in reality, *another mode* of preparation, one less bound to recieved ideas and ingrained practices and thus beautifully suited to a reinvention of cinematographic practice in Spain. Almodóvar's early efforts, usually taken as running from *Pepi, Luci, Bom* (but more rightly including his early Super-8 productions) to *What Have I Done to Deserve This?* (1984), though limited by the meager financial resources and, more generally, by a beleaguered and fragile national film industry, attest to the director's ability to overcome limitations and to develop artistic attitudes and cinematic techniques that promptly set him apart from other directors, Spanish or otherwise. The filming of *Pepi, Luci, Bom,* which went on for nearly a year owing to the aforementioned financial difficulties, drew on and expanded many of the techniques with which Almodóvar had been experimenting in his homey, extremely low-budget Super-8 shorts: a hyperattentive, even urgent sense of space; a marked stylization of set décor; a passionate presentation of characters; an almost fetishistic appreciation of costume and makeup, and a deployment of a welter of storytelling devices in the service of relatively free, often experimental, narrative material. These elements were integrated into a very personal artistic practice that has earned Almodóvar the status of auteur, a designation that, although itself marked by convention and a penchant for emphasizing individual talent that underestimates the collective aspects of filmmaking (precisely those that are at the center of the present article), arises as a generalized response to the hegemonic, often deeply moralistic formalization of cinema in Hollywood.

As scores of critics have noted, the sociopolitical context of Almodóvar's first film, a scant five years after the death of Franco, is marked by a dizzying transition to democracy and a giddy appreciation of new pop sensibilities. Almodóvar's response to the changes in Spanish society, loosely shared by a number of filmmakers, musicians, writers, and other artists who neither produced a manifesto nor articulated a specific ideology, *seemed* to arise almost spontaneously and was certainly indicative of the director's openness to different aesthetic possibililites. For all of its affinities to the raucous, urban cultural movement known as the *Movida,* Almodóvar's work was inflected from the very beginning by a deeply personal vision that entailed, as I hope to demonstrate, an acute awareness of technique. Understanding technique in the Heideggerian sense presented above, we move beyond any merely functional notion of artistic production and come to a poetic *perception* of spatiotemporal reality—here that of Spain in a global frame. If Almodóvar is arguably the most recognizable Spanish film director since Luis Buñuel, it is because his films, like Buñuel's, are distinguished by their own "quirky" or "idiosyncratic" cinematic codes that nonetheless appear to tap into something profound about the country, if not indeed the world, more generally.

One way in which an art form designated as "quirky" and "idiosyncratic" can come to represent an entire era—to wit, that of postdictatorial Spain— involves the *pars pro toto,* or "the part for the whole," which Sergei Eisenstein examined in his writings (8). In a long text dedicated to the evolution of the painted canvas in the history of art, Eisenstein pointed out how certain works, or certain aspects of certain works, outstrip the particular times and places in which they are produced and come to define, almost synthetically, the sensibility of an "entire" era. Without wishing to suggest any direct tie between two directors as different as Eisenstein and Almodóvar, one nonetheless encounters scenes and scenarios in the Spaniard's work that, as Eisenstein might have put it, outstrip a delimited, plot-bound functionality. A memorable example is the "mambo taxi" of *Women on the Verge of a Nervous Breakdown* (1988), a miniature, mobile shop of knicknacks that draws on stereotypically Hispanic modes of pastiche and kitsch to depict, ironically, a newly democratic and consumerist Spain and, more concretely, its capital and Almodóvar's adopted city, Madrid.

Writing and the City

The city of Madrid, that contested part of a national whole, has figured prominently in Almodóvar's cinema but also, and perhaps no less importantly, in his writings. Although writing is a solitary act for Almodóvar, as indeed it is for most people, it has assumed some rather spectacular public guises. During the early 1980s, Almodóvar expressed himself in writing through an erratic, provocative character named Patty Diphusa, whose name is a pun on the feminine form of the Spanish word *patidifuso*, which means "dazed," "bewildered," or "dumbfounded." In a manner not unlike that of Marcel Duchamp's Rose Sélavy, Patty Diphusa functioned as Almodóvar's alter ego in so-called underground circles in Madrid. From the incisive irony hidden in the folds of a wildly inauthentic feminine sensibility that in many respects was a male-inflected masquerade, the budding director put into writing, and on the public stage, a concept of life in which authenticity and inauthenticity, surface and masquerade, femininity and masculinity, and so on were blurred. As Almodóvar noted in the prologue to the first edition of *Patty Diphusa*, Patty, after having wandered through various fanzines and underground publications, found her most energetic platform in a now mythic monthly magazine called *La Luna* (The Moon), a veritable icon of the *Movida*.

In the early 1990s, influential editor Jorge Herralde proposed to Almodóvar that he gather his disparate chronicles of the wacky, wayward Patty into a book. Not only did Almodóvar accept the proposal, he also included new and previously unedited materials, in the process "reviving" Patty, a figure already famous for indiscreetly spilling into the public sector and impressing herself on the styles, attitudes, and gestures of any number of eager followers. As with the theatrical group Los Goliardos, with which Almodóvar played his first professional roles and met Carmen Maura, Patty became part of a series of campy, pop performances that included photo romances, comic books, and music. But film would also have its say, and in a manner that was intimately attuned, at least for a number of years, to the fervor of the street. Armed with a Super-8 camera and drawing on the character of Patty, Almodóvar created his first films to the delight of a small group of friends and artists.

As Pedro's brother and producer, Agustín, has repeatedly remarked, these early endeavors were more like loose *performances* or happenings than carefully orchestrated works of art. Be that as it may, not only did Almodóvar write his own stories, he also acted in them, designed the decor, filmed, edited, and chose the music for each scene. His main inspiration, as both he and his brother have said, was Spanish reality, especially that of Madrid, which found itself converted, after the long nightmare of Franco, into a quasi-heroic, quasi-burlesque setting for an entire generation. Almodóvar's "alter ego" expressed this generational sense on various occasions, especially in the chapter titled "Venir a Madrid" (Come to Madrid) from the book *Patty Diphusa*. In another chapter, titled "La vocación" (The Vocation), Patty summarized the excitement of the capital after the death of Franco as follows: "You've arrived in Madrid. Life isn't smiling down on you, but you are happy. So, finally, you begin to become part of a scenario that you had only seen on television or in magazines" (195). Madrid, the great scenario upon which Almodóvar projected his characters and stories, constituted, that is, an aesthetic realm in which reality itself seemed to be an effect of representation.

In order to have a more nuanced sense of how Almodóvar represents the city (and so much more), we might do well to attend to the fact that many of his critics have divided his cinematic work into three periods. Obviously, there is nothing definitive or discrete about these "periods," whose function is not to gainsay the often intense intertextual plays that occur between films from different historical moments but instead to shed light on, and perhaps to question, the notion of the director's "evolution" or "development." The first, as already indicated, runs from *Pepi, Luci, Bom* to *What Have I Done to Deserve This?* and is characterized by a penchant for biting or darkly humorous social commentary. The second phase runs up to *Kika* (1993), where we encounter a more self-conscious conception of filmmaking in which the director's versatility, his gift for drama as well as comedy, comes to the fore. The third phase runs, at least, to *Volver* (2006), a film, like those that immediately precede it, that points to what a number of critics have described, often quite tendentiously, as a more "self-reflective" and "mature" director who offers psychologically complex characters, intricately articulated stories (sometimes, as with *Bad Education,* to the point of confusion), and a self-conscious relation between form and content. Esther García, Almodóvar's production manager, speaks of *hondura,* or "depth," in relation to the more recent films of Almodóvar, part and parcel of what she calls a "change" in the director's life bound up in the passing of time. For her part, Lola García, Esther's sister and Almodóvar's personal assistant since 1989, explicitly refers to "maturation," the complex impact of aging on the director's understanding of art and life.

The early Almodóvar did indeed seem to live, work, and party according to the unwritten dictates of the moment. In the Madrid of the early 1980s, Almodóvar's involvement in various countercultural groups exposed him to a range of ideas and attitudes that would prove critical to his work. One of these groups was Casa Costus, so named for the "Costureras" (seamstresses), the collective nickname of two painters, Juan Carrero and Enrique Naya, both dead by 1989 (Enrique from AIDS-related complications and Juan, a month later, from suicide). Casa Costus was a studio situated in the heart of the popular Madrid neighborhood Malasaña that came to be emblematic of the *Movida* and that helped to form a number of other vibrant pop artists such as Guillermo Pérez Villalta and Sigfrido Martín Begué. In *Inside Almodóvar,* Begué, whose poster art figures prominently in *Bad Education* (2004), declares that, "the most extravagant characters that Madrid produced during those years paraded through Casa Costus. For example, you could find people who would dress up in crazy outfits but at the same time were so creative that they influenced contemporary fashion and, of course, Pedro."

A certain countercultural and underground stamp *a la española* permeates this and other declarations by Almodóvar's friends and collaborators. By the 1980s, Madrid, long a cultural backwater, had become a city where one could rub elbows with all sorts of different people, get lost in the crowd, and become familiar with alternative ideas and environments. The portraits of some of the characters of this period are suffused with proverbial, albeit postmodern, local color and, as is the case with local color in general, constitute quasi-caricaturesque reinventions of real people. In some respects, it is as if there were no mediation between the director and the city, as if his experience of it were direct—though, of course, Almodóvar has always been keenly aware of the multiple modes of cultural mediation that render experience at once suspect and artistically malleable. Be that as it may, the director's relation to Madrid, intensified in his relationships with Begué, the "Costureras," and others, has become more *obviously* mediated over time, no doubt in part because his fame no longer makes it possible for him to experience the city in the same unobtrusive ways as before.

The ability to disappear in the crowd, to submerge himself in the nightlife of the city, is, in other words, a thing of the past. Almodóvar is now a major public figure, and his relation to the everyday reality of Madrid and the rest of Spain has changed accordingly. In the face of fame and age, Almodóvar's way of working has become more reflective and allusive, more given to abstraction and stylization. Not surprisingly, the tone of his stories and the makeup of his characters have likewise changed, becoming on the whole more obscure, ambiguous, and enigmatic. His initial, almost intuitive take on the relations between character and location becomes, by dint of the elaborative process of filming, an increasingly *mediated* and self-conscious "intuition." The attention to urban spaces, which predominates in Almodóvar's films even though rural spaces punctuate them in critical ways, entails varying stylizations that are arguably less tethered to the particularities of place than to different moments in the director's life. The neorealist presentation of the working-class outskirts of Madrid in *What Have I Done to Deserve This?,* for example, stands in contrast with the fashionable, tourist-inflected presentation of the modernist center of Barcelona in *All about My Mother* (1999). The different presentation of the two cities is most likely an effect of the director's experience of them (a Madrid insider, Almodóvar is largely an outsider to Barcelona), but it is also surely an effect of changing attitudes and styles more generally.[3]

The numb anxiety that Carmen Maura, in the role of the overworked and underpaid housewife Gloria in *What Have I Done to Deserve This?,* projects onto the peripheral neighborhoods of Madrid is a far cry from the more meditative and self-reflective emotion of Cecilia Roth, who plays the grieving mother Manuela in *All about My Mother* and who moves across a broader Spanish landscape, encompassing Madrid, La Coruña, and, most notably, Barcelona. An arguably more intriguing contrast may be found, however, in the different modes of anxiety that the same actress, Maura, expresses as Gloria and, a few years later, as the professionally successful, but amorously challenged, Pepa in *Women on the Verge of a Nervous Breakdown.* Pepa enjoys a level of financial security about which Gloria, who pops amphetamines to keep on working for subsistence wages, can only dream. Centered on women from different socioeconomic classes, the films effectively thematize decor, makeup, and style in ways that at once remit to and derive from the realities of class difference in the city.

As Almodóvar's relationship to the city has changed, he has come to rely on someone who serves as an intermediary between the director and the city: the previously mentioned Lola García, whom Almodóvar has sometimes affectionately called a "slave of desire" [esclava del deseo] for her total dedication to him and his production company, El Deseo. A privileged inside observer, García has stressed the importance of the script in Almodóvar's cinematic process:

> I think that it is the writing that Pedro enjoys the most. That doesn't mean that he doesn't enjoy other moments of the film, most obviously the shooting. What happens is that these moments have so many external and complex components that it is very difficult for a miracle to happen. And when it does happen, it is wonderful.

According to García, the task of storytelling is the moment when the director is most immersed in a fictional universe and, not coincidentally, most prone to isolation. Accordingly, Almodóvar stays "connected" through a weekly diet of magazines, novels, or songs from different parts of the world. Reading and writing may well be the most constant source of stimulation for the director now that he no longer enjoys the relative anonymity of his early days. Perhaps this explains the texture of his latest stories, marked as they are by introspection, restraint, mystery, and solitude. Although *Volver* may mark a "return" to a lighter, more comic ethos (though rape, murder, and pain inflect it profoundly), Almodóvar has moved, in general, from writing in the service of the modish moment to a more deliberate sort of writing, turning inward from the street and acquiring in the process a more somber, though not necessarily less sumptuous, tone—as if his were now a heart in the shadows.

Artistic Creation: On the Concept of Style

Almodóvar's inward turn has, as intimated, a fractured prehistory. At the beginning of the 1980s, Almodóvar would get together with his friends in musician Bernardo Bonezzi's apartment in the Madrid Tower, one of the oldest skyscrapers in the center of the city. A major musical force in the *Movida*, Bonezzi composed, along with Carlos Berlanga, the music for Almodóvar and McNamara's recordings, but he also provided the space for innumerable gatherings with other unorthodox artists and musicians whose impact on Spanish cinematic history should not be slighted. As Sigfrido Martín Begué notes:

A very modest Spanish movie was made years ago in that very apartment. I think it was one of the worst films in the history of Spanish cinema. It was one of those films designated as *international intrigue*. The title of the film was *Chinos y minifaldas* [Chinese and Miniskirts] and we discovered that it had been filmed there, which for us was really hilarious.

In this same delirious setting, Almodóvar, along with Berlanga, Fabio de Miguel (aka Fabio McNamara), Begué, and Bonezzi gave free rein to their love of storytelling, improvising plots, playing roles, and parodying situations that in many cases would serve as fodder for future artistic creations, whether songs, theatrical performances, or films.

Martín Begué continues: "At that time [around 1980], Pedro was very interested in the films of John Waters, especially after having seen *Pink Flamingos* (1972) at the Filmoteca." Spanish cinema of the 1950s and 1960s, particularly that of Juan Antonio Bardem and Luis García Berlanga, had already influenced the budding director, John Waters, who also was fond of improvising with his friends, and came to embody for the Spaniards a sense of creative freedom and new artistic possibilities. Thus, even as Almodóvar turned to postdictatorial Spanish society for inspiration, he also turned to other societies, other cultural artifacts, far beyond his native land, not just the irreverent work of Waters but the more established work of the Hollywood studio system—seen, to be sure, through an often deliberately camp sensibility. A whole stylistic conception grew out of this personal synthesis of disparate cultural elements. The improvisations in Bernardo Bonezzi's apartment, drawing on Spanish, American, and other sources, were shared events, opportunities for experimentation that did not adhere to the typically isolated practices of reading and writing. These experiences, wavering between the solitary and the collective, have fueled, in the eyes of more than one of Almodóvar's critics, one of the most important and debatable aspects of his work, one that we have heretofore mentioned only in passing: to wit, intuition, an unmitigated, theoretically suspect quality that knows no laws or methodologies. What some have called the viscerality of Almodóvar's cinema is likewise related to this vexed yet resistant notion of intuition, that is to say to a concept of filmmaking that is not entirely regulated by preestablished technical and formal considerations.

The seemingly intuitive viscerality of Almodóvar's cinema—though lately challenged by a cerebrality that is particularly evident in *Talk to Her* (2002)—is related to the aforementioned sense of community, which, though varying over time, accompanies the act of making a film. One of the most unpredict-able members of this community was Fabio McNamara, Almodóvar's early artistic companion and one of the most notorious players in the *Movida*. Once again, Martín Begué proves insightful:

> many of the themes of our paintings, many of the lyrics of the songs by Olvido [Gara, aka Alaska] or by Pedro and Fabio, issued from moments of complete expressive freedom. At the time, anything could be of use to us. I remember the "calls" *[llamamientos]* that Fabio would make from the car in which he would zip around the city with Carlos [Berlanga], Bernardo [Bonezzi], Fabio, Pedro, and me. He would all of a sudden roll down the window and shout out to the passerbys, whoever they happened to be, improvising little speeches, always brimming with irony, imagination, and wordplays. Fabio brought a lot to us, not just themes and characters for Pedro's movies, but for all our work, work that could come about in the most unexpected of ways.

It was, you might say, an attitude toward life and art in which a certain "lack of respect" toward formally established procedures had some surprisingly fruitful consequences. This attitude, together with Almodóvar's limited finan-cial means, ensured that the first works were made in a rather haphazard way. An obvious example is *Pepi, Luci, Bom,* which was filmed for next to noth-ing on weekends and the occassional weekday over more than a year's time. According to Almodóvar's chief costume designer, José María de Cossío, during a visit to Los Angeles, Pedro, Agustín, and he ran into Jane Fonda, who, when told what *Pepi, Luci, Bom* had cost, asked in bemused astonish-ment: "Ah, but can you see and hear it?"

Almodóvar's accomplishments as a filmmaker have to do with talent, obviously enough, but also with his determination and capacity for work. His innovative conception of style was everywhere in evidence, especially in his recycling of existing cultural material, his ironic eclecticism, and his use of a wide array of subjects and situations that, while familiar to many Spaniards, had not been considered worthy of cinematic interest. Almodóvar's willing-ness, even eagerness, to appropriate and recycle, his ability to make a virtue out of necessity and to turn financial limitations to his advantage, though shared by a number of other young artists associated with the *Movida,* promptly morphed into a stylistic trademark. Recycling led to a cultural revival, one in which the director took neglected or denigrated materials of the 1950s and 1960s—popular, kitschy, and mass-produced—and trans-formed them into newly fashionable versions of their former selves. With the passage of time and the advent of fame and wealth, his sense of aesthetics, which had long relied on the recuperation of what had been overlooked or discarded, became increasingly more sophisticated and subtle.

Almodóvar's evolution, development, or maturation—if such teleologically fraught words are even appropriate—has been particularly noticeable in his use of dress for characterization. From his early collaborations with Spanish fashion designers Francis Montesinos and Jocomola de Sybila, up to his more recent collaborations with such internationally renowned designers as Jean-Paul Gaultier, Versace, Dior, Chanel, or Armani, Almodóvar has liberally put wardrobes together, almost always with the assistance of Cossío. Whenever designer-name clothing (obviously more prominent in the later films) did not fit into his vision of a particular film, then Cossío would take charge of the wardrobe. As Cossío put it in our interview:

> Pedro always needs at least three options for each scene and each character. It is not because he is undecided, but rather because he conceives of his scripts and his characters as living beings. And there are occasions when, even though the clothing for a character has already been decided, Pedro is interested in doing things differently and selects something else.

The search for a specific mode of presentation for each of his characters, even some of the most seemingly insignificant, is characteristic of the director's self-implicating approach to filmmaking. Cossío has said that even though he did not work on *Bad Education,* he is certain that Javier Cámara, who plays the relatively minor role of Paca/Paquito, was wearing at least three of Pedro's own shirts during the filming. Although such personal attention to detail may conjure up the image of a fetishistic investment à la Hitchcock, it more likely indicates the director's need to bring a character close to him in order to fit him or her into his idea of the story.

Another stylistic trait is his increasingly careful use of color. Almodóvar's initial reliance on the loud, bold, even garish colors of 1960s and 1970s pop art has gradually given way to a discerning deployment of softer hues and primary colors. In truth, however, all of his interiors are marked by a chromatic sophistication that spectators have come to associate, almost unconsciously, with the director's work. Reds, ochres, yellows, or oranges combine with ash or blue grey tones and different ranges of green in manners that vary significantly from one film to another. *Matador* (1986), for instance, draws heavily on the reds and golden yellows of the Spanish flag, in keeping with the bullfighting theme that is at its center; *All about My Mother,* which takes many of its dramatic cues from organ transplants, transfusions, and transmissions, draws on crimson and scarlet; *Talk to Her,* much more sober in tone, on the whites and blues of a hospital ward. As artistic director Antxón Gómez observes: "Pedro works with a very definite range of colors. He has trouble working with white, for example. He always says, 'I don't understand black and white.'" Although Almodóvar's chromatic conception of emotion is undeniable, he has indeed grappled—and to brilliant effect—with black and white in *The Shrinking Lover,* the silent film within *Talk to Her.* That said, what Gómez signals is *not* Almodóvar's lack of understanding of black-and-white film, but of black and white as decorative elements, as part of the decor.

Accordingly, color remains a dominant feature of Almodóvar's style, often functioning in concert with a neobaroque aesthetic that has enjoyed a place of prominence in Hispanic culture on both sides of the Atlantic. As Gómez notes:

> Minimalist language is something that doesn't go well with Pedro's formal vocabulary. He tends to opt for spaces that are full of objects, all of which have dramatic meaning. For example, when he described the character of Agrado to us during the preparation of *All about My Mother,* he said that she was someone who loved to accumulate things. This [little remark] provided us with an excellent clue [to the presentation of the character].

Although here explicitly linked to the character of Agrado, played by the extraordinary Antonia San Juan, symbolically charged objects are present in virtually all of Almodóvar's films and function on the level not only of characterization but of dramatic situation as well.

Conversations between a director and his team are, of course, standard fare in moviemaking, but with Almodóvar, Cossío, the García sisters, Gómez, Salcedo, and others they assume an almost family-like cast—at least if one understands the family in nontraditional ways. Typically, each new project begins with several meetings in which the script is read and the director explains the film, attending to details like the color of the city, the emotional tone of the interiors, and the placement and lighting of the actors. Not surprisingly, after the script has been discussed, the artistic work of the film is basically of a graphic nature, involving photographs, drawings, diagrams, or other visual props. As Gómez remarks: "Pedro has a big collection of interior design magazines and I have some as well. We look at the possibilities together and mark the ones that seem interesting to us. It is up to me to come up with a proposal based on the guidelines that Pedro has previously articulated."

As is usually the case, the artistic director has to start working long before the actual filming so that the director can visualize the set more fully. According to Gómez:

> sometimes we work with sketches of the decor; other times we work with 3D diagrams or models that help us visualize the movements of the characters and the development of the action. Pedro likes to see the set built, be in it, and try it out very much in advance. Often he rehearses with the actors on the nearly prepared set.

For films as intricately narrative as Almodóvar's, there is little room for improvisation, at least after the effusiveness of *Pepi, Luci, Bom* and *Labyrinth of Passion* (1982). The lack of improvisation may come as something of a surprise to all of those who, perhaps still under the spell of Almodóvar's early films, associate the director with spontaneity, implusiveness, and an unrepressed, and untheorized, "naturalness." And yet, as we have already indicated, Almodóvar has long controlled—or tried to control—even the smallest details of filmmaking. Still, the very complexity of the sets and locations makes it impossible for him to do so always. In the words of Gómez: "sometimes Pedro doesn't have time to supervise all of the sets. For example, in *Bad Education,* I prepared the sets in Galicia or Valencia and he was confident that I had done the work well." As commanding an auteur as Almodóvar can be, he necessarily entrusts certain aspects of his work to others, especially when he has forged a close relationship with them over time.

Filming: "A Pause in Our Lives"

The act of filming, the shoot, is, needless to say, often a moment of tension and potential conflict. The crew knows how demanding Almodóvar is during a shoot. According to Esther García, Almodóvar, in his meetings with the cast and crew (or, as Spanish would have it, the artistic and technical teams), repeatedly says that he wants them to make a "pause" in their lives and to dedicate themselves completely to the shoot. The person who is most familiar with Almodóvar's all-encompassing work ethic is, along with his brother Agustín, arguably Esther García herself, who has been the director's production manager for more than fifteen years, ever since *Tie Me Up! Tie Me Down!* (1990)—though she had worked with him freelance in previous films. Working as a production manager or producer involves many challenges, to be sure, but the challenges, and the benefits, are particulary acute when the director requires as high and prolonged a level of concentration and dedication as Almodóvar. Perhaps the most important discussions, prior to the formation of particular teams, take place in El Deseo between Almodóvar, his brother Agustín, and Esther García. As she says: "Pedro usually has a very clear idea about the casting and this helps us a great deal when it comes to determining the kind of film that he wants to make and to securing funding." García's expertise and professional experience are part and parcel of her intimate knowledge of virtually all aspects of Almodóvar's life and work. Accordingly, she is capable of deciphering what to outsiders might appear to be cryptic codes or meaningless gestures. As she puts it: "I am able to interpret when Pedro's 'yes' is actually a 'no.' He is an incredibly respectful person, and at times when we are working, it is difficult for him to change things that have involved much effort."

As García and others note, one of the most compelling aspects of Almodóvar's filmmaking lies in its planning, especially with regard to locations and rehearsals, which differs from that of other directors to the degree that practically everything is subordinated to the story. To quote Esther García once more:

> Pedro requests that, whenever possible, we shoot continuously, so that he can see the evolution of the characters as the story unfolds. As you can imagine, this complicates the work plan considerably, especially with regard to the locations. But after all these years, I can say that it is very important and that it helps Pedro very much to work this way.

Continuous, sequential shooting—that is to say shooting in the order that the scenes actually appear in the final film—is one of Almodóvar's trademarks and something that, for obvious financial and logistical reasons, few directors do. With Almodóvar, who has eschewed the big-budget productions of which Hollywood is so enamored (and which he has had more than one opportunity to do himself), both planning and shooting are in the service of an almost organic conception of narration, one in which a story appears, almost literally, to come to life. Almodóvar's work on both the script and the set thus follows a sort of developmental logic, even though, or perhaps precisely because, so many of his stories are full of twists and turns, doublings and coincidences. Little wonder, then, that he strives to be so thorough in his presentation of information, so careful in his management of times and spaces, and so attentive to the turns of language, gesture, and staging.

At times, indeed, Almodóvar has so internalized the dynamic of the stories that he brings into filmic being that he appears to be the only one who really knows where things are going. Indeed, the sense of internalization can at times be so intense that, as Cossío observes, "Pedro suffer[s] terribly during the shootings, surrounded by people, but, in the end, completely alone." A momentary lack of precision, a flash of doubt, or an impulsive feeling can alter even the best-laid plans and constitute particularly incisive challenges for so meticulous a director. As Esther García remarks, "Pedro always knows exactly what he wants. And it doesn't matter what has to be done in order to obtain it. What is important is that he never gives up, he never says, 'This is impossible.'" Not surprisingly, Almodóvar's rigor and demand have earned him a reputation as a temperamental artist who has great respect for his craft and who is not afraid of speaking his mind on matters ostensibly far beyond his craft—as his controversial public declarations on Spain's involvement in the U.S.-led war in Iraq and on the conservative government's response to the terrorist attacks in Madrid on March 11, 2004, have amply demonstrated.

Filming and Editing at the Same Time

The only technician who is still working with Almodóvar since the days of *Pepi, Luci, Bom* is film editor José (Pepe) Salcedo. This lengthy working relationship has enabled Salcedo to edit with confidence. Despite the undeniable changes in Almodóvar's cinema, which have led many critics, myself included, to speak of distinct periods and tendencies, in some profound respects Almodóvar's modus operandi, especially with regard to editing, has not changed substantially. Now as before, Almodóvar regularly visits the editing room to view the material that he has been shooting. If it is in the shoot that the story first "comes to life," then it is in the editing, of course, where essential elements of language, time, and space are finally arranged. Salcedo has underscored the aforementioned dependence of editing on storytelling as follows:

> [Almodóvar's] position as a filmmaker . . . was completely different from the norm in Spanish cinema. When he called me to edit *Pepi, Luci, Bom,* I was in Stockholm, editing a film for José Luis Borau. Some eight or nine months after the relatively spontaneous shooting of *Pepi* had come to an end, he called me again and I saw the material. I liked it very much; it seemed like something totally new.

The process that Salcedo here describes in relation to Almodóvar's first feature in many ways continues to hold. As is the case with many, if not most, directors, the process entails sending off the material that was filmed during the day (or evening) to a laboratory so that Almodóvar can review and work on it the next day, usually after more shooting. However much Almodóvar may have in common with other directors' modus operandi, from the perspective of his closest collaborators he continues to be exceptional. Salcedo, for instance, notes that "[h]is capacity for work is amazing. Even if it is eleven o'clock at night, Pedro always comes every day to the editing room to see what has been filmed. I think he needs to feel the story, how it is taking shape, how it becomes real from one day to the next."

Almodóvar is clearly an exacting director. According to Salcedo:

> Pedro doesn't usually do more than three takes per shoot and they are usually all very similar. Of course, there is usually one that is better, but the difference is usually just a question of nuance. At times, when we are in the projection room of the laboratory, I will tell him that I like a particular take and Pedro will say, "Let's use this one since Pepe likes it" and this gives me a lot of confidence.

At other times, however, there are decidedly more takes. As Brad Epps, who was on the set of *Volver* for a few days, reported, a brief scene that depicts the arrival of the three female protagonists (Penélope Cruz, Lola Dueñas, and Yohana Cobo) to the house of their elderly aunt (Chus Lampreave) required nearly ten takes.

Regardless of how many takes are required for a given scene, Salcedo, as editor, clearly enjoys the director's confidence. John Ford used to tell his editor that if he was having trouble with a scene, then it meant that the editor was not doing his job well. According to Ford, the editor only needed to find the first and the last clapperboards in order to orient himself because Ford maintained that he did not shoot anything that was not strictly for the film. Their obvious differences not withstanding, Almodóvar also follows a tight plan where there is little room for distractions and virtually no tolerance for confusion. Almodóvar tends to situate the axis of action, defines the shoot, and then "forgets" about the camera (in the sense that he does not remain obsessively attached to it, planted literally behind it, but attends instead to the set and the monitor), giving himself over to what Cossío calls, somewhat ponderously, "the interpretative truth of his characters." True, lately, as in the filming of *Volver,* Almodóvar seems to attend more closely to the monitor than to either the camera or the set (directly, that is), but, regardless, it remains the case that the vast majority of Almodóvar's work issues from a clear vision of the film before it is actually shot. As Cossío has said, "unlike other directors who can alter points of view in order to have various options for a single shot, Almodóvar tends to work with a very clearly defined approach."

The fact that Almodóvar directs his own scripts, some of which he has mused over for years, means that his work is marked by a certain conceptual and temporal ellipsis and hence by a communicative challenge: how he expresses or exteriorizes to his collaborators his "vision" of the film at hand. Almodóvar handles time gaps, which can be notoriously difficult, with considerable ease, usually after having already indicated them in the script and storyboard in such a way that the story "flows" even as it turns in and out of itself in the flashbacks and parallels that run from *Labyrinth of Passion* to *Talk to Her, Bad Education,* and *Volver.* Pepe Salcedo makes a similar point in reference to *Bad Education:* "a film in which three stories with different spaces and times occur simultaneously." As Salcedo readily admits: "I had to read the script several times in order to understand it. But Pedro told me, 'Don't worry, Pepe; everything will fit together.' Every day when I went to edit, we would compose the shoots and everything did indeed fit together perfectly." Although many critics would beg to differ, finding *Bad Education* exasperatingly torturous, Salcedo's assessment, colored as it is by feelings of personal loyalty and an understandably deep investment in the final product, reinforces an arguably counterintuitive view of Almodóvar as a meticulously commanding director whose confidence in his editor (and others) is a function of his confidence in himself.

Although Almodóvar's command of the cinematic apparatus is undeniable, and although he has long enjoyed the status of auteur, his collaborations with Salcedo, the two of them often alone together in the editing room for extended periods of time, are among the closest and most significant of his career. As if it were some ancient ritual, Salcedo requests, after the shooting is finally complete, two or three days to hole up with Pedro and the film in order to give it, in Pedro's own words, "a magical finish," removing some frames and adding others, attending to details that are at first blush almost unnoticeable but that usually result in what both the director and the editor perceive as a more rhythmic narrative flow. However "objective" their perceptions of their work may be, it may well be that there is no technical and creative collaboration in all of contemporary Spanish cinema as intense and fruitful as that of Pedro Almodóvar and Pepe Salcedo. Indeed, and at the risk of waxing hyperbolic, the mutual trust, affection, and deep collegiality that characterize Almodóvar and Salcedo's relationship constitute a paradigm that is comparable to only a very few other collaborations—one thinks of Sergei Eisenstein and Édouard Tissé—in the history of cinema.

Married to the Movies: By Way of a Conclusion

The technicians who have worked with Pedro Almodóvar do not hesitate to point out that he enjoys what he does so much that it is impossible to imagine that he could ever live without doing it. The cinema is his life, as Almodóvar is fond of saying. And lest the director's declaration be taken as a mere pose, those who have worked most closely with him are quick to agree. Cossío, who is one of the people who knows the Spanish director best, has gone so far as to declare that Almodóvar is "married" to the cinema. In this manner, he expresses to what extent the cinema has been, and continues to be, Almodóvar's reason for being, the love of his life. Perhaps it is only in the light of such passionate commitment to the cinema that we can begin to glimpse something like the truth and, dare I say it, the person of one of the most public yet private of fimmakers of our time.

NOTES

1. There are, of course, any number of ways of approaching the question of seeing, including seeing an era or a nation. To take a by now classic example, André Bazin, in his analysis of the "ontology of the photographic image," throws into relief the uncanny disposition of the cinematographic medium to provide a new formulation of the terrain of human, cinematic experience. Although Bazin's ontological conception of the cinema has been amply questioned, even rejected (a debate that exceeds the aims of the present essay), the new expressive territory that the cinema offers in its technologies and techniques and that profoundly marks contemporary reality might well be said to constitute an artistic truth, provisional and precarious as it may be, that can at once challenge the supposed ineluctability of historical time and shed light on it.

2. The present article draws on two documentary films of mine: *Almodóvar: Vanguard and Classicism* and, more recently, *Inside Almodóvar,* which consists of a series of interviews with some of Almodóvar's most important behind-the-scenes collaborators, from producers and editors to set and costume designers, musicians, and others. In the article, as in the documentary, I address some of the technical and interpersonal aspects of the creative process of a filmmaker who manages to remain at once attuned to cinematic conventions and extraordinarily independent. All quotes, unless otherwise indicated, are from the documentary *Inside Almodóvar.*

3. As Lola García notes in her filmed interview, Almodóvar's "relationship to the city [of Madrid] has changed because the city in which he once lived minute to minute and on which he drew to create his stories presents itself differently to him now that he is a public figure. He can no longer mingle freely with others or calmly observe the city around him while having a coffee."

WORKS CITED

Allinson, Mark. *A Spanish Labyrinth: The Films of Pedro Almodóvar.* London: I. B. Tauris, 2001.

Almodóvar, Pedro. *Patty Diphusa y otros textos.* Barcelona: Anagrama, 1991, 1998.

Bazin, André. "The Ontology of the Photographic Image." *What Is Cinema?* Trans. Hugh Gray. Berkeley: University of California Press, 1967. 9–16.

Eisenstein, Sergei. *The Film Sense.* Trans. Jay Leyda. New York: Harcourt, 1969.

Heidegger, Martin. "The Origin of the Work of Art." *Poetry, Language, Thought.* Trans. Albert Hofstadter. New York: Harper Perennial Modern Classics, 2001. 15–86.

Kinder, Marsha. "Pleasure and the New Spanish Mentality: A Conversation with Pedro Almodóvar." *Film Quarterly* 41.1 (1987): 33–44.

Oliva, Ignacio, dir. *Almodóvar: Vanguard and Classicism.* University of Castilla–La Mancha, Spain, 2000.

———. *Inside Almodóvar.* Univers Film-IDECA, Spain, 2005.

Smith, Paul Julian. *Desire Unlimited.* London: Verso, 1994.

Vernon, Kathleen M., and Barbara Morris, eds. *Post-Franco, Postmodern: The Films of Pedro Almodóvar.* Westport, Conn.: Greenwood Press, 1995.

Vidal, Nuria. *El cine de Pedro Almodóvar.* Barcelona: Destino, 1988.

15 Pepi, Patty, and Beyond
Cinema and Literature in Almodóvar

FRANCISCO A. ZURIÁN

TRANSLATED BY JESÚS PAZ-ALBO AND BRAD EPPS

For Francisco J. Sutil

The Task of the Storyteller

Pedro Almodóvar is a filmmaker consumed by a need to tell stories. His relation to narrative recalls Gabriel García Márquez's description of storytelling as a "bendita manía," a blessed madness, as well as Truman Capote's description of writing as an exacting gift. Drawing explicitly on Capote's *Music for Chameleons,* Almodóvar expressed his passion for narrative as follows in *All about My Mother* (1999):

> MANUELA (reading Truman Capote): Preface. I started writing when I was eight.
> ESTEBAN: You see? I am not the only one.
> MANUELA: Not knowing that I had chained myself for life to a noble and merciless master. When God hands you a gift, he also hands you a whip; and the whip is intended solely for self-flagellation. (Capote ix)

Almodóvar's self-declared need for understanding, expression, and communication is as vital as his self-declared need to overcome loneliness.[1] Writing, reading, and watching movies comprised a sort of safe haven for the director as a young man, but one activity outshone all others: telling stories. When he was a child, Almodóvar would tell his mother and his sisters about the movies that he had seen, often embellishing or reinventing the plots. By inventing his own story lines, he escaped, or at least assuaged, the gray and macho reality that surrounded him; in the process, he came to reinvent himself and his relations to others as well.[2]

In what follows I would like to offer a basic compendium of Almodóvar's autobiographically tinged views on narrative in order to illustrate the centrality of storytelling and literary expression in his work both in and out of the cinema. Although Almodóvar's accomplishments as a director have established his international reputation, his literary production has received relatively scant attention outside of Spain. By focusing on his written texts, I hope to make a case for the importance of Almodóvar's career as a writer, his experiments with storytelling in nonvisual media, and his literary presence in a Spanish cultural context. Much work about these dimensions of Almodóvar's oeuvre remains to be done; I aim, rather modestly, to identify some of the necessary directions for future research in this article.

For all of his technical accomplishments, for all of his attention to visual detail, Almodóvar is above all a storyteller who is especially committed to generating and communicating emotion:

> Since I was eight or nine years old, I was a great narrator, a great storyteller, in a way that already had much to do with movies. "Pedro, tell us about the movie we watched last night," my sisters would ask me. And I was delighted [to oblige them] because as I would begin to remember the story I would begin to invent it, and this spurred me on even more. In fact, it excited me so much that I would tell the story a different way each time . . . , but what I would recount to my sisters and my friends were movies, either totally outrageous or reworked into other movies, but always focused on stories aimed to entertain. At that, I was very good. (Harguindey 72)[3]

Almodóvar has spoken of his passion for telling stories many times—"passion" enjoys a place of privilege in Almodóvar's lexicon—and, despite his penchant for innovation and change, in a highly consistent manner: placing a premium on strong emotion, even sentimentality; underscoring the importance of friends and family, especially his mother; insisting on something like a generalized performativity in which people are personages and artifice is a natural act; and emphasizing the unorthodox, marginal, and alternative without losing sight of tradition, convention, and custom. As he insisted in a speech he gave when he was made Doctor *Honoris Causa* at the University of Castilla–La Mancha in 2000, he is "a storyteller by nature," one who "always wanted to tell stories" and who "did not wait to get permission to do so" ("Discurso de Investidura" 22).

And yet, for all the references to "nature," Almodóvar was also an avid reader, especially of works that were not likely to appear in the curriculum of a conservative religious school:

> I must have been nine when I bought my first book. . . . *The Devil's Advocate* by Lajos Zilahy, *Sinuhé the Egyptian* by Mika Waltari, books by Morris West or Walter Scott, and also *Steppenwolf* by Hermann Hesse and the famous *Bonjour Tristesse* [by Françoise Sagan] that made me cry out "My God, there are others like me, I'm not alone!" I didn't read Spanish literature; I began to do that when I was twenty and it fascinated me, especially the nineteenth-century realists. In high school, we didn't hear about Rimbaud or Genet, but I knew very soon that there was something interesting in them and I read them, and also some of "the damned poets." Since then, my relationship with literature was a passionate one, above all, thanks to the French authors. When I arrived in Madrid in 1968, there was a period of explosion of South

American literature throughout the world. I was reading compulsively, because I had many more things within my reach. (Strauss 15)[4]

Almodóvar's choice of reading materials is revealing. Along with the great, rambling, intricate plots of nineteenth-century realists, effervescent psychodramas (Sagan), radically alternative works of poetic density (Rimbaud, Genet), tales of antique adventure (Scott), and a variety of popular fiction comprised his library.

But, as bookish as he could and can be, Almodóvar has repeatedly and movingly stated that his seemingly unconditional love of narrative comes from his mother, Francisca Caballero, a major force in his life and work. At times, indeed, it seems that Francisca Caballero outshines and overshadows the greatest of the great actresses that Almodóvar has insistently honored, three of whom—Bette Davis, Gena Rowlands, and Romy Schneider—he explicitly mentions at the end of *All about My Mother*. In the words of famed Spanish novelist Juan José Millás, "Paca Caballero occupies so much space in Almodóvar's existence that there is almost no room left for his father.... Perhaps Pedro can address the world in a colloquial way because he addressed his mother in a formal one" (Millás 47).[5] Millás is here referring to the fact that Almodóvar always employed the formal *Usted* rather than the more common and informal *tú* when addressing his mother—something that does not quite jibe with the rather superficial image of the director as uncompromisingly irreverent. For the truth of the matter is that Almodóvar—in an almost stereotypically Spanish fashion that he is elsewhere so fond of parodying—has always held his family in high esteem.[6]

Almodóvar's mother made many cameos in her son's films and appeared in various documentaries about him before her death in 1999. But her presence can be felt in other, more subtle ways, for instance, in the director's understanding of color. As he said in the aforementioned speech: "I like to think that my passion for color is not merely a function of the baroque style of my characters, but that it is also my mother's answer to so many years of mourning [in which black was the dominant color]. I was her extravagant reaction to the stultifying and excessive tradition of La Mancha" ("Discurso de Investidura" 21).[7] Far from hiding his lack of formal cinematic training, Almodóvar has worn it as a badge of honor, persistently noting that he only had himself and his family to train him in the world of fiction and cinema:

Fiction for me comes from the world of the patio, my mother's friends in the neighborhood, my sisters taking sewing classes with their friends, the cats, the parties that would accompany the slaughter of certain animals, the Gypsies, the flamenco singers at the fair, the twist, the hanging from a grapevine of a still bleeding skinned rabbit, my mother chatting with neighbors outside the door, in the open air of long summer nights ... and the big screen of the outdoor movie theater. And a thick wall, the only fetish to which I am faithful.

My mother was the territory where everything happened.

I learned boldness from her, and something more: the need for certain doses of fiction so that reality can be better digested, better narrated, better lived. ... It was not a question of complacently accepting things, but of perfecting reality by adding a little bit of fiction. (Ibid. 17–18, 20, emphasis added)

Almodóvar finds the seeds of his vocation as a storyteller in the domestic space over which his mother reigned.[8] Narrative for him does not have watertight, intellectualized limits, but rather channels that flow, emotively, in and out of each other.

Nurtured on familiar, even traditional material, Almodóvar's understanding of narrative nonetheless veers into the postmodern in its blending of high and low cultural elements and in its appreciation of hybridity and pastiche. Much has been written about Almodóvar, Spain, visual culture, and postmodernity, but surprisingly little has been written about Almodóvar's writing, which he engages with considerable freedom and self-confidence. Almodóvar, unlike some of his actors, has largely resisted the allure of Hollywood and its penchant for big-budget blockbusters that subordinate story to action and emotion to special effects. Although his films are his principal claim to fame and his principal source of expression internationally, his writing is an indispensable part of his artistry, which also includes forays into music, acting, and, increasingly, photography.[9] Along with an impressive roster of original and adapted screenplays, Almodóvar's writing takes the form of short stories, chronicles, comics, and "photo-novels" as well. Upon his arrival in Madrid, this passion for telling stories issued in an assortment of filmic texts and literary texts in which the budding director *and* writer began to create a style, a poetics, an aesthetics, and, perhaps most important of all, a unique public persona.

Pepi and Patty: The Storyteller in the Movable City

Almodóvar's public persona is all but inseparable from a number of characters that he has created. Two of the characters, both female, who helped catapult Almodóvar to international fame are Pepi, the inventive protagonist of *Pepi, Luci, Bom* (1980), brilliantly played by Carmen Maura, and Patty

Diphusa, a sexually ambiguous literary character who, in her role as inter-national sex symbol and porn star, became an icon of the countercultural movement known as the *Movida*.[10] If Pepi is the first memorable manifes-tation of Almodóvar's directorial skills, Patty Diphusa—whose name is a play on the feminine form of the word *patidifuso,* which means "flabber-gasted," "dazed," or "dumbfounded"—is the first and most memorable mani-festation of his literary skills. Indeed, when Almodóvar presented his book *Patty Diphusa y otros textos* [The Patty Diphusa Stories and Other Writings] to the media in 1991, he gestured to Patty's place in his creative career: "If I have something, it's a literary vocation; I remember always writing, and it's a vocation prior to the cinema" (Rodríguez 32). *Patty Diphusa* brings together stories published serially in *La Luna de Madrid* between 1983 and 1984. One of the emblematic publications of the *Movida, La Luna de Madrid* was a monthly magazine that acquired cult status among those devoted to the city's "progressive" revival after the death of Franco and the establish-ment of democracy. Not quite "underground," but certainly at ease with the Spanish status quo, the magazine was an important venue for Almodóvar's early work as a writer.[11]

The first of Patty's stories—titled "I, Patty Diphusa"—was published in November 1983 to considerable expectation, at least in those circles in which Patty was already a minor celebrity. The character first came to public notice in 1982, when a photo-novel titled "Patty Diphusa en *Toda tuya*" [Patty Diphusa in *All Yours*] was published in *Víbora* magazine.[12] Fifteen years had elapsed since Almodóvar moved to Madrid in the now mythic year of 1968 and just over ten since he made his first incursions into Madrid's pop sub-culture, which had existed in a more or less precarious manner in the final years of Franco's dictatorship.[13] As Almodóvar told Frédéric Strauss in one of their many published conversations:

> I began in 1972. Before *Pepi, Luci, Bom,* I had already directed many Super-8 mov-ies.... I moved to Madrid in '68, but I didn't dare to take my first steps in the cin-ema until I had lived three years in this city that was for me still largely unknown, had surrounded myself with a group of friends, and had managed to save enough money working at Telefónica [the Spanish telephone company] to buy a Super-8 camera. (14)

If Almodóvar made his first moves as a filmmaker in 1972, he had started writing much earlier, becoming interested in literature, as noted, at around the age of eight—more or less the same age at which he became interested in film—and trying his hand at writing while in elementary school.

When he arrived in Madrid, reading and writing were indeed his first means of artistic expression. Once again, as he told Strauss: "I wrote [tales, stories] when I arrived in Madrid. . . . I was passionate about literature, and wrote all kind of stories, thinking that I would devote my life completely to writing until I discovered Super-8" (24). In 1978, Almodóvar published a compilation volume titled *Sueños de la razón* [Dreams of Reason—a title that recalls a famous etching by Goya], consisting of three stories: "La ausencia" [The Absence], "Las últimas palabras de Rosa" [Rosa's Last Words"], and "Anonadado (El origen del Dadá)" [Dumbfounded (The Origin of Dada)].[14] Not only did he write stories, comics, and photo-novels, he was also feverishly at work making short films and, more notoriously, composing and singing songs with the ebulliently gender-bending Fanny McNamara [Fabio de Miguel], with whom he released several albums and achieved much success with such songs as "Satanasa," "Voy a ser mamá" [I'm Going to Be a Mommy], "Gran Ganga" [Great Bargain], and "Suck It to Me," the latter two featured in *Labyrinth of Passion* (1982).

Almodóvar's performances at Rock Ola (sometimes spelled Rockola or Rock-Ola), one of the most important night spots of the *Movida*, garnered him increasing numbers of fans, captivated by his seemingly fearless desire to push at the boundaries of "polite" society and to experiment with a variety of creative forms.[15] In so doing, Almodóvar began to make his way in Madrid, honing his skills not just as an innovative artist but also, and perhaps no less importantly, as a skilled showman and savvy businessman:

> In the beginning, truth be told, I had to cut a path for myself in a very competitive manner that was not without a certain violence. I made my way with all the means that nature puts in your hands, however humble. [As a rule] I try to use whatever each age has to offer, and I get involved in it without thinking whether it is met with approval or not. But for me—and I don't really want to seem cliché—doing things my way has always been a way to have fun, to stay active, to have a full life. What I mean is that there was no real calculation or planning. When I would go onstage to sing with Fabio at Rockola, the two of us dressed like hookers, I would sing horribly, I know it, but the good thing about punk rock, what was truly liberating about punk, was that you didn't need to sing well because it was all sneers and growls, and your hair, your hair could be any which way. (Harguindey 70)

It was in just this raucous, punk-driven environment that Patty Diphusa emerged as one of the queens of the *Movida*.

Almodóvar himself has reiterated that Patty Diphusa was born and developed in the unpredictable and malleable context of the *Movida* and for the people—punkies, junkies, drag queens, and other divine creatures—who most actively participated in it. "Patty Diphusa is a cousin of the legion of misled girls that populate the films of the Warhol-Morrisey duo," he writes in the prologue of *Patty Diphusa* (xi). Almodóvar goes on to link Patty to "the early Divine" of John Waters's *Pink Flamingos* (1972) and *Female Trouble* (1974), Anita Loos's Lorelei, and Capote's Holly Golightly from *Breakfast at Tiffany's* and even states that he "would like to believe she has the amoral, ingenuous tone of Fran Lebowitz *(Metropolitan Life)* and even Dorothy Parker" (xii). Amid the references to other characters, Almodóvar also asserts Patty's singularity, calling her one of his favorite female characters:

> A girl with so much life in her that she never sleeps, naive, tender and grotesque, envious and narcissistic, friend of everyone and all pleasures, always ready to see the best side of things. Someone who, because she only thinks about situations super-ficially, ends up getting the best of them. Patty flees from solitude and from herself and she does so with a good dose of humor and a lot of common sense. (xii)

Patty's literary, cinematic, and cultural connections are perhaps no more diverse than Pepi's, but the very fact that Patty appears, disappears, and reappears over time, that she flees from solitude and herself, seems to make her star more seductive to follow, in no small measure because it shines in such a vast transcultural constellation in which Spain, the United States, and Latin America figure mightily.

Comparisons to countercultural movements abounded, then, but surely one of the most insistent had to do with Andy Warhol's New York studio known as The Factory, notorious for its melding of art, sex, drugs, and radicality. Almodóvar, who met Warhol in January 1983 after *Labyrinth of Passion* had hit the screens, has said that "[i]n the early eighties we lived in a permanent Warhol factory" (*The Patty Diphusa Stories* x). Although in many respects quite flattering, the comparison could become tedious and, not surprisingly, was not always to Almodóvar's liking:[16]

> I was constantly being introduced as the Spanish Warhol. The fifth time this hap-pened (at the home of the Marches, one of the wealthiest families in Spain), War-hol asked me why. Because nobody can think of another way to introduce me, I answered. At a glance, we don't look anything alike, he observed. He sported his famous platinum wig and I my natural jet black bush. It must be because I also have transvestites and drug addicts in my movies, I responded, ashamed, realizing that both the conversation and my role in it were pretty ridiculous. (*The Patty Diphusa Stories* xi)

Despite Almodóvar's professed feelings of shame (one might humorously speculate that perhaps it was because his hair was "natural," while Warhol's was wildly artificial), another reason for the comparisons with Warhol may have been Almodóvar's penchant for surrounding himself with coteries of friends and collaborators. Almodóvar's gregariousness also contributed to the formation of such constellations: he surrounded himself with friends—many of whom were engaged in various and sundry sorts of creative work in their own right—and led at the time a very active social life.

Almodóvar was a man of many hats in those years. During the day, he worked as an administrative assistant at the telephone company, and in the evenings and at night he wrote for and collaborated with magazines, preparing photo-novels that were published in a variety of ephemeral fanzines and alternative magazines in Madrid and Barcelona.[17] According to Almodóvar, "my mere presence in Telefónica was a scandal: I had long hair and didn't dress like the other employees. I actually had a double life: from nine to five I worked as an administrative assistant and at night I changed drastically" (Strauss 18). Almodóvar's "double life," consistent with his passion for storytelling, provided him with important lessons about Spanish society: "those years at Telefónica were very important for me because I learned about the Spanish middle class, which I'd never observed in any other place. This discovery marked my cinema, because up to then I only knew the poor and rural segments of society" (ibid.). The question of class is important, for although some of his early films, most notably *What Have I Done to Deserve This?* (1984), featured characters from the working class, many of his more recent films are firmly ensconced in a world of material privilege—a world into which the director was not born, but to which he has clearly come to have access.

Almodóvar's working-class origins are often forgotten or overlooked in critical work, but their importance should not be underestimated. The Spaniard's rise to international fame—and fortune—has certainly been spectacular, but it has also given the director insight into the power of money and the significance of economic stratifications. Almodóvar left the phone company—whose devices figure so prominently in *Women on the Verge of a Nervous Breakdown* (1988)—in 1981 to dedicate himself fully to *Labyrinth of Passion,* a more tightly structured, though still rambunctious, film than *Pepi, Luci, Bom* and his Super-8 ventures. But then, and before, Patty was still very much in the works and still very much on the rise, so much so that one of the emblematic magazines of the *Movida, Víbora,* entrusted Almodóvar with a photo-novel that would become one of the sources of *Pepi, Luci, Bom:*

> [At *Víbora*] they asked me to make another [photo-novel] that was very punk, very aggressive, very dirty, and very funny: such was the fashion. I wrote it and called it *General Erections* [in humorous allusion to the general elections by which Spain was marking its return to democracy]. The origin of the film is not only the photo-novel, but a comic book as well. . . . The fact that . . . it was a coarse and punk comic book ensured that the characters would be quite different [from what was then the norm]. (Strauss 24, 27)

Accordingly, even as Almodóvar was elaborating Patty Diphusa, he was also working on the character of Pepi, a woman who refuses to be victimized by rape and who transforms herself into a media-conscious entrepreneur.

Moving between a rather dizzying range of creative activities, Almodóvar made a virtue of necessity, working whenever he found the time and wherever he found the space: in friends' houses, in clubs, bars, and later on in art galleries, schools of photography, and even at the National Film Library. Hardworking as he was (amid all of the fun and games), Almodóvar also relied on youthful exuberance and sheer charm: "at that time [the early 1980s] I was irresistibly nice, and on the basis of personal charm, boldness, and tenacity, I found that even the most resistant of doors were opening. I remember that *Fólleme Tim* was shown for the very first time at a lavish party at [millionaire] Juan March's house" (ibid. 20).[18] Because *Fuck, Fuck, Fuck Me, Tim!* (1978) and other Super-8 productions were silent (adding sound was expensive and time-consuming), Almodóvar himself prepared the sound track and performed the voices of all the characters, who, despite the technical limitations, tended to talk as much as in his current films. Increasingly supported by wealthy figures like March (who apparently knew a rising star when he saw one), Almodóvar prepared these basically informal screenings as if they were commercial feature films:

> I would personally accompany the projection of the movie with all sorts of commentaries, and I would do the voices of all the characters. All live. I called it "Live Sound," from my mouth directly to the ear of my audience. My brother Agustín used to help me with the music; when I would give him the signal, he would start a cassette with music that I had previously selected. The screenings were a real party. A *happening*, as it was then called. I've never heard so many people laugh as during those screenings. (Ibid.)

Much of the laughter, to be sure, was the effect of a combination of derring-do and sheer silliness, provocation, and slapstick; the stories—whether of Patty, Pepi, or others—were always extreme, scathing, and irreverent.

For Almodóvar, the late 1970s and early 1980s, promptly codified as the "Transition," were years of intense, if erratic, self-training involving reading, writing, going to the theater (particularly low-budget, alternative fare), watching movies at the National Film Library, conversing with friends, and engaging in much self-reflection. In 1981, he published *Fuego en las entrañas* [Fire in the Guts], a collection of risqué tales illustrated with drawings by Javier Mariscal; in 1982, Almodóvar's second feature film, *Labyrinth of Passion*, premiered. In one particularly hilarious scene, Almodóvar plays the role of a photo-novel director, desperately trying to direct a shoot in which McNamara, insistently threatening to move out of frame, plays a quasi-transvestite figure in the style of Patty Diphusa. The scene, which highlights Almodóvar's happy travails as a director, remits to and replays the previously mentioned production of Patty for *Víbora*. To tighten the ties, the film also includes a brief scene in which the male protagonist, Riza Niro (Imanol Arias), is shown reading a Patty Diphusa text that had been published in *Star*.[19] These "appearances" set the stage, as already noted, for the publication

The cover of Almodóvar's collection of short stories Fuego en las entrañas *(Fire in the Guts), published in 1981 and illustrated with drawings by Javier Mariscal.*

Pedro Almodóvar, always the writer. Photograph by Jean-Marie Leroy. Copyright Jean-Marie Leroy/El Deseo.

of some of Patty's adventures in *La Luna de Madrid* in 1983. The stories became something of a sensation and Patty, whom more than one reader took to be real, became famous.

For all of the twists and turns in Almodóvar's literary and cinematic endeavors, it was not until 1983 that the first full-fledged literary character appears in a film: Sister Rat, played by the inimitable Chus Lampreave, in *Dark Habits* (1983). Of course, from the very beginning Almodóvar had populated his movies with characters related in one way or another to writing. For instance, and quite significantly, Pepi, whom we have been presenting as something of a filmic companion to Patty, devotes herself to writing. When her father admonishes her for being too old to not have a job, Pepi emphatically responds: "I already devote myself to do something! I write stories." She certainly appears to speak the truth, because she is repeatedly shown in front of a typewriter, and at one point even scolds herself for her lack of expertise: "Fuck, what a bad job I'm doing! If I want be a writer, I will have to learn."

The conjunction of a character and a typewriter is not incidental. In a number of Almodóvar's films, the typewriter functions almost as if it were another character. This is most dramatically in evidence in *Law of Desire* (1986), in which the typewriter of a successful film director named Pablo (Eusebio Poncela) binds people together in devastatingly intricate ways.[20] The typewriter's importance is made manifest at the end of the film, when Pablo, in a fierce reaction to the suicide of the man that he has come to love in spite of himself, hurls it out of the window. Landing in a large trash container, the typewriter explodes into flames. In the decidedly more tranquil, even understated *The Flower of My Secret* (1995), the typewriter and, more broadly, the act of writing are similarly important. The film's protagonist, Leo Macías (Marisa Paredes), is another one of Almodóvar's writer-characters, tied, like Pablo, to the typewriter, but in a way that glimmers with the possibility of a certain salvation. Leo's sense of literary salvation recalls García Márquez's assertion that a typewriter can be a very good thing to have: "I hold on to it like a shipwrecked person to a board, and I was happy to know that I needed only ink, tape and paper" (62). Leo, who writes romance novels under the name of Amanda Gris, at first also grabs on to the typewriter as if it were a life board that could keep her afloat while her marriage goes to ruin, but, like Pablo in *Law of Desire,* she soon comes to realize that writing can be an illusory means of salvation and ends up abandoning it in order to salvage something else. It is Ángel (Juan Echanove) who, as an expression of his love, ends up writing Amanda Gris's last novel. *The Flower of My Secret,* perhaps the director's most delicate and understated film, suggests that what really saves someone is not writing or artistic creation, but love, or at least friendship and brotherhood.

The parallels between such characters as Pablo, Leo, and, more recently, Enrique (Fele Martínez) in *Bad Education* (2004) and Pedro Almodóvar have not escaped the attention of critics. Then again, given the director's fondness for writing and speaking about his work and life, it would be curious if critics, and viewers in general, did not notice the parallels, misleading as some of them may be. For Almodóvar does indeed scatter pieces of himself in his characters. Among these partial alter egos, Pepi and Patty are arguably two of the freshest, simplest, and most innocent, despite—or, better yet, because of—the randy insouciance with which they articulate and assume their difference from established norms of behavior.[21] Both of these early female characters—for many a spectator increasingly tinged with a nostalgia for exuberance past—were and remain icons of the *Movida* and prototypes of a particularly pop Spanish postmodernism, where the speed of the "transition" from dictatorship to democracy generated a dizzying compression of modernity that became the very measure of postmodernity.[22] Pepi, like Patty, is, in the words of Almodóvar, "fun, audacious, corrosive, incorrect, modern, uneven, subversive and amoral" (Vidal 23). Made by Almodóvar, both are nonetheless self-made women, not unlike Agrado in *All about My Mother,* who rather matter-of-factly declares in her onstage monologue: "it costs a lot to be authentic, but one cannot be stingy when it comes to one's appearance. One is more authentic the more one resembles the self that one has dreamed about" (*Todo sobre mi madre* 104).

And dream Almodóvar's characters certainly do. As the irrepressible Pepi says to Luci and Bom: "Not only do you have to be yourself, but you also have to play [literally, 'represent'] your own character. And representation is always somewhat artificial." Almodóvar himself recognized as much in a much-cited interview with Nuria Vidal in 1988: "Superstitious or not, weak or not, with luck or without it, you always have to make yourself" (31). Later on, Almodóvar would make many significant changes in style and subject matter, moving from the hectic campiness of his first works to a certain "social realism" with *What Have I Done to Deserve This?* to an increasingly controlled and sophisticated demonstration of his artistry in such films as *Talk to Her* (2002) and *Volver* (2006). For all the changes, however, he has not entirely left behind the irony and *esperpento*—a self-consciously Spanish mode of the grotesque associated with the work of Ramón María del Valle-Inclán (1866–1936)—that characterized his earlier endeavors on both the screen and the page. What is more, even the "Almodóvar Factory" has not completely vanished, enduring as it does in a much more organized and elegant form in Almodóvar's production company, El Deseo.[23]

By the mid-1980s, with the growing success of his cinematic ventures, Almodóvar had stopped publishing serialized stories on Patty and had begun devoting himself less to writing for its own sake than to writing in the service of film. Patty did enjoy, however, a comeback—and a certain consolidation—with the previously mentioned publication of *Patty Diphusa* in 1991, a fact that led the newspaper *El Mundo* to propose to Almodóvar that he publish a sequel of sorts. Almodóvar accepted the proposal, and between April and June 1993 published four new stories, which were collected in a revised, expanded version of the book in 1998.[24] The year that saw the return of Patty also saw her departure; in 1993, Almodóvar stopped writing about Patty in order to concentrate his energies on *Kika* (1993), a film in which the ditzy yet resilient eponymous character, played by Verónica Forqué, bears more than a passing similarity to Patty Diphusa.

Patty herself is not exactly pleased with this turn of events (from writing to filming) and lets her reader, and her author, know so:

> I am very irritated. The days go by, and my author too. As Chavela Vargas would say, Don Pedro Almodóvar has abandoned me; he has left me for another woman, Kika....
>
> I get dressed and put my makeup on, ready to look for Pedro all over Madrid. The truth is that finding a simple but spectacular outfit takes me more time than planned....
>
> I catch Pedro's arm and drag him directly in front of the camera, trying not to let all my words go to waste, but possibly have them engraved on him eternally. Pedro pulls me out....
>
> Have you forgotten me? she reproached him. You've turned me into a lot of sheets of paper, dusty and forgotten on the shelves of a closed stationery store.
>
> Don't be melodramatic, Patty. It's not your style.
>
> That's the problem with authors; they know much more of you than yourself.
>
> When will you hand in my next chapter? ...
>
> There aren't more chapters for the time being. I have no time....
>
> That's because all your energy is taken by that bitch Kika!
>
> I say it loud so Verónica Forqué can hear me, I can see her coming toward us, dressed as a Versace shepherdess. (*Patty Diphusa y otros textos* 116–19)[25]

Patty was a character in Almodóvar's repertoire many years before she saw the light of day—and remains one long after she has faded from the daily press. Such comings and goings are not surprising, for Almodóvar *brews* his stories and films over time, moving from one to the other, mixing one with the other. His scripts often undergo many versions and at times are left to languish, or to ripen, while others come to the fore. *Pepi, Luci, Bom,* for instance, issues from a short story and a photo-novel, the previously mentioned "General Erections," which ends up appearing in only one scene (in one of its early incarnations, the film was called *El gran chasco* [The Great Disappointment]). Other literary and cinematic ties link Pepi, in her capacity as an advertising agent promoting "Ponte" panties (advertised in a cameo by Cecilia Roth), to *Fuego en las entrañas* and, more vividly, to the character of Tina in *Law of Desire* (also played by Carmen Maura), who is voluptuously hosed down by a street cleaner one sultry night in Madrid.[26]

Other written works and films are also intricately intertwined. A ten-page short story from the early 1970s titled "La visita" [The Visit] was the seed for *Bad Education,* where Juan, assuming the identity of his brother Ignacio, gives the director Enrique Goded a short story of the same name (Almodóvar, *La mala educación* 11). Another short story, "La bella durmiente de la clínica de El Bosque" [The Sleeping Beauty of the El Bosque Clinic], proved to be central to the script for *Talk to Her* (Almodóvar, "Mi otra cámara" 34). The more recent *Volver* is partly based on a story that Leo writes as Amanda Gris—and that her editor rejects:

> LEO: Did you get the novel I sent it to you last week?
> ALICIA *(serious)*: Yes, of course, we got it.
> LEO: And?
> ALICIA: Leo, what you sent wasn't a novel by Amanda Gris. What's up?

Carmen Maura as Tina in Law of Desire *(1987). Photograph by Jorge Aparicio. Copyright Jorge Aparicio/El Deseo.*

LEO: I guess I'm evolving.

ALICIA: I mean, why change if sales aren't down? *(Leo doesn't have time to answer.)* Leo, do you forget that the name of our collection is *True Love*? Why did you come up with a story about a mother who finds out that her daughter has killed her father after he tried to rape her? And her mother puts him in the freezer in her neighbor's restaurant so that nobody finds out.

LEO: It's not easy to get rid of a corpse, and the important thing for the mother is to save her daughter. Wouldn't you do anything to save your daughter? (Almodóvar, *La flor de mi secreto* 70–71)

Leo's final question, rhetorical as it surely is, finds its cinematic answer in *Volver,* in which the actress most closely associated with Almodóvar, Carmen Maura, also returns after a lengthy absence from the director's work. The Pepi of Almodóvar's first feature and the Pepa of his first box-office bombshell, the mother that Maura plays in *Volver,* is the mother whom Leo imagines, puts down on paper, and defends before her editor. What arises is a lush web of literary and cinematic images, situations, characters, and stories, those very stories that are at the heart of Almodóvar's creative passion.

If Almodóvar the writer and Almodóvar the filmmaker share anything, it is undoubtedly the passion for telling stories with passion, the same passion that appears printed on the screen at the very end of *Bad Education* as characterizing the movies of the writer-director-protagonist. We could say that Almodóvar *adapts* his own writing for the cinema, first composing the stories; then, sometimes, turning them into scripts; and, later, if other things are right, bringing them to the screen. An idea can percolate over months, years, even decades; it can rise and fall in his esteem; and it can often find itself modified or even displaced by another idea that the slightest and strangest of details can spark in him, details and ideas that come, more likely than not, from the world around him: a conversation, a sign seen in the street, a chance encounter, an old letter, a minor article in the daily news. In *Bad Education,* one of Almodóvar's most somberly personal films, Enrique cuts out newspaper articles as a source of inspiration for the story for a new film. What he writes is not so much a script as a short story, one that embroils a dizzying array of characters, each with his or her vast and variable set of emotions, one from which he cannot turn away and to which he returns, and rewrites, over and over again. Amid all these turns and returns, one thing nonetheless seems certain: Almodóvar is, as writer Juan José Millás so rightly says, "a filmmaker with a writer's mind."[27]

NOTES

1. As Almodóvar tells French film critic and historian Frédéric Strauss, he often felt alone while growing up: "Alone! Completely alone! I remember that at the age of ten I told my friends about [Ingmar] Bergman's *The Virgin Spring* [1960], which had a great impact on me. They looked at me at once terrified and fascinated, because it was something alien to them" (Strauss 15). To Strauss's question as to whether he thus lived "in a kind of parallel world," Almodóvar responds affirmatively (19).

2. See Almodóvar, *La mala educación. Guión cinematográfico*, 45. Like Ignacio and Enrique in *Bad Education*, the young Almodóvar found respite from the sad daily reality of Catholic school life in his visits to the local movie theater, which was also a place for erotic experimentation. As Ignacio-cum-Zahara says in *Bad Education*, "here [in the Olimpo theater] we watched the first of Sara's movies [in reference to Spanish screen icon Sara Montiel] and *Breakfast at Tiffany's*. Also here I touched Enrique up for the first time. Just thinking about it makes my knees start trembling."

3. In the words of one of Almodóvar's friends, renowned Italian writer Antonio Tabucchi: "I love Almodóvar's cinema because it moves me [mi da emozioni]" (v). Almodóvar himself has underscored the importance of emotion in his work: "For me, among other things, the cinema is just that: to make the unlikely seem natural, and to provoke in the spectator closeness and emotion—as much emotion as possible. This emotion achieved artificially is indeed real and truthful, and says more about my world and me than I myself could say. The emotion is very real, although the language is artificial" ("Discurso de Investidura" 20).

4. Even today Almodóvar devotes a great deal of his time to reading. According to his personal assistant Lola García, to whom we who work on Almodóvar owe so much, "Pedro can read four or five books in a week." The writer Juan José Millás notes similarly that "Pedro has been a voracious and a very original reader since he was twelve or thirteen years old. If we made an *Almodóvar Library*, with the fifty or hundred books [that he considers most important], we would have a bibliographic jewel" (47).

5. Juan José Millás is not merely one of Almodóvar's favorite writers, but is also a close personal friend. In *The Flower of My Secret*, Leo is briefly shown to be reading Millás's *Ella imagina* [She Imagines] (1994).

6. Although his mother does indeed loom large, Almodóvar's father, Antonio Almodóvar Trujillo, a mule driver affectionately known as "El Vinatero" for his devotion to wine, was also an enormously important figure in the director's life. As Almodóvar has told Millás: "My father looked at me with surprise and love. I didn't belong in his world. I resembled nothing of what he thought a man should be" (Millás 48). Antonio Almodóvar Trujillo died just before the premiere of his son's first feature film, *Pepi, Luci, Bom and Other Girls on the Heap*, at the San Sebastián Film Festival in 1980. When Millás recalled this fact in the course of a televised interview held shortly before the premiere of *Volver* (2006), the director could not keep himself from weeping with emotion.

7. Almodóvar writes: "When people asked me about my use of color, I would say that for me it was a natural drive. The plastic aspects of my films are based on instinct and intuition, not, in general, on conscious choice. But in the face of critical insistence, above all in France, I decided to improvise a theory because I had just remembered an anec-

dote involving my mother and color. During my gestation, my mother wore black. Since she was three, my mother went from one mourning dress to another, and thus for more than thirty years she always wore black. Even when she became pregnant she wore black. I didn't know this until I heard her tell someone about it while we were doing a dress rehearsal for *Women on the Verge,* in which she briefly appears. 'I don't want black,' she told the seamstress, to whom she proceeded to explain her long history with that color. The story really impressed me, because I didn't know anything about it at the time, and naturally, it stuck in my mind" ("Discurso de Investidura" 21).

8. For more on Almodóvar's gift as a storyteller, see Zurián, "Mirada y pasión," 21–22, and "Notas en torno a las relaciones cine-literatura en la obra almodovariana," 1.

9. With respect to acting, Almodóvar has made numerous appearances in his own films and has participated in Rafael Gordon's *Tiempos de constitución* [Constitution Times] (1978), Pedro Olea's *Un hombre llamado Flor de Otoño* [A Man Called Autumn Flower] (1978), and Iván Zulueta's brilliantly experimental *Arrebato* [Rapture] (1979). With respect to photography, his interest is more recent. Writing about an exhibition of his own photographs taken during the filming of *Talk to Her,* the director explains that this interest "has sprouted and developed in my maturity, I guess because I am now more aware of time and of the power that photographic images have to capture it and make it eternal. . . . In the last few years, I've taken thousands of pictures of objects and daily situations; sometimes I would simply stand in front of a mirror and shoot. I don't do it thinking only about the future, since for me it's also a way of living the moment" (Almodóvar, *Objetivo Almodóvar* 7).

10. *Patty Diphusa* has been reprinted many times—in 1998, it was "revised and updated"—and has been translated to a wide range of languages.

11. According to journalist Silvia Grijalba, in one of a series of six interesting reports on the *Movida,* Borja Casani, director of *La Luna,* remembers that the publication "came into being thanks to the now mythical Thursday meetings at the Galería Moriarty [an art gallery frequented by some of the movers and shakers of the *Movida*]." As Casani tells Grijalba: "A group of people with the same interests and similar tastes got together . . . [and] formed a society that we named *Per manjare* with 175,000 pesetas [a little less than two thousand dollars], and just like that, everything started. The idea was to do something in the line of the *Village Voice,* an urban newspaper that would talk about what was happening. Some people asked whether we were imitating [Andy] Warhol's *Interview,* but that wasn't the idea" (Grijalba, "25 años de la movida: 3. Publicaciones" 16).

12. The work, produced by Txomín Salazar, was written and directed by Almodóvar with photography by Pablo Pérez Minués and with Fabio de Miguel [aka Fabio McNamara] in the role of Patty.

13. As his official Web page notes: Almodóvar "was born in Calzada de Calatrava, in the province of Ciudad Real, the legal district of Almagro [where he filmed part of *Volver*], and the Archbishopric of Toledo. He migrated with his family to Orellana la Vieja, Extremadura, when he was eight. There he studied with the Silesian fathers and Franciscan friars." He stayed at a boarding school for part of his education, because at the time it was still common for friars and priests to recruit young people as candidates for the priesthood, offering them free education and lunch in the seminaries. Some of

these experiences inflect a number of Almodóvar's films, most notably *Bad Education.* "I was born during a very bad time for Spain, but a good one for the film industry," he goes on to say on http://www.clubcultura.com/clubcine/clubcineastas/almodovar/esp/cronologia.htm. Juan José Millás provides more bibliographic information for this highly autobiographical creator: "At seventeen, when Pedro moved to Madrid to 'do' the *Movida,* he shared an apartment in Canillas street, in the popular neighborhood of Prosperidad, with María Jesús [Almodóvar's second sister], who was at the time married to a member of the [highly militarized] civil guard (she is presently widowed). When [the couple had another child], the apartment was too small for them, and Pedro moved next door, although he really lived in both. It is difficult to imagine the Pedro Almodóvar of those crazy years of the *Movida* living with a conventional middle-class couple. When I asked María Jesús about it, she said that they never had any difficulty reconciling Pedro's life and theirs. What is more, the women's clothes that the filmmaker wore during his performances in *Las noches de boatiné* [nocturnal parties dedicated to humbly dressed housewives] at Rockola along with Fabio McNamara often came from Pedro's sister's closet, but also from his brother-in-law's, the *guardia civil,* whose regulation leather jacket and tights Almodóvar wore more than once onstage" (Millás 43).

14. For these stories, see Almodóvar's *Sueños de la razón,* which includes "La ausencia" (111–21), "Las últimas palabras de Rosa" (163–74), and "Anonadado (El origen del Dadá)" (197–99). He published a slightly altered version of "Dumbfounded (The Origin of Dada)" in *La Luna de Madrid,* no. 11 (October 1984): 86, with the shorter title "The Birth of Dada." The piece also appears in *Patty Diphusa* (160–63).

15. Silvia Grijalba quotes Fanny McNamara (Fabio de Miguel) as saying that "[b]eing at the Rock Ola was like being at Noah's Ark. . . . It seems as if the people outside were in the flood while those inside served to perpetuate the human race" (Grijalba, "25 años de la movida: 4. Locales" 16). Other clubs that Almodóvar frequented included Ras and Pentagrama (also known as El Penta). Youthful and countercultural as they were, some of the clubs, like Rock Ola, made millions of pesetas.

16. Grijalba, "25 años de la movida: 5. Cine, arte y moda" 16. See also Strauss 27–28.

17. Besides the previously mentioned *La Luna de Madrid* and *El Víbora,* two other significant magazines in which Almodóvar published were *Alphaville* and *Star.*

18. In 1978, Almodóvar shot his last short film, a 16mm piece titled *Salomé,* which runs only eleven minutes and stars his brother Agustín.

19. About the use of photo-novels, songs, and the idea of the grotesque in *Labyrinth of Passion,* see Zurián, "Mirada y pasión," 32.

20. In *Law of Desire,* Pablo has just released a film titled *The Paradigm of the Mussel* and is working on a theatrical adaptation of Jean Cocteau's *La Voix humaine,* which prefigured in many respects his subsequent film, the one that propelled him to international stardom: *Women on the Verge of a Nervous Breakdown.*

21. For more on Almodóvar's authorial alter egos, see Zurián, "Mirada y pasión," 21. Leo's case is particularly significant, sharing as she does with Almodóvar a maternally inflected childhood in a small town in La Mancha as well as the experience of emigration and a quasi-Arcadian return later in life.

22. According to an unsigned article in the *New Yorker* titled "Cocoon," "nostalgia is

a feeling that will come naturally to many who dip into [Almodóvar's] new book, *Patty Diphusa and Other Writings. . . .* The book intends to shock with a smile, but there are some canny observations. In a berserk 1988 piece called 'Styles and Customs in the Nineties,' Almodóvar predicts that 'all sorts of traffic problems' will result in people's being 'condemned to stay at home and do everything for themselves.' And that's exactly what has happened to Almodóvar and his gang: the movers and shakers of Madrid's mad eighties are now cocooning." See "Cocoon," *New Yorker,* 68.33 (Oct. 5, 1992): 59–61.

23. For more on *esperpento* in Almodóvar's work, see Zurián, "Mirada y pasión," 29–34.

24. The new texts are "El autobús desbocado" [The Uncontrolled Bus], which originally appeared in *El Mundo* as "Patty Diphusa, en el mundo de los vivos" [Patty Diphusa in the World of the Living]; "Bi," which first appeared as "El hijo del taxista" [The Taxi Driver's Son]; "Botines de punta chata" [Box Toe Ankle Boots], which was originally titled "Los botines" [The Ankle Boots], and "Yo y mi clon en una noche llena de incertidumbre" [My Clone and I in a Night of Uncertainty], which *El Mundo* published under the more laconic title "Patty y una noche llena de incertidumbre" [Patty and a Night of Uncertainty].

25. The expanded edition of *Patty Diphusa* also contains a section titled "Filler" and another, shorter one titled "Advice on How to Become an Internationally Famous Filmmaker."

26. *Fuego en las entrañas* includes the following description: "Two employees [from the Department of Sanitation] were hosing down the street. A youngster, called Mara, approached the jet of water, raised her dress, opened her legs and with moans of pleasure readied herself to receive a strong jet of water in her pussy. The man who was holding the hose played the game, and moved as if he were fucking her with the enormous jet of water" (38).

27. Millás made this remark at the presentation of the published version of the screenplay of *Talk to Her* on December 17, 2002, in the Madrid bookshop 8½ (Martín-Lunas 18).

WORKS CITED

Almodóvar, Pedro. *Carne trémula. El guión.* Barcelona: Plaza & Janés, 1997.
———. "Diario de campaña. Mi diario americano (1)." *El País Semanal* 1.222 (Feb. 27, 2000): 36–49.
———. "Diario de campaña. Mi diario americano (y 2)." *El País Semanal* 1.223 (March 5, 2000): 110–19.
———. "Discurso de Investidura." *Acto de investidura "Doctor Honoris Causa" del Excmo. Sr. Pedro Almodóvar.* Cuenca: Servicio de Publicaciones de la Universidad de Castilla–La Mancha, 2000. 17–22.
———. *La flor de mi secreto.* Barcelona: Círculo de Lectores, 1995.
———. *Fuego en las entrañas.* Barcelona: Ed. La Cúpula, 1981.
———. *Hable con ella. El guión.* Madrid: Ocho y medio libros de cine and El Deseo, 2002.
———. "Jet lag y papada. Diario pop americano." *El País Semanal* 1.377 (Feb. 16, 2003): 36–49.

———. *La mala educación. Guión cinematográfico*. Madrid: Ocho y medio libros de cine and El Deseo, 2004.

———. "Mi otra cámara." *El País Semanal* 1.326 (Feb. 24, 2002): 32–39.

———. *Objetivo Almodóvar. "Hable con ella" vista por su director. Catálogo de la exposición de fotografías*. Madrid: FNAC and El Deseo, 2002.

———. "Patty Diphusa en *Toda tuya*." *Víbora* 32–33 (1982): 21–37.

———. *Patty Diphusa y otros textos*. Barcelona: Anagrama, 1998.

———. *The Patty Diphusa Stories and Other Writings*. Trans. Kirk Anderson. Boston: Faber and Faber, 1992.

———. *Todo sobre mi madre. Guión original*. Madrid: El Deseo, 1999.

———. *Volver. Guión cinematográfico*. Madrid: Ocho y medio and El Deseo, 2006.

———, et al. *Sueños de la razón*. Madrid: Fernando de Polanco Editor-Titanic, 1978.

———, and Fermín Cabal. *Entre tinieblas. Libreto de la adaptación teatral*. Madrid: Fundación Autor (SGAE), 1993.

Capote, Truman. *Music for Chameleons*. New York: Vintage, 1994.

"Cocoon." *New Yorker* 68.33 (Oct. 5, 1992): 59–61.

García Márquez, Gabriel. *La bendita manía de contar. Taller de guión*. Madrid: EICT de San Antonio de los Baños & Ollero & Ramos, 1998.

Grijalba, Silvia. "25 años de la movida: 1. Historia." *El Mundo,* Feb. 7, 2005, 16–17.

———. "25 años de la movida: 2. Música." *El Mundo,* Feb. 8, 2005, 16–17.

———. "25 años de la movida: 3. Publicaciones." *El Mundo,* Feb. 9, 2005, 16–17.

———. "25 años de la movida: 4. Locales." *El Mundo,* Feb. 10, 2005, 16–17.

———. "25 años de la movida: 5. Cine, Arte y Moda." *El Mundo,* Feb. 11, 2005, 16–17.

———. "25 años de la movida: y 6. Qué fue de la movida." *El Mundo,* Feb. 12, 2005, 12–13.

Harguindey, Ángel Sánchez. "La vuelta de Almodóvar." *El País Semanal,* Dec. 23, 2001, 60–72.

Martín-Lunas, Milagros. "*Hable con ella,* el cine también se puede leer." *El Mundo,* Dec. 18, 2002, 18.

Millás, Juan José. "Almodóvar desconocido." *El País Semanal* 1.435 (March 28, 2004): 36–49.

Rodríguez, Emma. "El debut literario de Pedro Almodóvar." *El Mundo,* April 5, 1992, 32.

Strauss, Frédéric. *Conversaciones con Pedro Almodóvar*. Barcelona: Akal, 2001.

Tabucchi, Antonio. "La logica della vita." *Parla con lei* by Pedro Almodóvar. Turin: Giulio Einaudi editore, 2003. v–vii.

Vidal, Nuria. *El cine de Pedro Almodóvar*. Madrid: Ministerio de Cultura/Instituto de Cinematografía y de las Artes Audiovisuales, 1988.

Willoquet-Maricondi, Paula, ed. *Pedro Almodóvar: Interviews*. Jackson: University Press of Mississippi, 2004.

Zurián, Fran A. "Mirada y pasión: Reflexiones en torno a la obra almodovariana." *Almodóvar: El cine como pasión*. Eds. Fran A. Zurián and Carmen Vázquez. Cuenca: Ediciones de la Universidad de Castilla–La Mancha, 2005. 21–42.

———. "Notas en torno a las relaciones cine-literatura en la obra almodovariana." *Binaria. Revista de Comunicación, Cultura y Tecnología* 4 (2004): 1–12.

16 *Bad Education*
Fictional Autobiography and Meta–Film Noir
VÍCTOR FUENTES

I t almost seems as if Pedro Almodóvar, after the critical and popular success of *All about My Mother* (1999) and *Talk to Her* (2002), defies his
achievements by steering *Bad Education* (2004) toward the bizarre, tinted
with horror and largely bereft of the sense of human solidarity that characterized his two previous films. In some respects, the turn to darkness after
enjoying the bright lights of success is not new: after *Women on the Verge of
a Nervous Breakdown* (1988), an international sensation that remains one
of the highest-grossing films in Spanish history, Almodóvar explored the
bizarre and violent in *Kika* (1993) and, to a lesser extent, *Tie Me Up! Tie Me
Down!* (1990) and *High Heels* (1991). Although there may be no consistent
pattern of alternation in Almodóvar's cinematic trajectory, *Bad Education*
does depart from a mode of filmmaking that began with *The Flower of My
Secret* (1995) and peaked with *Talk to Her* and that the director, in the press
release of *Talk to Her,* a film set primarily in the caring space of a hospital, summarized as follows: "as far as content is concerned, I tend increasingly toward emotion and, as far as form is concerned, toward transparency." As indicated, this mode of filmmaking shines in *Talk to Her,* where
deep emotions of love and friendship and a transparency of form are conveyed through a profusion of windows, balconies, and glass doors that,
while at times impeding verbal communication, nonetheless facilitate visual
contact—so important in a film in which the blank eyes of comatose women
figure so prominently.

Bad Education, a film set primarily in the repressive space of a religious
school and the competitive spaces of the entertainment industry, though
also suffused with emotion, is marked, in contrast, by nothing so much as
violence and fear, darkness, confusion, mistrust, and crime. Its plot, moreover, is surely the most complicated, the least transparent, that Almodóvar
has ever written—more so even than such seemingly free-flowing early films
as *Pepi, Luci, Bom* (1980) and *Labyrinth of Passion* (1982). Tellingly, perhaps, the extraordinary box-office success and critical acclaim of *All about*

My Mother and *Talk to Her* did not accompany *Bad Education,* which was hardly awash with international awards and was practically ignored at the Goyas, the Spanish equivalent of the Oscars. In the light of such differences, some of which are of course beyond the director's control, it is tempting to venture that Almodóvar, at the peak of his glory, was willing to take a risk by reaffirming that his cinema was still dedicated to marginality and challenging, even "unredeemable," situations, and that its only law was the "law of desire," no matter how transgressive it may be.

In many respects, *Bad Education* is a noir return to *Law of Desire* (1986), for both films are metacinematic, centered as they are on the turbulent lives and loves of movie directors, and both, though especially *Bad Education,* showcase men rather than women. Compelling as the connections between *Bad Education* and *Law of Desire* are, the director from La Mancha also returns in *Bad Education* to aspects of film noir and the horror genre that he had deployed in *Matador* (1986) and in *Kika* and that provided him a way to get into what he has presented as the darkest part in all of us. All of these films, for all their differences, are similar in tone to *Bad Education* and deal with malicious, even criminal characters: there are no "Benignos" in them (Benigno is, of course, the name of the caretaker of the beautiful comatose young woman in *Talk to Her*). That said, what links all of the films is the director's refusal to judge his characters, to qualify them as "sick" or "evil"; indeed, in even the darkest of them—and *Bad Education* may well be the darkest—Almodóvar treats his characters with uncommon compassion. As he is reported to have said in an article by Lynn Hirschberg titled simply and significantly "The Redeemer": "My goal as a writer is to have empathy for all characters. In my films, I have a tendency to redeem characters" (38).

Although questions of genre, tone, and characterization are undoubtedly important, *Bad Education,* inasmuch as it focuses on a gay Spanish director who comes to fame during the raucous years of the Madrid *Movida* (as in *Law of Desire*), is also shot through with autobiographical references. Indeed, on the subject of *Bad Education,* Almodóvar has said that "everything that is not autobiographical is plagiarism" (Hirschberg 42), by which he does not seem so much to deride plagiarism per se as to signal a productive tension between it and autobiography. Within the "tradition of plagiarism" so present in Almodóvar's films, many of which are virtual palimpsests of classic Hollywood cinema of the 1940s and early 1950s, the intertexts of the autobiographically inflected *Bad Education* come mainly from film noir, which is manifested, as already intimated, in a metacinematic *mise en abîme*. As the author has explained: "*Bad Education* with its labyrinth-like construction and doomed characters was inspired by *noirish* movies like *Laura* and *Out of the Past*" (ibid. 26). In what follows, I will examine *Bad Education* with an eye to the interplays between autobiography and interfilmic borrowings or "plagiarisms" from film noir.

As important as intertextual or interfilmic references are, the starting point of *Bad Education* appears to be Almodóvar's own lived experience as passed through the sieve of his open and complex imagination. As noted, autobiographical tendencies are constant in his production, something that is evident from his first film, *Pepi, Luci, Bom,* in which the director makes an on-screen appearance as a nighttime entertainer. Almodóvar makes similar appearances in *Labyrinth of Passion* and *What Have I Done to Deserve This?* (1984), but it is in *Law of Desire,* which centers on the life of a gay director during the heady first years of Spanish democracy, that the autobiographical resonances are most compelling and complex. One sequence in *Law of Desire*—apparently derived from a real-life experience, duly fictionalized, to be sure—stands out because it is repeated in a more developed and complex form in *Bad Education.* The transsexual Tina (Carmen Maura) returns to the Catholic school that she attended as a young boy and confronts the priest who had been her choir director, spiritual counselor, and seducer, just as Juan-Ángel (Gael García Bernal), playing the role of his transsexual brother Ignacio (Francisco Boira), later does in *Bad Education.*

Like the young Tino (who is not depicted on-screen) and the young Ignacio (Ignacio Pérez), Almodóvar attended Catholic school and sang in the choir when he was a boy. Talking with Lynn Hirschberg, Almodóvar declares that, "he was a gifted soloist in his school choir" (43), like Ignacio, the young boy with the "white voice" in *Bad Education;* in another interview with the director, Suzie Mackenzie notes that Almodóvar's "main refuge was in music; he had a lovely voice, what they call a 'white voice' and he sang in the choir" (159). Of course, it is one thing to have a voice like an angel and to sing in the choir and another thing to suffer abuse, as Tino and Ignacio do, at the hands of a lecherous priest. Did the young Almodóvar have a similar experience? It may be impossible to know with certainty, whatever the director may say, but he has made more than one reference to something decidedly less savory than singing. In a conversation with pop cultural writer and journalist Maruja Torres, Almodóvar indicates that he lost his "religious fervor" for reasons similar to those that Ignacio expresses in *Bad Education*. As he rather perfunctorily, and enigmatically, puts it: "terrible things were happening to me. You already know what I mean" (12).

The project of giving artistic life to such a traumatic matter as the sexual abuse of schoolchildren by priests appears to have accompanied Almodóvar throughout his career. He first addressed the disquieting topic in the form of a short story from 1973, before he began to work as a filmmaker. It was, as he puts it, "a fierce story in which I took revenge on the religious education that I had received in a Catholic school twenty years before" (Almodóvar 11). In several interviews, some from many years ago, he alludes to this traumatic scenario of desire, abuse, and revenge that finally comes to the foreground in 2004. As already noted, Almodóvar's interest, if not "obsession," in the scenario, though apparently marked by direct personal experience, does not derive completely from it. As the director has reminded fans and critics: "*Bad Education* is not an autobiographical movie" (Hirschberg 43), it lies between autobiography and fiction, personal experience and partly "plagiarized" invention, and is more properly an autobiographical metafictional and a metacinematic movie. Still, it is interesting to note that before making the movie, the director did indeed allude, as noted, to lived experiences of abuse, but that after making the movie, and certainly after it was released, he insisted on his creed that what is important in a film is artifice, thereby avoiding, or at least striving to avoid, further questions about the links between the characters in the movie and himself.

Be that as it may, in the previously cited interview with Maruja Torres, conducted in 1982 on the subject of *Labyrinth of Passion*, Almodóvar responded to his interviewer's question as to whether the priests had ever "touched him" by "confessing" the following: "Yes, of course. . . . It was a shame, because sex should be discovered naturally, and not brutally, suddenly. For two or three years, I could not be alone, out of pure fear" (Torres 12). Twenty years later, in 2002, preparing for the filming of *Bad Education*, Almodóvar returned to the topic in Suzie Mackenzie's interview, titled "All about my Father." Referring to the Catholic school that he attended as a boy, he asserted that some 80 percent of the little boys, himself included, were sexually abused, and he recalled something that later appeared in *Bad Education*: "the dark, long corridors and running away—not that there was anywhere to run to" (Mackenzie 159). Indeed, in the interview from 2002, he essentially reiterated what he had already said in 1982: to wit, that "for years [he] was terrified of darkness."

In *Bad Education,* dark scenes of persecution and flight in which fear is dominant are interspersed with, and punctuated by, scenes in which music and song are prominent. The tensions between fear and music—and more precisely between music as a refuge for the child and as a fearfully erotic stimulant for the priests—are arguably at their most troubling, and touching, in the character of the child Ignacio, over and again the point of reference for discussions, and speculations, about the reality of sexual abuse. Beyond and beside the specifics, in the same interview, the Manchegan filmmaker also says something that has recently been widely confirmed, especially in the United States: "Abuse is an old problem that the Church does not want to face, but they have to face it now. It is impossible to contain. It will explode" (ibid. 158). Nevertheless, although the title, *Bad Education* (which in Spanish also means bad conduct), seems clear enough, and although the criminal practices of sexual abuse by priests have become part of daily news, it comes as somewhat of a surprise that the film does not overtly condemn such abuses or its practitioners. On the contrary, while in the news we read headlines such as "Pedophile priest to serve 12 to 15 years in prison" (regarding the defrocked Bostonian Paul Shanley), the pedophile priest is, for Almodóvar, "probably my favorite character in *Bad Education*" (Hirschberg 27).

Lest the more decisive moralists among us be scandalized by what might well appear to be a "shocking" statement, it is important to remember the obvious: that the pedophile priest in *Bad Education* is a character in a movie and not in real life—autobiographical aspects notwithstanding. It is also worth keeping in mind that the film may not dwell on such abuses precisely because the scandal that Almodóvar may have wanted to expose exploded onto the public stage before he made the movie. Anyone familiar with Almodóvar's work knows that, even at its most realistic or neorealistic (as with *What Have I Done to Deserve This?*), even at its most topical and timely, it passes quite evidently through the filter of fictional representation. In the metacinematic *Bad Education,* the filtering happens twice, representation through representation. The question that arises is whether such a filtered fictional representation overpowers what might otherwise have constituted a major cinematic reflection on the social and human repercussions of such a distressing practice as child abuse under the mantle of religious faith and devotion.

Although the film as a whole shies away from—or, better yet, is unconcerned with—an ethico-political meditation on child abuse, it does include several scenes and sequences that convey the stark reality of the phenomenon, especially when we hear the "white voice" of the abused child singing a Spanish version of "Moon River" and "Jardinero" and expressing, it appears, at once his innocence and bewilderment at the padre's "interest" in him (is there an obscure parody of *All about My Mother* here?). The scenes of the abuse that lies hidden in the daily practice of the church are nonetheless shot through with the expressive beauty of decoration and performance, communicating to the spectator the suffering and the trauma of the child. In this light, we might venture that the artist has managed, quite admirably, to sublimate his painful childhood experiences, leaving to the media the task that had apparently initially caught its imagination: telling furious stories of revenge and retribution, which recently have been full of media sensationalism.

Then again, *Bad Education* is also suffused with stories of revenge and retribution, albeit presented in a manner that eludes the more moralistic obviousness of most journalistic portrayals. The cagey articulation of autobiographical memory also entails a fairly romanticized celebration of the purity that characterizes the relationship of love and friendship between the two boys. Perhaps unwittingly, Almodóvar goes back to a theme treated by Antonio de Hoyos y Vinet, one of the precursors of Spanish homoerotic literature. In his short story "Eucaristía" (1911), Hoyos y Vinet presents a priest who makes two boys feel guilty about their friendship, similar in many respects to the one showcased in *Bad Education*. Almodóvar, who has repeatedly declared that he has overcome the feelings of guilt that the "bad education" of religious institutions forces on most children, appears more in tune to the Greek tradition rather than the Judeo-Christian one. Instead of guilt, he puts in the mouth of the child Enrique what he himself apparently discovered during adolescence: "I am a hedonist." When Ignacio asks the future director what "hedonist" means, Enrique responds: "Those who like to have fun. I read it in an encyclopedia."

When Almodóvar, in one of the previously cited interviews, recalls a relationship that he had with a classmate, he declares that the encounter had nothing to do with whatever may have happened with the priests, because there was mutual consent between two boys of the same age (Torres 12). In another interview from 1984, he says that his first love took place in a Catholic school in Cáceres, in largely rural Extremadura. It was a love "like in the movies, like Katharine Hepburn and Cary Grant." The interviewer, Ángel S. Harguindey, asks him if it might not have been more like Judy Garland and Mickey Rooney. With his characteristic nonchalance, Almodóvar laughs and adds: "Yes, those with Mickey Rooney and Judy Garland. Well, at any rate, in our case we were both either Cary Grant or Mickey Rooney" (Harguindey 38).

With its open-minded appreciation of desire, *Bad Education* gives a new spin to the theme of homoeroticism even as it revisits *Law of Desire*. Perhaps this relatively nonjudgmental spin is the reason why this movie has not been as popular as his previous ones. After all, it deals with a topic abhorred and criminalized in our societies: ephebophilia—which is the level at which Visconti kept his magnificent *Death in Venice* (1971)—transformed into pedophilia. In so doing, Almodóvar approaches a transgressive limit in his cinema, even though the transgression remains enmeshed, as intimated, in the mannerist web of the film. In contrast to the humorous or ironic work of the camera in many of his other films that touch on sexual taboos, in *Bad Education* the camera at times adopts the point of view of the pedophile priest, focusing on his strong libidinal desire toward the child: a risky move at a time when child pornography runs amok on the Internet.

As in his previous films (at least since *The Flower of My Secret*), in *Bad Education* Almodóvar once again proves himself to be a master of cinema, in total control of the cinematic apparatus. Nevertheless, his baroque mannerism here simultaneously hides and reveals, as with *Kika,* a *horror vacui* that is most fully conveyed to the spectator when the gate to Enrique's house closes in the last scene. In spite of its formal richness, emptiness and lack of true communication (we are at a far remove from the communication against all obstacles of *Talk to Her*) are the dominant characteristics of the film, the most pessimistic in all of Almodóvar's cinematography. The movie also reflects or expresses—indirectly, to be sure—a current crisis in the discourse of sexual liberation in the midst of disastrous processes of globalization. We might do well to keep in mind that the movie was made after 9/11 and was released on the eve of the devastating terrorist attack by Islamic extremists (in other films of Almodóvar, the subjects of campy comedy) in Madrid on March 11, 2004. In such a charged context, the subject of pedophilia, even when "elevated" to art, and of unchecked desire, ambition and greed leading to crime, could be seen as an aberrant index of a debased Western society. Maybe this is the reason, or at least one of the reasons, why Almodóvar talks about "playing with multiple mirrors" in the movie (Almodóvar 11), one of which functions in *mise en abîme:* the mirror of film noir. As is well known, film noir also developed at a time of deep social and moral crisis and was often produced and received as an allegory of social degradation.

It is within such a fraught international context that critical readings and reviews of *Bad Education* by Gustavo Martín Garzo (offered as a preface to the published screenplay), Lynn Hirschberg, and David Denby prove particularly insightful inasmuch as they point to an implicit ethical dimension in this film of abuse and crime. Denby, for instance, states that Almodóvar "is afraid of nothing" and "is a generous, playful, warm-spirited director—the last great humanist in cinema" (89). Although Denby is on solid ground when he designates Almodóvar as a humanist, it is also true that his humanism negotiates duality and duplicity. Central to film noir, duality and duplicity are omnipresent in *Bad Education,* so much so that when Paquito, a minor transsexual character played by Javier Cámara, asks the adult Ignacio (Juan/Ángel) for another line of coke, he does so by underscoring the symbolic importance of the number two: "Serve me another one, you know that I believe in couples! Two fucks, two lines, two friends." Duplicity implies conflict and ambiguity, just as the number 2, according to Cirlot's *Dictionary of Symbols,* "is as an image in the mirror, a symbol of consciousness, an echo of reality" (178). The structure of the film is marked by internal duplicity, underlined by the encompassing *mise en abîme* of film noir. Duplicity also marks the characters: Juan, the impostor who pretends to be his brother Ignacio; Ignacio, who "doubles" himself in the feminine as a transvestite and a transsexual; the priest Manolo, who later becomes Mr. Berenguer, the editor; and even Enrique, who recalls the film director in *Law of Desire* (Eusebio Poncela) and who can in many respects be considered to be the double of Almodóvar himself. Ángel S. Harguindey's final, off-the-cuff remark in his 1984 interview with the director has proved prescient indeed: "Some day he will have a chalet with a pool" (39), which is exactly what Enrique is shown as having in Madrid in the early 1980s.

The autobiographical element is also duplicated, embedded within the filmic narrative, as noted by Ángel/Ignacio/Juan, when he presents the story that he has written and that serves as the origin of the film within the film (yet another duplication): "One part is inspired in our childhood, but the other, when the characters grow, is fiction." Tellingly, these words are valid for the film as a whole, a work of autobiographical fiction that blurs the boundaries between reality and invention in a manner that remits in some fundamental respect to Don Quixote. Cervantine resonances aside, the duplicity and doubleness of the story and the characters contribute to a nonlinear cinematic experience, full of flashbacks and flash-forwards to different times (1964, 1977, 1980–81) and different places (Madrid, Valencia, Galicia), in which points of view proliferate and real and imagined events collide in ways seldom seen before on the big screen. Although the encapsulated stories that are superimposed on the door with which the film closes give the audience the sense that it has comes to understand the twists and turns of so many duplicitous, doubled, and redoubled identities, in actuality, the audience is more likely to be led to "revisit" the film (the name of the screenplay that Ángel brings to Enrique is "The Visit") in order to understand it. Inasmuch as Enrique is a director characterized by writer's block, uncertainty, and a lack of control that his desire to dominate Ángel only seems to exacerbate, it is perhaps not surprising that the "real" author, Pedro Almodóvar, works as if from on high, hiding or withholding from both the spectators and the characters crucial information that he does not reveal until the film's end— and even then not as clearly as the rather lapidary ending notes.

In contrast with *All about My Mother* and *Talk to Her,* where human communication involves the living and the dead, the conscious and the unconscious, *Bad Education,* once again not unlike *Kika,* insists on the lack of human communication and on the failure, if not impossibility, of relationships, especially between men. In *Bad Education,* the first piece of information that the audience receives about Ignacio's life is fictional (the "real" Ignacio, played by Francisco Boira, only appears in the last scenes of the film): in 1980, a man claiming to be Ignacio (Gael García Bernal) but insisting on going by the stage name of Ángel (but in "reality," Juan) visits film director Enrique (Fele Martínez) and presents him with a story, or screenplay, titled "The Visit." Although Enrique does not "see" in the man who calls himself Ignacio/Ángel the boy that he once knew and loved at the Catholic school, he takes the story home, where he reads it and, in good directorial fashion, visualizes it. Ignacio's story is presented on-screen as imagined— and later, as it turns out—filmed by Enrique. As we later find out, Enrique's suspicions are well founded, for the man who presents himself as Ignacio is actually being impersonated by his brother Juan, who is also his murderer— yet another twist that we discover toward the end of the film. Desirous to be an actor at any cost, Juan—who insists, as noted, on being called Ángel— studies transvestites in order to play the part of Zahara, who specializes in imitating Sara Montiel, and stars in what is revealed to be a movie (directed by Enrique) within the movie (directed by Almodóvar). In the movie within the movie, Ignacio plays a seductive transvestite who picks up a man who turns out to be Enrique, his classmate and first love in school, and they masturbate each other while watching a movie starring Sara Montiel in a small theater in a town in eastern Spain. As if to signal a gap between the director Enrique and the character Enrique, it is not the rather frail Fele Martínez but rather the hunkier Alberto Ferreiro who plays the part in the movie within the movie and who inflames Ignacio's desire. The two men have sex, at first somewhat mechanically, and later, once Ignacio discovers that the "sleeping beauty" is indeed Enrique (who had promptly passed out while Ignacio was performing fellatio on him), more passionately, at least on Ignacio's part (Enrique remains asleep). As the fairly tortuous attempt to put all of these comings and goings into writing indicates, these encounters are part and parcel of a complex multi-perspectivism. (This extremely convoluted, even neobaroque, story line with such complexity, may also have, well, "turned viewers off.")

The real Ignacio is the author of "The Visit," which his brother Juan usurps along with his identity. In the story, and in the movie based on the story, Ignacio idealizes his role as a beautiful transvestite, something else that we come to know later, when we finally see the real Ignacio: a bitter, broken, heroin addict who is far from being either handsome or beautiful. Before the moment when the real Ignacio appears, which is not part of the movie within the movie, Enrique artistically weaves together the scenes of the transvestite's performance and his, or rather their, (imagined) homoerotic encounters. As already noted, the impostor, Juan/Ángel, fulfills his dream of playing the role of his transvestite brother, Ignacio, whom he had earlier killed, in part because of his homophobic intolerance and in part because of his unyielding desire to have a part that would launch him into stardom. That his stardom would come by way of a transvestite performance on-screen, and homosexual relations with the director, Enrique, offscreen, is only one of many of the ironies of the vertiginous plot of *Bad Education*. Another irony is that Enrique, by way of an adult sexual relationship with a man pretending to be Ignacio, relives the loving relationship that he had with the real Ignacio when the two were boys. Although Enrique comes to be aware that Juan is playing at being Ignacio, the situation brings to mind the duplicitous Conchita in Buñuel's *That Obscure Object of Desire* (1977), played by two different actresses from two different countries, Carole Bouquet and Ángela Molina.

Without being aware of the violence that subtends the play of identities until nearly the end of film, the audience may well take the exuberant displays of nonnormative sexuality, both on the stage and in the bed, as yet another brilliant installment in the provocative world of Almodóvar's films.

Zahara's performance and other lush and lighthearted moments of the children at play at school, lighten and brighten this otherwise somber movie. The scenes that center on the transvestites also account for a connection between the neobaroque form of Almodóvar's latest films (amply evident in the sinuous plot structure) as well as the kitsch and camp stylistics of his previous ones. In reference to the scene in which Zahara incarnates Sara Montiel, for instance, the script notes read: "Her right hand holds a flower that she slowly passes around her body until both her face and her mouth form a beautiful kitsch image" (Almodóvar 34).

Amid all of the connections to prior films, *Bad Education* nonetheless adds something new to the leitmotif of the transvestite that runs throughout so much of Almodóvar's cinema. For the multiple duplicities of *Bad Education* also take aim at the gender divide (man and woman, man versus woman) that was one of the few stable features of film noir. Stunning and lethal like the femmes fatales of film noir, Juan/Ángel/Ignacio/Zahara is a masterpiece of multi-perspectivism. In the fictional part of the autobiographical story written by Ignacio and filmed by Enrique, Juan/Ángel, playing the role of Ignacio, returns to the town where the old school was located, masquerading as Ignacio's sister. There he visits Father Manolo in order to blackmail him and gain retribution and threatens the priest with publishing the story included in "The Visit." The text, then, is read by the fictional Father Manolo, but it is voiced over by the child Ignacio (Ignacio Pérez), who recounts the lived "real" part of the story.

In these sequences we again see and hear the extraordinary array of perspectives that converge in a whirlwind of inner duplicities. The memories, experiences, and feelings of both the children and the priest get entangled in Ignacio's writing, in Enrique's filming, and in Father Manolo's reading of the story. Enrique, possibly remembering how he was mistreated at the school, rewrites the ending of Ignacio's invented story, based on real events, and charges the Catholic church with being capable of anything, including murder. However Ignacio's story may have "really" ended, the ending that the director imposes occurs in the priest's office, where Ignacio is killed by "brother" José, who looks like a character out of some Gothic or expressionist film. In "real" life, as Berenguer recounts, Ignacio was killed by his brother Juan. From this point on (the third visit, which gives fuller meaning to the two previous ones), the story, marked by mystery, unfolds entirely within the domains of the gender of film noir, and in complicity with Berenguer (if not indeed from Berenguer's perspective), formerly the "real" Father Manolo, who appears as both a character in and spectator of the filming of the fictional killing of Ignacio.

Before filming this "ending," in a break that returns us to "reality" and to the diegetic present (1980), Enrique visits Ignacio's mother's house, tracking Ignacio/Ángel's secret all the way to Ortigueira, Galicia. Enrique discovers that Ignacio is in reality dead. He also discovers that Ignacio's brother Juan is training to be an actor under the name of Ángel. This sequence, the visit to a village colored with a patina of time gone by, is another of Almodóvar's leitmotifs: his cinema focuses on the city, but constantly reminds us of its popular, rural roots. The figure of the mother is another of his leitmotifs, filled with autobiographical resonances, and arguably uniquely important in the history of cinema. In several instances, as in this movie, she has the symbolic dimensions of the Pietà, extending love to her suffering, wayward children. In short, the sequence enables the audience to take an ethical "breath" in a film whose central themes are the sexual abuse of children, unchecked ambition, and murder.

Again, once the film within the film is finished, there is the third and final visit that issues in the denouement of the story and returns us to the "real" story of the characters. In a context of almost Byzantine decadence, it is significant that those parts related most closely to Almodóvar's lived experiences are presented as "fiction" and that those that are fictional appear as "real." The priest Manolo is now Mr. Berenguer, an editor of literary works by young authors—a subtle way of indicating that his interests have not entirely changed. And yet, much has changed. In another of the many splits and doublings of *Bad Education,* renowned Catalan actor Lluís Homar plays Berenguer, while Daniel Giménez-Cacho incarnates the "fictional" priest. After watching from the shadows the filming of the ending of "The Visit," Mr. Berenguer—who emerges from "out of the past," another film noir move enshrined in Jacques Tourneur's *Out of the Past* (1947)—pays a "visit" to Enrique in his office. He introduces himself as the *"malo,"* the "bad" or "evil" character of the film within the film that is *Bad Education.* The ex-priest reappears with a secular, sadomasochistic halo, which in some respects recalls the protagonist of Joseph Losey's *The Servant* (1963): a veritable master of desire run amok brilliantly played by Dirk Bogarde. From this point on, Enrique, the author and director, is made into a largely passive and suffering spectator, with the added twist that instead of possibly directing a story about a woman devoured by a crocodile in a zoo, as he had contemplated at the beginning of the film, he finds himself playing the role of the woman—and Juan the role of the crocodile. Although Enrique is not exactly an endearing character, Juan, as his mask falls, shows himself to be much worse, a veritable actualization of Cain. There is a certain playful irony in the play with bad characters and a bad education, because Almodóvar remains, as already noted, profoundly disinclined to resort to the facile, moralistic Manichaeanism by which characters and events are divisively qualified as "good" or "bad," let alone "evil." Be that as it may, given the film's focus on ecclesiastical settings and religious rituals, Almodóvar's exploration of the sinister side of humanity here includes satanic elements. Its plays with "devil" priests, "perverse" rituals, and implicit black masses pay homage to the late-nineteenth-century literature of Joris-Karl Huysmans and others, but also to the cinema of Buñuel, who admired the French decadent tradition. In this light, Satan, as the lord of evil and change, seems to preside over the multiple conversions in the film. Mr. Berenguer, a lay, miniversion of Satan, a true "poor devil," comes to tell Enrique the true story of Ignacio's death as a blackmailing drug addict killed by a lethal overdose of heroin that Berenguer and Juan, Ignacio's brother, acquire for him.

This new turn in the plot signals Juan's unchecked ambition and greed as the low passions that dominate the story, and the film, from the beginning, even though the audience does not fully realize this until the end. It seems that Almodóvar, the humanist, does seek some kind of retribution for such crimes. In his different roles and relationships, all of which prove corrupt, Juan personifies "ambition" in a figurative, obsolete sense registered by the dictionary of the Royal Spanish Academy (RAE), according to which *ambición* also means "of or related to the ivy and other similar climbing plants that entangle themselves with trees or other objects." The entanglement that characterizes *Bad Education* is also central to film noir, whose attributes, though present in the film from the first visit, come to the fore in the *mise en abîme* of the third visit, when the "real" ex-Father Manolo, remade into a publisher named Berenguer, visits the set of the film and tells his version of the story and of the real Ignacio's end.

From the very beginning of the film, the subdued lighting, dark setting, voice-over narration, and frequent flashbacks locate *Bad Education* in the genre of film noir. The elaborate neobaroque and expressionistic visual style indicates that, as in film noir, the meanings of the film will be shadowed by darkness. Gloomy shades and dark furniture reinforce the sense of a descent into the more somber territories of the human heart and psyche. The fade-to-black technique is used here, in keeping with cinematic convention, as a way to bring to the light, as it were, the troubling aspects of the images. According to the published screenplay: "The priest embraces him [the child Ignacio]; we do not see the rest, because at the time the camera offers a general shot of the priest's back and the screen is absorbed by the black of his cassock" (Almodóvar 78). The various passions that intricately bind together, and tear apart, the characters—desire, love, greed, jealousy, ambition—are likewise consistent with film noir, as is the previously acknowledged play of duplicity, and the generalized atmosphere of falsehood, possession, guilt, and debt that ensues. The desire to solve an enigma or mystery, which motivates the investigative acts of police and/or detectives in film noir, is displaced onto Enrique Goded's sexually charged desire to know Ignacio/Ángel/Juan. At the end, as the script says, "Enrique has no more energy. He does not care about Ángel. He already knows what he wanted to know" (ibid. 158).

The features of film noir are especially acute in the last visit, when Berenguer, through the very act of telling his tale, explores something like the psychology of the criminal mind, and when the voice-over narration jumps back to "real"-life 1977, and not to the fictional story imagined by Ignacio and filmed by Enrique. Ignacio has become a drug addict and tries to blackmail the former Father Manolo in order to get money for a sex-change operation that would improve his physical features. At Ignacio's home, Berenguer falls in love with Juan, who announces himself—as he had done when he first visited the adult Enrique—as an actor-to-be. The young actor takes advantage of Berenguer's uncontrolled infatuation, milking the former priest for as much as he can. Finally, both decide to get rid of Ignacio, who is a far cry from the glamorous, seductive Zahara, but is instead a haggard, angry drug addict struggling to free himself from heroin. The murder plot, which binds together the unlikely pair of Juan and Berenguer, is reminiscent of that of *The Postman Always Rings Twice* (1946), in which a voluptuous wife (Lana Turner) and her lover (John Garfield) murder her husband. After committing the crime, in order to "kill time," Berenguer and Juan/Ángel go to a movie theater where a film noir festival is being held. Two of Almodóvar's favorites are being shown: Marcel Carné's *Thérèse Raquin* (1953) and Billy Wilder's *Double Indemnity* (1944).

The screenplay makes the connections to film noir clear: as the murderous pair leave the theater, "Berenguer looks three times overwhelmed—by his own problems, those of Thérèse Raquin, and those of Raf Vallone," the famous Italian actor of the 1950s and 1960s who appeared in *Thérèse Raquin* (Almodóvar 148).

On-screen, in the two characters' own lived movie, we hear them comment: "it is as if the whole movie were about us!" In a previous scene, the two men try to pass unnoticed when they visit the Museo de Gigantes y Cabezudos (the Museum of Giants and "Big Heads") in Valencia, where Juan, according to the script, "covers his face with big dark glasses, paying homage to Barbara Stanwyck in *Double Indemnity*" (141). Of course, one could also say that Juan feels guilty and that he is implicitly paying homage to his brother. In this regard, when he cries in despair at the end of shooting "The Visit," whose ending the director Enrique has altered to be darker and more critical of the Catholic church, we experience, as Lynn Hirschberg has pointed out, a fleeting moment of redemption that is more visibly present in other films by Almodóvar.

Fleeting as the moment may be, a more enduring effect, at least upon a single viewing of the movie, is likely to be one of confusion: the last, "secularized" part of the movie, which is about half an hour in duration and which centers on events that appear to have taken place before the beginning of the filmed discourse, arguably only heightens the sense of confusion and lack of unity. And yet, as I have already pointed out, the final visit replays the previous two and intensifies the passions that move much of the film. In this light, it is significant that the last sequences of the film take place mainly in Valencia, a city famous for its *Fallas,* a festival in celebration of Saint Joseph dating from the Middle Ages and consisting of the ritual incineration of huge cardboard, papier-mâché, wood, and plaster figures or *ninots* (dolls), one of which is spared, by popular vote, and housed in a local museum. In *Bad Education,* Berenguer and Juan visit the Museum of Giants and Big Heads, where Juan, struck by the row of huge grinning faces asks: "What are they laughing at, these Big Heads?" "They are laughing at us," answers Berenguer, in a rare show of humor, bleak though it is. Almodóvar has said that he had planned to do only two visits, with a Grand Guignolesque tone (Almodóvar 11). But, not satisfied with two visits, and apparently wanting to mix even more genres, he included a third visit, in which the Grand Guignol—or the Spanish grotesque known as *esperpento*—is brought into play with film noir. What is more, Almodóvar, without ever showing the festival of the *Fallas* directly, nonetheless suggests a spectacular burning—or, if one prefers, a sort of tongue-in-cheek auto-da-fé—in which Juan, Ignacio, Manolo, Berenguer, and even Enrique are all, albeit differently, the victims.

In the end, Ignacio is dead, even double dead (murdered by Father Manolo's henchman, then murdered by Berenguer and Juan), but he remains tantalizingly alive on-screen in the character of Zahara, an important variation on the figure of the seductress who punctuates so many examples of film noir. To Joan Crawford, Jane Russell, Lana Turner, Barbara Stanwyck, and Rita Hayworth, we can now add Gael García Bernal as Zahara, diegetically imagined by Ignacio and Enrique and performed by Juan/Ángel. As in *Double Indemnity* and other masterpieces of film noir, the seduction entails the fall of a man, here Mr. Berenguer, running from his past "role" as Father Manolo. *Double Indemnity* becomes, in Almodóvar's hands, a play of double—indeed, multiple—identities in which the putatively natural coordinates of gender and sexuality are at once undone and done anew. Put a bit differently, the Manchegan director provides, in the person of Zahara, a cross-gendered, late-postmodern version of the femme fatale of film noir. The film concludes with a note about the three characters' destinies: Ángel Andrade (Juan, the killer) appears to get away with murder and becomes a sex symbol in the TV soap operas of 1990s; Father Manolo Berenguer (the priest and the publisher fused together) blackmails Juan, until the Dark Ángel kills him in a hit-and-run "accident" (could this "Exterminating Ángel" be another of Almodóvar's tributes to Buñuel?); and Enrique "continues to make cinema with the same passion." The word PASIÓN, so characteristic of Almodóvar's films, fills the screen, functioning as the final, closing message, one that seems to put into perspective the baser passions of envy, greed, jealousy, lust, and murder that have been highlighted during the film by alluding to the more generous passions of friendship, loyalty, care, sympathy, and solidarity that characterized his two previous films.

Considering this, one last question arises: has the time arrived for Almodóvar's cinema to return to comedy and humor? As with *Kika,* another violent, noirish film in which the death drive ends up devouring almost everything and everyone (except the title character, Kika, played by Verónica Forqué), Almodóvar seems to have realized with *Bad Education,* where Thanatos once again looms large, that he has reached a dead end. His pessimism in this film, made during Spain's involvement in the U.S.-led war in Iraq and released on the eve of the terrorist attack in Madrid, seems to parallel his disgruntlement with the policies of the Partido Popular (Popular Party) and José María Aznar's ultraconservative government, which fell from office about the time that the movie was released. Almodóvar himself, in public appearances at the University of Castilla–La Mancha, Harvard University, and elsewhere, noted that the return of the Socialist Party to power had filled him with hope and had reaffirmed his desire for lighter filmic fare after the somber experience of *Bad Education*. His latest film, *Volver* (2006), offers a return to the comically inflected female-centered cinemas of *Dark Habits* (1983), *Women on the Verge of a Nervous Breakdown,* and especially *All about My Mother,* where, though still present, autobiographical elements are less imposing. These are the films of yesterday, and today, films in which Eros presides over the screen, communicating an irrepressible joie de vivre, amid sorrow and suffering, to the spectators.

WORKS CITED

Almodóvar, Pedro. *La mala educación: Un guión de Almodóvar.* Madrid: Ocho y Medio/ El Deseo, 2004.

Cirlot, Juan-Eduardo. *Diccionario de símbolos.* Barcelona: Editorial Labor, 1985.

Denby, David. "In and Out of Love: The Films of Pedro Almodóvar." *New Yorker* 80.36 (Nov. 22, 2004): 84–89.

Harguindey, Ángel S. "Grab the Fame and Run." Willoquet-Maricondi 32–39.

Hirschberg, Lynn. "The Redeemer." *New York Times Magazine* (Sept. 5, 2004): 26–27, 38–45, 70.

Mackenzie, Suzie. "All about My Father." Willoquet-Maricondi 154–61.

Martín Garzo, Gustavo. "La piedad y el deseo." *La mala educación: Un guión de Almodóvar.* By Pedro Almodóvar. Madrid: Ocho y Medio/El Deseo, 2004. 7–10.

Torres, Maruja. "Pedro Almodóvar: Life Is a Bolero." Willoquet-Maricondi 9–16.

Willoquet-Maricondi, Paula, ed. *Pedro Almodóvar: Interviews.* Jackson: University Press of Mississippi, 2004.

Volver A Filmmaker's Diary

PEDRO ALMODÓVAR

Get Back to the Diary

1.

A man comes up to me while I am having breakfast in a bar. He tells me he's seen *Bad Education* three times. I thank him, as I normally do.

"The first time I fell asleep," the stranger explains.

"Did it bore you that much?"

"No, on the contrary," he says. "I was totally into it but I got sleepy and I let myself go. Then, of course, I went to see it again since the bit I had watched left me very intrigued."

"And?"

"I liked it better than the first time but, again, at one point I was so relaxed that I fell asleep once more. And the same thing happened the third time."

"So, you still haven't seen the whole film?"

"Actually, no, I haven't. Now I'm waiting for it to come out in DVD so that I can watch it calmly at home."

The man seems to be a little over fifty, without any particularly striking characteristics. I wouldn't know what a narcoleptic looks like, but he certainly doesn't look like he suffers from sudden sleep syndrome. And he doesn't seem to be joking either.

"Well, I don't know what to tell you," I say.

"Don't be offended," he adds, "it's just that when I like something a lot it relaxes me so much that I can actually go to sleep. It's a really pleasant feeling; I mean it as a compliment. And, also . . . I'm currently taking some medication to curb anxiety and the doctor warned me that it could make me sleepy."

"Then, there's no doubt," I tell him emphatically, "that that has to be the explanation. You are falling asleep because of the pills, not because of my film!"

"Don't you suffer from anxiety, anguish, or desperation?" he asks, unaware that his words are the lyrics of a bolero. "My psychiatrist told me that these problems usually arise when one is around fifty. And, to make matters worse, I'm also appallingly afraid of death."

I point to the newspaper. "I've just read an interview with Julian Barnes, the British writer, where he discusses his last book of short stories. Among other things, he says that the idea that maturity brings serenity is a lie. In reality, the opposite is more the case."

"I agree, what's the title of the book?"

"*The Lemon Table*. It's a collection of short stories about death and the failure of elderly people to achieve serenity."

"But I'm not old," he tells me.

"Nor am I," I say. "Or Julian Barnes. But the three of us think that the years haven't granted us that inner peace we heard so much about."

The spontaneous fan goes off to buy the book, and I leave for my office where I have a meeting with three women and a screenplay.

2.

The screenplay is called *Volver*, which means "to return," and is about death, though it deals with the subject in a less anguished manner than that of the man who fell asleep watching *Bad Education*. More than about death itself, the screenplay talks about the rich culture that surrounds death in La Mancha, where I was born. It is about the way (not tragic at all) in which various female characters of different generations deal with this culture.

On the other side of my desk, in my office in El Deseo, sit three of the actresses who will star in *Volver*. Each of them embodies an important return. The most anticipated is that of Carmen Maura, but there are two additional returns, full of sense and sensibility: Penélope Cruz, with whom I've worked twice before [in *Live Flesh* and *All about My Mother*], an actress and a woman whom I adore both on and off the set; and Lola Dueñas, with whom I worked in *Talk to Her* (she was a nurse, a fellow worker of Javier Cámara, and I felt like repeating the experience).

I am extremely agitated about the meeting. Despite the fact that the role assigned to me in this circus is that of the master of ceremonies, it doesn't mean that it's easy for me to break the ice. But that's what it means, among other things, to be a director—at least, in a European country. I'm the icebreaker, the chimney that warms the atmosphere, the mother-father-psychiatrist-lover-friend who, with a simple word, can help you regain your self-confidence.

The Spanish culture of death: the mourning women in Volver *(2006). Photograph by Emilio Pereda and Paola Ardizzoni. Copyright Emilio Pereda and Paola Ardizzoni/El Deseo.*

Films, the collection of all the processes that make up a film, entail a wide array of questions—hence the adventurous nature of a shooting. The adventure's worth isn't proportional to the number of answers one finds along the way, it is proportional to the resistance of the people involved. What happens is that the director is driving a train with no brakes, and his job is to make sure that the train doesn't derail. That's how Truffaut saw it.

My first question is always similar: Will I feel the same passion I felt the last fifteen times about the new story? Without an answer to this question, it is best to avoid getting involved in a new project.

With *Volver* the answer is certainly, "yes." Once again, I have the feeling of handling a story—a fable, a treasure, and a secret—in which I am anxious to engross myself.

I'm not conscious of it at the time but when I look at Carmen, Penélope, and Lola, I can't help but wonder if this trio of striking women will work as a family (Carmen's character is the mother of the other two). This sort of question doesn't need an answer. One must go ahead with the film in order to find out, but I look at them and it already feels as if they were mother and daughters. All three have in common the fact that they are not from La Mancha and have to act as if they were, and all three have a mad desire to get down to business. That energy is in itself a spectacle of which I am the first, and sometimes the only, spectator. I look at them and nothing is out of sync. That's enough. In this job, intuition is what rules.

I propose that we start reading the script so as to break the ice. Desk work, as theater people call it. I interrupt them sometimes in order to give them more details about the characters, real-life anecdotes on which I drew to create them. A reading isn't a rehearsal, but I always go beyond normal limits. Without being aware of it, I find myself telling them about tones, hidden intentions, and mysterious parallelisms. Carmen instantly picks up my hints.

The reading flows, it's like a canoe where the three actresses row at the same pace.

Penélope and Lola tackle it with ease and seemingly without fear. There is a lot of fear when the first words are initially spoken but I don't notice it, or I don't want to notice it.

I realize I'm finding the answer to a question that I hadn't even consciously asked myself: Will I share the same empathy with Carmen as I did back in the eighties? It's been a long time. Many things have happened to us since then. Chemistry, that elusive and miraculous quality—will we feel it again?

I listen to Carmen reading, integrating my observations, and I feel that we are just the same as when we did *Law of Desire*. I have to pat my belly to realize that time has passed. Seventeen years.

Carmen Maura as Irene and Pedro Almodóvar on the set of Volver. *Copyright El Deseo.*

Action

Before shooting I always fall ill. This is so recurrent that it has turned into a tradition: it means that everything is ready to start. This time I was beginning to worry, two days away from shooting and I was still in perfect health. Until yesterday, in Almagro, where part of the story takes place.

At night in the hotel I bent down to pick up something and then I couldn't stand up again: lumbago. Forty degrees in the shade and there was I, applying heat to my back. At last, we are ready to begin shooting.

By the time you read this, the film crew will have invaded—and left—the Granátula cemetery, where we shoot for the first two days. Penélope Cruz, Lola Dueñas, and Blanca Portillo, playing countrywomen, clean and spruce up their relatives' tombstones while Yohana Cobo looks on with adolescent indifference.

The crew will be roasting in the crucible of white walls that make up my homeland at this time of year.

Inevitably, I remember my childhood: the whitewashed streets, deserted until 8:30 in the evening, when we children used to discover the mysteries of the body while the rest of the family slept under the narcotic effect of the heat. I remember the red earth, the yellow fields, the ash green olive trees, and the patios, blooming with life, plants, neighbors, and secrets as deep as wells and loneliness. Female loneliness. (Thirty years had to pass before I faced male loneliness.)

The patio was the holy of holies, where life took place. In the patio, the woman making lace would work on, catching the sun's last rays with her bundle of wood bobbins. Plants were watered; women sewed, and time passed while sitting on rocking chairs in the shade.

In *Volver*, I've paid homage to the patios of La Mancha, less sensual, much more austere than the Andalusian ones, like everything in this region. There is also a tribute to the "neighbor." Female neighbors are an appendix to the family—a necessary and complementary appendix. Many of our mothers ended their lives in the company of such women because we children had other lives to live.

The neighbor lives embedded in the patio, and she sometimes has access to the higher and more private area of the house. In this case, the character of Agustina, played by Blanca Portillo, is the ultimate neighbor. She has absolutely no life of her own. She is a lonely spinster who has been taking care of her own grave in the cemetery for years, and each morning she raps on the window of a senile Chus Lampreave and refuses to move until the other woman answers.

The solidarity displayed between neighbors is a quality that all characters of *Volver* bring with them to the city. We talked about this and many other questions during the press conference held in Madrid on June 30 [2005]. It was a historic day, not because of our meeting with the press but because while our meeting was taking place, the Spanish parliament passed a law that allows people of the same sex to marry.

Since morning I'd felt like I was living a very special day. For a start, all the actresses (except the adolescent Yohana) had arrived dressed in white, without having arranged it previously. Pure chance. And that spontaneous and casual white connected very well with the white of the houses in La Mancha, with the white orange blossoms that adorn brides, and it also put all the actresses on a similar wavelength. The white of their dresses seemed to underline an event that will be a landmark in our society: whether the Holy Mother likes it or not.

The End.

Almagro

Without a doubt, the best thing is to take a stroll at night, on the way to the hotel, and to find that the villagers still sit on wicker chairs outside by their doors to get a breath of fresh air. I thought that the custom had almost vanished, but no, entire families still sit, almost in silence, enjoying the breeze that travels through the streets before and after midnight. Time stands still. We greet every family group that we encounter along our way, and they answer in one voice, infecting us with their soothing silence.

The first week of shooting is over. I came to Madrid on Friday, at the end of the day's work. The "girls" and most of the team stayed behind in Almagro. I miss them, and I like that. I can concentrate better in the solitude of Madrid and I prefer to feel homesick for the shoot and to see it from a distance, in perspective. I leave Almagro in order to miss it. I feel that my films are getting progressively more autobiographical. At least, I am much more aware of how my memories stroll along the sets, like the breeze along the streets of Almagro at night.

When I hear Chus Lampreave, I hear my mother. My sister María Jesús made the pastries that Chus gives to Lola Dueñas and Penélope Cruz for the road [in one of the first scenes of *Volver*]; she also made the ratatouille *[pisto]*. When I have any doubts, I call my other sister, Antonia, for whom the memories of our childhood remain spotlessly clear. I've even asked her about the kind of rags and brushes that the women normally take to the cemetery to clean the tombstones. My mother left her, as part of her inheritance, a deep respect for the social, religious, family, and neighborly rites that are traditional to La Mancha.

And yet, everything in *Volver* is fiction. But the best way to tell a fiction, at least in my case, is to dress it with reality. Reality and fiction come together without confusion. I feel that I can now hold a direct conversation with the film I am making. This is neither an endogamous nor a nostalgic feeling, but by now it is easier for me to accept that films are my life, that they arise from it and sometimes give rise to it.

Penélope gave me a very special present on the first day of shooting; she had told me about it some time ago. It's a book, perfectly bound and printed, covering the last five years in our relationship. It is called *Pedro and Me.* It has the shape and the volume of a coffee-table book, with more images than text. The texts are an anthology of the e-mails we have exchanged in the last years. The images represent our common history since we did *Live Flesh:* that winter night in Madrid, with Penélope giving birth in a bus with the help of Pilar Bardem. Our promotional tours. The Palm Springs desert where the old Hollywood stars ended their days, dried out by the sun. The strolls through Central Park. Our lunches at the Sunset Marquis with Billy Bob Thornton or Salma Hayek. Hugs and awards. Photos along Sunset Boulevard with its scattered billboards. Fantastic outfits—hers—and my faithful all-black Armani tuxedo. The smiling, tense hours inside the limousines. More hugs in Madrid, in New York, in L.A., in Paris, in Cannes. Cheek

Pedro Almodóvar with Penélope Cruz (as Isabel, giving birth on the bus) on the set of Live Flesh *(1997). Photograph by Daniel Martínez. Copyright Daniel Martínez/ El Deseo.*

to cheek. The passage of time is much more obvious in me; she starts out looking like a child and attains her current splendor.

Reading the messages gives me a strange impression. They are so real. She is concise, and it's obvious that she is prompting me to tell her more things because she plans to do a book. All my states of mind appear in my messages; she has censored some bits of gossip, in case someone reads them. But in those messages I manage to see myself with the eyes of a furtive spectator.

A wonderful present.

We leave Almagro today. I am writing from a patio that is swamped with electric material and rocking chairs with "No sitting" signs. It is one in the afternoon and all the shots we have to do today take place in the street and it's impossible to shoot until at least four because the sun multiplies on the white walls; the light is blinding and far too flat. We have to wait. The team has disbanded; at this point I like to stay in one of the lifeless interior sets and enjoy the solitude, the clutter of objects, and the silence.

During these two weeks, contact with the villagers has been wonderful. Both with those we cross in the streets and with those who have worked with us as extras. In most of the sequences of La Mancha there are groups of women and men, and, I must say, I've never had better extras. There is something priceless about them; everything that they are supposed to do in front of the camera mirrors their own lives. Their presence has given depth and truth to the sequences in which they participate. Women from this land know well what it is like to clean a tombstone, to pray at a wake, to greet the neighbors. And the faces of the men, slowly weathered by the sun and the wind, have a weight and an expressiveness that would be impossible to improvise.

Yesterday, when I was on my way to the catered lunch, I met a young man who wished me luck for the shoot. He seemed well informed, almost a specialist, I would say. He asked me if the film had anything in common with *Pedro Páramo*, Juan Rulfo's masterpiece [1955]. At first I thought of the title that includes my name and the word *páramo* ("wilderness" in Spanish), which in a sense evokes the flatness common in the landscape of La Mancha, particularly in the area where I grew up. And I also thought about Rulfo's other masterpiece, *El Llano en Llamas* [The Burning Plain, 1953]. In *Volver*, the main characters' parents die, burned to death in a fire caused by the east wind. The question surprised me but I answered anyway, flattered. Our dialogue was as follows: It could be that the story in *Volver* recalls that of *Pedro Páramo*, but my script has nothing to do with the novel, except that in both the living and the dead coexist, as well as the real and the unreal, the fantastic and the everyday, the imagined and the experienced, dreams and wakefulness. While watching the film (as when reading the book), I would like for the spectator to be overwhelmed by a permanent dreamlike feeling. I dream that the spectator, even while awake, feels trapped in a dream that is nothing other than my film. In any case, Rulfo's novel is furiously Mexican, while the script of *Volver* is furiously from La Mancha.

Do you like films with ghosts?

Not normally. I am interested in how Buñuel or Bergman treats the apparition of the dead without changing the light or resorting to special effects. Ghosts appear in front of the person who is thinking about them without pyrotechnical effects. They are inner ghosts. I like Hitchcock's *Rebecca* [1940] and *Vertigo* [1958]. And *Sunset Boulevard* [Billy Wilder, 1950], where the leading character, who is floating dead in the pool, talks about himself when he was alive, as if he were a ghost trapped by the desires of another ghost (Norma Desmond, who in turn is cared for by the phantasmagorical Erich von Stroheim). William Holden when alive is the ghost of the drowned William Holden. A wonderful use of the offscreen voice, endlessly imitated since then. I also like Tourneur, when he tells stories about beings of other species. In general, I don't like horror stories with ghosts (M. Night Shyamalan), or films with angels, or with U.S. presidents who keep on saving the world.

What ghost does *Volver* evoke?

It isn't a ghost, but the whole film is infused with the presence of my absent mother.

Were there any ghosts in *Bad Education*?

My childhood memory turned into legend. One of the actors also turned out to be quite ghostly, but that is a different kettle of fish.

And at this point I decide to end this dialogue that has become a monologue.

P.S. I feel that this entry in my diary has turned out a little softhearted. But I have really enjoyed the last two weeks and happiness is not a good muse. The actresses have delighted me, all of them. The beauty, freshness, and visceral nature of Penélope. The burning look of the adolescent Yohana Cobo. The intensity and truth of Lola Dueñas. The ease and precision of Carmen Maura, capable of giving a moving performance on the spot, without rehearsals or trial takes. And the powerful revelation, sublime and accu-

rate, of a true cinematographic animal: Blanca Portillo (a mixture between María Casares and the Gutiérrez Caba sisters). Thanks to all of them.

Doors and Cars: Scenes between Twos

This week is less intense; we are shooting many of those sequences necessary for credibility, where actors go in and out of houses, stop cars and park them, etc. Everything is important in a film, but these sequences, required to locate the action and establish its geography, are hard for me. In La Mancha there were doors also, but people left them wide open so they didn't interrupt action, but allowed it to flow instead. Those shots of entrances and exits from cars or houses are a requisite of film orthography, even if in quite a number of thrillers the screenwriter and the director decide to make characters appear at each other's spaces effortlessly, disregarding all obstacles. Take a look at *Basic Instinct* [Paul Verhoeven, 1992] and you will see what I mean. Characters show up inside other people's houses as if they walked through walls. And that's not right.

I like all film genres and I always say that I would like to touch all of them (without committing myself to their particular rules), but there are certain genres that I already know I will not tackle—for example, a big-budget war movie, with battles and crowd scenes. Nothing bores me more as a director than a big-budget film, with enormous amounts of people in front of, around, and behind the camera.

Nor am I interested in directing a remake of some Japanese horror film. Or a biopic, not even one of Liberace (which I was already offered). Or a car and motorbike story. I don't drive; I can't tell one car from another, and I don't know how to make a car act, I just know that in thrillers they are a good decorative element—cars are needed for getaways and for shootouts with other cars—and that they also go very well with the young rebel style. But if I must pick a fetish from among the props, I'd rather take the typewriter. Without taking anything away from Nicholas Ray, I prefer a violent screenwriter (Bogart in *In a Lonely Place* [1950]) to youngsters who worship cars as much as their genitals (*Rebel without a Cause* [1955]).

I will not do sequels, prequels, or remakes.

I will not do a musical without spoken dialogue (I love musicals but I like to make characters talk once in a while), nor an epic in which the president of my country saves the world, nor a buddy movie, nor an adaptation of a Tolkien novel.

I have nothing against the genres that I don't want to do, I simply don't want to tackle them myself. (For example, I won't do war movies, but I admire *Apocalypse Now* [1979], and I'd love it if Coppola shot a sequel, dealing with the Iraq war, of course.)

In general, I prefer working with scripts that have few characters, and I am particularly attracted to scenes with two or three characters, even at the risk of being slightly theatrical (I'm thinking of models such as Woody Allen, Bergman, Cassavetes). One can tell the story of the universe through scenes between twos. This is not a maxim. I guess one of the advantages of a diary is the right to be subjective. I like scenes where two characters confront each other. My films are full of them. And maybe that is the reason why students at Madrid theater schools (from what I have been told) often pick scenes from my films for their class exercises.

Scenes with couples have a special magic. The format in which I'm shooting (anamorphic widescreen, that is, in cinemascope) is the only one that enables you to have two characters together and in close-up. And if there is a man inspired while lighting shots of two faces, it is my director of photog-

Mother and daughter: Penélope Cruz as Raimunda and Yohana Cobo as Paula in Volver. *Photograph by Emilio Pereda and Paola Ardizzoni. Copyright Emilio Pereda and Paola Ardizzoni/El Deseo.*

raphy, José Luis Alcaine. We have already shot some of these scenes and, just as I expected, Alcaine has drawn from his magic wand the darkness and the lights that bind characters together.

Before beginning a film, the director of photography asks me for references, which are just a path to be followed in order to find your own path. I normally talk about photography in other films (I often speak about Jack Cardiff, thinking particularly about the films he made with Michael Powell) or about painters (I frequently mention Edward Hopper and Zurbarán, as well as pop artists) or I show him images that I have found in magazines or books.

When Alcaine asked me for references in order to create the texture and atmosphere of *Volver,* I couldn't think of any. It is a pop comedy (pastel colors wouldn't suit it); a false local film that involves a drama with surrealist elements; it isn't a horror film, but some characters inhabit the darkness within the houses, the dim back rooms. It is an intimate story, but with so much action that it seems like a domestic *Indiana Jones* (1981, 1984, 1989, 2008). I didn't tell Alcaine anything, I couldn't think of a single film with which to compare it. But, like the perfect artisan that he is, he has been able to wade into the story of *Volver* and reveal its images with the intensity and emotion of someone who is revealing an explosive and thrilling secret.

Crises and Lies

There is a moment, during each of the processes involved in making a film, when I go to pieces and think that I have irretrievably lost control of my movie. It happens when I write it, while we are shooting (when editing I suffer more that one crisis) and, certainly, when the film is ready and no one has seen it yet, that's when I truly shit myself.

In order for the crises to be short-lived, you need to have a very close relationship with what you are shooting. I know these crises; I've experienced them in every single one of my fifteen previous films. Always. As with all passions—and for me, making movies is essentially a passion—crises evaporate when one irrationally loves what one is doing. (And it has nothing to do with whether the film afterwards turns out to be good or bad, whether the crises were justified or not; often crises arise out of very specific problems. I'm talking about the crises that surface without a justifiable reason and still manage to drag you down into a sea of confusion.)

I am currently living one of those moments. I feel (and I am sometimes absolutely positive) that all I am doing is a mistake, including this "dear" diary. Experience tells me that the only thing that I can do is to take the plunge and closely watch every movement, every shot, every phrase, every pause, every tear, and every joke. I shouldn't be talking about this. A director's loneliness is sacred. And the director himself should be the first to respect it, without sharing it with you as I am doing right now.

You can take it as yet another contradiction. It's the problem of thinking/writing out loud. This diary is a monologue in shouts.

It's been twelve days since I wrote all of the above. I am a different person. I feel much more optimistic.

I think I've mentioned it before: a shooting is a closed home from which you do not leave until it is finished.

My existence in *Volver* is very poor in anecdotes not related to the shooting. I read at night, but I can't really grasp anything; I don't watch TV. I do listen to music during the long trips to the set. I don't see anyone; I don't go out. Sometimes someone comes to visit. There's not much worth mentioning, and that is why the rare things that leave an imprint and manage to captivate me acquire an enormous dimension, exaggerated for sure.

I'll mention some of them.

Music. For me, finding an album that moves me (or a book) is as tremendous and important as finding a good friend. This year I've discovered Antony and the Johnsons, Cat Power, Nouvelle Vague, Feist, Rufus Wainright, Julien Jacob, CocoRosie, M. Ward, and rediscovered my Brazilian classics: Elis Regina, Maysa Matarazzo, Tom Zé, the Gilberto family and the Veloso family, etc. Jobim and Mina, always. I recommend all of them. I cannot think of better company than what this music has provided me during the daily trips to the sets where we were shooting. With books and films I haven't been quite as lucky. I go to the cinema faithfully every Saturday, but I haven't seen anything interesting. My latest discovery is still Kim Ki-duk (*3-Iron* [2004], *Spring, Summer, Fall, Winter . . . and Spring* [2003]), but that was last year. The only thing I remember from this year is Park Chan-wook's *Oldboy* [2003] and Hirokazu Koreeda's *Nobody Knows* [2004], a title redolent of Cesare Pavese (*Lavorare stanca* [Work's Tiring, 1936]) and a story that grows with each passing day inside Juan José Millás's memory, as he himself confessed when he came to see us one day during the shooting.

Millás is the only author whose words have managed to captivate me during the summer exile in which I am still immersed. His photo captions in *El País* during August, as well as his columns, were widely discussed by the whole crew. They provide a critical and incisive mirror of Spanish reality.

Very inspired. (In my desk I have kept an article from August 22. The photo that Millás comments on depicts three Spanish bishops during the demonstration against the legalization of gay marriage and in defense of the traditional family. All three are dressed in black and wear sunglasses in a style between policemen and gangsters. The June sun hits them straight in the face and gives the three of them an extremely sinister expression. Juanjo Millás began the literary illustration of the photo like this: "If God had wanted his representatives on earth to be these three men in black, he wouldn't have put so much color in nature." Is there a better way to begin a text about the politicization of the Spanish Catholic church that has sided with the most brutish faction of the right wing?)

I have a debt toward Juanjo Millás, which I will settle right now. In one of the chapters of this diary, the one devoted to Almagro, I recounted a conversation I had with a stranger in the street about *Pedro Páramo* and its relationship with *Volver* or vice versa. In that conversation I shrewdly stressed the coexistence of the dead and the living both in *Pedro Páramo* and in *Volver*. The truth is I was lying. I wasn't the author of my words, Juanjo Millás was. It's true that I met a boy in the street who asked me whether *Volver* was inspired by *Pedro Páramo*. By chance, that same day I received an e-mail from Juanjo, who had just read my script and was telling me what he had thought about it. Among other compliments, Juanjo described the parallelism with Juan Rulfo's masterpiece, the latter being furiously Mexican and mine furiously from La Mancha. I stole some of Juanjo's words and inserted them into a conversation that never actually took place—but that almost did.

I lie very little when I talk about my films. During the promotion and the premiere, naturally I hide or conceal information about the crew, the actors, and my own assessment of the film. The level of concealment varies from 15 percent (in *Talk to Her,* for example) to 30 percent in *Bad Education.* So far in the shooting diary, my lies comprise no more than 5 percent. At the end I promise to say the exact percentage.

Juanjo visited us on a very special day, the day we shot what could be called the film's baptism. The moment when Penélope sings in an open-air restaurant the famous tango, "Volver," with a *bulería* rhythm. The voice that had fitted it perfectly when the song was recorded had been Estrella Morente's. I say, "had fitted" because when we shot the playback, Penélope made the song hers with such precision and passion that she left us all crying in admiration. I swear that what I'm telling you is 100 percent true,

Penélope Cruz is turning this film into a personal celebration. Watching her act every day is a true spectacle for the eyes of the face as well as the soul. We still have four weeks of shooting before us; I don't know who has taken over whom, the character over Penélope or Penélope over the character, but Penélope is Raimunda (the character in the film) as much as Raimunda is Penélope. And for me, being able to witness this fusion gives me a pleasure that I wouldn't know how to explain.

Drowsiness

I'm drowsy when I arrive at the shoot. We are in the eleventh week and a shower and coffee aren't enough to wake me up.

My body reaches the studio while my mind is walking around my house or is still on the way. I tell the first assistant director (the real arbiter in this whole setup) about the shot with which we are to begin the day's work. He informs the cameraman while the director of photography (owner of light but also of time) gets ready to direct a frenzied choreography in which the electricians become the dancers. Of all the crews that make up The Crew, the department of photography is the one whose members are most attractive; they work faster and harder than anyone else, and gobble up the greatest number of sandwiches. They have the kind of sturdy and "normal" build that is typical of soccer players.

While the electricians move cables, multiple socket adaptors, lights, screens, and so on, I withdraw to my dressing room in hopes that silence will place its soothing hand on my brow and illuminate me.

I wait, drowsy, for the cameraman to try out the movements with the camera and for the director of photography to create the atmosphere. Then, it's my turn. I come in and tell actors how they should move about the set and why; normally, I cling like a leech and move about with them. Afterwards, we read the text and I infuse them with my intentions, which often can only be read between the lines; I suggest the tone, and they follow my pointers attentively.

Each crew manager has a particular detail to correct at the last minute. Once again, I explain to the actors the music for each word, the length of the pauses, and the pitch of each phrase. I direct them as if they were sleep-walking singers in an opera whose sole music is that of words.

Just as one is unconscious of the precise moment when one falls asleep, I am not conscious of the moment when I wake up, but it always seems to be when the actors appear (actresses in this film) and I am working with them. Totally awake, I stand by the camera or in front of the video screen connected to it, where the images are reproduced. From that point onward, my body turns into a one hundred-kilogram block of adrenaline. I'm all eyes and ears, watching over the actors as they go about their delicate, neurotic, and moving game.

In the eleventh week of shooting, the only thing that manages to wake me is my work with the actors, utterly unique and nontransferable.

Actors' Eyes

Don't ask me why, but *Volver* is a story told through the eyes of the actors. From the beginning I felt that I needed to see them, and this impulse, somewhat abstract but very powerful, forced me to have the type of shot in which camera location and movements are hardly noticeable.

I realized this when I saw the edited material on Saturday with Alberto Iglesias, my composer. Proximity to the actors forces you to use a, let's say, classical method of shooting. To make myself clearer, it's the opposite of Dogma [the film collective Dogme 95] (and that doesn't mean I don't like their films. In fact, I like them all, but I hate those of their followers).

Monologue Night

In the script of *Volver* there is a long sequence that is practically a monologue since only one character talks, the one played by Carmen Maura. In that sequence, Carmen is telling her dearest daughter (Penélope) the reasons for her death and for her return to life. She does so through six intense pages and six shots that are just as intense. The sequence is one of the reasons why I wanted to shoot *Volver;* I've cried every single time I've corrected that part of the script. (I feel like the character played by Kathleen Turner in *Romancing the Stone* [Robert Zemeckis, 1984], a ridiculous writer of very kitsch romance novels who cried nonstop while she wrote them.)

The crew was aware of the importance of this scene since we began shooting and such intense interest made Carmen a little nervous. She wanted to tackle it as soon as possible in order to get the weight off her mind. We spent a whole night shooting it, and everyone, from the gofer to myself, was completely focused, with the concentration required by a truly difficult scene and which, precisely for that reason, becomes the easiest one since we are all working to the fullest of our potential.

Once again I sense that sacred complicity with Carmen, a marvelous feeling of being before an instrument that is perfectly tuned for me. All the takes are good, some even extraordinary. Penélope listens to her. In this film there is a lot of talking, a lot of hiding, a lot of listening, and, since it is supposed to be comedy, as the crew says, a lot of crying.

And it is during this complicated night that Cecilia Roth and Felicity Lott visit us. Both are performing at the Zarzuela Theater, Cecilia in Cocteau's *The Human Voice* and Felicity in Poulenc's opera based on the same text. Too many emotions for a night that could only hold one: Carmen's amazing monologue.

I talk with Cecilia about the importance of *The Voice* in my work. Carmen played it in *Law of Desire,* and how! It's wonderful to realize that from *Law* (in my opinion, the peak of her acting career) until now, Maura hasn't changed. She hasn't learned anything new because she already knew it all, but keeping that fire intact for two decades is an admirable and difficult task that not all the actors I've worked with have managed to accomplish.

Cecilia's presence, the accumulation of monologues, the night, and my own interior voice lead me to think about the last twenty years, about the time that has passed between *Law* and *Volver.* About how much we've changed, or, more to the point, about how much I've changed, because I think that, inside, Carmen has hardly changed at all. She is still the sweet chatterbox who refuses to complicate herself and lives her life with a relaxed and smooth humor. In comparison to her, I feel I have become heavier, and not just physically. Before, my load was lighter. Setbacks and problems lit up a wild spark inside of me that not only managed to defuse them but also, sometimes, actually turned them into an inspiration.

I remember, for instance, the day that we were going to shoot the scene of *The Human Voice* in *Law of Desire.* They had lent us the Lara Theater for just one day. When I arrived at eight in the morning and saw the decor onstage, I was furious. I didn't like it at all and we only had that day for shooting.

Even though it was early, I asked for an ax. Nobody seemed surprised; they brought me one. And as soon as I had it in my hands I began to hack away at the decor. We called Carmen and I handed her the ax. "When the scene starts," I told her, "you are completely deranged and while you wait for the call, you destroy the house that you shared with your lover." Carmen looked at me with the smile of a naughty girl, game for anything.

"Really?" she asked.

I gave her the ax and she energetically attacked her bedroom. I much preferred this to what I had originally planned when I prepared the scene.

God bless that ugly decor!

Nowadays, when I don't like a decor, I get an anxiety attack. Before, I solved the situation with wild humor and recklessness, and now I make do with breathing exercises and a tranquilizer or two. But I'm not complaining.

Filmography of Pedro Almodóvar

SHORT AND EXPERIMENTAL FILMS

These films have not been released in the United States.

Film político (Political Film), 1974. 4 minutes, Super-8.

Dos putas, o historia de amor que termina en boda (Two Whores; or, Love Story Ending in a Wedding), 1974. 10 minutes, Super-8.

El Sueño, o la estrella (The Dream, or the Star), 1975. 12 minutes, Super-8.

Homenaje (Homage), 1975. 10 minutes, Super-8.

La Caída de Sódoma (The Fall of Sodom), 1975. 10 minutes, Super-8.

Blancor (Whiteness), 1975. 5 minutes, Super-8.

Tráiler de *"Who's Afraid of Virginia Woolf?"* (Homemade trailer for *Who's Afraid of Virginia Woolf?*), 1976. 5 minutes, Super-8.

Sea caritativo (Be Charitable), 1976. 5 minutes, Super-8.

Muerte en la carretera (Death on the Road), 1976. 8 minutes, Super-8.

Las tres ventajas de Ponte (The Three Advantages of Ponte), 1977. 5 minutes, Super-8.

Sexo va, sexo viene (Sex Comes, Sex Goes), 1977. 17 minutes, Super-8.

Salomé, 1978. 12 minutes, 16mm.

Folle . . . folle . . . fólleme Tim! (Fuck, Fuck, Fuck Me Tim!), 1978. 90 minutes, Super-8.

FEATURE FILMS

Unless otherwise noted, all were filmed in 35mm.

Pepi, Luci, Bom, y otras chicas del montón (Pepi, Luci, Bom and Other Girls on the Heap), 1980. 82 minutes, 16mm blown up to 35mm.

Laberinto de pasiones (Labyrinth of Passion), 1982. 100 minutes.

Entre tinieblas (Dark Habits), 1983. 114 minutes.

¿Qué he hecho yo para merecer esto? (What Have I Done to Deserve This?), 1984. 101 minutes.

Matador, 1986. 110 minutes.

La ley del deseo (Law of Desire), 1987. 102 minutes.

Mujeres al borde de un ataque de nervios (Women on the Verge of a Nervous Breakdown), 1988. 90 minutes.

¡Átame! (Tie Me Up! Tie Me Down!), 1990. 111 minutes.

Tacones lejanos (High Heels), 1991. 112 minutes.

Kika, 1993. 114 minutes.

La flor de mi secreto (The Flower of My Secret), 1995. 103 minutes.

Carne trémula (Live Flesh), 1997. 103 minutes.

Todo sobre mi madre (All about My Mother), 1999. 101 minutes.

Hable con ella (Talk to Her), 2002. 112 minutes.

La mala educación (Bad Education), 2004. 106 minutes.

Volver, 2006. 121 minutes.

Mark Allinson is professor and associate dean of the Faculty of Humanities, Arts, and Social Sciences at Regent's College, London. His research and teaching interests are in Spanish cinema and theater. He has published three books: *A Spanish Labyrinth: The Films of Pedro Almodóvar, Spanish Cinema: A Student Guide* (with Barry Jordan), and *¡Te toca! A New Communicative Spanish Course* (with Richard Pym). He was a founding editor of *Studies in Hispanic Cinemas*.

Isolina Ballesteros is assistant professor at the Department of Modern Languages and Comparative Literature of Baruch College, CUNY. Her specialty is contemporary Spanish cultural studies, and she has published extensively on Spanish and Latin American women writers, the image of women in the post-Franco literature, and Spanish and European film. She is the author of two books, *Escritura femenina y discurso autobiográfico en la nueva novela española* and *Cine (Ins)urgente: textos fílmicos y contextos culturales de la España postfranquista*.

Leo Bersani is professor emeritus of French at the University of California at Berkeley. He works on nineteenth- and twentieth-century literature, psychoanalysis, literature and the visual arts, and cultural criticism. His publications include *A Future for Astyanax, The Freudian Body: Psychoanalysis and Art, The Culture of Redemption,* and *Homos.*

Ulysse Dutoit is lecturer of French at the University of California at Berkeley. He works on the visual arts, particularly film and painting. His publications with Leo Bersani include *The Forms of Violence: Narrative in Assyrian Art and Modern Culture; Arts of Impoverishment: Beckett, Rothko, and Resnais; Caravaggio's Secrets;* and *Forms of Being: Cinema, Aesthetics, Subjectivity.*

Marvin D'Lugo teaches Spanish and Latin American film at Clark University. He is the author of *The Films of Carlos Saura: The Practice of Seeing, Guide* *to the Cinema of Spain,* and *Pedro Almodóvar.* He has written extensively on the auteur tradition in Latin American cinema.

Brad Epps is professor of Romance languages and literatures and chair of Studies of Women, Gender, and Sexuality at Harvard University. He has published more than seventy articles on modern literature, film, art, photography, architecture, and immigration from Spain, Latin America, Catalonia, and France. He is author of *Significant Violence: Oppression and Resistance in the Narratives of Juan Goytisolo; Spain beyond Spain: Modernity, Literary History, and National Identity* (with Luis Fernández Cifuentes); and *Passing Lines: Immigration and Sexuality* (with Keja Valens and Bill Johnson González).

Peter William Evans is professor of film studies at Queen Mary, University of London. His publications include *The Films of Luis Buñuel: Subjectivity and Desire, Luis Buñuel: New Readings: Women on the Verge of a Nervous Breakdown, Bigas Luna: Jamón jamón,* and *Carol Reed.*

Víctor Fuentes is professor emeritus of Spanish, University of California, Santa Barbara. He has published fourteen books and numerous essays in prestigious journals in the United States, Spain, and Latin America. His books include *Bio-grafía americana; La marcha al pueblo en las letras españolas (1917–1936); El cántico material y espiritual de César Vallejo; Buñuel, cine y literatura; Antología de la poesía bohemia española; Antología del cuento bohemio español;* and *La mirada de Buñuel: Cine, literatura y vida.*

Despina Kakoudaki is assistant professor of literature at American University, where she teaches interdisciplinary courses in literature and film, visual culture, and the history of technology and new media. Her recent work involves robots and other versions of the mechanical body, as well as melodrama, the representation of race in disaster films, and the phenomenology of the body in early cinema.

Marsha Kinder is professor of critical studies in the School of Cinematic Arts at the University of Southern California. She is author of *Blood Cinema, Refiguring Spain,* and *Buñuel's The Discreet Charm of the Bourgeoisie,* plus many articles on Spanish cinema and other topics. Since 1997 she has directed The Labyrinth Project, a USC research initiative on interactive narrative, where she has produced a series of award-winning "database documentaries" as installations, DVD-ROMs, and Web sites. In recognition of her innovative transdisciplinary work, she was named a University Professor, an honor bestowed on only seventeen professors in USC's history.

Steven Marsh teaches Hispanic studies and film at the University of Illinois at Chicago. He is the author of *Popular Spanish Film under Franco: Comedy and the Weakening of the State* and joint editor of *Gender and Spanish Cinema* (with Parvati Nair). He is a coauthor of *The Mediation of Everyday Life: An Oral History of Cinema-Going in 1940s and 1950s Spain* and is writing a history of Spanish popular cinema of the sound period.

Andy Medhurst is senior lecturer in media, film, and cultural studies at the University of Sussex. He has published widely on sexuality, identity, and representation and is the author of *A National Joke: Popular Comedy and English Cultural Identities.*

Ignacio Oliva teaches film history and directing in the Faculty of Fine Arts in Cuenca at the University of Castilla–La Mancha. His publications include "La imagen sustantiva" on film art, "Eterno Eisenstein," and critical pieces at RESEÑA film review in Madrid. As a filmmaker he has directed more than twenty documentary works and short fiction films.

Paul Julian Smith is professor of Spanish at the University of Cambridge. He is the author of twelve books, including *Desire Unlimited: The Cinema of Pedro Almodóvar* and *Contemporary Spanish Culture: TV, Fashion, Art, and Film.* He is a founding editor of *Journal of Spanish Cultural Studies* and a regular contributor to *Sight and Sound,* the monthly magazine of the British Film Institute. His current research is on television in Spain. In 2008 he was elected a Fellow of the British Academy.

Kathleen M. Vernon is associate professor of Hispanic studies at SUNY Stony Brook. She is the editor of *Post-Franco, Postmodern: The Films of Pedro Almodóvar* and the author of numerous studies on Spanish cinema, culture, and literature. Her latest projects are *The Mediation of Everyday Life: An Oral History of Cinema-Going in 1940s and 1950s Spain* (as coauthor) and *The Rhythms of History: Cinema, Music, and Cultural Memory in Contemporary Spain.*

Linda Williams is professor of film studies at the University of California, Berkeley. Her books include *Hard Core: Power, Pleasure, and the "Frenzy of the Visible"* and *Playing the Race Card: Melodramas of Black and White from Uncle Tom to O. J. Simpson.* Her anthologies include *Reinventing Film Studies* (with Christine Gledhill) and *Porn Studies.*

Francisco A. Zurián was the academic coordinator of the International Forum Pedro Almodóvar at the University of Castilla–La Mancha from 2002 to 2006. He is assistant professor of cinema and television at the University of Carlos III in Madrid and the author of several publications on aesthetics and gender in contemporary Spanish cinema and narrative and the construction of personal identity in cinema. He serves as academic and scientific consultant for Almodóvar's production company, El Deseo.

INDEX

Abrazos rotos, Los. See Broken Embraces

Abril, Victoria: in *High Heels,* 42, 43, 46, 47, 85, 168, 174, 181, 190–91n12, 246, 366; in *Kika,* 42, 44, 47, 319; in *Tie Me Up! Tie Me Down!,* 42, 103, 111, 112, 164n17

abuse, 8, 60, 93–96, 101, 116, 131, 133–34, 268, 277, 283, 379; in *Bad Education,* 431–36, 440; in *Volver,* 341, 347, 350. *See also* incest; molestation

Academy Awards, 2, 11, 26, 28, 141

Acevedo-Muñoz, Ernesto R.: *Pedro Almodóvar,* 6

aesthetics: and desire, 23

AIDS, 8, 80, 93, 147, 245, 394

Alaska (Olvido Gara), 8, 72, 101, 398

Alcaine, José Luis, 26, 456–57

Aldrich, Robert, 290

All about Eve, 44, 48, 144, 148, 164n19, 241–42, 254, 259–62

"All about My Father" (Mackenzie), 432–33

All about My Mother, 8, 16, 17, 18, 21, 23, 32n17, 151, 222, 241–45, 249–50, 252–65, 395, 410, 420, 429–30, 466; Academy Award for, 2, 141; Almodóvar on set, 19; brain-dead trilogy, part of, 269; color, stylistic use, 399–400; as comedy and farce, 121, 122–24, 130, 445; communication in, 437; as drama therapy, 163; as melodrama, 141, 144–45, 145–51, 152, 158, 161–63, 188; music in, 53, 54, 57, 58; narrative in, 408; parody of, 434; as performative reflection on possibility of nonphantasmal imaginary, 263–64; performing identities, 78–84, 87, 89–90, 92–95; and purification of desire, 248; rehearsals and reality in, 319; stage environment, 163n11; and television, 38, 39, 40, 44, 45, 48

allegory, 63, 82, 94, 152, 154, 164n15, 210, 212–13, 223, 234, 381, 435

Allen, Woody, 13, 456

All I Desire, 144

Allinson, Mark, 20–21, 29, 37, 77, 115, 124, 154, 163n5, 163n11; *Spanish Labyrinth,* 5, 467

Almagro, 425n13, 450, 451–55, 459

Almodóvar, Agustín (brother), 2, 26, 38, 269, 274, 355n9, 393, 398, 401, 402, 416, 426n18

Almodóvar, Pedro, 1–34; alter ego, 4; artistic creation and style, 4, 396–401; as author (man of letters), 26–27, 408–28; cast as family, 400; as cinematic poet of fantasy, 116; cinematic self-consciousness of, 3, 141, 151, 195, 395; compassion and empathy for characters, 430; critical analyses and interviews, 5–6, 12–13, 14–15; critical canonization, 5, 20; directorial influences, 4; elusiveness in work, 15; feature films, 465–66; on female performance as preventative medicine, 144; filming, 401–3; filming and editing at same time, 403–6; filmography, 17, 25–26, 245, 268, 465–66; films, recently discovered and attended, 458; honorary degrees, 29, 409; informal

mediation of desire, 74–78; music in,
57–58; performing identities, 74–78;
poster art for, 314; spirituality of, 246
Da Vinci, Leonardo, 68n20
Davis, Bette, 97n3, 126, 148, 209, 242, 243,
288, 410
death: Spanish culture of in *Volver,* 30n10,
448; and violence, 247–48, 261. *See also*
murder; suicide
deathbed scenes, 173, 175, 177–81, 185,
187, 189
Death in Venice, 435
Death of a Salesman, 143
Death on the Road, 465
deceit: and violence, 96
Deleuze, Gilles, 298–99, 315, 331n6
Deleyto, Celestino, 29n1
Denby, David, 12, 436
Deneuve, Catherine, 225
De Palma, Brian, 277
Derrida, Jacques, 339, 340, 346, 347, 349,
354, 354n2
De Sica, Vittorio, 4, 341
desire: and aesthetics, 23; as artifact,
248; and brotherhood, 282–85; in
Matador, 300–18; modalities of, 21–22;
performance and mediation of, 74–78;
unhappy obsessive, 248; unlimited,
30n3, 173; and violence, 17. *See also*
sexual desire
Desire Limited. *See* El Deseo
Desire Unlimited (Smith), 5, 10–11, 50n1,
105, 174, 189–90n3, 189n2, 190n8, 197,
303, 304–5, 336n37, 336n40, 365–66,
369, 384n6, 469
Desmond, Norma, 454
Desperate Housewives, 271–72
destape, 9, 90
determinism, 197, 208, 227, 402
dialogism, 269
Diamond, Elin, 71, 72
Dickens, Charles, 206–8, 221, 225–26
Dickstein, Morris: *Great Film Directors,*
119

Dictionary of Symbols (Cirlot), 436
diegesis (telling), 20–21, 57, 65, 73, 85–86,
87–88, 95, 97n4, 107, 115, 144–45, 152,
154, 158, 162–63, 195, 200, 211–12,
215, 218, 221, 224, 230–31, 233,
236nn19–20, 263, 300, 307–8, 310,
313, 316, 340–41, 349, 356n15, 365,
378, 440, 444. *See also* melodrama,
limits of; mimesis (showing)
Dietrich, Marlene, 372
digital formats, 300–301, 332n9
Dior, Christian, 399
Diphusa, Patty (character and alter ego),
4, 27, 270–71, 392–93, 411–18, 420–21,
427n24. *See also Patty Diphusa*
distantiation, 163n9, 221, 225, 232, 233–34
D'Lugo, Marvin, 3, 12, 14, 24, 25–26, 29,
30n11, 94, 293n6, 332n10, 332n13,
467–68; *Pedro Almodóvar,* 5–6
Doane, Mary Ann, 24, 59–60, 65, 299, 314,
318–19, 331n4, 331n6
Dogme 95 (Dogma) (film collective), 28,
461
dominance, 102–3, 107, 111–13, 116, 225,
259, 303, 437
dominatrix, 114
Donapetry, María, 334–35n27
Don Quixote, 10, 436
*Dos putas, o historia de amor que termina
en boda. See Two Whores; or, Love
Story Ending in a Wedding*
Doty, Alexander, 66
Double Indemnity, 281, 442–44
drag, 18–19, 64–65, 71, 88–93, 98nn9–10,
99n12, 125, 126, 149, 151, 164n14,
167, 174, 176, 244, 281, 286, 360, 366,
374–75, 384n9, 413–14. *See also* cross-
dressing; transvestism
Dream, or the Star, The, 465
Dreyer, Carl, 343
drugs: in Almodóvar's films, 30n6
DuBois, Blanche (character), 79–80, 148,
222, 243, 245, 257, 259, 262
Duchamp, Marcel, 392